# THE EU CONSTITUTION:
# THE BEST WAY FORWARD?

ASSER INSTITUTE COLLOQUIUM ON EUROPEAN LAW
SESSION XXXIV – 13-16 OCTOBER 2004

T.M.C. ASSER INSTITUUT
The Hague

# THE EU CONSTITUTION: THE BEST WAY FORWARD?

edited by

Deirdre Curtin
Alfred E. Kellermann
Steven Blockmans

T·M·C·ASSER PRESS
The Hague

Published by T.M.C. ASSER PRESS
P.O. Box 16163, 2500 BD The Hague, The Netherlands
<www.asserpress.nl>


T.M.C. ASSER PRESS' English language books are distributed exclusively by

Cambridge University Press, The Edinburgh Building, Shaftesbury Road,
Cambridge CB2 2RU, UK,
or,
for customers in the USA, Canada and Mexico:
Cambridge University Press, 100 Brook Hill Drive, West Nyack, NY 10994-2133, USA
<www.cambridge.org>

ISBN 10: 90-6704-200-5
ISBN 13: 978-90-6704-200-0

**T.M.C. Asser Instituut - Institute for Private and Public International Law,
International Commercial Arbitration and European Law**
Institute Address: R.J. Schimmelpennincklaan 20-22, 2517 JN The Hague, The
Netherlands; P.O. Box 30461, 2500 GL The Hague, The Netherlands; Tel.: (31-
70)3420300; Fax: (31-70)3420359; URL: www.asser.nl.

Over thirty years, the T.M.C. Asser Institute has developed into a leading scientific research
institute in the field of international law. It covers private international law, public international
law, including international humanitarian law, the law of the European Union, the law of
international commercial arbitration and increasingly, also, international economic law, the
law of international commerce and international sports law. Conducting scientific research
either fundamental or applied, in the aforementioned domains, is the main activity of the
Institute. In addition, the Institute organizes congresses and postgraduate courses, undertakes
contract-research and operates its own publishing house. Because of its inter-university
background, the Institute often cooperates with Dutch law faculties as well as with various
national and foreign institutions. The Institute organizes Asser College Europe, a project in
cooperation with East and Central European countries whereby research and educational projects
are organized and implemented.

# SUMMARY TABLE OF CONTENTS

## PART I
### The Process and Impact of EU Constitution-making: Voice and Exit

## PART II
### Transparency and Legal Instruments in the EU Constitution

## PART III
### The Democratic Life of the European Union

# PART IV
## Expansion of Executive, Judicial and Legislative Powers

# PART V
## Access to Justice and the EU Constitution

# FOREWORD

I would like to compliment the Asser Institute on organising the 34th Session of the Colloquium on European Law, a major conference, during the Dutch Presidency of the European Union in 2004. It was a well-chosen moment to make a relevant and timely contribution to the ongoing debate about Europe's Constitution. This book brings together the work of scholars of exceptional calibre and high-ranking representatives of the European Union's institutions, national governments, legislatures, judiciaries and universities. It will no doubt become an authoritative reference work.

When so much knowledge and experience from Europe and beyond comes together in one place, it inevitably promotes lively and rewarding debate. And debate is precisely what Europe needs.

There is an anecdote about Georges Clemenceau, the French leader during World War One. The pre-war years saw a heated debate about the wealth of the Church. One wit, in a discussion with Clemenceau and others, was prompted to make the remark, 'I think there is a lot of money to be made from religion. I would like to start one of my own.' Once the laughter had died down, Clemenceau replied, 'it is not so difficult. All you need to do is be crucified and rise from the dead!'

Ironically, this is exactly what happened. Not to the wit in question, nor to Clemenceau, but to Europe. In the 20th century, Europe was indeed crucified. And it did rise from the dead. Not once, but twice. Partly, it should be said, because of the intransigence of Clemenceau himself. In the aftermath of '*la Grande Guerre*' he was determined to dictate harsh terms, and Europe was encumbered with the infamous Treaty of Versailles.

Europe's saviour was European integration. The European Union has succeeded in reconciling erstwhile archenemies France and Germany, and in uniting East and West. The internal market has brought us unprecedented riches. But we still lack true believers, true Europeans.

How can this be? The fatal flaw is that the EU lacks a cross-border political space, a European political arena, a transnational discourse. A place where European politics is made. This is why I say that Europe needs debate.

Debate across borders fosters a sense of a shared destiny. While the forum for debate is purely national, a shared sense of community will struggle to take root. Despite its great achievements, the Union has not made its people committed Europeans. 'We, the People of Europe' is a fiction. Nor will the Constitutional Treaty, as a symbol, engender a sense of community, just as the European flag and the European anthem failed to do in the past. But as a vehicle to bring Europe closer to the people, it has great potential. Even if the ratification process were to be derailed. As a catalyst for transnational debate, the Constitutional Treaty cannot fail to have an impact.

The Treaty forces us as Europeans to think about Europe and to express a view on its consequences. We will obtain a clearer picture of Europe in our minds. This does not mean that we will all become born-again Europeans. I, for one, would find that an alarming prospect. But greater engagement, be it positive or negative, is inevitable. And that is what we need.

As far as I am concerned, we will carry on being who we are: Irish, Poles, Greeks and so on. Twenty-five or more different nationalities with our own views, customs and characteristics. Yet, at the same time, we will feel more and more European. 'We, the Peoples of Europe.' That is an option.

So even before we know the outcome of the ratification process, one thing is clear. The Constitutional Treaty will bring us closer together as Europeans, regardless of whether we like what it says. However, that does not mean that I am indifferent as to the outcome; far from it. There are plenty of reasons why the Constitutional Treaty should rouse our enthusiasm.

The European Union has been carried forward on a tidal wave of change over the past fifteen years. The loose economic community of yesteryear has made way for a close-knit Union. A Union that plays a role in almost all areas of daily life, including those that used to be the exclusive preserve of the nation state, such as justice, external borders, foreign policy and monetary policy. At the same time, it has grown exponentially. Numbering twelve Member States when it came into being in 1992, it now has twenty-five and counting.

These tidal waves of change are testing the buoyancy of the Union to the limit. We need to stop and think about the future to prevent the vessel from capsizing, the crew from deserting or the passengers from being swept overboard. The European Convention on the future of the European Union was the unorthodox lifebelt that was thrown two and a half years ago.

At the Convention, for the first time ever, the discussion about the EU's principles, methods and objectives was left not to diplomats, but to representatives of national parliaments and the European institutions. This did not mean that the debate about the Union was entering calmer waters. At times, intergovernmentalists and supranationalists whipped up a real storm. But you will have realised by now that the rough seas of this kind of confrontation do not worry me. Especially since the debate was constructive. Despite their differences, the two sides were able to agree on a final text. And this text is no watered-down compromise, but a blueprint for a reformed Union. That is an impressive achievement.

The governments of the Member States were well aware of this. The outcome of the Convention put them under pressure to steer the Convention safely through the IGC. And although the voyage was again a stormy one, the ship sailed into port in June of this year.

The result of the deliberations is not a genuine constitution, nor is it an ordinary treaty. It is a Constitutional Treaty. Just like a constitution, the Treaty sets out the relative powers of the European Council, the European Commission and the European Parliament. It also includes a comprehensive catalogue of fundamental rights that binds the Union to the rule of law. But, unlike a constitution, the Treaty cannot be amended by a qualified majority of votes in parliament. It remains an agreement between independent states. And that is the hallmark of a treaty.

So while the term Constitutional Treaty may suggest an inherent contradiction, it does describe exactly how the Union is governed. The citizen and the state take turns at the helm of the Union, according to the policy area in question. Some decisions are taken by a qualified majority, others by unanimity.

This is not a sign of weakness. On the contrary, the duality in the system of the EU perfectly reflects the divided loyalty of its citizens which I mentioned earlier. Sometimes they consider their interests best represented at the national level, and sometimes at the European level. The success of the EU in the future will depend to a large extent on its ability to manage this duality. And the Constitutional Treaty is an excellent instrument for doing so.

Supranationalists see the Union as a community of citizens. Intergovernmentalists see it as a union of states. But in reality, the Union is both. And the Constitutional Treaty conveys this essential idea with remarkable clarity.

If we look at its potential to stimulate debate, its refreshingly unconventional origins and its appropriate duality, the Constitutional Treaty squares the circle. But, ultimately, it must prove its worth in practice. The key question is the following: will it help us to build a more prosperous, more democratic and more secure Europe? And despite its flaws and blemishes, my answer is an unqualified 'Yes, it will!'

The Union was created in a democratic vacuum. At the very least, the people were scarcely involved, if at all, in the establishment of the European Community. It is not in fact inconceivable that if they had been, the baby would have been smothered at birth. At any rate, it is to be feared that the deep-rooted anti-German sentiment that long prevailed across much of Europe would have seen to this.

However, although the democratic deficit initially helped breathe life into the European idea, as time went by it gradually became ever more stifling. The creation of the European Parliament in 1979 was an attempt to provide much-needed oxygen. Yet in subsequent years the air became even thinner, certainly after 1992, when the Community was transformed into the Union by the Treaty of Maastricht. The fact that the Treaty of Maastricht granted people EU citizenship, alongside their existing citizenship, entirely escaped most people's notice. And many of those that did take note dismissed it as a sop. Now Europe really was struggling for air.

Having said this, the Constitutional Treaty opens the window and lets the fresh air flood in. It truly makes the Union more democratic. First, it greatly extends the powers of the European Parliament. The main rule is that the European Parliament will have co-decision-making powers when it comes to the adoption of laws and framework laws. These powers may be extended without amending the Constitutional Treaty. In addition, the European Parliament will be given a full say over the annual budget. The Constitutional Treaty will also introduce an early warning system. Every new law conceived by Brussels will be submitted to national parliaments. If one-third of them believe that the EU is exceeding its powers with the new law, the Commission must go back to the drawing board. This will give national members of parliament an active role in patrolling the external boundaries of Brussels' power.

The Treaty also provides for a citizens' initiative. One million signatures from different Member States are enough to ask the Commission to initiate a law. In doing so the Treaty goes further than what is customary in many Member States. And the Union shows that it is open to other forms of democracy.

Finally, the Constitutional Treaty takes pioneering steps in the area of the protection of fundamental rights. It includes the full text of the Charter of Fundamental Rights of the European Union. This means that the rights and principles enshrined in the Charter will become legally binding. The Treaty also extends the jurisdiction of the Court of Justice, giving citizens a greater opportunity to bring appeals.

The Union is the result of changes made in fits and starts, as you can see in the treaties on which it is based. The complex pillar structure that we currently have is a good example of this. The Constitutional Treaty creates order out of the chaos. It makes the Union more transparent.

Some of you may well remember that a unitary structure was the goal of the Dutch EU Presidency in the run-up to the Treaty of Maastricht. What was swept from the table on that black Monday, 30 September 1991, has proved to be acceptable to all Member States thirteen years down the line. The Constitutional Treaty draws a line under the maze of treaty law consisting of the EU Treaty, the EC Treaty and an endless series of treaties making amendments.

And the Constitution not only tidies up the treaties. It also sweeps away the difficult distinction between Union and Community, thereby stimulating the integration of policy. For example, the Constitutional Treaty facilitates the strategic use of funds that are currently all too often tied to the individual pillars. Do we want to control migration flows and do we need third countries to help us to do so? One possible approach could soon be to combine internal market concessions with foreign policy pressure. This would be difficult to organise under the current treaties.

The Union will also gain greater internal cohesion. Because of the pillar structure, the Commission has had a tendency to view the Union's policy mainly from the perspective of the EU Treaty, under which it has primacy. Under the unitary structure it will automatically broaden its perspective, taking in justice, home affairs and external issues.

The unitary structure will also sweep away the current jumble of legal instruments. Six will remain, namely laws, framework laws, regulations, decisions, recommendations and opinions. That is quite sufficient.

More democracy and a simpler structure will undeniably help make the Union more effective in increasing Europe's prosperity and security. But the Constitutional Treaty will also promote progress in other ways. People in the EU may have reservations about Brussels, but when asked they often favour a European approach that goes even further than what their governments advocate. A common foreign and security policy is a case in point. The Constitutional Treaty contains major innovations in precisely this area.

The most striking of these is the creation of the office of Union Minister for Foreign Affairs. This person will be a member of both the Commission and the Council. This brings to an end the current situation, in which responsibility for foreign policy is shared by Commissioner Chris Patten and the High Representative of the Council, Javier Solana. Of course, combining these two posts does not mean that Europe will suddenly have a common foreign policy. But in my view it is beyond doubt that this construction will encourage Europe to speak with one voice.

People also expect Europe to act decisively when it comes to combating the negative effects of the free movement of people, goods and services, because they feel these effects just as keenly as the positive ones. A side-effect of the lifting of internal borders has been an upsurge in cross-border crime. Added to this, since the attacks in Madrid, is the real danger of terrorism.

Moreover, the end of the Cold War has triggered mass migrations of people seeking a better life. For many, Europe is the destination. Some obtain permission to stay here. But many do not. The lack of a strong common policy often condemns them to an exhausting odyssey through Europe. A journey that is doomed to end in failure.

The Constitutional Treaty, far more so than the current treaties, enables us – through the Union – to tackle these shared problems together, for example, by making qualified-majority voting the norm. This cannot fail to make Europe more effective in this area.

When the European Convention met for the first time, plenty of comparisons were drawn with the Constitutional Convention that drafted the American Constitution in 1787. Was this a new Philadelphia? If you make the effort to compare the text of the Constitutional Treaty with that of the American Constitution, there can be only one conclusion: Philadelphia was unique. The European text entirely lacks the conciseness, elegance and eloquence of the work of Alexander Hamilton, Benjamin Franklin and James Madison. After more than two hundred years, the words 'We, the People of the United States' have lost none of their force. But it would be a mistake to conclude from this that our Convention has failed. The Constitutional Treaty is not an end in itself. It is a means to an end. Just like the American Constitution, it draws the contours of future cooperation. How they will be shaded remains to be seen. Yet it seems certain that the spectrum will be broader and the colours more vivid.

There is no reason why Europeans have to be downcast. A little more American optimism would be justified. Because, on at least one crucial point, the Constitutional Treaty crosses a line from which its American counterpart shrank back: the right to withdraw from the Union. The Constitutional Treaty explicitly grants such a right, while its absence is the essence of the American Constitution. Who is showing more courage here?

The right to withdraw firmly establishes the EU as a federal union, rather than a federal state. It emphasises that the people of Europe have come together of their own free will. And it ensures that they must continually reaffirm their ties with Europe. This is an unprecedented sign of confidence that marks the Constitutional Treaty as unique and places the people in its debt. Europe has come of age!

Clemenceau once said, 'In order to act, you must be somewhat insane. A reasonable man is satisfied with thinking.' If this is the case, I am all for a little insanity in Europe. We have done the thinking. Now is the time to act. The Constitutional Treaty gives us every opportunity to do so.

In December last year, we saw tens of thousands of Ukrainian protesters camping out for weeks on Independence Square, in a peaceful campaign for democracy. Like the Serbs and Georgians before them, they were inspired by the European Union. Their campaign for democracy was a struggle to become European. But within the European Union, the idea of being European does not generate a lot of excitement. People are expressing more and more uncertainty about the Union. Is Brussels not becoming too powerful? Has enlargement not gone too far? Is there not too much disagreement within the EU? And are the Member States really living up to their promises?

Some call this criticism unacceptable. They point out that when the allies liberated Europe sixty years ago, they found a beat-up, burnt-out, run-down continent. It is because European countries decided to work together closely, without sacrificing their identities, that Europe rose again. I do not argue with that. Europe has changed from an arena of warlike nations to a place where war is inconceivable. Cruel dictatorships have become reliable democracies. A continent that was on the verge of bankruptcy has become a beacon of prosperity.

However, our admiration for the role of the Union as a catalyst of peace, freedom and prosperity must never degenerate into blind adoration. That would be most un-European. Criticism is a sign of maturity. For decades, it has proved impossible to sell the European Union to the public with flyers, a flag, a holiday or an anthem. Real commitment begins with real choices.

At this moment the peoples of the EU are faced with a very real choice: will they accept the Constitutional Treaty, yes or no. The people of France will vote in their referendum on this question on 29 May. On 1 June, the Netherlands will hold its first national referendum in almost 200 years on the same topic. The Union is not perfect. Nor will the Constitutional Treaty suddenly make it perfect. But I am perfectly sure the Constitutional Treaty is a clear improvement on the current treaties. I hope the peoples of Europe will agree.

ATZO NICOLAÏ
*Minister for European Affairs of the Kingdom of the Netherlands*

The Hague, 20 May 2005

# ACKNOWLEDGEMENTS

The T.M.C. Asser Instituut gratefully acknowledges the generous support it received for the financing and the organization of the 34th Asser Colloquium on European Law entitled 'The EU Constitution: the best way forward?', held from 13 to 16 October 2004 at the Kurhaus Hotel in Scheveningen (The Hague), and the publication of this book, from:

Ministry of Foreign Affairs, The Hague

Ministry of Economic Affairs, The Hague

Ministry of Justice, The Hague

Ministry of the Interior and Kingdom Relations, The Hague

Municipality of The Hague

Levi Lassen Foundation, The Hague

Houthoff Buruma, Brussels/Amsterdam

Goethe-Institut, Amsterdam

Freshfields Bruckhaus Deringer, Amsterdam

Barents & Krans, The Hague

M.A.O.C. Gravin van Bylandt Stichting, The Hague

the colleagues at the Conference Department for the logistical support before, during and after the Colloquium took place

and

Nicolette van der Hoek (deskediting) and Peter Morris (linguistic revision) who worked with great zeal on the technical realization of this book.

# DETAILED TABLE OF CONTENTS

PART II
TRANSPARENCY AND LEGAL INSTRUMENTS IN THE EU CONSTITUTION

PART III
THE DEMOCRATIC LIFE OF THE EUROPEAN UNION

PART VI
THE IMPACT OF THE EU CONSTITUTION ON SELECTED MEMBER STATES
AND NEIGHBOURING COUNTRIES

## ANNEXES

### I.   Speeches

### II.   Reports of the Discussions

# LIST OF ABBREVIATIONS

| | |
|---|---|
| AG | Advocate General |
| AJDA | l'Actualité juridique du droit administratif |
| Art. | Article |
| Arts. | Articles |
| CCBE | Council of the Bar Associations and Law Societies of the EU |
| CCP | Common Commercial Policy |
| CDE | Cahiers de droit européen |
| CEES | Common European Economic Space |
| CEPOL | Collège européen de Police |
| CEPR | Centre for European Policy Research |
| CEPS | Centre for European Policy Studies |
| CFI | Court of First Instance |
| CFSP | Common Foreign and Security Policy |
| CIS | Commonwealth of Independent States |
| CML Rev. | Common Market Law Review |
| COM | European Commission Document |
| CONEM | EU Committee of National and Ethnic Minorities |
| Coreper | Committee of Permanent Representatives |
| DG | Directorate-General |
| DR | Decisions and Reports of the European Commission of Human Rights |
| EC | European Community |
| ECB | European Central Bank |
| ECHR | European Convention for the Protection of Human Rights and Fundamental Freedoms |
| ECJ | European Court of Justice |
| ECOFIN | The Council of Economics and Finance Ministers of the European Union |
| ECommHR | European Commission of Human Rights |
| Ecosoc | Economic and Social Committee |
| ECR | European Court Reports |
| ECSC | European Coal and Steel Community |
| ECtHR | European Court of Human Rights |
| EFSA | European Food Safety Authority |
| EHRR | European Human Rights Report |
| ELR | European Law Review |
| ELRev. | European Law Reports |
| EMU | Economic and Monetary Union |
| ENP | European Neighbourhood Policy |
| EP | European Parliament |
| EPC | European Policy Centre |
| EPP | European Public Prosecutor |
| EPP-DE Group | Group of the European Peoples' Party (Christian Democrats) and European Democrats |
| ESC | European Social Charter |
| ESDP | European Security and Defence Policy |
| EU | European Union |

| | |
|---|---|
| Eurojust | European Judicial Cooperation Unit |
| EWHC | High Court of England and Wales (Administrative Court) |
| FPÖ | Freiheitliche Partei Österreich |
| Hand. I/II | Verslag der Handelingen van de Eerste/Tweede Kamer der Staten-Generaal |
| HLG | High-level Group |
| HR | High Representative |
| ICCPR | International Covenant on Civil and Political Rights |
| ICER | Interdepartementale Commissie Europees Recht |
| ICLQ | International and Comparative Law Quarterly |
| ICTY | International Criminal Tribunal for the former Yugoslavia |
| IGC | Intergovernmental Conference |
| ILO | International Labour Organisation |
| JHA | Justice and Home Affairs |
| JTDE | Journal des Tribunaux - Droit europeén |
| MEP | Member of the European Parliament |
| MFF | Multi-annual Financial Framework |
| MFN | Most Favoured Nation Treatment |
| NATO | North Atlantic Treaty Organization |
| Nyr | Not yet reported |
| OJ | Official Journal of the European Union |
| Para. | Paragraph |
| Paras. | Paragraphs |
| PCA | Partnership and Cooperation Agreement |
| QM | Qualified Majority |
| QMV | Qualified Majority Voting |
| RF | Russian Federation |
| SAA | Stability and Association Agreement |
| SaM | Serbia and Montenegro |
| SEA | Single European Act |
| SEC | Commission Staff Working Paper |
| SEW | Tijdschrift voor Sociaal Economische Wetgeving |
| SitCen | Situation Center |
| SME | Small and Medium-sized Enterprises |
| TCE | Treaty establishing a Constitution for Europe (CIG 87/2/04 REV 2, signed on 29 October 2004, *OJ* (2004) C 310/1) |
| TEC | Treaty on the European Community |
| TEU | Treaty on the European Union |
| UK | United Kingdom |
| UKHL | United Kingdom House of Lords |
| UNESCO | United Nations Educational, Scientific and Cultural Organisation |
| VCLT | Vienna Convention on the Law of the Treaties |
| VVDStRL | Veröffentlichungen der Vereinigung der Deutschen Staatsrechtslehrer |
| WHO | World Health Organisation |
| WRR | Wetenschappelijke Raad voor het Regeringsbeleid |
| WTO | World Trade Organisation |

# INTRODUCTION

The process involved in conceiving, planning, organising and hosting the conference, quickly followed by the process of pursuing contributors for their final texts by specific deadlines, as well as editing and producing the text of this book has some analogy with the Convention on the Future of Europe which prepared the Draft Constitutional Treaty for the European Union. It has been a relatively lengthy process, involving much deliberation by all involved; some multi-tasking on the organizational side but hopefully the book which has emerged will have a long and vigorous shelf-life.

When this project was originally conceived in the relatively heady days of 2003 the Convention had drawn to a successful conclusion and an IGC was scheduled to start. Spirits were high and the prospect of failure seemed remote indeed. Even when the Asser Conference itself was held in October 2004 the ink was barely dry on the final text to emerge from the IGC, but the mood was constructive and fundamentally positive. It was an occasion to analyse the complex provisions of the Constitutional Treaty from various angles, but especially from the institutional angle in terms of the roles of various institutions and, from the democratic angle, in terms of progress overall and in terms of both more legitimate inputs and outputs. The contributions were of a high-level and the audience were appreciative of the complexities unravelled. We hope that the contents of this book and the manner in which it has been organised will do credit in particular to the mammoth efforts made by our various contributors. We are in any event very grateful to them for their steadfastness of purpose, the high level of their contributions and their reliability.

As this project draws to a close, the tide has turned. On 29 May 2005 the French electorate will effectively decide the fate of the Constitutional Treaty as it was signed in October 2004. Three days later the Dutch electorate will add their verdict. The prospects of a 'no' verdict are, it seems, greater than that of a 'yes' verdict. If that proves correct no doubt many post mortems will be carried out. One problem has certainly been the failure of the governments in various Member States to get across in a clear and concise fashion what this effort to draft a 'Constitution' for the European Union has been all about. Another is the fact that the debate has often focussed on issues other than the specific content of the Constitutional Treaty and there has been much scaremongering and misrepresentation concerning both the *status quo* and extraneous issues such as the nature of the economic system, further enlargement of the EU, etc.

Irrespective of the result in the short or medium term, it can be recognised that this Constitutional Treaty is an important stage in the process of European integration. It has made visible certain institutional facts that were hitherto invisible at the level of the formal Treaty text. Moreover, it has conceptualised and made operational more divisions of power in the European Union than was hitherto the case, especially with regard to the legislative power and procedure. It has made its contribution to making law-making and rule-making in the European Union more democratic, more accountable and more efficient in a not insignificant manner. It has formalised the position of the European Council, created a Minister for Foreign Affairs and given the EU a new 'president' alongside the Commission President.

In all these senses, therefore, it has structured issues of government within the European Union and focussed the discussion, both for now and the future, on how that power must be held accountable. The solutions chosen do not reflect a grand scenario, a once and for all rewriting of the existing constitutional system of the EU, but rather some small and some larger incremental steps on the basis of the existing fairly unique system. It confirms irrevocably that the European Union is not only a fully-fledged and sophisticated legal system; it has a counterpart in an emerging and as yet partial political system. The whole is certainly too complex and at times too fragmented; the whole is nonetheless more than the sum of its parts.

We firmly believe that the Constitutional Treaty as discussed in the various contributions in this book represents the best way forward at this moment in time. It is definitely to be preferred to muddling through on the basis of the *status quo*. Moreover, we are convinced that the manner in which the various contributors have approached their subjects and have managed to put their specific subject into context will mean that they will constitute useful reference points for further debate, in the unlikely event (we hope) that the Constitutional Treaty does not enter into force as originally agreed.

We would like to thank all the contributors both jointly and severally for their indomitable efforts to produce their final texts on time. Moreover, much credit for the book in your hands lies with the internal editing team in the Asser Institute itself and especially to Nicolette van der Hoek who has been remarkably steadfast and professional in her efforts to have this book published in a very timely fashion and to Peter Morris for his careful linguistic revision.

Deirdre Curtin                                                        Alfred E. Kellermann
                                                                      Steven Blockmans


Utrecht School of Governance,
University of Utrecht                                                  T.M.C. Asser Institute

Utrecht                                                               The Hague

24 May 2005

# PART I

## The Process and Impact of EU Constitution-making:
## Voice and Exit

# ON THE POWER OF THE WORD: EUROPE'S CONSTITUTIONAL ICONOGRAPHY

**Joseph H.H. Weiler**[*]

Ladies and Gentlemen: I am honored to give this keynote lecture at the opening of the Asser Institute Conference on the European Constitution.

Now that the Constitutional Treaty has been finalized we have been told by our gracious host in his welcoming remarks, we must all turn to the job of convincing our fellow European citizens to ratify it.

With respect, that is absolutely not what this conference is or should be about. Individually, we will each have our views about the EU Constitution and about the role we would like to take in the ratification debate. But in the fine intellectual tradition of the Asser Institute, we are here to offer contrasting views, from different perspectives and with different normative inclinations on the Constitutional Treaty. We are, collectively, neither the *Bureau de Recherche* of the European Union, nor an extension of its Spokesman's Office.

## 1.     PREMISE

At the core of these remarks is a simple proposition: the defining feature of Europe's new Constitutional Treaty is a word, an appellation. It is not the content of the Treaty Establishing a Constitution for Europe (TCE) which gives it epochal significance but the (mere) fact that an altogether run-of-the-mill Treaty amendment has been given the grand name: Constitution.

The significance of this word is not monolithic. To capture the differing and often contradictory shades, the reader will have to keep several balls in the air at the same time. The word has had, and will continue to have, enormous political impact (ball one) on the process of adopting the Constitution (ball two) and on its subsequent life (ball three). Whether the impact is positive or negative depends, of course, on the set of values of the observer. Whatever those values, the impact will be shown to be both positive (ball four) and negative (ball five). It is

---

[*] University Professor and Jean Monnet Chair, Director of the Global Law School Program, NYU School of Law.

*D. Curtin, A.E. Kellermann and S. Blockmans, eds., The EU Constitution: The Best Way Forward?*
© *2005, T.M.C. Asser Instituut, The Hague.*

not only a political impact which the word imparts. It will become a tool for understanding some of the core conceptual implications (ball six) which Europe's particular constitutional choice implies.

As is my habit, I prefer in this type of essay to keep a narrative style rather than structure systematically the categories represented by the various balls. But the reader may wish to keep them in mind as, at least, the authorial intended interpretative key.


## 2.      A TREATY MASQUERADING AS A CONSTITUTION – PROCESS

This is what a semi-official narrative of the current constitutional circumstance in the history of European integration might read like:

> For decades the Community (as it was once known) and then the Union (as it later became) were powered by a Treaty-based system. Designed in the 1950s this system had many avant-garde features which served it well in its early 'economic' phase when it comprised six Member States. But as the Union grew from six to nine, to ten, to twelve and then to fifteen the original Model T(reaty) became increasingly creaky. Despite several facelifts, notably the Single European Act of 1986 and the Treaty of Maastricht of 1992, it was still the original power-train of Commission-Council-Parliament and the same supranational technology which sat under a body which had more than doubled from its original population size, almost tripled its original number of Member States and had vastly grown in political ambition in a post Cold War world. The pending Enlargement – by the accession of another ten Member State – would, it was widely believed, strain the extant operating system to implosion.
>
> The 1990s saw two last ditch attempts to adapt the system before Enlargement by the tried old and old tired Treaty Amendment process undertaken in two successive intergovernmental conferences (IGCs). The urgent rhetoric surrounding the very modest Treaty of Amsterdam became almost hysterical by the time the Treaty of Nice was negotiated. This would be the very last chance to put the European institutional and constitutional house in order before the expansion to twenty-five Member States. Nice, by most accounts, was a failure. The institutional architecture remained largely intact with some adjustments to the weighted voting power of the various Member States in the Council of Ministers – driven more by political grandstanding than by functional considerations of effective, accountable and transparent decision making in a Union of Twenty-Five Member States and over four hundred million citizens.
>
> In the wake of this failure a different approach was called for: no longer an IGC but instead a Convention with a broad based composition and a more transparent process. No longer a Treaty, but a Constitution. And this is where we stand now: a Treaty Establishing a Constitution for Europe – referred to by all but the most punctilious of lawyers as The Constitution – signed and sealed and awaiting ratification by the twenty-five Member States of the Union. A veritable 'constitutional moment'.

Even the most innocent of readers will now be suppressing a yawn, having guessed that this narrative has been set up in order to be knocked down. In academia, as elsewhere, some childhood games never lose their fascination.

Let us engage, then, in the following mental exercise: imagine the Document, as presented for ratification in the twenty-five Member States of the European Union, with the word 'Constitution' excised from all the places in which it appears. What is it we will find?

It does not look like a constitution: in its English version it weighs in at 66,497 words, which grow to 154,183 if the various annexes and declarations which, from a legal point of view are integral to the document, are added. For comparison sake, the American Constitution is 5,800 words long and the Charter of the United Nations 8,890. The actual weight of the official two-tome printed version is just under one kilogram.

It does not read like a constitution: constitutional opening phrases are typically of a magisterial style and make reference to the ultimate constitutional authority undergriding the document – the People. Thus, e.g.:

'We the people of the United States, in order to form a more perfect union (…).'

'Le peuple français proclame solennellement son attachement aux Droits de l'homme et aux principes de la souveraineté nationale tels qu'ils ont été définis par la Déclaration de 1789 (…).'

'Im Bewußtsein seiner Verantwortung vor Gott und den Menschen, von dem Willen beseelt, als gleichberechtigtes Glied in einem vereinten Europa dem Frieden der Welt zu dienen, hat sich das Deutsche Volk kraft seiner verfassungsgebenden Gewalt dieses Grundgesetz gegeben (…).'

The opening phrase of the Document now before Europe's peoples is equally revealing. It is the very same used since the very first treaty establishing the European Coal and Steel Community in 1951:

'His Majesty the King of the Belgians (…)!'

This is followed by the long list of Heads of State.

'The President of the Czech Republic [etc. who](…) Have designated as their plenipotentiaries (…) Guy Verhofstadt Prime Minister[,] Karel de Gucht Minister for Foreign Affairs [etc.](…). Who, having exchanged their full powers, found in good and due form, have agreed as follows (…).'

The non-initiated reader would be forgiven if he believed that he was reading the standard opening of an international treaty. He would be forgiven if the same opinion were formed by going to the conclusion of the Document. He will first find this:

'This Treaty shall be ratified by the High Contracting Parties in accordance with their respective constitutional requirements. The instruments of ratification shall be deposited with the Government of the Italian Republic.'

Followed by:

> 'IN WITNESS WHEREOF, the undersigned plenipotentiaries have signed this Treaty (...).'

*'Res Ipsa Loquitur!'*

What of the content of the document, its substance? It is for the most part, including the integration of the Charter of Fundamental Rights, the kind of content which one had hoped to see in the Treaty of Amsterdam and certainly in the Treaty of Nice in the countdown to Enlargement: A sensible though far from radical amendment of the Institutional architecture and decision-making processes of the Union; some meaningful but equally non-radical nods towards the further democratization of the above; the Charter (more about which below) and some sensible cleaning up of language. The Treaty revision procedures have been interestingly amended to provide a multi-tier process: Convention and Intergovernmental Process; Intergovernmental Process without Convention; decision of the European Council alone. But, significantly, from a constitutional point of view, all three processes are, in conventional thinking, not typical of constitutions but rather of Treaties. They all require unanimity among the Governments of the High Contracting Parties and ratification by national procedures in all Member States.

If you omit, then, the lexical addition to this document of the word 'constitution' you will find in front of you a post-Enlargement Treaty of Nice *bis*. Put differently, if the Nice IGC had come up with the identical material content of the EU Constitution, it would have been welcomed as a sensible adaptation of the Treaties establishing the European Union to Enlargement. No one would have used any superlatives to describe its content, it would have attracted very limited public attention or debate in most Member States, it would certainly not have generated the numerous referenda which are now planned in the Union, and there would have been no talk of the need for a Constitution (except, perhaps, among the European federalist fringe). No Convention, no European Philadelphia, no Constitutionspeak. At best, a good old treaty masquerading as a constitution.

Here is yet another way of making the 'what's all the fuss' point. For decades it has been common ground, that despite its formal treaty format, the structural architecture of the Communities and subsequent Union were better explained with a constitutional vocabulary than with an international law one. In the critical area (for lawyers, both constitutional and international) of the relationship between European law and Member State law, the Union has become, in this view, indistinguishable from a federal state, whereby the doctrines of direct effect and its derivatives, supremacy, and implied powers assure to the law of the Union the position enjoyed by federal law within a State – and not the position suffered by international law *vis-à-vis* a State. In a nutshell, long before Maastricht, Amsterdam and Nice, let alone the more recent Convention and ensuing 'Constitution' with its explicit Supremacy Clause, the law of the Union was the supreme law of the land within all Member States, invokable by individuals and accepted as such by Member State courts. The decisional and institutional architecture, one could further argue, had also become increasingly 'constitutional' in the growing prevalence of binding majority voting in the Council and the gradual empowerment of the European Parliament to the position of co-legislator with that Council. On this reading, all that the current 'Constitution' does it to codify the constitutional *status quo* and to formalize the hybrid extant arrangement of a Treaty with constitutional features. What's all the fuss?

3.    THE VICISSITUDES OF THE WORD IN THE ADOPTION PROCESS

The appropriate question might in fact be: 'Why all the fuss?' To this there is at least one answer which seems incontrovertible. The constitutional fuss was, it would appear, simply necessary for the Union to do what it was otherwise unable to do, namely to adapt its constituent treaties to the reality of Enlargement. Even if the current text is no more than Nice *bis*, the fact is that a Nice *bis* was necessary since Nice itself failed to deliver the goodies. And the only way to get there was to change the rules about change. No longer an IGC which failed to deliver both in Amsterdam and Nice, but the different constituted Convention which morphed into a hybrid IGC but which was, by 'consensus,' able to arrive at a text which the classical IGC might never have achieved. The text might be modest, but it is, its supporters argue with cogency, a lot better than nothing at all. It was not simply the composition of the Convention, the genius of the personalities which led it and its different decisional rules which account for the result. It was also its mission – drafting a Constitution – which explain a different internal dynamic, a sense of historical moment and a consequent grim determination to reach a result. The Members of the Convention, including the Foreign Ministers and the other powerbrokers who jumped in once it became apparent that this process was going to deliver something that the previous IGCs had failed to do and that once a text emerged it would be difficult to change it radically, believed, or had to make believe that they were not simply redrafting Nice but doing something far more transcendent. On this reading the Treaty had to masquerade as a constitution for the result to be achieved. Transcendence and 'make believe' can only explain so much. After all, with all the hype, the draft Constitution adopted by the Convention and submitted to the Heads of State and Government (un)ceremoniously failed to be approved in December 2003. It was the reality of Enlargement, it actually happened in May 2004, which forced the subsequent summit of Heads of State and Government in June 2004 to bite the bullet by accepting a materially somewhat watered down version of the institutional package that came out of the Convention. At the same time, in a mask-stripping exercise redolent with symbolism, the Intergovernmental Summit decided to excise from the text some of its most pompous constitutional majesty found in the text submitted by the Convention and to situate the presumed constitutional document firmly between the international law prologue of 'His

Majesty the King of the Belgians' and the epilogue of 'the Undersigned Plenipotentiaries'.

4.    IF ANY OF YOU KNOW CAUSE, OR JUST IMPEDIMENT, WHY
      THESE TWO PERSONS SHOULD NOT BE JOINED TOGETHER IN
      HOLY MATRIMONY, YE ARE TO DECLARE IT. THIS IS THE FIRST
      TIME OF ASKING...

It may be that a constitutional fuss was an indispensable element in arriving at an
indispensable text. It might be that it will also be the undoing of such a text. In
these fallen times one is reminded of a couple which have cohabited for years,
have begat a child or two, and now, with an enlarged family, have taken it into
their mind to solemnize their union by a very public and traditional wedding.
Why all the fuss, one might wonder staring at the invitation. Is it wise to put up
for solemn approval the banns of marriage and the vows of union one had already consecrated through the practice of living together? And what if someone
steps forward and asserts Cause or Impediment, just or otherwise?
    As argued above, the material content of the document now awaiting ratifica-
tion cannot explain the constitutional hoopla now in play. The decision to submit
the text to referenda in so many Member States is almost entirely a consequence
of the very same 'historical moment' which I have used to explain the dynamic
of the Convention rather than true constitutional exigency and so is the growing
popular call that such a process be followed in other Member States. A clear passage is likely in those States where ratification of the TCE will be in the hands of
governments which normally command a parliamentary majority. But as the
number of referenda grows, the chances of rejection in one or more Member
States is clear. And the reason for rejection would not, it is respectfully submitted, be linked to any specific provision of the new Constitutional Treaty, nor
even to its overall material content, but, I am arguing, such rejection may be associated with extraneous issues rooted in national politics, to a general 'anti-Eu-
rope' sentiment and most intriguingly not to the content of the new Treaty of
Rome, but to its very idea – that of a European Constitution. Thus the very same
symbolism which explained why the type of non-radical content was rejected by
the Amsterdam and Nice Intergovernmental Conferences but was able to gain
consensus within the Convention, might in an ironic constitutional twist, explain
eventual rejection by the peoples of Europe.
    Imagine a scenario whereby the EU Constitution is rejected by one or more
Member States. Could a rejection by, say, Malta and Estonia bring the constitutional edifice down? The legal rules of the game are clear enough. The extant
Treaties require unanimity for any amendment. The new Treaty requires unanimous ratification. Various legal constructs have been advanced as to how the
unanimity requirement for the modification of the extant Treaties may be by-
passed. On its own terms, the TCE does not, formally, constitute an amendment
of the current Treaty but its repeal.

'This Treaty establishing a Constitution for Europe shall repeal the Treaty establishing the European Community, the Treaty on European Union and, under the conditions laid down in the Protocol on the acts and treaties having supplemented or amended the Treaty establishing the European Community and the Treaty on European Union, the acts and treaties which have supplemented or amended them, subject to paragraph 2 of this Article.' (Art. IV-437(1) TCE).

And the new Union is conceptualized as just that, a new Union:

'The European Union established by this Treaty shall be the successor to the European Union established by the Treaty on European Union and to the European Community.' (Art. IV-438(1) TCE).

Thus, in the face of one or two recalcitrant Member States blocking the progress to the brave new constitutional order, one can imagine a construct whereby all 'forward looking' Member States withdraw from the old Union, leaving the laggards behind and then join this new Union. There are many variants to this reasoning, but none are particularly promising from a legal point of view. It is, to begin with, a construct which begs the question whether unilateral withdrawal is possible under the old Treaties by contrast with the new Treaty which has a specific clause regulating such unilateral withdrawal. It is an argument which runs up against the express unanimity requirement of the new Constitutional Treaty ex Article IV-447(1) TCE. It is also difficult to ground a legal theory which would require unanimity for small amendments to the current Treaties but which would dispense with that unanimity if the amendments were radical or simply deemed to be radical. It is, finally, a construct which would undermine constitutional confidence in the new Treaty which, itself, provides for unanimous amendment and, at most, provides the famous and enigmatic *passerelle*.

'If, two years after the signature of the treaty amending this Treaty, four fifths of the Member States have ratified it and one or more Member States have encountered difficulties in proceeding with ratification, the matter shall be referred to the European Council.' (Art. IV-443(4) TCE).

This construct would require us to accept that a new Constitution which provides in relation to its own amendment by way of Treaty which then fails to be ratified by a fifth of its Members for a mere reference to the European Council could come itself into being without unanimity.

Difficult as the unanimity avoidance legal argument might be, it will continue to lurk in legal drawers. Because the political rules of the game are almost as clear as the legal ones: all Member States are equal, but some are more equal than others. A rejection by Great Britain alone will, when all is said and done, amount to an act of British self-exclusion. A rejection by France alone, and the Constitution will have to be renegotiated. A rejection by Great Britain, Ireland and Denmark, would not thwart the Constitution. Add one or two 'Old Faithfuls' to the rejection front, and the Constitution sinks. Imagine a rejection by Poland alone and the Constitution lives. Add the Netherlands, and it dies. There is a powerful pedigree to this kind of political maneuvering: the American Articles of Confederation required unanimity to be amended. And yet not all thirteen colonies immediately ratified the new Constitution of the United States; a fact which did not prevent it from coming into force even in the face of abject illegality from the confederal perspective. It would seem that Original Sin is provoked not only by the drive of flesh and blood (especially flesh) towards carnal Union.

In the light of the above one might be tempted to draw the conclusion that if, indeed, the continued constitutional *talking up* of a document which in form is no more than a treaty masquerading as a constitution and which in substance does no more than codify the *status quo* will have contributed to its rejection, then Europe will have made a major blunder since not only will the constitution have failed, but the constitutional *status quo* would have been put in jeopardy.

This conclusion would, in my view, be short-sighted in terms of its own premises. Imagine each and every Member State deciding to hold a referendum increasing almost exponentially the risk of rejection. In fact, this will be a win-win-win situation for those who favor a constitutionalized Europe. There are three possible scenarios:

–   Scenario 1: a small and non-critical number of Member States reject the EU Constitution. Diplomacy and negotiation will most likely result in some cosmetic concessions followed by ratification in a second referendum. If rejection persists, Europe will not need to go to its legal drawer. It is almost certain that negotiation will lead to some form of special status to the non-ratifying Member State but that the rest will go ahead with the constitutional project. Although the *de jure* forms of unanimous ratification will have been respected, the all too clear message will have been that in a constitutionalized Europe there is some form of *de facto* constitutional majority convention. One will have achieved through praxis that which was impossible formally.

–   Scenario 2: the number and composition of the rejection front is such that the project is defeated. Pragmatically, the world will not have come to an end. After all, since May 2004 and for a considerable time yet to come, Europe is functioning under the Nice rules without major difficulty, let alone implosion. An interesting dynamic is in place which one observes from other organizations. Knowledge of the inadequate rules responsibilizes the players. Symbolically such rejection will be a huge victory for European democracy. For the project of elites to be rejected every now and again by popular will, can be a salutary experience. It will also constitute a lesson in one of the little understood disciplines of democracy, the need when qualified majority rules apply, as is almost always the case with constitutional amendment, for the majority to accept the need to convince a minority and not to ride over it roughshod.

–   Scenario 3: the Constitution secures ratification by referenda in all Member States. This would constitute yet another double ironic vicissitude in this complex constitutional saga. We noted above how the Member States encased the constitution within a frame which began with 'His Majesty the King of the Belgians' and concluded with the 'High Contracting Powers and their Plenipotentiaries'. We contrasted that with typical constitutional language which valorized '*le peuple français*' or '*das Deutsche Volk*' or 'we the people of the United States'. And yet, under this Scenario, 'the people' would, in the first ironic vicissitude, have had the last laugh, since a European instrument ratified constitutionally by referendum in all, or even a majority of Member States, will have the kind of democratic constitutional legitimacy which runs contrary to the spirit encapsulated by the international legal framing. Formally, this will be no more than a Treaty ratified in accordance with internal procedures of each Member State. But, which international treaty in Europe can claim to have been ratified by popular referendum in more than half the Member States? One does not have to be a card-carrying Legal Realist to understand the impact that this fact will have on the ensuing constitutional conversation including constitutional adjudication. The process will have become, willy-nilly, a constitutional process of ratification, and the peoples of Europe would have spoken at least in some sense as a *pouvoir constituant*. The second and final ironic vicissitude is that this elevated legitimacy and *de facto* constitutional status will have been given to an instrument the form and content of which hardly merits such constitutional resplendence.

## 5.   A CONSTITUTION MASQUERADING AS A TREATY – SUBSTANCE

I have argued above that merely the name of the document – 'constitution' – rather than its content has resulted in a level of public debate and political discourse, notably referenda, which define the process as never before in the course of European integration.

The same may be said of the life of the document should it come into force. The attempt to shackle the constitution within traditional treaty garb will, I predict, ultimately be defeated by popular and ubiquitous usage. At one level my point is simple enough. It is about the suggestive power of comparative lexical assimilation. The word 'constitution' has, of course, far from one political significance. As was pointed out facetiously in Great Britain, when the government was trying, for political reasons, to make light of its sudden support for the Constitutional project, every bowling club has a Constitution. No kidding. In the context in which the European discourse takes place, the word 'constitution' comes with a well determined set of associations derived from the context of national constitutionalism. When political actors of all walks of life think (if they do) or discuss, or form psychological reactions towards the EU Constitution, it is not a bowling club they have as their principle reference, but their own State constitution. Indeed, one of the reasons the constitutional debate in Great Britain is so fraught, lies in the fact that the very talk about a Constitution seems threatening to many in a national context which is often hostile to the very idea of a (formal) constitution.

If the varying interpretative communities – courts and jurists, politicians, administrators, most critically the media and through them the general public – will, as is certain to be the case, refer and think and henceforth relate to Europe through a constitutional lens, and inevitably that will shape the reality of the Constitutional understanding. I am not interested in predicting with precision the ensuing shape of that reality. Constitution and constitutionalism are understood in very different ways in different polities throughout Europe. There can be a messy cocktail. But one can predict without precision, that in this cocktail there will be many more flavors imparted by the statal context in which constitutionalism is normally understood. I can illustrate this by a proposition I made above. Simply calling it a Constitution will make it more difficult in, say, the case of a rejection by an individual Member State to enlist sympathy for such intransigence in the face of Europe's 'constitutional' will. Likewise, from time to time in the last half century their have been eruptions in Member States when faced with the reality of the already well established doctrine of supremacy and the need to bring national law, at times even of a constitutional nature, into compliance with Community or Union law. Again, simply calling the overriding canopy a 'constitution' is going to reshape and condition differently that debate.

In this part of the essay I wish, however, to turn the focus away from the political impact of the word and to concentrate instead on the conceptual significance. I want to relate the current constitutional circumstance of Europe to two theoretical propositions.

## 6.     'CONSTITUTIONAL TREATY', KELSEN AND SCHMITT AND THE PHENOMENON OF 'GLOBAL LAW'

I want to turn now to a different term – not Constitution, but Constitutional Treaty. Conceptually, the current circumstance of the European constitutional arrangement must be understood against a European constitutional discourse which for years has been dominated by a strange combination of Kelsen and Schmitt. It has been Kelsenian in its attempts, under many guises, to describe, define and understand the European *Grundnorm* – the source whence the authority of European constitutional disciplines derives. The search for this Kelsenian holy grail, whether or not acknowledged explicitly, underscores the great bulk of the academic literature theorizing European constitutionalism. And this Holy Grail has been, typically, understood in Schmittian terms: the search is for the *ultimate* source of authority, the one that counts in the case of extremity, of conflict. That is the true criteria of the real *Grundnorm*.

Early 'Europeanists' liked to argue that the *Grundnorm*, typically expressed in, say, the principle of the supremacy of European law over national law in case of conflict, had shifted to the 'central' or 'general' power: that is, to Europe. That view is less in fashion today and is contested by those who point out that, both in fact and in law, ultimate authority still rests in national constitutional orders which sanction supremacy, define its parameters, and typically place limitations on it.

According to this latter view, the statal *Grundnorm* would shift only if one were to take the existing constitutional precepts and enshrine them in a formal constitution adopted by a European 'constitutional *demos*' – the peoples of Europe acting on that occasion as one people – so that constitutional authority would in fact and in law shift to Europe. For the most part, both for friends and foes of European constitutionalism the debate is conducted on this Kelseno-Schmittian turf.

The debate Treaty-Constitution is a perfect example of this turf. What are typically suggested as the hallmarks of internationalism (treaty) rather than constitutionalism? The Amendment procedure, for example, which, much to the chagrin of many 'constitutionalists' in the Convention, was not amended into majoritarian constitutional mode and was retained in its pristine unanimous international treaty mode. It is a Treaty if ultimately the Member States and the Governments are the Masters of its content. This is a perfect example of a Schmittian exceptionalism type of thinking.

From this perspective, to say that the European Constitution is 'both' or 'hybrid' or words to that effect, is meaningless, because for the Schmittian construct that kind of hybridity is taken for granted and is the source of the question of what is the 'real' and 'essential' characteristic of the constitutional phenomenon in question. Exceptionalism, the exercise of power and the power to exercise in the exceptional moment is meant to define the true essence.

However, it is hybrid and that is its essence. The fact that in its quotidian constitutional existence Europe is constitutional and accepted as such, is in part explicable because of the ever more ephemeral safety net given by the exceptional constitutional moment when it 'reverts' to the international. At the deepest level the question is why should one privilege the exceptional moment as defining rather than the quotidian? What defines the essence of marriage – the exceptional possibility or impossibility of divorce or the reality of a life lived together? The two are not disconnected. The possibility or impossibility of divorce may have a (receding) impact on the quotidian reality of life lived together, but it is still that reality of the life lived together which does not only characterize a specific relation, but also is integral to understanding the institution itself. This is all the more so, as the exceptional power and power in the exceptional moment becomes more and more a theoretical prospect rather than a meaningful and realistic option. In the European landscape this hybridity is captured perfectly when we try to disentangle the significance of, say, Article I-60(1) TCE which provides as follows: 'any Member State may decide to withdraw from the Union in accordance with its own constitutional requirements' and the enmeshed reality of Union Membership.

I would like to take this point one step further. European hybridity, encapsulated in the term Constitutional Treaty is not, if I may spin a pun, a sign of European exceptionalism. It is, in my view, simply a very transparent example of a ubiquitous condition which one may call Global Law. This is not about universal international norms which prevail globally. It is about a condition in which legal normativity in an increasing number of fields, across most States, can only be explained by reference to a mélange of domestic (constitutional) and international sources. Moreover, the comforting Schmittian notion which locates sovereignty in the State, the constitutional law of which will determine the insertion of the international normativity, is losing its persuasive power not only in the highly formalized European context but more generally as the contexts of Global Constitutionalism spreads.

## 7.    THE FATE OF CONSTITUTIONAL TOLERANCE

The reason the question of *ultimate* authority and constitutional *Grundnorm* seems so important is that we consider the integrity of our *national* constitutional orders not simply as a matter of legal obedience and political power but of moral commitment and identity. Our national constitutions are perceived by us as doing more than simply structuring the respective powers of government and the relationships between public authority and individuals or between the state and other agents. Our constitutions are said to encapsulate fundamental values of the polity and this, in turn, is said to be a reflection of our collective identity as a people, as a nation, as a state, as a Community, as a Union. When we are proud and attached to our constitutions, we are so for these very reasons. They are about restricting power, not enlarging it; they protect fundamental rights of the individual; and they define a collective identity which does not make us feel queasy the way some forms of ethnic identity might. Thus, in the endless and tiresome debates about the European Union constitutional order, national courts have become in the last decade far more aggressive in their constitutional self-understanding. The case law is well known. National courts are no longer at the vanguard of the 'new European legal order', bringing the rule of law to transnational relations, and empowering, through EC law, individuals *vis-à-vis* Member State authority. Instead they stand at the gate and defend national constitutions against illicit encroachment from Brussels. They have received a sympathetic hearing, since they are perceived as protecting fundamental human rights as well as protecting national identity. To protect national sovereignty is *passé*; to protect national identity by insisting on constitutional specificity is *à la mode*.

Thus, on this new reading, to submit to the constitutional disciplines of Europe without a proper Kelsenian constitution, which formally vests in Europe Schmittian ultimate authority, is something that not only contradicts an orderly understanding of legal hierarchy, but also compromises deep values enshrined in the national constitution as well as a collective identity which is tied up with these values. Indeed, it is to challenge the idea of a constitution itself.

Miguel Maduro, one of the most brilliant of the new generation of European constitutional thinkers, gives eloquent expression to this concern:

'European integration not only challenges national constitutions (...) it challenges constitutional law itself. It assumes a constitution without a traditional political com-

munity defined and proposed by that constitution (...) European integration also challenges the legal monopoly of States and the hierarchical organisation of the law (in
which constitutional law is still conceived of as the 'higher law').'[1]

Is this challenge so threatening? In part it is. Modern liberal constitutions are, indeed, about limiting the power of government *vis-à-vis* the individual; they, too,
articulate fundamental human rights in the best neo-Kantian tradition; and they
reflect a notion of collective identity as a community of values which is far less
threatening than more organic definitions of collective identity. They are a reflection of our better part.

But, like the moon, like much which is good in life, there is here a dark side
too. It is, first, worth listening carefully to the rhetoric of the constitutional discourse. Even when voiced by the greatest humanists, the military overtones are
present. We have been invited to develop a *patriotism* around our modern, liberal, constitutions. The constitutional patriot is invited to *defend* the constitution.
In some states we have agencies designed to protect the constitution whose very
name is similar to our border defences. In other countries, we are invited to
*swear allegiance* to the constitution. In a constitutional democracy we have a
doctrine of a *fighting* democracy, whereby democratic hospitality is not extended
to those who would destroy constitutional democracy itself. To be a good constitutional liberal, it would seem from this idiom, is to be a constitutional national-
ist and, it turns out, the constitutional stakes are not only about values and limitations of power but also about its opposite: the power which lurks underneath
such values.

Very few constitutionalists and practically no modern constitutional court
will make an *overt* appeal to natural law. Thus, unlike the 'constitution' in the
parable, the formal normative authority of the constitutions around which our patriotism must form and which we must defend is, from a legal point of view,
mostly positivist. This means that it is as deep or shallow as the last constitutional amendment: in some countries, like Switzerland or Germany, not a particularly onerous political process. Consequently, vesting so much in the constitutional
integrity of the Member State is an astonishing feat of self-celebration and self-
aggrandizement, of bestowing on ourselves, in our capacity of constituent power,
a breathtaking normative authority. Just think of the near sacred nature we give
today to the constitutions adopted by the morally corrupted societies of the
World War II generation in, say, Italy and Germany and elsewhere.

---

[1] M. Maduro, *We the Court: the European Court of Justice and the European Economic
Constitution* (Oxford, Hart Publishing 1998) at p. 175. Maduro himself does not advocate a European
Constitution. I cite him simply for his striking diagnosis of the issue. It is superior to my own
clumsy attempt to formulate the dilemma as a 'Constitution without Constitutionalism', as 'do-
ing before hearkening'; J. Weiler, '"We Will Do, and Hearken" – Reflections on a Common
Constitutional Law for the European Union', in R. Bieber and P. Widmer, eds., *The European
Constitutional Area* (Zurich, Schulthess 1995).

A similar doubt should dampen somewhat any enthusiasm towards the new constitutional posture of national courts which hold themselves out as defending the core constitutional values of their polity, indeed its very identity. The limitation of power imposed on the political branches of government is, as has been widely noticed, accompanied by a huge dose of judicial self-empowerment and no small measure of sanctimonious moralizing. Human rights often provoke the most strident rhetoric. Yet constitutional texts in our different polities, especially when it comes to human rights, are remarkably similar. Defending the constitutional identity of the state and its core values turns out in many cases to be a defence of some hermeneutic foible adopted by five judges voting against four.

Finally, there is also in an exquisite irony in a constitutional ethos which, while appropriately suspicious of older notions of organic and ethnic identity, at the very same time implicitly celebrates a supposed unique moral identity, wisdom, and, yes, superiority, of the authors of the constitution, the people, the constitutional *demos*, when it wears the hat of the constituent power and, naturally, of those who interpret it.

It was Samuel Johnson who suggested that patriotism was the last refuge of a scoundrel. Dr. Johnson was, of course, only partly right. Patriotism can also be noble. But it is an aphorism worth remembering when we celebrate constitutional patriotism, national or transnational, and rush to its defence from any challenges to it. How, then, do we both respect and uphold all that is good in our constitutional tradition and yet, at the same time, keep it and ourselves under sceptical check?

The European constitution now before us does not introduce constitutionalism to the European construct. It is in fact a different form of European constitution from the constitutional architecture we already have. It might come with an intangible loss. The current constitutional architecture, which of course can be improved in many of its specifics, encapsulates one of Europe's most important constitutional innovations, the Principle of Constitutional Tolerance.

European integration has been, historically, one of the principal means with which to consolidate democracy within and among several of the Member States, both old and new, with less than perfect historical democratic credentials. For many, thus, democracy is the objective, the end, of the European construct. This is fallacious. Democracy is not the end. Democracy, too, is a means, even if an indispensable means. The end is to try, and try again, to live a life of decency, to honour our creation in the image of God, or the secular equivalent. A democracy, when all is said and done, is as good or bad as the people who belong to it. The problem of Haider's Austria is not an absence of democracy. The problem is that Austria is a democracy; that Haider *was elected democratically*, and that even the people who did not vote for him are content to see him and his party share in government. A democracy of vile persons will be vile.

Europe was built on the ashes of World War II, which witnessed the most horrific alienation of those thought of as aliens, an alienation which became annihilation. What we should be thinking about is not simply the prevention of another such carnage: that is the easy part and it is unlikely ever to happen again in Western Europe, though events in the Balkans remind us that those demons are still within the continent. More difficult is dealing at a deeper level with the source of these attitudes. In the realm of the social, in the public square, the relationship to the alien is at the core of such decency. It is difficult to imagine something normatively more important to the human condition and to our multicultural societies.

There are, it seems to me, two basic human strategies of dealing with the alien and these two strategies have played a decisive role in Western civilisation. One strategy is to remove the boundaries. It is the spirit of 'come, be one of us'. It is noble since it involves, of course, the elimination of prejudice, of the notion that there are boundaries that cannot be eradicated. But the 'be one of us', however well intentioned, is often an invitation to the alien to be one of us, by being us. *Vis-à-vis* the alien, it risks robbing him of his identity. *Vis-à-vis* oneself, it may be a subtle manifestation of both arrogance and belief in my superiority as well as intolerance. If I cannot tolerate the alien, one way of resolving the dilemma is to make him like me, no longer an alien. This is, of course, infinitely better than the opposite: exclusion, repression, and worse. But it is still a form of dangerous internal and external intolerance.

The alternative strategy of dealing with the alien is to acknowledge the validity of certain forms of non-ethnic bounded identity but simultaneously to reach across boundaries. We acknowledge and respect difference, and what is special and unique about ourselves as individuals and groups; and yet we reach across differences in recognition of our essential humanity. What is significant in this are the two elements I have mentioned. On the one hand, the identity of the alien, as such, is maintained. One is not invited to go out and, say, 'save him' by inviting him to be one of you. One is not invited to recast the boundary. On the other hand, despite the boundaries which are maintained, and constitute the I and the Alien, one is commanded to reach over the boundary and accept him, in his alienship, as oneself. The alien is accorded human dignity. The soul of the I is tended to not by eliminating the temptation to oppress but by learning humility and overcoming it.

The European current constitutional architecture represents this alternative, civilizing strategy of dealing with the 'other'. Constitutional Tolerance is encapsulated in that most basic articulation of its meta-political objective in the preamble to the EC Treaty: 'Determined to lay the foundations of an ever closer union among the peoples of Europe.' No matter how close the Union, it is to remain a union among distinct peoples, distinct political identities, distinct political communities. An ever closer union could be achieved by an amalgam of distinct peoples into one which is both the ideal and/or the *de facto* experience of most federal and non-federal states. The rejection by Europe of that One Nation ideal or destiny is, as indicated above, usually understood as intended to preserve the rich diversity, cultural and other, of the distinct European peoples as well as to respect their political self-determination. But the European choice has an even deeper spiritual meaning.

An ever closer union is altogether easier if differences among the components are eliminated, if they come to resemble each other, if they aspire to become one. The more identical the 'Other's' identity is to my own, the easier it is for me to identify with him and accept him. It demands less of me to accept another if he is very much like me. It is altogether more difficult to attain an ever closer Union if the components of that Union preserve their distinct identities, if they retain their 'otherness' *vis-à-vis* each other, if they do not become one flesh, politically speaking. Herein resides the Principle of Tolerance. Inevitably I define my distinct identity by a boundary which differentiates me from those who are unlike me. My continued existence as a distinct identity depends, ontologically, on that boundary and, psychologically and sociologically, on preserving that sentiment of otherness. The call to bond with those very others in an ever closer union demands an internalization – individual and societal – of a very high degree of tolerance. Living the Kantian categorical imperative is most meaningful when it is extended to those who are unlike me.

In political terms, this Principle of Tolerance finds a remarkable expression in the political organization of the Community and Union which defies the normal premise of constitutionalism. Normally in a democracy, we demand democratic discipline, that is, accepting the authority of the majority over the minority only within a polity which understands itself as being constituted of one people, however defined. A majority demanding obedience from a minority which does not regard itself as belonging to the same people is usually regarded as subjugation. This is even more so in relation to constitutional discipline. And yet, in the Community, we subject the European peoples to constitutional discipline even though the European polity is composed of distinct peoples. It is a remarkable instance of civic tolerance to accept to be bound by precepts articulated not by 'my people' but by a community composed of distinct political communities: a people, if you wish, of others. I compromise my self-determination in this fashion as an expression of this kind of internal – towards myself – and external – towards others – tolerance.

Constitutionally, the Principle of Tolerance finds its expression in the very arrangement which has now come under discussion: a federal constitutional discipline which, however, is not rooted in a statist formalized constitution. At least that is the argument.

Constitutional actors in the Member States accept the European constitutional discipline not because as a matter of legal doctrine, as is the case in the federal state, they are subordinate to a higher sovereignty and authority attaching to norms validated by the federal people, the constitutional *demos*. They accept it as an autonomous voluntary act, endlessly renewed on each occasion, of subordination, in the discrete areas governed by Europe to a norm which is the aggregate expression of other wills, other political identities, other political communities. Of course, to do so creates in itself a different type of political community one unique feature of which is that very willingness to accept a binding discipline which is rooted in and derives from a community of others. The Quebecois are told: in the name of the people of Canada, you are obliged to obey. The French or the Italians or the Germans are told: in the name of the peoples of Europe, you are invited to obey. In both, constitutional obedience is demanded. When acceptance and subordination is voluntary, and repeatedly so, it constitutes an act of true liberty and emancipation from collective self-arrogance and constitutional fetishism: a high expression of Constitutional Tolerance.

The Principle of Constitutional Tolerance is not a one-way concept: it applies to constitutional actors and constitutional transactions at the Member State level, at the Union level and among the Member States too. This dimension may be clarified by moving from concept to praxis, to an examination of Constitutional Tolerance as a political and social reality.

It is, in my view, most present in the sphere of public administration, in the habits and practices it instills in the purveyors of public power in European polities, from the most mundane to the most august. At the most mundane administrative level, imagine immigration officials overturning practices of decades and centuries and learning to examine the passport of Community nationals in the same form, the same line, with the same scrutiny of their own nationals. And a similar discipline will be practiced by customs officials, Housing Officers, educational officials, and many more subject to the disciplines of the European constitutional order.

Likewise, a similar discipline will become routine in policy-setting forums. In myriad areas – whether a local council or a parliament itself – every norm will be subject to an unofficial European impact study. So many policies in the public realm can no longer be adopted without examining their consonance with the interest of others, the interest of Europe.

Think, too, of the judicial function, ranging from the neighbourhood *giudice conciliatore* to the highest jurisdictions: willy-nilly, European law, the interest of others, is part of the judicial normative matrix.

I have deliberately chosen examples which are both daily and commonplace, but which also overturn what until recently would have been considered important constitutional distinctions. This process operates also at Community level. Think of the European judge or the European public official, who must understand that, in the peculiar constitutional compact of Europe, his decision will take effect only if obeyed by national courts, if executed faithfully by a national public official both of whom belong to a national administration which claims from them a particularly strong form of loyalty and habit. This, too, will instill a measure of caution and tolerance.

What defines the European constitutional architecture is not the exception, the extreme case which definitively will situate the *Grundnorm* here or there. It is the quotidian, the daily practices, even if done unthinkingly, even if executed because the new staff regulations require that it be done in such a new way. This praxis habituates its myriad practitioners at all levels of public administration to their concealed virtues.

What, then, of the non-Europeans? What of the inevitable boundary created by those within and those without? Does not Constitutional Tolerance implode as an ethos of public mores if it is restricted only to those chosen people with the violet passports? Let us return to the examples mentioned above such as the new immigration procedures which group all Community nationals together. What characterizes this situation is that though national and Community citizens will be grouped together, they will still have distinct passports, with independent national identities, and still speak in their distinct tongues, or in that peculiar Eurospeak that sometimes passes itself off as English. This is critical, because in the daily practices which I am extolling the public official is invited and habituated to deal with a very distinct 'other' but to treat him or her as if he was his own. One should not be starry-eyed or overly naïve; but the hope and expectation is that there will be a spill-over effect: a gradual habituation to various forms of tolerance and with it a gradual change in the ethos of public administration which can be extended to Europeans and non-Europeans alike. The boundary between European and 'non-European' is inevitable, dictated if by nothing else by the discipline of numbers. In too large a polity the specific gravity of the individual is so diminished that democracy, except in its most formal sense, becomes impossible. But just as at the level of high politics, the Community experience has conditioned a different ethos of intergovernmental interaction, so it can condition a different ethos of public interaction with all aliens.

To extol the extant constitutional arrangement of Europe is not to suggest that many of its specifics cannot be vastly improved. They can and should. The question is not about the need, nor the content, but about the form the necessary changes should take.

The final unanswered and unanswerable question is whether the discourse of formal constitutionalism, the very power of the Word outlined above will have the effect of eviscerating the constitutional voluntarism which has served Europe so well until now, will rob Europe of this ethos of tolerance which was its defining spiritual *Grundnorm*?

# THE PROCESS OF RATIFICATION AND THE CRISIS OPTIONS: A LEGAL PERSPECTIVE

**Bruno de Witte**[*]

## 1.    THE EMERGENCE OF THE NOTION OF A 'RATIFICATION CRISIS'

As the work of the Convention on the Future of Europe progressed, and as the Intergovernmental Conference was struggling to turn the Convention's Draft into a commonly agreed Treaty text, political attention came to be directed towards the conditions under which the Constitutional Treaty would enter into force and effectively fulfil the grand ambition of replacing the existing wordy and complicated Treaties with a reorganized and improved fundamental document. The text prepared by the Convention and adopted by the IGC contains a gigantic, but unavoidable gamble caused by the fact that the entry into force of the Constitutional Treaty is subject to the same rigid legal conditions as the previous Treaties of Maastricht, Amsterdam and Nice. Since the new Treaty is an amendment of the existing EC and EU Treaties (the Constitutional Treaty aims to repeal those treaties, but a repeal is just an extreme form of amendment), the revision procedure described in Article 48 TEU necessarily applies. In accordance with Article 48, the Constitutional Treaty will only enter into force, *normally speaking,* if it is approved by *all* the Member State governments within the framework of an IGC (which has now been done), and if it is ratified by *all* states according to their constitutional requirements (which remains to be done). The latter requirement multiplies the chances of an *accident de parcours* comparable to, or worse than, that which occurred with the Treaty of Maastricht in Denmark and with the Treaty of Nice in Ireland. Indeed, the question of what would happen if all Member State governments approve a revision treaty, but one of the countries is unable to ratify it, already arose concerning the Maastricht Treaty, after the first Danish referendum, and concerning the Nice Treaty, after the first Irish referendum. In neither of these two cases did the other Member States, or the EU institutions, officially argue that the other Member States could go ahead without the recalcitrant State. They managed to find a 'soft law' solution which did not mod-

---

[*] Professor of European Union Law at the European University Institute, Florence. The author wishes to acknowledge the fruitful exchange of ideas on this subject with Lucia Serena Rossi and Jo Shaw. See their publications mentioned in n. 16 *infra.*

ify the agreed text but enabled these two countries eventually to approve the revision treaty in a second referendum, so that the EU legal rules for entry into force were entirely respected.

This time around, the argument that the majority of states should be able to go ahead with a Treaty revision even in the absence of some countries' ratification has been openly made, on three different occasions: during the work of the Convention, after the European Council of December 2003 that failed to conclude the IGC, and after Tony Blair's announcement that the United Kingdom would submit the Constitutional Treaty to a referendum. I will briefly review the political considerations made on those occasions and then explore, in a second part, the legal scenarios that would be available in case a ratification crisis actually occurred.

Before looking at the most recent debates, it may be useful to recall an earlier example of a 'plan B', namely that proposed in the European Parliament's draft Treaty on European Union in 1984.[1] This document sought to bypass the EEC Treaty revision procedure by claiming that the new Treaty would be a fresh start setting up an entirely new organisation.[2] Its Article 82 provided that the proposed Treaty on European Union would enter into force if ratified by a majority of Member States representing two-thirds of the total population,[3] but it remained silent on what would happen if the non-ratifying states refused to accept the creation of this new organization and insisted on the preservation of the existing framework of the European Communities. As we know, the question remained entirely hypothetical at that time, because the Member State governments ignored the Parliament's Draft and set out to revise the Treaties according to a traditional intergovernmental conference providing for universal ratification of the revision treaty by all states. This traditional method was not only successful back in 1986 (with the adoption of the Single European Act) but was equally successful, formally at least, on three successive occasions, with the Treaties of Maastricht, Amsterdam and Nice. The fact that, each time, all Member States could eventually be kept on board, prevented a full-fledged confrontation with the non-ratification problem.

However, in the Draft Constitution adopted in 1994 by the Institutional Affairs Committee of the European Parliament, but not formally by the EP itself (the so-called 'Herman report'), it was stated, in Article 47, that those states failing to ratify the Constitution 'shall be obliged to choose between leaving the

---

[1] 'Draft Treaty establishing the European Union', *Bulletin of the European Communities* (February 1984, no. 2) pp. 8-26.

[2] See J.P. Jacqué, 'The Draft Treaty establishing the European Union', 22 *Common Market Law Review* (1985) at pp. 40-41. At that time, the various legal scenarios for dealing with not-ratifying states were examined in detail by J.H.H. Weiler and J. Modrall, 'Institutional Reform: Consensus or Majority?', 10 *European Law Review* (1985) pp. 316 et seq. Their study contains many valuable insights also for the current situation.

[3] See R. Corbett, *The European Parliament's Role in Closer EU Integration* (Palgrave, Macmillan 1998) at pp. 170-172.

Union and remaining within the Union on the new basis. Should one of these states decide to leave the Union, specific agreements shall be concluded, designed to grant it preferential status in its relations with the Union.[4] This idea resurfaced in the course of the constitutional Convention of 2002/3. Whether it was because of the large increase in national 'veto players' after the latest enlargement, or because of the ambitious nature of the Convention's work which seemed likely to cause parliamentary or popular opposition in one country or another, the fact is that already during the Convention's life a current of opinion developed that advocated a circumvention of the rigid amendment rules fixed by Article 48 TEU. One of the expressions of this unorthodox view was an editorial comment by Ferdinando Riccardi[5] in which he wrote that the Convention must affirm that 'the constitutional treaty will not need the ratification of all Member states to take effect between countries having approved it, as long as the latter represent a very high percentage (yet to be defined) of the total.' He added:

'It is indeed unthinkable that future Europe's essential project, and two years of negotiations, can end up in the "dustbin of history" because at the last hour the Parliament of a small country changes its mind, or because the Labour Party returns to power in Malta (...).'

Several of the private draft Constitutions presented during the Convention's work made the same point. Thus, for example, the Draft Constitution presented by the European Policy Centre stipulated, in its Article 77, that it would enter into force if supported 'by three quarters of the Member States of the Union representing three quarters of the population according to their own constitutional requirements.'[6] This view was shared by some central actors of the European constitutional debate. Giscard d'Estaing himself was quoted as agreeing with it, and to have offered the following tentative justification:

'The probability is that of 25 or 27 Member States [after EU enlargement] 23 would accept [the constitution] and two or three will refuse. (...) We have to abrogate the treaties that exist. If a country says that it does not like the new treaty, there's no existing structure for them to cling to, they cannot seek refuge in the old agreement.'[7]

So, in his view, the enactment of an ambitious constitutional treaty would be some kind of *refoundation* of the project of European integration rather than a *revision* of the existing Treaties. He reiterated this view more recently, stating ominously that if a large majority of the citizens of Europe and of the Member

---

[4] *OJ* (1994) C 61/155.

[5] F. Riccardi, *Bulletin Quotidien Europe* (29 October 2002).

[6] Available at: <http://www.theepc.be/Word/EUconst.doc>.

[7] D. Dombey and G. Parker, 'Europe: Tax Harmony is on EU agenda, says Giscard', *Financial Times* (11 November 2002) p. 4.

States approve the EU Constitution, problems will arise for the states that refuse to ratify it, and not for the EU Constitution itself.[8]

References to this question could also be found in documents of the European Parliament and the European Commission. In the European Parliament, a motion for a resolution presented by rapporteur Jean-Louis Bourlanges proposed the following new rule, which was similar to what was proposed in the EPC Draft Constitution:

> 'The ratification procedure should be revised with a view to ensuring that a small minority cannot block the ratification of the future constitutional treaty – for example, ratification could be secured by a dual qualified majority comprising at least three-quarters of the Member States representing at least three-quarters of the Union population – even if, in return, specific forms of cooperation must be negotiated with any Member State which does not ratify the Treaty.'[9]

However, this particular paragraph of the motion for a resolution was deleted by a vote of the plenary in its December 2002 session, and the resolution as adopted by the European Parliament does not refer at all to the question of the entry into force of the Constitutional Treaty.[10]

As for the European Commission, its official contribution to the Convention simply argued that entry into force is 'a matter to be studied in depth'.[11] However, the accompanying Draft Constitution of the same day (commonly known as 'Penelope') – which emanated from the Commission but was emphatically presented as *not* being the Commission's official opinion – made an elaborate proposal to facilitate the entry into force of the Constitutional Treaty.[12] Indeed, this is certainly the most sophisticated construction ever made in order to circumvent the unanimity rule for Treaty revision. The Penelope document proposes that the adoption of the 'Treaty on the Constitution' (as they call it) be accompanied by the simultaneous adoption of a separate short treaty called *Agreement on the Entry into Force of the Treaty on the Constitution of the European Union*. The sole purpose of this additional agreement would be to facilitate the entry into force of the Constitutional Treaty. The additional agreement, although adopted at the same time, would be ratified first, so that it could pave the way for the Constitutional Treaty. That Treaty would only enter into force one year after the additional agreement. The purpose of this delay is to allow each single Member State,

---

[8] V. Giscard d'Estaing, 'Vite, la Constitution de l'Europe!', *Le Monde* (10 July 2004).

[9] J.-L. Bourlanges, *Report on the Typology of Acts and the Hierarchy of Legislation in the European Union* (3 December 2002) Motion for a resolution, point 5.

[10] Amendment tabled by S.-Y. Kaufmann MEP and adopted by 266 in favour, 236 against with 4 abstentions (see *Agence Europe* (19 December 2002) p. 4).

[11] European Commission, *For the European Union – Peace, Freedom and Solidarity. Communication of the Commission on the Institutional Architecture*, COM (2002) 728 5 (December 2002) at p. 22.

[12] Penelope can be found on: <http://europa.eu.int/futurum/documents/offtext/const051202_en.pdf>.

when ratifying the additional agreement, to express a choice between either accepting the content of the Constitutional Treaty, or (while not accepting it) leaving the European Union if the Treaty is accepted by three-quarters of the Member States. If, at the end of the transitional year, it appears that at least
three-quarters of the States have indeed made the positive statement of acceptance, then the Constitutional Treaty enters into force between them and the other States comply with their earlier commitment to leave the EU, while starting
negotiations with the EU on the organisation of their future relations.

However, the rub with this 'gentle exit strategy' is that, as the Penelope study
accepts, the preliminary agreement should itself be agreed upon and ratified by
all Member States before it can enter into force and effectively replace the current revision procedure of Article 48 TEU. It seems quite likely, though, that a
Member State opposed to the *content* of the Constitutional Treaty would also
refuse to ratify an agreement that is designed to facilitate the *entry into force* of
that Constitutional Treaty, particularly if that could imply that it would be
'kicked out' of the European Union. Therefore, the Penelope group also included
a last resort clause: if by a given date, the preliminary agreement has been ratified by at least five-sixths of the Member States (so, presumably, 21 out of 25
States), then it will enter into force for all, disregarding the normal 'overall ratification' rule. So, when all is said, the Penelope Study *does* affirm the need to
adopt the 'constitutional rupture' approach, that is, the right for the overwhelming majority of States to move ahead with a Constitutional Treaty even against
the opposition of up to four countries.[13]

The Penelope mechanism was not inserted in the Draft Treaty proposed by
the Convention in July 2003. However, when the Intergovernmental Conference,
at the Brussels European Council meeting of December 2003, failed to reach
agreement on the text of a Draft Constitutional Treaty, the President of France
immediately recalled the idea of a two-speed Europe, in which a pioneer group
of countries led by France and Germany would show the way to the others. That
pioneer group could set out to achieve the ambitious objectives of the draft Constitutional Treaty proposed by the Convention on the Future of the Union, in the
absence of an agreement by all twenty-five national governments.[14] Approving

---

[13] The Penelope document argues (at p. XII) that the insertion of this 'last resort' clause would
itself require the agreement, at the time of *signature* (as opposed to ratification), of all the governments
and would therefore be a departure from Article 48 TEU that would be compatible with international
law (because all states would agree to substitute one revision rule by another). But, apart from
the fact that overall agreement to include such a clause seems politically very unlikely, the
replacement of Art. 48 TEU through an agreement between *governments* (without national
parliamentary approval) would be in clear violation of the constitutional law of most Member
States.

[14] For references to this aspect of the Brussels summit and some immediate reactions, see J.
Dempsey, 'Support for Two-speed Europe gathers Momentum', *Financial Times* (15 December
2003); 'Après le fiasco de Bruxelles, Paris relance l'idée d'une Europe à la carte', *Le Monde* (16
December 2003); 'Dutch lead Criticism of Two-speed Europe Plan', *Financial Times* (16 December
2003); H. Grabbe, 'The Siren Song of a Two-speed Europe', *Financial Times* (16 December 2003);

noises could be heard from the side of the German and Belgian governments. Strictly speaking, this was not a scenario for a ratification crisis, but a scenario for an 'adoption crisis'. Already in the spring of 2004, when agreement on the Treaty again became likely, France and Germany had buried any thought of setting in place a vanguard group. However, the prospect of a ratification crisis became very real once again when Tony Blair announced, in April 2004, that the Constitutional Treaty would be submitted to a referendum in the United Kingdom and opinion polls indicated that, if the referendum were to be held, then, it would result in an overwhelming 'no'. As more and more countries announced that they would hold a referendum as a binding or consultative part of their national ratification process, the likelihood of a ratification crisis increased further. By the time final agreement on the Constitutional Treaty was reached, in June 2004, it was at the forefront of all European Council members' minds, but it found only a feeble reflection in the texts which they agreed at the Brussels summit.

That feeble trace is the intriguing Declaration no. 30 *on the ratification of the Treaty establishing a Constitution for Europe* (to be annexed to the Final Act of the IGC):

'The Conference notes that if, two years after the signature of the Treaty establishing a Constitution for Europe, four fifths of the Member States have ratified it and one or more Member States have encountered difficulties in proceeding with ratification, the matter will be referred to the European Council.'[15]

At one level, this Declaration only states the obvious, namely that the European Council deals with any serious problem arising on the path of European integration. But at another level, it expresses the hope that, if such a situation will occur, the European Council will be able to devise a cunning plan to save the Constitutional Treaty despite the opposition expressed in some parts of the Union's territory.

Let us now assume that something indeed 'goes wrong' during the national ratification phase, in the sense that one or more Member States have 'difficulties' with the ratification process, because (presumably) the Treaty has been rejected in a referendum. For now, the most likely candidate for causing such difficulties is the United Kingdom, but since its referendum is scheduled only for 2006, it is quite possible that a ratification crisis may erupt earlier on in other countries. In view of the volatile nature of national electorates, there are in fact plenty of unknown national political constellations as regards the coming refer-

---

'Who killed the Constitution?', *The Economist* (20 December 2003); P. Ponzano, 'Après l'échec du Sommet de Bruxelles: Constitution européenne ou coopérations renforcées?', *Revue du Droit de l'Union Européenne* (2003) pp. 549 et seq.

[15] To be found in CIG 87/04 ADD 2 REV 2 of 25 October 2004. The Declaration corresponds, practically word for word, to what the Convention itself had proposed in an annex to its Draft Treaty.

endums. One of the questions arising then is whether any legal scenarios are available, under the present rules, for dealing with such a ratification crisis.[16] I will examine some of these potential legal scenarios in the following pages, on the basis of current EU law but also, more broadly, in the light of the notoriously flexible rules of international treaty law.

## 2. THE LEGAL SCENARIOS FOR DEALING WITH A RATIFICATION CRISIS

### 2.1 Some Legally Unavailable Options

#### 2.1.1 *Partial Entry into Force and the Creation of an 'Enhanced Union'*

It is by no means unusual for universal treaties to be subject to ratification in all participating states. The danger of excessive rigidity is, however, often countered by the fact that such treaties provide for their entry into force after a certain number of parties have ratified, with the other states having the option of joining the first group later on in the life of the treaty. So, for example, the Montego Bay Convention on the Law of the Sea entered into force after 60 ratifications had been lodged (12 years after its signature), the Vienna Convention on the Law of Treaties required 35 ratifications for its entry into force, which occurred 11 years after signature, and the Rome statute on the International Criminal Court came into force after 4 years, upon the 60th ratification.[17] It is therefore accepted, in international law, that many treaties remain 'limping' for many years after their adoption.[18]

Would this kind of 'layering of membership' be feasible in the case of the Constitutional Treaty? Would it be possible for the willing States to forge ahead with the Constitutional Treaty, and create an 'enhanced Union' between themselves, while also remaining members, together with the unwilling States, of the

---

[16] For an earlier discussion of such scenarios, see E. Philippart and M. Sie Dhian Ho, 'Flexibility and the New Constitutional Treaty of the European Union', in J. Pelkmans, et al., eds., *Nederland en de Europese grondwet* (Amsterdam, Amsterdam University Press 2003) at pp. 137 et seq. See also L.S. Rossi, *What if the Constitutional Treaty is not ratified?* (EPC Commentary (30 June 2004)) available at: <www.theepc.net> (click on 'Political Europe' and then 'Commentary'), and a longer article by the same author in *Revue trimestrielle de droit européen* (2005, forthcoming). Finally, a detailed analysis by J. Shaw, 'What happens if the Constitutional Treaty is not ratified?', in I. Pernice and J. Zemanek, eds., *The Treaty on a Constitution for Europe: Perspectives after the IGC* (Baden-Baden, Nomos 2005 forthcoming).

[17] I have taken these figures from P. Tavernier, 'Comment surmonter les obstacles constitutionnels à la ratification du Statut de Rome de la Cour Pénale Internationale', 13 *Revue trimestrielle des droits de l'homme* (2002) at pp. 547-548.

[18] The expression is used, and the phenomenon described, by A. Aust, 'Limping Treaties: Lessons from Multilateral Treaty-making', 50 *Netherlands International Law Review* (2003) p. 243.

old European Union and European Community? It is clear, on a moment's reflection, that such an option is not feasible for the European Treaties. European revision treaties deal with an organization that already exists, comprising Member States that have existing rights and obligations. Allowing for the partial ratification of a revision treaty (such as the Constitutional Treaty) would lead to different circles of members, some bound by the new and the old rules, and others by the old rules only. The EU institutions could not function under the new rules and the old rules simultaneously,[19] so the revision must necessarily apply to all States or to none of them. The intermediate option of partial entry into force is not available.

### 2.1.2 *Refoundation*

If a coexistence of the old and the new is impossible, could the 'Giscard' argument not be made, namely that signature of the Constitutional Treaty leads to the abolition of the old European Union, and 'refounds' the Union on an entirely new basis through the Constitutional Treaty. According to this view, the ratifying states would go ahead and, since the old regime is cancelled, the non-ratifying countries have nothing to hang on to and exclude themselves from the EU system, so to speak. It is clear, I think, that this reasoning reverses the legal reality. In fact, the states who want to move ahead have nothing to hang on to as long as the Constitutional Treaty itself has not properly entered into force in accordance with the rules of Article 48 TEU. The repeal of the old Treaties presupposes, and is preceded by, the entry into force of the new Treaty, not the other way round.

It is true that the Vienna Convention on the Law of Treaties allows for some of the parties to a treaty to decide to adopt another treaty modifying the first, without the participation of the other original state parties (a so-called *inter se* modification). However, this is only allowed if that modification does not affect the rights that the non-participating states draw from the original treaty. This is obviously not the case for the Constitutional Treaty whose enactment unavoidably affects and modifies the existing rights of all the EU Members. Therefore, under the current rules of Article 48 TEU, all the Member States must give their agreement to the changes.

### 2.2   The 'Nice Plus' Scenario

The most orthodox scenario in the case of a clear failure by one or more Member States to ratify the Constitutional Treaty is that the European Council acknowledges that the Constitutional Treaty will not enter into force and that the relations between the Member States (and the legal position of the EU institutions and the citizens) will continue to be governed by the EC and EU Treaty as last

---

[19] For some examples of this 'impossible cohabitation' between the old and the new system, see Rossi, *supra* n. 16, at p. 3.

amended by the Treaty of Nice and the Accession Treaties. However, the European Council would not have to leave it at this defeatist conclusion. It could decide to set in motion, immediately, a new Treaty revision process starting from scratch (which would obviously be governed by Article 48 TEU and not by the new revision clause provided by the Constitutional Treaty). In the meantime, there would be ample scope for tinkering with the current post-Nice Treaty regime, so that the contents of the Constitutional Treaty need not be completely dropped. This could be done in, essentially, two different ways which I will briefly elaborate below: through the application of parts of the Treaty by means of secondary law or mere institutional practice, and through the use of forms of closer cooperation.

### 2.2.1 *Informal Application*

With 'informal application' I mean the application of some of the institutional or substantive rules contained in the Constitutional Treaty without basing it on the formal authority that would have resulted from the entry into force of that Treaty. Today, we are already familiar with this phenomenon with regard to one important part of the Constitutional Treaty, namely the second part containing the text (with minor modifications) of the Charter of Fundamental Rights. This part of the Constitutional Treaty is already being applied by the political institutions of the Union (which committed themselves to do so when solemnly proclaiming the Charter in December 2000) and its content is effectively being used by the European Courts, although formally they continue to apply those rights as 'general principles of Community law'. A recent example of the formal enactment of a Constitutional Treaty innovation under current law is the establishment of the European Defence Agency.[20] More generally, a number of innovations contained in the Constitutional Treaty that are not incompatible with the present Treaties could be enacted. For example, the role of national parliaments could be enhanced by a combination of reforms in national laws and inter-institutional agreements between the EU institutions. The inter-institutional agreement is a legal instrument that has been used repeatedly in the past to anticipate later Treaty reforms, and could be used again to achieve a variety of reforms proposed in the Constitutional Treaty. The states could, similarly, agree among themselves to forego the use of their veto power in areas in which the Constitutional Treaty replaces unanimity by qualified majority voting. The Ioannina Agreement of 1994 could be invoked as a precedent for this: this was an informal agreement between governments dealing with the exercise of their voting rights in Council.[21] Finally, some of the new policy competences added by the Constitutional

---

[20] Council Joint Action 2004/551/CFSP of 12 July 2004 on the establishment of the European Defence Agency, *OJ* (2004) L 245/17. Recital 6 of the Joint Action mentions that the Agency 'is also envisaged in the draft Treaty establishing a Constitution for Europe'.

[21] See Editorial Comments, 'The Ioannina Compromise – Towards a Wider and a Weaker European Union?', 31 *Common Market Law Review* (1994) pp. 453 et seq.

Treaty could be exercised by using the residual powers clause of Article 308 TEC.

Obviously, such informal applications of the Constitutional Treaty would require the agreement of all the Member States. The government of a country that failed to ratify the Constitutional Treaty would have to tread with particular care for domestic constitutional and political reasons. And of course, the informal application of an unratified Constitutional Treaty would increase even further the present opacity of the EU system, and would therefore run counter to one of the main objectives which the Constitutional Treaty was set to achieve, that of increasing simplicity and transparency. So, it would not be satisfactory as a long-term solution.

### 2.2.2   Closer Cooperation

A second, complementary, way in which a Nice Plus scenario could be set in place is through increased recourse to forms of closer cooperation, both inside and outside the European Union system.[22] The *enhanced cooperation mechanism*, which exists since the Treaty of Amsterdam but has remained unused, could operate in order to perform one of its original aims, namely to allow 'willing and able' Member States to pursue deeper integration without passing through an intergovernmental conference.[23] In using the enhanced cooperation mechanism, the pro-Constitution states would be constrained by the numerous rules and conditions set by the Nice Treaty (even though that treaty relaxed the even more stringent rules set by the Amsterdam Treaty).[24] First, the Nice Treaty would not allow the 'pioneers' to select the members of the club, since enhanced cooperation regimes must be open to all states which want to participate. Secondly, the Nice rules require enhanced cooperation initiatives to be taken by at least eight countries, so that, for instance, an initiative of the six original Member States of the EC would not qualify. Thirdly, the Nice rules do not allow for enhanced cooperation in areas that are outside EU competences as defined by the

---

[22] For some stimulating recent reflections on this, see F. Dehousse, W. Coussens and G. Grevi, *Integrating Europe: Multiple Speeds – One Direction?* (European Policy Centre, Working Paper 9 April 2004) available at: <http://www.theepc.be/TEWN/pdf/992512761_EPC%20Working %20Paper%209%20Integrating%20Europe%20-%20Multiple%20Speeds%20One% 20Direction.pdf.>; and Philippart and Sie Dhian Ho, *supra* n. 16.

[23] A. Stubb, *Negotiating Flexibility in the European Union. Amsterdam, Nice and beyond* (New York, Palgrave Macmillan 2002) at p. 165.

[24] For comments on the enhanced cooperation rules as reformed by the Treaty of Nice, see J. Shaw, 'Enhancing Cooperation after Nice: Will the Treaty do the Trick?', in M. Andenas and J.A. Usher, eds., *The Treaty of Nice and Beyond. Enlargement and Constitutional Reform* (Oxford, Hart 2003) p. 207; H. Bribosia, 'Les coopérations renforcées au lendemain du Traité de Nice', *Revue du Droit de l'Union Européenne* (2001) p. 111; L.S. Rossi, 'Cooperazione rafforzata e Trattato di Nizza: quali geometrie per l'Europa allargata?', in A. Tizzano, ed., *Il Trattato di Nizza* (Milan, Giuffrè 2003) p. 41; F. Tuytschaever, 'Nauwere samenwerking volgens het Verdrag van Nice', 11 *SEW* (2001) p. 375.

Nice Treaty, and also expressly prohibit enhanced cooperation with military or defence implications. This means, for instance, that the Nice mechanism could not be used for the ambitious new defence policy delineated in the draft Constitution.

Hence, in view of the restrictions imposed by the Nice regime for enhanced cooperation, the states wishing to move ahead in accordance with the content of the Constitutional Treaty could also launch forms of cooperation between smaller groups of Member States *outside the EU institutional framework*. I have examined the legal issues raised by such partial agreements in another publication.[25] *Inter se* international agreements between two or more Member States of the EU are allowed, but only within the limits set by EU law obligations. Briefly said, this means that such agreements may not be concluded in areas of exclusive EU competence (e.g., in the field of trade or monetary policy), that they may not affect the normal operation of the EU institutional mechanisms (in view of the duty of sincere cooperation) and that they may not include any provisions that conflict with EU law or undermine existing EU policies, e.g., by discriminating on grounds of nationality in favour of citizens of some Member States only. If, for instance, Belgium and Germany conclude a cultural cooperation agreement on the basis of which they grant education scholarships to each other's nationals, then the citizens of the thirteen other Member States of the EU are excluded from the benefit of such a scholarship. This is in breach of EC law to the extent that citizens of other Member States, residing in Belgium or Germany, may not apply for a scholarship.[26]

Intergovernmental cooperation between a limited number of Member States of the EU is thus perfectly possible, but membership of the EU imposes certain legal constraints on the scope and content of such cooperation. The formation of a true core group, adopting binding laws in a large range of crucial policy areas, is hardly imaginable because it would unavoidably affect the rights which the other Member States and their citizens have under current EU law. Even a more limited regime of extra-EU closer cooperation, restricted for example to the area of defence, would have the negative side-effect of creating political fragmentation between Member States, and of undermining the institutional balance.[27] It would also add to the complexity and opaqueness of the EU system and reduce the scope for democratic control of the decision-making process.

---

[25] B. de Witte, 'Old-fashioned Flexibility: International Agreements between Member States of the European Union', in G. de Búrca and J. Scott, eds., *Constitutional Change in the EU – From Uniformity to Flexibility?* (Oxford, Hart 2000) p. 31. See also the study by L.S. Rossi, *Le convenzioni fra gli Stati membri dell'Unione europea* (Milan, Giuffrè 2000).

[26] These are the legal facts of the *Matteucci* judgment of the ECJ, judgment of 27 September 1988, Case C-235/87, *Annunziata Matteucci v. Communauté française of Belgium et al.* [1988] *ECR* 5589.

[27] This aspect is highlighted, from a Commission perspective, by Ponzano, *supra* n. 14, at p. 554.

## 2.3    Voice: The Renegotiation Scenario

Rather than admit defeat and proceed on the basis of the Nice Treaty, the European Council could also decide to face the misgivings emerging from a ratification crisis in one or more countries, while trying to keep the Constitutional Treaty alive. This is the 'voice' scenario, in which the views of the dissenters are taken into account by the supporters of the Constitutional Treaty with a view to achieving a mutually acceptable compromise.

The first option is to try to accommodate the dissenting State (or its dissenting electorate) within the bounds of the Constitutional Treaty as agreed by all governments at the IGC. This is, in fact, what happened after the unsuccessful Danish and Irish referendums earlier on. The diplomatic 'dialogue', in those two cases, was not aiming at a modification of the Treaty as signed, but at a separate legal or political agreement that could pave the way for a second referendum on that same treaty.[28] In the case of Denmark, this separate agreement was the Decision on Denmark approved during the European Council meeting in Edinburgh (December 1992), which was presented as a binding legal document, and therefore can best be qualified as an international agreement in a simplified form.[29] It did not purport to modify the Treaty of Maastricht, but only to offer a particular interpretation thereof. However, it is undeniable that the Decision on Denmark has cast its shadow on the European Union: it is directly responsible for the complicated and almost unworkable Protocol on Denmark agreed in connection with the Treaty of Amsterdam, and the Constitutional Treaty, again, contains a special Protocol on Denmark as well as a Declaration on that Protocol. So, one cannot deny that the negative Danish referendum in 1992 has affected every other state as well and has made the European Union more complicated than it would have been otherwise. In the case of Ireland, the effects of its first negative referendum on the Nice Treaty became less visible at the EU level. Common action at the European level took the form of two Declarations made at the European Council meeting of Seville (the 'Seville Declarations'),[30] one by the Irish government and one by the European Council as a body. Both stated that the Treaty of Nice would not prevent Ireland from preserving the essence of its neutrality despite the development of a common security and defence policy. However, the neutrality question was arguably not the central concern for most 'no' voters, and the main measures to convince the electorate to approve the

---

[28] See also the reflection on the legal ways of dealing with the Irish case, based on an analysis of the earlier Danish case, by W. Hummer and W. Obwexer, 'Irlands "Nein zu Nizza"; Konsequenzen aus dem negativen irischen Referendum vom 7. Juni 2001', *Integration* (2001) p. 237.

[29] See, on this legal qualification, A. Dashwood, 'States in the European Union', 23 *European Law Review* (1998) at p. 203; D. Curtin and R. van Ooik, 'Denmark and the Edinburgh Summit: Maastricht without Tears', in D. O'Keeffe and P. Twomey, eds., *Legal Issues of the Maastricht Treaty* (London, Chancery Law Publishing 1994) at pp. 353-358.

[30] Annexes III and IV to the Presidency Conclusions of the Seville European Council, 21 and 22 June 2002.

Nice Treaty in a second referendum were taken at the domestic level, namely the creation of a National Forum on Europe, and the strengthening of national parliamentary control mechanisms on Irish EU policy-making.[31]

Whether this 'vote-again scenario' could be repeated this time, in the case of a ratification crisis, depends very much on the circumstances. On those previous occasions, the crisis was caused by one single state, that happened to be a small state, and after rejection of the Treaty by a rather small margin of votes. If, this time, the Constitutional Treaty were to be rejected in a large Member State, or in more than one state, or by a huge majority of the electorate, then an easy accommodation would be more difficult. What one could envisage, then, is to go one step further and embark upon a true *renegotiation* of the Constitutional Treaty, whose object would be to accommodate the concerns that provoked rejection in one or more countries (provided one can identify such concerns with sufficient precision) by modifying the text of the Treaty. Since the Constitutional Treaty has come into legal existence upon its signature in October 2004, renegotiation would mean drawing up another treaty that would replace the Constitutional Treaty as well as revise the current EC and EU Treaties. That new treaty could either, if the disagreement relates to specific policies, provide opt-outs for the recalcitrant state(s) without modifying the content for the other states, or, if the disagreement relates to the general principles or the institutional reforms, it would have to change the relevant rules for all states.

All states would then have to lodge a new act of ratification in the international law sense, which would require a new approval by their national parliaments, but probably not a new referendum in countries where a referendum on the (original) Constitution had already been successful. Much would depend on the nature of the changes made to the original text (whether a mere opt-out for the dissenters or more), in the light of national constitutional requirements and national political dynamics.

The delay involved in all this could be mitigated, possibly, by resorting to the *provisional application* of the Constitutional Treaty as originally agreed at the IGC. According to Article 25 of the Vienna Convention on the Law of Treaties, a treaty or a part of a treaty may be applied provisionally, pending its entry into force, if the Treaty itself so provides (which is not the case with the Constitutional Treaty) or if the negotiating States have in some other manner so agreed. This device is often used in the European Community's external relations, particularly for mixed agreements, where provisional application allows for the 'EC part' of the agreement to be applied while the Member States are busy ratifying the 'Member State part'. The 'other manner of agreement', mentioned by the Vienna Convention, can also be expressed after signature. So, the Member States could, at the European Council ratification crisis meeting or afterwards, decide to apply

---

[31] See B. Laffan, *Ireland and Europe: Continuity and Change* (Notre Europe 2003) at pp. 22-26, available at: <http://www.notre-europe.asso.fr/IMG/pdf/Etud30-en.pdf>.

parts of the Constitutional Treaty provisionally – namely, those parts that are un-
controversial politically and from a domestic constitutional perspective, and have
not caused the rejection by the electorate in the country or countries 'with difficulties'. However, the provisional application of a treaty is supposed to be ...
provisional. If a contracting party is, or becomes, definitely unable to lodge its
ratification act, it cannot possibly agree to the provisional application of the treaty. So, provisional application must be coupled with ongoing negotiations to
save the essence of the Constitutional Treaty, otherwise it is nonsense.[32]

## 2.4    Exit: The Withdrawal Scenario

If the states who agree to ratify the Constitutional Treaty do not, or cannot, listen
to the 'voice' of the recalcitrant states, then the opposite scenario could be
considered, namely that of one or more (or most) states exiting from the European
Union as we know it, so as to enable the Constitutional Treaty to come into
operation.

### 2.4.1    *Voluntary Individual Withdrawal*

Article I-60 TCE allows for the unilateral withdrawal from the Union by a Member State, subject only to some procedural conditions.[33] This withdrawal clause
is, obviously, not applicable before the Treaty itself has entered into force and
would therefore not be available, as such, in the case of a ratification crisis. The
withdrawal from the European Union by a non-ratifying state is therefore a matter to be dealt with under current EU and international law. The European Treaties do not expressly allow for withdrawal by a member country. In the absence
of an express clause, the general rule of Article 56 of the Vienna Convention on
the Law of Treaties could be invoked. It holds that a treaty that contains no
express provision on withdrawal is not subject to withdrawal 'unless (a) it is
established that the parties intended to admit the possibility of denunciation or
withdrawal; or (b) a right of denunciation or withdrawal may be implied by the
nature of the treaty.' On that basis, many authors have argued that unilateral
withdrawal is not allowed in the case of the European Union,[34] but that is not
entirely evident. It could also be argued that the silence of the EEC Treaty (and

---

[32] See, for a more elaborate presentation of the international law background and conditions,
R. Lefeber, 'The Provisional Application of Treaties', in J. Klabbers and R. Lefeber, eds., *Essays
on the Law of Treaties: a Collection of Essays in Honour of Bert Vierdag* (The Hague, Nijhoff
1998) p. 81.

[33] For a discussion of this provision (which was numbered as Art. 59 in the Draft of 2003)
in a comparative perspective, see R.J. Friel, 'Providing a Constitutional Framework for Withdrawal
from the EU: Article 59 of the Draft European Constitution', 53 *ICLQ* (2004) p. 407.

[34] For example, L.M. Diez Picazo, 'Les pièges de la souveraineté', in R. Dehousse, ed., *Une
constitution pour l'Europe?* (Paris, Presses de Sciences Po 2002) p. 39, at pp. 59 et seq.

its subsequent revisions) on this matter leaves open the possibility of withdrawal given the very ambitious nature of the treaty. An element of state practice pointing in that direction is the fact that, when in 1975 the British government called a referendum on whether the UK should remain in the European Communities, none of the other Member States lodged a formal protest, and they acted as if they would accept the withdrawal that would result from a negative outcome of the referendum (in the end, of course, the question of withdrawal did not effectively arise).[35]

Apart from unilateral withdrawal, Article 54 of the Vienna Convention allows a country to terminate a treaty also if all its co-contracting parties agree so. This hypothesis is more likely to arise in the context of the Constitutional Treaty. If country X fails to ratify and declares its wish to leave the European Union, the other countries might agree with that intention. The withdrawal of country X would, however, not directly pave the way for the entry into force of the Constitutional Treaty. Indeed, Article IV-447 TCE makes entry into force conditional upon ratification by all the *signatory states*, and country X is a signatory state ... Therefore, what would be needed is a combination of two legal texts: an agreement in which all Member States accept the withdrawal of country X and organize the future relations between country X and the remaining states, and a treaty concluded between the remaining states in which they adopt Constitutional Treaty-bis, which is identical to the original Constitutional Treaty, with the exception of all the articles referring directly or indirectly to the withdrawing state. Both these legal texts would have to be approved by the national parliaments, but would probably not have to be submitted to a referendum.

This scenario does not seem very plausible. Why would a country decide to renounce the benefits of EU membership only because it does not agree with the reforms proposed in the Constitutional Treaty? The case of Norway is often cited to argue that a country can be strongly integrated into the EU's activities without being a full member, but, in fact, Norway's institutional position is rather unattractive, in that it must accept and enact many rules of European Union law without having a say in their formulation.[36]

### 2.4.2    *Forced Withdrawal (Exclusion)*

The previous option is based on the hypothesis that a non-ratifying state would be ready to exit from the European Union, if it could do so on sufficiently attractive terms. In fact, this is a hypothesis which some commentators have seen gaining consistency during the first stages of the UK referendum campaign. But

---

[35] Rossi, *supra* n. 16, at p. 7.

[36] See, for example, K.A. Eliassen and N. Sitter, 'The Quiet European – Norway's Quasi-Membership of the European Union', in P. Magnette, ed., *La grande Europe* (Brussels, Editions de l'Université de Bruxelles 2004) p. 351; 'The Norwegian Option', *The Economist* (9 October 2004) p. 34.

it is equally, if not more, likely that a non-ratifying state would not be prepared to leave the Union but rather stick to the current Treaties. Could that state then be forced out of the window by the other states?

This idea, that was openly mentioned in the spring of 2004 as 'the latest fashionable notion in Brussels',[37] has no basis whatsoever in European or international law. As was bluntly stated by a judge of the German Constitutional Court: 'The talk that a rejection of the Constitutional Treaty would lead to the respective state's exclusion from the Union is nonsense.'[38] The threatening words of Giscard d'Estaing, quoted above, that a non-ratifying state would create a problem for itself, and not for the Constitutional Treaty itself, are legally wrong and politically unjustifiable. It may seem difficult to accept that a small minority of the electorate of Denmark, Malta or even the UK could thwart the desire of the vast majority of European citizens to proceed with the Constitutional Treaty, but this is the rule of the game as it was agreed and re-agreed many times in the past, and which for every country has formed the basis of its membership. It cannot simply be set aside without the agreement of all Member States. So, excluding a country from the European Union because it fails to ratify the Constitutional Treaty is out of the question.

### 2.4.3 *Enhanced Union after Collective Withdrawal*

There is a third form of withdrawal, though, which could achieve the same results as the exclusion of the recalcitrant state but in a legally more orthodox (though highly acrobatic) manner. Faced with the inability of one or more states to ratify, the remaining states could decide to collectively withdraw from the European Union (including the European Community) and reconfigure a new organization, the Enhanced Union.[39] That would leave the original rump-EU unable to function in the absence of most of its Member States. The withdrawing states would have to justify their action on the basis mentioned in Article 62 of the Vienna Convention, namely that a *fundamental change of circumstances* makes it impossible for them to continue as parties of the original EU and EC Treaty.[40] More particularly, they would have to argue that the original objectives of the European Treaties can no longer be achieved under the current Treaties

---

[37] 'Make my day', *The Economist* (8 May 2004) p. 33.

[38] U. Di Fabio, 'The European Constitutional Treaty: An Analysis', 5 *German Law Journal* (2004) at p. 956, also available at: <http://www.germanlawjournal.com/pdf/Vol05No08/PDF_Vol_05_No_08_945-956_EU_DiFabio.pdf>.

[39] I have borrowed the term used by Philippart and Sie Dhian Ho, *supra* n. 16, for the sake of convenience. The new organisation would obviously not be called like this!

[40] This is also known as the *rebus sic stantibus* principle. See, Rossi, *supra* n. 16, at pp. 7-8. This legal argument is also mentioned by P. Demaret and D. Hanf, 'Le projet "Pénélope": un "Federalist Paper"? Quelques observations sur l'entrée en vigueur du nouveau traité constitutionnel et sur le futur des clauses de coopération renforcée', in A. Mattera, ed., *Penelope – Projet de Constitution de l'Union européenne* (Paris, Clément Juglar 2003) at p. 92.

and require the kind of *saut qualitatif* provided by the Constitutional Treaty. I would personally find this argument very dubious,[41] given the fact that the content of the Constitutional Treaty is not so radically different from the EC and EU Treaties in their post-Nice version: how could a Constitution, which is not that different from the existing treaties, permit states to achieve major objectives which the current treaties absolutely cannot achieve? However, the most compelling argument against the legal validity of this scenario is that it would allow, in an indirect but effective way, the objective of excluding the recalcitrant state to be achieved (something which I argued, above, to be unlawful). At the very least, the break-away states would have a duty to negotiate adequate terms for their future relations with the left-behind state(s), who could not be accused of having breached their existing treaty obligations.

3.    CONCLUSION

There are, thus, a number of ways to save the Constitutional Treaty, partly or wholly, in the case of a ratification crisis. None of those ways is easy and all of them require complicated legal arrangements that would be difficult to explain to the European citizens. The feasibility of the various options would depend on where the ratification crisis originates, and how many states and voters are involved. The fact that the legal scenarios strongly depend on the political constellation of the day explains why many commentators flatly distinguish between a *legal* and a *political* approach to this matter, as exemplified by the following words of Giuliano Amato:

> 'Si un de nos pays vote contre la Constitution, légalement cela signifiera qu'elle ne sera pas approuvée. Politiquement, rien n'empêchera ceux qui l'ont approuvée de signer entre eux un nouveau traité ayant le même contenu, en laissantles dissidents dehors. Ce serait très dur mais la seule solution possible.'[42]

Indeed, many of the statements calling for the Constitutional Treaty to go ahead in case of a ratification crisis indicate that such an initiative should not be stopped by 'legal technicalities'. In other words, the 'vanguard states' could also choose to 'ignore the law' and sweep away the current EU and international law rules if this were needed to extricate themselves from a ratification crisis. The countries willing to forge ahead would be prepared to break the law and explode the long-established institutional arrangements on the ground that the unreformed European Union no longer allows them to pursue their most cherished political goals and interests. Such a revolutionary move requires strong political

---

[41] See also the sceptical view of Shaw, *supra* n. 16.
[42] Joint interview with Giuliano Amato and Dominique Strauss-Kahn, *Le Monde* (30-31 May 2004).

resolve and close cohesion among the members of the break-away group. At the present time, neither the resolve nor the cohesion seem to be there. In the absence of this revolutionary spirit, it may be a good idea to keep an eye on the legal technicalities, and patiently explore the resources that these can offer.

# REFERENDUMS ON THE CONSTITUTIONAL TREATY 2004: A CITIZENS' VOICE?

**Anne Peters**[*]

## 1.    INTRODUCTION

The idea of a European referendum on a foundational document for Europe is not new. It has been heralded both by intergovernmentalists such as Charles de Gaulle[1] and by Euro-federalists such as Altiero Spinelli. The latter's project of a 'relaunch of the European unity' included as a possibility a 'constituent assembly which would formulate and pass a project of a federal constitution which would be submitted in every country to a referendum.'[2]

Today, the European polity possesses a new constitutional document, the Constitutional Treaty of 29 October 2004.[3] It has been hotly debated whether this Constitution should be subject to popular approval in the form of a referendum. As of December 2004, the prospects are that eleven out of the 25 Member States will hold a referendum on the EU Constitution,[4] and in two further Member States a referendum is likely.[5] In four Member States, a referendum seems unlikely,[6] whereas in the eight remaining States, the situation is unclear.

In this article, I will clarify the various referendum options and their legal bases (Part 2) and will then discuss whether the projected referendums will make the European Constitution more legitimate (Part 3). My conclusion is that legitimacy benefits are negligible.

---

[*] Prof. Dr. iur., LL.M. (Harvard), Chair of Public International and Constitutional Law, University of Basel, Switzerland. I thank my student research assistant, Simone Peter, for her excellent research.

[1] See Charles de Gaulle in a speech at Bordeaux on 25 September 1947: '*Moi, je pense que l'organisation de l'Europe doit procéder de l'Europe d'elle-même. J'estime que c'est un vaste référendum de tous les Européens libres qui doit lui donner le départ.*' Ch. de Gaulle, '*Discours et messages*', 2 *Dans l'attente* (Paris, Plon 1970) p. 304, at p. 309.

[2] A. Spinelli, 'Democratizzare le Comunità' [Democratizing the Community], in A. Spinelli, *Una strategia per gli stati uniti d'Europa* [A Strategy for the United States of Europe] (Bologna, il Mulino 1989) pp. 168-169. Original: 'Un' iniziativa italiana per l'Europa. Democratizarre le Comunità', *Quaderno del CIDE* no. 1, (Rome 1964) pp. 13-26. Translated by the author.

[3] CIG 87/2/04 REV 2 of 29 October 2004, available at: <http://europa.eu.int/constitution/constitution_en.htm>, visited on 10 November 2004.

[4] In Belgium, the Czech Republic, Denmark, France, Ireland, Luxembourg, the Netherlands, Poland, Portugal, Spain, and the United Kingdom.

[5] In Italy and Lithuania.

[6] In Cyprus, Germany, Greece, and Malta.

*D. Curtin, A.E. Kellermann and S. Blockmans, eds., The EU Constitution: The Best Way Forward?*
© 2005, T.M.C. Asser Instituut, The Hague.

2.  LEGAL ISSUES

## 2.1   Parallel National Referendums, but no European Referendum

The eleven referendums to come are parallel national referendums, but *no genuinely European referendum.*[7] A European referendum would have had its legal basis in EU law. Proponents of a European referendum on the Constitutional Treaty were – among others – (only) 97 of 210 members of the Convention,[8] academics,[9] judges,[10] politicians[11] and NGOs.[12] In theory, such a European referendum could have formed part of a European revolution. A revolutionary act could have established a genuinely new constitution in normative discontinuity to the existing treaties. A referendum would have been one option of approving the new, revolutionary constitution.

In reality, however, the Constitutional Treaty came into being by means of legal evolution in normative continuity to the existing law. The Constitutional Treaty is formally an amendment of the EC and EU Treaties (cf., also Art. IV-438 TCE on 'succession and legal continuity'). The revision procedure of Article 48 TEU has governed this amendment process. As a sole exception, the Constitutional Convention 2002/03 was introduced as a novel step without any formal legal basis. According to Article 48(3) TEU and Article IV-447 TCE, the ratification by all Contracting Parties in accordance with their respective constitution-

---

[7] See for overviews of the constitutional law and the political debate in the Member States: N. Hussain, et al., *Referendums on the EU Constitutional Treaty: The State of Play* (Chatham House, European Programme, October 2004, EP BP 04/01) available at: <http://www.riia.org/pdf/research/europe/BP-NHOct04.pdf>, visited on 21 December 2004; A. Maurer and A. Stengel, 'Ein Referendum für Europas Verfassungsvertrag?', *Stiftung Wissenschaft und Politik* (August 2004) available at: <http://www.swp-berlin.org/common get_document.php?id=1020&PHPSESSID=add6a08339d77a1d96efbf9f22b6c768>, visited on 17 December 2004; S. Hölscheid and I. Putz, 'Referenden in Europa', 56 *Die öffentliche Verwaltung* (2003) p. 737.

[8] 'Contribution submitted by several members, alternate members and observers: "Referendum on the European Constitution"' of 31 March 2003 (CONV 658/03), available at: <http://register.consilium.eu.int/pdf/en/03/cv00/cv00658en03.pdf>, visited on 23 September 2004.

[9] But see, critically, M. Zuleeg, 'Die Vorzüge der Europäischen Verfassung', in A. von Bogdandy, ed., *Europäisches Verfassungsrecht* (Berlin, Springer 2003) p. 931, at p. 952.

[10] See, e.g., Jutta Limbach, former President of the German Constitutional Court, statement in the *Frankfurter Allgemeine Zeitung* of 29 August 2002, p. 1; Günter Hirsch, President of the German Federal High Court (in an expert hearing of the German Federal parliament's committee for EU afffairs on 14 March 2001) available at: <http://www.bundestag.de/presse/hib/2001/2001_072/07.html>, visited on 8 August 2003.

[11] See, e.g., the Prime Minister of the German *Land* Bavaria in a speech at the Humboldt-University in Berlin on 8 November 2001, available at: <http://www.bayern.de/Presse-Info/Reden/2001/11-08.html>, visited on 21 December 2004; the Spanish Head of Government José Maria Aznar, *Neue Zürcher Zeitung* (14 April 2003) available at: <http://www.nzz.ch/2003/04/14/al/page-article8SNRJ.html>, visited on 21 December 2004.

[12] NGO referendum campaign, available at: <http://www.european-referendum.org>, visited on 21 December 2004.

al requirements is needed. Provided that all the instruments of ratification have been deposited, the Constitutional Treaty shall enter into force on 1 November 2006. As regards future amendments of the Constitutional Treaty, the ordinary revision procedure as foreseen in Article IV-443 TCE will consist in a Convention, which will issue a recommendation, a Conference of the representatives of the governments, and, finally, ratification by all Member States in accordance with their respective constitutional requirements.

To sum up, no legal basis for a European referendum exists in primary EC/EU law as it stands. Neither is a legal basis for a European referendum providable by secondary EC law, because a legal basis for a potential European Act which could foresee such a referendum is lacking.[13] And thirdly, even the Constitutional Treaty does not foresee a referendum for its own entry into force or for future amendments.

The projected Member States' referendums on the Constitutional Treaty will have their *legal basis in domestic law*. Member States' referendums on European issues already have a tradition. A total of 19 Member States' constitutions contain provisions on referendums, and 17 of the 25 Member States already have experience with referendums on European affairs. Since 1972, 33 such referendums have taken place. With regard to the Constitutional Treaty, the European Parliament explicitly called for Member State referendums.[14] Six Member States' constitutions, however, do not allow for referendums. Here, constitutional amendments or the enactment of a new bill on referendums are necessary in order to organize a referendum on the Constitutional Treaty.

## 2.2    The National Legal Bases for the Eleven Referendums on the European Constitutional Treaty

I will now briefly discuss the constitutional bases for the projected referendums on the Constitutional Treaty.[15] In at least nine of the eleven Member States which have so far announced a referendum ('Referendum States'), the envisaged referendum on the Constitutional Treaty is not mandated by the respective domestic constitution. However, the constitutional maneuvering space for the political actors differs.

---

[13] Hölscheid and Putz, loc. cit. n. 7, at p. 743.

[14] EP Resolution on the Draft Treaty establishing a Constitution for Europe of 24 September 2003, para. 40: 'Considers that Member States that hold referenda on the draft Constitution should if possible hold such referenda or ratify the Constitution in accordance with their constitutional provisions on the same day', *Doc. 11047/2003 - C5-0340/2003 - 2003/0902 (CNS)*, available at <http://ue.eu.int/uedocs/cmsUpload/European%20Parliament%20resolution.pdf>, visited on 9 November 2004.

[15] If not noted otherwise, the respective constitutional provisions are cited according to the English translations available on the website 'International Constitutional Law', 'Constitutional Documents', available at: <http://www.oefre.unibe.ch/law/icl/index.html>, visited on 17 December 2004.

In three of the eleven Referendum States (in France, Denmark and Ireland), the projected referendums are, although probably not strictly mandated by the national constitution, quasi-inevitable. In France, Article 11 of the French Constitution allows for a referendum on certain bills, including the ratification of a treaty which, though not unconstitutional, would affect the functioning of existing institutions.[16] However, according to a decision of the *Conseil Constitutionnel* of 19 November 2004, the implementation of various provisions of the Constitutional Treaty is not possible without an amendment of the French Constitution. Therefore, the authorisation to ratify the Constitutional Treaty requires a prior constitutional amendment.[17] The French referendum will consequently be a referendum under Article 89 of the Constitution. This provision mandates a referendum on any constitutional amendment, unless the president decides to submit the amendment to parliament, in which case a three-fifths majority for approval would be required.[18] Because of these high hurdles for the adoption of the Constitutional Treaty without a referendum, it seems fair to say that the French referendum under Article 89 of the French Constitution is 'quasi-mandatory'.

Article 20 of the Danish Constitution requires a referendum on the delegation of powers to an international authority if the very high majority of five-sixths of members of parliament is not obtained.[19] So this constitutional provision tilts in

---

[16] Art. 11(1) French Constitution of 4 October 1958:
'The President of the Republic may, on the proposal of the Government during sessions, or on a joint motion of the two Assemblies published in the Official Journal, submit to a referendum any bill dealing with the organization of the governmental authorities, entailing approval of a Community agreement or providing for authority to ratify a treaty which, though not unconstitutional, would affect the functioning of [existing] institutions.'

[17] Décision No. 2004-505 DC, available at: <http://www.conseil-constitutionnel.fr/decision/2004/2004505/2004505dc.htm>, visited on 10 December 2004.

[18] Art. 89 French Constitution of 4 October 1958:
'(1) The initiative for amending the Constitution shall belong both to the President of the Republic on the proposal of the Prime Minister and to the members of Parliament. (2) A government or a Member's bill to amend the Constitution shall be passed by the two assemblies in identical terms. The amendment shall have effect after approval by referendum. (3) Nevertheless, the proposed amendment shall not be submitted to referendum where the President of the Republic decides to submit it to Parliament convened in Congress; the government bill to amend the Constitution shall then be approved only if it is adopted by a three-fifths majority of the votes cast. The Bureau of the Congress shall be that of the National Assembly.'

[19] Art. 20 of the Danish Constitution of 5 June 1953 [Delegation of Powers]:
'(1) Powers vested in the authorities of the Realm under this Constitution Act may, to such extent as shall be provided by Statute, be *delegated to international authorities* set up by mutual agreement with other states for the promotion of international rules of law and co-operation. (2) For the passing of a Bill dealing with the above a *majority of five-sixths of the Members of the Parliament* shall be required. *If this majority is not obtained*, whereas the majority required for the passing of ordinary Bills is obtained, and if the Government maintains it, *the Bill shall be submitted to the Electorate for approval or rejection in accordance with the rules for Referenda laid down in Section 42*' (emphasis added, status of document in English translation: 1992).

favour of a referendum. Besides, Article 88 of the Danish Constitution mandates a referendum for constitutional amendments.[20] This means that the ratification of an international treaty which requires prior constitutional amendments in order to bring the Danish Constitution into conformity with that Treaty must be approved by a referendum.

Similarly, Article 46 of the Irish Constitution requires a referendum for any constitutional amendment,[21] whereas Article 27 of the Irish Constitution allows for an optional referendum on bills of national importance.[22] As of December 2004, no authoritative legal assessments of the impact of the Constitutional Treaty on the Danish or Irish Constitutions have been issued. It is therefore not yet clear whether these State Constitutions will have to be amended. In that case, the referendums (which will in any case be held) would fall within the category of a 'mandatory' referendum under the Danish or Irish Constitutions.

In Spain, the constitutional basis for the projected referendum hinged (as in France, Denmark, and Ireland) on the impact of the Constitutional Treaty on the domestic constitution. Under Article 167 of the Spanish Constitution, constitutional amendments must be approved by a three-fifths majority in both parliamentary chambers and are submitted to a binding referendum if so required by one tenth of the members of either parliamentary chamber.[23] In contrast, 'politi-

---

[20] Section 88 [Constitutional Amendments, Electors' Vote]:

'When the Parliament passes a Bill for the purposes of a new constitutional provision, and the Government wishes to proceed with the matter, writs shall be issued for the election of Members of a new Parliament. If the Bill is passed unamended by the Parliament assembling after the election, the Bill shall within six months after its final passing be submitted to the Electors for approval or rejection by direct voting. Rules for this voting shall be laid down by Statute. If a majority of the persons taking part in the voting, and at least 40 per cent of the Electorate has voted in favour of the Bill as passed by the Parliament, and if the Bill receives the Royal Assent it shall form an integral part of the Constitution Act.' (Emphasis added)

[21] Art. 46 of the Irish Constitution of 1 July 1937:

'(1) Any provision of this Constitution may be amended, whether by way of variation, addition, or repeal, in the manner provided by this Article. (2) Every proposal for an amendment of this Constitution shall be initiated in Dáil Éireann [House of Representatives] as a Bill, and shall upon having been passed or deemed to have been passed by both Houses of the Oireachtas [Senate], be submitted by Referendum to the decision of the people in accordance with the law for the time being in force relating to the Referendum.' (Available at: <http://www.taoiseach.gov.ie/upload/static/256.pdf>, visited on 21 December 2004. Emphasis added. Art. 46 Sec. 3-5 omitted). The technicalities of the referendum are regulated in Art. 47 Irish Constitution.

[22] Art. 27 [Request of Veto]:

'(0) This Article applies to any Bill, other than a Bill expressed to be a Bill containing a proposal for the amendment of this Constitution, which shall have been deemed, by virtue of Article 23 hereof, to have been passed by both Houses of the Oireachtas [Parliament]. (1) A majority of the members of Seanad Éireann [Senate] and not less than one-third of the members of Dáil Éireann [House of Representatives] may by a joint petition addressed to the President by them under this Article request the President to decline to sign and promulgate as a law any Bill to which this article applies on the ground that the Bill contains a proposal of such national importance that the will of the people thereon ought to be ascertained.' (Sec. 2 -6 of Art. 27 omitted).

[23] Art. 167(3) Spanish Constitution of 29 December 1978:

'(1) Bills on constitutional amendments must be approved by a majority of three-fifths of

cal decisions of special importance', but without legal effects on the Spanish Constitution may be submitted to a merely consultative referendum under Article 92 of the Spanish Constitution.[24] In a declaration of 13 December 2004, the Spanish Constitutional Court found that no contradiction exists between the Constitutional Treaty and the domestic constitution and that therefore Article 93 of the Spanish Constitution is a sufficient basis for the ratification.[25] The Spanish government could consequently pursue its initial plan to hold an optional referendum under Article 92. It took place on 20 February 2005 as the first referendum on the Constitutional Treaty.[26]

In Poland, three potential legal foundations for an optional referendum exist: Article 125 is a *lex generalis* allowing for a referendum on 'matters of particular importance to the state'.[27] More specifically, Article 90 of the Polish Constitution provides for an optional referendum for the delegation of authority to an International Organization.[28] The second special clause is Article 235 which empowers certain constitutional organs to require the holding of a 'confirmatory referendum' on a constitutional amendment if fundamental constitutional principles are affected.[29] The referendum on the Constitutional Treaty will be based on

---

members of each House. If there is no agreement between the Houses, an effort to reach it shall be made by setting up a Joint Committee of an equal number of Members of Congress and Senators which shall submit a text to be voted on by the Congress and the Senate. (2) If approval is not obtained by means of the procedure outlined in the foregoing subsection, and provided that the text has been passed by the overall majority of the members of the Senate, the Congress may pass the amendment by a two-thirds vote in favour. (3) Once the amendment has been passed by the Cortes Generales, it shall be submitted to ratification by referendum, if so requested by one tenth of the members of either House within fifteen days after its passage.' (English translation on the official Spanish website, available at: <http://www.constitucion.es/constitucion/lenguas/ingles.html>, visited on 10 December 2004.

[24] Art. 92 of the Spanish Constitution of 29 December 1978:
'(1) Political decisions of special importance may be submitted to all citizens in a consultative referendum. (2) The referendum shall be called by the King on the President of the Government's proposal after previous authorization by the Congress. (3) An organic act shall lay down the terms and procedures for the different kinds of referendum provided for in this Constitution.'

[25] Tribunal Constitucional, DTC 1/2004, available at: <http://www.tribunalconstitucional.es/Stc2004/DTC2004-001.htm>, visited on 15 December 2004.

[26] Participation: 42,32%; yes: 76,73%; no: 17,24%; blank votes: 6,03%. Source: <http://www.constitucioneuropea.es/index.jsp>, visited on 22 February 2005.

[27] Art. 125(1) Polish Constitution of 2 April 1997: 'A nationwide referendum may be held in respect of matters of particular importance to the State.'

[28] Art. 90(3) Polish Constitution of 2 April 1997:
'Granting of consent for ratification of such agreement may also be passed by a nationwide referendum in accordance with the provisions of Article 125.'

[29] Art. 235(1) and (6) Polish Constitution:
'(1) A bill to amend the Constitution may be submitted by the following: at least one-fifth of the statutory number of Deputies; the Senate; or the President of the Republic. (...) (6): If a bill to amend the Constitution relates to the provisions of Chapters I, II or XII, the subjects specified in para. 1 above may require, within 45 days of the adoption of the bill by the Senate, the holding of a confirmatory referendum. Such subjects shall make application in the matter to the Marshal of the Sejm, who shall order the holding of a referendum within 60 days of the day of receipt of

Article 90, because it implies a delegation of authority to the new EU, but does not affect constitutional fundamentals.[30]

Under Article 115 of the Portuguese Constitution, a referendum may be convened on an international convention, if it concerns a 'matter of national interest'.[31]

In Luxembourg, Article 51(7) of the Constitution allows for a referendum under conditions to be determined by law.[32] Similarly, Article 10a of the Czech Constitution (on the transfer of powers to an International Organization) foresees that a constitutional Act may require a referendum.[33] Such an act has, however, not yet been enacted by parliament. In Belgium and in the Netherlands, the State Constitutions do not even contain any legal basis for referendums. They will be based on *ad hoc* laws in both countries.

---

the application. The amendment to the Constitution shall be deemed accepted if the majority of those voting express support for such amendment.'

[30] See on the Polish referendum of 7 and 8 June 2003 on the accession of the country to the EU, the judgement of the Polish Constitutional Court (Tribunal) K 11/03 of 27 May 2003, English summary available at: <http://www.trybunal.gov.pl/eng/index.htm>, visited on 22 February 2005 and generally S. Biernat, 'The Openness of the Constitution of the Republic of Poland Towards European Integration', in G. Amato, et al., eds., *The Constitutional Revision in Today's Europe* (London, Esperia Publications 2002) p. 339.

[31] Art. 115(1) Portuguese Constitution of 20 September 1997:
'Citizens having the right to vote who are registered in the national territory may be called upon to express their opinions directly, and in a binding form, through a referendum, on the decision of the President of the Republic following a proposal by the Assembly of the Republic or by the Government, on matters relating to their respective competence, in the circumstances, and subject to the provisions, prescribed by this Constitution and the law. (2) A referendum may also be held on the *initiative of citizens*, directed to the Assembly of the Republic, which shall be presented and considered under the terms and within the periods determined by law. (3) The only subjects for a referendum shall be those *matters of national interest* in respect of which the power of decision rests with the Assembly of the Republic or the Government through the *approval of an international convention* or the enactment of legislation.' (emphasis added) [cl. 4 spells out issues which can not be the subject of a referendum]. See also Arts. 162, 167 Portuguese Constitution.

[32] Art. 51(7) Luxemburg Constitution of 17 October 1868: 'The electors may be requested to pronounce themselves by way of a referendum in cases and under conditions to be determined by law.'

[33] Art. 10a of the Czech Constitution of 16 December 1992, introduced on 18 October 2001: '(1) Certain *powers* of Czech Republic authorities may be *transferred by treaty to an international organization* or institution. (2) The ratification of a treaty under paragraph 1 requires the consent of Parliament, unless *a constitutional act provides* that such ratification requires the approval obtained in a *referendum*.' (Emphasis added).

3.    POLICY AND FAIRNESS ISSUES

## 3.1    The Legal and Political Quality of the Constitutional Treaty does not compel its Adoption by Referendum

The desirability of a European referendum or of parallel referendums in the Member States might depend on the legal quality and on the political importance of the text which is at issue. According to Article I-1 TCE 'this Constitution' reflects 'the will of the citizens and the States of Europe'. In this quotation, two assertions are relevant for the issue of referendums. The first is its auto-qualification as a constitution, the second is the text's reference to the will of the citizens.

The qualification of the text of 29 October 2004 as a constitution is appropriate, although the document is technically speaking a hybrid between a contract and a constitution. On the contract side, we note that the text comes in the form of an interstate treaty under public international law, and that it is based on an unanimous agreement between the contracting parties. Its ratification and future amendments are subject to procedures which are normally applied to treaties.

On the other hand, the text also has constitutional qualities.[34] The document of 29 October 2004 fulfils typical functions of a constitution, such as the organization of the polity, the containment of political power, and the embodiment of basic values. It contains some typical constitutional contents such as rules on the powers of the institutions, programmatic provisions on the objectives of the Union, and justifying principles such as fundamental rights, democracy, and transparency.

Moreover, the document has some political significance. The text is an important consolidation and clarification of the law. Also the Convention process as a novel, relatively transparent and parliamentary procedure, which actually produced good results, was important and functional. In substance, the Constitutional Treaty introduces a number of institutional reforms, formalizes the Charter of Fundamental Rights, expands majority voting in the Council, modifies the scope of decision-making modes, introduces a new hierarchy of norms, reforms the budget provisions, confers legal personality to the EU, and more. And finally, the new provisions imply substantial new transfers of sovereignty to the European level (notably in home and justice affairs). Taken together, these features justify the denomination of the new document not only as a Constitutional Treaty, but as a Treaty Constitution, in short: as a 'European Constitution'.

However, neither the legal qualification as a constitution, nor the text's reference to the will of the citizens as its normative basis requires those citizens to pronounce their will by means of a European referendum. Throughout history, only very rarely have State constitutions been approved directly by the people.

---

[34] This qualification is of course based on the premise that constitutional law can be conceptualized beyond the State and that a European Constitution does not imply European statehood.

A different, though related, issue is the following: the legal qualification of the document of 29 October 2004 as a constitution does not necessarily mean that its adoption requires an amendment of the adopting Member States' constitutions. This is important, because in many Member States a constitutional amendment must be approved by a mandatory referendum (e.g., in Denmark and Ireland). [35] However, the assessment whether the adoption of the Constitutional Treaty requires a national constitutional amendment, is for the Member States to take individually and depends on the national constitution.

In sum, neither the text's legal quality, nor its substance, nor its political and symbolic value as a European Constitution compels resorting to a European referendum or to parallel Member States' referendums for its adoption.

## 3.2    Basic Arguments on Direct versus Indirect Citizens' Participation

Any assessment of the fairness and political soundness of the referendums on the Constitutional Treaty must start from general considerations on the merits of direct and indirect democratic participation, because in all Member States, the ratification of the Constitutional Treaty involves at least the national parliaments. This ensures an indirect approval of the Constitutional Treaty by the citizens via the ordinary channels of representative democracy. In contrast, the additional (or alternative) national referendums in eleven States ensure a direct democratic foundation of the Constitutional Treaty in those countries. In both cases, however, the phase of national ratification is a 'receptive', not creative one and an all or nothing decision. The Constitutional Treaty can only be accepted or rejected in its totality (by parliaments or by the citizens), and amendments are no longer possible.

In a general legitimacy perspective, a merely indirect participation of the citizens in the adoption of legal norms, including a new constitution, may even be preferable to the direct involvement of the citizens. It is often argued that lawmaking by the representatives of the citizens is more rational than decisionmaking by the citizens themselves. Referendums are ostensibly more prone to abuse and manipulation. Finally, it is pointed out that the ordinary people do not have the necessary expertise.

However, these standard arguments in favour of a purely representative democracy are hardly supported by empirical data. Moreover, the claim that the people is too stupid is not a permissible argument in a democracy. And emotions may also be positive for the polity due to their integrative effects.

Another classical argument against referendums is the danger of their manipulation through the formulation of the question. Throughout history, this danger did materialize, for instance in the German plebiscite under Hitler on the 'unification' of Austria with the German *Reich*. But in functioning democracies this

---

[35] Section 88 of the Danish Constitution, *supra* n. 20; Art. 46 of the Irish Constitution, *supra* n. 21.

danger can be met with procedural safeguards. Many European countries have enacted specific laws which precisely regulate the referendum process, e.g., with regard to the length of the debate, the financing and other important issues.[36] As a controlling body, special commissions are frequently installed in order to supervise the entire referendum process.[37] The Portuguese situation is a case in point. The Portuguese Parliament had suggested the following referendum question on the Constitutional Treaty: 'Do you agree with the Charter of Fundamental Rights, the rule of qualified majority voting and the new institutional framework of the EU, as defined by the European Constitution?' In December 2004, the Portuguese Constitutional Court ruled that this question was not objective, precise and sufficiently clear.[38] It will therefore have to be formulated in a more objective fashion. This example illustrates that appropriate safeguards may prevent manipulation and abuse. Anyway, the problem of a preselection of the issues is not specific to referendums, but exists also in relation to ordinary elections. Here, the political parties themselves have defined the issues and have preselected the candidates. The voters can only choose between those alternatives presented to them.

A further general objection raised against referendums is that their outcome is strongly influenced by extraneous factors such as the general political situation in the State and voters' satisfaction with their national government. But this seems true also for elections.

On the other side, various policy arguments are made in support of the citizens' direct participation in the form of referendums. Frequently, but misleadingly, it is asserted that a direct citizens' vote is somehow 'more democratic' and thus a more legitimate mode of expression of popular sovereignty than a merely indirect participation of the citizens in politics. However, representative democracy is an equivalent type of democracy. It is not 'less' democratic, but simply different from direct democracy. The claim of the superiority of direct democracy is based on a romantic and holistic mystification of 'the' people. In reality, even the direct vote does not manifest a more genuine, uniform will of the people, but reflects diverging interests and competing parties, just as they come into play in decision-making in a representative democracy.

In terms of democratic ideals, referendums on the Constitutional Treaty could be viewed as a natural continuation of the (comparatively) transparent constitutional debate. They therefore contribute to the fulfilment of the Laeken mandate, namely the improvement of democracy, transparency and the closeness of the

---

[36] See for example the British Political Parties, Elections and Referendums Act, available at: <http://www.hmso.gov.uk/acts/acts2000/20000041.htm>, visited on 22 December 2004; the Portuguese *Lei orgânica do regime do referendo* [Law on referendums] of 3 April 1998, available at: <http://www.cne.pt/Eleicoes/dlfiles/legis_lorr2002.pdf>, visited on 22 December 2004.

[37] In Portugal, a *Commisão Nacional de Eleiçöes*, in Ireland the Referendum Commission, in the UK an Electoral Commission.

[38] Acórdão No. 704/2004 of 20 December 2004, available at: <http://www.tribunalconstitucional.pt/tc/acordaos/20040704.html?impressao=1>, visited on 22 December 2004.

EU to the citizens.[39] However, in the logic of a model of deliberative democracy, the inverse can also be argued: because of the citizens' opportunity to participate in the Convention deliberation, an additional, formal citizens' vote is not required.

An important argument in favour of direct democracy is based on the observation that in a parliamentary democracy, government and parliament are closely tied up. Direct democracy allows other actors to come in and break up this alliance. Therefore, referendums, especially if they can be initiated by the citizens themselves or by a parliamentary minority,[40] can compensate for deficiencies in the parliamentary system such as purely party-oriented politics and power cartels.

Additional positive aspects of direct democracy are that referendums may encourage citizens' engagement and identification with the polity. Direct democratic decision-making may have stronger integrative effects than a purely representative system. In the current situation and with regard to the Constitutional Treaty, this is an important plus factor, because the European identity is still embryonic and precarious. Moreover, the referendum debate has indeed fostered the European political space by forging a transnational NGO coalition, the European referendum campaign. Generally speaking, direct democracy may also encourage more substantial communication (less ideology), may cut back the influence of interest groups, and may ultimately allow for more social learning.

Overall, both a representative procedure of decision-making and a direct vote by the citizens have specific strengths and shortcomings. A referendum is not *per se* a superior or more democratic type of procedure. Therefore, the question whether a popular vote on the Constitutional Treaty is preferable to the mere parliamentary approval of the EU Constitution should not be answered on the basis of a presumption in favour of direct participation, but with a view to the political context and to reasonably foreseeable legitimacy benefits in the concrete case.

### 3.3 Political Tactics

It would be naïve to blend out that the political decision to organize a referendum on the Constitutional Treaty (if not mandated by the national constitution), did not depend on theories of legitimacy, but primarily on the State's tradition and experience with referendums on Europe, on its political stability, and on the current political atmosphere in general.

Especially the timing depended on political factors. For example, in Portugal, the President dissolved the parliament in December 2004, which prompted gen-

---

[39] Laeken Declaration on the Future of the European Union of 15 December 2001, Part I: 'Europe at the Crossroads', with the sub-title: 'The democratic challenge facing Europe'. Part II: Challenges and Reforms in Renewed Union: 'The Union need to become more democratic, more transparent and more efficient.' Available at: <http://europa.eu.int/constitution/futurum/documents/offtext/doc151201_en.htm>, visited on 22 February 2005.

[40] See on this important point *infra* 3.5.

eral elections. The unintended consequence was that the scheduled Portuguese referendum on the Constitutional Treaty had to be postponed, because the Portuguese Constitution forbids referendums between the date for calling and carrying out a general election.[41]

Last but not least, proponents and opponents of European referendums on the Constitutional Treaty were driven by tactical considerations. In Poland, whose people is highly sceptical of the Constitutional Treaty, the announcement by the Polish Head of government, Miller, in October 2003 that a referendum would be organized was used in order to exert pressure in the Intergovernemental Conference so as to achieve modifications of the Constitutional Treaty in favour of the Member State. In Germany, which on the federal level is a strictly representative political system, a referendum was propagated because of expected spill-over effects for the introduction of direct democratic elements in the domestic realm. In Great Britain, both Conservatives and the Green Party favour referendums in the desire to delay or even block the ultimate coming into force of the Constitutional Treaty.[42] In the same vein, the referendums may be used as an instrument of protest against European integration as such. Popular disapproval in only one Member State (e.g., in the United Kingdom or in Poland) will most likely provoke a crisis for the entire integration process. Rejection of the Constitutional Treaty might trigger those States' withdrawal from the Union under Article I-60 TCE. More generally, popular disapproval in one Member State might pave the way for a Europe of two speeds.

Moreover, the referendum issue was tied to internal politics. In Germany, the Social Democrats' proposal to hold a referendum was used as a manoeuvre to divert from internal political difficulties. In France, the call by some parts of the socialist party to reject the Constitutional Treaty in the French referendum is motivated by personal questions in domestic politics and has nothing to do with the substance of the European Constitution or with the progress of European integration.

A final practical consideration is that the referendums on the Constitutional Treaty will result in a significant delay in the ratification process. However, the European Constitution-makers themselves have anticipated such a delay. According to the Declaration on the ratification of the Treaty establishing a Constitution for Europe, the matter will have to be referred to the European Council if within two years after signature (that is in October 2006), four fifths of the Member States have ratified it, but one or more Member States encounter difficulties.

---

[41] Art. 115(7) Portuguese Constitution of 20 September 1997:
'Referenda shall not be called or carried out between the dates for calling and carrying out a general election for the organs with supreme authority or the organs of self-government of the autonomous regions or of local government or for the European Parliament.'

[42] Cf., Charlemagne, 'The Ultraliberal Socialist Constitution', *The Economist* (18 September 2004) p. 42.

### 3.4  Parallel Member States' Referendums (as opposed to a European Referendum): Unequal Standards and Pseudo-Federalism

In terms of legitimacy, it is very important that the referendums on the Constitutional Treaty have their legal basis in the (constitutional) law of the Member States. They may have the same objective, but they differ with regard to timing and procedure. These procedural and technical details, notably the right of initiative[43] and the thresholds, are important factors which may secure or prevent legitimacy benefits through referendums. They are in numerous countries regulated in special statutes.[44]

One pre-condition of legitimacy gains is that a sufficiently long democratic debate must take place before the referendum. Equal access to media sources must be granted and a balanced dissemination of information must be possible. Moreover, financial transparency in the referendum campaign must be guaranteed. However, European-wide fair financial conditions can probably be realized only with the help of European directives. Also, the referendum should not be combined with national votes or elections on the same day. For example, the Polish referendum on the Constitutional Treaty is planned for 2005 in connection with the Polish presidential elections. The government's justification for this timing is that thereby a higher turnout will be secured. The drawback is, however, that voter behaviour tends to be influenced strongly by the national question at issue. Good practice also requires an opportunity to appeal against the referendum in the case of alleged procedural errors or fraud which may have affected the outcome.

A final and important element of good referendum practice are reasonable voter turnout thresholds, because excessive thresholds provoke boycott strategies. Such moderate voter turnout thresholds are established by the Danish Constitution (thirty percent, but for a constitutional amendment forty percent of the persons entitled to vote)[45] and the Irish Constitution (33.3 percent of the voters on the register).[46] In contrast, high thresholds are required by the Portuguese

---

[43] See *infra* 3.5.

[44] See, e.g., in the United Kingdom the Political Parties, Elections and Referendums Act, *supra* n. 36, in Portugal *Lei orgânica*, *supra* n. 36.

[45] Art. 42(5) of the Danish Constitution [Referendum]:

'At the Referendum votes shall be cast for or against the Bill. For the Bill to be rejected a majority of the electors taking part in the voting, however, *not less than thirty per cent of all persons entitled to vote*, shall have voted against the Bill.'

Art. 88 Danish Constitution [Constitutional Amendment]:

'When the Parliament passes a Bill for the purposes of a new constitutional provision, (...) the Bill shall within six months after its final passing be submitted to the Electors for approval or rejection by direct voting. (...) If a majority of the persons taking part in the voting, and at least *forty per cent of the Electorate* has voted in favour of the Bill as passed by the Parliament, and if the Bill receives the Royal Assent it shall form an integral part of the Constitution Act.' (Emphasis added).

[46] Art. 47(2.1) of the Irish Constitution of 1 July 1937:

Constitution (more than half of the persons entitled to vote must participate)[47] and by the Polish Constitution, where the result of a referendum is binding only if the minimum turnout rate is at least 50 per cent of the eligible voters.[48] Overall, it must be concluded that due to diverging national legislation, the projected referendums on the Constitutional Treaty will not equally satisfy the requirements of a good referendum practice.

Most importantly, the legal force of the referendums will not be identical. In seven out of the eleven Member States which have so far announced a referendum, the referendum will be binding,[49] namely in Denmark, France, Ireland, Luxembourg, Poland, Portugal and in the United Kingdom. A merely consultative (non-binding) referendum is foreseen by three States, namely by Belgium and by the Netherlands (on the basis of ordinary legislation in these states), and by Spain.[50] Arguably such consultative referendums do not provide any kind of legitimacy, because their results can be discarded or used as window-dressing by the governments.

These divergencies mean that less European guidelines exist and probably less uniformity will be present than with regard to the elections of the representatives of the European Parliament under Article 190 TCE. These inequalities raise the problem of the equal treatment of EU citizens. *Prima facie* there is no rational basis for the different opportunities to participate in a referendum or not, depending on the Member State one lives in.

On the other hand, parallel nationwide referendums arguably have the advantage of avoiding a potential political conflict in Members States which must anyway hold a mandatory referendum based on the national constitution.[51] In legal terms, European law claims priority over the national constitutions of the Member States. This would mean that an overall positive result of a hypothetical Eu-

---

'Every proposal, other than a proposal to amend the Constitution, which is submitted by Referendum to the decision of the people shall be held to have been *vetoed by the people if* a majority of the votes cast at such Referendum shall have been cast against its enactment into law and if the votes so cast against its enactment into law shall have amounted to *not less than thirty-three and one-third per cent of the voters on the register.*' (Emphasis added).

[47] Art. 115(11) of the Portuguese Constitution: 'A referendum shall only have binding force where the number of voters is greater than one half of the voters registered in the census.'

[48] Art. 125(3) of the Polish Constitution of 2 April 1997: 'A result of a nationwide referendum shall be binding, if more than half of the number of those having the right to vote have participated in it.' See for details on the problem of minimal turnout rates, A. Albi, 'Referendums in the CEE Candidate Countries: Implications for the EU Treaty Amendment Procedure', in C. Hillion, *EU Enlargement: A Legal Approach* (Oxford, Hart 2004) p. 57, at p. 66 with table 2.

[49] In total, 12 of the 25 Member States' constitutions allow for binding referendums.

[50] The binding character of the Spanish referendum depended on the constitutional basis of the referendum. While Art. 167 of the Spanish Constitution foresees a binding referendum, the referendum which took place under Art. 92 is only 'consultative' (see the text of Art. 92 *supra* n. 24).

[51] Maurer and Stengel, loc. cit. n. 7, at p. 5.

ropean referendum would overrule, e.g., a Danish 'no'. However, notably the Danish Superior Court explicitly denies that European law supersedes the national constitution.[52] In consequence, Danish courts would most likely give priority to the results of the national vote on the EU Constitution. In the light of this danger, parallel national referendums instead of a European referendum appear pragmatic and sensible.

A final consideration is that parallel referendums (as opposed to a genuinely European referendum) are some kind of a federalist solution, because the parallel referendums register approval or disapproval. This seems appropriate, because the EU is a transnational federal polity, and consequently, the decision-making process must include federal elements in order to take national identities into account.

A classic example of a federalist element in a popular vote is the Swiss scheme. In Switzerland, a proposal for a constitutional amendment must in the mandatory referendum be approved by 'the people and the Cantons.' The result of a popular vote in a Canton determines the vote of that Canton.[53] The requirement of approval in the sub-entities is an anti-majoritarian element in relation to the entire polity, because the voters in one or several sub-entities may be able to overrule the overall majority.

The fact that only parallel Member States' referendums (no European referendum) on the Constitutional Treaty will take place can be viewed as a *de facto* realization of the federal concern: votes will be counted separately per State, and disapproval in one country will block the entry into force of the Constitutional Treaty. However, the federal concern is exaggerated, because the population of only one single country, e.g., Denmark, which constitutes a very small minority of the entire EU citizenry, possesses the veto power. This comes close to a tyranny of the minority. In conclusion, parallel national referendums are saddled with serious policy and legitimacy shortcomings.

## 3.5    The Deplorable Absence of 'Bottom-Up Referendums'

The most important legitimacy gain of a referendum on the Constitutional Treaty is its *preventive effect*. The mere existence of this option functions as a 'Damocles sword'. If the political actors negotiating the text are aware of the need to gain approval in a referendum for this text, its contents will come out differently. But this preventive mechanism functions only if the referendum is mandatory[54] or if it can be triggered bottom-up through a *citizens'* initiative or at

---

[52] Danish Supreme Court, *Carlsen* v. *Rasmussen*, decision No. 361/1997 of 6 April 1998, available at: <http://www.eu-oplysningen.dk/dokumenter/traktat/amsterdam/bilag/grundlov/>, visited on 17 December 2004; the English translation can be found in 37 *CMLRev.* (1999) p. 854.

[53] Art. 140(1) lit. a); Art. 142(2) Swiss Constitution. English translation by the Embassy of Switzerland in Washington DC, available at: <http://www.admin.ch/ch/itl/rs/1/c101ENG.pdf>, visited on 21 December 2004.

[54] If the Member State's constitution mandates the referendum, the 'initiative' has already

the request of a parliamentary *minority*. Only in that case does the referendum function as an instrument of the opposition. The conferral of the right to initiative to a (parliamentary) minority is important, because in a parliamentary democracy, the parliamentary majority will generally take the identical position as the Government when it comes to deciding whether a referendum should be held. (Therefore there is hardly any political difference whether the right to initiate a referendum is vested in the Government or in Parliament deciding by majority vote, as we will see below.)

A referendum definitely has no preventive or oppositional function if it can only be triggered by the *executive branch* alone. For example, the French President may submit to a referendum any bill providing for authority to ratify a treaty which, though not unconstitutional, would affect the functioning of existing institutions.[55] A monopoly of initiative on the part of the executive branch is a 'plebiscitary trap', because the referendum will take place only if the executive branch anticipates a favourable outcome. In this case, the popular approval serves as window-dressing for political decisions taken by the President.

The preventive and oppositional function is likewise absent when the executive branch may take a political lead which must be formally approved by Parliament. This scheme is more or less functionally equivalent to an initiative by the legislative branch, because in both situations, a *parliamentary majority* must be secured in order to make the referendum happen. In the eleven Referendum States, seven national referendums had to be set up by a parliamentary majority, with or against the executive branch: in the United Kingdom, Prime Minister Tony Blair announced to Parliament that the Government plans a referendum on the Constitutional Treaty: 'Once agreed, (...) Parliament should debate it [the Treaty] in detail and decide upon it. Then let the people have the final say.'[56] This plan of the executive branch has to be implemented by the British Parliament, because specific legislation in this sense is required.

Just like the United Kingdom, Belgium does not have any constitutional foundation for a referendum. Nevertheless, Prime Minister Guy Verhofstadt announced that a non-binding referendum would be held on 1 June 2004. But, as in Britain, this must be legally implemented by Parliament. Currently, the Belgian Parliament is still undecided in this matter.[57]

In Luxembourg, Prime Minister Jean-Claude Juncker announced that a referendum would be held on 28 June 2003. Under Article 51(7) of the Constitution of Luxembourg 'the electors may be requested to pronounce themselves by way

---

been taken by the constitution-maker. An example is the Irish Constitution which requires a referendum for every constitutional amendment (Art. 46(2) Irish Constitution of 1 July 1937, *supra* n. 21).

[55] Art. 11(1) French Constitution of 4 October 1958, *supra* n. 16.

[56] Speech of 20 April 2004, available at: <http://www.number-10.gov.uk/output/Page5669.asp>, visited on 10 November 2004.

[57] Information based on the Government policy statement of 12 October 2004: *La déclaration de politique fédérale*, at p. 35, available at: <http://premier.fgov.be/fr/politics/20041012-pol-declar-fr.pdf>, visited on 10 November 2004.

of a referendum in cases and under conditions to be determined by law.'[58] A respective parliamentary motion was passed by a huge majority.[59] Although a Luxembourg bill to introduce a citizens' initiative is currently under consideration,[60] the projected referendum on the Constitutional Treaty was not initiated by the citizens.

In the Czech Republic, the ratification of an international treaty requires a three-fifths majority in Parliament.[61] Because of strong political opposition against the Constitutional Treaty in the Czech Parliament, Prime Minister Vladimir Spidla announced in October 2003 that a referendum would be held. This referendum would need a legal basis in a special constitutional act. Such a constitutional act can be adopted only with a three-fifths majority in Parliament.[62] It cannot therefore be introduced by the parliamentary opposition.

In the Netherlands, no constitutional foundation for a referendum exists. Although a temporary Act on Referendums allowed citizens to initiate nationwide non-binding referendums,[63] this Act cannot be the legal basis for a referendum on the Constitutional Treaty, because it does not apply to the implementation of international decisions or to constitutional amendments. Instead, it was the Dutch Parliament which voted in November 2003 in favour of holding a referendum on the Constitutional Treaty. This decision was taken against the wishes of the Prime Minister and despite the fact that all the major political parties declared their support for the EU Constitution.[64] Legally, the referendum will be based on an *ad hoc* law which is actually under consideration in Parliament.

According to the Constitution of Poland, a referendum on 'matters of particular importance to the State' or on 'granting of consent for ratifications of international agreements' is possible when a majority of at least 50 per cent of the Members of the parliament vote in favour of a referendum.[65] In Spain as well,

---

[58] Constitution of 17 October 1868, *supra* n. 15.

[59] For further details see <http://www.european-referendum.org/up/up44.html>, visited on 10 November 2004.

[60] In 1999, a Governmental declaration on the general extension of the referendum practice was issued. In December 2003, Luxembourg's Prime Minister submitted a law reform project which includes the introduction of the popular law initiative (10,000 electors) and the popular initiative to submit a law project to a consultative referendum (25,000 electors). See *Le referendum au Grand-Duché de Luxembourg*, available at: <http://www.gouvernement.lu/dossiers/elections/referendum/>, visited on 3 November 2004.

[61] See Art. 39(4) Czech Constitution of 16 December 1992: 'An approval of a three-fifths majority of all Deputies and of a three-fifths majority of Senators in attendance is required to pass a constitutional Act, as well as to approve the ratification of an international agreement stipulated in Section 10a, Subsection 1.', *supra* n. 15.

[62] Art. 39(4) Czech Constitution, *supra* n. 61.

[63] 'Tijdelijke referendumwet' [temporary Referendum Act] of 16 July 2001, *Staatsblad* (2001) p. 388, available at: <http://www.eerstekamer.nl/9324000/d/270/w27034st.pdf>, visited on 21 December 2004. The Act was in force from 1 January 2002 until 1 January 2005, and its validity was not extended into 2005, see <www.referendumwet.nl>, visited on 22 February 2005.

[64] Hussain, et al., loc. cit. n. 7, at p. 3

[65] The legal basis of the referendum on the Constitutional Treaty is Art. 90 of the Polish

the decision to hold the referendum depends on parliamentary approval.[66] In Ireland, the power to trigger a referendum is vested in both parliamentary chambers which must act jointly through a majority of the members of the Senate and not less than one-third of the members of the House of Representatives.[67]

A genuine *bottom-up referendum* is only possible in very few European countries: in Denmark, one sixth of the Members of Parliament can block a bill delegating powers to international authorities, which must then be submitted to a referendum.[68] The Portuguese Constitution confers the initiative for a referendum not only to the Government and to the parliamentary majority, but also to the citizens. [69] With regard to the Constitutional Treaty, the decision-making process was, however, not a bottom-up process. It was the Portuguese Prime Minister who decided to hold a referendum.[70]

To conclude, most of the eleven referendums on the Constitutional Treaty were initiated either by the government or by the majority in parliament. They therefore do not have a really critical function (and certainly no preventive effect), but they rather serve as an acclamatory tool.

## 3.6　Genetic Legitimacy versus Legitimacy through Performance

My crucial argument against referendums on the Constitutional Treaty is the observation that a popular vote confers a purely *'genetic' legitimacy,* which is, as a matter of principle, weak. This objection starts from the idea that constitutions are living instruments. Therefore, constitution-making does not happen in one big bang, but is a process through time. In contrast, the formal act of (popular) approval relates only to the *status quo*. Consequently, this isolated act cannot justify a constitution (for all times to come). If the constitution's contents do not prove to be good, or if circumstances change, the past single act of approval is no longer relevant. Even assuming that an act of popular approval is apt to justi-

---

Constitution of 2 April 1997, *supra* n. 15. Art. 90(3) refers to Art. 125:

'(1) A nationwide referendum may be held in respect of matters of particular importance to the State. (2) The right to order a nationwide referendum shall be vested in the Sejm [House of Representatives], to be taken by an absolute majority of votes in the presence of at least half of the statutory number of Deputies, or in the President of the Republic with the consent of the Senate given by an absolute majority vote taken in the presence of at least half of the statutory number of Senators.'

[66] Art. 92 of the Spanish Constitution of 29 December 1978, text *supra* n. 24.

[67] Art. 27(1) of the Irish Constitution of 1 July 1937, text *supra* n. 22.

[68] Art. 20 of the Danish Constitution of 5 June 1953, text *supra* n. 19. See also the more general provision in Art. 42(1):

'Where a Bill has been passed by the Parliament, *one-third of the Members of the Parliament* may within three week-days from the final passing of the Bill request of the President that the Bill be subjected to a Referendum. Such request shall be made in writing and signed by the Members making the request.' (Emphasis added).

[69] Art. 115(1) and (2) of the Portuguese Constitution, text *supra* n. 31. See for details the *Lei orgânica, supra* n. 36.

[70] See <http://www.european-referendum.org/up/up41.html>, visited on 15 November 2004.

fy a constitution, this does not hold true for future generations, who have not consented.[71]

The most important factor of the legitimacy of a constitution is not its mode of creation, but its performance and continuing popular support. Both can be verified only *ex post*. 'Social legitimacy' in the sense of acceptance and diffuse support, and output legitimacy, that is the actual performance of the constitution and the fulfilment of constitutional functions, do not (directly) depend on the genesis of the constitution. For example, the German Basic Law suffers from various 'birth defects': there was no public debate, no referendum by the German people and instead the Allied Powers exercised a strong influence by issuing guidelines, by requesting to be consulted and, finally, by their formal approval of the constitution. Nevertheless, the German Basic Law is a legitimate constitution.

Therefore my overall conclusion is that the parallel referendums will not contribute much to the legitimacy of the Constitutional Treaty. In the perspective of constitutional theory, we can well do without.

---

[71] T. Paine, 'The Rights of Man' (orig. 1792), in M.D. Conway, ed., *The Writings of Thomas Paine, Vol. II* (London, Routledge/Thoemmes Press 1996) p. 278:
'Every age and generation must be as free to act for itself in all cases as the age and generation which preceded it. (...) Man has no property in man; neither has any generation a property in the generations which are to follow. (...) It is the living, not the dead that are to be accommodated'.

Thomas Jefferson answered the question 'whether one generation of men has a right to bind another' in the negative and concluded that a constitution is valid only for one generation: '[N]o society can make a perpetual constitution, or even a perpetual law. The earth belongs always to the living generation. (...) Every constitution then, and every law, naturally expires at the end of 19 years', 'letter of 6 September 1789 to *Madison*', in M.D. Peterson, *The Portable Thomas Jefferson* (New York, Viking Press 1977) p. 444 (445 and 449).

Art. 28, sentence 2 of the French Constitution of 24 June 1793 which never entered into force proclaimed: 'Une génération ne peut assujettir à ses lois les générations futures.' (available at: <http://www2.toulouse.iufm.fr/defi/citoyenn/declarat/autres/1793.htm>, visited on 17 December 2004). Pertinent is also David Hume's famous critique of John Locke's theory of the social contract. This theory 'supposes the consent of the fathers to bind the children, even to the most remote generations, (which republican writers will never allow)', D. Hume, 'Of the Original Contract', in *idem*, 'Essays: Moral, Political, and Literary', T.H. Green, et al., eds., Vol. I (London, Longman 1898 (1748)) p. 447.

# FLEXIBILITY AND THE TREATY ESTABLISHING A CONSTITUTION FOR EUROPE

## Jo Shaw[*]

### 1. INTRODUCTION

'Flexibility' is one of the favourite words of a certain type of politician whose first instinct is always to ask how the European Union fits with his or her country, rather than to pose the same question the other way round. Not all of these politicians are British of course, but a good number of them are. One of the headlines of the September 2004 United Kingdom Government White Paper on the Treaty establishing a Constitution for Europe, which fired the long awaited opening shots in what will be a long-drawn-out ratification (and referendum) debate in the United Kingdom, argues that the Constitutional Treaty helps to make the European Union more 'flexible'.[1] What exactly does this mean? Is the White Paper correct in making this judgement?

Even though it is so frequently used in the EU context, those who adopt the term 'flexibility' and seek to apply it to the EU rarely specify precisely what they mean. What exactly do politicians mean when they ask for the EU to be more flexible? It seems unlikely that many politicians actually want to see a wholesale retreat from binding rules guaranteeing freedom of trade or movement between the Member States in favour of a discretionary system of open borders where Member States can pick and choose whether to apply EU law. If this 'pick 'n' mix' formula were to be adopted for the EU, many observers think that this might well spell the end of the EU as it exists at present. Consequently the call for the unravelling of the EU is not widely supported, except by certain types of Euro-sceptic voices.

Or does the invocation of 'flexibility', especially in the UK's relations with the EU, simply mean that politicians prefer an EU in which the UK can continue to opt out of two key dimensions of the continued integration project, namely Economic and Monetary Union and the single currency, and the Schengen area

---

[*] Senior Research Fellow at the Federal Trust for Education and Research, London and Salvesen Chair of European Institutions at the University of Edinburgh. This is a slightly updated and expanded version of a paper published in *European Current Law* (October 2004) pp. xi-xvi.

[1] Foreign and Commonwealth Office, *White Paper on the Treaty establishing a Constitution for Europe*, Cm 6309 (September 2004).

*D. Curtin, A.E. Kellermann and S. Blockmans, eds., The EU Constitution: The Best Way Forward?*
© 2005, T.M.C. Asser Instituut, The Hague.

of open borders? If so, their concerns are probably misplaced. None of the key parties within the negotiations on the EU Constitution – whether in the Convention of 2002-2003 or in the subsequent Intergovernmental Conference which concluded in June 2004 – seriously suggested that these opt-outs should be removed as part of the package of changes introduced. This is despite the unpopularity of the Schengen opt-out arrangements (given that they differ for the United Kingdom/Ireland and for Denmark, and given that they give rise to a high level of complexity in application) especially amongst EU insiders and many close observers of the EU and its workings. For example, in its so-called Penelope paper presenting an alternative schema for constitutional reform to the Convention,[2] the Commission loudly bemoaned the extent of disintegration within the EU legal order and suggested the elimination of key opt-outs. Despite this, economic and political realities at the present time, combined with the essentially immutable facts of physical geography, appear to suggest that these elements of differentiation with the EU 'core' will continue for the time being. Differentiation also applies in respect of the new Member States, although all ten are expected to join both the euro and Schengen in due course. These forms of flexibility at the point of accession are, therefore, by definition temporary in nature.

There is another idea of flexibility which is quite frequently evoked by politicians, which is the mirror image of the dominant UK conception of flexibility as a restrain on integration. This is the idea of the 'pioneer group', which was evoked on a number of occasions during the whole 'Future of the Union', Convention and IGC reform process, in particular at points when progress appeared to be stalling such as at the very beginning when the Treaty of Nice was casting a rather large shadow over the debate and more recently after the initial failure of the Italian Presidency to bring the IGC to a successful conclusion in December 2003.[3] In the latter context it was evoked as a threat to those blocking progress on the negotiation of the Constitutional Treaty, e.g., by insisting on the Nice Treaty arrangements on the form of qualified majority voting. Those Member States (and their politicians) which had felt particularly thwarted in their political objectives as a result of the collapse of the talks, which resulted from what appeared to be irreconcilable differences between France, Germany, Poland and

---

[2] European Commission, 'Feasibility Study: Contribution to a Preliminary Draft Constitution of the European Union', 4 December 2002 (presented on 5 December 2002) Working Document, available at: < http://europa.eu.int/futurum/docinstcomm_2002_en.htm>.

[3] See B. de Witte, 'Future Paths of Flexibility: Enhanced Cooperation, Partial Agreements and Pioneer Groups', in J. de Zwaan, et al., eds., *The European Union: An Ongoing Process of Integration. Liber Amicorum Alfred E. Kellermann* (The Hague, T.M.C. Asser Press 2004) pp. 141-152 with references to relevant press reports; see also F. Dehousse and W. Coussens, 'Flexible Integration: What could be the Potential Applications?', in F. Dehousse, W. Coussens and G. Grevi, *Integrating Europe: Multiple Speeds – One Direction?* (European Policy Centre, Working Paper 9 April 2004) pp. 4-38, available at: <http://www.theepc.be/TEWN/pdf/992512761_ EPC%20Working%20Paper%209%20Integrating%20Europe%20-%20Multiple%20Speeds% 20One%20Direction.pdf.>

Spain over the question of the definition of what constitutes a qualified majority vote in the Council of Ministers, (re)turned to the debate about a flexible Europe.

As often occurs at moments of crisis and turmoil regarding the possible stalling of the integration process, politicians turned in their rhetoric to invoking the possibilities of a hard-core proceeding with further integration as a reaction to the failure to achieve consensus amongst the twenty five Member States. The idea of such a re-formed Union often engages speculation about leaving behind Member States which are both unwilling and unable to proceed more quickly with integration, and the creation of a leaner, fitter hard core. In the context of the failure of the IGC, Grevi describes these moves as tactical rather than principled, concerned with pushing all Member States back to the bargaining table, rather than raising real possibilities of dramatic change.[4] However, as the Irish Presidency moved swiftly and skilfully to bring the parties back to the negotiation table, references to core Europe and pioneer groups disappeared as swiftly as they had appeared in the press. Bruno de Witte highlights very effectively the chimerical nature of these ideas by likening the pioneer group to a very famous myth:

'The pioneer group idea is like some kind of Loch Ness monster of the European integration process, rearing its curiously shaped head at irregular intervals but disappearing again shortly afterwards, leading observers to doubt the reality of what they have seen and to wonder whether the monster will reappear again in the future.'[5]

Thus debates about a hard core have largely disappeared again since early 2004, even though the Treaty itself is still lauded as a triumph of flexibility.

This paper highlights the protean nature of the 'flexibility' concept, which often provides a language for politicians with dramatically differing conceptions of both the ends and the means of European integration to converse with each other within the confines of European institutions such as the European Council, the Convention or the IGC, whilst maintaining the purity of their respective positions especially with a view to reassuring national political audiences. Flexibility in the EU context speaks more often to a pragmatic tradition of problem solving on a collective basis than it does to questions of principle about the nature of the integration project, although there is no reason why it could not be related in important ways to the latter.[6] Overall, flexibility plays an important role – but one which is often difficult to pin down – in the equally pragmatic *constitution composée* of the European Union, a Constitution comprising hitherto 'bits and pieces' of Treaty provisions, judgments of the Court of Justice, and a variety of other

---

[4] G. Grevi, 'Flexible Means to Further Integration', in Dehousse, et al., loc. cit. n. 3, at pp. 38-67.

[5] De Witte, loc. cit. n. 3, at p. 141.

[6] See generally the contributions to G. de Búrca and J. Scott, eds., *Constitutional Change in the EU: from Uniformity to Flexibility* (Oxford, Hart Publishing 2000) and B. de Witte, D. Hanf and E. Vos, eds., *The Many Faces of Differentiation in EU Law* (Antwerp, Intersentia 2001).

constitutional documents which will largely be gathered together and codified in the event that the Constitutional Treaty comes into force if it is ratified by all current twenty-five EU Member States.

This paper is limited in its coverage to reviewing actually existing cases of flexibility and specific mechanisms for facilitating flexibility under the Constitutional Treaty signed on 29 October 2004.[7] However, it takes as its starting point the proposition that flexibility will continue to be at least as important as it presently is for the future European Union, and that indeed it might conceivably become more important if the revised legal frameworks offered by the Constitutional Treaty, especially in the domain of defence and security policy, prove to be useful for the Member States. Overall, the Constitutional Treaty is unlikely to dispel the impression that the agenda of flexibility is, above all, one driven by the dominance of national interests, and that sometimes it is hard to see how instances of flexibility pursued within the framework of European integration directly foster the collective or 'European' interest.

## 2.    FLEXIBILITY UNDER THE EC AND EU TREATIES

In addition to cases such as Schengen and EMU, often called predetermined flexibility, the EU Treaties already currently provide for – or allow the existence of – several other types of flexibility. The most important in terms of practical application involve the Member States taking action outside the scope of the Treaties (the original basis for the Schengen agreements on border-free travel) and micro-flexibility through flexible approaches to regulation (e.g., minimum harmonisation of national law through directives and flexible soft governance approaches such as the Open Method of Coordination). In both cases, the overall constitutional framework of the EU sets constraints upon the freedom of action of the Member States and the EU institutions.[8] The Member States are free to conclude treaties under international law, but so far as these lead to obligations or effects which are not compatible with their responsibilities under the EU Treaties, they could be subject to enforcement actions brought by the Commission under Article 226 TEC for breach of the EC Treaty. In relation to flexible governance mechanisms, key principles concerned with the internal market and non-discrimination will set limits, especially where the measures in question are justifiable before national courts or the Court of Justice.

The Treaties also provide for so-called 'enhanced' or 'closer' cooperation under which groups of Member States are given formal consent by the Council of Ministers to pursue a path of closer integration in certain spheres of EU law and

---

[7] See the final agreed (and renumbered) text: CIG 87/2/04 REV 2, 29 October 2004.

[8] See B. de Witte, '"Old Flexibility": International Agreements between Member States', and G. de Búrca, 'Differentiation within the "Core"? The Case of the Internal Market', in De Búrca and Scott, loc. cit. n. 6.

policy, provided this does not undermine the core values of the European integration process, such as non-discrimination or the operation of the internal market. Three different sets of structures and conditions exist for the three pillars of
the Treaty on European Union – under the EC Treaty, in relation to police and
judicial cooperation in criminal matters, and in relation to the Common Foreign
and Security Policy. These mechanisms, although widely discussed by academics and practitioners alike, have never in fact been used, although they were introduced by the Treaty of Amsterdam back in 1999 and further 'tweaked' by the
Treaty of Nice in 2003 to make them more usable as instruments of EU governance.[9] Sometimes the use of enhanced cooperation has been threatened by the
majority of Member States in order to obtain agreement on the part of reluctant
Member States to measures which require a unanimous vote (e.g., in the case of
Italy and the European Arrest Warrant in late 2001). It will be interesting during
the latter part of 2004 and early 2005 to see whether preliminary studies amongst
a working group of Member States in favour of creating a common base for corporate taxation (a move opposed by the United Kingdom, Ireland, Slovenia, Estonia and Malta) will result in the first practical application of the enhanced cooperation provisions.[10]

3.      FLEXIBILITY AND THE EVOLUTION OF THE CONSTITUTIONAL
        TREATY

Despite the importance of these diverse cases of flexibility to the EU, the subject
was not at the forefront of the reform and renewal debates which triggered the
work of the Convention and the subsequent IGC. It was the topics of simplification and 'closeness of the EU to the citizen' which dominated the debates about
the future of the EU which intensified after the conclusion of the (unsatisfactory)
Treaty of Nice and the adoption of the Declaration on the Future of the Union, as
well as the subsequent Laeken Declaration which led to the establishment of the
Convention. Indeed, when preparing some suggestions on how flexibility might
be treated in what was then the proposed Constitutional Treaty at the beginning
of 2003, I found that there had been almost no direct treatment of the question
within the workings of the Convention up to that point (whether in plenary or in

---

[9] For commentary on Nice, see J. Shaw, 'Enhancing Cooperation after Nice: will the Treaty
do the Trick?' in M. Andenas and J. Usher, eds., *The Treaty of Nice and the EU Constitution*
(Oxford, Hart Publishing 2003) pp. 207-237; A. Stubb, *Negotiating Flexibility in the European
Union* (London, Palgrave 2002) esp. Ch. 6 'Assessing the Flexibility Clauses'; H. Bribosia, 'Les
coopérations renforcées au lendemain du traité de Nice', 1 *Revue du Droit de l'Union Européenne*
(2001) pp. 111-172; T. Jaeger, 'Enhanced Cooperation in the Treaty of Nice and Flexibility in
the Common Foreign and Security Policy', 7 *European Foreign Affairs Review* (2002) pp. 297-
316.
[10] S. Castles, 'Britain objects to Harmonised Tax Rate', *The Independent* (13 September 2004)
available at: <http://news.independent.co.uk/europe/story.jsp?story=561014>.

the working groups), and almost no external commentary upon the question in the specific context of the process of renewal offered by the Convention and the IGC which was to follow.[11] Consequently, my contributions to this topic necessarily consisted in reflection from first principles about what role flexibility might play in a reorganised and simplified treaty.[12] In fact, the first substantial contribution on flexibility – and specifically on the mechanism of enhanced cooperation – was not issued by the Presidium of the Convention until late May 2003, well into the last two months of the Convention's life span of nearly eighteen months.[13]

Yet despite this initial neglect of the topic within the formal confines of the Convention, flexibility did still emerge as a rather significant *Leitmotiv* of the proposed Constitutional Treaty and the debates which have surrounded it. This was in part because, in the end, the draft prepared by the Convention – and largely approved by the Intergovernmental Conference in this as in other respects – did make some small but significant steps towards the further constitutionalisation of flexibility within the EU. These involved further changes to the Amsterdam/Nice enhanced cooperation provisions, and a significant extension of the types of flexibility that can be applied in relation to the emergent European Security and Defence Policy (ESDP), and especially in relation to defence. However, the overall structure for flexibility under the Treaties remains the same. Flexibility also came more to the forefront of debate and concerns as the negotiations moved closer to a conclusion, because a conclusion to negotiations necessarily meant moving to the next and perhaps most tricky phase of ratification. In that context, many have become convinced that even though the Constitutional Treaty as a whole may founder, various aspects of flexibility, including enhanced cooperation and action, outwit the framework of the Treaties and could assist the process of putting at least some of the innovations in place.[14]

The most prominent provision on flexibility in the Treaty establishing a Constitution for Europe (TCE) comprises the general framework for enhanced coop-

---

[11] For an exception see E. Philippart, *A New Mechanism for Enhanced Cooperation for the Enlarged European Union* (Notre Europe 2003) available at: <http://www.notre-europe.asso.fr/IMG/pdf/Etud22-en.pdf>.

[12] See J. Shaw, 'Flexibility in a "Reorganized" and "Simplified" Treaty', in B. de Witte, ed., *Ten Reflections on a Constitutional Treaty for Europe* (Robert Schuman Centre for Advanced Studies, European University Institute 2003) available at: <http://www.iue.it/RSCAS/e-texts/200304-10RefConsTreaty.pdf>, and developed in more detail in J. Shaw, 'Flexibility in a "Reorganized" and "Simplified" Treaty', 40 *Common Market Law Review* (2003) p. 279. Specifically, I suggested that six different clauses should be separated out in the enhanced cooperation context: (a) definition and constitutional enabling; (b) conditions; (c) exclusions; (d) institutional arrangements; (e) consequences; (f) triggering and implementation.

[13] Conv 723/03, 23 May 2003.

[14] J. Shaw, 'What happens if the Constitutional Treaty is not ratified?', in I. Pernice and J. Zemanek, eds., *The Treaty on a Constitution for Europe: Perspectives after the IGC* (Baden-Baden, Nomos 2005, forthcoming); E. Philippart and M. Sie Dhian Ho, 'Flexibility and the New Constitutional Treaty of the European Union', 1 *WRR Paper* (The Hague, May 2003).

eration (Art. I-44 TCE).[15] It is notable that this is the *only* substantial reference to flexible frameworks for the development of policy and practice which appears in Part I, the section which purports to set out the most important constitutional principles for the EU. This is ironic given that enhanced cooperation has never (yet) been used. The important practical instances of flexibility, especially the arrangements on EMU and Schengen, are not regulated in the main body of the TCE, but in protocols and other annexes which essentially reproduce the existing EU *acquis*. The only reference to the fact that the euro is not the single currency for the *whole* EU[16] appears in Article I-13(1)(c) TCE which states that monetary policy is a form of exclusive competence only for those Member States which 'have adopted the euro'. Article I-18 TCE is headlined 'flexibility clause', but closer inspection shows that it is in truth the familiar residual legal basis provided in the current EC Treaty by Article 308, allowing measures to be taken by unanimous vote in the Council of Ministers where no other legal basis is available, provided the measure to be adopted falls within the overall competences of the Union and is necessary to attain one of the objectives of the Treaty. Traditionally EU law scholarship has subsumed the discussion of this under the headings of competence and implied powers, not flexibility.

Article I-44 TCE stands alone in a separate chapter III of Title V on the Exercise of Union Competence. Thus it is not treated as a separate form of competence, but as an addendum to the normal exercise of competence. Antonio López-Pina goes so far as to refer to it as a 'European form of government', to emphasise its autonomous nature.[17] It is in turn subject to those normal conditions, such as the new typology and hierarchy of legal acts established in the Constitutional Treaty. Enhanced cooperation effectively allows the sub-groups of Member States to borrow the institutions, procedures and practices of the EU in order to pursue their common objectives, namely closer integration. Subject to specific conditions laid down in relation to security and defence matters, and to a lesser extent the Common Foreign and Security Policy, enhanced cooperation can now be applied in the same manner and under the same conditions to all areas of EU policy-making, provided the basic conditions are applied. There are no longer any separate rules for justice and home affairs. The enhanced cooperation mechanism can only be applied in areas of non-exclusive competence (i.e., shared competences and areas where the Union's action is supporting or complementary in relation to that of the Member States). Only bare details of how the mechanism operates can be found in Article I-44 TCE, and in truth it really must

---

[15] For further analysis see also B. Donnelly and A. Dawes, 'The Beginning of the End or the End of the Beginning? Enhanced Co-operation in the Constitutional Treaty' (Federal Trust European Policy Brief, No. 7 (October 2004)) available at: <http://www.fedtrust.co.uk/admin/uploads/PolicyBrief7.pdf>.

[16] Art. I-8 TCE states that the euro is the currency of the Union.

[17] A. López-Pina, 'Enhanced Cooperation as a European Form of Government', in I. Pernice and M. Maduro, eds., *A Constitution for the European Union: First Comments on the 2003-Draft of the European Convention* (Baden-Baden, Nomos 2004).

be read in conjunction with the more elaborated provisions of Articles III-416 to III-423 TCE which set out procedures and conditions. The specific provisions on flexibility in relation to the European Security and Defence Policy also deserve separate attention.

It is arguable that the topic of enhanced cooperation is one of the fields in which the Convention's objective of making Part I a stand-alone and comprehensible statement of constitutional principles is simply not achieved (and probably could never be in relation to what is necessarily a complex idea of allowing subgroups of Member States to go it alone without the rest). 'Enhanced cooperation', like 'legal personality' perhaps, is simply not a commonsense idea. Thus, general readers of the EU Constitution, and indeed many lawyers, are unlikely to be greatly illuminated by what they read in Article I-44 TCE, any more than they would be by the bare statement in Article I-7 TCE that the Union 'shall have legal personality'.[18]

The key principles to be found in Article I-44 TCE are that enhanced cooperation is a last-resort mechanism, requiring the participation of at least one third of the Member States, which must aim to further the objectives of the Union, protect its interests, and reinforce its integration process. It must be open to all Member States at all times. Authorisation is given by the Council in the form of a European decision, indicating that the Constitutional Treaty's default decision-making formula of qualified majority voting will apply. Measures adopted within the framework of enhanced cooperation will be decided upon only by the participating Member States, although the non-participants may deliberate alongside the participants in the Council. Article I-44(4) TCE makes it clear that acts adopted in the context of enhanced cooperation are not part of the *acquis* which a new Member State must adopt on accession.[19] It is significant that this core statement of enhanced cooperation *does not* include any reference to the roles of the European Parliament and the Commission. In fact, closer inspection of Articles III-416 to III-423 TCE makes it clear that these two institutions are in fact given significant roles in relation to enhanced cooperation, a point which is important because they act as crucial binding elements within the institutional structures of the EU.

Article III-416 TCE specifies further conditions for enhanced cooperation, such as the obvious point that it must comply with the EU Constitution and with other provisions of EU law. Enhanced cooperation must not undermine the internal market or economic, social and territorial cohesion, it must not constitute a barrier to or discrimination in trade between Member States, and it must not distort competition between them. Article III-417 TCE keeps the participating and

---

[18] See a similar argument in relation to legal personality by B. de Witte, 'The Constitutional Law of External Relations', in Pernice and Maduro, loc. cit. n. 17, pp. 95-96.

[19] It should be noted that in Case T-135/96, *UEAPME* v. *Council* [1998] *ECR* II-2335, the Court of Justice concluded that a measure adopted within the framework of the UK's Maastricht social policy opt-out by the other Member States was a 'normal' part of Community law for the purposes of the application of general principles.

non-participating Member States apart by requiring the former to respect the competences, rights and obligations of the latter, and the latter not to impede the implementation of enhanced cooperation by the former. These are, in essence, simplified statements of principles originally articulated in the Amsterdam and Nice Treaties.

One novelty of the Constitutional Treaty provisions, as compared to those earlier versions of enhanced cooperation, is a reference in Article III-418 TCE to possible 'conditions of participation' in an instance of enhanced cooperation. This seems for the first time to open the door to enhanced cooperation being used by Member States which are willing *and able* to proceed with further integration in particular areas (e.g., environmental policy), with the door closed as a result of objective conditions to those Member States which are willing *but not able*. No reference is made to countervailing measures of assistance which might be used to enable those who are willing but not able to pass the threshold for participation. On the contrary, access will be policed both at the point of initiation, and at subsequent points of potential entry by non-participating Member States, with regard to whether such 'conditions' are satisfied. This could be a divisive force within the future (and ever more diverse) EU. On the other hand, it is none the less the clear task of both the Commission and the participating Member States to promote participation in any instance of enhanced cooperation.

The procedure for triggering enhanced cooperation (Art. III-419 TCE) requires a request by the Member States wanting to cooperate to the Commission to submit a proposal. Thus the Commission can block enhanced cooperation because authorisation can only be given by means of a European decision adopted by the Council on the basis of a proposal from the Commission. The Commission does not have to accede to the request for it to make a proposal. The European Parliament likewise has blocking powers as it must give its consent before the decision can be adopted. In contrast, in the normal case, no individual Member State has blocking powers, as the Council must act by a qualified majority. This is in contrast to the original position under the Amsterdam Treaty where every Member State was able to apply an emergency brake. That requirement was dropped already in the Treaty of Nice.[20] The Commission also has significant gateway powers in relation to a subsequent request by a Member State to join in an existing instance of enhanced cooperation (Art. III-420 TCE).

In common with the general tendency of the Constitutional Treaty to remove major distinctions between the old 'Maastricht' pillars of the EU, the instances of special procedures for the triggering of enhanced cooperation are reduced to a minimum. In the case of Common Foreign and Security Policy, the request to proceed with enhanced cooperation is forwarded to the Council. The Union Minister of Foreign Affairs is asked for an opinion as to whether it would be compatible with the Union's Common Foreign and Security Policy, and the Commis-

---

[20] See Shaw, loc. cit. n. 9, containing tables at pp. 224-225, 227 and 230-231 highlighting the differences between the Amsterdam and the Nice clauses.

sion is asked for an opinion on whether it is compatible with the Union's other policies. The European Parliament is merely informed. Authorisation is given by the Council acting unanimously.[21] The Council also polices the subsequent entry of non-participating Member States into an existing instance of enhanced cooperation.

An important gesture to those Member States which felt that the Constitutional Treaty as a whole has been unambitious in relation to the extension of qualified majority voting is that the enhanced cooperation provisions contain a *passerelle* clause allowing the Member States participating in an instance of enhanced cooperation to decide by unanimity to shift to qualified majority voting and to the ordinary legislative procedure for policy-making (Art. III-422 TCE). This obviously bypasses the full Treaty amendment procedure. The application of the *passerelle* clause is excluded in the case of measures having military or defence implications (Art. III-422(3) TCE). These provisions mirror a similar *passerelle* clause applicable to the CFSP as a whole under Article I-40(7) TCE, as well as the simplified revision procedure in relation to amendments to Part III, set out in Article IV-444 TCE. However, in contrast to the latter, no provision is made in Article III-422 TCE for national parliaments to enter objections to the application of the revision procedure, as is possible under Article IV-444 TCE.

The provisions which the Constitutional Treaty introduces in relation to possible flexible solutions to some of the complex and divisive issues raised by defence and security policy would on their own merit separate treatment if they were to be considered in full. There are additional specific provisions on the possibility of (permanent) 'structured cooperation' for groups of Member States whose military capabilities fulfil higher criteria and which wish to make binding commitments to each other (Art. I-41(6) and Art. III-312 TCE)[22] and on the possibility of the Council entrusting the implementation of defence-related tasks (e.g., peace-keeping or conflict prevention) to specific groups of Member States (Art. I-41(5) and Art. III-310 TCE). Flexible participation in the new European Defence Agency is also provided for, and general provision is made for so-called constructive abstention whereby a Member State's failure to vote does not preclude the adoption of a measure where unanimity is required to apply within the CFSP generally, and in particular in the context of security and defence policy. This is to prevent blockages in decision-making whilst at the same time respecting national sovereignty and distinctive national interests.

The proliferation of provisions in these areas in the Constitutional Treaty is testimony to the fertile nature of the field of security and defence policy for flex-

---

[21] The text prepared by the Convention was somewhat ambiguous on this matter: Art. III-325(2), *OJ* (2003) C169/01 (now Art. III-419 TCE). See Dehousse, et al., loc cit. n. 3 at p. 12.

[22] For a brief comment, see W. Wessels, 'A "Saut Constitutionnel" out of an Intergovernmental Trap? The Provisions of the Constitutional Treaty for the Common Foreign, Security and Defence Policy', in J.H.H. Weiler and C. Eisgruber, eds., *Altneuland: The EU Constitution in a Contextual Perspective* (Jean Monnet Working Paper 5/04, at pp. 14-15) available at: <http://www.jeanmonnetprogram.org/papers/04/040501-01.html>.

ible solutions to the challenge of proceeding further in this field, given the very diverse interests and approaches of the Member States (some are members of NATO, some are not; a minority are neutral states, etc.). However, under the Treaty of Nice, failure to resolve the disagreements amongst the Member States meant that areas with military and defence implications were completely excluded from the possible application of enhanced cooperation. As Thomas Jaeger noted, the exclusion of defence-related matters from the Nice settlement was not a matter of 'unmoveable principle'.[23] This was clear given that the Member States went quite far down the road to agreement during the IGC, but lacked the time to reach a conclusion. The reflection time provided by the Convention, which had a Working Group on Defence where flexibility issues were discussed, and subsequently by the IGC, provided the framework within which agreement could be reached on some quite far-reaching new arrangements. The changes introduced in the Constitutional Treaty represent an important achievement of the Convention and the IGC, and it is clear from developments from mid-2003 onwards, with the EU's Security and Defence Strategy and rapid moves to establish an armaments agency, that the Member States are set on a pre-emptive and anticipatory application of these particular provisions of the Constitutional Treaty, without waiting for the formalities of ratification.[24]

A generally warm welcome must be given to the endeavours of those who drafted the Constitutional Treaty to 'improve' the existing arrangements in relation to flexible integration, without completely altering the conditions under which – for example – enhanced cooperation could operate. The Constitutional Treaty does not provide a revolutionary change in the balance between the integrative and disintegrative elements of the enhanced cooperation mechanism. It no more attempts to define or encapsulate the concept of flexibility than do its predecessors as the founding Treaties of the EU. This remains disappointing, as does the unfortunate failure to provide a user-friendly definition of enhanced cooperation in Part I. Reading between the lines, however, it is clear that the Constitutional Treaty continues to recognise flexibility as a pragmatic response to the challenges of both widening and deepening in the EU context. It will, consequently, be an important – if always contested – aspect of the EU's future. It is bizarre, of course, to see that the enhanced cooperation provisions might end up being amended twice before they are ever used in practice. However, it is one of the ironies attaching to many of the provisions of the EU Treaties that they appear in general to be more easily amendable if they are of more recent vintage. It is some of the key provisions dating from the 1957 Treaty of Rome which are perhaps most in need of amendment, but which are in turn the most resistant to change.

---

[23]  See Jaeger, loc. cit. n. 9, at p. 307.
[24]  For the pre-emptive establishment of the Agency, see Council Joint Action 2004/551/CFSP of 12 July 2004 on the establishment of the European Defence Agency, *OJ* (2004) L245/17.

It would be good to think that the flexibility elements of the Constitutional Treaty might indeed strengthen the case for ratification especially if one looks at this from the perspective of upcoming UK debate including the prospective referendum. In fact, the UK White Paper quite soberly points out the precise areas in which it sees flexibility being offered by the Constitutional Treaty, although some of the features it identifies have in fact existed within the Treaties for some time. Sadly, it seems unlikely that the UK referendum debate will be conducted in the sober terms of the White Paper; rather the heightened and often misleading rhetoric of the United Kingdom's tabloid press will predominate. In that context, the niceties of enhanced cooperation seem unlikely to feature prominently in the debate, even if they now offer some subtle and interesting governance possibilities for the future EU.

# THE PROCESS AND IMPACT OF EU CONSTITUTION-MAKING: 'VOICE AND EXIT'

## Peter-Christian Müller-Graff[*]

The process and impact of EU Constitution-making in the light of having a 'voice' and providing the possibility of a possible 'exit' refers to two rather abstract and essayistic categories of self-determination, which have gained certain attention for structuring debates on the degree of influence in an organisation.[1] This contribution focuses on three aspects of this subject and develops three theses thereon: first, on the approach of the Treaty establishing a Constitution for Europe[2] (TCE) to the relation between the concept of a constitution and having the possibility to exit (1), second, on the specific exit option of non-ratification and its legal and political exit effects (2) and, third, on the basic relation between having a voice and providing the possibility of a possible exit within the projected new European Union in the case of ratification (3).

## 1. THE RELATION BETWEEN THE CONCEPT OF CONSTITUTION AND EXIT

The first thesis is that the Constitutional Treaty masters the conceptually paradoxical task of combining the idea of a constitution with the idea of exit. Three lines of thought lead to this result.

### 1.1 The Basic Contradiction between Constitution and Treaty

It is evident that the creation of a text which uses in one part of its self-description the word 'constitution' (*Verfassung*; Art. I-1 TCE) raises expectations which are different from those connected to a Treaty even if the text, in legal terms, projects a Treaty which is explicitly spelled out by its Title (*Vertrag über eine*

---

[*] Professor at the University of Heidelberg and Director of the Institute of European Law and Economic Law.

[1] See as the starting point for these categories: A. Hirschmann, *Exit, Voice and Loyalty - Responses to Decline in Firms, Organizations and States* (Cambridge, Harvard University Press 1970).

[2] CIG 87/2/04 REV 2, signed on 29 October 2004.

*D. Curtin, A.E. Kellermann and S. Blockmans, eds., The EU Constitution: The Best Way Forward?*
© 2005, T.M.C. Asser Instituut, The Hague.

*Verfassung für Europa*) and its legally essential fourth part (Arts. IV-437 et seq. TCE). While a Treaty like a private contract emphasizes the idea of voluntary self-binding and also implies, notwithstanding the basic principle *pacta sunt servanda*, the possibility of a potential exit at least in cases of important changes, the idea of a 'constitution' in the context of public powers stresses the notion of a durable collective polity with original public powers (*'Gemeinwesen'*),[3] the orientation to a common public good as mentioned, e.g., in Article I-26(1) TCE (*'Gemeinwohl'*),[4] solidarity and a common destiny (*'Schicksalsgemeinschaft'*) *without* a legitimate exit.

Hence the *combination* of both terms (Constitution and Treaty) will be and is already a source for permanent misunderstandings in the public perception of the text, but also in parts of the scholarly approaches to its categorisation[5] into the choice of 'relevant topics'[6] and into shaping and founding arguments in debates on the nature of the new European Union.[7]

## 1.2    The Tradition of the EC Treaty as a Constitutional Treaty

Nevertheless, the idea of a constitutional Treaty is not necessarily a paradox in *legal perception*, but a *correct description* of the creation and control mechanisms of public powers by an international Treaty. Hence this understanding of the primary law of the European Community as a constitutional Treaty with primacy over secondary law[8] and national law[9] has been present in parts of the legal doctrine for a long time[10] and in particular in Germany with its constitutional

---

[3] See P.-C. Müller-Graff, 'Europäische Verfassungsordnung – Notwendigkeit, Gestalt, Fortentwicklung', 5 *Europäisches Wirtschafts- und Steuerrecht* (2002) p. 206, at p. 209; *idem*, 'Verfassungsziele der EG/EU', in M. Dauses, ed., *Handbuch des EU-Wirtschaftsrechts* (Munich, C.H. Beck 2000) A I at no. 73.

[4] See for this idea, e.g., W. Brugger, 'Gemeinwohl als Ziel von Staat und Recht an der Jahrtausendwende – Das Beispiel Europäische Gemeinschaft', in P.-C. Müller-Graff and H. Roth, eds., *Recht und Rechtswissenschaft – Signaturen und Herausforderungen zum Jahrtausendbeginn* (Heidelberg, C.F. Müller 2000) pp. 15 et seq.; P.-C. Müller-Graff, *Unternehmensinvestitionen und Investitionssteuerung im Marktrecht* (Tübingen, Mohr 1984) pp. 355 et seq.

[5] In particular when the text is viewed in a one-sided perception as a constitution in the etatistic tradition.

[6] See in particular contributions which emphasize in particular state-analogous topics such as the protection of human rights or the creation of a common identity of the citizens as the most prominent future constitutional challenges.

[7] E.g., when the text is criticised for not corresponding to the form and the content of a national constitution.

[8] See, e.g., ECJ, judgment of 20 April 1987, Cases C-80/77 and C-81/77, *Société les Commissionaires Réunis* v. *Receveur des Douanes* [1978] *ECR* 927; order of 3 April 2000, Case C-376/98, *Germany* v. *European Parliament and Council* [2000] *ECR* 5525.

[9] See, e.g., ECJ, Case C-6/64, *Costa* v. *ENEL* [1964] *ECR* 1251.

[10] See, e.g., H.P. Ipsen, *Europäisches Gemeinschaftsrecht* (Tübingen, Mohr 1972) p. 64; R. Bieber and J. Schwarze, *Verfassungsentwicklung in der Europäischen Gemeinschaft* (Baden-Baden, Nomos 1984) p. 20; P.-C. Müller-Graff and E. Riedel, 'Gemeinsames Verfassungsrecht in der Europäischen Union', in P.-C. Müller-Graff and E. Riedel, eds., *Gemeinsames Verfassungsrecht in der Europäischen Union* (Baden-Baden, Nomos 1998) pp. 11 et seq.

court system[11] and its federal tradition.[12] This perception has even surfaced in an early judgement of the *Bundesverfassungsgericht*[13] and, more recently, in an opinion of the European Court of Justice.[14] However, this was never meant to be equated with a process of self-constitutionalisation at the European level.[15]

Therefore the creation of a Treaty establishing a Constitution for Europe implies no categorical novelty in this legal perspective. The word 'constitution' could be skipped and it would still be a constitutional treaty. On the other hand, it would be misleading to consider the Constitutional Treaty as the first non-state constitution in history, since neither is this Treaty a constitution in a state sense of original public power and common destiny nor is a constitutional Treaty currently lacking for the European Community. On the contrary, the Treaty establishing the European Community, apart from shaping the transnational substantive topics of objectives, transnational market freedoms, policy competences and other federal-like elements, necessarily covers classical constitutional issues such as institutions,[16] decision procedures,[17] implementation instruments,[18] the budget,[19] judicial review[20] and legitimacy for the European level.[21]

---

[11] See for the constitutional court system, e.g., E. Friesenhahn, *Die Verfassungsgerichtsbarkeit in der Bundesrepublik Deutschland* (Cologne, Heymanns 1963); K. Schlaich, 'Die Verfassungs-gerichtsbarkeit im Gefüge der Staatsfunktionen', 39 *Veröffentlichungen der Vereinigung der Deutschen Staatsrechtslehrer* (1980) pp. 99 et seq.

[12] The German federal tradition quickly recognized the European Economic Community in view of its competences as an organisation with federal-like elements; see, e.g., P. Badura, 'Die "Kunst der föderalen Form" – Der Bundesstaat in Europa und der europäische Föderalismus', in P. Badura and R. Scholz, eds., *Wege und Verfahren des Verfassungslebens, Festschrift für Peter Lerche zum 65. Geburtstag* (Munich, Beck 1993) p. 369; for a more recent appraisal, e.g., M. Herdegen, '"Föderative Grundsätze" in der Europäischen Union', in H.-J. Cremer, et al., eds., *Tradition und Weltoffenheit des Rechts. Festschrift für Helmut Steinberger* (Berlin, Springer 2002) pp. 1281 et seq.; H.-P. Schneider, 'Föderative Gewaltenteilung in Europa. Zur Kompetenzabgrenzung zwischen der Europäischen Union und ihren Mitgliedstaaten', *idem*, pp. 1401 et seq.

[13] See *Bundesverfassungsgericht* E 22, 293.

[14] See ECJ, Opinion 1/91 *European Economic Area I* [1991] *ECR* I-6079.

[15] See, e.g., P.-C. Müller-Graff, 'Europäische Föderation als Revolutionskonzept im europäischen Verfassungsraum?', 3 *Integration* (2000) p. 157, at pp. 162 et seq.

[16] See, e.g., Arts. 189 et seq. TEC.

[17] See, e.g., Arts. 251 et seq. TEC in combination with the respective empowerment clause such as, e.g., Arts. 94, 95 and 308 TEC.

[18] See, e.g., Art. 249 TEC.

[19] See Arts. 268 et seq. TEC.

[20] See in particular Arts. 230 and 234(1) TEC.

[21] See in particular for the European legal level, e.g., Arts. 313 TEC and 48 TEU for primary law and the empowerment provisions in combination with the procedural provisions of the TEC for secondary law.

## 1.3    The Exit Option in the Constitutional Treaty

It is well known that current primary law does not explicitly meet the requirement of an exit, although it is, in its structural types, a relational long-term[22]
(and – in addition – corporation-like)[23] Treaty. However, neither the applicability
of the principle of *'clausula rebus sic stantibus'* in international law nor the implications of Article 56 Vienna Convention could be convincingly excluded in
relation to the EC Treaty.[24] In a complicated reasoning the *Bundesverfassungsgericht* pointed to this shaky ground of primary law with a view to the fact that the
Monetary Union would deviate from the ratified path of stability.[25]

Now the Constitutional Treaty presents the utmost clarity in this respect for
the projected new Union and masters the *political challenge* posed to the 'makers' of the Constitutional Treaty to *combine* both core elements: voluntary adherence *and* (at least) a potential for a collective destiny. On the one hand, the new
text serves the latter by its enforced state-analogous language[26] and topics[27] and
by its polity potential as laid down in its existing and new provisions. On the
other hand, the idea of voluntary adherence is served by an explicit exit device,
namely the right of voluntary withdrawal from the Union without any legal requirement to provide substantial reasons for such a move (Art. I-60 TCE), although its real value is open to speculation. The new text also continues the basic
technique of amendments to primary law by the Member States[28] and the possibilities for reinforced cooperation between groups of them.[29]

## 2.    THE EXIT OPTION OF NON-RATIFICATION

The second thesis is that the exit option of non-ratification is full of paradoxes
and incalculable effects. Three observations point in this direction.

---

[22] See for the terminology and the implied distinction of relational contracts and transactional
contracts I.R. MacNeil, 'The Many Futures of Contracts', 47 *Southern California Law Review*
(1973) pp. 691, at p. 720.

[23] The *tertium comparationis* is the pursuit of common objectives as the structurally characteristic feature; for German law, see para. 705 *Bürgerliches Gesetzbuch*.

[24] See for the possibility of withdrawal under Art. 56 Vienna Convention, the article by Bruno
de Witte on p. 34 of this book, 'The Process of Ratification and the Crisis Options: A Legal
Perspective'.

[25] See *Bundesverfassungsgericht* E 89, 155.

[26] In particular the continuous use of the term 'constitution' in the first three parts, although
legally it is a Treaty as spelled out in the fourth part.

[27] See, in particular, the provision on the 'symbols' of the Union (Art. I-8 TCE).

[28] See Art. IV-443 TCE, but also the enhanced emphasis on the protection of human rights
(see P.-C. Müller-Graff, 'Die Kopfartikel des Verfassungsentwurfs für Europa – ein europarechtlicher
Vergleichsblick', *Integration* (2003) p. 111, at pp. 120 et seq.).

[29] See Art. I-44 TCE.

## 2.1    The Choice between Consent and Exit

In the projected ratification procedure[30] the reasonable unanimity principle gives every State the choice between consent or exit concerning the establishment of the new Union. Hereby the inclusion of the voice of the citizens convincingly depends upon the specific constitutional requirements of every State and hence it can vary.[31] This is a rational consequence of the basic concept that the Constitutional Treaty does not imply a self-constitutionalisation of a European polity, but is a Treaty.[32]

## 2.2    The Paradoxical Legal Effect of the Exit Option

In *legal* terms the exit option in the ratification procedure is limited and paradoxical. The rejection of the Constitutional Treaty, which in huge parts is only the repackaged *acquis*, does not end the adherence to the *acquis* of the Community and the Union as it exists. In particular the provisions on the very first path of realising the objectives of the present EC Treaty, namely the provisions on the internal market remain basically unchanged in the new text.[33] The same is true for the provisions on the Economic and Monetary Union[34] and for the array of other (in large parts flanking) policies.[35] Hence those who reject the Constitutional Treaty will find themselves legally bound by the core content of the rejected text.

## 2.3    The Incalculable and Ambiguous Political Effect of the Exit Option

However, in *political* terms the exit option by means of non-ratification is incalculable and ambiguous in its consequences in the long run.[36] This opens up a wide field of speculation with many unknown and varying factors.[37]

The rejection of the new text by a State may entail or generate internal political pressure in the respective State to leave the present European *acquis*. It will be gradually perceived that the issue of ratification is different from the alternative 'ratification vs. non-ratification'. Rather the core of framing the adequate

---

[30] See Art. IV-447 TCE.

[31] For a thorough analysis of this differentiated legal situation, see the article by Anne Peters on pp. 39-57 of this book, 'Referendums on the Constitutional Treaty 2004: A Citizens' Voice?'

[32] See P.-C. Müller-Graff, 'Strukturmerkmale des neuen Verfassungsvertrags für Europa', *Integration* (2004) p. 186, at pp. 189 et seq.

[33] See in particular Arts. III-130 et seq. TCE.

[34] See Arts. III-178 et seq.; and III-185 et seq. TCE.

[35] See Arts. III-203 et seq. TCE.

[36] See also De Witte, *supra* n. 24, at pp. 21 et seq.; J. Shaw, 'What happens if the Constitutional Treaty is not ratified?', in I. Pernice and J. Zemanek, eds., *The Treaty on a Constitution for Europe: Perspectives after the IGC* (Baden-Baden, Nomos 2005, forthcoming)

[37] See Shaw, *supra* n. 36.

referendum question is the alternative between ratifying the new Treaty or leaving the Union.

On the other side the rejection may indeed entail not only efforts for 'Nice plus' arrangements[38] or for accommodations in the tradition of prior failings of referendums,[39] but also recommendations[40] from other Member States to the respective State to look for a negotiated different status in the architecture of Europe outside the path of the Constitutional Treaty. It is easy to see that the factual weight and value of this exit option from the future and present Union may differ between the different States. For some few core countries probably no exit option will be seriously considered at all, while other States may, in the case of the failure of their ratification, come into a different and difficult political situation.

3.    RELATION BETWEEN VOICE AND EXIT IN THE PROJECTED NEW UNION

The third thesis is that in the case of ratification of the Constitutional Treaty the existence of the device of voluntary withdrawal can have an ambiguous effect on the voice of a Member State. Again three aspects are relevant in this respect.

### 3.1    The Impact of Voice and Exit in General

The impact of the so-called 'constitution-making' procedure on the future political reality, when seen in the light of 'voice and exit', may materialize in the degree of implementation and durability of the new text. Both depend upon the seriousness of the involvement of the claimed sources of legitimacy and addressees (citizens and States according to Art. I-1 TCE) in the 'making' period. In general one specific relation can be assumed: the stronger the voice of the Member States and the citizens within three areas of decisions, namely within the 'making' period, within the new framework of decision-making and within the amendment procedures of the Constitutional Treaty, is provided for and perceived by the addressees, the more durable the impact of the new text on political reality can be expected.

---

[38] For this scenario, see the article by De Witte, at pp. 28 et seq.

[39] See De Witte, at pp. 32 et seq.; for the Danish experience see H. Rasmussen, 'Europäische Integration durch Referenden? – Dänische Erfahrungen', in P.-C. Müller-Graff, ed., *Europäisches Recht im Querschnitt – Heidelberger Jean-Monnet-Vorlesungen zum Recht der Europäischen Ingegration* (Heidelberger Schriften zum Wirtschaftsrecht und Europarecht, Band 10, 2003) pp. 87 et seq.

[40] As a matter of course a non-ratifying State could not legally be forced to exit from the present European Union; see in this sense also De Witte, at pp. 35 et seq.

## 3.2    The Differentiated Channels of Voice

It is already well known that there are many differentiated channels and weights of voice on all three mentioned levels: within the 'making' period, within the new framework of decision-making and within the amendment procedures of the Constitutional Treaty.

a)    In the three-phase 'making' period (Convention, Intergovernmental Conference, ratification) the voice of the single Member State and its citizens, when seen in legal terms, *changes* in the different stages of the 'making'. It is visible that a *differentiated weight* of the 'voice' is inherent in the process. In general, the 'voice' was weaker in the Convention period than in the Intergovernmental Conference and the ratification period.

During the basic text-shaping Convention period which took place outside the present primary law scheme for amendments[41] every State (in conformity with the principle of equality of any State in international law) had the voice of the Convention Member, who represented its government, within the 'consensus' procedure pursued by the Presidency of the Convention, which, however, was no formal unanimity requirement.[42] The voice of the citizens in this 'consensus' procedure was represented by different mediatized channels: via the national government, via the representatives of the national parlaments and via the Members of the European Parliament.

During the period of the Intergovernmental Conference every State held a strong voice rooted in the unanimity requirement which gives the power to block the adoption of an amendment or repeal of the Treaties on which the Union is founded (Art. 48 TEU) and, by that, the potential for an exit from the procedure to establish a new binding text among all present Members. It is well known that this means was used by Spain and Poland in December 2003 and only withdrawn after negotiations had led to the final text which was adopted by the Intergovernmental Conference in June 2004. In this period the voice of the citizens was represented only by their national governments.

In the projected *regular ratification procedure* (Art. IV-447 TCE) again the unanimity principle gives every State the choice between consent or exit, while the method of including the voice of the citizens on the new legal conditions for the transnational polity depends upon the constitutional requirements of every State. However, it is visible that the unanimity principle implies an unproportional strong weight for any State

---

[41] The Convention method for amendments is introduced only by the Constitutional Treaty itself for the future; see Art. IV-443(2) TCE.

[42] For this understanding of 'consensus' see now the rule on the decision-making procedure within the European Council in Art. I-21(4) TCE which avoids the term 'unanimity'.

insofar as it has the potential to hinder the vast majority of other States to set the Constitutional Treaty into force.

b)  Within the *projected new framework of decision-making* in the new Union the weight of the voice of a national government depends upon the different modes of decision within the Council and the European Council. In the newly defined qualified majority voting it holds one vote and the weight of the size of the population represented by it.[43] This combination optimally fulfils the legitimacy requirements both of international law (equality of States) and of democracy (equality of citizens).[44] It is difficult to see how legislation[45] (the adoption of 'European laws'[46] and 'European framework laws'[47]) on the basis of qualified majority voting in the Council could be justified without fully taking into account the equality of citizens in this vote, as long as the concept of the European Parliament as embodied in the Treaty does not sufficiently fulfil this requirement of democratic legitimacy. This would prolong this specific democratic legitimacy problem for European legislation which has not been sufficiently resolved by the amendments of the Treaty of Nice.[48]

The weight of the voice of the citizens within the projected new framework of decision-making is determined by three devices: in a *government-mediatized* way by the national governments within the Council and the European Council (Art. I-46(2) TCE); in a *parliamentarian representative* way by the European Parliament (Art. I-46(2) TCE) and, in certain cases of legislation, by national parliaments (Protocol on Subsidiarity, Art. IV-444(3) TCE); and in a *direct* (although tamed) way by the possibility of a citizens' initiative (Art. I-47 TCE).

c)  Within the projected *different amendment procedures* (on the European level: Convention and Intergovernmental Conference,[49] Intergovernmental Conference alone[50] or European Council[51]) the voice of *any State* is guaranteed by different forms of the unanimity principle. The States are

---

[43]  See Art. I-25 TCE.

[44]  See P.-C. Müller-Graff, 'Systemrationalität in Kontinuität und Änderung des Europäischen Verfassungsvertrags', *Integration* (2003) p. 301, at p. 308 and 310.

[45]  For the topic of its substantial quality see A.E. Kellermann, et al., eds., *Improving the Quality of Legislation in Europe* (The Hague, Kluwer Law International 1998).

[46]  See Art. I-33(2) TCE.

[47]  See Art. I-33(1) subsection 2 TCE.

[48]  Art. 205(4) TEC tackles this problem, but is only inserted as a means of destruction, not of construction. In particular the ponderation of votes in Art. 205(2) TEC (e.g., Italy 29; Spain 27) lacks rational legitimacy.

[49]  See Art. IV-443(2) and (3) TCE.

[50]  See Art. IV-443(2) subsection 2 TCE.

[51]  See Arts. IV-444(1) and (2), IV-445(2) TCE.

protected by the requirements of ratification,[52] consent[53] or non-objection of the national Parliament.[54] The voice of the *citizens* can unfold in the ordinary amendment procedure through the channels of the 'consensus' procedure[55] of the Convention, the unanimity requirement of the Inter-governmental Conference[56] and the ratification in accordance with the respective national constitutional requirements.[57] Specific and differentiated safeguards apply within the *special* amendment procedures.[58]

## 3.3    The Ambiguous Effect of the Voluntary Withdrawal Option on the Weight of the Voice

However, for a complete picture of the voice in the projected framework of decision-making within the Union the new provision which grants the right of voluntary withdrawal of a State (Art. I-60 TCE) has to be taken into consideration. This right implies the most extreme form of expressing the voice of rejection. Its existence may have an ambiguous consequence for the political weight of the voice of a Member State. On the one side it may enhance its weight as long as the other Member States are willing (or eager) to continue the concrete member configuration of the Union in any case. If not, then the existence of the exit option may cause other Member States to give less political weight to the voice of a certain Member State in the long run by implicitly or even explicitly pointing to the possibility of voluntary withdrawal provided for by the Constitutional Treaty. This situation, on the reverse side, may, paradoxically, shape an overall prudent use of the voice of a State in the regular procedures of decision-making and hence contribute to the stability of the member configuration of the European Union also in the future.

---

[52] See Art. IV-443(3) subsection 2 TCE.
[53] See Art. IV-445(2) subsection 2 TCE.
[54] See Art. IV-444(3) TCE.
[55] See Art. IV-443(2) TCE.
[56] See Art. IV-443(3) TCE.
[57] See Art. IV-443(3) subsection 2 TCE.
[58] See Arts. IV-444 and 445 TCE.

# THE CONSTITUTIONAL TREATY AND THE NATURE OF EUROPEAN CONSTITUTIONALISM: THE TENSION BETWEEN INTERGOVERNMENTALISM AND CONSTITUTIONALISM IN THE EUROPEAN UNION

Miguel Poiares Maduro[*]

## 1.    INTRODUCTION

The currency of constitutionalism has become the dominant currency of the debates on European integration. But do we really know what we mean by constitutionalism in the European Union? We have moved from talking about a process of constitutionalisation to the question whether such a process represents a European Constitution (does Europe have a Constitution?). We have then discussed whether the Union requires a formal Constitution (does Europe need a Constitution?). Two issues underlie the discussion on both of these questions: whether constitutionalism is the best form of power[1] for the European Union and whether the European Union has the constitutional authority (in the form of a *pouvoir constituant*) to adopt this form of power. These constitutional questions can also be linked to two different types of legitimacy identified by Bellamy and Castiglione: regime and polity legitimacy.[2] The first relates to the legitimacy of

---

[*] Advocate General at the Court of Justice of the European Union. The views expressed are, naturally, purely in a personal capacity. I would like to thank Kieran Bradley and Carlos Closa for comments on this paper. This is a slightly adapted and shorter version of a paper entitled 'How Constitutional can the European Union be? The Tension between Intergovernmentalism and Constitutionalism in the European Union' originally published in J. Weiler and C.L. Eisgruber, eds., *Altneuland: The EU Constitution in a Contextual Perspective* (Jean Monnet Working Paper 5/04) available at: <http://www.jeanmonnetprogram.org/papers/04/040501-18.html>.

[1] The definition of constitutionalism as a form of power belongs to Francisco Rubio Llorente, *La forma del poder* (Madrid, Centro de Estudios Constitucionales 1993).

[2] The distinction between regime legitimacy and polity legitimacy (see below) was advanced by Bellamy and Castiglione. See R. Bellamy and D. Castiglione, 'Normative Theory and the European Union: Legitimizing the Euro-Polity and its Regime', in L. Tragardh, ed., *After National Democracy: Rights, Law and Power in the New Europe* (Oxford, Hart, forthcoming, cited in Neil Walker) and this was recently also used by Neil Walker, 'The White Paper in a Constitutional Context' (part of the Jean Monnet Working Paper no. 6/01) available at: <http://www.jeanmonnetprogram.org/papers/01/011001.rtf>. The meaning in which these expressions will be used here does not totally coincide with the meanings attributed to the expressions by these authors.

---

*D. Curtin, A.E. Kellermann and S. Blockmans, eds., The EU Constitution: The Best Way Forward?*
© 2005, T.M.C. Asser Instituut, The Hague.

the institutional and procedural mechanisms through which power is exercised in a polity. The second refers to the need to justify the existence of that polity.[3] In part, the Constitutional Treaty aims to provide the Union with these two forms of legitimacy. The way in which one answers these different questions in the context of the European Union is, in turn, influenced by the way we conceive constitutionalism in general (what does constitutionalism serve?) and the notion of a political community we embrace (what kind of social and political relationship must it contain?). Understood as a normative theory,[4] constitutionalism has been conceived as a set of legal and political instruments limiting power (constitutionalism as a limit to power). But it has also been conceived as a repository of the notions of the common good prevalent in a certain community and as an instrument to organise power so that it pursues that common good (constitutionalism as a form of polity expression). In between, it is possible to stress, instead, the role of constitutionalism in creating a framework in which competing notions of the common good can be made compatible or arbitrated in a manner which is acceptable to all (constitutionalism as a form of deliberation).[5]

Those three core conceptions of constitutionalism and their partial affinity with certain notions of polity allow me to present the key purpose of this paper: to identify the changing nature of European constitutionalism and its relationship with the intergovernmental aspects of power in the European Union. My argument will be that the role of constitutionalism is changing in the European Union and that its function depends on the relationship between the constitutional regime and polity legitimacy and, more generally, between constitutionalism and intergovernmentalism. The prevailing character of European constitutionalism has, so far, been determined by its instrumental relation to intergovernmentalism. However, this relationship may have to be changed in light of the regime changes introduced by the current constitutional processes of the European Union. For these purposes, a distinction will be made between constitutionalism (where individual interests are directly aggregated and deliberation is based on

---

[3] See also Neil Walker's five orders of constitutional pluralism questions. See N. Walker, 'The Idea of Constitutionalism', 65 *Modern Law Review* (2002) pp. 317-359.

[4] With this I mean a notion of constitutionalism that embraces a particular form of organizing power and not a neutral label for any fundamental document setting the organizational principles of a particular system or organization (in this latter sense, one can find constitutions in the most diverse settings from the United Nations Charter to the statutes of a golf club as a conventioneer at the Convention on the Future of Europe remarked).

[5] These notions of constitutionalism can, *prima facie*, be linked to different conceptions of polity. The first appears to correspond to the liberal emphasis on the protection of freedom and private autonomy. The second to the communitarian assumption of a thick form of association capable of supporting a notion of the common good. The third to a republican ideal of a contestatory and fully deliberative polity whose identity is secured by engagement in its permanent discussion. Such associations should not, however, be overemphasised. It is possible, for example, to adopt the last-mentioned version of constitutionalism in the context of a liberal polity. Moreover, constitutional reality often presents us with a mix of those different constitutional and polity conceptions.

the promotion of universal rules guaranteed, *ex ante*, by its generality and abstraction and, *ex post*, by non-discrimination) and intergovernmentalism (where
interests are aggregated through the State and deliberation does not aim at universal rules based on the individual status of citizens but reflects the bargaining
power of States and generates accommodating agreements between their perceived conflicting interests).

I will start by identifying the polity challenge faced by the European Union
and will relate it to the nature of European constitutionalism. It is in the light of
this that the question of whether the European Union needs a European Constitution and what type of constitutional authority that entails must be addressed.
After presenting this crisis, I will discuss the nature of the Convention process
entrusted with the resolution of this crisis. It is in the light of this discussion that
I will review the main changes introduced by the new Constitutional Treaty paying attention to the relationships between regime and polity legitimacy, and
between constitutionalism and intergovernmentalism. My overall argument is
that there is a paradigmatic tension between constitutionalism and intergovernmentalism embodied in the Constitutional Treaty.

## 2.    THE CONSTITUTIONAL QUESTION

Joseph Weiler famously described a process which he called the 'transformation
of Europe'.[6] This process included both a dynamic of constitutionalisation and of
Europeanisation leading to what could be described as a claim by Europe to normative and political authority, expressed in the doctrines of supremacy and direct
effect and its emergence as a community of open and undetermined political
goals. The legitimacy of this process was founded on a functional understanding
of the original Communities and was linked to a limited form of constitutionalism (focusing on the first form of constitutionalism mentioned above). But this
process did not affect the deliberative nature of the European Communities that
remained predominantly intergovernmental. The constitutional form of power
adopted was strictly limited to the adoption of those instruments of constitutionalism necessary to limit and, at the same time, legitimise the constitutional
authority claimed, but did not affect the nature of political deliberation. Its polity
legitimacy was either ignored, inspired by references to private autonomy, or
functionally linked (in different ways) to that of the States. As a consequence, its
regime legitimacy was dominated by the form of constitutionalism as a limit to
power and its polity legitimacy by private autonomy and functional legitimacy.

This was a consequence of the lack of constitutional authority. The Union
was not perceived as having the *pouvoir constituant* of a *demos*. In his contribution to this volume Joseph Weiler describes, in effect, the tensions arising
between constitutionalisation and the lack of a European *pouvoir constituant*.

---

[6] J. Weiler, 'The Transformation of Europe', 100 *Yale Law Journal* (1991) pp. 2403-2483.

It would appear that the clarification of the question of the nature of the authority of the European Union would required either a strict separation of
competences with the States (therefore limiting the political authority of the
Union) or a clear definition of the constitutional authority of the European Union
with regard to the Member States. For the second view, the Union should assume
a form of *pouvoir constituant*. Only this would clarify the extent of its constitutional authority and solve the problems raised by the normative and political
authority it already has. In my view, however, and in this I agree with Joseph
Weiler, it is in the nature of European constitutionalism itself that the question of
constitutional authority should remain open.[7]

One of the conclusions to be drawn from the current constitutional debates is
how difficult it is to establish the polity legitimacy of the European Union, but
also how strongly that is required to answer many of its current challenges. At
the same time, it is also clear that such a European polity cannot and ought not to
replace national polities. This requires the project of European integration to be
able to secure a delicate balance between the authority of national and European
polities. It is in this context that the concept of constitutional pluralism appears
particularly appropriate to describe this emerging relationship between a plurality of constitutional forums.[8] But this constitutional pluralism must not simply be
about regulating the question of the ultimate authority between national and EU
constitutions. It must be grounded on a particular understanding of the normative
value to be derived from this plurality of constitutional sources and of the relationship between EU and national political communities.

Gradually, some visions have been put forward that attempt to find, concerning the constitutional relationship between EU and national political
communities, the source of legitimacy for the emerging European polity.
Weiler's principle of constitutional tolerance is a good example. The EU would
be legitimated by openness to the other and the tolerance it would impose on
States, limiting the communitarian dangers inherent in the Nation State.[9] Christian Joerges' work also pays a great deal of attention to the legitimating power of
the inclusion of the other in national political processes promoted by EU law.[10]
Another trend includes multi-governance scholars such as Jo Shaw and republi-

---

[7] See Contrapunctual Law; M.P. Maduro, *Sovereignty in Transition* (Oxford, Hart Publishing
2003) pp. 501-537.

[8] See N. Walker, 'The Idea of Constitutional Pluralism', 65 *Modern Law Review* (2002) pp.
317-359.

[9] J.H.H. Weiler, 'Federalism and Constitutionalism: Europe's Sonderweg' (Jean Monnet Working
Papers, no. 10/00) available at: <www.jeanmonnetprogram.org/papers/index.html>. See, also, J.
Weiler's article on pp. 3-20 of this book.

[10] C. Joerges, 'European challenges to Private Law: On False Dichotomies, True Conflicts
and the Need for a Constitutional Perspective (Annual Conference of the Society of Public Teachers
of Law on 17-20 September 1997 at Warwick) 18 *Legal Studies* (1998) pp. 146-166; *idem*, 'Taking the Law Seriously: On Political Science and the Role of Law in the Process of European
Integration', 2 *European Law Journal* (1996) pp. 105-135.

can scholars such as Bellamy and Castiglione who stress the role of the EU in promoting the permanent contestability of democratic deliberations which, in turn, feeds the legitimacy of political communities.[11]

In previous works, I have argued for the legitimacy of the European Union grounded on its constitutional and democratic added value in reforming national political processes (with regard to external and internal democratic deficits) and in allowing a choice between polities.[12] There are at least three forms of national democratic deficit with regard to which European constitutionalism may bring an added value to European citizens. Firstly, national political processes no longer control many decision-making processes which impact on the national polity but take place outside its borders. In many cases, these are transnational processes (such as those of regulatory competition) that escape national democracies. Secondly, it has always been true that national democracy excludes from partici- pation and representation in the national political process many interests which are affected by its decisions. Elsewhere, I have presented this as the paradox of polity: a polity is both a condition for democracy and a limit on democracy (by limiting those that participate in the democratic process).[13] This difficulty is compatible with the claims of the modern citizen to have a voice in any polity that affects him or her and even to have a choice between different polities.[14] In this respect, national democracy cannot cope with our desire to be involved in different polities and does not legitimise the different decision-making processes that affect our lives. Thirdly, even from an internal perspective there is a grow- ing perception concerning the institutional malfunctions of national democracies. The recognition that the political process may be captured by small concentrated interests is one of the examples of the challenges facing traditional democratic models through parliamentary representation. But that is also the case with the recognition that collective decision-making often takes place outside the political process or that representation and participation depends on a set of variables much more complex than simply political participation through elections. In some cases, national political processes have become embedded with certain val- ues and assumptions that are no longer subject to deliberation. However, these values and assumptions are frequently the expression of particular interests.[15]

---

[11] J. Shaw, 'Process and Constitutional Discourse in the European Union', in C. Harvey, J. Morison, and J. Shaw, eds., *Voices, Spaces, and Processes in Constitutionalism* (Oxford, Blackwell 2000) pp. 4-37; Bellamy and Castiglione, op. cit n. 2.

[12] M.P. Maduro, *We the Court, The European Court of Justice and the European Economic Constitution* (Oxford, Hart Publishing 1998) and *idem* 'Europe and the Constitution: What if this is as good as it gets?' in: J.H.H. Weiler and M. Wind, eds., *European Constitutionalism beyond the State* (Cambridge, Cambridge University Press 2003).

[13] Ibid.

[14] See L. Pires, *Introdução ao Direito Constitucional Europeu* (Coimbra, Almedina 1997) at p. 67, who argued that national democracy is no longer able to satisfy the needs of the new 'multiple and supranational individual' which corresponds to the 'modern citizen'.

[15] These democratic problems can perhaps also be related to what Habermas described as the

Economic protectionism and the frequent 'hijacking' of the powerful concept of national interest are typical examples of these limits on the truly deliberative character of national democracies. European constitutionalism can be of added value to the citizen with regard to these different democratic deficits of national political communities. But it can also provide a new dimension to citizenship. Not only because it provides a new sphere of deliberation for problems we can no longer fully address at the national level, but also because it provides us with a kind of meta-democracy: the possibility to choose between different political communities.

This path for providing legitimacy to a European polity is however also linked to the regime developments undertaken by the European Union. The institutional regime depends on the polity legitimacy attributed to the Union and its relation with national polities. The definition of the competences of the Union also depends on its perception as a polity and the same could be said of the discussion on the goals of European integration. The reverse is also true, however. Some regime developments may require giving the Union a certain form of polity legitimacy. Certain majoritarian developments, for example, presuppose a form of democracy that requires a particular form of polity. The redistributive consequences of certain policies may also only be fully legitimated by a criterion of distributive justice agreed within a polity.

The extent and difficulty of the constitutionalism challenge faced by the Union derives from the fact that while European constitutionalism must have polity-building capacity, it must, at the same time, preserve polity diversity. In the first place, the ideal of political pluralism inherent in European constitutionalism extends itself to the question of the polity itself. In the second place, the maintenance of polity diversity in the context of an emerging polity creates a tension between the constitutionalism required by the latter and the intergovernmentalism imposed by the former. So far, this tension has been solved by keeping constitutionalism outside the deliberative process. The policies of the European Union are limited and constrained by constitutionalism, but they are still largely decided under the logic of intergovernmentalism. The extent to which this limited constitutionalism is compatible with the polity and regime developments of the Union is unclear.

---

relationship between life's world and system (J. Habermas, *Theory of Communicative Action*, Vol. 2 (Boston, Beacon Press 1973)). Systems are 'genetically' embodied with certain values and assumptions that are excluded from communicative action (that is, discourse, which is, according to Habermas, the most common way to legitimise moral statements and acts). What happens is that systems have taken control of life's world (where communicative action and rationality now predominate, albeit based on a set of common understandings and culture), in this way reducing the area of life and normative action subject to discourse. In other words, reducing the scope of democracy.

## 3.      THE CONSTITUTIONAL MOMENT

Many perceived the tensions created by the challenges highlighted as requiring a clearer definition of the *ethos* and *telos* of European integration to be expressed in the form of a new and fully assumed political contract.[16] In stark contrast, European constitutionalism has evolved as a simple functional consequence of the process of market integration without a discussion of the values it necessarily embodies. In other words, it was presented as a logical constitutional conclusion without a constitutional debate. In this respect, the current debate on the future of Europe was presented as a departure from the traditional way 'of doing constitutional business' in Europe. It was, first of all, presented as a constitutional moment.[17] To use the words of the Laeken declaration: 'the Union stands at a crossroads. A defining moment in its existence.'

To legitimate the constitutional exercise necessary to answer this moment, a different procedure was set up, one that comes closer to the idea of constitutional deliberation. The basis for this constitutional procedure was the Convention model, already adopted in what we could qualify as the pre-constitutional moment of the Charter of Fundamental Rights. Such a model appears to be closer to a traditional process of constitution-making than to the classic inter-governmental model that has so far dominated the revision of the Treaties.

However, what makes such a process more 'constitutional'? And how does it impact on the constitutional outcome? Usually, stress is placed on the broader scope of representation and the direct legitimation entailed in such a method. The Convention is composed of representatives of the EU institutions, national parliaments and national governments. In particular, the role played by national parliaments and the European Parliament was aimed at expressing a more direct link with the European citizens. These institutions (notably, national parliaments) are seen as expressing a form of direct representation that national governments lack. In this sense, the Convention method, by comparison with the inter-governmental method, appears to be closer to a Constitutional convention with direct representatives of the people reflecting the different social interests. But also the representatives of the national governments reflected a pattern of representation different from the classical intergovernmental process. In some cases, though not in all, they were independent personalities selected in view of their technical and/or political experience and not as representatives of the State. It is curious to note, however, that the number of independent personalities called in to represent the States decreased considerably from the Convention on the Charter of Fundamental Rights to the Convention on the Future of Europe. Regarding the former, national governments probably did not fully grasp the po-

---

[16] See N. Walker, 'After the Constitutional Moment' (Federal Trust Online Paper no. 32/03, The Federal Trust for Education and Research, 2003) available at: <http://www.fedtrust.co.uk/constitutionalpapers>.

[17] Whether or not it can, in fact, be described as a constitutional moment is much more doubtful.

tential impact of the Convention. Once it became obvious, after the example of
the Charter, that the Convention results would become, in practice, highly binding for the Intergovernmental Conference (due to its perceived reinforced
legitimacy), many national governments decided to send their ministers of foreign or European affairs as their representatives at the Convention. The
Convention was, in this respect, partly intergovernmentalised.

The Convention is also presented as promoting a broader participation from
the so-called 'civil society' (though the extent to which it did so successfully is a
cause of dispute).[18] At least theoretically, civil society participation was fur-
thered and a great deal of stress was placed on making the debates more
transparent for public opinion. This mirrors an idea of constitutional deliberation
for Europe: constitutional moments are identified with a much broader
mobilisation of society and a higher degree of direct participation by citizens.[19]
The deliberative process on the Constitutional Treaty would enhance Europe's
constitutionalisation by promoting such broad involvement which, at the same
time, would help to legitimate its final outcomes.

The constitutional character of the Convention method must, however, be discussed not only in the light of its scope of representation but also by taking into
account the character of its deliberative process. The second major difference
brought about by the Convention method concerns, precisely, the way in which
deliberation is expected to take place and the nature of the contract arising there
from. Intergovernmental conferences have as their purpose the production of an
agreement between States. A forum of intergovernmental bargaining is expected
to reduce information and transaction costs between States facilitating the adoption of cooperative decisions. Each state departs from a predefinition of the
national interest that it attempts to promote and harmonise with the interests of
the other States. This intergovernmental bargaining is quite different from the
nature of the deliberative process usually identified with the framing of Constitutions. In the latter, the vision of a social contract appears with its universal
ambitions. Deliberation is seen as an agreement among individuals on the basis
of universally constructed rules under a hypothetic veil of ignorance. The fram-
ers of a Constitution are seen as rational actors in search of universal rules that
can best satisfy everyone's future interests.

This form of constitutional deliberation is substantially different from intergovernmental bargaining even when we realise that every constitutional
deliberation is shaped and influenced by the specific interests of the participants
and the context they are in. The difference arises from four elements that the

---

[18] Regarding the Charter of Fundamental Rights see J. B. Liisberg, 'Does the EU Charter of
Fundamental Rights threaten the Supremacy of Community Law?', 38 *CMLRev.* (2001) p. 1171,
namely at p. 1182.

[19] For an in-depth analysis, see B. Ackerman, *We the People – Foundations*, Vol. 1 (Cambridge, Harvard University Press, 1998).

Convention method imperfectly expressed. First, the expectation is that an over-all political contract will be produced and not simply a particular negotiation on certain opposing interests; this helps to detach participants from their contextual stand-points and to take an overall long-term perspective that is more conducive to the universal rules typical of a Constitution. Second, the creation of a forum of stable medium-term deliberation, instead of the short-term highly concentrated (though previously prepared) intergovernmental conferences, shifts the attitude of participants towards the process of deliberation itself and promotes greater mutual trust, stronger involvement and a more rational engagement between the participants. Thirdly, the participants in the Convention are expected to consist of more independent individuals, more committed to certain rational conceptions of the common good than to pre-established assertions of national interest. Even when that is not the case, because, for example, national governments appoint public officials as their representatives in the Convention, the Convention method still promotes a more open deliberation on the part of the participants. This is due to the circumstance that the 'national interest' is not represented by a particular single representative at the process of negotiation. The variety of na-tional participants both releases them from being the individual guardians of a predefined national interest and challenges their respective notions of that na-tional interest. There is no single representation of the national interest. There are, instead, different conceptions of the national interest. This also promotes transnational interests to emerge through strategic coalitions between different sub-national groups. The fourth and final element conducive to a more constitu-tional characterisation of the Convention's deliberative method concerns its potential higher transparency. The subjection of the deliberative process to higher transparency requires arguments to be put forward in terms of universal rules of a social contract and not as a defence of the national interest. This change in the character of the arguments that participants can use will end up be-ing reflected in the agreements that they will reach.

It is wrong, however, to adopt an idealist perspective of the Convention method. On the one hand, this process entrusts a great degree of authority to those that shape the agenda and provide the required technical expertise and le-gal drafting. The 'independence' and the lack of in-depth expertise of many of the participants make them much more dependent on EU technocracy. At the same time, in such a large scale and comprehensive project the *Praesidium* and *Secretariat* assume a key role in setting the agenda, processing the different amendment proposals, drafting final versions and 'establishing' the consensus. In the case of the Convention on the Future of Europe one of the more frequent criticisms has been, precisely, that the entire scope of views expressed in the Convention has not, in reality, been reflected in the final document. This was also visible, in part and in a different way, in the process of drafting the Charter and namely in the tremendous impact that the EU technocracy and the Praesidium had on the final versions of the more contentious provisions, particu-

larly when compared with the degree of incorporation of the amendments proposed by other participants at the Convention and civil society.[20]

The third change in the nature of Europe's 'constitution making' introduced
by the Convention method regards the reinstatement of political control over the
constitutional development of European integration. As said above, it has often
been remarked that the constitutionalisation of EU law has been, to a considerable extent, a judicially-driven process. This has opened the constitutional
growth of the Union to legitimacy challenges and the Court itself has appeared,
at times, to expect the political process to take a more clear direction concerning
the constitutional development of the Union. The Charter of Fundamental Rights
and its legal status can be seen as an example of this. The Court is, in fact, often
placed in the difficult position of being asked to intervene in filling the constitutional vacuum left by the EU political process in not reaching a clear agreement
as has been the case with the legal status of the Charter.

The Convention and the larger constitutional process initiated with the Declaration on the Future of Europe can be seen as signalling a move away from the
judicial process towards the political process in the development of European
constitutionalism. There are important consequences that can be expected in the
outcomes arising from these two different processes once both representation
and the form of deliberation differ between them. It also impacts on the sources
of law and its process of discovery that have dominated the European Constitution. In the absence of a written Constitution, the Court of Justice has
constitutionalised the European Communities (now the EU) by reference to the
constitutional principles of its Member States. The EU Constitution becomes, in
this light, mainly a product of both the EU Treaties and national constitutions
and it is upon these sources that the constitutional values of the emerging polity
are to be found by the Court. Once the EU political process takes over, EU constitutional values become a product of a transnational deliberative process that
takes place at the EU level. The dynamics of this new constitutional political
arena are bound to determine a different set of constitutional values.

This formalisation and politicisation of the EU Constitution do not necessarily determine a lower importance for the role to be played by the European Court
of Justice in the context of European Constitutionalism. It is not so much a difference in relevance as it is mainly a change in the nature and character of the
role to be played by the Court. The emphasis will no longer be on establishing
the normative authority of EU law and creating a legally dogmatic constitutional
architecture to control that authority. Greater emphasis will have to be given, instead, to secure and clarify the constitutional conditions inherent in the political
community necessary to support the constitutional architecture set up by the
Constitutional Treaty. A major challenge will also be that of guaranteeing the
constitutional coherence of a document where constitutional ambitions are mixed

---

[20] See Liisberg, loc. cit. n. 18, at p. 1178.

with classical intergovernmental bargaining. These two logics (that of universal rules associated with a political contract among individuals and that of *ad hoc* agreements resulting from bargaining between States) do not necessarily fit together very well and will give rise to increased legal conflicts between, on the one hand, constitutional principles and fundamental rights and, on the other, intergovernmental agreements.

What has been said highlights that the Convention and the IGC were, in fact, a very peculiar form of constitutional moment: They did not completely adopt a form of constitutional deliberation. Nevertheless, that did not prevent the use of constitutional language to mould the new founding document of the European Union. It is wrong, however, to assume that the agreement on the use of constitutional language also entails an agreement on what constitutionalism means for the Union. In reality, there are two very different conceptions of constitutionalism underlying the apparent agreement on the use of the word Constitution and its associated concepts. One is the conception of constitutionalism as a limit to power. This grows upon the previous limited constitutionalisation of the Union and uses constitutionalism as much to protect the normative authority of the Union as to guarantee that such authority would not threaten the constitutional values of the Member States. The other is the conception of constitutionalism as a form of polity expression. This reflected the more ambitious views aiming to use constitutionalism as an instrument for building a political community in the EU. At the extreme, the expectation was even that such a process could be endowed with *pouvoir constituant* and serve to fully establish the constitutional authority of the Union.

A review of the four main constitutional issues of the Constitutional Treaty will help to highlight those two different conceptions. As will be discussed later, however, the notion of constitutionalism as a form of political deliberation remained absent from the debate. This, together with the conflicting influences exercised by those two notions of European constitutionalism, means that the tension between intergovernmentalism and constitutionalism will be reinforced.

## 4.   THE CONSTITUTIONAL TREATY: FOUR UNEASY PIECES

Several strategies have been presented to face the challenge of legitimacy in Europe. Many of them were actually reflected in the agenda for the 'Constitutional' Convention and have spilt over into the Constitutional text. Next, I will assess what are, in my view, the four core issues addressed by the Constitutional Treaty and their connected strategies of legitimacy for Europe. I will try to show that the legitimating power of these strategies depends both on different conceptions of constitutionalism and its relation with intergovernmentalism. In my view both those different conceptions and the tension between constitutionalism and intergovernmentalism is reflected in the constitutional text. I will also highlight the fact that albeit the focus of the Constitutional Treaty appears to be on improving regime legitimacy, this may not be possible without facing the question of polity legitimacy.

## 4.1   The Importance of being called a Constitution

The Constitutional form assumed by the Constitutional Treaty appears, in the first place, as the essential element of a strategy that appeals to the legitimating power of constitutionalism. There are several possible advantages entrusted in this formal constitutionalisation. A less ambitious thesis foresees the process of formal constitutionalisation as an opportunity to codify and clarify Europe's constitutional principles, fundamental rights and political organisation. But this is not seen simply as an exercise in tiding up. It is expected to have important consequences due to the mobilisation of political and legal discourses that will be promoted by a clearer exposition of the EU Constitution. The EU Constitution might not change much, but it would no longer be implicit. It will be there for citizens to discuss and engage and this, apart from its immediate legitimating value, could have important future political and legal spill-overs in the constitutional development of the Union.

A more aggressive version of the codification strategy argued for such an opportunity to be used in order to introduce a new set of constitutional foundations for the Union: a catalogue of fundamental rights, a clear allocation of competences, a 'truly' democratic institutional system for the Union. The formal constitution was presented as the instrument by which to advance these changes. But there are other arguments that have been put forward in favour of a formal constitution.[21]

First, the EU Constitution was expected to clarify the present constitutional system and its relationship with national constitutions and, in this process, to confirm the normative authority of the EU Constitution *vis-à-vis* those national constitutions. Second, the process of drafting a formal constitution was expected to constitute a polity-building process. It would finally give European citizens control over constitution-making in Europe. The mobilisation promoted by the constitutional process would, in itself, help to generate a European *demos*. In this light, it would be the exercise of *pouvoir constituant* at the European level that would lead to a European *demos* and not the reverse. For this view, constitutional authority, in line with the traditional conceptions of *pouvoir constituant*, is inseparable from the adoption of a Constitution. The adoption of a European Constitution would, as a consequence, be both the instrument by which to grant to the Union constitutional authority and evidence that the Union has it. But this link between the EU Constitution and its assumption of *pouvoir constituant* can be criticized in both normative and descriptive terms. It has been questioned, in

---

[21] For a critical summary of the arguments in favour of a European formal constitution, see also Weiler, loc. cit. n. 9.

the first place, whether the Union should and can assume a form of constitutional authority tantamount to a *pouvoir constituant*, mainly because that would entail replacing the national polities with the European polity and it could destroy the present plural relationship between the European and national constitutions. As mentioned above, such plural constitutionalism is a particular trademark of European constitutionalism and there are strong normative reasons to protect it. It reflects the nature of European constitutionalism as being founded on the competing claims of the European and national political communities.

The argument opposing a formal constitution asserts, instead, that such a constitution reflects a particular model of constitutionalism, that of national constitutionalism, that is associated with a state and an ultimate sovereign authority. It reflects a form of constitutionalism that is not and ought not to be that of European constitutionalism.

I agree with the concerns regarding any move that could allocate final constitutional authority to the EU. This does not mean, however, that the European Union ought not to have a constitutional future. The value of European constitutionalism lies precisely in its pluralistic form and the permanent dialogue it establishes with national constitutionalism. In this light, I nevertheless believe that the Union should adopt some form of constitutional document. The Union should have a Constitution.[22] Not as an expression of a constitutional authority which is supreme over the constitutional authority of the States, but as an expression of the adoption of constitutionalism as the form of power in the EU and of the polity-building character of the project of European integration.

The fact that the Union does not have a *pouvoir constituant* should not be confused with a lack of normative authority. Union norms can and must have normative authority (supremacy and direct effect) over national constitutional norms (that is an existential requirement for a single and coherent EU legal order), but that does not entail that the Union's normative authority amounts to the authority to create a Constitution independently from national political communities and to be imposed on such national communities. Constitutional authority (in the sense of a *pouvoir constituant*) is still, ultimately, in the hands of the national political communities,[23] (and) but once it is jointly exercised at the European level it becomes autonomous from the national polities to embody a European polity that is granted both normative and political authority.

---

[22] In his contribution to this volume J. Weiler correctly states that I did not find it necessary for the Union to have a Constitution. I still oppose the adoption of an EU Constitution expressing a form of constitutional authority similar to that of the *pouvoir constituant* in a state. However, I now accept that the particular form of European Constitutionalism may be reflected in some form of constitutional document such as a Constitutional Treaty. This may help in reinforcing the authority of constitutionalism in the European Union without changing the nature of its constitutional authority.

[23] That is why the Constitutional Treaty allows the possibility for a State to withdraw from the Union.

The importance of a formal Constitution is twofold: first, the process of drafting a constitutional document and, now, of debating it will, itself, help to develop a European political identity; second, that constitutional document will be the basis for a permanent European-wide discourse that would sustain a European public sphere and its polity-building dynamics. These are, in my view, essential elements for the polity legitimacy that the European Union currently requires. A political community needs a permanent public and reflective discourse on its political values. Constitutional texts normally provide the basis for that discourse. They provide a common platform of agreement on the basis of which political conflicts assume the nature of competing rational arguments on the interpretation of shared values and not the character of power conflicts without mutually accepted (albeit not agreed) solutions. Text does matter in this context. But what is not required is for such a text to take the nature of a formal constitution adopted in the way national constitutions normally are and expressing the ultimate authority of a European *demos*.

What has been said can be related to two different constitutional dimensions on the basis of which we can assess the true constitutional nature of the Treaty instituting a European Constitution. One has to do with the constitutional authority of the document and the other with the degree to which it adopts constitutionalism as the form of government.

If the current process would have abandoned the requirement of unanimous ratification by the States, it would be recognising an independent constitutional authority for the Union. In other words, the Union would not simply have normative authority over national legal orders but that authority would be the result of a constitutional authority independent from the States or the peoples of Europe. Its future would be decided by a single European polity and not by an agreement between all national polities. Having a European Constitution would then be a decision to be taken by the European people and no longer by the peoples of Europe. For some, this exercise of *pouvoir constituant* at the European level was what was needed to legitimate the European Union. In this light, what Europe lacks is not a people but simply a true exercise of constitutional power by that people. For others, any such European constitutional exercise is illegitimate precisely because it implies a European *demos* that does not exist.

The Constitutional Treaty did not assume a true *pouvoir constituant*. Instead, the constitutional authority of the Union will continue to be a mixed product of the formal constitutional authority of national polities complemented by an incremental or reflexive constitutionalism[24] that flows from the deliberative mechanisms set up by the EU Constitution and upon which the polity itself is in the process of being built. In this respect, the Constitutional Treaty appears to respect the canons of the constitutional pluralism upon which the Union has evolved.

---

[24] This expression belongs to Neil Walker (in an unpublished text).

This is not to say that the adoption of a formal constitutional text will have no effect whatsoever. On the contrary, it will have two types of profound effects. First, its will generalise the use of constitutionalism as the language of political and legal claims in the European Union and, as stressed above, will provide the basis for the rationalisation and arbitration of political conflicts that characterises successful political communities. This impact will not simply be a consequence of the symbolic and codification value of a European Constitution. It will arise from the role of a constitutional text in reconciling political pluralism (different visions of Europe) with the viability of a European project deliberated around a shared constitutional platform. Second, the Constitutional Treaty will confirm the adoption of constitutionalism as the form of power. In this respect, the question becomes that of determining the extent to which the formal adoption of constitutionalism is reflected in the deliberative logic of the entire polity and its regime. The limited conception of constitutionalism that I have identified as being dominant in European constitutionalism up until now is challenged by this broader constitutional ambition.

## 4.2    Fundamental Rights: An Instrument for or a Limit to European Integration?

The different conceptions of constitutionalism underlying the European constitutional debate were already particularly relevant in the Charter of Fundamental Rights which now integrates the Constitutional Treaty. From the outset, the instrumental role of the Charter in providing legitimacy for the project of European integration was conceived in two very different ways. One discourse places the Charter at the centre of the political building of Europe and foresees it as a dynamic element for further constitutionalisation. Another presents it as a limit to the political growth of Europe and conceives it as a tool for the protection of national constitutional values.[25]

The original aim entrusted to the Charter appeared to fit better with the second perspective. The goal ascribed to the Convention entrusted with the drafting of the Charter was not to alter the substance of fundamental rights protection in the Union but to make that protection clearer for European citizens. That was expected to promote a more effective application of those rights and, at the same time, to reinforce the legitimacy of the integration process. It is this that also explains why the attribution of legal binding effect was not considered to be a priority. However, the final product is much more complex. The duplicity of constitutional discourses on the Charter comes to light in its catalogue of rights that is broader than what would simply result from the consolidation of previous

---

[25] I develop this analysis in 'The Double Constitutional Life of the Charter of Fundamental Rights', in E. Eriksen, et al., eds., *The Chartering of Europe: the European Charter of Fundamental Rights and its Constitutional Implications* (Baden-Baden, Nomos 2003).

Community legislation, Treaty provisions and the Court's case law. In fact, the Charter constitutes the most comprehensive catalogue of rights adopted in many years.[26] At the same time, some of the rights may not create new competencies but may nevertheless give rise to new claims both under the existing competences and with regard to future constitutional developments. This dimension is reflected in the higher expectations that some deposit on the Charter as the basis for a strategy of legitimacy based on an understanding of the Charter as a centre for continuous discourse and deliberation that would lead to both a constant affirmation and redefinition of European political identity.[27] This identity could even be affirmed in the internal sphere of the States. In this respect the Charter could provide a yardstick to be applied to Member States in defining a common set of European political values that all have to respect.[28]

On the other hand, the Charter's scope of application is substantially limited in its horizontal provisions, thereby limiting its polity-building ambitions. First, the Constitutional Treaty even reinforces the limits on the use of the Charter's rights to expand the competencies of the Union. At the same time, the provision limiting the application of the Charter to the classical scope of EU law limits the potential for the incorporation of European political values in the Member States' domestic orders. In that regard, it is well known that the general catalogue of EU fundamental rights does not, in general, apply to acts of States, and the Charter remains cautious in that regard.

There is another dimension that a European Charter of Fundamental Rights could assume: that of a Charter of European citizenship focused on a new set of rights granted to individuals *vis-à-vis* all national political communities (including their own and others) and transnational processes. In other words, the rights linked to a new form a citizenship relevant in the context of a plurality of political communities and a growing deterritorialisation and atomisation of power.[29] That could be a privileged path for legitimacy in the European Union but, to argue this, one must first discuss the *telos* of European integration and the nature of the European political community. The difficulty with this endeavour explains why both the Charter and the Treaty Constitution have not paid much attention to European citizenship and the set of rights and duties that could be attributed thereto.

---

[26] G. Sacerdoti, 'The European Charter of Fundamental Rights: From a Nation State Europe to a Citizens Europe', 37 *Columbia Journal of European Law* (2002) at p. 43.

[27] Ibid.

[28] There are increased political claims, even in the domestic spheres of the States, that appeal to such values. Academically there are also numerous projects that promote such a dimension by comparing the status of the different fundamental rights incorporated in the Charter in different Member States.

[29] Gustavo Zagrebelsky talks about a pluralist revolution of power in *Il diritto mite* (Turin, Einaudi 1992) notably pp. 4-11 and 45-50.

The primary goal of the Charter appeared limited to the more classical dimension of constitutionalism in the European Union: to guarantee that the assumption of European powers will not challenge the standards of fundamental rights protection granted to European citizens in their States. But the logic of a Charter of fundamental rights and its placing at the core of a comprehensive constitutional project for the Union immediately adds a polity perspective to that more limited role: the exercise of defining the common political values justifying the recognition of those rights and the debate that will be generated in the interpretation and application thereof will both legitimate and promote polity-building dimensions. It is thus difficult to clearly establish the nature of the relationship between the Charter and European constitutionalism. It shares the same ambiguous constitutional character of the other pillars of the Constitutional Treaty, reflecting an agreement inherent in the use of the language of constitutionalism in European integration without agreeing on the conception of constitutionalism underlying such language. For some, the Charter is the foundation upon which to build a true constitutional project for the European Union. It will promote the construction of a European political identity and mobilise European citizens around it. For others, the Charter is simply a constitutional guarantee that the European Union will not threaten the constitutional values of the States. It is a constitutional limit to the process of European integration.

## 4.3    Competences: Constitutional Limits to Integration or the Promotion of a European Public Sphere?

Another dominant topic of the constitutional debate concerns the setting up of clearer limits on EU competences. It was natural, therefore, for it to be the object of particular attention by the Convention. The issue of competencies normally focuses on a clearer delimitation of the competences given and/or exercised by the EU. In this respect, the Constitutional Treaty both addressed this concern (through a new classification of the different EU competences and a clear affirmation of the principle of conferred competences) and recognised the limits to establishing a clear separation of competences between the Union and the States (by maintaining a flexibility clause and not adopting a strict catalogue of competences). There are both normative and pragmatic reasons that explain the difficulties involved in attempting to make a clear-cut division of competences.

From a normative standpoint it is, first of all, quite contestable that there can be, in abstract, an ideal allocation of competences between the States and the Union. The allocation of competences is often better made by taking into account the real world contexts of participation in the different institutional alternatives available to exercise those competences. For example, it is often proclaimed that competences should be exercised as close as possible to the affected interests. However, it is, in fact, misleading to assume that the institutions closer to the affected interests are always more apt to exercise the competences affecting those interests. It may be the case that those same circumstances facilitate the capture of those institutions by concentrated interests against the interests of a dispersed majority. In the real world, more distant institutions may perform better in regulating local interests where the local institutions are particularly susceptible to be captured by regulated interests. That may not always be the case, but this simply serves to prove the point that an abstract allocation of competences ignores these institutional dynamics and therefore presents serious normative problems.

A strict delimitation of competences would also work against the normative goal of democratic deliberation inherent in the role played by the Union in providing an alternative deliberative and political setting for national actors which find little voice in domestic politics. As mentioned above, one of the democratic values provided by the Union is linked to the idea of democracy as being founded on permanent contestation and deliberation. The European Union is, in this case, a source of contestation and redeliberation of national policies, keeping national democracies 'alive' and providing alternative viewpoints in their political debates.

It is also quite debatable whether there is, or even that it should exist, an agreement on what competences should belong to the Union and what competences should be left to the States. Though the question of competences is often presented as an issue of simply determining who is more efficient or effective in exercising certain competences, in reality it often hides profound different conceptions of the polity and the common good it should pursue. Our stance on the allocation of redistributive policies exclusively to the States depends on whether or not we believe that a polity such as the European Union should pursue objectives of solidarity and distributive justice between its citizens. Underlying the discussions on competences are, therefore, different conceptions of the European political community and the nature of the political and civic links between its citizens. In the light of this, it is in normative terms more appropriate for the Union to maintain an organisation of its competences that leaves room for pluralism in the discussion of alternative visions of the common good associated with the European polity and its policies.

From a pragmatic perspective, it is also quite difficult to devise a workable general and abstract criterion that can provide a clear allocation of competences between the States and the Union. The history of federal systems tells us how ineffective it is to trust to either a catalogue of competences or an abstract criterion the role of clearly allocating competences between different levels of government. The same can be said about the practice of European integration and the limited effect of the principle of subsidiarity. Once the threshold of simple intergovernmental cooperation and limited competences is passed the idea of a clear allocation of competences is surpassed by the dynamics of political action and institutional interpretation. Once we have a new level of independent political power, this level is bound to be used by any social actor that is not satisfied with the national or local resolution of a certain policy issue. The substantive policy discussion rapidly overcomes the debate on what level is more appropriate to pursue that policy.

In this context, the question of the allocation of competences really comes down to a question of who should allocate those competences[30] and how its exercise ought to be politically controlled by the citizens (accountability). Who should decide on who can better exercise a certain competence? And to what kind of institutional constraints should the exercise of that competence be subject? These are questions that depend largely on the practice of political action and judicial interpretation.

In the context of a multi-level system of governance, competences cannot be *a priori* rigidly divided and codified in the Constitution. The Constitutional Treaty appears to have recognised this complexity. Some of the most positive reforms introduced by the project of the Constitutional Treaty with regard to EU competences are, in reality, measures addressing accountability and transparency in the exercise of those competences. The mechanism of control by national parliaments, on the application of the principle of subsidiarity, introduced in the Constitutional Treaty is a good example. Its merit and effect does not lie so much in a possible blocking right of national parliaments in the adoption of EU legislation. It lies instead in the higher scrutiny by national parliaments over the role played by their respective national governments in the adoption of such legislation. At the same time, the increased discussion of EU legislative acts in national parliaments might subject EU legislation to greater public scrutiny through the different national public spheres. Increased accountability will be the consequence. Not only with regard to European institutions but also with regard to the role of national governments.[31] National parliaments become, in the light of this, catalysts for an emerging European public sphere. This is also improved by further elements of transparency in the legislative process. The openness of the Council's deliberations when adopting legislation is a good, albeit limited, step forward.

The treatment of the question of competences as a question of transparency and accountability also shifts its constitutional role from that of a limit to European integration into an instrument for the development of more European deliberation with enhanced citizenship participation. It becomes a question of democratic accountability in a context of constitutional pluralism that reinforces democratic deliberation.

## 4.4   Institutional Reform: Intergovernmental Majoritarianism?

The core of the constitutional debate was, however, institutional reform. In this respect, there were four main goals enshrined in the agenda of the Convention:

---

[30] The control over competences is normally transferred in this case to the institutional mechanisms of participation in the definition and exercise of those competences. That was expressly recognized by the American Supreme Court in *Garcia* v. *San António* [469 U.S. 528].

[31] This decreases the risk of the EU being 'used' to pass unpopular legislation at the national level transferring, therefore, the political costs of such measures to the European level.

first, higher transparency and simplification; second, stronger democratic legiti-macy; third, effectiveness and operationality; fourth, the promotion of political leadership. In part, these goals reflected the old normative problems of the Union. In another part, they were made more visible and acute by the enlarge-ment of the Union. But addressing these goals entailed a reorganisation of the balance of power with the Union. One of the problems was that the move to-wards a more effective, operational and stronger European Union would not be compatible with the continuation of the traditional institutional balance. This bal-ance satisfied different national States and EU institutions, by diffusing power to such an extent that it affected the operationality and effectiveness of the Union or the degree of political leadership we could expect from this. In this way, for example, the aim of providing stronger political leadership enters into conflict with the goal of maintaining the current institutional balance as it will require empowering one of the institutional pillars. The same occurs with the claims for higher democratic control or effective decision-making in an enlarged EU. The pursuit of these goals requires abandoning an institutional system whose legiti-macy basis, as referred to above, is deeply dependent, on the one hand, on the degree of voice given to the States in its decision-making processes and, on the other, in a partial delegation of power to a technocratic institution, independent from the States (the Commission) and which is conceived as functionally legiti-mated and pursuing efficiency goals. A stronger and 'more democratic' executive would require politicizing the Commission but this goes against its perceived technocratic and independent legitimacy.

There is nothing scandalous about a Constitutional Convention being domi-nated by concerns over the distribution of power. On the contrary, that is a key concern of constitutions. The problem with the Constitutional Convention was the lack of a constitutional theory of power (or a debate between competing con-stitutional theories of power) to frame its intended reorganisation of power within the Union. Instead of the discussion being framed by a previous clarifica-tion of the political characterisation of the Union and a debate on the principles of representation and separation of powers to be taken into account in its in-stitutional and political reform, the path followed was that of a piecemeal intergovernmental bargain whose impact on the constitutional principles legi-timating and organising power will largely be a product of unintended consequences. Moreover, the choice of the political system of the Union (mainly its added majoritarian elements) is more a consequence of practical pressures (how to work with 25 or more Member States) than of real normative ideals on the nature of or representation and participation in the EU.

There is much in these practical concerns that is unavoidable, but the conse-quence is a further reinforcement of the tension between constitutionalism and intergovernmentalism in the European Union. The Constitutional Treaty rein-forces certain majoritarian elements of the institutional system without having fully addressed the requirements necessary to legitimise such a system in both normative and social terms, particularly because it ignores the relationship be-tween majoritarianism and constitutionalism. By a majoritarian political system

I mean, in this context, a system where decisions in a particular jurisdiction are taken, in an open and undetermined sphere of competences, in accordance with the majority view of its citizens and which can be effectively pursued by the legitimated authority of that jurisdiction. Such a system implies an effective executive, a system of decision-making dominated by majority vote, increased proportional representation and an open and undetermined field of competences. The Union already fulfilled some of these requisites and they are being enhanced by the forthcoming institutional changes. One of the aims of the current reform is the emergence of a true executive power through a variety of means: a President of the European Council, reinforcing the authority of the Council and the accountability of the Commission to the Parliament. Majority decision-making is also being extended, albeit not as much as some would like. Proportional representation, too, has been a key feature underlying many of the current debates and was quite visible in the stress placed by the president of the Convention on legitimacy having to be assessed by the support of the majority of the European population and not the majority of the States. Proportional representation to the population has been reinforced in the Council with the Nice Treaty and it is developed with the new Constitutional Treaty. It will also increase via the extension of the co-decision procedure (since the Parliament is thought to be closer to such a principle of representation). A paradox emerging from this development is that majoritarianism is developed while, at the same time, intergovernmentalism is reinforced. However, while majoritarianism is normally legitimated by reference to a single polity (we are bound by that to decisions taken by a majority, although we disagree), intergovernmentalism is based upon the competing interests of different but equal polities.

The move towards a majoritarian system may be unavoidable in a Union entrusted with a broad scope of undetermined and flexible competences and including an increased number of participants in its decision-making processes. Even if we would depart from the assumption that the acquiescence of all participants (unanimity) will be, in normative terms, the normative ideal for collective action in the context of the EU, we would have to recognise, as Buchanan and Tullock have taught us,[32] that with 25 Member States the costs of deciding will be so high that they justify the adoption of majority decision-making as being second best. Once we do that, the question becomes the criteria to be adopted in determining the relative power of the different participants and this requires elements of proportional representation in balancing between equality between States versus equality between citizens. We will then also have to define appropriate mechanisms of separation of powers and political accountability which requires a stronger distinction between the executive and the legislative, allowing stronger political leadership but subject to more intense democratic scrutiny.

---

[32] J.M. Buchanan and G. Tullock, *The Calculus of Consent: Logical Foundations of Constitutional Democracy* (Ann Arbour, University of Michigan Press 1965).

The development of a majoritarian system is inextricably linked to the scope of the political ambitions that the European Union has assumed and the costs of decision-making increased by the enlargement process.

In these circumstances, it becomes crucial to discuss what kind of requirements a majoritarian system must fulfil and how are they to be guaranteed in the European Union. The move towards a majoritarian system, in the context of a polity of increased open and undetermined goals, entails, first of all, a move from what, adopting the categories of Hirschman,[33] we could define as a system of allegiance based on voice (secured by the high degree of relative power of all States in the decision-making process and the issue of the linkage between different policy decisions of the Union compensating different States) to a system based on loyalty (where citizens will feel bound even by decisions of the majority to which they do not belong). One of the first priorities of the current constitutional reform should therefore be that of establishing the conditions for the political loyalty of all European citizens towards the majoritarian decisions of the Union. This requires polity and not simply regime legitimacy.

Second, any majoritarian system must establish a framework guaranteeing the universality of its policies and mechanisms of deliberation. These are the conditions of constitutionalism as a form of deliberation (opposed to the nature of intergovernmental bargaining). This requires, in the first place, the protection of minorities and, above all, the prevention of permanent and insulated minorities (*net losers*). Instrumental to this goal is the promotion of mobility between the majority and minorities (guaranteeing that those one day in the minority may be part of the majority in the other) and a deliberative system that tends to disseminate the patterns of vote and not to promote the aggregation of rigid majorities or the creation of pivotal players. This guarantees, at the same time, the prevention of zero-sum decisions (since those which compose the majority know that they can, in another instance, be part of the minority and have, therefore, an incentive to create mechanisms of compensation for the losing minority). Constitutionalism as a form of deliberation also requires the majority decisions always to comply with a principle of universality in their translation into policy-making and rules. Policies are framed under the criterion of universal application that determines that they are applicable to all citizens fulfilling the same requirements. In this way, it becomes more difficult for a particular group to concentrate the benefits or costs of a certain policy. This is also why rules are subject to requirements of generality and abstraction. In this way, they have to be drafted in light of conditions that can be potentially applicable to anyone and it is more difficult to draft them along the lines of particular interests. They provide a kind of *ex post* consequence that obliges decision-makers to internalize a certain form of a veil of ignorance. It is easy to see how the logic of constitutionalism tends to conflict, in this case, with the EU patterns of intergovernmental deliberation.

---

[33] Applied by Weiler to the previous stages of European integration.

Unfortunately, the naturally compromise and ambiguous nature of the Constitutional Convention and the Constitutional Treaty means that its fulfilment of the requirements of both political loyalty and constitutionalism is not clear at all. Some help can be obtained from the general principles of the EU Constitution but that, in effect, is strictly linked to assessing the extent of constitutionalism envisioned by the Constitutional Treaty. To what extent does it entail a move from intergovernmental deliberation to universal deliberation (where interests are to be aggregated between individuals and not simply between States) and from intergovernmental policies to universal policies (where policies are drafted along universal conditions referred to all European citizens and not dependent on the borders of the States)? EU policies would have to move into a framework of universality, satisfying substantive, and not simply formal, conditions of generality and abstraction and where their redistributive impact is determined by the individual conditions of EU citizens. This requires constitutionalism to become, to a substantial extent, the form of political deliberation in the Union and no longer simply an instrument to solve conflicts of normative authority and establish the limits to such authority. In other words, constitutionalism would also have to frame the form of political deliberation in the Union. The extent to which the Constitutional Treaty really embodies such a choice is open to debate.

The creation of political loyalty would also require a much stronger emphasis on enhancing European citizenship and mechanisms of distributive justice than, indeed, it was the case at the Convention and the IGC. It would require further discussion on the link between the polity legitimacy of the Union and the rights of its citizens and how it can further the debates of competing visions of the common good without, at the same time, endangering the project of integration itself.

A majoritarian political system needs a political community that guarantees the legitimacy of such system and secures the necessary safeguards to prevent its risks. Securing political loyalty, changing the character of political deliberation and universalising its policies, ought to be the priorities of any constitutional reform of the European Union that takes seriously its democratic rhetoric and the need for social legitimacy. But this requires European constitutionalism to fully embrace a discussion of its polity legitimacy and to adopt a truly constitutional form of deliberation for the EU political process.

## 5.  CONCLUSION: WHAT DOES CONSTITUTIONALISM MEAN FOR THE EUROPEAN UNION?

At the moment, the future of the Constitutional Treaty remains in peril: we do not really know what will be the results of the lengthy process of ratifying the Treaty. The current constitutional process may still tilt in two opposing directions: it may promote a genuine deliberative debate on Europe's political identity and even, as some would like, to provide it with some form of constitutional authority, but it may also lead to the opposite result of not only refusing the

Constitutional Treaty but the idea of European constitutionalism itself. Whether it will be one or the other does not depend on the idealist conceptions of broad public involvement in direct constitution-making that the current rhetoric of openness and civil society appears to assume.[34] It depends much more on tackling the issues that may mobilise the peoples of Europe to engage in the creation of that political identity. It is not that such political identity is a necessary precondition for a constitutional project: a Constitution both assumes and promotes a political community (it is both an arrival point and a point of departure in the construction of a political identity). Instead, that constitutional project must fulfil two polity-building conditions: first, it must generate the right incentives for European citizens to embark on such a constitutional project; second, it must provide an adequate framework for European citizens to engage in the construction of a common political identity. In other words, it must secure the political loyalty necessary to the subsistence of a political community, particularly of a majoritarian type. And it must guarantee to all members of that political community that they are treated as equal citizens and not as members of insulated and discrete groups. This is what I have described as the need for polity legitimacy and deliberative constitutionalism.

Until we fully address the need to legitimate the polity and not simply the regime we will not get satisfactory answers to the constitutional challenges faced by the Union. It is not necessary, however, that we fully agree on what makes a European polity legitimate. We only have to agree on having that debate and how we are going to have it. In other words, we must agree to discuss different conceptions of the common good relevant at the European level and we must accept a common framework for that discussion. It is here that deliberative constitutionalism becomes relevant. Once the polity becomes increasingly majoritarian in its regime, it becomes quite difficult to conciliate those developments with the continuing intergovernmental character of deliberation. A majoritarian and increasingly redistributive polity is not very compatible with the low intensity form of constitutionalism that has helped to legitimate the Union so far. It needs to add to the dimension of constitutionalism as a limit to power, its polity expression and deliberative dimensions. How to do this without affecting the constitutional pluralism upon which the Union has been founded is the challenge.

---

[34] J.H.H. Weiler, 'A Constitution for Europe? Some Hard Choices', 40 *Journal of Common Market Studies* (2002) p. 563.

# WINE-BOTTLING LEGITIMACY OR EU LEGITIMATION BY A WRITTEN CONSTITUTION

## Evgeni Tanchev*

### 1.    INTRODUCTION

In this contribution some problems of the legitimacy and legitimation of the Treaty establishing a Constitution for Europe (TCE) are reviewed and various ways of legitimation are outlined.

The Constitutional Treaty, being the first non-state constitution in human civilization, is often compared to the fully-fledged constitutionalism of nation states and particularly the drafting of Central and Eastern European constitutions in the last decade of the 20th century.

This contribution attempts to survey some legitimacy problems in the context of the two levels of modern constitutionalism – the nation state and the European Union (EU) as a non-state supranational entity, a polity in the making and consisting of nation states and peoples.

Theoretical issues of legitimacy, legitimation and legality have been the object of a vast political discourse throughout previous centuries, starting with the adoption of nation-state written constitutions. The debate intensified and triggered a proliferation of concepts and constructs tackling the democracy deficit and the legitimacy crisis in the EU, especially since the beginning of a new stage of integration marked by the Treaty of Maastricht.

The EU Constitution and the greatest enlargement in the history of European integration more than quadrupling the number of founding nation states, pose new challenges to the EU polity in the making and the issue of legitimacy in particular. The Constitutional Treaty has been a tremendous step forward as regards improving legitimacy; however, its entry into force after a successful ratification process will not bring about a panacea and an optimal solution to legitimacy at the supranational level.

Due to limited space the theories of legitimacy and legality and their constitutional safeguards cannot receive the profound and the exhaustive treatment that they certainly deserve. Hence the objectives of this contribution are reduced to a

---

* Judge at the Constitutional Court of the Republic of Bulgaria.

*D. Curtin, A.E. Kellermann and S. Blockmans, eds., The EU Constitution: The Best Way Forward?*
© 2005, T.M.C. Asser Instituut, The Hague.

modest presentation of the approaches to these problems and no attempt is made to provide final answers.

So much has been written on the deficits of democracy and legitimacy, so many interesting proposals have been tabled and so little has been done that it seems that EU legitimacy issues are reaching a stage where public receptiveness has become somewhat stale. To put it simply, it seems like everything has already been said already but not by everybody.

The main conclusion is that it would be inadequate to build the foundations of legitimacy around unprecedented developments, which the EU and the Constitutional Treaty undoubtedly are, as they challenge the well established patterns of constitution-making, the ideas derived from 18th century political theory or having to rely on participatory democracy and active citizenship in the republican tradition alone. Rather, the EU legitimacy crisis should be approached with other legitimation sources and instruments developed by recent political and legal achievements.

With a clear intention to present the academic discourse on legitimacy in a non- academic manner and to avoid further complicating the complexities, I have chosen the old and simple wine and bottle metaphor to address the various legitimacy issues in the nation-state and in the EU.

2.     THE TYPICAL WINE-BOTTLING PROCESS DURING THE LAST
        THREE CENTURIES OR THE EVOLUTION OF THE CONCEPTS OF
        LEGITIMACY, LEGALITY AND LEGITIMATION WITHIN THE
        NATION-STATE

It is common to discuss legitimacy, legality and legitimation within the framework of the principles of the rule of law (the *Rechtsstaat* doctrine) and popular sovereignty, although the concepts of legitimacy and legality evolved at a much earlier stage of civilization.

The main reason for the legitimacy and legality interrelationship is their subordination to hierarchy and while legitimacy transcends the legal system with the law being inferior to values preceding the legal system and being metalegal foundations of the legal order, legality reflects the preservation of a hierarchy within the legal system. If the logic of the legal system has been penetrated with the same set of values and principles which are the foundation of the legal system, then observing legality is instrumental to preserving legitimacy. Legality in government might be the source that generates legitimacy, especially when value systems are compatible. Historically, the incompatibility of these two concepts has led to the reverse constellation – legitimacy did not produce legality and neither of the two concepts went hand in hand with democracy. Legality cannot survive by ignoring legitimacy for a relatively long period of time and the breakdown of one leads to the breakdown of the other.[1] Constitutional democracies are

---

[1] According to J. Blondel, Tsarist Russia at the time of World War I is a typical example of

built on the coexistence of legitimacy, legality and popular sovereignty providing citizen support for the government. Legality seems to be the best principle for safeguarding a legitimate constitutional government. Legality produces legal certainty and citizens' legitimate expectations lead to trust in the government and public support for a democratic political system is thereby increased.

Higher law was regarded as the foundation of the ancient and medieval legal systems created by rulers and a moral source mobilizing obedience towards democratic republican governments by citizens in Greece and Rome or the king's subjects within monarchies. Even in premodern societies and even in despotic forms of government, the effective performance of state power depended not on resorting to the state's monopoly of violence alone, but on the moral and just grounds of governmental action. So the prototype for the modern concept of legitimacy can be traced back to antiquity and medieval times and has been associated with higher, immutable law, divine will, morality or reason which have justified the established political system and have persuaded people to abide by the law on a voluntary basis.[2] That the legal order and the political system were in accordance with natural law began to be regarded as a basic source of legitimacy during the period of the Enlightenment.

The roots of legality might be traced to the organic growth of the law in antiquity and the Middle Ages when, within monarchical sovereignties, the law evolved as one king added to the legislation of his predecessors.[3] Within the English legal system, statutes began to recognize that they should conform to the Magna Carta.[4]

---

a state observing legality having lost its legitimacy. It is possible that a new regime established at the start of the transition period could have been legitimate without observing the imperatives of legality. However, a conflict between legitimacy and legality cannot result in the stability of political regimes even if the government mobilizes propaganda and attempts to manipulate public opinion through legitimating or justifying deviations from legality. See J. Blondel, *Comparative Government: An Introduction*, 2nd ed. (London, Prentice Hall 1995) pp. 62-66.

[2] See E.S. Corwin, 'The "Higher Law" Background of American Constitutional Law', in R. Loss, ed., *Corwin on the Constitution* (Ithaca, Cornell University Press 1981) pp. 79-140. Exploring the rudimentary forms of legitimacy during premodernity and absolutism is related to the reason of state doctrine, see F. Meinecke, *Machiavellianism, the Doctrine of Raison d'Etat and its Place in Modern History* (London, Transaction Publishers 1998); C.J. Friedrich, *Constitutional Reason of State: The Survival of the Constitutional Order* (Providence, Brown University Press 1957) pp. 4-5.

[3] H.J. Berman, *Law and Revolution, the Formation of Western Legal Tradition* (Cambridge, Harvard University Press 1983) pp. 536-537.

[4] In 1368 Edward the Third's 42nd statute provided that the Magna Carta 'be holden and kept in all Points; and if there be any statute, made to the contrary, it shall be holden for none', cited in A.E.D. Howard, *The Road from Runnymede, Magna Carta and Constitutionalism in America* (Charlottesville, University of Virginia Press 1968) p. 9. In Tudor times the Magna Carta became dormant and the king did not aspire towards the conformity of his acts with the Magna Carta, see also A.E.D. Howard, *Magna Carta, Text and Commentary* (Charlottesville, University of Virginia Press 1999) p. 25. It would take centuries, however, to establish the principle by Sir E. Coke in the Bonham Case in 1610 that the common law is superior and should be observed

The first generation of written constitutions, created after the origin of the modern nation-state subsequent to the Westphalian Treaty in 1648, starting with the constitutions since 1776, contain the first set of legitimacy and legality safeguards.[5]

Political legitimacy was expanded to new moral and rational grounds by Rousseau, Montesquieu and Sieyes. In fact, building theoretical constructions of the ideal legal and political system, founded on social contract, popular sovereignty, separation of powers and juridical equality, was an implicit refutation of the legitimacy of the ancien regime. The contractarian school of the time focused the legitimacy debate on the process of formation, representing the will of the governed and governmental performance.[6] The legitimacy and legality debate developed within the discourse on the 'rule of law', the *Rechtstaat* and the *Etat de droit* principles. Although having different origins in the history of the main legal families in the world, these concepts have been united by the common approach of framing political power within the limits of valid legal rules.[7] Within the Anglo-American legal system the rule of law always acquired the meaning of establishing a certain set of liberal democratic values for the political system which had to be present in the institutional design, as a precondition for the legitimacy of the government, which exercised its powers by observing legality.

The German doctrine of *Rechtsstaat* was established by R. von Mohl in the first half of the 19th century.[8] Initially, the idea was founded on Kantian liberal-

---

as a prerequisite for the validity of all legal acts, see Bonham case of 1610, reproduced in M. Cappelletti and W. Cohen, *Comparative Constitutional Law: Cases and Materials* (Charlottesville, Bobbs-Merrill 1979) pp. 9-10.

[5] A different approach to the problem of constitutional safeguards for legitimacy and legality might be developed if we look at constitutions through the concept developed by conservative theory where the concept of the real constitution has been associated with the specific conditions, mentalities, inclinations, the moral, civil and social habits of the people, which predated the formation of the nation-state, E. Burke, *Selections* (London, 1914) p. 263; J. de Maistre, *Considerations on France* (Montreal, McGill-Queen's University Press 1974) p. 92.

[6] It might be interesting to note that within the contractarian school early antecedents proposed to safeguard legitimacy by extralegal methods ranging from justifying the murder of tyrants and withdrawing support for the ruler to popular resistance against unjust government and civil disobedience.

[7] The laconic statement of basing the state on the principle of the rule of law and not of men which has been attributed to J. Adams and J. Locke was used in antiquity and can be traced back to Aristotle. The common feature shared by all the national models of the classical and modern rule of law concepts within the common law system is the compatibility between legitimacy and legality.

[8] This expression was used for the first time by C.T. Welcker in 1813 and R. von Mohl further developed the idea in 1829. On the history and the evolution of the concept see E.-W. Böckenförde, *State, Society and Liberty, Studies in Political Theory and Constitutional Law* (Oxford, Berg 1991) pp. 47-70; O. Kirchheimer, 'The Rechtsstaat as Magic Wall, in Politics, Law and Social Change', in F.S. Burin and K.L. Shell, *Politics, Law, and Social Change: Selected Essays of Otto Kirchheimer* (New York, Columbia University Press 1969) pp. 429-452; R. Grote, 'Rule of Law, Rechtsstaat, and "Etat de droit"', in C. Stark, ed., *Constitutionalism, Universalism and Democracy – A Comparative Analysis* (Baden-Baden, Nomos 1999) pp. 269-306; J-Y. Morin, 'The Rule of Law and

ism and was expounded as a principle having both material and formal dimensions. The perception that the state is based on reason, on collective will, that governmental functions are limited to the protection of liberty, security and property and even the goal of policing and using violence is to remove hindrances to individual self-fulfilment and autonomy. Having both material and formal aspects the *Rechtstaat* met the standards of legitimacy and legality. The *Rechtsstaat* was affirmed as an antipode to despotism by including the legitimate values of juridical equality, the protection of human rights against state encroachment on liberty, governmental action in accordance with the law and self-government based on popular sovereignty and representative government.[9]

In the context of conservative theory the *Rechtsstaat* received another connotation. It was reduced to a formal concept and by accepting a value-neutral approach to the political and the legal system it was reduced to the supremacy of parliamentary statutes which bind administrative bodies.[10]

The conservative concept of practical implications led to the affirmation of legality, but by ignoring the substantive requirements of legitimacy, it limited the content of the principle as a procedural one. What is even more important, divorcing legality from legitimacy justified different forms of trespassing upon the concept of legality itself.[11]

Totalitarianism marked the end of the *Rechtsstaat*, but, to some extent, reducing the principle to legality had undermined the *Rechtsstaat* long before then, thereby decreasing the democracies' possibility for self-defence and paving the way for dictatorships.

In political and legal theory, legitimacy has been defined by using different approaches. In the context of justifying constitutional democracy legitimacy has

---

Rechtsstaat Concept: A Comparison', in E. McWinney, J. Zaslove and W. Wolf, *Federalism-in-the-Making* (Dordrecht, Kluwer Academic Publishers 1992) pp. 60-85.

[9] For contributions by L. von Stein, O. Mayer, R. Gneist and other liberal exponents of the principle see Böckenförde, op. cit. n. 8, at pp. 52-58.

[10] Severing ties between legitimacy and legality is obvious in Stahl's definition which states that the *Rechtsstaat* does not implement moral ideals and its substance is not the essence of governmental function and actions but only the manner, method and nature of their realization. A conservative interpretation of the principle had two immediate consequences:

- safeguarding the legality of the administration, which is bound by general and rational law, making state interference in the sphere of individual liberty and property predictable and calculable;

- independence from the aims, values and forms of the state.

See F. Neumann, *The Rule of Law, Political Theory and the Legal System in Modern Society* (Oxford, Berg 1986) pp. 182-183.

[11] Theoretically overcoming legitimacy by legality was possible through Kelsen's legal normativism and by C. Schmitt's political decisionism, although on the eve of the Nazi takeover he held the view that it was illegitimate and unconstitutional under the Weimar constitution to appoint a Nazi or a Communist chancellor. C. Schmitt, *Legalität und Legitimität*, 2nd edn. (Berlin, Duncker und Humblot 1968) p. 61; H. Kelsen, *General Theory of Law and State* (Cambridge, Harvard University Press 1945) p. 117.

been considered as a formula for a moral, ideological or philosophical identity and the self-image of a political system.[12] The emphasis on political behaviour led to the description of legitimacy as a capacity of the system to engender and maintain the belief that the existing political institutions are the most appropriate for society.[13]

Legitimacy has been defined as the people's support for the government and their willingness to accept domination, irrespective of the specific beliefs on which their acceptance rests. Legitimacy has been confined to compliance with the political system, values which it safeguards, and the obedience of the majority of citizens by their passive tolerance or their active support.[14] From a decision making perspective, it is a generalized degree of trust on the part of the address-ees of the decisions toward the political system, though not necessarily linked to parliamentary government or democracy.[15] Legitimacy has been associated with the shared expectation among actors in a specific arrangement of asymmetric power so that the actions of the rulers are voluntarily accepted by the ruled due to the conviction that these actions are in conformity with pre-established norms. Legitimacy converts power into authority and simultaneously establishes an obligation to obey and a right to govern.[16]

The political and the legal system's adherence to different conventions has been used to define different types of legitimacy. According to the classic three-fold classification of legitimate domination and obedience, three claims of legitimacy have been extrapolated and defined as traditional, charismatic or personal and domination by virtue of legality or a belief in the valid and rational impersonal rules created by the competent authorities.[17]

Legality ensures the obedience of the legal subjects through law enforcement which might be realized when the citizens do not abide by the law or undertake unauthorized actions; contra legem acts on the part of the government and the administration have thereby been produced. The optimal situation according to the rule of law in a constitutional democracy is voluntary obedience with the law due to the belief of all the legal subjects in the legitimacy of and compliance with the legal norms which safeguard society's well-being. The legitimacy of the legal order is a sine qua non for the effectiveness of legality.[18] However, the le-

---

[12] C. Schmitt, 'The Legal World Revolution', 72 *Telos* (1987) Special Issue on C. Schmitt.
[13] S.M. Lipset, *Political Man: The Social Bases of Politics* (New York, Doubleday 1960) p. 77.
[14] J.L. Quermonne, *L'Europe en quête de légitimite* (Paris, Presses de Sciences Po 2001) p. 13.
[15] M. Jachtenfuchs, 'Democracy and Governance in the EU' (ELOP 1997/002) 6.
[16] Ph. Schmitter, 'What is there to legitimize in the EU... And how might this be accomplished?' (Jean Monnet Working Paper No. 6/01 (2001)) available at: <http://www.jeanmonnetprogram.org/papers/01/011401.html>.
[17] M. Weber, *Economy and Society: an Outline of Interpretive Sociology*, vol. I, ed. by G. Roth and C. Wittich (New York, Bedminster Press 1968) p. 215.
[18] Other possible ways of looking at legitimacy might emphasize that legitimacy is a quali-

gitimacy of the legal and political system is best protected by the democratic and rational juridically-institutionalized procedures for legality, thereby providing, as a result of the legal discourse, that the valid law produced justifies the different interests and opinions in the process of drafting impartial rules.[19]

These rational institutionalized legal procedures concern the three branches of power and their relationship to the people. The most important of these rational institutionalized procedures have been enshrined in the modern written nation-state constitutions as constitutional safeguards for legality and legitimacy.

All fourth-generation democratic constitutions drafted after World War II, and especially Germany's 1949 *Grundgezetz* proclaimed and reaffirmed both the substantive and formal contents of the *Rechtsstaat* principle based on the legitimacy and legality of the political and legal systems. The post-communist drafting of constitutions during the 1990s provided a laboratory for building a new legitimacy and legality and paved the way for the transformation of emerging democracies into fully-fledged democracies in Europe. However, no matter how quickly this transformation took place, it can be seen as an exercise in legitimacy-building on the part of pre-existing polities and the pre-established nation-state.

The nation-state constitutions provide a list of safeguards in order to maintain legality and legitimacy in the polity where homogeneity and constitutional consensus are achieved by democratic procedures. A brief restatement of these safeguards would include:

- constituent authority residing in the sovereign people and being exercised by the nation directly or through elected representatives.[20] The supremacy, stability and longevity of the national constitutions will result from them being drafted, revised and amended by the constituent power. The constitutional consensus provides for non-amendability clauses which defend constitutional democracy;[21]

---

tative, substantial and broader concept relating to the substance of legal rules and the political system, while legality is a more quantitative, formal idea, directly concerning the legal system. Legitimacy has been treated as a political capacity, a fountain of political power, as a value and principle by which to justify political authority, a way of governmental authorization. See D. Radev, 'Legitimnost i legalnost' [Legitimacy and Legality], *Savremeno Pravo* [Contemporary Law] No. 6 (1992) pp. 53-57.

[19] J. Habermas, 'Wie ist Legitimität durch Legalität möglich?', 20 *Kritische Justiz: Vierteljahresschrift* (Heft 1 (1987)) pp. 1-16.

[20] On constituent power see U. Preuss, 'Constitutional Powermaking for the New Polity: Some Deliberations on the Relations between Constituent Power and the Constitution', in M. Rosenfeld, *Constitutionalism, Identity, Difference, and Legitimacy* (Durham, Duke University Press 1994) pp. 143-164. Recourse to popular sovereignty is a *sine qua non* of constitutional amendments resulting from public consensus and the super-majority's agreement to transform the rules established for the constituted powers.

[21] The non-amendability clauses in some of the constitutions serve as limitations on constituent power and preclude the destruction of the legitimacy of the transition through abolishing basic

– founding the constitutional framework on democratic values and principles such as human dignity, equality, inclusion, social solidarity, popular
sovereignty, separation of powers, political pluralism, the rule of law and
the supremacy of international law;

– formation, performance and distribution of powers between different
branches of government by opting for a rationalized parliamentary or
semi-presidential system of government;[22]

– stimulating citizens' involvement in political decision-making through direct participation, deliberation concerning political decisions or publicly
controlling the government;

– proclaiming universal human rights and establishing social and legal
mechanisms for their protection, especially through the system of judicial
review governmental action;

– the Constitutional courts protecting against unconstitutional statutes which
preserve the constituted powers within the legitimate will of the constituent power; and

– recourse to justice through the Administrative courts which can repeal administrative acts which infringe upon legality.[23]

---

values by constitutional amendment. Non-amendability clauses are the outcome of Western
constitutionalism's experience in creating safeguards for the preservation of constitutional democracy against authoritarian encroachment or a totalitarian takeover. The German 1949 *Grundgezetz*
proclaims the inadmissibility of constitutional amendments to federalism and the democratic and
social character of the Republic, to the basic constitutional principles of popular sovereignty, the
constitutional supremacy of the legislature and the fact that law and justice is a task of the executive. Furthermore, it condemns those who wish to abolish the constitutional order and it protects human dignity and the inviolability, inalienability and direct enforceability of human rights
(Art. 79(3); Art. 20; Art. 21). Following a tradition established by the 1875 Third republic, the
1958 Constitution of the Fifth French Republic provides in Art. 89 that the republican form of
government shall not be subject to amendment. According to Art. 148 of the 1991 Romanian
Constitution the national, independent, unitary, and indivisible character of the state, the republican form of government, territorial integrity, the independence of the judiciary, political pluralism, the official language, and human rights freedoms and their guarantees cannot explicitly be
the subject of constitutional revision.

[22] On the differences between these models of government see D.V. Verney, *The Analysis of
Political Systems* (London, Routledge and Kegan Paul 1959) pp. 17-56; A. Lijphart, *Parliamentary and Presidential Government* (Oxford, Oxford University Press 1992) pp. 118-127 and pp.
142-151; G. Sartori, *Comparative Constitutional Engineering* (New York, New York University
Press 1994) pp. 83-196; J. Linz and A. Valenzuela, ed., *The Failure of Presidential Democracy*
(Baltimore, John Hopkins University Press 1994) pp. 91-162; M. Duverger, *Echec au roi (les
regimes semipresidentiels)* (Paris, A. Michel 1977).

[23] The evolution of administrative justice since the 19th century in France has been outlined

The procedural safeguards for constitutional legitimacy concern those procedures in the relationship between citizens and the government which are designed to protect individual freedom and maintain people's trust in the government, being the cornerstone of support for democratic regimes. A democratic deficit and a lack of legitimacy might lead to the citizens' distrust in the government as the latter would be using unfair procedures.[24] Just like inter-institutional procedures, legal relations between individuals and institutions should be founded on impartiality and non-partisan decision-making.

Constitutional democracy provides for legal procedures for civil servants and governmental responsibility.

Deliberative democracy is based on citizen involvement as a legitimacy-building method based on popular sovereignty. It acquires different shapes – expressing one's political persuasion and attachment, forming public opinion in order to influence and control governmental actions, participation in decision-making through free elections and direct democracy.

Openness in governmental proceedings and transparency are indispensable for the citizens' formation of opinions and providing the information which is instrumental to combating the manipulation of public opinion. Authoritarian regimes are always inclined to apply the paraphrased version of Bentham's panopticon effect of transparency – the government can observe citizens at all times without the possibility of being seen by the public.[25] Avoiding transparency and openess in government leads to the state power's loss of publicity and legitimacy.

Access to governmental rulings and proceedings might be limited by *arcana imperii*, but it cannot be denied to the citizens. Secrecy undermines legitimacy by depriving the public of information as a premise for partaking in public dis-

---

as a peculiarity in the context of the European rule of law, placing limits on constitutional review and a basic safeguard for legality. See O. Kirchheimer, 'Legality and Legitimacy in Rule of Law under Siege', in W. E. Scheuerman, ed., *Selected Essays of F. Neumann and O. Kirchheimer* (Berkley, University of California Press 1996) pp. 44-63, at pp. 46-47.

[24] From a political science perspective there are four ways of signaling fairness by the state and producing trust in government: 1. coercing the non-compliant; 2. the universalistic (non-partisan, impartial) recruitment of civil servants; 3. establishing credible courts for arbitration and conflict resolution; 4. the citizens' involvement in politics see M. Levi, *A State of Trust* (Florence, Working Paper EUI – Robert Schumann Centre, No. 96/23 (1996)) pp. 13-15.

[25] By the late 1790s J. Bentham had developed a utopian scheme for a self-sufficient social system built on his prison building plans. According to his theory criminals should be imprisoned in a tower with each chamber having two opposite windows – one for the light to come in and the other for constant supervision. A. Bentham, 'Reader', in M. Mack, ed. (New York, Western Publishing Co 1969) p. 19. For a detailed description of the panopticon effect see M. Foucault, *Surveiller et punir. Naissance de la prison* (Paris, Gallimard 1975) ch. 3; see also M. Foucault, 'L'oeil du pouvoir', in M. Foucault, *Dits et Ecrits* (Paris, Gallimard 1994). In Bobbio's words the panopticon effect as applied to the government creates an all seeing and invisible government and people that are blind but visible. By the panopticon effect public government might be easily transformed into a form of crypto-government, N. Bobbio, *Il futuro della democrazia* (Turin, Einaudi 1994) p. 14.

cussion. Instead of deliberative or discursive democracy,[26] where support for governmental policies evolves in robust public discussion, direct democracy might be instrumental to authoritarianism by faking the legitimacy of plebiscite political regimes.

Considering these circumstances, as well as the political tradition and legal culture in the new democracies, one should not be overwhelmed by the appeal of direct democracy, but should adopt a more reasonable approach.

The new constitutions of the emerging democracies in Central and Eastern Europe and the independent republics of the former Soviet Union drafted in the 1990s are typical examples of building a new legitimacy since they were adopted as a result of the crisis of legitimacy experienced by the old regime and the collapse of the communist system.[27] The building of a new legitimacy by these constitutions has marked the emergence of a new statehood in the world community. The new constitutions established a foundation for the transformation of the legal, political and social systems based on the rule of law, parliamentary democracy and a market economy. By providing a new legitimacy and an implicit refutation of the legitimacy of the ancien regime, the new democratic constitutions have been typical examples of reactive fundamental laws.[28] The adoption of the constitutions can be seen as successful legitimacy-building within the boundaries of the nation-state. However, this new legitimacy-building has taken place within pre-existent polities and has been interpreted as a direct democratic renewal of polity legitimacy.

3.      ACADEMIC RECIPES TO ENHANCE LEGITIMACY-BUILDING IN THE EU

The legitimacy-building challenge in the EU might be given a somewhat simplified presentation by several variants of the wine bottling metaphor.

---

[26] On deliberative democracy see J. Cohen, 'Deliberation and Democratic Legitimacy in Deliberative Democracy', in J. Bohman and W. Rehg, eds., *Deliberative Democracy: Essays on Reason and Politics* (Cambridge/Massachusetts, MIT Press 1997) pp. 67-91.

[27] In general the crisis of legitimacy has been defined as a transition to a new social structure when the status of political institutions is threatened by change or some political groups are excluded from the political system, Lipset, op. cit. n. 13, at p. 78. However, this concept has been challenged by at least two contemporary developments. In fact the erosion of the legitimacy of the communist regimes took place long before the beginning of the system's collapse in 1989. The EU's current stage of development and the transformation of the nation-states in Europe at the turn of the 21st century have been treated as a deficit of both legitimacy and democracy in the EU's institutional framework.

[28] In contrast to derivative constitutions which are the result of the evolution of national constitutional development, reactive constitutions mark a new beginning or break the ties with the constitution they are replacing. For an extensive treatment of reactive constitutions see the introductory essay in V. Bogdanor, *Constitutions in Democratic Politics* (Aldershot, Gower 1988).

## 3.1 Old Wine in Old Bottles

This approach to the EU legitimation problems and the legitimacy crisis is the best weapon available to any Eurosceptic scholar. The nation-state is conceived not as the best, but as a sole locus of legitimacy. The conclusion that the nation-state is the sole model for legitimacy excludes any other entity from claiming legitimacy.

Probably the best proof for this mode of thinking is the famous Chinese no precedent and irrevocable laws argument, so eloquently described by J. Bentham in his famous *Handbook of Political Fallacies*.[29]

Scholars of this theory will always tailor their arguments to prove that, as an international organization, the EU is not and cannot become a repository either to constitutional democracy or to legitimate governance.

Without a direct polity legitimacy for the EU institutions in the same manner as it exists in an idealized vision of this phenomenon in the nation-state, there cannot be any sort of legitimacy. This negative justification tends to prevail and has been garnished with negative arguments of different kinds. Starting with the famous non-existent European demos thesis, the objections tend to boil down to no European civil society, no European public space, no common identity, no accountability, no openness and no responsibility in governance in order to prove that there can be no legitimate EU governance.[30]

In a milder form some of the champions of European integration have made attempts to solve the legitimacy crisis in the EU by transposing the classic legitimation methods of governmental power within a nation-state to the EU polity in the making. However, this approach leads to inadequate proposals since not only is the EU conceived in a static manner and compared to a nation-state, but also the current legitimacy crisis within the nation-states is largely underestimated.

Moreover, legitimacy itself is a dynamic concept and the same methods of legitimation might lead to different degrees of legitimacy for similar institutions, even within the context of national political and legal systems.[31]

---

[29] J. Bentham, *The Handbook of Political Fallacies* (New York, Harper 1962) pp. 43-75.

[30] For a summary see H. Dahlsson and D. Staun, 'The EU State Constitution – A Critical Analysis' (TEAM Working Paper, No. 1 (2002)) available at: <http://www.teameurope.info/wp-constitution.nr1.pdf>.

[31] As M. Troper notes in a recently published article, any institution or policy can be held to be legitimate in a given nation at a given moment and illegitimate in another place and time depending on the value system entrenched in the constitution. M. Troper 'The Logic of Justification of Judicial Review', 1 *International Journal of Constitutional Law* (2003) pp. 99-121, at p. 101.

## 3.2    New Wine in Old Bottles – Elaborating New Legitimacy Concepts to enhance the Legitimacy of the EU

The EU legitimacy crisis might be approached on the basis of recent theoretical developments.

Although theoretical issues of legitimacy, legitimation and legality have been the object of extensive political discourse over the last few centuries, starting with the adoption of nation-state constitutions, during the last decade academics have come up with a plethora of new ideas concerning these subjects. The debate intensified and triggered a proliferation of concepts and constructions to tackle the democratic deficit and the legitimacy crisis in the EU, especially since the new phase of integration marked by the Treaty of Maastricht.

At present the concept of measuring legitimacy as developed by Beetham and Lord during the last decade is almost universally accepted. According to them there are three criteria which measure legitimacy and serve as a test for any legitimate political system.

Legality means that political authority is acquired and distributed and that it functions according to the adopted constitutional rules. However, the rules have to meet the requirement of *normative justifiability* or to correspond to the socially accepted beliefs concerning the correct form of authority, its standards and proper means of government. The legitimation of authority should be achieved by confirmation, explicit approval by subordinates and it should be recognized by other legitimate authorities.[32]

Studies differentiating, supplementing and explaining the parallel functioning of legitimacy in constitutional pluralism have emerged since the Maastricht Treaty and they provide a new impetus for EU constitutionalism and are now flourishing by adding the dimension of global governance.

In Walker's words, there are 'many ways to cut the conceptual cake of legitimacy in the European Union.'[33]

Leaving aside the differences between a philosophical and a utilitarian connotation of legitimacy which would take the analysis towards speculative grounds, I will proceed to briefly describe the basic dichotomies recently outlined by academia.

Differentiating between input and output legitimacy has been developed during the last few decades by F. Schrapf and is almost universally agreed upon at present.[34] Input legitimacy is based on popular sovereignty, majority rule, direct

---

[32] D. Beetham and C. Lord, *Legitimacy and the EU* (London, Longman 1998) p. 37.

[33] N. Walker, 'The White Paper in Constitutional Context', in *Symposium: Mountain or Molehill, A Critical Appraisal of the Commission White paper on Governance* (Jean Monnet Working Paper No. 6/01 (2001)) available at: <http://www.jeanmonnetprogram.org/papers/01/011001.html>.

[34] F. Scharpf, 'Interdependence and Democratic Legitimation' (MPIfG Working Paper No. 98/2 (September 1998)) available at: <http://www.mpi-fg-koeln.mpg.de/pu/workpap/wp98-2/wp98-2.html>; F. Scharpf, 'Problem Solving Effectiveness and Democratic Accountability in the EU' (MPIfG Working Paper No. 03/1 (February 2003)) available at: <http://www.mpi-fg-koeln.mpg.de/

participation and citizen involvement in governmental decision-making. These methods of legitimation were moderately balanced with the rule of law by G. Buchanan in Scotland[35] or vigorously supported by radical democratic thinkers since J.J. Rousseau. Output legitimacy is related to the separation of powers and the principles of rule of law acting as safeguards against encroachment on liberty and abuse of power. Output legitimacy is measured by governmental effectiveness and efficiency.

Internal or social legitimacy is related to support, based on trust in the government and popular consent, and stands in contrast to external or normative legitimacy measured by the effectiveness of external standards and the merits of just and democratic government.[36] Internal legitimacy relates to the socially accepted norms, while external legitimation is based on formally established rules.[37]

An analysis of the justification of state power, which has provided support to governments since the Middle Ages, contributes to understanding the dichotomy between ascending and descending legitimacy.[38]

This type of differentiation depends on the nature of the external source for justifying the governmental structure. Governmental power possesses descending legitimacy which is due to a general principle or higher force, while ascending legitimacy is ascribed to the agreement or approval of the people.

Descending legitimacy was inherent in monarchical sovereignty and might be observed in regimes where authority is exercised by charismatic leadership. Popular sovereignty mechanisms like elections, referendums, plebiscites, initiatives, recalls and, last but not least, different patterns of constituent authority provide for ascending legitimacy.

Direct versus indirect (representative, derivative or deliberative) legitimacy has at least two connotations depending on the modes of legitimation.[39] While in

---

pu/workpap/wp03-1/wp03-1.html>; See also J. Thomassen and H. Schmitt, 'Democracy and Legitimacy in the EU', 45 *Tidsskrift for Samfunnsforskning* (2004) pp. 377-410.

[35] See G. Buchanan, *The Powers of the Crown in Scotland* [transl. of De Jure Regni Apud Scotos, printed in 1579] (Austin, the University of Texas Press 1949).

[36] Walker, *supra* n. 33, at p. 4. For a slightly different version see R. Bellamy and D. Castiglione, 'Normative Theory and European Union: Legitimising Euro-polity and its Regime' (Queen's Papers on Europeanisation, No. 13/2001) available at: <http://www.qub.ac.uk/schools/SchoolofPolitics InternationalStudies/FileStore/EuropeanisationFiles/Filetoupload,5283,en.pdf>.

[37] Bellamy and Castiglione, *supra* n. 36, at p. 27.

[38] E.L. Rubin, *Rethinking Politics and Law for the Administrative State* (Princeton, Princeton University Press 2005) Ch. 5: 'From Legitimacy to Compliance', available at: <http://www.law. buffalo.edu/research/workshops/Rubin.pdf>, pp. 1-7.

[39] E. Eriksen and J. Fossum, *The EU and Postnational Legitimacy* (Arena Working Paper No. 00/26) available at: <http://www.arena.uio.no/publications/wp00_26.htm>; see also their 'Democratic or Technocratic Governance' (Jean Monnet Working Paper No. 6/01 (2001)0); V. Schmidt, 'The European Union: Democratic Legitimacy in a Regional State?', 91 *Reihe Politikwissenschaft* (Vienna, Institute for Advanced Studies 2003) available at: <http://www.ihs.ac.at/ publications/pol/pw_91.pdf>.

the EU nation-states direct legitimation comes from the people, EU governance derives its legitimacy from the legitimacy of Member State governments. The other meaning of this legitimacy dichotomy is based on the presence or absence of the people's will.[40] Direct legitimacy is the outcome of the people's participation in governmental decision-making. Indirect legitimacy occurs as a result of representation or deliberation in which people's preferences are brought into the decision-making process. Legitimation based on free and robust discourse requires that people arrive at a decision by agreement and reach a consensus so that dissenters are those who have a defective judgment. Active civil society is an indispensable ingredient for deliberative democracy.[41] Deliberative democracy adds a new dimension to the classic Lincoln formula of popular sovereignty known as government by the people, of the people and for the people. Participation by deliberation adds to the popular sovereignty principle the notion of government with the people.[42]

Although discussions on the dichotomy between substantive and procedural legitimacy started at the beginning of the 20th century, it was only finally clarified during the last two decades. The basic contents of substantive legitimacy mean that governments derive their support from promoting the interests of the governed. Better political performance on the part of governmental institutions is evaluated according to popular preferences. The more effectively they discharge their responsibility, the more legitimate the political system.[43] Procedural legitimacy is achieved by legally institutionalized procedures providing that, in the outcome of the discourse, the valid law produced serves to justify the different interests and opinions in the process of drafting impartial rules.[44]

Depending on the scope of the entity – a nation-state, the EU or global governance – different types of legitimacy were dealt with. According to the object to be justified and in order to receive public support, the diffuse concept of legitimacy opposed the specific concept. When the legitimation concerns the whole government, diffuse legitimacy is observed, but when the justification relates to a special institution or a policy, then specific legitimacy occurs.[45]

---

[40] R. Dehousse, 'European Governance in Search of Legitimacy: The Need for a Process-based Approach', in O. de Schutter, et al., *Governance in the European Union* (Luxembourg, Office for Official Publications of the European Communities 2001). See also in 'Constitutionalism and Democratic Representation in the EU' (Vienna, Austrian Academy of Sciences, ICE Research Unit for Institutional Change and EU Integration, Final report 2003) available at: <http://www.tamilnation.org/conflictresolution/countrystudies/europe/project.pdf>.

[41] See D. Curtin, 'Non-Governmental Representation v. Civil Society Deliberation: A Contemporary EU Governance Dilemma', available at: <http://www.arena.uio.no/events/Conference2002/documents/Curtin.doc>.

[42] Schmidt, *supra* n. 39.

[43] A. Weale, 'Democratic Legitimacy and the Constitution of Europe', in R. Bellamy, D. Castiglione, and V. Buffacci, eds., *Democracy and Constitutional Culture in the Union of Europe* (London, Lothian Foundation Press 1995) pp. 81-94, at p. 86.

[44] Habermas, loc. cit. n. 19.

[45] D. Easton, *A Systems Analysis of Political Life* (Chicago, Chicago University Press 1965) pp. 286-310.

Recently the legitimacy of performance, the regime and polity have all been distinguished.[46] Performance legitimacy might develop in every political system and relates to its efficiency and effectiveness. Regime legitimacy concerns the established and functioning institutional framework. Polity legitimacy refers to the citizens' feeling of belonging to the polity, solidarity and mutual commitments.

There are five legitimating vectors in the EU, being themselves complementary to conflict minimization in order to close the legitimacy gap. International legitimacy can be indirect or derivative, depending on the legitimacy of the states in question. It will always require states' authorization on the input side and the delivery of state preference on the output side. Parliamentary legitimacy reflects this dual legitimation based on the EU double reference – individual rights and the rights of the people – and presupposes the input of elections and the delivery of voters' preferences on the output side. Technocratic legitimacy takes place through the empowerment of independent actors which have a primary interest in performing their tasks with maximum efficiency and this requires expertise on the input side and efficiency on the output side. Based on the input of the treaties and the delivery of rights on the output side, legal and procedural legitimacy adds the virtues of the rule of law to transparency, motivation, the balance of interests and participation. Corporate legitimacy concerns negotiating a policy with those whose compliance it needs and this concerns consultation on the input side and compliance as far as output is concerned.[47]

Legitimacy should not be considered in all or nothing terms. Within the nation-states and EU governance different degrees of legitimacy can be observed when evaluating the performance of the system, institution or a policy. So it will always be more precise to scale legitimation accordingly and to consider different degrees of legitimacy. However, applying the new theoretical developments of legitimacy to an EU perceived as something which is not like any other known phenomenon is totally inefficient as far as solving EU legitimacy problems is concerned.

### 3.3    Old Wine in New Bottles – The Classic Methods of Legitimation in the Nation-State transposed to the EU

In pure abstract terms scholars belonging to this school of thought propose different constructions for the EU in which they attempt to apply the classic methods of legitimation, legality and legitimacy that were devised for nation-

---

[46] Bellamy and Castiglione, loc. cit. n. 37; and Walker, loc. cit. n. 36, pp. 5-8. See also C. Jetzlsperger, 'Legitimacy through Jurisprudence? The Impact of the European Court of Justice on the Legitimacy of the European Union' (EUI Working Paper Law, No. 2003/12) pp. 11-13.

[47] C. Lord and P. Magnette, 'Notes towards a General Theory of Legitimacy in the European Union' (ESRC Working Papers, No. 39/02) available at: <http://www.one-europe.ac.uk/pdf/w39lord.pdf>.

state democracy and which have acquired their contemporary shape after more than three centuries of evolution. As has been noted these scholars take as their benchmark the national form of democracy and are unable to reinvent different concepts of constitutionalism in order to apply them to a new form of political community.[48]

However, there are at least two difficult problems which require a solution before the methods of legitimation in the nation-state can be transposed to the EU and before they can adequately fulfill the task of providing the necessary means to overcome the EU legitimacy crisis. The first problem is to provide some kind of identity to the EU and the second is to solve the problem of translating the nation-state apparatus to a system of governance beyond the nation-state.

There is consensus in academia, with Eurosceptic scholars being the only exception, that in general it is easier to identify what the EU is not rather than to define the nature of the EU.

According to the Eurosceptics, the present and future institutionalization of the European integration process should preserve the shape of an international and a functional intergovernmental organization.[49] The anticipated limitations on the sovereignty of the nation-state feed apprehensions and reaffirm notions of realism and new functionalism, which have had their adherents among politicians and the academic community during all the stages of the European integration process.[50]

The European integration process, which started in the second half of the 20th century as a regional economic organization with the three communities being founded in the 1950s and which evolved into a *sui generis* international organization, became a special supranational entity which, in the words of Jacques Delors, has turned into an Unidentified Political Object. The evolution and simultaneous functioning of the community, intergovernmental and federal

---

[48] M. Maduro, 'Where to look for Legitimacy?', available at: <http://www.arena.uio.no/events/Conference2002/documents/Maduro.doc>.

[49] In modern times confederalism was relatively unstable leading to a dissolution of the union or its evolution into a federal state in the USA, Switzerland 1815-1848, and Germany 1815-1866-1867. See for more details, J.F. Aubert, 'The Historical Development of Confederations', in G. Malinverni, ed., *The Modern Concept of Confederation* (Strasbourg, Venice Commission, Council of Europe) pp. 17-39; E.B. Haas, *Technocracy, Pluralism and the New Europe* (Berkeley, University of California 1964) pp. 64-66; E.B. Haas, *The Uniting of Europe: Political, Social, and Economic Forces 1950-1957* (Stanford, Stanford University Press 1958).

[50] Genetically, the integration was a victory for functionalism over federalism. European integration has been a voluntary unification of the economic sector and not a political union which has been the foundation of federalism. The snowball effect and the resulting spillover has brought about the situation that even before the Maastricht Treaty, the communities engaged in intergovernmental forms of political cooperation. According to federalists the action has always been quicker than the thought, thereby producing chaos, and this might be interpreted as a concession to the predominance of functionalism in the process of integration.

methods in the integration process has not been instrumental to identifying the nature of the EU as a supranational body.[51]

After half a century, the European integration process has not created a federal state identical to the known models of federalism in the world.[52] None of the confederations ever created resembles the EU at the present stage of its development. In contrast to federalism and confederalism, political integration in the EU is lagging behind in the two intergovernmental pillars added by the Treaty of Maastricht.[53] Clearly, the EU does not have all the features of a prefederal or confederal state, but it has surpassed the international organizations so far known throughout history. Although being an important step, the EU's legal personality in the EU Constitution would not fully resolve the inherent ambiguity.

The arguments of the federalists traditionally follow several lines of thought. Some place a great deal of effort into proving that our scientific apparatus produces inadequate means to explain the current state of the integration process. They insist upon the notion that the EU has surpassed the orthodox precept of an international organization and is evolving into a quasi-confederal structure or a non-state entity uniting sovereign states, an international organization *sui generis*, a prefederal union or non-state association of states with its own rational evolution, creating unique structural and constitutional features.[54] Globalization

---

[51] For a federation founded on the principle of tolerance see J. Weiler, 'Federalism and Constitutionalism: Europe's Sonderweg' (Jean Monnet Working Paper No. 10/00 (2000)) available at: <http://www.jeanmonnetprogram.org/papers/00/001001.html>.

[52] See Д.Дж. Элейзер, Сравнительный федерализм, Полисñ[D. Elazar, *Comparative Federalism*, Polis] (1995) No. 5, pp. 106-115; For classifications of dichotomy see W.H. Riker, *Federalism: Origin, Operation, Significance* (Boston, Little, Brown and Co. 1964) or other classifications, A. McWhinney, *Comparative Federalism: States' Rights and National Power*, 2nd edn. (Toronto, Toronto University Press 1965) pp. 16-17; D. Kommers, 'Federalism and European Integration: A Commentary', in M. Cappelletti, M. Seccombe and J. Weiler, *Integration through Law*, Vol. 1, book 1 (Berlin, De Gruyter 1986) pp. 603-616; K.C. Wheare, *Federal Government* (Westport, Greenwood Press 1980) pp. 35-39.

[53] Confederalism is founded on an international treaty as a union of sovereign and equal states, sharing common values and striving to achieve common political goals. The confederation member states preserve their legal personality under international law. Compared to federalism the institutional structure of a confederal state remains quite limited, including a representative institution for common policy, but does not envisage a fully-fledged separation of powers, G. Malinverni, 'The Classical Notions of Confederation and of a Federal State in the Modern Concept of Confederation' (Strasbourg, Venice Commission, Council of Europe 1995) pp. 39-51, at p. 40.

[54] See G. Schuppert, 'On the Evolution of a European State: Reflections on the Conditions of and the Prospects for a European Constitution in Constitutional Policy and Change in Europe', in J.J. Hesse and N. Johnson, eds., *Constitutional Policy and Change in Europe* (Oxford, Oxford University Press 1995) pp. 324-368, at p. 330 and pp. 344-348. For the German doctrine treating the EU as a functional international organization, being a regime and not a federation or concordat interlocking system see R. Hrbeck, 'Federal Balance and the Problem of Democratic Legitimacy in the European Union', 50 *Aussenwirtschaft* (1995) pp. 43-66, at pp. 46-49; M. Zuleeg, 'The European Constitution under Constitutional Constraints: The German Scenario', 22 *European Law Review* (1997) pp. 19-34, at pp. 20-21.

and the transitory nature of the nation-state and state sovereignty have also been highlighted by some authorities in order to emphasize that the EU will need a written constitution.[55] Bringing new features of statehood besides the territory and the nation into the institutional structure and the functioning of the European Union and speculation as to the crisis concerning the territory and nation as statehood elements have been another set of arguments raised in the discourse.[56] The reconsruction of traditional forms of the state has given rise to some speculation that the EU is a unique postmodern state.[57]

Conceptualizing the EU in terms of existing constructions has given rise to the interesting concept of an emerging regional state with divided sovereignties and governance on national and supranational levels, variable boundaries concerning policies which have not yet been geographically determined, and a composite culture and nationhood identity.[58] Another way of looking at the EU within the state context is to define the Union as a regulatory state. The present EU template, even after the drafting of the TCE, does not take the form of a super-state, nor is it an intergovernmental entity of nation-states but rather a supranational union of citizens, peoples and states. As has already been argued, contemporary multilevel constitutionalism in Europe is founded on the EU functioning not as a state-like entity but as a supranational system of governance in response to and compensating for the nation-states' political and economic failings in the globalized world.[59]

---

[55] N. MacCormick, 'Beyond the Sovereign State', 56 *Modern Law Review* (1993); N. MacCormick, 'Sovereignty: Myth and Reality', 11 *Scottish Affairs* (1995); *idem*, 'Sovereignty, Democracy and Subsidiarity' in Bellamy, et al., loc. cit n. 43; C.M.G. Himsworth, 'In a State no longer: The End of Constitutionalism?', *Public Law* (1996) pp. 639-660; V. Schmidt, 'The New World Order, Incorporated: The Rise of Business and the Decline of the Nation-State' (Working Paper EUI – Robert Schumann Centre No. 95/5 (1995)); For a criticism of sovereignty in public international law see L. Henkin, 'International Law: Politics, Values and Functions: General Course on Public International Law', 216 *Recueil des cours* (Dordrecht, Nijhoff 1989) pp. 44-49. See J. Habermas, 'Citizenship and National Identity', in J. Habermas, *Between Facts and Norms: Contributions to a Discourse Theory of Law and Democracy* (Cambridge, Polity Press 1996) pp. 490-515

[56] Globalization has placed a new focus on territory as the basic element of the state. In the ideas of Poggi this constellation has been developed as a crisis of territoriality, G. Poggi, *The State, its Nature, Development and Prospects* (Cambridge, Polity Press 1990) pp. 183-189. The power of transnational organizations has been as if it were separated (severed) from the state territory and the decisions within the legal boundaries of action have had a direct impact on national legal persons within the Member States, see Schmidt, loc. cit., n. 39.

[57] See extensively J. Caporaso, 'The European Union and the Forms of State: Westphalian, Regulatory, or Postmodern?', 34 *Journal of Common Market Studies* (1996) pp. 29-52.

[58] Schmidt, loc. cit. n. 39.

[59] S. Weatherhill, 'Is Constitutional Finality Feasible or Desirable? On the Cases for European Constitutionalism and a European Constitution' (Constitutionalism Web-Papers, ConWEB No. 7/2002) p. 5, available at: <http://www.qub.ac.uk/schools/SchoolofPoliticsInternationalStudies/FileStore/ConWEBFiles/Filetoupload,5315,en.pdf>.

Scholars proposed a different set of new constructs, but none of them fitted into the mould of the classic apparatus of federations, unions, confederations and confederacies, networks and multilevel systems of governance.[60]

A modern approach within these current attempts to apply not the classic, but the newest methods of legitimation developed in the democratic nation-states in Western Europe after the end of World War II, such as some of the attributes of deliberative democracy.[61]

The other problem when addressing the EU legitimacy crisis in terms of power legitimation within the nation-state constructs has been the possibility of adapting modes of legitimacy to different contexts of governance. The issue of the compatibility of the nation-state apparatus with EU governance has been dealt with by J. Weiler and N. Walker using the metaphor of translation and applying it to the transplantation of legal ideas into a different contextual setting. Without a doubt, the question of whether it is legitimate even to attempt to translate the language and normative concerns of constitutionalism from the state to the non-state domain has given rise to new academic debate.[62] The use of constitutional translation as a dynamic process should be internalized in each constitutional area and should not be perceived as a bundle of keys for opening the doors to all governance areas.

### 3.4 Replacing the Bottled Wine with a Soft Drink – From Legitimacy to Compliance

The legitimation crisis in the modern nation-state has encouraged scholars to look for other sources to justify and secure support for governmental power.

One of the most interesting constructions has been the effort to replace the problem of legitimacy with the idea of citizens complying with the government.[63] This alternative model of support for state authority is based on people's ordinary reactions to signals from various institutions of government. The citizens' inclination to comply with government commands, suggestions and

---

[60] For a brief overview of the nature of the EU as multi-level governance or polity, a mixed commonwealth, *condominio consortio*, partial polity, etc., see E. Ericksen, J. Fossum and A. Menedez, 'On Constitution Making and Democratic Legitimacy', available at: <http://www.arena.uio.no/events/Conference2002/documents/ErikFossMen.doc>. See also E. Ericksen and J. Fossum, 'Europe in Search of Legitimacy: Assessing Strategies of Legitimation' (Arena Working Papers, WP 02/38) available at: <http://www.arena.uio.no/publications/wp02_38.pdf>.

[61] A. Peters, 'A Plea for a European Semi-Parliamentary and Semi-Consociational Democracy', 7 *European Integration Online Papers* (2003) available at: <http://eiop.or.at/eiop/> under 'archives'.

[62] J. Weiler, *The Constitution of Europe: 'Do the New Clothes have an Emperor?' And Other Essays on European Integration* (Cambridge, Cambridge University Press 1999) p. 270; N. Walker, 'Postnationalist Constitutionalism and the Problem of Translation (IILJ Working Paper 2003/03 (History and Theory of International Law Series)) (2003) available at: <http://www.iilj.org>.

[63] Rubin, op. cit. n. 38.

requests is related to the self-interest involved in obtaining benefits from the government in exchange for their obedience. Individuals comply with governmental decisions not only because of their material interest but also due to affection, cooperation and concurrence.

The compliance model breaks down the legitimacy concept into particular justifications which facilitate a microanalysis of each citizen's relationship with the government.[64] Proponents of trading legitimacy for compliance conclude that compliance is best suited to the modern state. They also think that citizens form global judgments relating to the government depending on the mix of self-interest, loyalty, cooperation and concurrence that determine their more individual reactions. However, these theoretical constructs should first be approved based on the nation-state experience for which they were intended. Attempts to impose the compliance model on EU governance in contrast to the EU member states based on legitimacy might have a devastating effect as far as EU legitimacy-building is concerned. It is simply not at all certain that the majority would prefer a soft drink to the real wine.

### 3.5    Maturing the New Wine in the New Bottles – Towards the Invention of Universal Criteria for Governance Legitimacy (Ph. Schmitter, T. Herbst)

The EU legitimacy crisis has led to attempts to elaborate a universal theory of legitimation which is valid for nation-states and post-national governance. Instead of looking at how to synchronize various modes of legitimacy, which differ according to the multilevel structure, scholars tend to look for the criteria which are applicable to governance within and beyond the nation-state framework. These efforts mark a radical break with tradition based on rationalist thinking in order to solve future problems with the well known traditional solutions of the past.

The point of departure is that post-national legitimacy goes beyond the nation-state as the natural and exclusive source of governance and that sub- and supranational polities have a sufficient degree of autonomy in order to take and implement collective decisions.[65] In Schmitter's words the complete and immediate democratization of the EU is neither possible nor desirable for not only do the politicians not know how to do this, but there is no compelling evidence that Europeans want such democratization and the citizenry are not prepared to exercise this power.[66] Legitimacy-building will be founded on new innovative practices in the EU governance arrangements concerning their chartering, com-

---

[64] Ibid.

[65] Ph. Schmitter, 'What is there to legitimize in the European Union and how might this be accomplished?' (Jean Monnet Working Paper No. 6/01 (2001)) available at: <http://www.jeanmonnetprogram.org/papers/01/011401.html>.

[66] Ibid.

position and rules rather than transposing the methods of nation-state legitimation to the EU level.

Another interesting idea of creating the legitimacy of postnational governance is based on a critical reconstruction of E. Sieyes' and C. Schmitt's concepts of legitimate constitution-making.[67] Instead of classical theories of legitimacy within the nation-state, three founding principles of the Constitutional legitimation of governance have been proposed:

- protection of freedom;
- collective autonomy; and
- ability to uphold durable consensus.[68]

### 3.6     Complications in the Wine-Bottling Process or applying New Legitimacy Constructions to the New EU Identity

Even the best restatement of theoretical approaches cannot provide a pool for picking the best recipe to resolve the EU's legitimacy gap. A general review, however, is instrumental to understanding the complexity of EU legitimacy-building.

Comparisons between legitimacy within a nation-state and EU governance should be used with care and with the proviso that purely classical methods of legitimation cannot be mechanically transposed to the EU and that nation-state legitimacy options cannot provide terms of reference for solving the EU's legitimacy crisis. Moreover, in modern times there is a legitimation crisis within the nation-state as well.[69] Especially at the beginning of the 21st century, globalization has integrated a democratic deficit within the borders of the nation-state. As a keen observer M. Maduro has proved that transnational processes cannot be contained by the nation-states and legitimized with direct or indirect popular control. National polities, traditionally regarded as a precondition for legitimacy and constitution-making, have come to limit direct participation by restricting political decision-making to citizens. On the national scale corporatism has led to the distortion of parliamentary representation and the malfunctioning of the democratic process.[70]

---

[67] T. Herbst, *Legitimation durch Verfassungsggebung, Ein Prinzipienmodell der Legitimität staatlicher und supranationaler Hoheitsgewalt* (Baden-Baden, Nomos 2003).

[68] Ibid. at pp. 103-122.

[69] Among the abundance of legal literature on this subject one should not overlook an early contribution by J. Habermas, *The Legitimation Crisis* (Boston, Beacon Press 1975).

[70] M. Maduro, 'How Constitutional can the European Union be? Reconciling Intergovernmentalism with Constitutionalism in European Constitutionalism', available at: <http://www.jeanmonnetprogram.org/conference_JMC_Princeton/NYU_Princeton_Maduro.rtf>; Schmidt, loc. cit. n. 39.

It seems that EU legitimacy-building is a much more complicated and differentiated process which takes place in parallel with the dynamically evolving multilevel governance of the EU.

Even without a detailed analysis, the explorer of EU legitimacy should be aware of at least three complications when providing solutions to resolve the legitimation crisis. The first relates to the dimensions of and the criteria for legitimacy:

- the interplay of the criteria for legitimacy and their malfunctioning due to insufficient legality;

- normative justifiability (a feeling of belonging, the content and performance of the electoral system, representation, accountability, established structures and competencies); and

- inadequate direct or indirect social legitimation.[71]

The second complication depends on the simultaneous actions of methods of legitimation and the possible collision between them which would lead to ineffectiveness.[72]

The third is implied by the integration methods. In the EU, as a system of multilevel governance, different modes of legitimation lead to various legitimacy models depending on the parallel functioning of community, intergovernmental and federal methods which establish different hierarchies of power in government.[73]

In a world of constitutional pluralism, legitimation follows many tracks and abundant locations of governance beyond the nation-state will bring about plural legitimacies. Concurrent legitimacies are supposed to act simultaneously and will be attributed to different locations of government. The overall picture should not be oversimplified – the growth of one legitimating mode should not be interpreted at the expense of another. Also, it should not be expected that the diminishing of one method of legitimacy should lead to the growth of other forms of legitimacy.

Perhaps it might be appropriate to draw a comparison with M. Maduro's concept of hierarchy within contra punctual constitutionalism and legitimacy within the national, EU and global constitutionalism. In our contemporary globalized age constitutional pluralism is at a stage where separate constitutional locations

---

[71] M. Kelstrup, 'Legitimacy and Institutionalisation in the European Union: Dilemmas and Institutional Policies' (Paper presented at NOPSA, Alborg University (2002)) draft available at: <http://www.socsci.auc.dk/institut2/nopsa/arbejdsgruppe16/kelstrup.pdf>; M. Horeth, 'No Way for the Beast? The unsolved Legitimacy Problem of European Governance', 2 *Journal of European Public Policy* (1999) pp. 249-268.

[72] Lord and Magnette, loc. cit. n. 47.

[73] See V. Roben, 'Constitutionalism of Inverse Hierarchy: The Case of the European Union' (Jean Monnet Working Paper No. 8/03 (2003)) available at: <http://www.jeanmonnetprogram.org/papers/03/030801.html>.

have reached a different level of hierarchy within the legal order. The weakest of all has been the global constitutionalism where different currents mark the emerging priorities of governance and the legal order. In contra punctual constitutionalism harmonizing the different loci of constitutionalism should be done in a harmonious manner. Harmony, however, would require certain premises to be observed. For example, simultaneous melodies in music should be performed within one key and should not be sung in an *a capella* fashion. Hierarchies and legitimacies in national, EU and global constitutionalism should be built on the consensus concerning some democratic values and should not be aimed at repetition, although with a different consequence.[74]

The heterogeneity of governance modes in the EU requires the use of all avenues of legitimacy available to the various modes of governance.[75] One should not fear that in this way complex and differentiated legitimacies will be the result. There are at least two reasons for this. The first relates to the fact that even within the nation-state a differentiated legitimacy exists when comparing the general legitimacy of the political system with the legitimacies of parliament, the executive branch, the courts, etc.

The second, but no less important reason, is that building a hierarchy of legitimacies based on their relation to democracy would be inefficient and counterproductive. Scholars often have preferences and are tempted to recognise the superiority of direct or input legitimacy over the other modes of legitimation. The strong aspiration of more legitimacy drawn from direct citizen participation through elections and referendums has to acknowledge the double citizenship in the EU. Observing the principle of legality and the supremacy of the EU Treaty and after the ratification of the Treaty establishing a Constitution for Europe, the legality ingredient of the legitimacy content should be observed on an equal basis with efforts to gradually introduce elements of input legitimacy in the EU. EU citizenship, which is not intended to destroy national citizenship, has moreover been introduced and is based on national citizenship. Admitting that EU citizenship actually exists based on the prerequisite of citizenship of one of the member states of the Union automatically means the direct participation of EU citizens, thereby creating input legitimacy, but this should not be seen as more valuable or impairing the indirect or output legitimacy of intergovernmentalism, as within the nation-state this is built on the direct participation of the people in government elections. Therefore the conclusion that there should be a prevalence of one mode of legitimacy in the EU above all others seems to be somewhat misleading.

---

[74] See for contrapunctual constitutionalism, M. Maduro, 'Europe and the Constitution: What if this is as good as it gets?', in J.H.H. Weiler and M. Wind, eds., *Rethinking European Constitutionalism* (Cambridge, Cambridge University Press 2000). Also available at: <http://www.umich.edu/~iinet/euc/PDFs/2002%20Papers/Maduro.PDF>.

[75] See R. de Jonghe and P. Bursens, 'The Quest for more Legitimacy in the EU as a Multi-level Political System' (Paper for ECPR Congress in Edinburgh 28 March – April 2003).

Within different EU governance methods various types of legitimacy will un-doubtedly prevail. For example, intergovernmental legitimacy will be based on indirect and output legitimacy, while direct and input legitimacy will normally develop more efficiently at the supranational level of community and federal methods of integration. This does not exclude other methods of legitimation, however.

4.    THE EU CONSTITUTION: ITS LEGITIMACY AND LEGITIMATING
      THE UNION BY MEANS OF A WRITTEN CONSTITUTION OR
      BOTTLING THE WINE BY THE ADOPTION OF THE
      CONSTITUTIONAL TREATY

### 4.1    The Constitutional Treaty's Legitimacy Implications

During the first stages of the European Community's evolution, for more than three decades after the Treaty of Rome a metaphoric use of the term constitution encompassing primary law would have had nothing more than a symbolic sig-nificance which can be compared to qualifying the structure of the Christian Church as a constitution during the Middle Ages. For half a century the evolu-tion of constitutionalism has been incremental, bottom up, developing step by step and driven by a judicial process.[76] Characterized as low intensity constitu-tionalism it has led to the emergence of an unwritten constitution of the EU.
Compared to the UK Constitution with its uncodified constitutional norms, the EU Constitution was identified in a single document as an unwritten constitu-tion.

Being the matriarch of Western democracy, Great Britain still has an unwrit-ten constitution, although during the revolution it was the first to create an Instrument of Government. It has been a common approach to compare EU pri-mary law to the UK's unwritten constitution comprising a set of charters, bills, declarations, parliamentary statutes and constitutional conventions containing fundamental legal norms. Along these lines the founding treaties, especially after Amsterdam, were considered by some authorities to be the EU's unwritten con-stitution.[77]

---

[76] Maduro, op. cit. n. 70.
[77] J. Shaw, *Law of the European Union* (London, Macmillan 1996) pp. 63-66; D. Curtin, 'The Constitutional Structure of the Union: A Europe of Bits and Pieces', 30 *Common Market Law Review* (1993) pp. 17-69; W. van Gerven, 'Toward a Coherent Constitutional System within the European Union', 2 *European Public Law* (1996) pp. 81-103; M. Zuleeg, 'The European Constitution under Constitutional Constraints: The German Scenario', 22 *European Law Review* (1997) pp. 19-34, at pp. 20-21;  Л.Ферайоли, Отвъд суверенитета и гражданството. За един световен конституционализъм, Съвременно право, кн.6, 1995, 70-78. [L. Feraioli, 'Beyond Sovereignty and Citizenship for a World Constitutionalism' in *Contemporary Law* No. 6 (1995) pp. 70-78].

The unwritten constitution is a poli-constitutional act, comprised of provisions, and which is contained in the founding treaties and some of the decisions of the ECJ which have a constitutionalizing effect. Although this unwritten constitution is more difficult to understand since its provisions are contained in the founding treaties and in ECJ decisions, it does meet most of the formal requirements of the norms of the nation-state constitutions as a higher law.[78]

Why, then, was a new written EU constitution considered necessary? What is the added value for the EU of a documentary (written) constitution or a Treaty establishing a Constitution for Europe? How does the nation-state constitutional theory fit such a meta-constitutional document which the Constitutional Treaty undoubtedly is?

It is a well-known fact that a written constitution belonging to the modern nation-state is an offspring of the people and national sovereignty in that nation-state and is regarded as a universal and free association of the citizens living within a certain territory. The constitutions are indispensable in providing limited and responsible government, determining the political power structure, dividing the powers between the constituted political institutions and protecting human and citizens' rights. The constitutions are created by a constituent power and draw their legitimacy from popular sovereignty and basic human rights. In principle, a democratic constitution is an undisputed prerequisite for the rule of law and a cornerstone in building legitimate government in the nation-state.

Since antiquity at least two meanings of the concept of a constitution have evolved.[79] The real (functional or material) constitution has been present since ancient times and is still a feature of every state and even organized human organizations and corporations. The real constitution refers to the institutionalized

---

[78] For the evolution of the higher law concept in antiquity and after the drafting of the written constitutions see Capelletti and Cohen, op. cit. n. 4, at pp. 5-11; C.J. Friedrich, *The Philosophy of Law in Historical Perspective*, 2nd edn. (Chicago, Chicago University Press 1963) pp. 12-26.

[79] In *Politics* Aristotle used the term polity which has been translated into English as a constitution, meaning real constitution, since it concerns the organization and division of political power between the institutions and not a higher law or a supreme legal act. Aristotle, *Politics*, Book IV, Ch. 1 (Baltimore, Penguin books 1970) p. 151; Contemporary authorities in the field differentiate 3 meanings of a constitution. According to F. Snyder *empirical* constitutions refer to the way in which a state is organized; *material or substantive* constitutions are sets of fundamental legal norms determining the legal order of the state; *instrumental* constitutions are written documents or fundamental legal acts which lay down the principal constitutional legal norms. See F. Snyder, 'General Course on Constitutional Law of the European Union', *Collected Courses of the Academy of European Law*, Vol. VI, Book I (Dordrecht, Nijhoff 1991) pp. 41-155, at p. 53. Blondel adds to the real and legal (written) constitution the prescriptive constitution referring to doctrines, values, goals and ideals, including a limited constitutional government. See J. Blondel, *Comparative Government: An Introduction* (London, Prentice Hall/Harvester Wheatsheaf 1995) pp. 217-218. See also V. Bogdanor, 'Constitutions', in V. Bogdanor, ed., *Constitutions in Democratic Politics* (Aldershot, Gower 1988) pp. 5-7; Ph. Allott, 'The Crisis of European Constitutionalism: Reflections on the Revolution in Europe', 34 *Common Market Law Review* (1997) pp. 439-490, at pp. 468-469; N. Walker, 'European Constitutionalism and European Integration', *Public Law* (Summer 1996) pp. 266-290, at p. 270.

forms of different associations and is related to the structure and functioning of the institutions and their relationship with the members of the collective body. In this train of thought one cannot deny that the EU has a real constitution, consisting of a governmental structure and a predefined relationship with the member states and their citizens.

Modern written constitutions appear at a much later stage in the evolution process, although some of the acts of Roman emperors were called constitutions. A written constitution is a charter, a higher law comprising a set of norms providing for the organization, separation and functioning of political power, protecting the basic rights of man and citizen in order to prevent abuse and concentration of absolute power, to guarantee civil, political and economic liberties.[80]

Referring to the method of adoption, F. Snyder added another meaning to the concept of a constitution which is relevant to its legitimacy by relating the constitution to a written document that has been deliberated by the citizens or by their representatives.[81]

At first glance, the Constitutional Treaty does not exemplify a typical constitutional moment of discontinuity and transformation in terms of the construction by B. Ackerman and N. Walker.[82] It does not fall within the category of reactive constitutions drafted in Central and Eastern Europe as a radical break with the past.[83] It would have been much more comfortably situated within the concept of the growth of a constitution as developed by K. Llewellyn in the US school of legal realism. It bears similarities to constitutional serialism regarding its continuity, but differs with respect to transformation which is inherent in the growth of the constitution concept.

It seems that it might be more appropriate not to use the constitutional moments concept but to refer instead to the constitutional 'weather forecast' which produces the prognosis for evaluating the prerequisites for drafting a constitution and calculating when this should be dome. The EU constitutional climate for a fully-fledged written constitution exemplified by the Constitutional Treaty was indeed ripe, considering the pending issues that could certainly not be postponed. The biggest enlargement in history – nearly doubling the number of EU Member States and more than quadrupling the European Community's founding states – saw to it that the EU could not be run with a governance framework designed for

---

[80] Written constitutions acquired their meaning as fundamental laws and took their contemporary shape after the adoption of the fourth-generation constitutions after World War II. There are more than 180 constitutions belonging to sovereign states today and the constitutions drafted since 1970 outnumber those created before that date.

[81] F. Snyder, 'The unfinished Constitution of the European Union: Principles, Processes and Culture', in J.H.H. Weiler and M. Wind, eds., *European Constitutionalism beyond the State* (Cambridge, Cambridge University Press 2003).

[82] N. Walker, 'After the Constitutional Moment' (The Federal Trust, Online Paper No. 32/03 (2003)) available at: < http://www.fedtrust.co.uk/uploads/constitution/32_03.pdf>.

[83] See Bogdanor, *supra* n. 79, at p. 7.

six Member States and which was subsequently developed to run the EU consisting of fifteen Member States. The willingness of some countries to proceed at a greater speed towards enhanced cooperation before the others would be ready to join this momentum also increased the pressure to draft a constitution. It now seemed that the question posed by J. Weiler – do the new clothes have an emperor? – should be answered to the effect that the emperor is in need of new clothes.

Looking at the Constitutional Treaty from a legitimacy prospective, however, raises some new issues. The first set of open questions concern the legitimacy of constitution-making in a non-state entity. What is the true nature hidden behind the hybrid and the ambivalent title of the Treaty establishing a Constitution for Europe? What lies behind the dubious label of the Europe Convention – a treaty or a constitution?

The Constitutional Treaty has been interpreted as both a constitution and a treaty. Some have questioned the constitutional character of the Constitutional Treaty. They claim that the Constitutional Treaty, although having some specific constitutional features, should be given a treaty status.[84] However, the importance of calling the Constitutional Treaty a constitution has been emphasized by many distinguished scholars.[85] Analyzing the mixed features of the Constitutional Treaty J. Weiler labeled it a treaty masquerading as a constitution and a constitution masquerading as a treaty.[86]

Most of the controversial issues might be resolved by looking at the procedure which was followed in the adoption of the Constitutional Treaty and which will be used to enact the Constitutional Treaty on the one side, and its functions, on the other. The answers to both questions are related to legitimacy, but in the first case it concerns how the EU has created the legitimacy of the new constitution and, in the second, it relates to the effect which the constitution's legitimacy has on the EU's legitimacy.

The creation of the Constitutional Treaty might be laconically presented with the use of O. Neurath's building the ship at sea metaphor.[87] It is a normal out-

---

[84] P. Elefteriades, 'Constitution or Treaty' (The Federal Trust, Online Paper No. 12/04 (2004)) available at: <http://www.fedtrust.co.uk/constitutionalpapers>.

[85] J. Habermas, 'So, why does Europe need a Constitution?' (Florence, Policy Papers on Constitutional Reform of the European Union, EUI – Robert Schuman Centre, No. 2001/02 (2002)); A. Follesdal, 'Drafting a European Constitution – Challenges and Opportunities' (Constitutionalism Web-Papers ConWEB No. 5/2002); L.M. Diez-Picazo, 'Treaty or Constitution: The Status of the Constitution for Europe' (2004).

[86] J. Weiler, 'Hard Choices' available at: <http://www.law.nyu.edu/clppt/program2003/readings/weiler.pdf>. For more arguments on the dual nature of the Constitutional Treaty see also A. von Bogdandy, 'The Preamble', in B. de Witte, ed., *Ten Reflections on the Constitutional Treaty for Europe* (Florence, EUI 2003) p. 4; P. Craig, 'Constitutions, Constitutionalism and the EU', 7 *European Law Journal* (2001) pp. 25-150.

[87] 'We are like seafarers, who must rebuild their ship in open sea, without being able to take it apart in a dock and build it up of its best constituents from the bottom up', cited in Follesdal,

come of top to bottom constitution-building by a gradual low intensity constitutionalism marked in the end by a drafted written document following the constitution-making procedure in the nation-states and reflecting the peculiarities of the EU as a non-state entity.

Traditional democratic constitution-making within the nation-state has always followed the traditional pattern that the '*demos*' can be the only source by which to shape the '*polis*'. People elect a representative body, endowed with constituent authority, and by arriving at a consensus this body drafts a constitution that is accepted by the citizens as a valid and legitimate supreme legal act and this is then directly or indirectly ratified by the people. This constitution-building process blends several equally important elements – constituent assembly, legitimately elected by the people, consent for a written constitution.[88]

What was the procedure applied in the EU constitution-making process, considering that the EU '*demos*' and a European state were lacking? The adoption of the Constitutional Treaty had to comply with the TEU amendment procedure. Legality and legitimacy implied that the voluntary adoption of the Constitutional Treaty would be better fitted to the treaty amendment procedure if the legal term 'treaty' appears in the title of the new EU written constitution.

The Eurosceptics go further and refute the legitimacy of the Constitutional Treaty as a written constitution due to the fact that a non-constituent authority in a non-demos entity has adopted a constitution for a non-existing EU state. Of course, interpreting the constitution as a treaty has been seen as the only logical explanation for the Constitutional Treaty which is consistent with the traditional theory of democratic constitution-making.

However, the Constitutional Treaty's adoption procedure has a constitutional context as well. In fact, in order to adopt the Constitutional Treaty, a three-stage constitution-making procedure was invented in order to overcome the lacking elements in the traditional nation-state constitution-drafting procedure and to reinforce the legitimacy of the EU's written constitution with a combination of devices which are common to all forms of EU governance.

The Convention on the Future of Europe was the first stage in preparing the Constitutional Treaty. Certainly there were weaknesses in this convention reflecting community governance, but they are outweighed by the successful outcome. Although it was strongly criticized with regard to the method of formation and the procedures that were followed,[89] the Convention proved to be an

---

op. cit. n. 85, at p. 1. For a commentary see J. Shaw, 'Process, Responsibility, and Inclusion in EU Constitutionalism' (The Federal Trust, Online Paper No. 01/02 (2002)) available at: <http://www.fedtrust.co.uk/constitutionalpapers>.

[88] Principles generating consensus – by bargain, by argument, by commitment or mystification – have a further impact on the life expectancy and legitimacy of the constitution, once it has been enacted. See M. Müller and G. Schaal, 'The Relevance of a Constitution for Europe', available at: <http://www.epsnet.org/2004/pps/Müller.pdf>.

[89] For a detailed list of the Convention's demerits see A. Coughlan, 'A Critical Analysis of the EU Draft Constitution' (Brussels, TEAM Working Paper No. 10 (2003)).

autonomous and representative body with sufficient internal dynamics, open to deliberation, receptive to the new proposals and efficient in integrating the communicative process within the framework of decision making.[90]

Although there is resemblance in substance and as its title tends to suggest, the Convention on the Future of Europe has not been a typical example of the representative constituent assemblies that have drafted the nation-state constitutions. Only a comparison between the unlimited authority of the constitutional conventions and the assigned tasks of the Convention on the Future of Europe, which was a mandated body, gives rise to substantial differences. For example, the 1787 Philadelphia convention intended to propose amendments to improve the Articles of Confederation in order to prevent the break up of the loose and fragile confederal union of states. By adopting a completely new federal constitution, the founding fathers exceeded their mandate. The voting procedure in Philadelphia was kept secret as a safeguard against the unpopularity of their endeavour.[91] The voting was conducted under the confederal principle of one state one vote, but when the draft was completed it was only signed by 39 delegates out of the 74.[92] If this principle had to be applied to the final voting on the draft it would have led to 6 state delegations voting in favour, which was a minority of the 13 states. The signature of 39 founding fathers overcame this shortcoming, however.

Instead of starting debates after the constitutional drafts have been introduced, as was the case in Philadelphia, the French or any other constituent assemblies, the Convention on the Future of Europe began with the reports of the working groups on controversial issues and voting on the proposed solutions tended to do away with any potential conflicts which the draft might have and which could have led to disruption.

The Convention on the Future of Europe should be seen as an indispensable stage, as an element, but not as the whole constituent authority and the sole repository of constituent power.[93] The Convention on the Future of the EU was assigned by the Laeken declaration and was never intended to copy the constitutional conventions in the nation-state context, nor has it ever aspired to assume

---

[90] Shaw, op. cit n. 87, at pp. 12-26.

[91] The founding fathers retained their notes pertaining to the convention debates, but agreed not to publish them during their lifetime. The most accurate account was that by J. Madison and this was bought from the contents of his inheritance after he was the last of the delegates to pass away in 1836 and it was subsequently published in 1840. By that time the Federal Constitution had been in force for more than five decades, securing the foundations for an effective constitutional government evolving into a constitutional democracy. F. Lundberg, *Cracks in the Constitution* (Secaucus, L. Stuart 1980) p. 133.

[92] After waiting for 10 days for the majority of the delegates to appear in Philadelphia 29 delegates started the meeting, see M. Farrand, ed., *The Records of the Federal Convention of 1787*, Vol. I (New Haven, Yale University Press 1966) pp. 1-2.

[93] For an historical overview of conventions in the constitution-drafting process see H. Dippel, 'Conventions in Comparative Constitutional Law' (College of Europe, Research Papers in Law, No. 4/2003 (2003)).

such an elevated role. Moreover, trespassing on the path of constituent assemblies the EU convention should have produced an illegitimate Constitutional Treaty. That is why the comparative constitutional approach, which is used as a criticism of the Convention, seems to be inconsistent since it cannot be criticized for not meeting the features it was not intended to meet.

With the requirement that the Constitutional Treaty has to be adopted by the IGC, the intergovernmental method has been included in the process for adopting the EU Constitution. The consent of Member State governments at the IGC might be seen as the second stage in drafting the constitution or as an integral part of the constituent authority in drafting the EU Constitution.

The ratification process by the Member States is the third stage in the procedure of exercising constituent authority in the adoption of the EU Constitution.

At first glance the ratification stage is the typical procedure for the adoption of treaty amendments or for the entry into force of completely new treaties. In the light of EU constitution-making when the final product to be submitted for ratification is the Constitutional Treaty (or a treaty containing a written constitution), this stage acquires another meaning. It can be seen as the third element in or the third phase of constituent authority. It is during ratification that the 'no European *demos*' objection[94] can be successfully invoked, to be eventually superseded by the consent of the European '*demoi*' for the EU Constitution. [95]

The ratification adds to the EU Constitution's legitimacy as it has gained the support of the peoples in the EU Member States. This stage of constituent authority can be regarded as EU constitutional '*demoi-cracy*' as EU governance is already a reality. Its significance might be downgraded to the entry into force of an international or an EU Treaty. While this stage or part of the constituent authority functions at the national governance level, it should not be forgotten that in all federal constitutions the constituent authority has always included the ratification of a totally new treaty or amendments to an existing constitution at the level of the Member States. So the ratification acquires a double entendre of national participation in the constitution-drafting process and as an indispensable stage of federal constituent authority.

Thus the two-sided nature of supranationalism has been preserved in the constitution-making process – in order to be legitimate the EU Constitution has to be produced by 3 levels or stages of constituent authority. In compensating for the lack of legitimacy in the constitution-drafting process when compared to the constituent authority in the nation-state, each part of the threefold constituent authority has added and will add its own legitimacy, thereby securing the legitimacy of the EU's written constitution. Beyond any doubt, when a legiti-

---

[94] This thesis has many adherents in academic circles and has been extensively expounded by Judge P. Kirchoff of the German Constitutional Court in the famous Brunner case, *BVerfGE* 89, p. 155.

[95] K. Nicolaïdis, 'The New Constitution as European Demoi-cracy?' (The Federal Trust, Online paper No. 38/03 (2003)) available at: <http://www.fedtrust.co.uk/constitutionalpapers>.

mate constitution is adopted after its ratification, it will have a tremendous effect on the EU's legitimacy.

The constituent authority in the EU Constitution has, to date, successfully exploited the building of a ship at sea metaphor. Instead of following the '*demos*' – constituent power – constitution – polity sequence it has adopted a different route – a constitution built by constituent authority to be ratified by the European '*demoi*' and attaining a new EU polity. Here lies the real constituent power as some have looked at the impact of the constituent power on the political and social system. The genuine impact of the constituent power leading to the adoption of a written constitution has been defined as the creation of a new polity *ex nihilo*.[96]

The other reason for applying the threefold constituent procedure is due to the fact that the Constitutional Treaty is the first written constitution in the EU's history. While the Constitution is in the process of being adopted, the primary EU treaty law and the unwritten EU Constitution will remain in force. So legality and the rule of law require that this procedure should be followed in order to bring the Constitutional Treaty into existence and to give birth to the EU's written constitution. A successful transition from the EU's unwritten to the EU's written constitution had to be anchored in the existing treaty amendment system.

However, the Convention as the first stage in the drafting process is not a typical think-tank working group preparing a draft for an IGC decision within which ratification is integrated, thereby upgrading the EU treaty system. The threefold constituent authority both had to comply with the requirements which are in force for an entity founded on treaties and to comply with constituent power which transforms primary EU law into a written constitution. Thus, subject to the requirement that the constituent power has to be legitimate, the adoption of the EU Constitution had to faithfully follow the treaty amendment procedure and, by observing the treaty amendment procedure supplemented by a successful convention, the drafting of the constitution has given rise to legitimacy stemming from three sources of the existing different methods of governance in the EU. The threefold constituent power and the requirement of having to reach a consensus have predetermined the Constitutional Treaty's content.

A legitimate constitution has many implications for the EU, but one such implication is directly related to the topic being considered in this report. The Constitutional Treaty has given rise to legitimation and will lead to boosting the EU's legitimacy, which is one of the best ways to rectify the present democracy and legitimacy deficit.

The merits of a written constitution extend far beyond the simplification and codification of the complex primary EU law structure and content which will be

---

[96] Constitutions are adopted as the outcome of gradual development or as a revolutionary act. 'The constituent power is the power to create a political order *ex nihilo*'. See U.K. Preuss, 'Constitutional Powermaking for the New Polity: Some Deliberations on the Relations between Constituent Power and the Constitution', in M. Rosenfeld, ed., *Constitutionalism, Identity, Difference and Legitimacy* (Durham, Duke University Press 1994) pp. 143.

easier for the EU citizen to understand. The advantages of the Constitutional Treaty cannot be confined to channeling the distribution of power, ensuring a horizontal and vertical separation of power by pooling sovereignties. In a broader context the Constitutional Treaty creates the framework for a European public sphere;[97] it does not establish a European 'super state', but maintains the delicate balance between the EU constitutional order and the Member States' national constitutions.[98] A written constitution provides concrete validity and by its supremacy it excludes recourse to regression in justifying governmental actions and human rights.[99]

However, the most important of a new constitution's functions has been legitimization.

Within the nation-states, besides the normative, integrative and framing functions which the constitutions perform, the legitimation by which they justify the democratic values and virtues of the established form of government creates a feeling of attachment as far as citizens are concerned thereby promoting their support for the constitutional government. Constitutional supremacy is the prime safeguard of legal security and respect for legitimate social expectations. The adoption of a written constitution functions as a birth certificate for constitutions in that it establishes a new regime and political legitimacy. In this context the Constitutional Treaty is a method of regime legitimacy[100] and it legitimates the creation of the new polity.[101] The Constitutional Treaty bridges the community, intergovernmental and national legitimation by anchoring the EU governance framework in the consent generated in the community governance method, intergovernmentalism and the national Member States' constitutional orders. The difficulties inherent in consent-building predetermine the contents of the Constitutional Treaty. As was noted in the Constitutional Treaty there is as much 'stateness' as has been specifically laid down in the constitution, as much power as has been conferred by the constitution and as much unity as is necessary to preserve specific identities.[102] The written EU Constitution can be seen as a catalyst for deepening and strengthening mutual trust and promoting a common attachment to shared European values.[103] Constitutional legitimacy by means of

---

[97] Habermas, loc. cit. n. 85.

[98] J. Shaw, 'The Draft Treaty establishing a Constitution for Europe' (Malta, Paper prepared for the Conference 'Value of Constitution for Europe' (2004)).

[99] H. Kelsen, 'The Function of the Constitution', in D. Lloyd and M.D.A. Freeman, eds., *Lloyd's Introduction to Jurisprudence*, 5th edn. (London, 1985) pp. 379-385, at p. 385.

[100] A. von Bogdandy, 'The European Constitution and European Identity: Potentials and Dangers of the Draft Treaty establishing a Constitution for Europe' (Jean Monnet Working Paper No. 5/04 (2004)) available at: <http://www.jeanmonnetprogram.org/papers/04/040501-07.html>.

[101] N. Walker, 'Europe's Constitutional Momentum and the Search for Polity Legitimacy' (Jean Monnet Working Paper No. 5/04 (2004)) available at: <http://www.jeanmonnetprogram.org/papers/04/040501-01.html>.

[102] Cited in R. Goring, 'Requirements for the emerging European Constitution' (WHI Working Paper No. 2/03) available at: <http://www.whi-berlin.de/goring.htm>.

[103] N. Walker, op. cit n. 82, at p. 10.

the Constitutional Treaty is instrumental in resolving the missing element of a nation, a gap in the EU Constitution by the creation of a new polity when compared to states constitutions. However, the claim that a fully-fledged postnational constitution should meet all the features of a nation-state constitution would be a simplification.

Constitutions confer legitimacy, but they cannot be considered as a 'cure all' for legitimacy crisis problems. The legitimating function of the Constitutional Treaty should not be overestimated as it does not contain universal solutions for a democracy deficit. This feature is common to a postnational constitution and to a nation-state constitution as well. Constitutional legitimation cannot be tied to the content-based concept of the binding nature of constitutions.[104] The dynamic nature of legitimacy will require that EU governance will be based on and will be exercised within the EU Constitution, although this in itself will certainly not be enough to automatically bestow legitimacy on multi-centred governance in Europe.

## 4.2 Are Referendums a Must for the Fine Wine-Bottling of EU Legitimacy?

A tremendous effect of the legitimation of the Constitutional Treaty of the EU would have been a decision to hold a European-wide referendum. The ratification by means of a single European referendum conducted on the territories of the Member States would have had a positive impact on the common feeling of belonging as the voters might have had the opportunity to transcend their identity as nationals and would have voted with their conscience and values as EU citizens. In a long-term perspective it might not be an exaggeration to claim that a European-wide referendum on the Constitutional Treaty would have had a positive influence on the gradual formation of the European '*demos*' by raising citizens' EU awareness. No doubt, the symbolic function of a written constitution would have mobilized the feeling of community among EU citizens and would have steered the further development of the European public sphere. Direct participation in the ratification process would affirm the EU citizens' belief in the benefits of further integration and would promote their trust and support which would mean that the constitution-making process would have a most profound impact as far as the EU's legitimacy is concerned. Last but not least, EU citizens would have the opportunity to look at the new constitutional EU garments in one mirror which reflects their preferences in the same light and size and minimizes any distortions based on the different national settings of the ratification arrangements. No doubt, a European-wide referendum would minimize the possibility of the Constitutional Treaty's ratification becoming bogged down in national issues.

---

[104] See F. Michelman, 'Constitutional Legitimation for Political Acts', 66 *Modern Law Review* (2003) pp. 1-15, at p. 14.

This fact has been well recognized by some politicians and NGOs.[105] Respected members of the academia have emphasized the constructive role which the EU polity can play in the '*demos*' formation and the great legitimacy advantage of holding an all-European referendum on the EU constitution.[106]

Instead the decision was taken that the ratification process should be decided by the nation-state governments, with each one opting for direct or parliamentary voting on the Constitutional Treaty. Of course, this decision was not prompted by logistical reasons. At first glance it encapsulates the democratic ratification procedure in the nation-states and makes it dependable on the different '*demoi*' in the EU Member States. However, it is this form of ratification that is in harmony with the amendment/drafting a new treaty procedure and the eventual ratification by the nation-states opting for different procedures is the sole option for legality. In this way, the legitimation of the EU Constitution is sanctioned by observing legality, while in the referendum on ratification it rests on popular sovereignty.

There are other arguments against holding a European-wide referendum. The first relates to the responsibility of political leaders. Is a referendum a weapon by which to hold political leaders accountable, or are leaders capable of proceeding with a policy which is beneficial to the common well-being without having to resort to a referendum? Might not the excuse of consulting the people be a way of avoiding responsibility as far as the government is concerned? What if in this referendum the participation is so low that it cannot be representative of the people's will? And what impact on the future European integration will an all-European referendum have if the majority of EU citizens vote against the creation of the Convention on the Future of Europe? Of course, a Eurosceptic radical democrat would say that the EU will remain where it was before the Convention with the unwritten constitution that it already has, but the important thing is that it is what the people want. However, it is not possible to go back, or at least going back after a negative popular vote would have a devastating effect on the EU's future. An enlarged EU having 25 and later more Member States would be extremely difficult to manage even with an enhanced institutional framework initially designed for regional cooperation between six states.

Here, then, is where the phenomenon of the legitimacy of governance transforms itself into the non-legitimacy of governance. Does democracy then mean a preference for a legitimacy crisis which certainly cannot be eliminated once and for all by means of a referendum when compared to a crisis in EU governance which will certainly follow the defeat of the Constitutional Treaty in an all-European referendum?

Beyond beating around the bush concerning the technicalities of referendum devices and the legitimacy wording, a return to the logistics of holding a referen-

---

[105] B. Berg, 'Transnational Referendums Plans (20 September 2002) available at: <http://www.euobserver.com>.

[106] See Weiler, loc. cit. n. 86, at pp. 6-7.

dum in the context of the national constitutional arrangements will provide an insight which is hostile to the European-wide referendum.

From a comparative perspective the constitutions of the Member States are of three kinds depending on the provisions for holding a constitutional referendum. Some of them do not envisage holding a nationwide referendum at all. Others, like Germany, consider an amendment to their constitution as making it possible to hold a referendum. Still others, exemplified by the Irish and Austrian constitutions, contain provisions which create an obligation to hold a nationwide referendum on ratification. There is also a third group where the holding of a nationwide referendum on constitutional ratification is an option, but the choice to make use of this possibility instead of parliamentary ratification lies in the hands of the national political elite.[107]

The middle ground compromise has been to hold simultaneous referendums in the EU Member States according to their national constitutional arrangements.[108] This method, however, does not provide the stimulus for EU polity and 'demos' and will be merely mechanical support for the Constitutional Treaty from the European 'demoi' – each one acting within the national context and in different constitutional houses. Simultaneous national referendums might have boosted national loyalty as far as the feeling of European belonging is concerned. What is even more important is what the national setting will bring to the different mirroring process which might even distort or at least make less comparable the preferences of the citizens of the EU Member States.

The great advantage of a European-wide referendum is that a Constitutional Treaty defeat in one or even in 5 of the 25 Members is not an overall Constitutional Treaty defeat and it might still survive even with the majority support of 20 Member States so as to be considered in the European Council.

Under Article 48 TEU, any amendments to existing treaties require the unanimity of all the Member States. The adoption of the Constitutional Treaty requires the existing treaties to be substantially amended with each Member State having a veto on the adoption of the Constitutional Treaty.

The Constitutional Treaty recognises this in Declaration No. 30 annexed to the Final Act (Declaration on the ratification of the Treaty establishing a Constitution for Europe) providing that if, after two years, any Member State has not ratified the Constitutional Treaty, the Constitution will be returned to the European Council – where again, each Member State has a veto. So a Member State which chooses not to ratify the Constitutional Treaty will be in a very strong position to negotiate a new 'associate membership', which might provide for a free trade area or other options which seem to be the opposite of the enhanced coop-

---

[107] According to the latest data, 9 Member States have decided to hold a referendum, Malta has ruled out the possibility of a referendum and the other 15 Member States are still undecided (2004).

[108] 'MEPs Call for Synchronization of Referenda Timetable' (2 September 2004) available at: <http://www.euobserver.com>.

eration in the Constitutional Treaty. Other possible scenarios might include inter-governmental renegotiation in the European Council or the community option of redrafting the Constitutional Treaty by means of a new convention.

Considering the direct ratification method, some other referendum implications should not be ignored. The number of referendums on EU accession and the ratification of EU treaty amendments since 1972 and until the last EU enlargement in 2004 is 40. It is worth noting that of the last ten countries that acceded to the EU only Cyprus decided, for well-known specific reasons, not to hold a referendum. Almost all were decisive referendums with a 'yes' or 'no' voting option for the nationals taking part, with most of them being sovereignty referendums facilitating the transfer of external sovereignty.[109]

Are the nation-state experiences and particularly the constitutionalism of the 1990s relevant to the ratification of the Constitutional Treaty by means of national referendums? Can the constitutional experiences of emerging democracies be regarded as a laboratory for referendum implications to be used at the EU level? What lessons can be drawn from the experiences of the new democracies? Can referendums be regarded as a *panacea* for legitimation?

Besides the well-known abuse of direct democracy leading to a plebiscite effect which has had a long tradition in France, referendums have sometimes served as an antipode of deliberative democracy, circumventing the parliament in order to reinforce authoritarianism and legitimate totalitarian regimes.[110] Referendums were also used as a means of avoiding responsibility by political leaders or to resolve deadlocks in governance or to submit unpopular issues to be decided by a popular vote. In some cases the majority decisions in a referendum have led to infringing minority rights.

Over exaggeration and excitement concerning the democratic virtues of direct governance has often been based on the underestimation of their role in the decision-making process. With a consultative referendum the citizens can come up with proposals, but their vote has no mandatory effect when the decision is taken by parliaments or presidents. In binding referendums although the peoples' vote cannot be appealed against or changed, the citizens' vote has only a 'yes' or 'no' alternative on an issue that might have already been pre-decided by the formulation of the question submitted by the representative assembly.

---

[109] Between 1791 and 1999 over 1,090 referendums were held worldwide and in Switzerland from 1866 to 1993 414 forms of direct democracy have been used. Nearly 40% of all referendums were on constitutional issues. Sovereignty referendums have been of six kinds – affirming nation-states' independence, settling border disputes, determining the status of territories, facilitating the transfer of sovereignty, deciding on the secession or cession of territories and the incorporation of territories. In Europe 33 out of 88 sovereignty referendums were on the transfer of sovereignty. See G. Sussman, 'When the Demos shapes the Polis – The Use of Referendums in settling Sovereignty Issues', available at: <http://www.iandrinstitute.org/Studies.htm>.

[110] In his time C. Schmitt has forcefully shown how misleading the traditional argument is on the benefits of direct democracy by emphasizing the negative impact of plebiscite legitimacy on the legality of parliamentary statutes in the German Weimar Constitution. See C. Schmitt, 'Legality and Legitimacy' (Durham, Duke University Press 2004) pp. 59-66.

All of the post-totalitarian constitutions provide for different forms of direct democracy channelling public opinion and citizen involvement in governmental decision-making.

National and local referendums have been provided in most of the constitutions as a form of recourse to the public will, an expression of popular sovereignty, and which is considered as the ultimate legitimate source of authority. Some of the constitutions contain other direct democracy forms like popular initiative, a constitutional or confirmatory referendum, which in Poland has been shaped along the lines of the ratification referendum in Italy.[111]

Constitutions provide content limitations as regards the legislation's subject matter and they subject financial matters, budgetary and taxation issues to a referendum.[112] These issues might lead to complicated consequences and should be decided on the basis of an agreement resulting from a robust parliamentary debate considering different opinions, including safeguarding minority interests and freedoms.

Constitutional courts have been charged with maintaining constitutional supremacy as the ultimate legal expression of legitimacy, reached by fundamental consensus, and protecting it from any encroachment by the institutions and direct democracy as well. Subjecting issues to be decided by a referendum to a constitutional review has been another precaution against undermining legality and legitimacy by direct democracy.[113] Radical democratic arguments stemming from popular sovereignty, from the thesis that the people are the best guardians of their rights, cannot overrule the need to protect constitutional legality and legitimacy. The conclusion that a constitutional review trumps legality over legitimacy is certainly incorrect. When the Constitutional court acts to preserve legality, this is the best safeguard for legitimacy in the democratic systems. Along these lines, a constitutional review of the issues submitted to referendums should be viewed as a check on institutions sometimes using referendums to avoid deadlocks in politics, to escape responsibility or to acquire more power.

---

[111] A ratificatory referendum is a brand of the classical, but outdated, institution of the popular veto. Referendums can be initiated by Parliaments, by Presidents or by the voters when they meet the requirement of having collected a certain number of signatures. In the 1997 Constitution of Poland (Art. 125) the Parliament is to submit an issue to a national referendum by absolute majority decision, the President with the consent of the absolute majority in the Senate. The result of the Referendum is binding if at least half of the voters have taken part. The Supreme court has been charged with determining the validity if the referendum concerns certain specified issues.

[112] The longest list is to be found in the 1998 Albanian Constitution and includes issues related to territorial integrity, the limitation of fundamental rights and freedoms, budgetary issues, taxes, financial obligations of the state, the declaration and abrogation of a state of emergency, the declaration of war and peace, as well as amnesty (Art. 141).

[113] For specific forms of constitutional review of the issues submitted to referendums in Hungary, Lithuania, Poland, Russia, Slovakia and Western Europe see 'Constitutional Justice and Democracy by Referendum' (Strasbourg, Council of Europe Publishing, Science and Technique of Democracy No. 14 (1998)).

Under the limited, responsible constitutional government, constituted powers are circumscribed to the constitutional limitations set by the constituent power, as the ultimate expression of popular sovereignty. Hence, the intervention of the constitutional courts in order to preserve legality is an effective safeguard for the hierarchy and compatibility of two forms of legitimacy emanating from constituent and constituted powers. A legitimate decision reached through direct democracy has to be according to the will of the people as expressed in constitutional legitimacy and legality and not an ineffective instrument for resolving deadlocks between the institutions and political elites.[114]

5.      CONCLUDING REMARKS OR ADVICE ON SEALING THE WINE IN A
        BOTTLE THAT MIGHT NOT BE USED

This overview of EU legitimacy issues should not cast any doubt that the EU as a union of constitutional democracies in Europe would itself become a constitutional democracy with the adoption of the Constitutional Treaty.

However, there might be no doubt that a difficult ratification path lies ahead for the Constitutional Treaty. A failure to ratify by even one Member State will throw new controversies on the pile of unsolved problems. Will this be due to the fact that legitimacy crisis issues were not handled on time or will it be due to the issue of legitimacy obsession? Only the future can tell us.

Here I would like to share some ideas that would have made the ratification process easier on the one hand, and more open and deliberative on the other, thereby increasing the Constitutional Treaty's overall legitimation effect on the EU.

It seems that constructing the highway for a vanguard of Member States driving towards integration at great speed was not the only option compared to driving safely along a common road at a more moderate speed. Certainly, the enhanced cooperation in the Constitutional Treaty is a good thing, although to be sustainable, it requires a higher level of legitimacy than ordinary cooperation. It might have been better if the founding fathers of the Convention for the Future of Europe would have foreseen another level which is different from regular integration and being an antipode to the enhanced cooperation which I will call a slow dance. Supplementing the regular and enhanced cooperation with an integration which reflects the pre-Constitutional Treaty state of integration would have opened the possibility for some Member States to ratify. Having designed an integration along the lines of the three-gear model, the Convention might have increased the possibility of ratifying the Constitutional Treaty with some Member States willing to preserve the first-gear cooperation instead of opting not to ratify.

---

[114] See H. Brady and C. Kaplan, 'Eastern Europe and Former Soviet Union', in D. Butler and A. Ranney, eds., *Referendums around the World* (Washington, The AEI Press 1994) pp. 174-215, at p. 210.

In the context of modern democratic constitution-drafting and legitimacy-building the Constitutional Treaty's ratification process should be perceived not as a formal legal requirement for completing the treaty amendment procedure alone, but should be considered in terms of a constitutional discourse securing deliberative democracy.

Has the already decided ratification procedure facilitated the Constitutional Treaty's enactment and legitimation impact? Does it provide the necessary flexibility and conditions for constitutional discourse?

At first glance, opting for binding referendums has been the most democratic ratification method proposed in the Convention and this has been decided in nearly half of the Member States at present. In fact, most of the current ratification procedures instead of elevating citizens and national parliaments to a position of participants in the constitutional discourse during the ratification process, treat the ratification as a 'take it or leave it' deal where with the participation of the people or parliaments' political elites would like to avoid taking responsibility for decisions.

Another option which increases the possibility of ratification might have been the simultaneous use of a consultative referendum where citizens might propose amendments to the Constitutional Treaty supplemented with ratification by the national parliaments combining an affirmative ratification vote with the proposal for amendments to the Constitutional Treaty to be considered at the European Council.

A three-stage constitutional discourse would have been a better solution during the ratification process. Consultative referendums would have been instrumental for citizens to make different propositions and not to provide a 'yes' or 'no' decision, which should then be deliberated in the national parliament and taken into account when deciding whether or not to ratify the Constitutional Treaty. The third stage, which would take the national constitutional discussions on the Constitutional Treaty to the supranational intergovernmental level, would have been an option for the national parliaments to ratify the Constitutional Treaty with some reservations and to propose amendments to be discussed in the European Council. Being aware that one of the most often taught lessons in history has been that no one learns from the experiences of others, it might be of no help to reiterate that this was the key to the ratification of the US 1787 Federal Constitution where support in most of the states was based on certain proposals leading to the adoption of the Bill of Rights. But what is much more important is not learning lessons from the historical experiences of others, but providing a ratification process taking into account the citizens' legitimate opinion, arriving at a decision after deliberating the issues in the national parliaments which instead of a 'yes' or 'no' alternative would have the option to ratify by making proposals to improve the Constitutional Treaty. In this way the ratification process would benefit from being an inclusive constitutional discourse engaging the participation of most of the constitutional actors – the citizens, parliaments and governments.

However, what use is there in making proposals concerning decisions which have already been taken? No use at all in the case of a happy ending for ratification, which I would gladly prefer. And unfortunately a great deal of use if the failure to ratify the Constitutional Treaty will lead to new decisions on building support for the EU written constitution.

# DISCOURSE, AUTHORITY AND THE MAKING OF THE EU CONSTITUTION

**Siniša Rodin**[*]

## 1. INTRODUCTION

As it stands Article 1 of the Nice Treaty, the Treaty '(...) marks a new stage in the process of creating an ever closer union among the peoples of Europe, in which decisions are taken as openly as possible and as closely as possible to the citizen.'[1] Joseph Weiler has added a grain of salt to this visionary comittment when he observed that 'no matter how close the Union, it is to remain a union among distinct peoples, distinct political identities, distinct political communities.'[2] Indeed, like in any non-unitary structure based on pluralism, those who interpret the law are by necessity confronted with disagreement about competing definitions of basic constitutional concepts, such as the good, the equal or the just.[3] The peoples and polities of Europe, being different from each other, contribute to the building of the common meaning of the European Law, the legal order, and ultimately the EU Constitution. Their individual understandings are

---

[*] Professor of Law, Department of European Public Law, University of Zagreb, Faculty of Law.

[1] One of the early versions of the Draft Treaty establishing a Constitution for Europe specified in the Preamble: 'The peoples of Europe, in creating an ever closer union among them, are resolved to share a peaceful future based on common values.' Provisional consolidated version of the draft Treaty establishing a Constitution for Europe (Brussels, 25 June 2004) (OR. fr) CIG 86/04. The final version was changed and reads:

'Convinced that, thus 'United in diversity', Europe offers them the best chance of pursuing, with due regard for the rights of each individual and in awareness of their responsibilities towards future generations and the Earth, the great venture which makes it a special area of human hope.' *OJ* (2004) C310/1.

[2] J.H.H. Weiler, 'Federalism and Constitutionalism: Europe's Sonderweg' (Jean Monnet Working Paper No. 10/00 (2000)) also in K. Nicolaïdis and R. Howse, eds., *The Federal Vision: Legitimacy and Levels of Governance in the US and the EU* (Oxford, Oxford University Press 2001)

[3] This led Rosenfeld to propose that legal interpretation in pluralist societies is in crisis. M. Rosenfeld, 'Pragmatism, Pluralism and Legal Interpretation: Posner's and Rorty's Justice without Methaphysics meets Hate Speech', 18 *Cardozo Law Review* (1996) p. 97; see also G. Teubner, 'De Collisione Discursuum: Communicative Rationalities in Law, Morality and Politics', 17 *Cardozo Law Review* (1996) p. 901. Teubner draws attention to the '(...) fragmentation of universal rationality into a disturbing multiplicity of discourses.' (p. 901).

---

*D. Curtin, A.E. Kellermann and S. Blockmans, eds., The EU Constitution: The Best Way Forward?*
© 2005, T.M.C. Asser Instituut, The Hague.

communicated among qualified audiences across Europe and are attributed meaning. Law, including the EU Constitution, lives through interpretation – the assignment of meaning to black-letter words. To have a say means to have power.[4] Yet, the starting positions of actors from the old and new Member States of the EU contributing to the constitutional discourse are different in terms of legal and political culture – while one is of democratic pluralism, the other was dominated by past communist ideology.[5] The legitimacy of any democratic legal order requires a broad agreement that goes beyond mere compliance.[6] The same is true for the European order. Such an agreement has to be reached through assigning meaning to basic notions that define the political or legal culture, and it is built into the interaction between different actors.

I am starting from a realist position, claiming that reality is constructed and construed socially, through interaction, and that the social construction of reality depends on the intensity of the power that is delivered to the debate by each respective participant. It seems to me that in a Europe of 25 or more states, the fundamental semantic building blocks of the EU Constitution will necessarily continue to reflect the positions which have been crystalized so far by traditional actors, but will not necessarily be identical to those positions. Namely, the discoursive and procedural nature of European constitutionalism by necessity allows elements of political and legal heritage that still persist in the legal and political culture of the new Member States to contribute to the definition of the EU Constitution.[7]

In this article I will first give some thought to the pluralist-realist[8] stance in an attempt to explain how political and/or legal reality depend on a qualified agreement between discourse participants.[9] I will further proceed by highlighting some fundamental differences in understanding constitutionalism and the law in the former communist countries as opposed to the long established liberal democratic Member States. These differences, I will claim, have their origin in the different development and social function of authority and discourse in communist and liberal democratic states. Finally, I will argue that the unity of and loyalty to

---

[4] P. Kirchof, 'Das Sagen-haben bedeutet Macht haben', in H.-P. Mansel, et al., eds., *Recht wirkt durch Sprache, Festschrift für Erik Jayme*, Band 2 (Munich, Sellier European Law Publishers 2004) p. 1167.

[5] Sometimes there is little agreement on both libertarian and egalitarian ideas even among the old Member States which is demonstrated by their widely diverging social policies and agendas.

[6] J. Habermas, 'On Law and Disagreement. Some Comments on 'Interpretative Pluralism', 16 *Ratio Juris* 2 (June 2003) p. 187. Habermas speaks about the legitimacy of a democratic order. I am of the opinion that the same holds true from a legal point of view.

[7] It is popular to say that the Moon revolves around the Earth. However, the fact is that both, the Moon and the Earth, revolve around a common centre of gravity.

[8] Habermas, *supra* n. 6, at p. 189. Realism proposes that reality (truth) is socially construed under the influence of the most authorative actors.

[9] A qualified agreement is an agreement between the parties concerned to agree on a certain interpretation of social factors.

the European constitutional framework, in the European Union of 25 or more Member States, can only be secured by a discursive construction of the meaning of constitutional choices, principles and rules.

## 2.     DEMOCRATIC PLURALIST LEGAL CULTURE

Legal pluralism is understood as one of the underlying concepts of post-modern legal scholarship. According to the pluralist proposition, no one can claim privileged access to the truth of constitutional or legislative matters within the institutional framework of democracy. This understanding breaks with the traditional Kelsenian understanding of a legal system as a hierarchy of legal rules, and introduces a '(...) conception of different legal spaces superposed, interpenetrated and mixed in our minds (...)'.[10] In methodological terms, legal pluralism marks a departure from understanding a legal order exclusively as an objective reality, and proposes a subjective approach according to which the law amounts to an outcome of 'cognitive fermentation' that takes place at individual level and influences law-making through discourse. As far as the legal order defines individual action, it is individual action which, by communication, defines the legal order.[11] In such circumstances the meaning of law depends not on an ultimate and undisputed authority, for example, 'the command of the sovereign', as proposed by John Austin,[12] but on the outcome of the discursive process, an outcome which is itself subject to permanent reinterpretation.

Realism, on the other hand, proposes that reality (truth) exists outside and beyond individual convictions and understandings and is socially construed under the influence of the most authoritative actors. Accordingly, reality depends on the discursive inputs of participants having different social 'weight'. Confronted with reality, individual interest is best served by adjusting action to predictions of what the law actually is.[13]

Briefly stated, the pluralist-realist position assumes that:

–   law is defined not by its black letter but by its meaning;

–   the definition of what the law is (the meaning of law) is a function involving the interaction of multiple actors;

---

[10] B. de Sousa Santos, 'Law: A Map of Misreading. Toward a Postmodern Conception of Law', 14 *Journal of Law and Society* (1987) pp. 279 and 293.

[11] As Teubner put it, 'Legal pluralism is then defined no longer as a set of conflicting social norms in a given social field, but as a multiplicity of diverse communicative processes that observe social action under the binary code of legal/illegal.' G. Teubner, 'The Two Faces of Janus: Rethinking Legal Pluralism', 13 *Cardozo Law Review* (1992) pp. 1443, 1451.

[12] J. Austin, *The Province of Jurisprudence determined*, 1st edn. (Cambridge, 1832).

[13] According to Holmes, law is '(...) prediction of incidence of public force through the instrumentality of the courts (...)'. O. Wendell Holmes, 'The Path of the Law', 110 *Harvard Law Review* (1997) p. 991.

- the discoursive definition of law results in the 'politicization' of the law by bringing regulatory purposes and policies into the legal analysis;

- participants in the discourse have different strengths and faculties to contribute to the definition of law;

- once defined, law is subject to permanent reinterpretation through legal and social discourse.

European constitutionalism has been growing out of rational discourse which, as suggested by Alexy, assumes that conditions of communication prevent the irrational termination of argumentation, secure freedom of choice concerning topics, equal conditions for participants, and exclude coertion.[14] In circumstances of such rational discourse a broad and qualified consensus between discourse participants is attained, from time to time, as to the meaning of legal rules, principles or legal concepts. Due to a general agreement about their meaning, such rules, principles or concepts become difficult to redefine and thus become constitutionalized landmarks of a given legal system. Such landmarks are sometimes enacted by *pouvoir constituant*, sometimes they are merely internalized by discourse participants, and sometimes both.[15] So the Draft Constitutional Treaty[16] has been developed from a complex web of extended communication in which definitions were made and agreed to. Finally, those definitions were solemnized in the final act of signing and expected ratification by all Member States.

Examples of the described constitutional developmens are many, and we can simply mention constitutional principles of direct effect and the supremacy of Community law, principles of the four freedoms, fundamental rights, etc. The development of gender equality law in the European Union provides a good example of pluralist-realist assumptions at work.

The original text of Article 119 of the Treaty establishing European Economic Community laid down an obligation for each Member State to ensure that the principle of equal pay for male and female workers for equal work is applied. This simple provision developed into an area of law covering a wide range of

---

[14] R. Alexy, *A Theory of Legal Argumentation*, transl. by R. Adler and N. MacCormick (Oxford, Clarendon Press 1989). As Habermas encapsulated:

'In rational discourse, we assume that conditions of communication obtain that (1) prevent a rationally unmotivated termination of argumentation, (2) secure both freedom in choice of topics and inclusion of the best information and reasons through universal and equal access to, as well as equal and symetrical participation in, argumentation, and (3) exclude every kind of correcion – whether originating outside the process of reaching understanding or within it (...)'.

See J. Habermas, *Between Facts and Norms: Contributions to a Discourse Theory of Law and Democracy* (Cambridge, Polity Press 1996) at p. 230.

[15] As Rosenfeld has put it, '(...) so long as the consensus holds, there may be no awareness of prevailing philosophical inconsistancies and no need to fill existing theoretical gaps.' Rosenfeld, *supra* n. 3, at p. 108.

[16] Draft Treaty establishing a Constitution for Europe, Provisional consolidated version (Brussels, 25 June 2004) (OR. fr) CIG 86/04.

individual rights, policies and social choices pursued by the Community and its Member States. As was stated by the ECJ in the *Defrenne II* case,

> '(...) it is impossible not to recognize that the complete implementation of the aim pursued by article 119, by means of the elimination of all discrimination, direct or indirect, between men and women workers, not only as regards individual undertakings but also entire branches of industry and even of the economic system as a whole, may in certain cases involve the elaboration of criteria whose implementation necessitates the taking of appropriate measures at community and national level.'[17]

By making the equal pay provision part of Community social policy, the ECJ legitimized a wide range of actors to participate in the law-making process. Furthermore, attempts to affect the development of law by test cases contributed to the development of the concept of 'equal pay'. When the Equal Treatment Directive was passed in 1976,[18] it became clear that the meaning of equality reaches far beyond the concept of equal pay and embraces the principle of equal opportunities for men and women. The principle was subsequently constitutionalized by the Maastricht Treaty and further developed by the ECJ, notably in the landmark cases of *Kalanke*[19] and *Marschall*.[20] Both cases came to the ECJ as requests for preliminary rulings from the German courts which were in active dialogue both with national legislatures (the parliaments of the respective *Länder*) and the ECJ. The meaning of the equal opportunities concept[21] that emerged from the discourse was a result of dialogue between national legislative authorities, national courts, the ECJ, the law-making institutions of the EU, notably the Parliament and the Council, and last but not least, individuals and NGOs. Each of them participated within their respective position of authority, contributing different political and legal angles. The mentioned dialogue brought into play a number of other concepts, some of which were broad, such as gender mainstreaming, empowerment, positive action, while others were technical, such as 'the saving clause'. Each concept enriched the discourse and streamlined the meaning of the equal opportunities principle. Finally, these concepts stabilized in time and gained widespread recognition. Their constitutional significance is entrenched in the *expectations* of individuals that authority created in pluralist discourse will be enforced.

---

[17] ECJ, judgment of 8 April 1976, Case C-43/75, *Gabrielle Defrenne* v. *Société anonyme belge de navigation aérienne Sabena* [1976] *ECR* 455.

[18] Council Directive 76/207/EEC of 9 February 1976 on the implementation of the principle of equal treatment for men and women as regards access to employment, vocational training and promotion, and working conditions (*OJ* (1976) L 39/40-42).

[19] ECJ, judgment of 17 October 1995, Case C-450/93, *Eckhard Kalanke* v. *Freie Hansestadt Bremen* [1995] *ECR* I-3051.

[20] ECJ, judgment of 11 November 1997, Case C-409/95, *Hellmut Marschall* v. *Land Nordrhein-Westfalen* [1997] *ECR* I-6363.

[21] That women who have equal qualifications to men may be given priority in employment but not automatically and mechanically, but subject to a 'saving clause'.

To emphasize once again, the *authority* of constitutional principles, such as the one relating to gender equality in the EU, was created through and owes its legitimacy to a qualified *discourse*[22] in which the participation of widely legitimized actors was ensured.[23] Finally, *language* is created as a methodological tool that facilitates the discourse and expresses our human self[24] in the relevant field. Such authority created in discourse, and for the purposes of this paper we can call it *discoursive authority,* rests on expectations that the enforcement of the underlying qualified agreement will be based on values and oriented towards ends that are universally acceptable,[25] without having to waste time on resolving conflicts between formalistic, scientific or logical artifice.


3.      AUTHORITARIAN LEGAL CULTURE

While the above-mentioned pluralist-realist assumptions are very well established in Europe's West, and are even described as banal on the other side of Atlantic,[26] they have little practical, theoretical or cultural underpinning in postcommunist Europe. Political realities that defined fundamental concepts such as constitutionalism, the rule of law, equality or fundamental rights, created an entirely different language in which the meaning of rules was being determined by the authority of naked power in the absence of rational discourse as understood by Alexy. Instead of rational discourse that shaped the legal and institutional landscape of Europe's West, the discourse that was dominant in Central and East Europe was authoritarian.[27] The main characteristic of such *authoritarian dis-*

---

[22] It is easy to agree with Habermas that sound procedures guarantee:
'… the certainty of law at a different level. Procedural rights guarantee each legal person the claim to a fair procedure that in turn guarantees not certainty of outcome but a discursive clarification of the pertinant facts and legal questions.' See Habermas, *supra* n. 14 at p. 220.
See also, H. Baxter, 'Habermas' Discourse Theory of Law and Democracy', 50 *Buffalo Law Review* (2002) pp. 205, 302.
[23] While institutional discourse means primarily a discourse between institutions, separate discourses are taking place within each of them. In that sense, national judges, parties to the proceedings, and Advocates General, participate in intra-institutional discourse.
[24] R. Rorty, 'Consequences of Pragmatism', at xxxvii, quoted from Rosenfeld, *supra* n. 3, at p. 126.
[25] For Habermas values are teleological and reflect intersubjectively shared preferences. Habermas, *supra* n. 14 at p. 255.
[26] See R. Rorty, 'The Banality of Pragmatism and the Poetry of Justice', 63 *Southern California Law Review* (1990) p. 1811, at p. 1812: 'Even under this broader definition of formalism, however, it is not so easy to find a good example of a formalist among legal theorists'; and T. Grey, 'Holmes and Legal Pragmatism', 41 *Stanford Law Review* (1989) pp. 787, 814.
[27] The phenomenon of authoritarian discourse results partly from communist ideology and partly from decades-long exclusion from mainstream legal discourse. Nevertheless, due to its deductive nature it has managed to persist, at least for a limited time in an ideology-free environment. Paradoxically, the unconditional acceptance of the *acquis communautaire* as a 'take it or leave it' deal in membership negotiations by definition excludes discourse. See, e.g., W. Sadurski,

*course* is the proclamation and imposition of one truth as universal and final. Such discourse was authoritarian since it purported to have a social monopoly in determining the meaning of legal and political language at the political top and of communicating it downwards. It was, nevertheless, a discourse, since the communication of meaning defined in an authoritarian way was indespensible to support the claim of universal acceptance, the maintenance of which is a condition for the integrity of the system. Certainly, while authority generated in rational discourse is necessarily inductive and inclusive, making the creation of new categories possible, the model of authoritarian discourse is deductive, based on definitions that may or may not correspond to reality, and it transmits them to the lower levels of thesocial or professional hierarchy.

In the post-communist countries of Eastern Europe the deductive transmission of the prescribed meaning was, and to a large degree still is, present in all spheres of life: legislation, adjudication, legal scholarship, education. The government is understood as the mere transmitter of parliamentary will,[28] the function of adjudication is understood as 'applying the law' and not as solving disputes between parties.[29] Legal scholarship was not expected to be critical but descriptive and appologetic, while the function of education was understood as the transmission of uncontested ultimate truth from teachers to disciples: *magister dixit, discipulus scripsit*.

The language of law and legal concepts as developed under conditions of authoritarian discourse did not miraculously disappear with the fall of the Berlin wall. They outlasted communist ideology in corroboration of what Max Planck wrote in his Scientific Autobiography: that new scientific truth does not triumph by convincing its opponents and making them see the light, but rather because its opponents eventually die, and a new generation grows up that is familiar with it. Indeed, old language and concepts created significant problems when confronted with the need to integrate and apply legal rules developed within a system that is defined by rational discourse, such as that of the European Union.

As far as the harmonization of law is concerned, even in cases of the literal transcription of legal rules of Community law, they are attributed different meaning and are applied by the courts in different ways. In other words, since knowledge (knowledge of the law included) is context sensitive, legal rules necessarily have different meaning in different contexts with regard to knowledge stan-

---

'Accession's Democracy Dividend: The Impact of the EU Enlargement upon Democracy in New Member States of Central and Eastern Europe', 10 *European Law Journal* (2004) pp. 371 and 382. In other words, the meaning of legal rules that has been developed gradually and over the years in the EU, is being served to candidate countries on a silver plate of authority. Ćapeta holds that legal formalism will actually help judges in new and prospective Member States to apply Community Law. See T. Ćapeta, *Preparing New European Judges: The Case of Croatia,* forthcoming in 1 *Croatian Yearbook of European Law and Policy* (2005).

[28] In the former Yugoslavia the government was officially called the 'Federal Executive Council'.

[29] In fact, it was taken as ideologically given that socialist society knows no disputes which exist only between social classes in bourgeois societies.

dards.[30] This means that elements of normative language are not to be expected to have a standard meaning in every Member State. More importantly, where applied, the model of authoritarian discourse, being inherently deductive, does not consider new knowledge ascriptions to be legitimate, and treats them as exceptions, and does not permit normative language to have any other meaning than the standard meaning, which is, to reiterate, determined at the top. Needles to say, the meaning of funamental legal concepts in Europe's East and West differed dramatically. The more fundamenal the legal concept – the greater the semantic dissonance.

Examples of semantic dissonance are sometimes striking. For instance, the rule of law, or the *Rechtstaat* principle, is understood not as government limited by law, but as naked state power to enforce laws, even in the face of fundamental rights violations.[31] Furthermore, the EU Constitution is generally not understood as a legal instrument but as a political declaration. The criticism of such an understanding is emerging only slowly,[32] primarily among legal scholars and rarely among practitioners. Nevertheless, the denial of the legal nature of the EU Constitution can still be found in legal textbooks.[33] The non-application of the EU Constitution by the courts and the public administration can not be explained by the self-referential nature of statutes,[34] but by the dominance of the regulatory state relying on subregulation which is often arbitrary.[35] Even the concept of individual public rights (*subjektive öffentliche Rechte*) as a defence against the state is not conceptualized. The Constitutional Court protects individual rights in constitutional complaint procedures, but the ordinary courts rarely do so, if at all.[36]

---

[30] T. Hofweber, 'Contextualism and the Meaning-Intention Problem', in K. Korta, et al., eds., *Cognition, Agency and Rationality* (Dordrecht, Kluwer Law Publishers 1999).

[31] One of the drastic examples of such an understanding is the often repeated statement by Slobodan Miloašević from the 1980s that the public protests of the Albanian population must be crushed by means of the *Rechtstaat* (*sredstvima pravne države*), meaning by naked police force.

[32] T. Ćapeta, *Preparing New European Judges: The Case of Croatia*, see *supra* n. 27. Similar arguments were presented by Branko Smerdel at the annual conference of the Croatian Judges Association (Zagreb, July 2004).

[33] E.g., I. Borković, *Upravno pravo*, 8th edn. (Zagreb, Informator 1997) at pp. 59, 90 and 91. Borković maintains in eight editions of his standard textbook on administrative law that the Constitution provides for a set of abstract principles that have to be concretized by administrative law.

[34] D. Caruso, 'The Missing View of the Cathedral: The Private Law Paradigm of European Legal Integration', 3 *European Law Journal* (1997) p. 3, quoted from M. W. Hesselink, *The New European Legal Culture* (Deventer, Kluwer 2001) fn. 10 at p. 11.

[35] The situation seems to be similar in Romania. As G. Andreescu has emphasised, Romanian judges reluctantly apply the Constitution.

'(…) in the absence of an express article allowing the rights provided for by the Constitution to be directly enforced, the Romanian courts are extremely reluctant to consider them as such and have always asked for ordinary laws to include and develop such provisions with procedural terms.' G. Andreescu, *Right-Wing Extremism in Romania* (Cluj, Napoca, Fundatia CRDE 2003) at p. 56.

[36] Ordinary courts have power to stay proceedings and to institute a constitutional review of

As far as the *separation of powers* is concerned, past communist concepts are still alive in the law and legal culture. Suffice it to mention just a few examples.

The dominant dogma of the socialist era was that parliament is an instrument of the 'dictatorship of the working class' and that the communist party, as the avant-garde of the working class has a monopoly of power and the last say in determining policy. Two sets of consequences flow from this legal heritage. First, the communist party controls the legislative process and other agencies of the unitary system of power and, second, the courts are subservient to parliament and have very little judicial discretion, if at all. The law has to be applied as written. Possible lacunae are not to be filled by methods of statutory construction, but by recourse to so-called authentic interpretation that can be obtained either from parliament, or sometimes, from the government. Elements of this understanding, now void of communist ideology, still persist today, e.g., in the parliamentary rules of procedure that provide for a so-called 'authentic interpretation' of laws[37] which clearly amounts to retroactive legislation and is prohibited by the Constitution.

The participation of the courts in the legal discourse is hampered by a well established regulatory practice of the Supreme Court within the framework of a general meeting between the judicial departments (civil and criminal). At such meetings the judges of the Supreme Court take positions on controversial issues of law and such positions carry significant weight and are followed in practice.[38] While it is sometimes objected that this amounts to the impermissible involvement of judges in law-making and violates the Constitutional separation of powers, the real problem concerning such a practice is that legal positions are not being developed through the process of solving actual controversies, but through abstract law-making which is detached from practical experience.

Furthermore, as a result of the post-communist inertia that perpetuates the concept of unity of power, the Parliament purports to strongly control not only the judicial but also the executive branch. Attempts to limit the self-executing

---

legislation if they have to apply constitutionally suspect legislation. However, since the Constitutional Act on the Constitutional Court was adopted in 1991, there are no instances of such a review. A recent example of the ignorance of the ordinary courts relates to the amendment of rules concerning family violence. Due to the restructuring of legislation, family violence is no longer criminalised by Article 362 of the Family Act (*Narodne novine* [Official Gazette] No. 162/1998 as amended, *Narodne novine* [Official Gazette] No. 116/2003), but by the Protection against Family Violence Act (*Narodne novine* [Official Gazette] No. 116/2003). Due to a technical error, there was a one-week gap between the effective dates of the two acts, creating a period during which family violence was not criminalised at all. This resulted in a massive dismissal of cases (more than 2,000 cases), rationalized by the principle of *nullum crimen sine lege*. Not a single court has ever instituted the constitutional review procedure in order to challenge this obvious error on constitutional grounds.

[37] Arts. 176-178 of the Rules of Procedure of the Croatian Parliament, *Narodne novine* [Official Gazette] No. 9/2001 of 2 February 2001.

[38] For example, the Supreme Court adopts 'framework criteria' for the compensation of damages.

character of the Stabilization and Association Agreement[39] by enacting implementing legislation seeking Parliamentary ratification for the effectiveness of
secondary Association Law[40] and a subsequent interpellation addressed to the
Government seeking a Parliamentary mandate for the negotiation of additional
protocols to the Agreement are good examples of the understanding that, arguably quite opposite to the Constitutional intention, the Government does not have
independent constitutional authority to act in European affairs, but has to execute
the will of the legislature – once the Socialist Assembly, today the Parliament.[41]

Needles to say, the described understanding of the separation of powers differs significantly from the meaning that is ascribed to this concept in Europe's
West. However, even more importantly, it is a headwind to the emerging self-
awareness of the judicial branch, it suppresses discourse, delegitimizes both
judges and litigants as discourse participants and locks the judiciary into the
*bouche de la lois* role now abandoned even by French scholarship,[42] thereby
sending a clear signal that the courts remain instrumental and have to restrict
their interpretative role.[43] Certainly, in such circumstances any dialogue between
institutions and the discursive creation of the meaning of legal rules is not possible.

The lack of rational discourse alao affects the process of adjudication. Not
surprisingly, it can be described as formalistic, immune to policy considerations,
characterized by circular reasoning and heavily dependant on subregulation. The
Constitution is rarely applied and even when it is, it seldom serves as a legal basis for the decision.[44]

---

[39] Stabilization and Association Agreement between the European Community and its Member States and the Republic of Croatia, *Narodne novine* [Official Gazette], Međunarodni ugovori,
No. 15/2001.

[40] Zakon o provedbi Sporazuma o stabilizaciji i pridruživanju, *Narodne novine*, Međunarodni
ugovori, No. 15/2001. [Law on Implementation of the Stabilization and Association Agreement,
*Official Gazette*, International Treaties No. 15/2001].

[41] A shift of powers from the legislative to the executive branch is a well known phenomenon both in Member States and Candidate Countries. See e.g., Sadurski, *supra* n. 27 at p. 382.
Arguably, in circumstances of permissive political consensus, negotiation on membership is primarily
an administrative task. Excessive control by the legislature over the executive can slow down the
negotiating process. However, in Croatia the problem is wider and refers to the entire understanding of the parliamentary system and the allocation of constitutional powers.

[42] See, e.g., the Opinion of AG Leger in Case C-224/01, *Gerhard Köbler* v. *Republik Österreich*:
'Thus the national judge is no longer necessarily, as Montesquieu was able to say in earlier times,
"the mouthpiece of the law,"' at pt. 59 of the Opinion.

[43] Compare O. Wendell Holmes, 'Theory of Legal Interpretation', 12 *Harvard Law Review*
(1898-1899) pp. 417, 420 at p. 42:

'In this country, at least, for constitutional reasons, if for no other, if the same legislature that
passed it should declare at a later date a statute to have a meaning which in the opinion of the
court the words did not bear, I suppose that the declaratory act would have no effect upon inter-
vening transactions unless in a place and case where retrospective legislation was allowed.'

[44] For example, in case no. II Kž-888/03-3 of 7 January 2004, the Supreme Court stressed
that the Croatian courts have an obligation to apply statutes, regardless of whether the concrete
legal basis for detention is harmonised with international treaties or the Constitution. The

## 3.1  Formalism

Not unlike the legal systems of some other post-communist states of Central and Eastern Europe, the Croatian legal system is a formalistic one, generally believed to be based on good traditions from the times of the Habsburg era, but which is, in fact, deeply rooted in socialist legal culture. The demise of the extreme formalism of the *Begriffsjurisprudenz* and the limited success of reconstruction by the *Freie Rechtschule* that took place in Europe in the late 19th century,[45] due to historic circumstances[46] never really occurred in Eastern Europe, and where it did, it came as a result of reception instead of genuine development.[47] It is worth mentioning that, as a rule, the reception of law was limited to the reception of codes, and only rarely included judicial practice that has been developed. Also, during fifty years of socialist rule, the original formalist assumptions, such as objectivity, coherence and the systemic nature of the law eroded into a vulgar, textual formalism, sometimes extending beyond good taste.[48]

## 3.2  Policy Considerations

The idea that every piece of legislation rests on a certain underpinning policy probably originates from Rudolph von Jhering and is encapsulated in his famous maxim – *Keine Handlung ohne Zweck.*[49] Since the end of the 19th century this understanding has caught a much firmer hold on the American side of the Atlantic where it fuelled the rise of American legal realism. However, even in Europe it was gradually becoming clearer that a narrow and formalistic interpretation of the law was becoming increasingly useless when dealing with complex issues of law posed by the rising interventionist state of the 20th century. The linkage of legal problems with economic and social realities redefined the task of lawyers, particularly judges, during the 20th century. Legal logic became meaningless in the absence of policy considerations. As it was brilliantly put by John Dewey taking the example of the famous syllogism,[50] '(...) the issue is not whether Socrates was mortal, the point is whether this mortality would or should occur at a specified date and in a specified way.'[51]

---

Supreme Court did not even try to apply constitutional or international standards directly.

[45] See Hesselink, *supra* n. 34, at pp. 29-32.

[46] The First World War, the subsequent dictatorship of King Alexandar Karađorđević, the Nazi denial of the rule of law and Josip Broz Titos socialism.

[47] The impact of *Begriffsjurisprudenz* on judges and scholars in Russia and elsewhere in Eastern Europe is even described as enormous. See G. Ajani, 'By Chance and Prestige: Legal Transplants in Russia and Eastern Europe', 43 *The American Journal of Comparative Law* (1995) p. 93.

[48] For example, one attorney invoked the principle of *nullum crimen sine lege*, based on the fact that the name of the drug 'ecstasy' had been misspelled in the list of prohibited drugs. Attorney Borislav Kraljevski in Večernji List, 15 February 2004.

[49] R. von Jhering, *Der Zweck im Recht*, 4th edn. (Leipzig 1904).

[50] Socrates is a man, all men are mortal, thus Socrates is mortal.

[51] J. Dewey, 'Logical Method and Law', 10 *Cornell Law Quarterly* (1924) p. 17.

Policy arguments are used both by the political and judicial branch of government. Ronald Dworkin understood them as those that '(...) justify a political decision by showing that the decision advances or protects some collective goal of the community as a whole.'[52]

While the policy component of laws is slowly starting to emerge in Croatia, there is still a wide consensus that judges should base their decisions on a strict reading of legal texts and their *scientific* analysis. According to the prevailing position, all legal answers can be found by reference to legal rules and principles, and it is the task of the courts, typically the Supreme Court, to proclaim *urbi et orbi* what the law is. Commenting on non-final judicial decisions is a criminal offence[53] and the criminalisation thereof is supported by the legal profession.[54] Denying the existence, not to mention the justification, of judicial policy is deeply rooted in the legal culture of the East European legal profession. The refusal of judges to admit that their decisions have social consequences[55] and, at least incidentally, create policy, makes adjudication non-transparent, the prediction of outcomes difficult.[56] and this opens the door to undeclared policies pursued sporadically by the courts[57] or even individual judges.

---

[52] R. Dworkin, 'Hard Cases', 88 *Harvard Law Review* (1975) p. 1057, at p. 1059. The complete quote reads as follows:

'Arguments of policy justify a political decision by showing that the decision advances or protects some collective goal of the community as a whole. The argument in favor of a subsidy for aircraft manufacturers, that the subsidy will protect national defense, is an argument of policy. Arguments of principle justify a political decision by showing that the decision respects or secures some individual or group right. The argument in favor of anti-discrimination statutes, that a minority has a right to equal respect and concern, is an argument of principle.'

[53] As Ćapeta noted, there is no tradition of publishing judicial decisions in full and on a regular basis while commenting on judicial decisions that are not final is a criminal offence. Art. 309 of the Criminal Law (*Narodne novine* [Official Gazette] No. 110/1997) criminalises commenting on judicial decisions that are not final subject to a punishment of six months imprisonment. T. Ćapeta, *Preparing New European Judges: The Case of Croatia*, unpublished. See *supra* n. 27. This provision was amended in 2003, only to be more severely criminalised (*Narodne novine* [Official Gazette] No. 111/2003). Although there there are no officially reported cases, this crime has already become part of the public discourse. See, e.g., the statement by Vlado Madunić, president of the Municipal Court in Split, Slobodna Dalmacija, 3 January 2001; the statement by Aleksandra Kolarić, spokeswoman of the Croatian Government, Vjesnik 23 January 2001. The only case reported by the local press was decided by the Municipal Court in Daruvar. The Defendants, a representative of a local trade union and a journalist, were acquitted as they had commented a non-final judicial decision after the first instance court had delivered its decision.

[54] The Croatian Judges Association recently called on the State Attorney to institute proceedings against a journalist who had commented on a non-final decision of the Municipal Court in Senj. See Jutarnji list (14-15 August 2004).

[55] E.g., framework criteria for compensation of damages as adopted by the Croatian Supreme Court. While these criteria provide for guidelines for compensation concerning a wide range of damages, they do not refer to damages incurred in sexual harassment cases. However, this is not understood by judges to be a policy choice.

[56] Concerning the lack of transparency see Hesselink, *supra* n. 34, at p. 74.

[57] A good example of judge-made criminal policy can be found in criminal proceedings against

To put it succinctly, judicial decisions are rarely informed by policy and seek justification in the text, rather than in its meaning and legal logic. Such an attitude renders the application of policy-oriented concepts, such as, e.g., 'equal opportunities' or 'indirect discrimination', difficult if not impossible.[58] The meaning of these and other similar concepts necessarily depends not only on the final outcome of judicial decisions – the result of judicial thinking, but also on the policy that these decisions are based on. The textual interpretation of legal rules, so widely accepted in Croatian legal culture, creates semantic confusion and hinders a discursive definition of the meaning.

## 3.3    Circular Reasoning

This can typically be identified in judicial decisions that apply certain standards prescribed by law, without any substantive underpinning of their application to a pending case. For example, a case has been reported[59] where the Supreme Court referred to the constitutional principle of the non-retroactivity of laws, but in the same breath it upheld the retroactivity of Article 10(3) of the Civil Procedure (Amendment) Act, treating it as a constitutionally permissible exception. While the Constitution provides that an exception may be permissible for 'specifically justified reasons', the Supreme Court did not elaborate any grounds or principles for granting an exception to the non-retroactivity rule. Accordingly, an exception to the non-retroactivity rule was justified because it is permissible for specifically justified reasons, and specifically justified reasons are those which are permissible. Examples of circular reasoning can also be found in legal scholarship, methodology and taxonomy. So the specific *sedes materiae* of administrative

---

Stanko Bubić, reported in Slobodna Dalmacija (26 March 2004). The Supreme Court reversed the judgment of the County Court in Split, Croatia, which had seized certain financial proceeds of a convicted drug dealer which had been generated by dealing in heroin. As the Supreme Court explained, the court below did not take into consideration the money that had been invested in the purchase of heroin. Accordingly the amount to be seized was decreased by the 'purchase price.'

[58] One of the objections of the Parliamentary Committee on Legislation to the concept of indirect discrimination introduced into the Croatian legal system by the Draft Gender Equality Act was that 'judges will not know how to apply it.'

[59] Judgment of the Supreme Court, No. Rev-2471/00-2 of 7 October 2003:

'Although the principle of non-retroactivity of laws is proclaimed by the Constitution, the Constitution, nevertheless, permits the possibility of the retroactivity of individual provisions of laws in Art. 89 (5) providing that "(...) individual provisions of laws may have retroactive effects subject to specifically justified reasons". This is the case with Art. 10 (3) of the Civil Procedure (Amendment) Act, and objections of the plaintiff concerning the prohibition of non-retroactivity are unfounded.' *(Iako je načelo zabrane povratnog djelovanja zakona proklamirano Ustavom Republike Hrvatske* (Narodne novine [Official Gazette] *broj 41/01 pročišćeni tekst), ipak Ustav dopušta mogućnost povratnog djelovanja pojedinih odredaba zakona odredbom članka 89. st. 5: 'Iz posebno opravdanih razloga samo pojedine odredbe zakona mogu imati povratno djelovanje, što je slučaj i s odredbom članka 10. st. 3. ZIDZPP-a, pa su prigovori tužiteljice o zabrani povratnog djelovanja zakona neosnovan').*

law is defined by the jurisdiction of the administrative courts while the administrative courts have jurisdiction in administrative matters.

## 3.4    Reliance on Subregulation

Reliance on subregulation is a direct function of textual positivism. However, the problem is double-sided. On the one hand, the courts prefer to look into legal rules which are as concrete as possible. On the other hand, the Parliament and the Government erode the authority of laws by excessive subregulation, sometimes reversing the higher norm.[60] Although the courts are authorized to institute a concrete constitutional review of suspect legislation or even to set aside unconstitutional secondary legislation (*exceptio illegalitatis*), the Constitutional Court has only heard one such case since 1991.

## 4.    LEGAL CULTURE AND MAKING OF THE EU CONSTITUTION

Although many examples used in this paper originate from Croatian experience, the scope and proportions of semantic dissonance in other post-communist states of Central and Eastern Europe[61] do not seem to be significantly different.[62] While examples rooted in national experience may vary, the lowest common denominator for all post-communist countries of Eastern Europe was the absence of freedom of dialogue, the inequality of discourse participants, and state/party coertion – all being essential constituents in the lacking rational discourse.

---

[60] See, e.g., Government Regulation amending the Law on the Recognition of Foreign Qualifications (*Uredba o izmjeni zakona o priznanju inozemnih obrazovnih kvalifikacija*) of 18 December 2003, *Narodne novine* [Official Gazette] No. 198/2003. There are 36 Regulations adopted on the basis of 'empowering legislation' based on Art. 88 of the Constitution. Such empowering legislation authorizes the Government to regulate 'commerce'. However, the Government often uses it for other regulatory purposes, such as the recognition of diplomas, the regulation of misdemeanors, taxation etc. There is no explicit Constitutional authorization to amend laws. However, it has become a regular practice.

[61] The same seems to hold true for countries in Europe's West. Compare Ajani, *supra* n. 47, fn. 70 at p. 116: 'As it is known, even in countries sharing the same fundamental *legal culture*, identical laws, adopted as a result of legal transplant, generate in the long run different interpretations...' Such interpretations differ because of the different meaning ascribed to them.

[62] Z. Kühn, 'Application of European Law in Central European Candidate Countries', 28 *European Law Review* (2003) p. 551; E. Evtimov, 'Integration of the International Agreements into Bulgarian Law', in A. Ott and K. Inglis, eds., *Handbook on European Enlargement* (The Hague, T.M.C. Asser Press 2002); F. Emmert, 'The Independence of Judges – A Concept often Misunderstood in Central and Eastern Europe', 3 *European Journal of Law Reform* (2002) pp. 405-409; Andreescu, *supra* n. 35. The specific situation in Croatia and other post-Yugoslav states is that certain political and legal concepts were not entirely absent from the discourse. In such cases, solving semantic dissonance is more difficult than in cases of a complete absence of discourse.

Bearing the described situation in mind, what are the consequences of the Eastern enlargement for European constitutionalism, and how will semantic dissonance affect the meaning of the EU Constitution? As I have explained earlier, instances of semantic dissonance range from a different understanding of overarching concepts, such as the rule of law, fundamental rights, separation of powers, constitutionalism, property, liberty, to more concrete ones, such as equal pay, equal treatment, the non-retroactivity of laws, proportionality, delegation of powers, discretion, state subsidies, etc. Yet the entire problem of adjusting national law to the *acquis communautaire* is being presented as one of harmonization of legal rules, while the adjustment of their meaning[63] is left for the future.[64] Once that day arrives, the first step in resolving the problem of semantic dissonance, I believe, will beg an answer to the question of 'how the meaning of legal rules and principles has been arrived at.'

In this respect, I maintain that the method of 'getting to the meaning' in Europe's post-communist states has to go through a paradigmatic shift from authoritarian to rationally discoursive, and in terms of legal analysis – from formal to substantive. However, even so, another problem remains. On the basis of what values or criteria will semantic dissonance be solved, and what sort of interpretative theory will be necessary to accommodate legal tradition, coherence and policy in an Europe of 25 or more states, without creating a system where legal certainty is replaced by a 'semantic lottery'?[65]

There are two possible answers to this question. First, experience shows that post-communist societies that have succeeded in becoming members of the EU voluntarily accepted, during the process of integration, the method of communication that Paul Feyerabend calls *guided exchange*. In such a form of communication, '(...) some or all participants adopt a well specified tradition and accept only those responses that correspond to its standards.'[66] The problem emerges in a situation where one side, explicitly or implicitly, refuses to accept the standards of another legal tradition and insists on *free exchange*, i.e., on such communication where '(...) the participants get immersed into each other's ways of

---

[63] Certainly there are instances of plain meaning that need no further elaboration. See e.g., Holmes, *supra* n. 43, at p. 420:

'I do not suppose that you could prove, for purposes of construction as distinguished from avoidance, an oral declaration or even an agreement that words in a dispositive instrument making sense as they stand should have a different meaning from the common one; for instance, that the parties to a contract orally agreed that when they wrote five hundred feet it should mean one hundred inches, or that Bunker Hill Monument should signify Old South Church.'

[64] One of the functions of Association Agreements is semantic harmonization. The same can be said for the process of negotiations for accession. There needs to be some minimum threshold of agreement concerning the meaning of rules before a candidate country can accede to the EU.

[65] A term used by Lord Nicholls in *Ghaidan* v. *Godin-Mendoza* [2004] UKHL 30, *The Times* (24 June 2004): '(...) a meaning which departs from the unambiguous meaning the legislation would otherwise bear (...) would make (...) something of a semantic lottery'.

[66] P. Feyerabend, *Science in a Free Society* (London, NLB 1978) at p. 29.

thinking, feeling, perceiving to such an extent that their ideas, perceptions, world views may be entirely changed.'[67] I find it important that, due to the nature of European Law which does not apply to *purely internal situations* in Member States, a complete guided exchange between the EU and the candidate countries is not possible, and that one part of the interaction between the EU and its Member States will always remain in the form of a free exchange.

While the outcome of a guided exchange in the process of European integration seems to be given, a semantic harmonization in conditions of free exchange probably depends on whether, to paraphrase Rorty's words, Europe's constitutional reality has an intrinsic nature which we must try to discover, or are all possible descriptions of reality equally relational and extrinsic?[68] If the latter is correct, as I suspect, it is quite possible, even probable, that the meaning of law as developed by jurists from post-communist countries will contribute, at least to certain extent, to shaping the understanding of the European Constitution. I dare to propose that, in order to minimize the impact of the meaning developed in authoritarian discourse, a broad agreement on ends, as Rosenfeld suggested, may obviate the need to examine or justify antiquated legal concepts and keep the focus of interpretation on workable legal solutions. In this sense the programmatic provision envisaging an 'ever closer Union' could be understood in instrumental terms, as a cannon of construction, meaning much more than a political declaration or wishful thinking.

---

[67] Ibid.

[68] R. Rorty, 'Pragmatism and Law: A Response to David Luban', 18 *Cardozo Law Review* (1996) p. 75.

# PART II

# Transparency and Legal Instruments in the EU Constitution

# DRAWING THE THREADS TOGETHER FROM PARTS I AND III OF THE EU CONSTITUTION

## Jan Wouters[*]

### 1. INTRODUCTION

A little booklet, like the U.S. Constitution, that could fit into the pockets of European citizens and be carried close to their hearts – that was what Valérie Giscard d'Estaing had in mind for the EU Constitution. However, from the outset it was clear that the simplification requested in the Nice Treaty and in the Laeken Declaration with a view to obtaining 'a Constitution for European citizens'[1] was not going to result in a 'lilliput' type of constitution that would make enjoyable reading for all EU citizens. Nevertheless, even in the preliminary draft Constitutional Treaty, which the Praesidium of the Convention circulated by the end of October 2002, a basic division was proposed between a part one, entitled 'constitutional structure', and a part two (the Charter had not yet been inserted in between) called 'Union policies and their implementation'. The former part would contain provisions 'laying down the institutional architecture'[2] (definition, legal nature, values and goals, citizenship, competences, institutions, democratic life of the Union, finances, external action); the latter 'would contain the legal bases. For each area it should specify the type of competence (…) and the acts and procedures (…) to be applied, in line with what is decided for Part I'.[3] This treaty architecture was favourably received at the Convention's plenary session.[4]

In the end-product of the Convention and in the final 'Treaty establishing a Constitution for Europe' ('the EU Constitution') agreed upon by the Intergov-

---

[*] Professor of International Law and the Law of International Organisations, Leuven University; *Of Counsel,* Linklaters De Bandt, Brussels.
[1] 'Laeken Declaration on the Future of the European Union' (*Bull. EU* I.27 (2001)) also available at: <http://ue.eu.int/en/Info/eurocouncil/index.htm>.
[2] CONV 378/02, p. 1.
[3] CONV 369/02, p. 17.
[4] See CONV 378/02, p. 13:
'the structure of the Treaty was deemed good while its essential features, namely its constitutional nature, the fact that it was a single Treaty, the explicit conferral of a single legal personality and the clarity and readability of the 'backbone' of the draft were commended by the members as a bold approach which met the expectations of both the Convention and Union citizens.'

*D. Curtin, A.E. Kellermann and S. Blockmans, eds., The EU Constitution: The Best Way Forward?*
© 2005, T.M.C. Asser Instituut, The Hague.

ernmental Conference ('IGC') and signed in Rome on 29 October 2004, this basic architecture has been upheld, even though, remarkably enough and unlike the other parts, Part I no longer has a name, whereas Part III is called 'the policies and functioning of the Union'. Even though it is nameless, it is clear that Part I is conceived to be the most fundamental part of the EU Constitution. With its 60 articles, starting with the Union's establishment, core values and objectives, to the notorious voluntary withdrawal clause, it does indeed constitute a mini-constitution in its own right – which does not mean that it makes easy reading for Europe's citizens. Part III for its part is most of all about '[t]he scope of and arrangements for exercising the Union's competences'.[5]

In this contribution I propose to address two main questions concerning the relationship between Parts I and III of the Constitution: (a) have the Constitution's drafters been consistent in their decisions to put certain matters or aspects in Part I or III rather than the other way around; and (b) does the place of one or the other provision in Part I rather than Part III (or the reverse) legally make a difference?

2.      THE CHOICE FOR HAVING CERTAIN PROVISIONS IN PART I
        RATHER THAN IN PART III OR *VICE VERSA*

Although the rationale of the EU Constitution's structural division between Part I and III may be apparent from the above, it is by no means always crystal clear why, concretely, certain provisions do appear in Part I rather than in Part III or *vice versa*. In its IGC opinion of 17 September 2003, the Commission noted rather critically that 'the choice between which provisions have to feature in Part I of the Constitution and those which can be contained in Part III is not always balanced.'[6] It offered the following example: in Part I it is stated how many times the European Council is to meet every year, whereas essential rules on the decision-making by the European Parliament and the Commission are laid down in Part III.[7]

One can come up with many more examples of such questionable choices. Let us first consider a number of institutional matters, by comparing Title IV of Part I on 'the Union's institutions and bodies' with chapter I ('provisions governing the institutions') in Part III's Title VI on 'the functioning of the Union'. It makes sense to spell out in Part I the essential features and mission of each institution, but does that mean that all the complexities of the appointment procedure

---

[5] Quoted from Art. I-12(6) TCE.

[6] Commission of the European Communities, 'A Constitution for the Union. Opinion of the Commission, pursuant to Article 48 of the Treaty on European Union, on the Conference of Representatives of the Member States' governments convened to revise the Treaties', COM (2003) 548 final, pp. 11-12, para. 21.

[7] Ibid., n. 8.

of the Commission (including transitional arrangements)[8] had to be added to that Part, whereas for the composition and designation of Members of the Committee of the Regions and the Economic and Social Committee reference is simply made to Part III?[9] Consistency is not the strongest side of the EU Constitution in this respect: on the one hand, the eligibility criteria for Members of the Commission are mentioned in Part I,[10] on the other hand, those for judges and Advocates-General are laid down in Part III.[11] Why is a crucial body like the European Investment Bank not at least mentioned, as far as its key role is concerned, in Part I?[12] Speaking of essential features of the institutions, why does Part I of the EU Constitution not take over the 'constitutional' elements of the Act concerning the election of the representatives of the European Parliament by direct universal suffrage, such as the independence of Members of the European Parliament and the list of incompatibilities (which does not even figure in Part III now), whereas the independence of Members of the Commission, judges and Advocates-General and of the ECB are explicitly emphasised in Part I? Why is the independence of Court of Auditors' members only mentioned in Part III?

For substantive issues, too, the division of matters between Part I and Part III is not always obvious. Was there a need for the rather detailed provisions on the common foreign and security policy ('CFSP') and the common security and defence policy ('CSDP') in Articles I-40 and (especially) I-41 TCE rather than in the Title on the Union's external action in Part III? Compare this to the concise reference of just one line to the core fundamental freedoms of the internal market in Art. I-4 TCE and one can see the lack of balance in this. Of course, the length of the aforementioned provisions indicates that the Convention and the IGC have paid – rightly – particular attention to these areas, but that does not make for a more balanced Part I. Regarding fundamental market freedoms, the question of the relationship between the various parts of the EU Constitution is still more complicated, as it is not only mentioned in Part I and (in explicit detail, with their traditional provisions) in Part III, but also – as far as EU citizens as beneficiaries are concerned and with the exception of the free movement of capital – in Article II-75(2) TCE, i.e., in Part II in which the Charter of Fundamental Rights has been incorporated.[13]

---

[8]  See Art. I-26 TCE.

[9]  See Art. I-32(5) TCE.

[10]  Art. I-26(4) TCE.

[11]  Art. III-355 TCE. Art. I-29(2) TCE, third para. only mentions the 'independence beyond doubt' requirement.

[12]  Art. I-34(3) TCE only mentions the European Investment Bank in passing, referring to specific cases in which European legislative acts may be adopted at the request of, *inter alia*, the European Investment Bank. The basic provisions on the European Investment Bank can be found in Arts. III-393 and III-394 TCE.

[13]  Much more can be said about the relationship between Parts I and III on the one hand, and Part II on the other. For instance, the very fact that Part II has kept its own preamble which does not wholly match the Constitution's preamble is rather remarkable.

Overall, both for institutional and substantive matters, it is hard for a user of the EU Constitution who wants to obtain a complete oversight of, and an insight into, the manner in which the EU Constitution deals with a certain point, to avoid a 'ping-pong' experience, being thrown from Part I to Part III and back. Although, obviously, more detailed requirements had to be dealt with in Part III, the legibility of Part I suffers needlessly from an overkill of cross-references such as 'for the aspects defined in Part III', 'in accordance with Part III', 'under the conditions laid down in Part III' and 'except in the cases referred to in Part III'.

Something should also be said about the drafting quality of Part III. In its IGC opinion the Commission has been roundly very critical of this Part. Apart from the areas rewritten by the Convention (such as, e.g., on the EU's external action and the area of freedom, security and justice), the Commission found that the provisions on policies in Part III were rather unbalanced:

> 'In certain areas, the text dates back to the 1957 Treaty of Rome. In others, it has been amended repeatedly, which does not make it any more accessible. The result is that the provisions on policies as featured in Part III of the draft Constitution (apart from the areas rewritten by the Convention) form a lengthy, uneven and complicated whole which is drafted in a variety of styles and, above all, has been superseded by the reality of current policies. The provisions on agriculture thus reflect the ideas of the 1950s on growth and security of supply, and are far removed from the key elements of the CAP reform designed to encourage production of high-quality food whilst respecting environmental imperatives and developing the countryside by means of diversification. The concept of sustainable development – which the Convention highlighted as one of the Union's aims – does not appear in the provisions on environmental policy. By contrast, the draft Constitution contains a number of provisions that are obsolete or irrelevant.'[14]

The Commission concluded by stating that, failing a complete overhaul, the IGC:

> 'should at least clarify some provisions and should make all the Constitution's provisions consistent, particularly by reflecting fully the provisions of Part I, on which the Convention focused a great deal of attention, in Part III, which it did not revise.'[15]

---

[14] *Supra* n. 6, pp. 12-13, para. 22. The Commission gives the example of Art. III-141 and Art. III-56(2)(c) (in the final text: Art. III-243 and Art. III-167(2)(c) TCE), on the division of Germany, and of Art. III-109 (in the final text: Art. III-215 TCE) which provides that the 'Member States shall endeavour to maintain the existing equivalence between paid holiday schemes.' It should be noted that in the EU Constitution's final version (not in the Convention's draft, on which the Commission commented), both Arts. III-243 and III-167(2)(c) contain a last sentence pursuant to which five years after the entry into force of the EU Constitution, the Council (on a proposal from the Commission) may adopt a European decision repealing this exception.

[15] *Supra* n. 6, p. 13, para. 23.

However, even this has not been done in a systematic manner during the IGC. There are many examples of this. Just one: Part I makes in Article I-3(3) TCE 'a highly competitive social market economy' an objective of the Union. This notion appears nowhere in Part III, which in Article III-178 TCE still speaks of 'the principle of an open market economy with free competition, favouring an efficient allocation of resources' for the conduct of economic policy by the Member States and the Union.[16] In the light of this and other cases one may agree with the Commission that:

> '[t]his situation constitutes one more important reason for enabling the Constitution to be revised more flexibly (…). If the provisions on policies are not rewritten at this time, the Union should be given the possibility of doing so in coming years. If the rules were too inflexible, much of the Constitution, the Union's flagship text, would carry these defects for many years to come.'[17]

## 3. DOES IT LEGALLY MATTER WHETHER CERTAIN PROVISIONS APPEAR IN PART I RATHER THAN PART III OR *VICE VERSA*?

As such, the answer to this question is 'no', as far as the hierarchy of norms is concerned. Given the close links between Parts I and III in many instances and the many cross-references between these parts, it seems very difficult to draw any overall legal consequences from the fact that one provision of the Constitution carries a Roman figure 'I' before it and the other a Roman figure 'III' (or II or IV, for that matter). This being said, it is obvious that the European Court of Justice will be inclined to interpret the EU Constitution's provisions – as it has always done with the EC Treaty – in the light of the overall objectives of the EU.

What, then, about the procedure for the revision of these parts? One would have expected the Convention to develop different methods of amendment for Parts I and III: more difficult for the 'foundational' principles, more flexible for the 'policies' Part III.[18] However, in the end – and to the disappointment of many[19] – the Convention did not propose this, because 'some of the provisions of Part III were closely linked to the provisions of Part I and should therefore be subject to the same amendment procedure'; and 'laying down different amend-

---

[16] See also Art. III-177, first and second paras and Art. III-185(1) TCE on the European System of Central Banks.

[17] *Supra* n. 6, p. 13, para. 22 *in fine*.

[18] See already the hint in the Laeken Declaration, *supra* n. 1:

'Should a distinction be made between a basic treaty and the other treaty provisions? Should this distinction involve separating the texts? Could this lead to a distinction between the amendment and ratification procedures for the basic treaty and for the other treaty provisions?'

[19] See, for instance, the Commission's IGC opinion, *supra* n. 6, p. 8, para. 10:

'This state of affairs could lead to total paralysis of the Union and eventually to a loss of interest on the part of the Member States and citizens as regards this form of integration, in favour of less effective models of cooperation or even cooperation between only some Member States.'

ment procedures would mean re-opening discussion on the structure of the EU Constitution and would give rise to requests for certain areas of Part III to be moved to Part I.'[20]

This has remained so in the final Constitution text adopted by the IGC.[21] However, there is an important nuance: two simplified revision procedures have been provided for, in Article IV-444 and IV-445 TCE respectively, each of which refers to certain provisions of Part III. In spite of its title ('Simplified revision procedure'), the former article contains a number of cases which, *stricto sensu*, do not amount to real treaty changes although they do have their importance in terms of efficient decision-making. For instance,[22] Article IV-444(1) TCE makes it possible for the European Council to adopt a European decision authorizing the Council for areas or cases for which Part III provides for unanimous decision-making – with the exception of decisions with military implications or in the defence area – to act by a qualified majority. This is, in essence, a revamped version of the '*passerelle*' provisions that were a familiar – but never used – technique in the Maastricht and Amsterdam Treaties. There are two caveats, though: the European Council has to act unanimously, and even if a decision is taken, it can be easily neutralized: if a national parliament opposes such a European Council decision, it 'shall not be adopted' – *causa finita*.[23]

The procedure laid down in Article IV-445 TCE is more aptly named a 'simplified revision procedure concerning internal Union policies and action'. It provides for the possibility for any national government, the European Parliament or the Commission to submit to the European Council proposals for revising 'all or part of the provisions of Title III of Part III on the internal policies and action of the Union'. This comprises the internal market, economic and monetary union and a whole variety of policies in other areas, from certain shared competences[24]

---

[20] CONV 728/03, p. 10.

[21] For a discussion of the proposals of the Italian presidency of the IGC in this respect, see K. Lenaerts and D. Gerard, 'The Structure of the Union according to the Constitution for Europe: The Emperor is getting dressed', 29 *European Law Review* (2004) p. 289, at p. 305.

[22] I will not dwell on Art. IV-444(2) TCE, which makes it possible for the European Council to adopt a European decision allowing for European laws or framework laws to be adopted in accordance with the 'ordinary legislative procedure' (i.e., co-decision) instead of the 'special legislative procedure' (i.e., consultation). The same restrictions apply as with regard to Art. IV-444(1) TCE.

[23] See Art. IV-444(3) TCE, first para.

[24] This includes, as far as shared competences are concerned: social policy; economic, social and territorial cohesion; agriculture and fisheries; environment; consumer protection; transport; trans-European networks; energy. It also includes two areas which are not, or not strictly, catalogued as areas of shared competence in Art. I-14(2) TCE, namely employment (categorized as 'coordination of economic and employment policies' in Art. I-15 TCE) and research and technological development and space (mentioned in Art. I-14(3) TCE, with the specificity that the exercise of Union competence does not result in Member States being prevented from exercising their competences). Note that an area of shared competence mentioned in Art. I-14(4) TCE, namely development cooperation and humanitarian aid, is not a part of Title III of Part III, but of its Title V ('the Union's external action'), more in particular in Arts. III-316-318 and III-321 TCE re-

and the area of freedom, security and justice to 'areas of supporting, coordinating or complementary action'.[25] That is quite substantial. However, the manner in which this simplified revision procedure is regulated, is not extremely flexible, to say the least: it presupposes a unanimous European decision of the European Council; the changes can only enter into force after approval (note: not 'ratification') by all Member States according to their constitutional systems and no measure is foreseen in the event of a blockade at this juncture;[26] and, quite importantly, such European decision may not increase the competences conferred on the EU. The fact that this procedure does not cover the titles of Part III on the EU's external action and on the functioning of the Union, including the institutional provisions of Part III, makes it, in the end, limited in scope.

## 4.    CONCLUDING REMARKS

My conclusion is brief: the relationship between Parts I and III of the EU Constitution is not what it could have been. On the one hand, Part I provisions are sometimes needlessly long and detailed, and some of them could easily have been inserted in Part III. On the other hand, Part III of the EU Constitution is a rather strange compilation of entirely rewritten or new provisions and age-old articles, some of which are, in any event, outdated or even completely obsolete. In that respect, Part III is also a missed opportunity for another kind of constitutional exercise, namely a consolidation and updating of some of the Union's (nowadays: the Community's) core provisions in light of their interpretation by the Court of Justice.

---

spectively. For these areas, and more in general for all areas of the Union's external action, the simplified revision procedure is not available.

[25] Thus the title of Art. I-17 TCE; compare the title of Chapter V of Part III's Title III: 'areas where the Union may take coordinating, complementary or supporting action'. This includes the areas of public health; industry; culture; tourism; education, youth, sport and vocational training; civil protection; and administrative cooperation for the effective implementation of Union law by the Member States.

[26] Compare, under the ordinary revision procedure, Art. IV-443(4) TCE.

# *LA LOI EUROPEÉNNE*: PROMISE AND PRETENCE

## Armin von Bogdandy and Jürgen Bast[*]

I.  INTRODUCING 'EUROPEAN LAWS' – MERE SYMBOLIC CONSTITUTIONALISM?

For the Anglo-Saxon world, the quantum leap which the Constitutional Treaty plans for the European Union is best symbolised by the term 'constitution'. From the perspective of continental legal scholarship, the projected leap is perhaps even more evident in the use of the term 'law' (*loi, legge, Gesetz*) for Union legislation. On the continent it evokes some of the deepest presumptions and expectations that the English term 'law' – given different constitutional paths in the Anglo-Saxon world – does not carry.[1] Whereas the term 'constitution' is not totally uncommon for founding documents of transnational organisations (for instance, the ILO, the UNESCO, or the WHO), the term *loi* or *Gesetz* has never been used for measures enacted by such organisations. Hence, employing the term *loi européenne* for certain acts of the Union is far from a merely technical move. The concept is loaded with historical experiences and civic expectations, and it is strongly linked with certain premises of constitutional theory, in particular the democratic ideal of the will of the people (*volonté générale*).[2] The citizen's perception of the Union's activity could alter significantly.

Our contribution will discuss to what extent *la loi européenne* meets these presumptions and expectations. Does the Constitutional Treaty keep the promises it makes by employing the term 'law', or does this lexical revolution form part of a purely symbolic constitutionalism? More specifically, how does the concept of *loi européenne* introduced in Part I of the Constitutional Treaty (Arts. I-33 et

---

[*] Armin von Bogdandy is director at the Max Planck Institute for Comparative Public Law and International Law, Heidelberg and Jürgen Bast is a research fellow at the same institute.

[1] Compare, e.g., J.H.H. Weiler, U. Haltern and F.C. Mayer, 'European Democracy and Its Critique', 18 *West European Politics* (1995) at p. 4.

[2] See A. Ross, *Theorie der Rechtsquellen* (Leipzig, Deuticke 1929, reprint 1989) pp. 34 et seq.; R. Carré de Malberg, *La loi, expression de la volonté générale* (Paris, Librairie du recueil Sirey 1931); J. Habermas, *Faktizität und Geltung* (Frankfurt am Main, Suhrkamp 1992).

*D. Curtin, A.E. Kellermann and S. Blockmans, eds., The EU Constitution: The Best Way Forward?*
© 2005, T.M.C. Asser Instituut, The Hague.

seq. TCE) relate to its Part III, which contains almost all of the empowering provisions and therefore the real 'power map'[3] of the Constitutional Treaty?

### 2.   DOUBLE-CHECKING THE CONSTITUTIONAL TREATY – WHAT DOES THE *LOI EUROPÉENNE* PROMISE?

In order to check the 'honesty' of the Constitutional Treaty we have to translate the civic expectations, mentioned above, into legal terms. The following discussion offers a – certainly non-exhaustive – list of legal characteristics which a 'law' is expected to demonstrate. These attributes may help to profile 'European laws' and 'European framework laws', which Article I-33 TCE defines as the two 'legislative' instruments under the Constitutional Treaty.[4]

### 2.1   **Act of Parliament**

First, a 'law' is generally expected to be an Act of Parliament. A 'law' derives its claim to higher legitimacy from its conceptual assignment to a parliamentary procedure. In this respect, the Constitutional Treaty fares quite well as far as the so-called ordinary legislative procedure is concerned. It defines, as a rule, that the Parliament and Council co-decide upon a legislative act (Art. I-34(1) TCE). This follows the bicameral approach gradually developed since the Maastricht Treaty and reflects the two strains of democratic legitimacy of the Union.[5] Had the Convention (and the ensuing IGC) stopped at that point, it would have proposed a convincing classification based on a procedural concept of 'law'. But the rule has various exceptions called 'special legislative procedures' (Art. I-34(2) TCE). Whenever the Constitutional Treaty, in Part III, so provides, the Council acts as a legislator that does not necessarily need to reach agreement with the Parliament. The 'special' law-making procedures vary considerably. In some cases Parliament is required to give its assent; in others it is only consulted.[6] It follows from this approach that, concerning the voting procedure, there need not be any difference between a European law and a European regulation of the Council. For a legal act to qualify as a 'law' under the Constitutional Treaty, it does not have to pass through parliamentary co-decision.

---

[3] I.D. Duchacek, *Power Maps: Comparative Politics of Constitutions* (Santa Barbara CA, ABC-Clio Press 1973).

[4] As opposed to the non-legislative acts, the list of legislative instruments is exhaustive, see Art. I-33(2) TCE.

[5] Affirmed by Art. I-46(2) TCE.

[6] Most problematic are 'special legislative procedures' which combine qualified majority voting in the Council with mere consultation of the Parliament, as stipulated in, e.g., Art. III-127 TCE and Art. III-251(3) TCE.

## 2.2    Supremacy of Laws

Second, a 'law' is supposed to meet the expectation of being the (almost) supreme law of the land, ranking only below the Constitution, but prevailing over
other instruments enacted under that Constitution. This aspect is very much connected to the law's procedural legitimacy, since the basic decisions of a body
politic, acting through its elected representatives, should not be called into question by any later act of a less legitimate authority. In the European Convention
and its Working Group on 'Simplification', this aspect was repeatedly referred to
as the (alleged) need for establishing a hierarchy of norms. A hierarchy of legal
instruments is, to date, essentially foreign to secondary Union/Community law.[7]
The Union is based on the premise that each institution shall act within the limits
of the powers conferred on it in the Treaties. Seen from that perspective, all rule-
making institutions and rule-making procedures are equal.[8] The respective scope
of action for each institution is defined and delimited by the relevant empowering provisions of the Treaties. Within that system, a hierarchy of norms is not
required since possible conflicts of norms are, at least in principle, already
solved by the horizontal order of competences.

According to a widespread view, this system will be overthrown by the concept of European laws.[9] Granted, given its traditional meaning, one expects a
'European law' (no matter whether 'ordinary' or 'special') to prevail over any
'European regulation', including Council regulations with a legal basis directly
in a constitutional provision. Yet, on closer inspection, no indication is found
that such a revolution will occur. There is no provision in the Constitutional
Treaty stipulating a general hierarchy of instruments, and the Convention's Praesidium rejected requests from the floor to include such an article.[10] Consequently, the division of powers within the Constitutional Treaty is still governed by
the individual empowering provisions of Part III. For example, when Part III empowers the Council to adopt European regulations on fixing prices, levies, aid

---

[7] For details, see J. Bast, 'On the Grammar of EU Law: Legal Instruments', in A. von Bogdandy
and J.H.H. Weiler, eds., *New German Scholarship* (Jean Monnet Working Paper no. 9/03) available at: <http://www.jeanmonnetprogram.org/papers/03/030901-05.pdf>.

[8] ECJ, judgment of 6 July 1982, Cases C-188/80–190/80, *France et al.* v. *Commission* [1982]
*ECR* 2545, para. 6; ECJ, judgment of 2 October 1997, Case C-259/95, *Parliament* v. *Council*
[1997] *ECR* I-5303, para. 27; see R. Bieber and I. Salomé, 'Hierarchy of Norms in European
Law', 33 *Common Market Law Review* (1996) at pp. 915 et seq.

[9] See, e.g., F.J. Carrera Hernández, 'Simplifición de los instrumentos jurídicos en el Proyecto
de Tratado constitucional', 16 *Revista de Derecho Communitario Europeo* (2003) pp. 1058 et
seq.; J. Schwarze, 'Ein pragmatischer Verfassungsentwurf', 38 *Europarecht* (2003) at p. 554;
K. Lenaerts, J. Binon and P. Van Nuffel, 'L'Union européenne en quête d'une Constitution: bilan
des travaux de la Convention sur l'avenir de L'Europe', 11 *Journal des tribunaux – Droit européen*
(2003) at p. 293.

[10] See, e.g., 'Suggestion for amendment of Article: I-32' by Dr. Silvia-Yvonne Kaufmann,
available    at:    <http://european-convention.eu.int/Docs/Treaty/pdf/24/24_Art%20I%2032%
20Kaufmann%20DE.pdf>.

and quantitative restrictions relating to the common agricultural policy (Art. III-231(3) TCE), the Constitutional Treaty voluntarily forecloses these issues from the reach of the European laws establishing the common organisations of the agricultural markets (Art. III-231(2) TCE). Within the scope of their respective competences, European regulations prevail over interfering European laws. Overall, the persistence of European regulations and decisions directly based on constitutional provisions (Art. I-35(2) TCE) militates against the alleged supremacy of European laws and framework laws.

## 2.3    Domain of the Law

A further aspect of what a 'law' is commonly expected to entail is the legal concept which the French call *domaine de la loi*, the Italians *riserva di legge*, and the Germans *Gesetzesvorbehalt*. The 'domain of the law' is formed by subject areas reserved for rule-making by way of laws (that is, as described above, mostly for parliamentary law-making). The definition of this 'domain' varies significantly between the respective state constitutional orders. Within German constitutional law, for example, all 'essential' decisions have to be made by the Parliament. Other constitutional orders are more relaxed, leaving a wider scope for the rule-making of the executive branch. Yet, it is a common characteristic of these nationally defined domains that they include constitutionally protected individual liberties: interference with these fundamental rights is only permissible on the basis of, or by order of, a law.

Reading the text of the Charter of Fundamental Rights, which now forms Part II of the Constitutional Treaty, suggests the existence of such a domain of the European law formed by individual liberties. According to Article 52 of the Charter, now Article II-112(1) TCE, 'any limitation on the exercise of the rights and freedoms recognised by this Charter must be *provided for by the law* [emphasis added]'. Granted, there is a presumption of consistency telling us that the term 'law' in Part II has the same meaning as in Part I. Regarding the general clause on permissible restrictions on fundamental rights, however, there are good reasons to support a different construction. Firstly, one may point out that the phrase 'provided for by the law' was taken from similar formulae in the European Convention on Human Rights.[11] This militates *prima facie* for the same meaning as under this Convention.[12] The Strasbourg Court, in its settled case law, rejects the idea that the phrase was drafted in order to guard the prerogatives of a

---

[11] E.g., Art. 8(2) ECHR: 'in accordance with the law'; Arts. 9(2), 10(2) and 11(2) ECHR: 'prescribed by law'.

[12] See Art. 52(3) of the Charter, now Art. II-112(3) TCE.

[13] ECtHR, judgment of 16 April 2002, Appl. No. 37971/97, *Societe Colas Est* v. *France* [2004] 39 *EHRR* 17, para. 43; for further references, see J.A. Frowein, 'Vorbemerkung zu Art. 8-11', in J.A. Frowein and W. Peukert, *Europäische MenschenrechtsKonvention: EMRK-Kommentar*, 2nd edn. (Kehl, Engel 1996) before Arts. 8–11, paras. 2 et seq.

certain branch of government. Rather, it aims to protect the individual in guaranteeing a certain degree of foreseeability, notwithstanding the instrument chosen. Hence, the term 'law' is to be understood in its substantive sense, not its formal one.[13] Secondly, there is an argument *ad absurdum* demonstrating that 'the law' also includes 'non-legislative' instruments like the European regulation. If the institutions of the Union could only interfere with constitutionally protected fundamental rights by using a European law, any such interference would be excluded in areas where the European law is not at the disposal of the institutions. Take, for example, competition law. There are no provisions conferring a competence to adopt European laws in order to establish the competition rules for the internal market (see Arts. III-161 et seq. TCE). Rather, the Commission is empowered to make European regulations and decisions, and the Council is, in the form of European regulations, empowered to set up a legal framework, regulating, in particular, the relevant administrative procedures.[14] There is no doubt that these regulations and decisions (directly based on the EU Constitution) potentially interfere with the rights and interests of private subjects. If that kind of action were lawful only when it takes the form of a European law, Part III of the Constitutional Treaty would then provide a competence which Part II intends to suppress. That construction would make no sense.

Overall, one may designate the sum of the empowering provisions of Part III of the Constitutional Treaty which provide for European laws and framework laws as 'the domain of the law' under the Constitutional Treaty. This notion, however, does not meet the expectation that the 'domain of the European law' should extend to an area of specifically protected fundamental rights. In European constitutional law the chapter on legal instruments is still not interlinked with that on fundamental rights protection.

## 2.4    Shielding against the Judiciary

In most national constitutional systems, the 'law' enjoys a high degree of shielding against the judiciary. If not excluded completely, the right to declare an act of parliament void (or inapplicable) is most often reserved to a special procedure or a special court. In Community law this conception is unknown. An action for annulment can be brought against 'all measures adopted by the institutions, whatever their nature or form, which are intended to have legal effects'.[15] Even for an action brought by a private applicant, the legal form of the contested act is not decisive. Despite the wording of Article 230(4) TEC, all instruments are subject to legal review if the contested provisions are of direct and individual con-

---

[14] On the Council's powers, see Arts. III-163 and III-169 TCE.

[15] ECJ, judgment of 31 March 1971, Case C-22/70, *Commission* v. *Council* [1971] *ECR* 263, paras. 38/42.

[16] ECJ, judgment of 18 May 1994, Case C-309/89, *Codorniu* v. *Council* [1994] *ECR* I-1853, para. 19.

cern to the plaintiff.[16] The ECJ carefully takes notice that the scope of legal review does not depend on the instrument chosen by the enacting institution.

The Constitutional Treaty clearly supports this conception of the Court, in particular by replacing the term 'decision' in Article 230(4) TEC with the term 'act' in the relevant provision of the Constitutional Treaty, thereby finally clarifying the neutrality of legal protection regarding the choice of instrument. But the Constitutional Treaty raises new questions about linking legal instruments with legal review: henceforth, an individual action for annulment could be admissible, even though the individual concern requirement is not met, if the contested measure is a 'regulatory act' (Art. III-365(4) TCE). Since this notion is neither defined nor used elsewhere in the Constitutional Treaty, its content is fairly difficult to determine. Some authors construe it along the lines of the similar term 'European regulation'.[17] They conclude that the streamlined conditions for legal protection against a 'regulatory act' should not apply to a legislative act, i.e., European laws and framework laws. We prefer a different view. The Constitutional Treaty's provisions on legal protection should be construed in the light of the right to an effective remedy (Art. II-107 TCE). One has to recall that the very moderate extension of legal standing was meant to close a serious gap between decentralised legal protection by the national courts and centralised protection by the ECJ. This gap pertaining to so-called self-executing EC regulations[18] would continue to exist if the liberalised standing provisions were limited to non-legislative acts. Consequently, any act of general application should be considered as possibly constituting a 'regulatory act' – including European laws.[19] This interpretation of Article III-365 TCE, admittedly, misses an opportunity to link the concept of European laws with expectations drawn from national experience. Yet, the right to an effective remedy should prevail over the idea of immunising European laws against the judiciary.

---

[17] F.C. Mayer, 'Individualrechtsschutz im Europäischen Verfassungsrecht', 119 *Deutsches Verwaltungsblatt* (2004) at pp. 610 et seq.; J. Temple Lang, 'Declarations, Regional Authorities, Subsidiarity, Regional Policy Measures, and the Constitutional Treaty', 29 *European Law Review* (2004) at pp. 102 et seq.; W. Cremer, 'Der Rechtsschutz des Einzelnen gegen Sekundärrechtsakte der Union gem. Art. III-270 Abs. 4 Konventsentwurf des Vertrags über eine Verfassung für Europa', 31 *Europäische Grundrechte-Zeitschrift* (2004) at p. 582.

[18] Recently discussed in ECJ, judgment of 1 April 2004, Case C-263/02 P, *Commission* v. *Jégo-Quéré*, nyr; CFI, judgment of 3 May 2002, Case T-177/01, *Jégo-Quéré* v. *Commission* [2002] *ECR* II-2365; for an overview, see J. Schwarze, 'The Legal Protection of the Individual against Regulations in European Union Law,' 10 *European Public Law* (2004) p. 285.

[19] S. Flogatis and A. Pottakis, 'Judicial Protection under the Constitution', 1 *European Constitutional Law Review* (2005) at p. 109: 'the term seems to leave the Court ample room for manoeuvre'; see also R. Barents, 'The Court of Justice in the Draft Constitution', 11 *Maastricht Journal of European and Comparative Law* (2004) at p. 134.

## 2.5    Openness to the Public and Transparency

That having been said, what are the legal characteristics distinguishing a European law (or framework law) from other legal instruments, which the Constitutional Treaty classifies as 'non-legislative'? In fact, the Constitutional Treaty rather sparingly attaches legal consequences to its 'legislative' acts exclusively. Such consequences do, however, exist. Constitutional rules applicable solely to 'legislative acts' concern the transparency of the rule-making process, its openness to the public. Not only the Parliament but also the Council shall deliberate and vote in public session when exercising legislative functions, i.e., deciding upon a draft European law or framework law.[20] Likewise, under the Protocol on the role of the national parliaments a 'draft legislative act' shall be forwarded to the national parliaments. The Protocol on the application of the principles of subsidiarity and proportionality establishes an early warning mechanism involving the national parliaments in order to foster subsidiarity compliance, which, again, is only applicable when a 'draft legislative act' is at issue. A law under the Constitutional Treaty is, one can conclude, an act which is subject to special public scrutiny, since certain rules ensuring the transparency of the proceedings of the Union's institutions are mandatory (only) for legislative acts. Organised actors, including political parties in national parliaments, as well as individual Union citizens are better enabled to control and perhaps involve themselves in the process of European law-making.[21] The introduction of 'the law' in Union affairs is aimed at selecting those rule-making projects being of major relevance to the citizenry and the polity as a whole[22] and concentrating public attention thereon. Here a surprising parallel with the national constitutional system appears. On the national plane as well, the concept of a domain of the law ensures that, by requiring a parliamentary procedure, public deliberation is enabled, and at the same time that public attention – a scarce resource in contemporary societies – is focussed on issues of major importance.[23]

Hence, the thin line which the Constitutional Treaty draws between legislative and non-legislative acts really does matter, both in legal and in political terms, since this delimitation is about the appropriate level of public scrutiny.[24]

---

[20]  Arts. I-24(6) and I-50(2) TCE.

[21]  The national parliaments, here, serve as a link between the Union institutions and the citizens.

[22]  See Art. I-36(1) TCE, stating that the 'essential elements of an area shall be reserved for the European law or framework law'.

[23]  A. von Bogdandy, *Gubernative Rechtsetzung* (Tübingen, Mohr Siebeck 2000) pp. 199 et seq.

[24]  In this context, Art. I-21(1) TCE provokes critical questions in stating that the European Council 'shall not exercise legislative functions'. Taken as a description of the constitutional role of the European Council, this simply is a semantic dishonesty. It holds normative truth insofar as the European Council, while adopting European decisions, escapes the public scrutiny mechanisms which are applicable only to legislative acts expressly so-called. Moreover, in Arts. III-136, III-270 and III-271 TCE the European Council is directly involved in a legislative procedure.

Consequently, it is not for the institutions to decide whether an act is legislative or non-legislative in character – the decision is already made by the Constitutional Treaty itself by way of classifying the respective legal basis. This being true, then, only a careful analysis of Part III of the Constitutional Treaty can determine whether the distinction between legislative and non-legislative acts is based on reasonable criteria. Astoundingly, there was hardly any debate within the Convention about which empowering provisions of Part III should form part of the domain of the European law, and which of them could, alternatively, be assigned to European regulations and decisions of the Council. The outcome is, to put it mildly, not in all cases convincing. Is the Council really adopting an act of a 'non-legislative' nature when:

- laying down the general rules on competition, e.g., pertaining to state aids control (Art. III-169 TCE)?

- the Council defines the legal framework for administrative co-operation in the area of freedom, security and justice, e.g., for cross-border police co-operation (Art. III-263 TCE)?

- it establishes the limits and conditions for the power of the ECB to impose sanctions on undertakings (Art. III-190(3) TCE)?

- it lays down the rules governing the languages of the Union's institutions (Art. III-433 TCE)?

All this appears, as Dougan correctly notes, 'rather arbitrary'.[25] Bypassing the higher level of public scrutiny and of parliamentary involvement (both European and national) is precisely what seems to have motivated the drafters of the Constitutional Treaty in excluding those competences from the domain of the European law.[26]

## 3.    CONCLUSION: AN EDUCATIONAL CONCEPT

We arrive at a mixed conclusion. Those who expected the twofold *loi européenne* – European laws and framework laws – simply to replicate the laws of the national constitutional orders become disappointed, or may even have the dim feeling of being cheated, since the new instruments are basically the old ones renamed. As in most other sections of European constitutional law, the pro-

---

[25] M. Dougan, 'The Convention's Draft Constitutional Treaty: Bringing Europe closer to its Lawyers?', 28 *European Law Review* (2003) at p. 784.

[26] K. Lenaerts, 'A Unified Set of Instruments', 1 *European Constitutional Law Review* (2005) at p. 61.

posed reform of the legal instruments heralds no revolution but mainly rests on established constitutional structures. However, the Constitutional Treaty brings about a significant change insofar as it uses legal instruments to decide on the applicability of certain transparency rules and to guide public discourse: European laws and framework laws are adopted under mechanisms of enhanced public scrutiny and are aimed at attracting a higher degree of attention. This approach is to be welcomed, because it rests on the democratic ideal that a law shall be reserved for issues of major importance, and intense public debate is, therefore, worthwhile. But the distinction between legislative and non-legislative acts established in Part I is only as reasonable as the provisions of Part III which ultimately give meaning to it. Here the Constitutional Treaty certainly has its weaknesses, since important empowering provisions are classified as 'non-legislative' on a rather arbitrary basis, let alone the activities of the European Council and the Council in the Common Foreign and Security Policy, which are completely excluded from the domain of the European law.

The tensions between the promises in Part I and the normative reality in Part III are quite significant. With this in mind, do we have to regard *la loi européenne* as an element of what Karl Loewenstein in the 1950s called a 'semantic constitution', i.e., a constitution that is unwilling to effectively shape and limit public power, constituted elsewhere?[27] Of course, an isolated reading of Parts I and II of the Constitutional Treaty is misleading. Since the real 'power map' of the Constitution is drawn in Part III, the Constitutional Treaty is, to a certain degree, 'dishonest towards its own contents'.[28] On the other hand, the Constitutional Treaty nevertheless has the potential to bring the Union closer to that form of polity for which *la loi* as a political idea stands. Introducing a demanding concept like the *loi européenne* has a normative potential which transcends the current regime of Part III. Attaching certain public scrutiny mechanisms to 'legislative' instruments may, in retrospect, prove to have marked only the beginning of a lasting development. Perhaps the Constitutional Treaty is neither a fully 'normative' nor a merely 'semantic' constitution. Perhaps it resembles the 'nominal' type, which Loewenstein related to hopeful post-colonial constitutions of his time: 'the primary objective of the nominal constitution is educational, with the goal, in the near or distant future, of becoming fully normative and actually governing the dynamics of the power process instead of being governed by it.'[29]

---

[27] K. Loewenstein, *Political Power and the Governmental Process* (Chicago, Chicago University Press 1957) pp. 147 et seq.; K. Loewenstein, *Verfassungslehre*, 4th edn. (Tübingen, Mohr Siebeck 2000) pp. 153 et seq.

[28] C. Möllers, 'Pouvoir Constituant – Constitution – Constitutionalisation', in A. von Bogdandy and J. Bast, eds., *Principles of European Constitutional Law* (Hart Publishing, Oxford 2005).

[29] Loewenstein (1957), *supra* n. 27, at p. 149.

# CONTROL OF EXECUTIVE ACTS: THE PROCEDURAL SOLUTION. 'PROPORTIONALITY, STATE OF THE ART DECISION-MAKING AND RELEVANT INTERESTS'

Michelle Everson[*]

## 1.   INTRODUCTION

How best to control the executive acts is a complex question that has long occu-pied a central place within academic legal debate. Authoritative executive acts, whether they are of a preparatory or implementing nature, present modern state theory with one of its greatest conundrums. The modern state, with all its pre-tence to a legitimacy that is comprehensively rooted in the expressed will of the people, is, if it hopes to fulfil its commitments to that people, inevitably reliant upon a small army of bureaucrats, experts and policy makers: which state can protect its citizens from intricate hazards or provide its citizens with comprehen-sive welfare provision without recourse to an extensive executive, or even a 'regulatory',[1] branch acting outside the traditional legislative mandate? With this, however, the essential paradox of the modern state becomes apparent: founded within the legislative will of the people, it is nonetheless functionally dependent upon non-majoritarian bodies and technocrats who, in exercising power outside the legislative process, are a simple anathema to democracy.

The imperative of state recourse to executive action and the resultant tension between legislative and executive arms of government has, in its turn, forced law and lawyers to engage with the tricky task of establishing the boundaries be-tween the legislature and the executive and to ensure that the circle between legitimising majoritarian will and efficiency-ensuring executive action is squared. At state level, the primary plank in this mission to control and democratise an anti-democratic executive has been a principle of 'non-dele-gation' partnered by a 'transmission' model of administration that determines, first, that the executive should be conceived of as the handmaiden rather than the principal of the democratic (legislative) process, and seeks, secondly, to entrench handmaiden executive status through the strict delineation of executive competences and the policing of that delineation through the rule of law.[2] At Eu-

---

[*] Birkbeck College, University of London.
[1] With more extensive powers of policy-making of its own.
[2] See only, R. B. Stewart, 'Administrative Law in the Twenty-First Century', 78 *New York University Law Review* (2003) p. 437.

*D. Curtin, A.E. Kellermann and S. Blockmans, eds., The EU Constitution: The Best Way Forward?*
© 2005, T.M.C. Asser Instituut, The Hague.

ropean level, however, this widely accepted transmission-belt model of executive action and control has always been and still remains a subject of fierce controversy.[3]

The primary distorting factor in any attempt to transfer transmission-belt models of administration to EU level must be identified as a trend in 'governance' that has witnessed the transfer of competences, including executive and regulatory competences that were once held to be integral to the national polity or the nation state, to international organizations and bodies whose own democratic nature, or structure of democratic control, remains experimental or highly contested. Whilst the European Union has undertaken evermore the tasks once reserved to its Member States, it has nevertheless struggled to reproduce the constitutional symmetries of the state. This process has inevitably raised questions about the control of executive acts at post-national level. First, as the EU has long seemed to privilege non-majoritarian governance mechanisms and regulatory institutions (such as agencies and comitology established within the Commission's institutional umbrella) above more democratically legitimated governing forms (acts in Council); and secondly, since the *sui generis* governing and legal structure of the Union has made the application of the traditional transmission-belt model of administration to Union acts incongruous, if not impossible – it is thus, for example, very difficult to identify a single majoritarian will within the European Union.

Within this context, the efforts of the Constitutional Treaty to simplify the governing structures of the Union might and must also be investigated for their impact upon the control of executive acts within Europe. The question of whether this new Treaty will improve the control of executive acts within the European polity nonetheless remains a vexed one. Concentrating analysis upon the endeavour to establish a clear hierarchy of norms within the Union in Articles I-33 to I-39 TCE, and more particularly the distinction made between executive and non-executive acts, it is apparent that the contested tensions within the EU polity will survive any passage into force of the EU Constitution and will continue to raise doubts about the simple application of a traditional transmission-belt model of administration to the EU. Specifically, for all of the EU Constitution's declared commitment to representative (legislative) democracy (Art. I-46 TCE) and for all of its efforts strictly to strengthen European notions of a separation of powers, and thus to delineate and control delegation to non-majoritarian institutions (Art. I-36 TCE), the apparently streamlined vision of administration presented by the Convention and IGC still contrasts with the Commission's broader commitment, expressed in its White Paper on Governance,[4] to the maintenance of 'good' governance through its widespread reliance

---

[3] See, M. Everson, 'Administering Europe', 36 *Journal of Common Market Studies* (1998) pp. 195-216.

[4] See only, Commission of the European Communities, 'European Governance. A White Paper', COM (2001) 428 final.

on regulatory mechanisms and institutions such as comitology and agencies that are themselves governed not by a transmission logic, but by the triadic principles of 'efficiency, effectiveness and economy'.[5]

In this atmosphere of a contested and complex European polity, it is the contention of this paper that we can no longer, as lawyers, restrict our efforts to control the executive acts of the EU through any unthinking reflex reliance upon a traditional paradigm of transmission administration. Instead, and in the light of continuing doubts about the nature of the EU polity, European law would be well advised to establish its own more procedural mechanisms of executive control. Strictly delineated principles of non-delegation, together with their partner mechanism of a strictly policed rule of law, would no longer seem to be the appropriate legal mechanisms to secure the transparency, accountability and effectiveness of EU executive acts. Instead, we should begin to sketch out a framework of legal control over executive and regulatory acts within the Union, which is broad enough to ensure that the will of the European polity be done, even where European institutions of non-majoritarian governance are engaged in more than a simple transposition of a legislative will.

## 2.    EUROPE'S CONTESTED PUBLIC 'INTERESTS'

In a simple restatement of the elements of the transmission-belt model of administration, it is readily apparent that such a model derives from a conception of the general public interest that deems the legislative will of a polity to be paramount and that seeks to protect that will from any interference or subversion by its executive 'servants'. The establishment of a strict separation of powers between legislative and executive arms of government, the establishment of a non-delegation principle and the dedication of administrative courts to ensuring that the administration neither steps outside its legislatively delineated sphere of operation (notions of *ultra vires*) nor encroaches upon individual rights, confirms the liberal state's commitment to *polity facilitation*. Not only shall the common will of a polity be done, even if executed by a potentially disruptive administration, but also the core of that polity will always be protected, at least to the degree that its individual rights of expression are also subject to legal protection within the rule of law.

Within the process of European integration, however, this model has been placed under enormous strain. For all the efforts of the European Court of Justice, with its *Meroni* doctrine,[6] to establish a strict principle of non-delegation

---

[5] In other words, the 'Three E's' identified by Harlow, see C. Harlow, *Accountability in the European Union* (Oxford, Hart Publishing 2002). The three 'E's' are designed to serve the need to secure the functional legitimacy of EU institutions. In other words, they relate to 'output' legitimacy within the evolutionary EU.

[6] ECJ, *Meroni* v. *High Authority* [1957-8] *ECR* 157, establishing a principle of non-delega-

within the EU, the simple functional imperatives of European integration have seen the wide-scale delegation of powers from the Council, initially to the Commission, and subsequently to its myriad of committees and agencies, established on an *ad hoc* basis and without a firm basis within the European Treaties. At the same time, for all the efforts of both the European Court of Justice and its Court of First Instance to expand the rights of private standing of individual Europeans, the rule of law policing mechanism remains somewhat weak at EU level.[7] On this score, then, various of the efforts of the Constitutional Treaty might, at a first reading, be viewed as an attempt to strengthen an existing, though institutionally weak, EU interest in polity facilitation. Nevertheless, such initial impressions must also be balanced, both against contradictory visions found within that Treaty and against strong indications within existing executive and regulatory authorities within the Union, more particularly the Commission's agencies, that the guiding EU public interest is somewhat more complex than a simple legal dedication to the ensuring of the paramount nature of the legislative will of Europeans.

## 2.1    Transmission confirmed?

The clearest indication of a desire within Europe to establish more conventional notions of democratic primacy and a transmission-belt model of executive action comes in the distinction made in Article I-33 TCE between 'legislative' (European Laws and European Framework Laws) and 'non-legislative acts' (Decisions and Regulations), as well as the efforts found in Article I-36(1) TCE to establish a definitive principle of non-delegation within the EU:

> '1. European laws and framework laws may delegate to the Commission the power to adopt delegated European regulations to supplement or amend certain non-essential elements of the law or framework law.
>
> The objectives, content, scope and duration of the delegation of power shall be explicitly defined in the European laws and framework laws. *The essential elements of an area shall be reserved for the European law or framework law and accordingly shall not be the subject of a delegation of power.*' (emphasis added).

Combined with the potential powers of the Council and Parliament to revoke any delegation of powers (Art. I-36(2)(a) TCE), Articles I-33 to I-39 TCE thus not only appear to establish the Union's very own and very explicit 'hierarchy of norms', but also intimate an endeavour to clarify a separation of powers between

---

tion on the basis of a notion of a balance of powers within the EU that restricts European institutions to acting within their own institutional powers.

    [7] See only, A. Ward, 'The Draft EU Constitution and Private Party Access to Judicial Review of EU Measures', in T. Tridimas and P. Nebbia, eds., *European Law for the Twenty-First Century* (Oxford, Hart Publishing 2005).

legislative and executive branches within the Union. At the same time, these provisions seem to direct the EU towards a traditional transmission-belt model of administration.

Explaining this point in some more depth, it thus appears that the Union's traditional commitment to a 'balance of powers' founded on the notion that no Community institution should encroach upon the powers of any other institution,[8] is now to be complemented by a principle of the separation of powers, which, in the spirit of polity facilitation, gives explicit primacy to legislative-type activities within the Union (the passing of legislative acts by Parliament and Council) over the executive-type activities (the exercise of delegated powers) of the Commission and at the same time subjects such activities to a potential legislative recall (Art. I-36(2)(a) TCE). The whiff of transmission and the apparent relegation of the Commission and its administrative satellites to the status of a handmaiden of the European polity is likewise confirmed by the EU Constitution's commitment in Article I-46 TCE to 'representative democracy', a notion which, with all its connotation of an assembly of European representatives giving voice to the common legislative will of Europeans, would seem at last to lay the grounds for the firm majoritarian basis upon which an EU transmission-belt model of control over non-majoritarian executive bodies might be founded.

Nevertheless, even within the Constitutional Treaty, there also exist various indicators suggesting that any celebration of the establishment of a transmission-belt model of administration at EU level would be premature. Thus, for example, individual standing before European Courts, for all of the admission of a catalogue of fundamental rights in Section II of the EU Constitution, remains weak, especially in relation to executive acts that have an impact far beyond their addressees (Art. III-365 TCE).[9] More important than this apparent limitation on the policing powers of the European judicial system, however, is the equal commitment in Article I-47 TCE to notions of 'participatory democracy' and the clear failure of the EU Constitution explicitly to bring those more nebulous of EU executive, or indeed regulatory, bodies such as agencies and committees, within the Union's nascent hierarchy of norms and scheme of transmission administration.

In short, it would thus appear that the constitutional primacy of a single European legislative 'will' within the Constitutional Treaty remains in doubt. 'Participatory Democracy' is a mechanism that has long been deployed within the contested European polity to give a remedial sense of legitimising democratic input to executive institutions that seem to have challenged the Union's existing and somewhat unclear scheme of legitimacy (or, the legitimacy derived from the 'masters of the treaties'). Thus, the Commission has often made recourse to the

---

[8] A balance of powers that is particularly important in relation to the maintenance of equity between Community and nation interests. See, C. Joerges, 'The Law's Problems with the Governance of the European Market', in C. Joerges and R. Dehousse, eds., *Good Governance in Europe's 'Integrated' Market* (Oxford, Oxford University Press 2002) pp. 3-34.

[9] See *supra* n. 7.

views of interest groups and activists for the purpose of the subsidiary but directly democratic legitimation of agencies and committees within its scheme of governing, where those agencies and committees would seem to be exercising functions far in excess of those foreseen by the European Treaties. Seen in this light, the historic reliance of the Union upon participatory democracy and, more pertinently, its reappearance within a Constitutional Treaty would seem to indicate that Europe's proposed public interest is far more complex than its hierarchy of norms would initially suggest.

Equally, however, the continuing failure of proposed primary European law explicitly to draw the major motors of European executive and regulatory action (agencies and committees) within the hierarchy of norms and its concomitant return to more nebulous notions such as 'transparency' (Art. I-50 TCE), 'openness', 'efficiency' and 'independence' (Art. III-398 TCE) in the matter of the legitimation of the activities of such bodies, also intimates that something is rotten in the hierarchy of European norms. Surprisingly, the Constitutional Treaty does not contain a legitimating basis for, or indeed an explicit description of the legitimate character and structure of the agencies and committees that the Commission has historically deployed to meet the functional need for administration within Europe and, more particularly, within the integrated European market. Instead, such committees and agencies appear to remain *ad hoc* creatures of regulatory need whose forays into executive action can only be legislatively controlled through indirect and *ex ante* Council and Parliamentary oversight of powers that have been delegated to the Commission. Equally, where the Treaty does mention such bodies, they are not directly linked with the non-delegation principle encapsulated within Article I-37 TCE, and instead the old style schemes of 'efficiency' and 'transparency' step up to continue their role in furnishing some form of direct oversight over such bodies as a European Ombudsman (Art. I-149 TCE), as well as the Court of Justice (Art. III-365(1) TCE), are exhorted to review their workings on this basis.

Stated briefly then, a degree of uncertainty still exists as to the exact nature and role of executive action within Europe. Accordingly, such conflict and doubt determines that the European public interest may not reside solely in the pursuit of a single European legislative will safeguarded by a European rule of law dedicated to the policing of transmission.

## 2.2    Transmission rejected?

The search for the appropriate rationale behind a scheme of control over executive acts within the EU must thus perforce lead us more closely to examine the existing normative structure and *modus operandi* of executive structures within the Union. Where the Constitutional Treaty is normatively incoherent or even silent on the exact nature of executive bodies within the EU, it would seem to confirm that the EU polity continues to be a polity in contested flux. As such, it proves illuminating to return to the Commission's competing vision of legitimate governance within Europe established within its White Paper[10] and the forms of European public interest that the executive and regulatory bodies (more particularly, European agencies), which it has established in the wake of that paper, seem now to embody.

Article 37(1) of Regulation 178/2002 of the European Parliament and of the Council,[11] establishing the general principles and requirements of food law and a European Food Safety Authority (EFSA) thus declares confidently that: 'the members of the Management Board, the Advisory Forum and the Executive Director [of the EFSA] shall undertake to act independently *in the public interest.*' The second paragraph of Article 37(1), making it clear that members 'shall make a declaration of (…) interests indicating (...) the absence of any interests which might be considered prejudicial to their independence', indicates that this provision was included within the Regulation in an effort to reproduce, at European level, the traditional ethos of civil service and administrative impartiality historically present at national level. Nonetheless, the partnership within this article of notions of 'independence' and 'service to a public interest' might also be argued to be indicative of the normative and factual peculiarities that mark a nascent European 'regulatory' executive; peculiarities that become evermore apparent if the slightly contrasting provisions of Article 37(2), applying to members of the Scientific Committee, are also considered: 'the members of the Scientific Committee and the Scientific Panels [of the EFSA] shall undertake to act independently *of any external influence.*' This provision, shielding scientific experts from any 'undue' influence, and even from the influence of a public interest that might express itself as 'public opinion', immediately confirms the technocratic character of a tier within a European regulatory executive, which owes a duty *only* to the pursuit of 'scientific truth'. By contrast, Article 37(1), applying to the governing bodies of EFSA, and demanding independence (presumably also from the named treaty institutions of the EU) in the service of a public interest, would seem to suggest some form of 'direct' (whether normatively, politically or socially-flavoured) interaction between a further governing tier within an emergent European regulatory executive and a wider European public.

It is not only the tiered nature of the administration within Europe, but rather this apparent 'direct' connection, or establishment of a 'duty' as between the European regulatory executive and a wider European 'polity', that seems to make it distinct from traditional administrative structures to be found at the national level. Executive legitimation in this analysis is not to be mediated through the legislature, but is instead to be located in a direct relationship between the executive and the polity. Certainly, the differentiation in duties owed, either to the public or to scientific truth, could be explained by the differences in the tasks given to Management Boards, Executive Directors, Advisory Councils and Scientific Committees. Thus, as a preamble to the Regulation explains, 'the

---

[10] See *supra* n. 4.
[11] *OJ* (2002) L 31/16.

scientific and technical issues in relation to food and food safety are becoming increasingly important and complex' (preamble (33)). Food law aimed at combating risks to health is accordingly broken down into a technically-refined process of 'interconnected' risk analysis, risk management and risk communication (preamble (17)), wherein: (a) risk analysis is a wholly apolitical task to be assigned to independent scientific committees; (b) risk management may be affected by non-technical issues such as 'societal, economic, traditional, ethical and environmental factors', as well as, 'the feasibility of controls' (preamble (19)) and as such is devolved to 'politicised' Community institutions and national authorities; whilst (c), risk communication, the transparency of which is vital to ensure 'consumer confidence and the confidence of trading partners' within the internal market (preamble (22)), becomes a task for the administering institutions of the EFSA. Nonetheless, and in the light of the preamble's equal recognition that tasks of risk assessment, management and communication are 'interconnected', although the non-scientific management bodies of the EFSA cannot be described as possessing political powers to intervene in regulation for, say, ethical or social reasons, they do have a vital agenda-setting role within food law, both through their structuring and oversight of independent scientific experts and through their ability to control the dissemination of information on risks.

Accordingly, it appears appropriate for the Regulation to establish firmly that such a potentially agenda-setting role must be exercised in accordance with the public interest. However, by the same token, the recognition of the interconnected, possibly even indivisible, nature of risk analysis, management and communication, not only raises the character of EFSA managing bodies above the status of simple technocrats, but also undoubtedly heralds a final departure from the notion that legitimate government entails the *ex priori* setting of a political agenda, the transmission of a political will to a neutral executive, and the final *ex ante* execution of a political mandate by the administration.[12]

In other words, constant monitoring of scientific risks, post-market control and the brief of the EFSA to supply independent scientific information on demand to the institutions of the Community and the authorities of the Member States, entail a recognition that, beyond general commitments to the maintenance of a 'high level of protection for health and safety', food law, and its administration, is not a *proactive* matter of the formulation of detailed policy and its application within the market. Instead, food law and food policy is a *reactive* matter of responding to the sometimes foreseeable and sometimes unforeseeable risks that may arise within modern production processes. Seen in this light, the institutionalisation of a monitoring authority as an agency embodies a simple practical acceptance that executive functions are not merely about implementation, but are also, however indirectly, about the day-to-day formulation of policy

---

[12] Stewart, see *supra* n. 2.

and regulation in the light of prevailing market conditions. Structuring of research and future research demands, shaping of the modes of the communication of risks, as well as the stimulation of public discussion on particular issues; all can contribute to the manner in which we as a polity respond to individual issues arising in food markets, and all can consequently have a major impact on everyday policy-making. Accordingly, Article 37(1), or what may initially be regarded as a simple measure to secure the impartiality of the administration, may also be argued to be a normative guarantee, given to the European polity as a result of a fundamental upheaval in the manner in which administrations are conceived of, and as a consequence of the recognition that a clear distinction can no longer be made between legislative and executive governance functions.

## 2.3    European Public Interests in 'Polity Restraint' versus 'Polity Facilitation'?

The existing and readily apparent challenge to the transmission-belt model of administration and the direct dedication of the EFSA to the independent service of the European public interest, however, also raises further fundamental questions about the place of executive and regulatory European agencies within European governance. The concept of 'public interest' is thus far from being a neutral normative term. Rather, lying at the core of the liberal constitutional settlement, the notion of public interest may be understood as an expression of the differentiated underlying rationales of entire schemes of governance, as well as a reflection of the substantive or institutional aims to which such governance schemes are dedicated.

In its simplest form, an appeal to the public interest may thus embody no more and no less than the substantive conviction that the will of the polity, democratically expressed, should be executed without any deviation or room for executive manoeuvre.[13] Alternatively, the public interest may also lie in measures designed to 'restrain' the powers of the polity, whether for liberal reasons of the protection of individual autonomy and minority rights,[14] or for more functional reasons, such as the constituting and protection of an autonomous and functioning market sphere.[15] Finally, in a more complex institutional and procedural reading, the public interest can also be located within the maintenance of the principles and norms which seemingly underpin the liberal constitution; principles and norms, such as deliberation, solidarity and universality.[16] What then is

---

[13] Harlow, see *supra* n. 5.

[14] S. Holmes, *Passions and Constraints* (Chicago, University of Chicago Press 1995).

[15] E.-J. Mestmäcker, 'On the Legitimacy of European Law', 58 *Rabels Zeitschrift für ausländisches und internationales Privatrecht* (1994) p. 615.

[16] J. Habermas, 'Der Demokratische Rechtsstaat – eine paradoxe Verbindung widersprüchlicher Prinzipien', in *idem, Zeit der Übergänge* (Frankfurt am Main, Suhrkamp 2001) pp. 133-154.

the public interest which the EFSA and a European executive in general[17] are required 'independently' to serve?

At one level, the particular public interests which individual agencies are required to serve are easily identified within founding regulations. The European Environmental Agency (EEA), for example, is dedicated to the restraint of a European polity with regard to ensuring that Community legislation does not unnecessarily impact upon the maintenance of an environmental quality, which has been given quasi-constitutional status within the European Treaties. The Agency is thus required to furnish Community institutions and the Member States with:

> '[O]bjective and comparable information at European level enabling them to take the requisite measures to protect the environment, to assess the results of such measures and to ensure that the public is properly informed about the state of the environment.'[18]

The apolitical provision of information, it is thus hoped will have a restraining effect on general legislative programmes, ensuring that such programmes are also governed by the polity's normative commitment to the preservation of the environment. By the same token, the public interest to which EFSA would seem to be dedicated entails further restraints on a European polity, particularly with regard to the functioning of the internal market:[19]

> 'The free movement of safe and wholesome food is an essential aspect of the internal market and contributes significantly to the health and well-being of citizens and to their social and economic interests.' (preamble (1)).

Further,

> 'There are important differences in relation to concepts, principles and procedures between the food laws of the member states. Where member states adopt measures governing food, these differences create unequal conditions of competition, and may thereby directly affect the functioning of the internal market.' (preamble (4)).

Certainly, the quality of food and the health and welfare of individual citizens of the EU are aims in themselves within the overall canon of European legislation. Nonetheless, the pursuit of health and welfare is also a matter of the restraint of fragments of the European polity (Member State authorities) which might inadvertently do damage to the smooth functioning of the market through their uncoordinated pursuit of welfare aims. Likewise, a diverse consumer interest, to the

---

[17] Interestingly enough, direct reference to service to a public interest is a new feature within European agency design.

[18] Council Regulation No. 1219/90 on the establishment of the European Environment Agency and the European Environment Information and Observation Network (*OJ* (1990) L 120/1) Art. 2.

[19] See *supra* n. 11.

protection of which EFSA is also dedicated, is inexorably linked to the smooth functioning of the internal market: 'it is necessary to ensure that consumer *confidence* and the confidence of trading partners is secured through the open and transparent development of food law' (preamble (22)). The maintenance of consumer confidence *in* the autonomous working of the market, rather than the securing of political sovereignty *over* the market, would seem to be the aim of the institutionalisation of the oversight of EU food law within a semi-autonomous agency.

All this would appear to support a characterisation of European agencies as the institutional expression of the desire of the European polity to limit its political sovereignty with regard to particular goals and aims that have been given a higher normative status and recognition; to wit, the smooth and autonomous functioning of the internal market and the protection of the European environment. Seen in this light, a 'European public interest' cannot simply be found within the forms of *polity facilitation* suggested by the Constitutional Treaty, or within any simple notion of transmission administration within Europe. Instead, a European public interest might *also* be thought to lie in the concept of *polity restraint*; polity restraint with regard to individual rights (the right to a good environment or, indeed, the right to economic autonomy), or restraint with regard to particular functional needs (the need to ensure the smooth functioning of the internal market).

3.  PUBLIC INTEREST(S), THE POLITICAL ADMINISTRATION AND THE NEW PUBLIC LAW

Clearly, to the extent that the Constitutional Treaty both appears to confirm a public interest in polity facilitation, and leaves much room for the Commission to pursue its historical administrative commitment polity to polity restraint, Europe remains a contested polity in which executive action may be controlled either through a transmission-belt model or through more flexible means, such as ensuring the transparency and efficiency of regulatory authorities. In a final analysis, however, the conflict between the EU's public interests and uncertainty about the appropriate nature of legal control over administrative acts is nothing new.[20] Rather, at a national level, a transmission-belt model has always also masked conflicts between notions of democratic primacy within the national polity and the nation state's parallel commitment to polity restraint, more specifically in areas such as the pursuit of a rational economic policy, that can legitimately and sensibly be protected from often exhibited tendencies towards political expediency – independent central banks should thus be remembered, with all their

---

[20] See, M. Everson, 'Review Article: Accountability and Law in Europe: Towards a New Public Legal Order?', 67 *Modern Law Review* (2004) pp. 124-138.

rejection of democratic control, are an invention, not of the EU, but of nation states, such as the Federal Republic of Germany. The importance of controversy within a European public interest is thus not a *new* phenomenon, it is rather a readily apparent phenomenon. Nation states have always sought to delineate areas of executive action: in some there is a greater degree of protection for the executive from political actors; in others, there is a greater degree of direct public involvement in delegated decision-making – in many such areas, transmission is thus practically if not normatively obsolete. The only difference within an EU context is the fact that the Constitutional Treaty does not hide behind simple notions of transmission to disguise this fragmentation in a public interest, but instead, in all its contested nature, makes it clear that control of executive acts cannot always be appropriately achieved through simple principles of non-delegation and recourse to the policing functions of the rule of law.

Seen in this light, however, the European Union's partial withdrawal from the model of transmission-belt administration and its final admission of the enduring fragmentation of public interests and polities possesses serious consequences of its own:

–   An increased commitment to polity restraint is not immediately congruent with an acceptance of the apolitical primacy of a 'regulatory state' or 'fourth branch of government'.[21] Rather, where the ongoing and conditional character of the discourse on the appropriate nature of the public interest to be pursued is recognised, regulatory authorities located outside traditional institutional frameworks of politics are placed under a far greater onus, *politically*, to justify their operations *beyond* accepted standards of democratic legitimacy. In short, and in recognition of fragmented polities and public interests, the resurrection of the largely discredited term, *Politische Verwaltung*, may be justified. Not since it reproduces the welfarist aim to subordinate economic organisation to material standards of welfare. But since a modern *political administration* must continually justify and found its pursuit of, say, economic rationality or environmental integrity, in the face of equally valid 'public interest' claims (especially within schemes of 'good governance') for corrective (democratically legitimated) political action.

–   Where the executive is no longer committed to polity facilitation and is further required to continue, *politically*, to justify its actions outside a conventional non-delegation method of legal control, the law itself must take care, not only to evolve its own novel modes of review, but also to

---

[21] In other words, a regulatory executive that has very widespread powers of policy-making and is given a large degree of independence of protection from the political process. Such protection is justified by the nature of tasks which such authorities undertake. See, G. Majone, 'The European Community, an Independent Fourth Branch of Government?', in G. Brüggermeier, ed., *Verfassungen für ein ziviles Europa* (Baden-Baden, Nomos 1994) pp. 23-44.

find some form of constitutional legitimation for that oversight. In brief, a new *public law* charged with the task of evolving modes of oversight over executive and regulatory acts within a contested polity cannot simply rely on the (contradictory) provisions of the Constitutional Treaty to give such measures concrete legitimacy. Instead, where the constitutional polity remains contested, the law must take care to develop politically neutral (procedural) modes of oversight that are flexible enough to ensure constant legitimacy within a constantly shifting constellation of executive and regulatory action.

## 4. 'PUBLIC LAW' OVERSIGHT OF THE EU'S 'POLITICAL ADMINISTRATION'?

Finally then, the question must be answered: how best might we control this contested EU administration? How best might we construct a scheme of law to control a variety of executive acts within Europe, each perhaps owing to different and sometimes conflicting notions of the correct public interest that Europe must pursue? Clearly, under such conditions of contingent uncertainty, the answer to this question will not easily be found. However, at the outset, the question can be broken down into two subsidiary parts, the first concerning issues of the institutional design of executive institutions within the EU, and the second touching upon the scheme of judicial oversight applied to such institutions and their acts. Equally, even though the question of the control over executive acts within a contested polity might pose unprecedented problems to law in general, European Courts and European law have long been concerned with such issues. In short then, existing European jurisprudence has already begun to develop those mechanisms that might form the core of a novel European approach to the control of executive acts through procedural law.

### 4.1 Political Administration

#### 4.1.1 *Independence?*

As noted, the Constitutional Treaty calls upon the various bodies of EU administration, including European agencies, to act 'independently' in pursuit of their tasks (Art. III-398 TCE). Equally, however, existing jurisprudence on the balance of powers under the *Meroni* doctrine,[22] plus a restated principle of non-delegation within the Constitutional Treaty (Art. I-36 TCE), also militate against full independence within a European executive. As a consequence, both Member States and Parliament retain much oversight over and presence within existing bodies of EU administration, more particularly, within the management boards of EU agencies.

---

[22] See *supra* n. 6.

Now, where the talk is of a 'political' administration, a 'close' relationship between political actors and executive or regulatory authorities is not necessarily a de-legitimising factor and may even be a vital aid in the maintenance of a discourse dedicated to constant review of the appropriate pursuit of variable public interests. Nonetheless, given the potential *raison d'être* of executive authorities and, more particularly, the fourth branch of government as guardians of a public interest in polity restraint (in pursuit either of economic rationality, or, indeed, at another level, of environmental integrity), the lack of formal institutional guarantees for regulatory autonomy appears incongruous. By this same token, it is possible to conceive of the 'contingent' European public interest in terms that support greater regulatory autonomy for the executive since the regulation it promulgates is recognised as being worthy of protection from potentially disruptive social and political interests. In this regard then, current trends, such as the increased degree of practical independence afforded the European Food Standards Agency[23] may well be justified.

### 4.1.2 Political 'Accountability'

Independence for an EU executive within a contested European polity can nonetheless never be construed as being commensurate with a lack of political accountability. Instead, and within the context of intense debates on 'good' European governance,[24] a 'political' administration must maintain its links with a social and political sphere within which valid demands for social justice and political action are formulated. In practice, such a stipulation surely extends far beyond a demand that accountability be secured through the application of the tried and trusted mechanism of control over a fourth branch of government established, for example, within the US regulatory sphere (for example, mechanisms such as parliamentary review of agency budgets). Rather, where final acceptance is made of the conditional nature of public interests, this issue is no longer a simple one of whether an independent executive is 'efficiently and effectively' performing its allotted role. Instead, it also entails the continuing political justification for such roles.

This is perhaps the most demanding of challenges facing a European executive. At its core, the challenge would thus appear to be wholly counter-intuitive: if independent executive action is in large part justified by its *apolitical* pursuit of economic rationality or environmental integrity, how can a political character be legitimately reintroduced to such action? Importantly, this is not a matter for the *authoritative* involvement of politically-legitimated actors from Council or Parliament within, say, agency operations; such involvement can only reduce the

---

[23] To wit, a lesser role for Member States within its management board.

[24] See *supra* n. 4: whilst the Commission is cognizant that its *ad hoc* institutions of market management upset traditional schemes of executive control, it is nevertheless concerned to identify some form of legitimacy for those institutions.

efficiency and effectiveness of executive acts and fatally conflate and obscure the pursuit of conflicting public interests. Instead, the issue is far more one of establishing systems whereby the breadth of executive mandates may constantly be reviewed, and unexpected issues of social regulation be tackled with an eye to continual readjustments in public interests and still valid demands for social and political justice.

The reintroduction of politics into an autonomous apolitical sphere of economic regulation is accordingly a multi-level problem, involving the creation of political and social links between a fragmented and contested polity and the 'political' administration; links that neither politically compromise executive acts, nor artificially reestablish the myth of a single, normatively determinative, public interest. At its core, the issue is one of the redefinition of European politics to ensure that whilst axiomatic constructions of social 'solidarity' (a potential cloak for the pursuit of particularist political interest) are absent from the executive sphere, a measure of 'informed' political contention between conflicting public interests is a feature of executive decision-making:

- *Limited governance*: at one level the Constitutional Treaty provides a vibrant new mechanism to aid in maintaining the political accountability of an apolitical EU executive. Thus, Article I-36(2)(a) TCE offers Parliament and Council an unprecedented opportunity to monitor the acts of an apolitical executive and to ensure that it never strays too far into social and political activities by virtue of their new power to recall delegated powers. Nonetheless, the anchoring of the EU executive within a political environment might also be achieved through renewed emphasis upon an ancient principle of 'limited government'. Alternatively, where the current and future design of a European executive might potentially be led by a preoccupation with the identification of 'narrow' regulatory mandates (Art. I-36(1) TCE), an obsession potentially undermining efficient and effective regulation,[25] the issue should instead be redefined as one of the establishment of the normative conditions for the exercise of governance restraint within *appropriate* regulatory competences. Where possible and appropriate, a European executive should possess a pre-emptive regulatory competence. Nonetheless, pre-emption should likewise be governed by *wise* self-restraint on the part of that executive; by a secession of decision-making to social and political centres of power and influence where this seems to be more appropriate (for example, where issues of seemingly technical regulation are deemed to entail redistributive competences in the manner, say, of essential facilities doctrines).

---

[25] Recall only the complexities inherent within the regulation of food, and the subsequently wide powers delegated to the EFSA in the matter of the definition of the problem of health and safety within the EU.

- *'Deliberative' decision-making*: following on from this, however, a further question arises as to the possible character of the governing principles which might effectively regulate discourse between social, political
  and economic values, where each value is seen as being equally valid.
  Clearly, within this construction, the search is on for a mode of regulating
  interaction within a contested polity, within which the governing normative basis for action is no longer always the primacy of an imputed (common) legislative will, but rather the context-specific 'rationality' of any
  form of decision-making. Which values should prevail, when and why?

In this regard then, normatively-founded politics (democracy) can and have been
redefined as a deliberative process,[26] whereby the functional act of effective
problem-solving becomes the leading criterion for decision-making, whilst parties to the decision are subject to a duty to justify their arguments that is founded
in a proven eschewal of all personal (non-rational) interests. Within a context of
'arguing' rather than 'bargaining', a political administration might thus identify
the appropriate basis for regulatory self-restraint; the context-specific primacy of
competing public interests. In short, 'effective problem-solving' is a criterion
that matches the Commission's desire to ensure the factual legitimacy of a European executive through the three 'E's' of efficiency, effectiveness and economy,[27] whilst deliberation augments the normative legitimacy functions of
political 'accountability' and 'transparency', especially as regards the adequate
representation of all civil society interests and 'participatory democracy' (see below).

## 4.2    Legal Oversight

Finally, some thought should also be given to the role that European law does or
could play in the oversight of a European political administration.

### 4.2.1   *Public Law*

A primary point to remember, here, however, is the fact that, with the primacy of
a transmission-belt model of executive control in doubt, courts of review find
themselves in the uncomfortable position of no longer being able to review executive decisions with simple recourse to tried and trusted mechanisms of oversight, such as a principle of delegation or notions of *ultra vires*. In other words, a
new European public law must find novel mechanisms and values to ensure the
accountability and transparency of a European executive (Art. I-50 TCE).

---

[26] O. Cohen and C.F. Sabel, 'Directly-Deliberative Polyarchy: An Institutional Ideal for Europe?',
3 *European Law Journal* (1997).
[27] See *supra* n. 5.

### 4.2.2 A 'Modern' Proceduralism

Now, in this regard, the interesting point for this paper is not the manner in which such values might be evolved with regard to any future European 'political' administration, but is instead, the degree to which a *sui generis* European law has already evolved its own form and mode of procedural review that is supportive of political and executive deliberation, rather than merely reflective of outdated adherence to simple schemes of executive oversight that have little relevance within the contested European polity.

Certainly, European law does display weaknesses in relation to the oversight (and design) of the European executive. Most particularly, the *Meroni* doctrine seems to continue to stand in the path of truly effective delegation, whilst restricted bases for judicial review under Article 230 (Consolidated Treaty) seem currently to foreclose one of the most important bases for legal oversight over the political administration. Nonetheless, the current genius of European law lies in the fact that, in view of the lack of conventional Constitution settlement, it has never be able simply to refer to outdated and inappropriate legal doctrines within its judgments, but has instead always been required to respond to the political complexities of the Union with its own evolving and functionally appropriate mechanisms and doctrines of control. Most importantly, European law has already begun to evolve a series of procedural doctrines that seem to support the ongoing process of adjustment between equally valid public interests in policy facilitation and restraint through political deliberation:

–   *Proportionality*: by far the most important doctrine in this respect, that derives from a need to maintain judicial independence while facilitating societal interaction and decision-making, is that of proportionality. The demand that all decision-making be fully justified both in relation to its necessity and with regard to the appropriate means used to solve problems currently plays a crucial role in setting a workable balance between the national and European jurisdictions. In the future, a mechanism that calls on all bodies to review the grounds for their decision-making within an independent forum, could surely also play a primary role in policing 'limited government', or decisions on how, when and where to use or restrict the pre-emptive regulatory powers of the political administration.

–   *State of the art decision-making*: a further deliberation-ensuring doctrine, informed by ancient legal values of *ultra vires* decision-making, has been the insistence of the European Court of Justice upon the quality of the information used to reach executive and regulatory decisions. Again, where all decisions are to be reviewed in the light of independent procedural criteria on the character of the information that feeds those decisions, the danger that bargaining replaces arguing as personal interests are cloaked as values is lessened.

- *Relevant interests*: importantly, the ECJ has also recently sought to develop subtle means to maintain ancient legal notions of 'equity' within a modern European legal system.[28] In particular, the notion of equity dictates that no decision should be taken in a manner that leaves any parties affected by that decision without a means to register their views or interests. Seen in this light, such a line of European law could both allow for the extension of individual standing under Article 230 (and in the future under Art. III-365(4) TCE) and go some way to answering one of the primary conundrums that decision-making within a contested polity faces; that is, the identification of instruments that compensate for consequent restrictions in political representation.

In other words, one of the most immutable barriers to increased delegation of powers must be the claim that delegation would leave policy and decision-making open to domination by a minority of public interests. In this regard, for example, the presence of social interests within the management or advisory boards of agencies is to be prized. Nonetheless, any claim that these interests represent an adequate cross-section of civil society is surely illusory. However, where, and to the degree that, the law of review is tailored to ensure that all relevant interests might participate in decision-making, either through a widened basis for *locus standi* or through the 'deliberative' stipulation that all relevant interests are reviewed during decision-making, the lack of direct representation within the contested polity presents a lesser problem. Instead, the focus of legitimation shifts to the maintenance of 'participatory democracy' within the EU (Art. I-47 TCE). Appropriate 'participation' can thus be assured either at the stage of the proper executive consideration of the views of 'participants' who may not even be present during the decision-making process, or within an *ex ante* judicial review procedure where concrete voice might be given to initially absent participants to demand renewed deliberation of their regulatory concerns.

## 5.  CONCLUSION

In final summary then, still torn, even following an extensive process of attempted constitutionalisation, between competing visions of the legitimate nature of the EU polity, the European Union and its Constitutional Treaty continues to challenge our traditional perceptions, not only of the control of executive action, but also of the very character and function of the executive. To a degree, at least, the EU would appear to be seeking a traditional model of administration, based on a separation of powers between the legislative and executive and a strict nondelegation principle. At the same time, however, the Union is also still largely

---

[28] See, in particular, the Social Insurance Cases, above all *Albany*, with, *Drijvende, Bokken* and *Bretjens*, Joined Cases C-115/97, C-116/97, C-117/97, and C-219/97 [1999] *ECR* I-6025 and [1999] *ECR* I-6121.

dependent on its own existing mechanisms and institutions of administration; mechanisms and institutions that appear to enjoy a far greater degree of autonomy than any traditional transmission-belt model of administration might admit. Although the Constitutional Treaty does not specifically approve of such institutions and their operations, it nevertheless does not preclude their continuing existence in their current form and, indeed, in approving alternative modes of institutional legitimation, such as 'transparency', 'independence' and 'participatory democracy', which appears to contain at least a tacit acceptance of the need within notions of 'good' governance to maintain a more fluid attitude towards institutions that can meet the flexible functional demands of the European Union for efficient, effective and economic regulation.

At one level, such a degree of uncertainty within the Constitutional Treaty can be regretted. At yet another level, however, it should also be welcomed as a manifestation of a modern form of governance that is more accepting of the imperative need to make distinctions between the various and varied purposes pursued by a modern executive, and indeed for the normative case for either restricting an executive mandate or curbing a legislative will, if and when the circumstances justify it. In this regard then, mechanisms of control over a European executive must also be flexible. European law has however already begun to cater for such needs. Old mechanisms such as a non-delegation principle and a policing-oriented rule of law are not always appropriate control instruments within the EU setting. Instead, more flexible and refined modern methods of procedural control over executive action should and have been developed within the European forum.

# OPERATIONAL COLLABORATION ON JUSTICE, SECURITY AND POLICING IN THE CONSTITUTIONAL FRAMEWORK

## Steve Peers*

## 1. INTRODUCTION

Is the Constitutional Treaty the best way forward as regards operational cooperation on internal security? The starting point for analysis of this subject is the need to ensure accountability over the operations of police or other law-enforcement services, in the form of effective judicial, parliamentary or other supervision and control, whether in the national or international context. Within the EU framework, the current level of accountability of such operations is clearly insufficient: this can be termed the accountability deficit. As we will see, the Constitutional Treaty would improve the current situation in some respects, but there would remain important limitations and uncertainties regarding the effectiveness of the provisions concerning accountability. Furthermore, the new Treaty would create certain new risks of insufficient accountability of operational cooperation.

## 2. BACKGROUND: EU INTERNAL SECURITY OPERATIONAL COLLABORATION

Currently the EU has two frameworks for operational collaboration on internal security: a framework for cooperation between national authorities and a framework for cooperation within EU-level agencies and entities. The framework for national operational cooperation is contained in the Schengen *acquis*,[1] supplemented by EU measures, which addresses issues such as hot pursuit, surveillance, exchange of information and undercover operations. At EU level, a police agency (Europol), a prosecutors' agency (Eurojust), a border police agency and meetings of EU police chiefs provide a framework, along with a Framework Decision on joint

---

* Professor University of Essex.
[1] Arts. 39-119 of the 1990 Schengen Convention, *OJ* (2000) L 239.

---

*D. Curtin, A.E. Kellermann and S. Blockmans, eds., The EU Constitution: The Best Way Forward?*
© 2005, T.M.C. Asser Instituut, The Hague.

investigation teams.[2] It is obviously necessary to ensure effective systems for accountability at both levels, although the specific rules could be differentiated.

3.    ACCOUNTABILITY OF CURRENT EU INTERNAL SECURITY
      OPERATIONS

The 'accountability deficit' of EU operational cooperation on internal security results from: limited parliamentary supervision of operational activity; the absence of any regular public reports on operational cooperation within the EU framework; limited parliamentary involvement in the relevant EU legislation; limitations on judicial control by the EU's Court of Justice; the absence of bodies permitting the public to complain about the activities of the EU bodies, or requirements for Member States to establish such bodies to hear complaints against their national agencies which are involved in cross-border activity; the insufficient accountability of Europol's extensive international activities; the unclear extent of control or direction of Europol activities by the Council; and the limited provisions governing data protection.

To take these issues in turn, the first two points are linked because the absence of regular public reporting inhibits both the possibility of public debate concerning the effectiveness and merits of operational cooperation within the EU and the effectiveness of parliamentary supervision of operational activity (whether by the European Parliament or national parliaments). Although Europol and Eurojust are subject to reporting requirements, there has been no regular reporting on police cooperation between national authorities since a prior practice of regular reporting on Schengen police cooperation was discontinued in 1999.[3] As for the reports by Europol and Eurojust, there is insufficient information in each report in order for a parliament to assess the effectiveness and appropriateness of these bodies' activities. A Protocol to the Europol Convention signed in 2003 only marginally increases the role of the EP or national parliaments, despite intensive discussion of the issue.[4] There has been no independent assessment of the operation of these bodies, despite a general belief that Europol is not operating as effectively as the Member States had hoped.[5]

Also, the EU has established a task force of police chiefs, meeting since 1999, but has never established any formal rules concerning the establishment, operation or accountability of this meeting. The opportunity to do so was ignored

---

[2]  The legislation can be accessed at: <http://www.europa.eu.int/comm/justice_home/doc_centre/police/doc_police_intro_en.htm>.

[3]  The last report was for 1998 (Council doc. 8744/99 (2 June 1999)).

[4]  For details, see S. Peers, 'Governance and the Third Pillar: The Accountability of Europol', in D. Curtin and R.A. Wessel, eds., *Good Governance and the European Union: Reflections on Concepts, Institutions and Substance* (Antwerp, Intersentia 2005) pp. 257-259 and 269-273.

[5]  See the Commission Communication on EU policing and customs cooperation, COM (2004) 376 (18 June 2004) p. 19.

when the role of the task force was reviewed in 2004. Instead the Council adopted conclusions conferring even further responsibilities upon the task force.[6]

Next, parliamentary involvement in the relevant EU legislation is limited by the current legal framework for the adoption of measures concerning police co-operation and judicial cooperation. The current legal framework for Europol presently comprises a Convention, amended by means of various Protocols, along with implementing measures adopted by the Council. National parliaments had power over ratification of the Europol Convention and retain power over ratification of subsequent Protocols to amend that Convention, *if* national procedures require parliamentary assent to such measures. But there is no such inherent control over implementing measures adopted by the Council, unless national law exceptionally gives national parliaments a power to control national executives' votes on such measures. In any event, national parliaments have no prior power to become involved in the *negotiation* of Conventions, Protocols or implementing measures, only the potential power to withhold consent after such measures have been negotiated by executives. As for the European Parliament, it must be consulted on all Conventions and Protocols since the entry into force of the Treaty of Amsterdam according to Article 39 EU, and the Europol Convention in conjunction with Article 39 EU requires it to be consulted on most implementing measures.[7] But the consultation is advisory only.

Next, the Europol Convention (with its Protocols) sets limitations on judicial control by the EU's Court of Justice, permitting Member States to opt out of the Court's jurisdiction over dispute settlement and references from national courts and excluding the Court from jurisdiction over the Protocol on privileges and immunities of Europol staff.[8] Furthermore, the latter Protocol initially extended sweeping immunity to Europol officers,[9] although a subsequent Protocol to the Convention will require a waiver of this immunity when Europol officers participate in joint investigation teams.[10] These limitations and exclusions obviously stand in the way of uniform interpretation of the Europol Convention and of effective judicial control of Europol, in particular in cases of abuse of power by Europol officers. As for Eurojust, Member States are able to opt out of the Court's jurisdiction as regards third pillar measures adopted since the Treaty of Amsterdam, and nearly half have done so;[11] this prevents effective judicial control and uniform interpretation of the provisions of the decision establishing Eurojust.

---

[6] See JHA Council press release (19 November 2004).

[7] See Peers *supra* n. 4.

[8] *OJ* (1995) C 316; on the Court of Justice and references from national courts, see *OJ* (1996) C 299.

[9] *OJ* (1997) C 221. For details, see Peers *supra* n. 4, pp. 260-262.

[10] *OJ* (2002) C 312. For details, see Peers *supra* n. 4, pp. 269-273.

[11] See Art. 35 TEU. Twelve of the first fifteen Member States (all except the UK, Ireland and Denmark) have opted in, as has the Czech Republic.

Although the accountability of operations can only be enhanced by the creation of a complaints authority, whether integrated into the judicial system or with a non-judicial remit, there are no such systems applicable to Europol and Eurojust and no requirements or even soft law relating to their establishment and functioning at national level in order to ensure accountability of cross-border national police operations.

Europol has agreed many treaties with non-EU countries and organisations, many of them providing for the exchange of personal data, but there is no effective system of accountability as regards these treaties. Very few have been published in the EU's *Official Journal* and the treaties only became available on Europol's website early in 2005.[12] Eurojust now appears set to follow in Europol's footsteps.[13]

The next problem is the unclear extent of control or direction of Europol activities by the Council. Although the Hague Programme attempts to address this issue, by providing for the Council to establish yearly strategic priorities for Europol,[14] so far these provisions have not been put into practice, as the Council had provided no input into the functioning of Europol as of April 2005.

Finally, the limited provisions governing data protection in EU measures are a lasting concern. The relevant measures provide for extensive scope to refuse access to data on security grounds, and there is no strong single authority with powers to consider complaints by data subjects and order the release, deletion or correction of data.[15]

## 4.    CONSTITUTIONAL TREATY

To what extent would the proposed Constitutional Treaty affect operational police and justice cooperation within the EU? First of all, the 'legal bases' relating to that cooperation would be clarified, along with changes to decision-making (entailing qualified majority voting in the Council and co-decision for the European Parliament) and to the forms of legal act used (using EC legislative measures instead of special third pillar acts).[16] The jurisdiction of the Court of Justice would be extended so that its 'normal' jurisdiction applies to this area, although

---

[12] The treaties with the new Member States have become redundant following all new Member States' ratification of the Europol Convention. The remaining treaties are with Bulgaria, Romania, Norway, Iceland, the USA, Switzerland (not found on the Europol website), Colombia, Russia, Turkey, Eurojust, the EU Central Bank, the European Commission, OLAF, the EU drugs agency, Interpol, the World Customs Organisation, and the UN Office on Drugs and Crime. For more on these treaties, see Peers, *supra* n. 4, pp. 262-269. For the texts, see: <http://www.europol.eu.int/index.asp?page=agreements>.

[13] See Eurojust treaty with Norway (Council doc. 11641/04 (23 July 2004)).

[14] *OJ* (2005) C 53, point 2.3.

[15] For example, see Arts. 102-118 of the 1990 Schengen Convention (*supra* n. 1).

[16] Arts. III-270-277 TCE (*OJ* (2004) C 310/1).

it would still not have jurisdiction over 'the validity and proportionality of operations carried out by the police or other law-enforcement services of a Member State' or the exercise of Member States' responsibilities regarding 'the maintenance of law and order and the safeguarding of internal security'.[17]

Many of the specific concerns identified above would be addressed by the Constitutional Treaty. First of all, there are specific provisions on EP and national parliamentary supervision of Europol's activity and evaluation of Eurojust.[18] However, the details of such measures remain to be adopted, and there is no provision for adopting such rules as regards national cross-border action, or requiring the EU to produce regular public reports on all forms of operational cooperation within the EU framework.

Secondly, as noted already, the European Parliament would have 'co-decision' powers in most areas, with the exception of the creation of a European Public Prosecutor (where it would have the power of assent), measures on operational police cooperation and rules on cross-border activities of police forces.[19] However, the EP would not have co-decision or assent powers over administrative cooperation between national administrations, or national administrations and the Commission. Such measures would be adopted by a qualified majority vote in the Council with mere consultation of EP.[20] If the powers conferred by the 'administrative cooperation' clause were interpreted broadly, this would be an unacceptable approach to democratic scrutiny and control of EU action, in light of the exclusion of both national parliaments and the EP from effective control of the Council. But given the specific legal bases for border control and judicial and police cooperation found in the Constitutional Treaty, the administrative cooperation clause should be interpreted as a narrow *lex specialis* which cannot apply to the adoption of rules on practical operational cooperation.

On the other hand, national parliaments would lose the powers they possess to control ratification of Conventions and Protocols and would be unable to control their Member State's delegations in the Council effectively whenever qualified majority voting applies. They could retain such power, depending on national arrangements, only in the cases where unanimity still applies to Council voting, with the further possibility that Member States' executive might accept a formal or informal role for national parliaments in pulling the 'emergency brake' applicable to the adoption of certain criminal law measures.[21]

Next, most of the concerns about limitations on judicial control by the EU's Court of Justice would be removed, subject to the question of how to interpret the limitation of its jurisdiction set out above (which appears in the present Art. 35(5) TEU). If this limitation is read broadly, the Court's jurisdiction over opera-

---

[17]  Art. III-377 TCE.
[18]  Arts. III-273(2) and 276(2) TCE.
[19]  Arts. III-274, 275(3) and 277 TCE.
[20]  Art. III-263 TCE.
[21]  Arts. III-270(3) and 271(3) TCE.

tional actions will have little practical effect. However, there are strong arguments for a narrow interpretation of this exception.[22]

As for police complaints bodies, the Constitutional Treaty would not require them to be established, so it can only be hoped that the powers of the Union are interpreted and applied to give effect to the need to create such authorities at EU level and ensure their creation at national level.

Next, the insufficient accountability of Europol's extensive international activities and the unclear extent of control or direction of Europol activities by the Council could be addressed when adopting the European law that would govern Europol in future. The Hague Programme calls for the adoption of this legislation by the start of 2008.[23] But there is no guarantee that sufficient safeguards would be put into place.

The provisions currently governing third pillar data protection would be replaced ultimately by the provisions to be adopted pursuant to Article I-51 TCE, which would confer power (by use of the co-decision procedure and QMV) to adopt measures governing data protection within the EU institutions and the Member States, applying to the entire scope of the Constitutional Treaty (therefore, to all three of the current pillars). But a declaration to the Constitutional Treaty concerning Article I-51 TCE suggests that specific provisions in this future measure could still exempt the exchange of policing and operational data from sufficient safeguards.[24]

Several new accountability issues would arise from specific provisions of the Constitutional Treaty. Article III-258 TCE would confer power on the European Council to establish legislative *and operational* guidelines as regards criminal law, policing and border control. However, the Treaty would not provide for any effective public input into or control of European Council activity.

A bigger concern is Article III-261 TCE, which provides that a standing committee would be set up 'within the Council to ensure that operational cooperation on internal security is promoted and strengthened'; it 'shall facilitate coordination of the action of Member States' competent authorities'. It is apparent from a discussion paper drafted by the Luxembourg Council Presidency[25] that the notion of 'internal security' would likely be defined widely, to at least include:

– 'the prevention and combating of crime,
– the prevention of the terrorist threat, the protection against a terrorist attack and the assistance in the event of a terrorist attack (terrorism solidarity clause),
– intelligence exchange,
– public order management,
– the prevention and combating of criminal offences such as illegal immigration and trafficking in persons,

---

[22] See S. Peers, 'Who's judging the Watchmen? The Judicial System of the "Area of Freedom, Security and Justice"', 18 *Yearbook of European Law* (1998) pp. 409-412.

[23] See *supra* n. 14.

[24] Declaration 10 in the Final act to the Constitutional Treaty.

[25] Council doc. 6626/05 (21 February 2005).

– the provision of an integrated management system for external borders as a major factor for preventing (certain) forms of crime within the EU,
– and crisis management with cross-border effects within the EU (including the disaster solidarity clause).'

While 'the future committee is not directly *in charge of conducting* operational activities', it would ensure that operational cooperation is promoted and strengthened by 'providing the appropriate framework, tools, policy, implementation and evaluation to allow / oblige the competent authorities to cooperate in areas of common interest or threat, covering all subjects which are relevant for internal security'. The facilitation of:

'coordination of the action of Member States could be defined as provide [*sic*] the appropriate EU bodies and support required to guarantee the success of Member States' contributions at a trans-national level. This includes coordinating the contribution of actors such as Europol, Eurojust, European Border Agency, SitCen, CEPOL, Commission/OLAF (…)'

In turn, this would entail a monitoring, measuring and evaluation function, including 'the mandate to direct action in order to address these shortcomings.'

Article III-261 TCE provides that the EP and national parliaments would be informed of the work of the committee. Obviously, it is possible that the information given to these parliaments would be insufficient to enable them to engage in any effective scrutiny of the standing committee's activities. On this point, it is unfortunate that the early discussions of the role of the Committee pay no attention at all to this issue.


5.     CONCLUSIONS

There is presently insufficient accountability of operational cooperation within the EU framework, and the problems grow more intractable as the EU develops further forms of such collaboration and devotes insufficient attention to the need to ensure parliamentary, judicial or other forms of supervision and control. Even if the Constitutional Treaty enters into force, the European Parliament's increased powers and the Court of Justice's increased jurisdiction could be negated by uncertainties about the use of the EP's powers in practice and the limitations which would remain on the Court's jurisdiction. Furthermore, a new factor would be the creation of a powerful new committee dealing with operational cooperation, with early signs already indicating that the Council is concerned only about its effectiveness. The battle for the accountability of EU operational cooperation is set to continue over the years to come, whether the Constitutional Treaty is ratified or not.

# TRANSPARENCY IN THE EXERCISE OF POWER IN THE 'CONSTITUTIONALIZED' UNION: THE PROBLEM OF DIFFUSED LEADERSHIP AND RESPONSIBILITY

Jörg Monar*

## 1. TRANSPARENCY IN THE EXERCISE OF POWER AS A 'CONSTITUTIONAL' REQUIREMENT

From the perspective of a realist school approach to international relations the European Union's Treaty establishing a Constitution for Europe (hereinafter referred to as the 'Constitutional Treaty') can be viewed as a treaty whose primary purpose it is to define rules regarding the exercise of power in a system of states where pooled powers exercised by common institutions coexist with powers which remain completely under national control. The exercise of power in such a system is necessarily more complex than that in a traditional international organisation/state alliance system or a state. As the Union clearly exercises real powers over European citizens – some of which will be increased by the Constitutional Treaty – transparency in the exercise of these powers can be regarded as a fundamental 'constitutional' requirement. In its decision on the Treaty of Maastricht of 12 October 1993 the German Constitutional Court declared transparency in the exercise of power to be one of the essential conditions for the democratic legitimacy of the EU's institutional system. According to the Court this includes the need for the decision-making procedures and the aims of the institutions exercising public power to be 'generally visible and intelligible'.[1] Arguably, such transparency should be all the more ensured in the context of a 'Constitution' which the Constitutional Treaty, reaffirming all the democratic aspirations of the Union, claims to establish. The European citizen, over whom the Union – directly or indirectly – exercises a range of real powers, should clearly be put into a position to understand the extent of the Union's powers, the way in which these powers are exercised (procedures and instruments) and who actually

---

* Professor of Contemporary Studies and Co-Director of the Sussex European Institute at the University of Sussex (Brighton, United Kingdom).
[1] 'Dazu gehört auch, daß die Entscheidungsverfahren der Hoheitsgewalt ausübenden Organe und die jeweils verfolgten politischen Zielvorstellungen allgemein sichtbar und verstehbar sind', *Bundesverfassungsgericht*: *BVerfGE* 89, 155 <185> BVerfG, 2 BvR 1877/97 of 31 March 1998, para. 78, available at: <http://www.bverfg.de/>.

*D. Curtin, A.E. Kellermann and S. Blockmans, eds., The EU Constitution: The Best Way Forward?*
© *2005, T.M.C. Asser Instituut, The Hague.*

decides on the actual use of these powers, thereby assuming the role of political leadership and responsibility normally assigned to governments in a state-like political system. The last point is of particular importance from a transparency perspective as knowing who is ultimately 'in charge' is crucial for the citizens' understanding of the executive in their political system and their ability to hold the executive accountable.

In the following we will briefly evaluate some of the progress and deficits the Constitutional Treaty brings with regard to this 'constitutional' requirement.

## 2.    ELEMENTS OF PROGRESS

In several respects the Constitutional Treaty marks some forward steps as regards transparency in the exercise of power: the prominent reaffirmation of the principles of conferral, of subsidiarity and proportionality (Art. I-11 TCE and the Protocol on the application of the principles of subsidiarity and proportionality) and the introduction of the three different categories of competences (Arts. I-12 to I-15 TCE) are clearly aimed at giving a generally 'intelligible' (in the sense of the German Constitutional Court's *dictum*) answer to the question of the extent and limits of the Union's powers. It is true, of course, that one needs to read rather carefully the detailed provisions of Part III to arrive at a better understanding concerning the extent of Union powers in the different policy-making fields listed under the categories of competences in Articles I-13 to I-15 TCE, concerning the fact that the Common Foreign and Security Policy has ended up in a rather undefined separate category of competence (Art. I-16 TCE) and concerning the new, rather unhelpful reference to the 'respect' of essential functions of the state (Art. I-5(1) TCE) which can be open to a rather wide range of different interpretations. Yet, still, it can be argued that at least a greater effort than ever before has been made to bring more clarity into the contentious issue of the division of powers between the Union and the Member States.

One can also say that the Constitutional Treaty brings some clear progress in respect of the way in which these powers are exercised. One example of this is the reduction in the number of different decision-making procedures and the establishment of one procedure, the 'ordinary' legislative procedure as set out in Article III-396 TCE. It is true that there are important exceptions to this 'ordinary' procedure (Common Foreign and Security Policy, co-ordination of economic policies, judicial co-operation in criminal matters, for instance). Nevertheless, there is now at least one 'standard' procedure for the whole Union system with exceptions which are clearly identifiable as such, and this constitutes, arguably, a step forward as regards transparency.

Another example is that of the set of reforms regarding the legal instruments. Here the existing jungle of different types of legal acts has to some extent been cleared through a reduction in Article I-33 TCE to four legally binding acts.[2] It is

---

[2] European laws, European framework laws, European regulations and European decisions.

true that not everything is as clear and convincing as one might have wished. Not only is the Common Foreign and Security Policy still a domain apart with its own range of instruments, but also the way in which the distinction between 'legislative' (European laws and framework laws) and 'non-legislative' binding acts (European regulations and decisions), as introduced in Article I-33 TCE, is applied in Part III is in several cases rather questionable. It is rather puzzling, for instance, that non-legislative instruments are to be used with regard to the adoption of rules on state aid (Arts. III-167 to III-169 TCE) and on the methods and procedure whereby own resources budget revenue is made available to the Commission (Art. III-413 TCE). Nevertheless, there is real progress in transparency as regards the legal instruments, and this is not only because there are now only four types of legally binding acts left, but also because the adoption of two of them – the European laws and European framework laws – are now subject to additional procedural requirements which are likely to enhance public and parliamentary scrutiny: one innovation is that the Council has to meet in public when deliberating and voting on a draft 'legislative' act (Arts. I-24(6) and I-50(2) TCE). The other major innovation is that, according to the Protocol on the role of the national parliaments and the Protocol on the application of the principles of subsidiarity and proportionality, each draft 'legislative' act has to be forwarded to the national parliaments which can – under what is usually known as the 'early warning mechanism' – forward a reasoned opinion to the Presidents of the European Parliament, the Council and the Commission on whether a draft European legislative act complies with the principle of subsidiarity and may even force a 'review' of the draft act if one third of them take the view that there is a case of non-compliance.[3]

As a result of the above reforms the exercise of legislative power in the Union is likely to become more transparent than ever before. Yet, as the following section will show, the same cannot be said as regards the exercise of executive power.

## 3.     THE DIFFUSION OF THE LEADERSHIP FUNCTION OF EXECUTIVE POWER

It can be argued that even under the Constitutional Treaty the Union does not have any executive power in the traditional sense as none of its institutions have been vested with any power of law enforcement and that the Union continues to

---

Art. I-33 TCE also maintains, however, the two non-binding instruments of recommendations and opinions.

[3] Protocol on the role of national parliaments in the European Union, Arts. 2 and 3, and Protocol on the application of the principles of subsidiarity and proportionality, Arts. 4, 5, 6 and 7, *OJ* (2004) C 310/204 and C 310/207.

be dependent in that respect on the executive powers of the Member States.[4] Even the regulatory activities of the European Commission and of the EU's growing number of regulatory agencies are ultimately all implemented and enforced by national administrative authorities. Yet the exercise of law enforcement powers is only one among a range of other functions which the executive branch of government normally assumes in political systems. Other key functions commonly associated with the role of the executive are what Jean Blondel has called the conversion of inputs into outputs, i.e., the transformation of demands into policies,[5] the co-ordination of policies and the conduct of external relations. In a simplifying perspective these and a number of other governmental functions may be regrouped under the heading of the 'leadership function' which the executive has to exercise in respect of both internal and external policies. This function of the executive is crucial to the transparency of a political system and is probably the most visible aspect of public authority, both internally and internationally. It is well known that at elections citizens tend to vote for whom they want to entrust with this leadership function rather than the vote being swayed by precise political programme elements. The leadership question therefore goes to the very heart of the role of the executive: in very basic terms transparency in the exercise of executive power can ultimately be reduced to the question of who is ultimately 'in charge' of deciding for which objectives the available power is to be used. The answer to this question is also of major importance from the perspective of accountability.

There can be little doubt that a 'leadership function' of the executive is required in the Union: after all the Union has put into place and keeps developing a number of policies (some of which the Constitutional Treaty will allow to strengthen) which need to be co-ordinated in order to be effective and the Union has developed an increasingly sophisticated and wide-ranging system of external relations well beyond its original primarily economic scope. But who actually exercises this leadership function of the executive in the Union, who is actually 'in charge' of providing direction to the Union, its development and policies? The Constitutional Treaty makes it more difficult than ever before to answer this question.

According to Article I-21(1) TCE it is the European Council which shall 'provide the Union with the necessary impetus for its development and shall define the general political directions and priorities thereof'. Furthermore, according to Article III-293(1) TCE it 'shall identify the strategic interests and objectives of the Union' in the CFSP domain and pursuant to Article III-258 it 'shall define the strategic guidelines for legislative and operational planning within the area of freedom, security and justice'. This already gives the European Council

---

[4] A point underlined in P.-C. Müller-Graff: 'Strukturmerkmale des neuen Verfassungsvertrages für Europa im Entwicklungsgang des Primärrechts', 3 *Integration* (2004) p. 190.

[5] See J. Blondel, *Comparative Government*, 2nd edition (London, Prentice Hall 1995) pp. 268-269.

what can be termed as a strategic political leadership role. Yet the Constitutional Treaty strengthens the position of the European Council even further: in several fields (social security, Art. III-136 TCE; judicial co-operation in criminal matters, Arts. III-270 to 271 TCE) the newly introduced referral procedure (often referred to as the 'emergency brake') gives the European Council the possibility – on the basis of an appeal by a single Member State – to examine a draft piece of legislation and to decide whether the normal legislative procedure regarding its adoption should be resumed or whether, instead, it should be considered as not having been adopted and that a new proposal should therefore be drawn up. It should be noted that this gives the European Council a decision-making power over the outcome of a current legislative process, a power which it never had before. A similar position of 'supreme arbiter' is given to the European Council in the case of a Member State objecting 'for vital and stated reasons of national policy' to a European decision to be adopted by qualified majority in the CFSP domain (Art. III-300(2) TCE). It also has the power to decide – if national parliaments do not object – on the use of the *passerelle* provided for by Article IV-444 TCE both in respect of passing to qualified majority voting by the Council in areas subject to unanimity and to the ordinary legislative procedure in areas to which the special legislative procedure applies. Finally, it is also entrusted with the decision-making power on a number of other matters of constitutional importance, such as the composition of the European Parliament (distribution of seats among the Member States, Art. I-20(2) TCE and the Council configurations and their rotating presidencies, Art. I-24 TCE). All this adds to the leadership role of the European Council which obviously is a collective leadership as the Heads of State or Government have to act as a body when exercising any of the above described powers.

This collective leadership of the European Council, however, has some serious limitations. One is that its direct impact on the actual elaboration and implementation of Union policies continues to be limited because:

–   it does not directly control decision-making in the Council which depends to a considerable extent on initiatives by an institutionally independent Commission and complex bargaining between the responsible national ministries which often are not 100% in line with the positions adopted by their respective Head of State or Government in the Council, and

–   it does not control the Union's administration, which is provided by a Commission which – apart from its appointment – remains independent from the European Council.

A second limitation stems from the fact that, of course, the European Council is essentially a non-permanent body which according to Article I-21(3) TCE meets only once per quarter which amounts to around one week in total per year (if one does not count potential special meetings). This is clearly not ideal for a body entrusted with supreme leadership which would normally require a higher degree of continuity.

The new position of a permanent European Council President elected for two and half years (Art. I-22(1) TCE) would seem to give to the European Council a strong element of continuity which it has so far lacked and additional weight in terms of political leadership. Yet Article I-22(2) TCE, which defines the new President's role, is full of ambiguities. While it is said that he shall 'chair and drive forward' the Council's work (Art. I-22(2)(a) TCE) no formal powers of execution/implementation are given to the President, and some of the provisions point to a much more modest role of the President such as 'endeavouring to facilitate cohesion and consensus' within the European Council (Art. I-22(2)(c) TCE). No power whatsoever is assigned to the President as regards the operation of the Council which – as in the past – will be the key institution for implementing European Council decisions. It is true that Article I-22(2) TCE provides for the President to 'ensure the external representation of the Union' on Common Foreign and Security Policy (CFSP) issues, but this 'without prejudice' to the role of the Union Minister for Foreign Affairs whose position is obviously of major importance in this domain.

There is clearly a problem of leadership and transparency here: the Treaty assigns very considerable powers of political leadership to the European Council collectively, but no real power at all to the President of the European Council who – as its only permanent emanation and actual 'face' – has good opportunities to become identified as the visible 'top' of the Union's executive. To confuse matters even further, the European Council President will, of course, not be the only 'President' on the Council side as there are still the various Presidents of the Council (of ministers) formations: the Union Minister for Foreign Affairs in the case of the Foreign Affairs Council and Member States' representatives on the basis of 'strict rotation' in the case of other Council formations (Art. I-24(7) TCE). Presidencies of the Council have so far wielded considerable influence – and occasionally real leadership. While this may decline slightly as a result of the new rotation system, they are still likely to play an important role as regards agenda setting, brokering compromise packages and as collective representatives of their ministerial colleagues.[6] How does this relate to the leadership of the President of the European Council? The Treaty does not subordinate the Council Presidencies to the European Council and the Presidency of the European Council. There is only a vague reference in Article I-24(2) TCE to the General Affairs Council 'preparing and ensuring the follow-up' to meetings of the European Council 'in liaison' with the European Council President and the Commission. This suggests that the European Council President is not in a formally stronger position whatsoever as regards the conduct of the General Affairs Council's business when compared to the President of the European Commission. As a re-

---

[6] On these functions generally, see F. Hayes-Renshaw and H. Wallace, *The Council of Ministers* (Basingstoke, Macmillan 1997) pp. 145-150.

sult there is no clear-cut hierarchical link between political leadership at the European Council and at the Council level. In the past some hierarchical link was at least provided by the fact that the President of the Council was the Head of State or Government of the country whose ministers were also the Presidents of the individual Council formations. But this will no any longer be the case under the new 'constitutional' regime. As a result of these various structural deficits the Union system of leadership as far as the Council is concerned is not only likely to be exposed to friction and reduced efficiency, but also to a considerable price in terms of diffusion of leadership and transparency: from the perspective of the non-expert citizen there will not only be still the same bewildering range of EU Councils but also two new and additional Presidential roles (European Council President and Union Minister of Foreign Affairs) and other Council Presidents now no longer coming from one country but from several, each being responsible for different areas.

The strengthening of the European Council's role and the introduction of a permanent European Council President are likely to further weaken the institution which has traditionally been most identified with the leadership role in the European Construction: the European Commission. However, because of its key roles in both the initiation and implementation of measures in a range of key policy-making areas the Commission will clearly retain some elements of leadership, and Article 26(1) TCE explicitly mentions its important roles in ensuring the application of the Constitution and Union law, the execution of the budget and co-ordinating, executive and management functions. As the 'promoter of the general interest of the European Union' entrusted with the task to 'take appropriate initiatives to that end' (Art. I-26(1) TCE) the Commission arguably also retains some strategic political leadership role for the development of the Union as a whole. Especially the latter is potentially in conflict with the leadership role assigned to the European Council (see above), and the Constitutional Treaty does not provide for any clear division between these two leadership functions or even co-ordination between the two institutions. There can be little doubt – if one compares the wording of Articles I-21(1) and I-26(1) TCE – that the Treaty reserves the more prominent leadership function to the European Council, but at least in principle the Commission retains enough autonomy and a mandate of its own to dissociate itself from the European Council's leadership, so that potential competition is not excluded.

In terms of the Commission's actual capacity to exercise this leadership one has to note that in accordance with Article I-26(5) TCE it will consist, until 2014 (at least),[7] of one member per Member State which – if only Bulgaria and Roma-

---

[7] Art. I-26(6) TCE provides for a reduction in the number of members to that of two thirds of the number of Member States with the second incoming Commission after the entry into force of the EU Constitution (i.e., 2014). Yet Member States can alter this number by unanimity. It cannot be excluded that Member States might wish to maintain the one member per Member State principle even after 2014.

nia will have joined by then – will mean a team of 27. As most of the leadership function can only be exercised collectively – the collegiality principle will still fully apply – this means a rather large body for assuming this role. Experience has shown that the risks of the emergence of factions and lines of division within the Commission have increased with its growing membership. The unity and coherence necessary for effectively exercising the Commission's political leadership is therefore likely to depend more than ever before on the leadership provided by President of the Commission within the college.[8] The President's role is clearly strengthened by the Constitutional Treaty as Article I-27(3) TCE gives him – on top of its existing guidelines and organisation competence – the power to ask a member of the Commission to resign. Yet the Treaty does not fully develop this logic of the members being subordinated to the President as he can only select the other members by 'common accord' with the Member States (Art. I-27(2) TCE).[9] This aspect of the appointment procedure, which was also one of the contributing factors in the 'Buttiglione crisis' in October 2004, clearly limits the sway the President can hold over the members of the college. The Commission remains therefore a half-way house between a strong prime ministerial type of organisation of leadership and a more collective one. This will make its actual leadership capabilities depend very much on the personality of its President and its internal dynamics. In practice leadership might well fluctuate between the President and the college as a whole, which does not contribute to transparency either.

As if all this diffusion verging on confusion would not be enough, the Constitutional Treaty creates one further position which will surely enter the competition for the leadership function in the Union: the Union Minister for Foreign Affairs, surely one of the most curious creations of the new 'constitutional order'. According to Article I-28(2) TCE the Minister has 'to conduct' the Union's Foreign and Security Policy and Common Security and Defence Policy, contribute through his proposals to the development of these policies and carry them out as mandated by the Council. This is strong language and suggests a substantial leadership role in these domains. Yet immediately some questions arise: as already mentioned the President of the European Council has been assigned the task 'to ensure the external representation of the Union on issues concerning the foreign and security policy' (Art. I-22(2) TCE) which clearly provides potential room for friction between the holders of those two positions. The provision that the President of the Council shall do so 'without prejudice' to the powers of the Union Minister for Foreign Affairs is unlikely to exclude such friction in practice. Article I-26(1) TCE identifies the European Commission as a body (not its

---

[8] On the issue of presidential leadership within the college see J. Peterson, 'The College of Commissioners', in J. Peterson and M. Shackleton, eds., *The Institutions of the European Union* (Oxford, Oxford University Press 2002) pp. 85-86.

[9] See on these points also W. Wessels, 'Die institutionelle Architektur der EU nach der Europäischen Verfassung', 3 *Integration* (2004) pp. 171-172.

President) as being responsible for ensuring the Union's external representation 'with the exception of the common foreign and security policy' and other cases provided for in the Constitution. This sounds fine in theory but, as past experience has shown, the borderlines between the Foreign and Security Policy and other politically relevant aspects of Union external relations (such as trade policy) are often difficult to draw, which generates a rich potential for friction and confusion.

It is true, of course, that the Constitutional Treaty addresses the problem of consistency in the conduct and representation of Union external relations through the 'double-hat' position of the Union Minister for Foreign Affairs who in accordance with Article I-28(3) and (4) TCE is both President of the Foreign Affairs Council and a Vice-President of the Commission with responsibility for external relations and for co-ordinating other aspects of the Union's external action. In principle this could give the Minister a strong position for providing leadership in both the CFSP/ESDP domain and all other domains of Union external relations. Yet his position is clearly an extremely hybrid one: whereas as President of the Foreign Affairs Council and representative of CFSP/ESDP he will clearly be subject to the mandate and discipline of the Council, he will be bound by Commission procedures in the exercise of his functions within the Commission.[10] As a result there is obviously a considerable risk of the Union Foreign Minister being exposed to serious tensions between external relations objectives and priorities defined in the Commission by decisions of the college and those defined in the Council by the Member States. If in these circumstances the Union Foreign Minister arrives at exercising any sensible form of leadership in the conduct and representation of Union external relations at all – a big 'if' indeed – it is most likely to be a rather confusing one both from the perspective of the citizens and third countries as it will be partially leadership from within and through the Council and partially from within and through the Commission. On top of that surely the European Council President will clearly wish to play his own role in the external relations domain (for which he has an explicit mandate) and it is most unlikely that any President of the Commission will totally refrain from making his voice heard and his influence felt in this domain either. The diffusion of leadership could hardly have been taken to a greater extreme.


## 4.    THE DIFFUSION OF RESPONSIBILITY

The drastic reduction of transparency which the above-described diffusion of the leadership function in the Union entails is only part of the problem. Political leadership in a democratic system – which the Union after all claims to be –

---

[10] Art. I-28(4) TCE explicitly states that this subordination to Commission procedures does not apply to his functions in the Council context in accordance with Art. I-28(2) and (3) TCE.

should go hand in hand with responsibility. Yet in the case of a 'constitutional-ized' Union the diffusion of political leadership goes hand in hand with the dif-fusion of political responsibility. Surely the European Council is in a position to exercise strategic political leadership, but as it is neither responsible for this be-fore the European Parliament nor has any direct executive power over the Coun-cil (of ministers) and the Commission the corresponding responsibility is rather elusive. In addition, the European Council is not a body which by any means can be forced out of office or to resign, although with its President (responsible only to the European Council) there is for the first time the (faint) possibility of a po-tential scapegoat in case of a major political failure. The situation is very similar in the case of the different Council formations and their Presidencies. One might object, of course, that both in the case of the European Council and the Council (of ministers) the individual members are responsible to their own parliaments and electorates, but the difficulties for national parliaments to effectively scruti-nize collective decision-making by their representatives at the Union level are well known, and outside of the legislative domain national parliaments have most of the time to content themselves with general statements of government policy before political leadership decisions are taken at the EU level and general statements on outcomes after they have been taken, with parliamentary majori-ties expected to 'rubber-stamp' those in one way or another. Looking at it criti-cally one could say that responsibility in the context of collective Council leader-ship is assumed rather than real and certainly not compatible with that which national constitutional frameworks normally provide for.

The position of the European Commission as far as responsibility for political leadership is concerned is a difficult one: on the one hand, it shall be 'completely independent' in carrying out its responsibilities (Art. I-26(7) TCE) and in this sense is fully responsible for any of its actions before the European Parliament which has to approve it and can dismiss it from office through a vote of no-con-fidence (Art. I-26(8) TCE). Yet it can be argued that in line with the general trea-ty and institutional framework the Commission remains subject to the 'general political objectives and priorities' defined by the European Council in accor-dance with Article I-21(1) TCE, and the Commission has so far always largely complied with those. This means, however, that it becomes quite difficult to hold the Commission responsible for any leadership it exercises in order to implement guidelines and priorities defined by the European Council. It currently also regu-larly occurs – and will, no doubt, continue to occur under the Constitution – that the Commission takes a lead on a new compromise package in the Council which in fact reflects the objectives and priorities of a majority of the Council members rather than the Commission's original intentions. Quite often the 'com-promise brokering' of the respective Presidency plays a major role in defining the content of such compromise packages. Where does the ultimate responsibili-ty for political leadership lie in such cases? Clearly it is diffused between the Commission, the Presidency and the Council as a collective body.

The diffusion of leadership responsibility reaches a new peak in the position of the Union Minister for Foreign Affairs: he is responsible to the Council for his tasks regarding the CFSP and ESDP and to the Commission for his respective tasks as Vice-President responsible for external relations. This divided responsibility in an area where borderlines between CFSP and other EU external relations aspects are often difficult to draw is already a challenge in its own right. Yet Article I-28(4) TCE confers upon him responsibility for ensuring 'the consistency of the Union's external action', and no doubt this is an issue on which real leadership is required in the Union system. The rest of this paragraph all deals with his responsibilities within the Commission, but surely this is a responsibility which also applies to his CFSP/ESDP 'hat'. But to whom is he responsible for this general consistency function? To the Council, to the European Council with his overall guidelines function or to the Commission (as the context of the paragraph suggests)? The answer is probably that the Minister will be responsible to all of them to a varying degree depending on the subject-matters on which 'consistency' needs to be ensured. And what about parliamentary responsibility? Unlike the other members of the Commission the Union Foreign Minister is both appointed and dismissed by the European Council, with the agreement of the Commission President. He is only responsible to the European Parliament as far as his membership in the European Commission and his tasks within this institution are concerned. This means that, if the Commission resigns or has to resign because of a vote of no confidence by the European Parliament, he remains European Union Foreign Minister but has to resign from his responsibilities within the Commission (Art. I-26(8) TCE). As he is not a ministerial representative of any Member State when exercising his functions in the Council context either, there will also not be any national parliament to which he will be ultimately responsible. All this leaves one of the potentially most important leadership functions in the 'constitutionalized' Union in an extraordinary mixture of divided and non-defined responsibilities.


5.    CONCLUSIONS

Although the Constitutional Treaty brings some progress as regards the clarification of the extent and the limits of Union powers and the simplification of the instruments and procedures through which this power is exercised, the political leadership and responsibility functions normally associated with the executive in constitution-based political systems is more diffused – and even confused – than ever before. This leaves the Union, enlarged to 25 and more Member States and, through the Constitution, an again widened set of objectives and tasks, with a singularly diffused answer to the question of who exercises power and leadership in the system. It will be more difficult than ever before for the citizen to understand who is actually 'in charge' in this system, and the polyphony of voices speaking in the name of the Union will increase rather than decrease. The Constitutional Treaty thereby not only maintains but even increases the existing problem of transparency, and it is a serious one: how can one expect citizens to support a 'constitution' which does not give a clear answer to who is actually 'in charge' and bears overall responsibility for the Union's development and policies? How can the citizen identify himself with a 'constitutionalized' political system in which various overlapping leadership roles are claimed by a puzzling variety of Presidents and Councils, with the Commission and a hybrid Union Foreign Minister as leading competitors too? The (in more than one respect) deficient context of parliamentary responsibility in which this diffused leadership is exercised raises a further question mark in this respect.

One reason for this diffusion of leadership and responsibility is clearly the fact that, ultimately, some or even most of the national governments have no real interest in creating a single strong centre of executive power in the Union. As the controversies over the introduction of a European Council President have shown, even those which are in favour of strengthening the efficiency and continuity of the executive branch in the Union system regularly disagree on whether this should be done in a more supranational (Commission) or more intergovernmental (European Council/Council) context. The other reason, however, is that this Constitutional Treaty no less – and in some respects more – than the Nice, Amsterdam and Maastricht Treaties tries to patch over fundamental disagreements over the nature and the objective of the European construction by an institutional engineering which adds more complex features to an already hybrid system just in order to prevent it from grinding to a halt and to satisfy, as far as possible, all diverging interests. The results of this institutional engineering might be intelligible and – in spite of all its dysfunctional aspects – still acceptable to the practitioners involved in the process on an almost daily basis. As 'insiders' of the system they have learned to live with it and to more or less effectively operate in this context. It might even be the same for the quite considerable number of academics who have become used to looking at the evolution of the EU system very much 'from within', being all too familiar not only with its complexities but also the particular constraints under which this evolution has and is taking place. While often being critical enough concerning many aspects of its functioning, they have nevertheless developed an understanding for the Union system which can verge on connivance. Yet the non-insider citizen looks at the system necessarily more from without, and what the Constitutional Treaty will present him with in terms of political leadership and responsibility in the Union is at best bewildering and confusing, and at worst perfectly incomprehensible and alienating. Quite a number of citizens in the Union will be asked to vote on the Constitutional Treaty in the context of public referendums. Many of them are likely to cast their votes (or not to vote at all) for totally different reasons. Yet those who might take a serious look at what is presented to them in terms of political leadership and responsibility in the 'constitutionalized' European Union may be forgiven for either not bothering to vote or to reject it. One could at least have spared the European citizens from having this construction presented to them as a 'constitution'.

# PART III

## The Democratic Life of the European Union

# THE ROLE OF PARLIAMENTS IN THE
# EU CONSTITUTIONAL FRAMEWORK:
# A PARTNERSHIP OR RIVALRY?

Heidi Hautala[*]

We are made aware of the two sources for the democratic legitimacy of the European Union at the very beginning of the Treaty establishing a Constitution for Europe: the Constitution reflects:

> 'the will of the citizens and States of Europe to build a common future, this Constitution establishes the European Union, on which the Member States confer competences to attain objectives they have in common'(Art. I-1(1) TCE).

The EU Constitution brings the citizens – through the European Parliament – and states close to an equal footing in most fields of decision-making, as the ordinary legislative procedure (Art. III-396 TCE) will be generalized with fewer exemptions than the present co-decision procedure.

However, the Convention has also strengthened the possibilities of the national parliaments, in particular encouraging them to scrutinize their respective governments when the ordinary legislative procedure is applied. The EU Constitution amplifies the parliamentary dimension of EU decision-making. The Union is understood, more so than earlier, as a 'bi-cameral system' even if no second parliamentary chamber has been created.

The parliaments representing citizens from 'constitutional regions' also demand recognition. Arrangements have been made by some national governments so that they can take part in EU policy-making. However, it is left to the Member States to decide how they engage the regional parliaments in national EU decision-making. This has been explicitly confirmed by the Convention in its deliberations on the role of national parliaments and on monitoring the principle of subsidiarity.

In several European Council meetings beginning with Maastricht, national parliaments have been recognized as a source of democratic legitimacy. In their Laeken Declaration of December 2001 the heads of EU States 'stressed the need to examine their role in European integration'. The question concerning the need

---

[*] Member of the Finnish Parliament.

*D. Curtin, A.E. Kellermann and S. Blockmans, eds., The EU Constitution: The Best Way Forward?*
© 2005, T.M.C. Asser Instituut, The Hague.

for 'preliminary checking of compliance with the principle of subsidiarity' by parliaments was evoked, and whether the national parliaments 'should be represented in a new institution, alongside the Council and the European Parliament'.

In the Convention these questions have been handed to two working groups.[1] The deliberations resulted in two protocols, one on the role of national parliaments in the EU and the other on the application of the principles of subsidiarity and proportionality. The protocols were originally introduced in the Amsterdam Treaty and amended in the EU Constitution.

The principles of subsidiarity and proportionality are defined in the EU Constitution as fundamental principles: 'the limits of Union competences are governed by the principles of conferral. The use of Union competences is governed by the principles of subsidiarity and proportionality' (Art. I-11(1) TCE). The subsidiarity principle applies in an area of joint competence:

'(…) the Union shall act only if and insofar as the objectives of the proposed action cannot be sufficiently achieved by the Member States, either at central level or at regional and local level, but can rather, by reason of the scale of effects of the proposed action, be better achieved at Union level (…).' (I-11(3) TCE).

The Convention has provided a positive answer to the question posed by the heads of states concerning the preliminary checking of compliance with the principle of subsidiarity. On the basis of its working group I, the Convention has established an *ad hoc* mechanism for the *ex ante* monitoring of subsidiarity involving the national parliaments. The working group defined subsidiarity as being mainly political, taking note of the fact that the principle leaves considerable discretion to the institutions. With a view to the *ex post* judicial monitoring of subsidiarity the Convention has broadened the conditions for referring suspected cases of non-compliance to the Court of Justice.

The new 'early warning system' of subsidiarity monitoring involves, for the first time, the national parliaments themselves. According to the protocol, the Commission shall send all its legislative proposals to the national parliaments, and they are also entitled to receive the legislative resolutions of the European Parliament as well as the Council positions on legislative acts. The national parliaments can publicly notify the EU institutions and their own governments of any proposal which they think does not comply with the subsidiarity principle. If one third of the parliaments (involving both eventual chambers) share the same view, the Commission must review its proposal. In the case of the Area of Freedom, Security and Justice the required threshold is one quarter. The Commission, however, has no obligation to change its proposal, but certainly the new mechanism increases its awareness of the principle of subsidiarity as it drafts legislation. The mechanism is aimed at involving the national parliaments at an early stage of the legislative process.

---

[1] I – The Principle of Subsidiarity, CONV 286/02 and IV – The Role of National Parliaments, CONV 353/02.

As for the judicial control of subsidiarity, the parliaments may, via the governments of the Member States, refer a case to the Court of Justice for non-compliance with the principle of subsidiarity. In fact, also the judicial monitoring will prove to be of a political nature, as only governments are entitled to present cases to the Court of Justice. All the same, the national parliaments are encouraged to fulfil their natural role in the scrutiny of their respective governments.

In its 32nd meeting held in November 2004 in The Hague, COSAC[2] decided to begin an 'experiment' with regard to the new monitoring system. The third railway package was proposed by the French National Assembly and was selected by COSAC as a test case. The national parliaments are invited to scrutinize this legislation with a view to compliance with the principle of subsidiarity.

It may prove to be very rare that a legislative act can be directly challenged on the ground of non-compliance with the principle of subsidiarity. As subsidiarity is not easy to define, it also serves the purposes of those in the Members States who do not want 'Brussels' to have a say, but rather call for renationalisation. Quoting Commissioner Chris Patten on what he called 'UK virtual reality', at the time of his leaving office:

'Why should our partners in the EU let us simply jack out of anything we don't like but let us stay for the ride where we think it suits us. Are we prepared to let the French and the Germans off the hook on state aids or aspects of the single market of competition policy?'[3]

According to Chris Patten, 'repatriating fish policy' would imply 'teaching fish only to swim in our (UK) territorial waters'.

It will be interesting to see how the monitoring of subsidiarity works in reality. One cannot help thinking that a Member State and its parliament might rather need to refer to non-compliance with the principle of proportionality. A piece of draft legislation may propose a measure which is clearly too intrusive in relation to its objective. The protocol of the Constitution in question does deal with the principle of proportionality, but it does not allow for any new mechanism for the national parliaments to control compliance with this other fundamental principle. The desire that national parliaments could also scrutinize proportionality side by side with subsidiarity was in fact expressed by the working group on national parliaments. Again, the chances are that the national parliaments will learn to make sure, when exercising their general scrutiny, that their governments do not agree in the Council with legislation which clearly does not comply with proportionality. One could conclude that monitoring proportionality may be indirectly enhanced with the EU Constitution.

The protocol guarantees the national parliaments a better dissemination of information. The Commission will send all of its green and white papers and com-

---

[2] *Conférence des organes specialisés dans les affaires communautaires*, the permanent body of EU national parliaments and the European Parliament.
[3] *The Independent* (11 October 2004).

munications at the time of their publication. It will send its annual legislative and working programme and all documents relating to its legislative planning and policy strategy etc. directly to the national parliaments at the same time as to the European Parliament and Council. The legislative resolutions of the European Parliament and Council positions on legislative acts, agendas and minutes of Council meetings and the annual report of the Court of Auditors will also be sent.

According to the Amsterdam Treaty, a six-week period shall elapse between the time when a legislative proposal is made available to the institutions and the national parliaments, and the date on which the proposal or a position under the legislative procedure is placed on the agenda of the Council. Few exceptions are allowed. The proposal or position may not be adopted until a minimum period of ten days from its placing on the agenda has elapsed. These stipulations are repeated in the Constitution and should encourage the national parliaments to invite their respective governments to inform them swiftly.

The protocol on national parliaments does not as such bring much that is new. The legislative proposals and green and white books are already (since the Seville Council (2002)) sent to the national parliaments. They are already available on the Internet and in the *Official Journal*. The amount of information flowing from the Commission and other institutions to the national parliaments will invariably increase. The question then arises how the national parliaments will learn to set priorities and select the relevant items from the flow of paperwork.

In 2003 the Commission published 1100 documents (27,000 pages) which, according to the EU Constitution, would need to be sent to the national parliaments. Some 770 of them are documents relating to legal instruments. The Finnish Parliament, to take an example, decided that only 100 of these documents were of direct interest as they require a decision by Parliament, in other words, which influence the rights and duties of citizens, or of which Parliament has not delegated powers to the government or ministries. Out of the 700 legal proposals mentioned another 100 were of further political interest. Less than one-fifth of the original Commission documents were selected for parliamentary scrutiny in the Finnish Parliament.

The national parliaments will need to select the relevant items and to be proactive. The EU committees of the UK Parliament, for example, select 20-40 issues of major importance which are subject to public hearings and extensive reporting. The UK Parliament, however, does not possess mandating powers of the government. This may partly explain why it has developed its own method of scrutiny.

As the annual legislative and working programme of the Commission becomes more binding – and realistic – it will become a key instrument for the selection of priority items. The European Parliament has for a number of years already devoted more attention to the annual legislative and working programme of the Commission. COSAC, in its 33rd meeting in November 2004, called on the national parliaments to hold debates on the annual legislative and working programme of the Commission 'during the same week'. It remains to be seen whether this suggestion will be taken on board by the national parliaments, but it would certainly allow for the earliest possibility to identify key items in the Commission's preparations. The parallel national parliamentary debates would also help the national parliaments to exchange information with each other on the most important items and would maybe also feed into joint debates within COSAC.

To sum up, the chief merit of the 'early warning' mechanism and a better dissemination of information may generally improve the scrutiny of the governments by the national parliaments if it leads to a general increase in self-awareness in each of them. The EU Constitution primarily provides a political impulse in this direction. This objective is fully in line with the thinking of the two Convention working groups which discussed the role of the national parliaments.

As reiterated in the preamble of the protocol on national parliaments, the way in which the national parliaments scrutinize their governments' EU activities is a matter for the constitutional system and practice of each Member State. The way in which each national parliament can participate more fully in EU decision-making essentially depends on what kind of constitutional arrangement and practice it has developed with its own government.

The national parliaments are indeed involved in EU policy in variable degrees. On examining recent developments, it can be seen that 'mandating' arrangements are increasing, i.e., the government may only take a position in the Council of Ministers after it has received a mandate to that effect from the national parliament. This has been the case in Finland, Denmark, Austria and Sweden. Many new Member States have followed suit. There has been a tendency to involve the sectoral committees in this process. In this way EU business becomes the normal work of all parliamentarians. Parliaments are realizing that they can already start their work parallel to when Council working groups are holding their first discussions.

A further challenge is how to increase the openness of EU policy-making in national parliaments, e.g., by more plenary debates instead of committee meetings behind closed doors. The UK and Irish examples show that committee meetings can be open to the public. And in the European Parliament closed committee meetings are very rare examples, anyway.

A prerequisite for a more transparent manner of dealing with EU affairs in national parliaments is to open up the procedures in the Council of Ministers. The Convention working group on national parliaments stated that this:

'was essential to facilitate and improve the active involvement of national parliaments in the EU (...) the Council should legislate with open doors. Policy coordination as well as other activities should also be carried out with open doors as much as possible.'[4]

---

[4] The Role of the National Parliaments, CONV 353/02.

In this respect the point of view of the European Parliament is no different to that of the national parliaments. The European Parliament has regularly and persistently reiterated that in particular the Council must further improve the transparency of its deliberations. The latest resolutions of the Parliament were adopted upon a recommendation to the Council and the European Council on the future of the Area of Freedom, Security and Justice (14 October 2004) and in the context of the investiture of the Barroso Commission (18 November 2004).

According to the Nice Treaty, the Council Rules of Procedures should be amended so that the Council:

> '(…) shall define the cases in which it is regarded *as acting in its legislative capacity*, with a view to allowing greater access to documents in those cases, while at the same time *preserving the effectiveness of its decision-making process.* In any event, when the Council acts in its legislative capacity, the results of votes and explanations of vote as well as statements in the minutes shall be made public.' (Art. 207(3) ECT, emphasis added.)

However, when one looks at Council internal decisions, one should note that the emphasis on co-decision is found identically in the two Convention protocols which are relevant to national parliaments. In their wording, co-decision is replaced by the ordinary legislative procedure.

However, the requirements on openness and transparency do not prevail outside the ordinary legislative procedure. The EU Constitution allows the Council to continue to use procedures whereby decisions are taken behind closed doors and without a co-decision by the European Parliament. They are called 'other than legislative procedures' or 'special legislative procedures'. A number of European regulations and decisions thus fall into the category of 'non-legislative' decisions. This is not helpful to parliamentary scrutiny, whether by the European or national parliaments.

The much publicised abolition of the pillar structure of the present Treaties in the EU Constitution is of a lesser importance to public and parliamentary scrutiny as the new division of legal instruments into 'legislative' and 'non-legislative' in fact rather cements it. The special legislative procedures and non-legislative documents will prevail in matters belonging to the present second and third pillars, keeping them within the inter-governmental domain of decision-making. The Area of Freedom, Security and Justice provides a safe haven for large parts of the present third pillar. It is going to deliver many non-legislative *and* binding decisions. Even fundamental rights may be limited without considering Part II of the EU Constitution. The limitations on fundamental rights and freedoms contained therein may only be delimited by law (Art. II-112 TCE).

As Armin von Bogdandy and Jürgen Bast show:

> '(…) the distinction between legislative and non-legislative acts established in Part I is only as reasonable as the provisions of Part III which ultimately give meaning to it (…) important empowering provisions are classified as 'non-legislative' on a rather arbitrary basis, let alone the activities of the European Council and the Council in the

Common Foreign and Security Policy, which are completely excluded from the domain of the European law.'[5]

It can be argued that the EU Constitution only improves the transparency and openness of the Union in a very limited way. This mostly occurs with the shrinking number of exceptions to the ordinary legislative procedure. For the rest, future struggles will have to be fought.

The Parliament and Council Regulation regarding public access to European Parliament, Council and Commission documents contains a more helpful definition of legislative documents: '(…) that is to say, documents drawn up or received *in the course of procedures for the adoption of acts which are legally binding in or for the Member States* (…)'[6]

A similar definition can be found in the Council Rules of Procedures:

'The Council acts in its legislative capacity within the meaning of the second subparagraph of Article 207(3) of the EC Treaty *when it adopts rules which are legally binding in or for the Member States*, by means of regulations, directives, framework decisions or decisions, on the basis of the relevant provisions of the Treaties, with the exception of discussions leading to the adoption of internal measures, administrative or budgetary acts, acts concerning inter-institutional or international relations or non-binding acts (such as conclusions, recommendations or resolutions) (…).'(Art. 7, emphasis added).

This is surprising, since the decisions of the Council, according to the Seville Council conclusions presented by the Secretary-General, Javier Solana, concentrated any measures on more openness and transparency in co-decision – and even then as and when selected as key instruments by the Council itself on a semi-annual basis. It may be noted that there is a direct link here with the thinking behind the division into legislative and non-legislative instruments according to the Constitution.

The Convention paid hardly any attention to the importance of a 'constitutional' way of defining legislation; the highest norms will follow from the Constitution. A possible remedy is to try to defend the wider definition of legislation as suggested in the two above-mentioned instruments. The European Parliament has already started to produce an own-initiative report to amend Regulation 1049/01 to prepare for the Constitution.

Many other aspects of the democratic deficit relate to the exceptions to the principle of openness and misuse of procedures. An effective way to avoid public debate and scrutiny is to agree on a legal instrument at the level of Coreper and to adopt it without debate in one of the consequent Council meetings as an A-point on the agenda.

---

[5] See the article by A. von Bogdandy and J. Bast on pp. 171-179 of this book.

[6] Parliament and Council Regulation 1049/01, Art. 12(2), *OJ* (2001) L 145/43-48, emphasis added.

The Council still refuses to publish the national positions, even in the co-decision procedure, until the end of the proceedings by referring to the need for 'preserving the effectiveness of its decision-making process' in Art. 207(3). This resembles Regulation 1049/01 which states that documents relating 'to a matter where the decision has not been taken by the institution, shall be refused if disclosure of the document *would seriously undermine the institution's decision-making process*'.[7] It becomes very clear that if the Council is to become worthy of the 'ordinary legislative procedure' of the EU Constitution and leave behind its character as an inter-governmental diplomatic organization, this exception to access to documents must be abolished, e.g., by amending Regulation 1049/01, Art. 4(3).

Parliaments often have special constitutional or institutional arrangements concerning access to information from their own executives. In the absence of public scrutiny through general access to information, by means of special rules parliaments can exercise their scrutiny of governments. For instance, the Constitution of Finland (2000) gives the bodies of Parliament unlimited access to documents, including classified documents, under Articles 97 and 47. The Grand Committee which has the overall responsibility of scrutinizing EU policy is handed and may request non-public documents and, upon reception, must guarantee discretion (Art. 50 of the Finnish Constitution).

With the emergence of the European Security and Defence Policy, since 2000 the European Parliament has initiated long-lasting negotiations with the Council of Ministers on its right of parliamentary scrutiny of Council activities in this domain, including its access to classified information. The Parliament and Council finally agreed on establishing a special committee in the Parliament with only a few members. Unlike the Finnish Parliament's unlimited rights to access information, according to the inter-institutional agreement between the Council and Parliament, the final decision on which information will be delivered to Parliament lies with the Council.

The parliaments of the European Union have many reasons to amplify their cooperation and take a quantum leap from the current, rather ceremonial, six-monthly meetings of COSAC. Parliaments, through COSAC, have on many occasions emphasised the need to exchange information in the less transparent domain of EU decision-making, and the need to disseminate best practices of parliamentary scrutiny. The European Parliament occupies a privileged position and is expected to co-host special meetings at the level of sectoral committees just as before, but in a more equal spirit.

A useful precedent was provided by the European Parliament when its LIBE committee[8] was dealing with the well-known case of Passenger Name Record, i.e., the right of US authorities to have access to information on passengers arriv-

---

[7] Art. 4(3), emphasis added, see *supra* n. 5.

[8] The LIBE Committee is the Committee on Citizens' Freedoms and Rights, Justice and Home Affairs (of the European Parliament 1999 2004).

ing from the EU. The rapporteur of the dossier, Ms. Johanna Boogerd-Quark, requested every national parliament to explain their position on the matter, before drafting her report in the committee.

The role of COSAC has until recently been disputed. Such national parliaments as the French National Assembly have previously argued for the institutionalization of COSAC into a kind of third chamber of the Union – perhaps as compensation for its lack of powers *vis-à-vis* its own government. The (French) President of the Convention, Giscard d'Estaing, wanted to create a 'People's Congress', an assembly of members of the European and national EU parliaments. This was not adopted by the Convention, however.

At the other end of the spectrum, the parliaments of the most federalist Member States such as Italy and the Netherlands have tended to reduce the role of COSAC altogether, and so has the European Parliament. These parliaments have tended to interpret that there is no space in the institutional architecture of the Union for national parliaments and that they would only disturb the European Parliament.

A rather significant change has, however, taken place during the last few years. This change is expressed in the report of the Convention working group on national parliaments:

'(…) the issue was not one of competition between national parliaments on the one hand and the European Parliament on the other hand. Each had its distinct role but both shared the common objective of bringing the EU closer to citizens and thus contributing to enhancing the democratic legitimacy of the Union.'[9]

On the one hand, there is a clear need for the national parliaments, hopefully inspired by the EU Constitution, to take their place in the EU parliamentary system, mandating their governments in the Council. Best practices are spreading from one parliament to another. Perhaps the newly created constitutional framework is now best seen in Slovenia – a new Member State. More so than in other parliaments, EU matters are debated in open plenary sessions. Perhaps many of the parliaments of the old Member States will soon follow suit.

On the other hand, the European Parliament has learned that it not only has a part in cooperation with national parliaments. It may also profit therefrom. Understanding the impact of European law at the level of 25 Member States is crucial in order to create better legislation, an endeavour which binds all EU institutions. And it may discover that the prevailing lack of transparency and openness in Council activities may partly be compensated by aligning with national parliaments. The representatives of the citizens should be alerted to the fact that, quite unexpectedly, the EU Constitution may make the public and parliamentary scrutiny of EU policy-making more demanding than it already is.

---

[9] The role of the national Parliaments, CONV 353/02.

# THEORY AND REALITY OF PUBLIC ACCESS TO EU INFORMATION

## Lorenzo Cotino[*]

1. TRANSPARENCY AND THE RIGHT OF ACCESS UP TO THE ENTRY INTO FORCE OF THE EU CONSTITUTION

### 1.1 Before the Constitutional Process

It is not possible to detail here the process of the legal recognition of transparency and the right of access from the Declaration attached to the Treaty of Maastricht of 1992 until the new constitution. At present, Article 255 TEC and Regulation (EC) No. 1049/2001 of 30 May 2001[1] govern public access to Council, Commission and the European Parliament documents. Apart from some specific points, the general view on these rules is largely positive.[2]

From the point of view of the subjects, the important progressive role of case law[3] cannot be forgotten (Court of Justice[4] and, mainly, the Court of First Instance[5]) and neither should the progressive influence of the European Ombudsman be forgotten either.[6]

---

[*] Professor of Constitutional Law at the University of Valencia.

[1] *OJ* (2001) L 145/43.

[2] See, for example, M. Maes, 'The "New" Regulation on Access to Documents', in V. Deckmyn, ed., *Increasing Transparency in the European Union?* (Maastricht, European Institute of Public Administration 2002) pp. 199-208; and S. Peers, 'The New Regulation on Access to Documents: A Critical Analysis' (Queen's Papers on Europeanisation, No 6/2002) available at: <http://www.qub.ac.uk/schools/SchoolofPoliticsInternationalStudies/FileStore/EuropeanisationFiles/Filetoupload,5277,en.pdf.> Recently, also, M.E. de Leeuw, 'The Regulation on Public Access to European Parliament, Council and Commission Documents in the European Union: are Citizens better off?', 28 *European Law Review* (2003) pp. 324-348. In Spanish, see my monograph: *Teoría y realidad de la transparencia pública en la Unión Europea* (forthcoming, 2005).

[3] On case law, see, S. Peers, 'From Maastricht to Laeken: The Political Agenda of Openness and Transparency in the European Union', in Deckmyn, ed., *supra* n. 2, at pp. 7-32; and C. Naôme, 'The Case-Law of the Court of Justice and of the Court of First Instance of the European Communities on Transparency: From Carvel to Hautala II (1995-2001)', *idem*, at pp. 147-198.

[4] See, ECJ, judgment of 22 January 2004, Case C-353/01 P, *Mattila* v. *Council and Commission*, nyr.

[5] To date, it has delivered 19 judgments in this field.

[6] I. Harden, 'The European Ombudsman's Efforts to increase Openness in the Union', in Deckmyn, ed., *supra* n. 2, at pp. 123-146.

---

*D. Curtin, A.E. Kellermann and S. Blockmans, eds., The EU Constitution: The Best Way Forward?*
© 2005, T.M.C. Asser Instituut, The Hague.

Likewise, mention must be made of the horizontal extension of public access that is now enshrined in the EU Constitution. Also, the vertical enlargement of public access has been expanded – vertically – to traditionally opaque committees, groups, and comitology. Furthermore, there has been significant progress in case law and the establishment of norms.[7] Finally, regarding transparency, mention should be made of the publicity surrounding the meetings of the Council in its legislative activity; this was formalised by means of a Council Regulation after the Council of Seville of 2002.[8]

## 1.2    Transparency and Public Access in the Constituent Process

In December 2000 the 'right of access to documents' was recognized in Article 42 of the Charter.[9] This article has been amended in the second part of the EU Constitution by extending it to all the institutions, bodies, offices and agencies of the EU and access to documents 'whatever their medium', as in Regulation 1049/2001 on public access. Finally, the right has been recognized in Article II-102 TCE:

> 'Any citizen of the Union, and any natural or legal person residing or having its registered office in a Member State, has a right of access to documents of the institutions, bodies, offices and agencies of the Union, whatever their medium.'

After the inclusion of this right in the Nice Bill of Rights, it must be remembered that the Council of Laeken in 2001 precisely ordered the Convention to achieve a 'more democratic, more transparent, and more efficient EU'. The White Book of Governance in Europe (in 2001) said its 'ethos' was transparency.

A year later,[10] in the Draft of The Constitutional Treaty of 28 October 2002,[11] a Title VI was included: 'On the democratic life of the EU'. It contained five articles, limited only to naming the themes. An article on 'Transparency of the legislative debates of the EU' was included in Article 36. After this first draft, the article on transparency took shape in Article 87 of the studies ordered by Prodi, in December 2002.[12]

---

[7] Decision 1999/468 of 28 June 1999, *OJ* (1999) L 184/23 replaced former Decision 87/373 EEC of 13 July 1987, *OJ* (1987) L 197/33. In the same sense, CFI, Case T-188/97, judgment of 19 July 1999, *Rothmans International BV* v. *Commission* [1999] *ECR* II-2463.

[8] Regulation by the EU Council, approved by a Decision of Council of 22 August 2002, 2002/682/EC, Euratom. Its Art. 8 concerns 'open deliberations of Council to the public and public debates', as well as Art. 9 on 'Publicity of the votes, explanations of vote and proceedings'.

[9] See <http://www.europarl.eu.int/comparl/libe/elsj/charter/art42/default_en.htm >.

[10] Peers, *supra* n. 2, at pp. 7-32, p. 30.

[11] See, Preliminary draft project of Constitutional Treaty, Secretary of the European Convention, Brussels, 28 October 2002, (OR fr), CONV 369/02, by the Presidium, to be presented in the full session of 28 October 2002, available at: <http://european-convention.eu.int/docs/sessPlen/00369.en2.PDF>. This was an articulate skeleton but it was not completed.

[12] Article 87 of this study (draft with articles) dedicated to transparency consisted of:

After the work of the Convention,[13] reflected in the Draft of July 2003, versions of the text of the IGC (November 2003) and, finally, the IGC agreement of 18 June 2004 should be mentioned. The changes made regarding transparency and the right of access throughout these stages are basically semantic and formal, without altering the substantive content contained in the Draft of July 2003. It could be said that in the constituent process it was intended to guarantee with greater legal precision not only the right of access but also the autonomous principle of transparency (which includes that right), while at the same time extending it horizontally (as seen in Art. III-399 TCE).

## 1.3    The Final Content of Transparency and Public Access in the EU Constitution

The Preamble to the TCE affirms that 'Europe (...) wishes to deepen the democratic and transparent nature of its public life'. A symbolic value is expressed – beyond the merely legal – that is granted to transparency and, as a consequence, to the right of access.

The First Part, Title VI, is on 'The democratic life of the EU'[14] with the final Article I-50 TCE dealing with the 'Transparency of the proceedings of Union Institutions, bodies, offices and agencies'.[15] This article declares:

'1. In order to promote good governance and ensure the participation of civil society, the Union institutions, bodies, offices and agencies shall conduct their work as openly as possible.[16]
2. The European Parliament shall meet in public, as shall the Council when considering and voting on a draft legislative act.[17]

---

– broad reception of the right of access (1st para, first sentence; 3rd para, final sentence).
– the remission to European law for principles and limits (paras. 1 and 4)
– the consecration of the Parliament's and Council's publicity in their legislative activity (2nd para., also at the end).
See, 'Feasibility Study Contribution to a Preliminary Draft Constitution of the European Union Working Document', at the request of President Prodi by F. Lamoureux and others (4 December 2002).

[13] The text of all the thirty-six amendments presented on Art. I-49 (former 36 in the first draft project and, at the end, Art. I-50) in the Convention process, can be followed at: <http://european-convention.eu.int/Docs/Treaty/pdf/36/global36.pdf >.

[14] Now it is in Arts. 45-52 TCE: Democratic equality (Art. I-45 TCE); Representative democracy (Art. I-46 TCE), participative democracy (Art. I-47 TCE); Social partners and autonomous social dialogue (Art. I-48 TCE); the European ombudsman (Art. I-49 TCE), as well as data protection (Art. I-51 TCE) and Status of churches and non-confessional organisations (Art. I-52 TCE).

[15] In the project only the 'Institutions'.

[16] Adding 'offices' to agencies introduced by the IGC of November 2003.

[17] Modification introduced by the IGC of November 2003; in the project the 'Council of Ministers' was also discussed. Also, in the IGC the open meetings were changed from the time when the Council should 'examine or adopt a legislative proposition' (Project) to when the Council should 'deliberate and vote'. Besides, the final text includes 'project of legislative act' and not the former 'legislative proposition'.

3. Any citizen of the Union, and any natural or legal person residing or having its registered office in a Member State shall have, under the conditions laid down in Part III, a right of access to documents of the Union institutions, bodies, offices and agencies, whatever their medium.[18]
European laws shall lay down the general principles and limits which, on grounds of public or private interest, govern the right of access to such documents.[19]
4. Each Institution, body, office or agency shall determine in its own rules of procedure specific provisions regarding access to its documents, in accordance with the European laws referred to in paragraph 3.'

Likewise, in this title various references to transparency and openness are reiterated as, for example, in Article I-46 TCE (the openness principle) and in particular in Article I-47 TCE (transparent dialogue).

Finally, Article III-399 TCE (common rules of management of EU institutions, organs and agencies and offices):

'1. The institutions, bodies, offices and agencies of the Union shall ensure [20] transparency in their work and shall, pursuant to Article I-50, determine in their rules of procedure specific provisions for public access to their documents. The Court of Justice of the European Union, the European Central Bank and the European Investment Bank [21] shall be subject to the provisions of Article I-50(3) and to this Article only when exercising their administrative tasks.[22]
2. The European Parliament and the Council shall ensure publication of the documents relating to the legislative procedures under the terms laid down by the European law referred to in Article I-50(3).'[23]

In conclusion, the following may be emphasized with regard to the text of the EU Constitution:

–   Transparency is legally consolidated as an autonomous principle, from which the right of access (Art. III-399 TCE) and the public meetings of the Parliament and the Council (in its legislative activity) are derived as an essential nucleus. The rule of openness and publicity is also essential to this principle.

---

[18] There is a slight change with the omission of the reference to 'the Constitution' (in Part III), as well as the term offices added to 'agencies'. Likewise, as in Art. II-102, the access is to documents 'whatever their medium'.

[19] There is a variation of style in relation to the project of the Convention and the IGC, but without any material alteration. The variation is the change to the paragraph number, it is now 3 (before it was 4). There is a mistake in Article III-399 TCE caused by this. Also, it can be mentioned that now 'European laws' are referred to, before it was 'a European law'. The regulation, for that matter, could be disseminated, but not necessarily in a law on public access.

[20] It is pertinent to indicate that the July 2003 project used the term 'recognise the importance'; this was amended by the IGC of November 2003.

[21] This Bank is only included in the last version of the approved text.

[22] This reference to management functions has been added by the IGC of November 2003. Similarly, in the final version it is stressed that they are 'only' subdued to Art. I-50 TCE.

[23] The reference to Art. I-50(4) TCE was included by the IGC of November 2003.

–   The presence of transparency and access is across the spectrum of the EU Constitution; it is not only present in its functional Part IV.

–   There is an excessive amount of repetition concerning the recognition of transparency and access. The right of access is recognized on three different occasions, sometimes with internal and reciprocal omissions (Arts. I-50 and II-102 TCE reiterate the right; Arts. I-50 and III-399 TCE had a crossbred remit, even with mistakes[24]). Legally, these repetitions do not seem to make any sense.

–   The importance of transparency and access goes beyond the purely legal aspect, with the importance that is implied by repetition and the guarantee, its presence across the spectrum of the EU Constitution, and its proclamation in the Preamble.

–   The regulation on access to the different institutions, organs, agencies, and offices will not be regulated by a single European law, but by separate laws.

–   Finally, the nature of the right of access as a fundamental right will be confirmed when the Constitution becomes effective, but not before then.

The practice of institutions, organs, agencies, and offices, as well as the case law of the Courts will be confirmed if legally and politically we are facing something which is so fundamental. Nevertheless, the effective exercise of this right of access and transparency in Europe will be what is revealed if they really are decisive and fundamental for the democratic development of the EU, as has been hoped over the years.

On this point, the remainder of the present study will attempt to show, very briefly, what the reality of the right of access and transparency exactly is after ten years' experience in the Council and the European Commission.

## 2.   FORMAL AND REAL ACCESS TO INFORMATION IN THE EU

### 2.1   **Reality of exercising the Right of Access: From Scepticism to Hope**

Examining the data available from the Commission and the Council, there can be a new analysis of exercising the right to access from 1984 to the end of 2003.[25] We should note the following:

–   Until 2002 (before it was possible to access the Registry on the Internet) six out of every ten requests were addressed to the Council (6,742; 59%)

---

[24]  Art. III-399 TCE refers to the European law cited by Art. I-50(4) TCE. However, this cross-reference should have been to para. 3.

[25]  Council and Commission annual reports since 1994 have been studied. Some of the data do not incorporate the last reports from 2003 (published in April and May 2004).

and four to the Commission (4,713; 41%). In addition, almost nine out of ten documents requested were from the Council (87.25%), and only one in ten from the Commission (13.75%).

- There is a clearly sustained growth in exercising the right of access. In the last few years, this growth has been linear (from 431 documents requested in both 1994 and 1995, to 11,467 in 2002). Nevertheless, this progression stabilized in 2003, probably due to the introduction of online access to the Council Register of documents.[26]

- With the implementation of online access to The Council Register,[27] the number of downloads of the Council's documents multiplied forty times (not 40%!) in 2002.[28] These numbers increased by 25% in 2003 with 467,532 online downloads of the Council's Register, 37 times greater than the number of documents accessed, but not on-line.

- Moreover, if an estimate is made of users and the number of screens accessed, then online access is 400 times that of non-virtual access. In 2002 900,000 people accessed the Council Register Internet site and consulted 4,600,000 screens (electronic documents).[29] In 2003 181,317 different users paid 768,725 visits – 800 per day – and accessed 5,928,096 screens.[30]

- University researchers are the most frequent visitors (27.5%), followed by lawyers (16.5%), and the industrial sector (10%), which mostly visit the Commission (16.6% as against 7.1% for the Council). Industry is closely followed by pressure groups (9.9%). Journalists take a surprisingly modest position (just 6.6%) and more to the Council than to the Commission. Members of Parliament and their associates represent a mere 2.5% of those seeking public access to documents.

- In terms of countries, Belgium is the country which exercised the right the most, just under one in three requests are from there (27.2%). With the exception of the Netherlands, where the access exceeds its correlative population, the rest of the member countries are more or less on a par.

- There is a high proportion of success as regards requests. Approximately eight out of ten are successful (80.9% Council; 81.8% Commission). The

---

[26] According to the data from 2003 (published in April 2004) the growth has stabilized: from 11,467 documents in 2002 to 14,118 requested documents in 2003 (1,523 Commission; 12,595 Council).

[27] From 2001 access online was made possible to the Commission Register and, more so, to the Council Register. In December 2002, less than half the documents of the Council were directly accessible online (44.95%) and only 0.07% were classified. In 2003 53% of the Council documents were accessible online (349,935 of 467,532).

[28] In 2002 9,349 documents were accessed not online, there were 375,155 documents accessed online (40.12 times more).

[29] See the First Annual report of the Council of 2002 on the application of Regulations 1049/2001, loc. cit. n. 1, without more precision.

[30] Reference is made to the Second annual report of the Council of 2003 (May 2004).

evolution in the Council is noticeable, from 58% access (1994-1995) to 87% in 2003. Nevertheless, the Commission has gone from 92% in 2002 to 70% in 2003 (due mainly to access requested by lawyers concerning questions of competence). There are two reasons for rejection by both institutions: the secrecy of the deliberations (43.4%) and for reasons of public interest (30.6%), in particular, investigations and infringement procedures. The latter reason has been used increasingly by the Commission in recent years.

Thus, in spite of non-stop growth – almost linear – in the exercise of this right, until online access was available, absolute numbers proved that the exercise of formal access was practically anecdotal. If the access request numbers are used in relation to the population of the EU, then one in thirty-three thousand citizens have exercised that right to date.[31] Without wishing to sound like a demagogue, obviously if only one in a hundred vote in elections, it would be invalid to argue that the rest have had the opportunity to do so. This very reduced use of exercising the right of access contrasts with the high legitimizing expectations that public access and transparency represent.

Thus, we wonder if so much baggage was needed for this trip, with such great normative and institutional effort to constitutionalize and fundamentalize this right. Likewise, we should consider the profile of the people who make use of this right (university researchers, libraries, students, lawyers, and industrial-

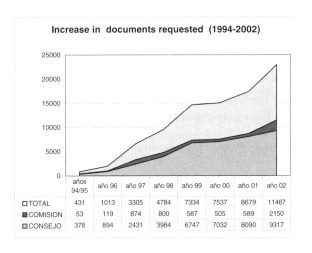

**Increase in documents requested (1994-2002)**

| | años 94/95 | año 96 | año 97 | año 98 | año 99 | año 00 | año 01 | año 02 |
|---|---|---|---|---|---|---|---|---|
| ☐ TOTAL | 431 | 1013 | 3305 | 4784 | 7334 | 7537 | 8679 | 11467 |
| ■ COMISION | 53 | 119 | 874 | 800 | 587 | 505 | 589 | 2150 |
| ☐ CONSEJO | 378 | 894 | 2431 | 3984 | 6747 | 7032 | 8090 | 9317 |

*Table. Evolution of the number of requests to Council and Commission*[32]

---

[31] Thus, for 378 million inhabitants of the EU (before the enlargement), taking into account a total of 11,455 access requests to the Commission and Council. 0.003%, 1 in every 33,000 people, exercise this fundamental right of access.

[32] The table comes from L. Cotino, *Teoría y realidad de la transparencia pública en la Unión Europea* (Valencia, INAP-Tirant lo Blanch, forthcoming 2005).

| Requests | 1994 | 1995 | 1996 | 1997 | 1998 | 1999 | 2000 | 2001 | 2002 | 2003 | Total |
|---|---|---|---|---|---|---|---|---|---|---|---|
| Council | 71 | 71 | 169 | 282 | 338 | 889 | 1294 | 1234 | 2394 | 2831 | 9573 |
| Commission | 320 | 320 | 322 | 745 | 676 | 408 | 481 | 450 | 991 | 1523 | 6236 |
| Total | 391 | 391 | 491 | 1027 | 1014 | 1297 | 1775 | 1684 | 3385 | 4354 | 15809 |

| Documents requested | 94/95 | 1996 | 1997 | 1998 | 1999 | 2000 | 2001 | 2002 | 2003 | Total |
|---|---|---|---|---|---|---|---|---|---|---|
| Council | 378 | 894 | 2431 | 3984 | 6747 | 7032 | 8090 | 9317 | 2936 | 41809 |
| Commission | 53 | 119 | 874 | 800 | 587 | 505 | 589 | 2150 | 12595 | 18272 |
| Total | 431 | 1013 | 3305 | 4784 | 7334 | 7537 | 8679 | 11467 | 15531 | 60081 |

*Table. Evolution of the number of documents requested from Council and Commission*

ists). They are people not necessarily linked to the idea of participation in the general interest.

The data on the poor use of the right of access can be interpreted as criticism of the emergence, proclamation, and constitutionalizing of transparency as part of a strategy of the rhetorical legitimizing of the EU. I consider this to be an important part of the phenomenon.

However, a more optimistic interpretation is possible if we take into account the most recent electronic accessibility of the Registers of documents by means of the internet, in particular that of the Council. These Registers allow direct access. Thus, with the data for the years 2002 and 2003, each year there were 800,000 accesses online to 350-470,000 documents and 4.5-6 million screens. There are forty times more online accesses than ordinary (non-virtual) accesses. There are about 400 times more accesses to electronic documents (screens). These numbers are not to be looked down upon.

Perhaps the internet leads to the people's perception that the public powers are being effectively monitored by the public. Nevertheless, the absence of journalists, Members of Parliament, associations, NGOs, and private individuals as visitors is a detail that does not suggest a political legitimisation of the EU system thanks to this right of access and transparency.

## 2.2    Real Access to Public Information through the 'Europa' Website

Electronic access to the Registers has been studied. Now, it is possible to analyse access to general information on the website 'Europa' (www.europa.eu.int). And the data[33] confirm the above-mentioned desire for 'electronic transparency' to be actually exercised by the public.

---

[33] The 'Europa' server has monthly statistics on access to the website. See <http://europa.eu.int/survey_es.htm> accessed on 25 August 2004.

[34] From 1998 to 2003 there were around two thousand seven hundred million yearly accesses to 'documents' (web pages with text). From 1998 to 2003 the level of access was multiplied 12 times, from 80 million accesses to documents in 1998, it was one billion in 2003. In other words: in 1998 an average of 225,000 documentary daily accesses was achieved. At the end of 2003 there were two and a half million documentary daily accesses.

The data are convincing: in 2003 already two and a half million 'documents' (web pages with text) were accessed every day, a billion a year.[34] Furthermore, these numbers have doubled annually.

| Site 'Europa' | Million docs/day | Million docs/year | Increase/year (%) |
|---|---|---|---|
| 1998 | 0,223 | 80 | — |
| 1999 | 0,486 | 177,6 | 197% |
| 2000 | 0,869 | 318,3 | 178% |
| 2001 | 1,314 | 479,4 | 156% |
| 2002 | 1,678 | 612,8 | 127% |
| 2003 | 2,322 | 1000 | 163% |

Although it is comparing apples and pears (access to documents or access to information on Web pages), if the important thing is to eat fruit, then there is 1 pear to every 60,000 apples![35]

In spite of the inappropriateness of comparing this data, the number of electronic accesses makes us reflect on the institutional efforts which have been accomplished to obtain the legal recognition of the formal right of access, and perhaps the relative ignoring of the real access by means of the internet for the sake of effective transparency in the EU. At this point, as Curtin insists,[36] the overload of information is as dangerous as the lack thereof and it has generated the paradox of disinformation by product saturation. Besides, it is the emitter who selects the information and who makes it more or less accessible in real parameters (difficult to control legally), with all the after-effects that that entails.

Thus, we need to know what kind of information there is and how to find it, especially in the decision-making process[37] and its preparatory phases.[38] Due to this certain policies have been embraced such as *euroactiv*.[39] In order to make electronic government become more transparent government, it is not enough just to make information available; this information should rather follow the parameters of 'accessibility': recognizability and localizability, availability, man-

---

[35] Between 1994 and 2001 (available data) 44,550 documents were requested formally from the Council and from the Commission and about 40,000 documents were effectively accessed while, in the same period 1994-2001 1,055 million 'documents' were accessed online. In this way, for every document that was accessed by means of using the formal right of access, some 24,000 documents (23,681) were accessed by means of the internet. And this number would be very much more concerning the data from 2003, arriving at an average of one formal access to every 60 thousand documents accessed online.

[36] D. Curtin, 'Citizens' Fundamental Right of Access to EU Information: An evolving Digital *Passepartout?*', 37 *Common Market Law Review* (2000) pp. 7-41, at p. 40.

[37] Ibid., p. 18.

[38] D. Curtin and I.F. Dekker, 'Governance as a Legal Concept within the European Union: Purpose and Principles', 4 *International Law FORUM du droit international* (2002) pp. 134-148, at p. 141.

[39] See, W. Baker, 'How Information Technology can further Transparency: Euroactiv.com', in Deckmyn, ed., loc. cit. n. 2, at pp. 241-242.

ageability, affordability, reliability, clarity, and accessibility to handicapped people.[40]

Given that formal and real access (the right of access and access to online information) seems to be an important *lever* for legitimizing the political system of
the EU (and one of the apparent causes of constituent process), the possibility for
control that the electronic government of the EU has and whether this also implies effective transparency has to be studied. While attention and constituent efforts are concentrated on the possibility of formal access to a few thousand documents – perhaps the most important ones – the public information that is
disseminated by the internet is not supervised in practice. For that reason, some
isolated demands by Curtin are of interest, for example, the possibility of enlarging the jurisdiction of the European Ombudsman as an independent guarantee of
access to public information by the different public powers of the EU.[41] These
functions are in fact exercised by the Information Commissioner or Information
Tribunal in various countries from the English-speaking world such as Australia,
the United Kingdom, Ireland, Canada, and South Africa.[42] In the EU, the person
in charge should create and apply standards of accessibility to information, not
only technical standards, but standards created from the political and democratic
point of view, taking into account the importance that transparency seems to
have for the EU. The Inter-institutional Group on Information[43] that exists in the
EU is not designed to fulfil these needs.

The data on the profiles of the users of the 'Europa' website have not been
sufficiently updated. They only indicate that the majority of users are men (as in
general on the Internet) and also that they are university students, civil servants,
members of public administrations, agencies and multinationals, followed by

---

[40] On this, one should follow the principles of 'accessibility' determined in the conclusions
of the e-democracy GOL project by G-7. VV. AA, *Online consultation in GOL countries. Initiatives to foster e-democracy* (Government Online International Network project report 6 December 2001) available at: <http://www.governments-online.org/articles/18.shtml> accessed 21 December 2001.

[41] Curtin and Dekker, loc. cit. n. 38, at p. 142 mentions this possibility.

[42] See in general, <http://www.law.utas.edu.au/foi/bookmarks/FOI_index.html>.

[43] The Inter-institutional Group on Information is a mixed working group made up of Members of Parliament and the Commission (the Council is not a part of this for the moment). Its
initial mandate was restricted to the Prince campaigns. It was subsequently widened to cover all
of the activities concerning information and communication. This group supervises the correct
functioning of cooperation among the Institutions, on an annual basis, and it evaluates progress
and determines policy on the general and specific activities of information when the Parliament
and the Commission cooperate. Also, it has responsibility in choosing the priority areas for the
activities concerning information, the general objectives that must be attained and the strategy to
be followed; as well as the determination of the instruments that must be utilized (Prince, other
important campaigns, etc.). It also has to recommend agreements for the control and evaluation
of the resulting impact. See the Communication entitled 'A New Frame to the Cooperation in
Activities on the Information and Communication EU Policy' by the Commission to the Council,
EP, ECS, and RC (COM (2002) 354 final (26 June 2002)).

NGOs, lawyers, academics, secondary school students, and small businesses. That is why a considerable number of requests are for students (23%), although it is most used by professionals (47%).

Issues searched by citizens on the Internet are: six out of ten search EU News (61%) and official documents (49%), rules (47%) and detailed information on policies (46%). A third of the hits are from outside the EU.


3.    CONCLUSION

Transparency is advanced for two basic reasons: as much to be able to control the government and the administration as to be able to participate in such a system of governance. Article I-50(1) TCE expresses the latter.

The EU has made transparency sacred. We can see it in Laeken's declaration that transparency was one of the three reasons for drafting a Constitution (a more transparent EU) and which can be seen in the Preamble to the EU Constitution. However, although constitutionalisation is praiseworthy, transparency has been proclaimed in the EU without its necessary complement: the recognition of concrete rights of participation.[44] As Frost indicates referring to the earlier legislation, it is 'a notable absence'[45] that the right of access is not accompanied by the right of participation, so that transparency is almost merely symbolic.[46]

It reveals a 'reality': 'transparency has become the leading candidate to represent the EU's public image'.[47] If in the USA transparency 'is perceived as just one more of the good government practices, in the EU it is seen as a constitutional pre-requirement of democracy'.[48] It is one thing to regard transparency as a principle of good government and the premise for participation in a democracy,[49] while it is another very different thing to consider transparency as a *magic ointment*, which when rubbed into the EU solves all its evils.

Berdin indicates that the citizen, now without God, without a mother country, without beliefs, without doctrines, in a society without a project, sees truth as a 'last virtue', thus the 'cult of transparency' in the modern society is the last refuge of a democracy that has lost its beliefs and illusions, a democracy that only has the ideal of a world of truth.[50] Carcassone considers that we have passed from an excess of secrecy to the transparency nebula,[51] and he insists on the

---

[44] See, A. Frost, 'Restoring Faith in Government: Transparency Reform in the United States and the European Union', 9 *European Public Law* (2003) pp. 87-104.

[45] Ibid., p. 98.

[46] Ibid., p. 96.

[47] Ibid., p. 95.

[48] Ibid., p. 101.

[49] For instance, Curtin, loc. cit. n. 36, at p. 8.

[50] J.-D. Berdin, 'Secret, transparence et démocratie', 97 *Pouvoirs* (2001) pp. 5-16, at p. 11.

[51] Ibid., p. 18.

common confusion of ends and means; transparency is not a goal but merely an instrument for the superior purposes of the democratic ideal.[52]

Transparency definitely, but always as an instrument, complementing and supplementing, without distracting attention and effort from other problems of democratic deficits in the EU which are just as or more important. Transparency definitely, but with its complement of democratic participation clearly and legally guaranteed.

The fundamentalisation and constitutionalisation of transparency and the right of access and their formal institutionalisation have been seen as 'theory' and as 'reality', the real importance thereof being together with the observation of the exercise of the right of access. Moreover, the proclamation of transparency and public access has been interpreted as an attempt to legitimize the EU which lacks real democratic legitimisation.

Regarding the effective exercise of transparency, a first appreciation tends to confirm the idea that the proclamation of transparency conceals an attempt to legitimize an EU which is difficult to legitimize democratically. In this sense, it has been observed that in spite of its formal appearance, the exercise of the right of access has been insignificant and almost anecdotal in its first ten years of life. It can hardly serve to legitimize the EU.

Nevertheless, on the phenomenon of the Internet, the analysis of the data is more hopeful, at least quantitatively. Online access to the Registers of documents, just as much as the information available on the 'Europa' website, suggests that we are facing really transparent public European power. In any case, the study has ended noting that if transparency is so important then it will be necessary to control the institutions that provide the information themselves.

---

[52] G. Carcassonne, 'Le trouble de la transparence', 97 *Pouvoirs* (2001) pp. 17-24, at pp. 18 and 19.

# EUROPEAN CITIZENSHIP: ORIGIN, CONTENTS AND PERSPECTIVES

## Jaap W. de Zwaan[*]

### 1. INTRODUCTION

In this contribution the origin, contents and perspectives of European Citizenship, the concept introduced by the Treaty of Maastricht,[1] will be discussed. First, the contents of Part II of the EC Treaty where the arrangements concerning European Citizenship are to be found will be examined. Then an analysis of the case law of the Court of Justice, more in particular with regard to the right of EU citizens to travel and reside freely within the territory of the Member States, will be made. Thereafter the approach taken by the Treaty establishing a Constitution for Europe, signed on 29 October 2004 in Rome, regarding European Citizenship and the Citizen's Europe will be discussed. A further aspect concerns the question of whether nationals of third countries lawfully residing in the EU, either in their capacity as family members of EU citizens or as holders of an autonomous right of residence in one of the Member States, should not be granted certain civil or political rights on the same footing as EU citizens. Finally, some concluding remarks will be made.

### 2. CONCEPT AND CONTENTS

'European Citizenship' is a concept which was introduced by the Treaty on European Union, the Treaty of Maastricht, which entered into force on 1 November 1993. The contents of European Citizenship are dealt with in Part II of the EC Treaty.[2]

---

[*] Professor of the Law of the European Union, Erasmus University Rotterdam, the Netherlands and Jean Monnet Professor and Vice-President of the Executive Board of the T.M.C. Asser Institute.

[1] See for a recent publication on European Citizenship the book published after the 33rd session of the Asser Institute Colloquium on European Law on 12 September 2003, *Europees Burgerschap* (The Hague, T.M.C. Asser Press 2004). The book contains contributions from several authors and references to further literature.

[2] Arts. 17-22 TEC. Whereas, according to the text of Art. 17 TEC, citizenship is connected

*D. Curtin, A.E. Kellermann and S. Blockmans, eds., The EU Constitution: The Best Way Forward?*
© 2005, T.M.C. Asser Instituut, The Hague.

According to Article 17(1) TEC every person who has the nationality of a Member State shall be a citizen of the Union. It is recalled in the second sentence – an addition introduced by the Amsterdam Treaty – that citizenship of the Union complements but does not replace national citizenship.[3]

The primary substance of European Citizenship is to be found in Article 18(1) TEC where it is said that every citizen of the Union has the right to move and reside freely within the territory of the Member States. As is recalled in Article 18(1) TEC, this right to move and reside freely is 'subject to the limitations and conditions laid down in the Treaty and the measures adopted to give it effect'. We will discuss in a moment what the concrete meaning of these restrictions is in practice.

Apart from the right of free movement and residence, Part II of the EC Treaty provides for several specific rights and privileges. These concern:

–   the right to vote and to stand as a candidate in municipal elections in the Member State of residence as well as in elections to the European Parliament (Art. 19(1) and (2) TEC);

–   the right to enjoy, in the territory of a third country in which the Member State of which EU citizens are nationals is not represented, the protection of the diplomatic and consular authorities of any Member State (Art. 20 TEC);

–   the right to petition the European Parliament, the right to apply to the European Ombudsman, and the right to address the institutions and advisory bodies of the Union in any of the Community's languages and to obtain a reply in the same language (Art. 21(1)-(3) TEC).

Finally, it is said in Article 22 TEC that the Commission shall report to the European Parliament, the Council and the Economic and Social Committee every three years on the application of the provisions regarding European Citizenship.[4] On this basis the Council, acting unanimously on a proposal from the Commission and after consulting the European Parliament, may adopt provisions to strengthen or to add to the rights of European Citizenship. Such a Council decision has to be adopted by the Member States in accordance with their respective constitutional requirements.[5]

---

to the 'Union', it is included in the EC Treaty. The explanation for this is that the merits and substance of European Citizenship are essentially linked to the EC Treaty objective regarding the Internal Market. Therefore citizenship is better placed in the EC Treaty compared to the EU Treaty where, indeed, no references to specific rights and facilities for the ordinary citizen can be found.

[3] This phrase was added in order to ease concerns in Denmark where the Maastricht Treaty in the first instance was rejected during a popular vote expressed in a referendum.

[4] The last, fourth, report, COM (2004) 695 final.

[5] On the one hand, the procedure to add new EU citizens' rights to the catalogue of Part II of the EC Treaty is relatively simple because the relevant decision is taken by the Council, albeit by unanimity. On the other hand, the procedure is a labourious one because the Council decision

Clearly the right to travel and reside freely in the territory of the Member States – the subject-matter of Article 18 TEC – connected to the principle of equal treatment as laid down in Article 12 TEC, is the 'core business' of European Citizenship. Still, originally European Citizenship, as it was proposed by the Spanish delegation and the Commission during the Maastricht negotiations, was looked upon as a purely 'political' concept. It was said and thought that, apart from a few civil rights such as the right to vote and to stand as a candidate for municipal elections in the Member State of residence, European Citizenship did not bring anything new. This, more in particular, was especially so in the context of the free movement of persons. Indeed, because Article 18(1) TEC – as has already been reminded – refers to 'limitations and conditions' laid down in the Treaty or secondary legislation, it was said that this treaty provision in fact refers to the existing directives and regulations.[6] Furthermore, it was thought that Article 18(1) TEC has no direct effect. To that extent the idea was that European Citizenship was only intended to confirm the *acquis* so far.

3.     CASE LAW OF THE COURT OF JUSTICE

In fact it took the Court some time to give European Citizenship, notably the free movement dimension thereof, a proper dimension. This, however, not so much with respect to *economically active* EU citizens. Indeed, their situation is already governed in clear terms by the rules of the internal market, notably the provi-

---

concerned needs to be approved by national parliaments. In fact this amounts to a procedure comparable to the treaty amendment procedure of Article 48 TEU. Certainly the sensitive nature of the subject of European Citizenship must be taken into account here. This being said, in view of the importance of this treaty concept, one could have hoped that a lighter procedure would have been included in the treaty.

  [6] Such as Regulation 1612/68 (*OJ* (1968) L 257/2) on freedom of movement for workers within the Community; Directive 64/221 (*OJ* (1964) L 56/850) on the coordination of special measures concerning the movement and residence of foreign nationals, which are justified on grounds of public policy, public security or public health; Directive 68/360 (*OJ* (1968) L 257/13) on the abolition of restrictions on movement and residence within the Community for workers of the Member States and their families; Directive 72/194 (*OJ* (1972) L 121/32) extending to workers exercising the right to remain in the territory of a Member State after having been employed in that State within the scope of Directive 64/221; Directive 73/148 (*OJ* (1973) L 172/14) on the abolition of restrictions on movement and residence within the Community for nationals of Member States with regard to establishment and the provision of services; Directive 75/34 (*OJ* (1975) L 14/10) concerning the right of nationals of a Member State to remain in the territory of another Member State after having pursued therein an activity in a self-employed capacity; Directive 75/35 (*OJ* (1975) L 14/14) extending the scope of Directive 64/221 to include nationals of a Member State who exercise the right to remain in the territory of another Member State after having pursued therein an activity in a self-employed capacity; Directive 90/364 (*OJ* (1990) L 180/26) on the right of residence; Directive 90/365 (*OJ* (1990) L 180/28) on the right of residence for employees and self-employed persons who have ceased their occupational activity; and Directive 93/96 (*OJ* (1993) L 317/59) on the right of residence for students.

sions of the EC Treaty and secondary law concerning the free movement of workers and the right of establishment for independents.[7]

No, the developments initiated by the Court of Justice concern the scope of – what is called – *non-economic* EU citizens who claim a right of residence in another Member State, in conjunction with a flexible interpretation of the requirement – which has to be met in order to be allowed to reside in the host Member State – regarding the possession of one's *own resources*. The Court's case law has dealt with certain categories of persons such as:

– persons whose status under Community law is not clear;
– job seekers;
– students; or
– family members.

Some examples of the Court's case law can illustrate these developments.

### 3.1    Persons whose Status is not clear and Job Seekers

In the case *Martinez Sala*[8] the Court was of the opinion that the dossier did not provide sufficient information to enable the Court to determine whether the person concerned was covered by the scope *ratione personae* of Article 39 TEC and of Regulation 1612/68 or of Regulation 1408/71.[9] However, in this case where a national of a Member State was lawfully residing in the territory of another Member State, the Court recalled the importance of Article 12 and – since 1 November 1993 when the Treaty on the European Union entered into force – of Article 17 TEU.[10] The Court concluded that Community law precludes a Member State from requiring nationals of other Member States authorized to reside in its territory to produce a formal residence permit issued by the national authorities in order to receive child benefit, whereas that Member State's own nationals are only required to be permanently or ordinarily resident in that Member State.

A similar principle was confirmed in the cases *Trojani*[11] and *Baumbast and R.*[12] a citizen of the EU who does not enjoy, or no longer enjoys, a right of residence in the host Member State under Articles 39, 43 or 49 TEC may, simply as a citizen of the Union, enjoy a right of residence in that Member State by the direct application of Article 18(1) TEC. The Court added to this that, although the exercise of the right of residence referred to in Article 18 TEC is subject to

---

[7] Arts. 39 and 43 TEC. See for the relevant secondary law provisions *supra* n. 6.
[8] ECJ, judgment of 12 May 1998, Case C-85/96, *Martinez Sala* [1998] *ECR* I-2691.
[9] Paras. 29-45.
[10] Para. 59.
[11] ECJ, judgment of 7 September 2004, Case C-456/02, *Trojani*, nyr.
[12] ECJ, judgment of 17 September 2002, Case C-413/99, *Baumbast and R.* [2002] *ECR* I-7091.

the limitations and conditions referred to in that provision, the competent authorities and, where necessary, the national courts must ensure that those limitations and conditions are applied in compliance with the general principles of Community law, in particular the principle of proportionality.[13] Thus the Court concluded, for example in the *Trojani* case, that, once it is ascertained that a person is in possession of a residence permit, he or she may rely on the principle of equal treatment laid down in Article 12 TEC in order to be granted – in that particular case – a social assistance benefit.

## 3.2  **Students**

In cases concerning students the Court has developed specific rules and principles that imply that the requirement concerning the possession of one's own resources in the host Member State must be interpreted in a flexible manner.

For example, the Court concluded in the case of *Grzelczyk*[14] that Articles 12 and 17 TEC preclude the entitlement to a non-contributory social benefit from being made conditional, in the case of nationals of Member States other than the host Member State where they are legally present, if they fall within the scope of Regulation 1612/68 when no such condition applies to nationals of the host Member State. In its reasoning the Court referred to Directive 93/96 on the right of residence for students.[15] More in particular, the Court found that it follows from Directive 93/96 that Member States must grant a right of residence to student nationals of a Member State who satisfy certain requirements. In this context the Court recalled that Member States may require that students should satisfy the relevant national authorities that they have sufficient resources to avoid becoming a burden on the social security system of the host Member State during their period of residence; that they be enrolled in a recognized educational establishment for the principal purpose of following a vocational training course there; and that they be covered by health insurance in respect of all risks in the host Member State.[16] However, as regards more specifically the question of resources, the Court recalled that (Art. 1 of) Directive 93/96 does not require resources of a specific amount, nor that they be evidenced by specific documents. The article refers merely to a *declaration* which enables the student to satisfy the national authority concerned that he has, for himself and, in relevant cases, for his spouse and dependant children, sufficient resources to avoid becoming a burden on the social security system of the host Member State during his/their stay. Therefore, by merely requiring a declaration, the Court concluded that Directive 93/96 differs from Directives 90/364 and 90/365, which namely do indicate a specific – minimum – level of income that persons wishing to avail themselves

---

[13] Para. 34 of the *Trojani* decision, and para. 91 of the *Baumbast and R* decision.
[14] ECJ, judgment of 20 September 2002, Case C-184/99, *Grzelczyk* [2002] *ECR* I-6193.
[15] Para. 35.
[16] Para. 38.

of those directives must have. That difference is explained by the special characteristics of student residence in comparison with that of persons to whom Directives 90/364 and 90/365 apply.[17] Moreover, the Court added that whilst Article 4 of Directive 93/96 does provide that the right of residence will exist for as long as the beneficiaries of that right fulfill the conditions laid down in Article 1, the sixth recital in the directive's preamble envisages that the beneficiaries of the right of residence must not become an *unreasonable burden* on the public finances of the host Member State. Directive 93/96, the Court said, thus accepts a certain degree of financial solidarity between nationals of a host Member State and nationals of other Member States, particularly if the difficulties which a beneficiary of the right of residence encounters are only temporary.[18]

Another fine example of the Court's approach to students is the judgment in *D'Hoop*[19] where the Court established that Community law, more in particular Article 17 TEC, precludes a Member State from refusing to grant a subsistence allowance to one of its nationals, a student seeking her first employment, on the sole ground that that student had completed her secondary education in another Member State (and, therefore, had exercised her right of free movement to another Member State).

The *Bidar* case,[20] which at the time of writing this article is still pending, is another case where the position of students in the Member State of study is at stake. In this case the discussion centers around the question of whether a visiting student must be granted a scholarship by the authorities of the host Member State subject to the same conditions as local students. However, it seems that in view of the facts of the case it is not even clear whether Bidar is to be considered as a student or a worker (or, even, a provider of services).[21]

### 3.3    Family Members

The case of *Garcia Avello*[22] is an example of a case where the Court addressed the situation of family members, in this case minor children, also clearly a category of non-economically active persons. In this decision the Court applied the principle of equal treatment in the sense that different situations should not be treated in the same manner. Another important feature of this case was that the minor children in question, having dual nationality, were born and continued to live in one of the Member States of which they had the nationality. Confronted with the view expressed by a number of governments that the situation of the children was not covered by Community law, the Court ruled that, although citi-

---

[17] Para. 41.
[18] Para. 44.
[19] ECJ, judgment of 11 July 2002, Case C-224/98, *D'Hoop* [2002] *ECR* I-6191.
[20] ECJ, Case C-209/03, pending.
[21] See for the *Bidar* case also *infra* para. 4.
[22] ECJ, judgment of 2 October 2003, Case C-148/02, *Carlos Garcia Avello* v. *Belgian State* [2003] *ECR* I-11613.

zenship of the Union is not intended to extend the scope *ratione materiae* of the Treaty also to internal situations which have no link with Community law,[23] a sufficient link with Community law does exist with regard to persons in a situation such as that of the children of Mr Garcia Avello, who are namely nationals of one Member State lawfully resident in the territory of another Member State.[24] A similar approach has been followed in a recent case, the *Chen* decision delivered by the Court on 19 October 2004.[25]

The substance of the case *Garcia Avello* concerned national legislation governing a person's surname, a subject clearly falling within the scope of the competences of the Member States. Nonetheless, the Court found that Articles 12 and 17 TEC preclude the administrative authority of a Member State – in this case Belgium – from refusing to grant an application for a change of surname made on behalf of minor children resident in that State and having the dual nationality of that State and of another Member State, in a case where the purpose of that application is to enable those children to bear the surname to which they are entitled according to the law and tradition of the second Member State.[26] A striking decision indeed, to the extent that the Court in fact forces a Member State in an area which clearly falls within its own competence, to apply the system of another Member State. Apparently, however – this at least follows from the facts as reflected in the decision[27] – the Court was irritated by the fact that the Belgian authorities reacted so reluctantly to the request concerned and, more generally, because of the restrictive practices in Belgium concerning surnames in general.

### 3.4 Summary of the Court's Reasoning

By way of a summary, in its case law the Court underlines, first of all, the effect of possessing the nationality of a Member State. Because of this fact the citizen concerned can, as a citizen of the Union, enjoy a right of residence in another Member State and may rely on Article 12 TEC, the principle of equal treatment (see the judgment in the *Trojani* case). For this to occur in certain circumstances it is not even necessary that the EU citizen concerned has exercised his/her right of free movement to another Member State (see the judgments in the *Garcia Avello* and *Chen* cases). In this context the Court also found that Article 18 TEC has direct effect (see the judgment in the *Baumbast and R.* cases).[28] By so argu-

---

[23] Para. 26. Here the Court referred to its decision in the joined cases C-64/96 and C-65/95, *Uecker and Jacquet* [1997] *ECR* I-1371, para. 23.

[24] Para. 27.

[25] ECJ, judgment of 19 October 2004, Case C-200/02, *Zhu and Chen*, nyr. See in particular paras. 18 and 19.

[26] Para. 45.

[27] See more in particular paras. 33, 38 and 44.

[28] This conclusion had not yet been reached in an earlier decision of the Court: the judgment of 21 September 1999, Case C-378/97, *Wijsenbeek* [1999] *ECR* I-6207.

ing, the Court certainly respects the fact that the exercise of that right of residence is subject to limitations and conditions (such as the possession of one's
own resources and health insurance); however, it states that national authorities
and national courts must ensure that those limitations and conditions are applied
in compliance with the general principle of Community law, in particular the
principle of proportionality (see the judgments in the *Grzelczyk* and *Trojani*
cases).

All in all, it is striking to note that the Court, once it has ascertained that a
person is a EU citizen and is in possession of a right of residence or a residence
permit in the host Member State, accepts that he or she may rely on Article 12
TEC, the principle of equal treatment, in order to be granted certain financial al-
lowances or benefits. On the other hand, it is only in exceptional circumstances
that the Court accepts that national legislation makes the entitlement to an allowance conditional on a residence requirement. For example, in the *Collins* case[29]
(where the appellant was a jobseeker) the Court found that the right to equal
treatment laid down in Article 39(2) TEC, read in conjunction with Articles 12
and 17 TEC, does not preclude national legislation which makes entitlement to a
job-seeker's allowance conditional on a residence requirement, in so far as that
requirement may be justified on the basis of objective considerations that are independent of the nationality of the persons concerned and proportionate to the
legitimate aim of the national provisions.

Be that as it may, it follows from the Court's case law that 'European Citizenship' has now clearly been given a proper meaning. Articles 17 and 18 TEC,
to be read and applied in close connection with Article 12 TEC, have clearly
proven to represent an added value compared to the existing traditional arrangements, for economically active EU citizens, in the framework of the internal
market.

4.      DIRECTIVE 2004/38 OF 29 APRIL 2004

The rules on the free movement of persons as they result from the EC Treaty,
secondary legislation, the Court's case law interpreting these acts of legislation
as well as the Court's case law on European Citizenship, have been laid down
in a *consolidated* text of a directive, Directive 2004/38/EC of the European
Parliament and of the Council of 29 April 2004.[30] As a consequence, all existing
and well known legislative instruments on the free movement of persons, including

---

[29] ECJ, judgment of 23 March 2004, Case C-138/02, *Colllins*, nyr.

[30] Directive on the right of citizens of the Union and their family members to move and reside
freely within the territory of the Member States amending Regulation 1612/68 and repealing
Directives 64/221, 68/360, 72/194, 73/148, 75/34, 75/35, 90/364, 90/365 and 93/96. The directive is published in *OJ* (2004) L 158/77.

the three directives on the free movement of non-economically active persons (90/364, 90/365 and 93/96), have been repealed. The title and contents of the new instrument even centre around the notion 'citizens of the Union'. The directive entered into force on the day of its publication, which was 30 April 2004. The implementation period runs for a period of two years.[31]

Article 6 of the directive provides for the modalities of the right of residence in another Member State for up to three months. Article 7 deals with the right of residence for more than three months. Article 16 states – as a 'general rule' for Union citizens and their family members – that Union citizens who have resided legally for a continuous period of five years in a host Member State, shall have the right of permanent residence there.

However, the precise modalities of free movement and the consequences related thereto as to the personal and substantive scope of the directive, are still subject to discussion. Some discussion, for example, is taking place with regard to the interpretation of the principle of *equal treatment*, more particularly – which is obviously relevant in the context of European Citizenship – in situations of the movement of non-economically active persons. An important example here is the case of *Bidar*, already mentioned[32] and presently pending before the Court of Justice. In this case the question has arisen whether a student can claim access to a scholarship in the Member State of study subject to the same conditions as local students. Apart from arguments based on European Citizenship, the interpretation of Directive 2004/38 is at stake, and this in a situation where the deadline for the transposition of the directive has not yet expired. The relevant provision is Article 24(2) where it is said that a host Member State:

'shall not be obliged to confer entitlement to social assistance during the first three months of residence (...) nor shall it be obliged, prior to acquisition of the right of permanent residence, to grant maintenance aid for studies, including vocational training, consisting in student grants or students loans to persons other than workers, self-employed persons, persons who retain such status and members of their families.'

Obviously the condition, to be fulfilled in order to enjoy a right of residence in the host country, regarding the possession of one's own sufficient resources, is relevant here. Also the nuance expressed in the *Grzelczyk* case[33] that a student should not become an 'unreasonable' burden on the public finances of the host Member State may be of importance. This nuance seems to be more crucial in a situation where the student concerned has the obligation to reimburse, at a given moment, the scholarship or loan which has been granted to him or her. Yet, as observed earlier, it seems that, *inter alia*, it is not clear whether Bidar is to be considered as a student, a worker or, even, a provider of services.

---

[31] Art. 40(1).
[32] *Supra* para. 3.2.
[33] *Supra* para. 3.2.

## 5.    NEW CITIZEN'S RIGHTS: EXTENSION OF THE RIGHT TO VOTE?

When one poses the question of what new rights are imaginable for EU citizens it is striking to note that – so far – no concrete proposals have been made in this respect, also not by the Commission in its reports by virtue of Article 22 TEC. However, on the basis of an analysis of the existing text of Part II of the EC Treaty, one could think of widening the scope of the right to vote and the right to stand as a candidate: Article 19(1) TEC.

Indeed, whereas the right to vote and to stand as a candidate is at present restricted to *municipal* elections, one wonders whether such a right of EU citizens should not be extended to *regional* elections and, even, to elections at the *national* level, eventually subject to conditions such as a minimum period of lawful stay – 5 or even 10 years? – in the Member State of residence. Because is it not true that granting such a right can only contribute to the process of integration, by the EU citizen and his/her family members, in the host Member State?[34]

Certainly, politically such an idea may be difficult to accept. Generally speaking, Member States are of the opinion that persons must have – or should accept – the nationality of the country where they are living and have their residence, before being entitled to vote or to stand as a candidate for elections at the regional or national level. However, such a requirement seems to be increasingly contrary to the idea that EU citizens, when moving from one Member State to another, should be in a position to retain their *identity*. Indeed, does 'United in diversity', which is the motto of the EU as reflected in Article I-8 TCE, not imply that persons moving from one Member State to another should not be forced to change their nationality? Therefore, there clearly are arguments to widen the scope of the right to vote (and to stand as a candidate).

## 6.    EU CONSTITUTION

Be that as it may, the EU Constitution has not taken up this idea, and neither has the Hague Programme which is the new long-term programme to strengthen the area of freedom, security and justice.[35] In this programme it is only said in abstract terms that the citizen's participation in public life will be promoted and facilitated.[36]

---

[34] In fact, a similar idea is expressed in the Fourth Report of the Commission on Citizenship of the Union of 26 October 2004, already referred to, see section 3.3 and the Conclusions. However, the Commission refers to petitions, questions and correspondence, without expressing its own opinion on this idea.

[35] The reference is to Annex I in the European Council's conclusions of 4/5 November 2004, doc. 14292/1/04 of 8 December 2004, pp. 11 et seq.

[36] Para. III.1.1 of the Hague Programme (doc. 14292/1/04) p. 16.

On the other hand, the EU Constitution[37] offers some new insights as to the legal context and scope of European Citizenship. In this context it is observed that 'European Citizenship' is referred to in the EU Constitution in different places: twice in Part I (Art. I-10 and Title VI TCE), in Part II (Title V TCE) and twice in Part III (Title II and Title VI, Chapter I TCE).

In Article I-10 TCE a summary of the rights as presently included in Part II of the EC Treaty is provided. Article I-10 TCE forms part of Title II called 'Fundamental Rights and Citizenship of the Union'. Therefore, although in essence the present legal situation is reflected and consolidated in Article I-10 TCE, an interesting finding is that citizenship is now linked to the fundamental rights dimension of the EU Constitution.

Secondly, Title VI of Part I of the EU Constitution presents citizenship in the context of the 'Democratic Life of the Union'. Although the concept of 'European Citizenship' is not directly referred to, it follows from the title of Title VI TCE that the EU Constitution presents the ordinary citizen as a partner in an organization which aims to operate according to democratic principles. In this context mention is made of respectively the principle of democratic equality (Art. I-45 TCE), the principle of representative democracy (Art. I-46 TCE),[38] the principle of participatory democracy (Art. I-47 TCE),[39] the social partners and social dialogue (Art. I-48 TCE), the European Ombudsman (Art. I-49 TCE), transparency (Art. I-50 TCE),[40] the protection of personal data (Art. I-51 TCE)[41] as well as the status of churches and non-confessional organizations (Art. I-52 TCE).[42]

---

[37] Reference is made to the final version as published in *OJ* (2004) C 310/1.

[38] Para. 2 states, on the one hand, that citizens are directly represented at Union level in the European Parliament. On the other hand, it is said that the Member States are represented in the European Council by their Heads of State and Government and in the Council by their governments. Para. 3 includes the phrase, presently referred to in Art. 1(2) TEU, that decisions of the Union shall be taken as openly as possible and as closely as possible to the citizen. Para. 4 mentions the idea, at present included in Art. 191(1) TEC, that political parties at the European level contribute to forming European political awareness and to expressing the will of Union citizens.

[39] According to para. 1 the institutions shall give citizens and representative associations the opportunity to make known and publicly exchange their views in all areas of Union action. Para. 4 includes the so-called 'peoples' right of initiative', according to which no less than one million citizens from a significant number of Member States may take the initiative of inviting the Commission, within the framework of its powers, to submit any appropriate proposal on matters where citizens consider that a legal act is required for the purpose of implementing the Constitution. A European law has to be established in order to determine the provisions for the procedures and conditions required for such a citizen's initiative, including the minimum number of Member States from which such citizens must come.

[40] This provision deals not only – in para. 3 – with the principle of access to documents, which is presently included in Article 255 TEC, but also – in para. 1 – with the principle concerning the openness of the work of the institutions, bodies, offices and agencies of the Union. In this respect para. 2 specifies that the European Parliament shall meet in public, as shall the Council when considering and voting on a draft legislative act.

[41] The subject-matter at present dealt with in Art. 286 TEC.

[42] According to para. 1 the Union respects and does not prejudice the status under national law of churches and religious associations or communities in the Member States.

The third reference, which is Title V of Part II TCE,[43] concerns 'Citizen's Rights'. Partly the rights at present included in Part II of the EC Treaty are mentioned here.[44] However, also new, additional, citizen's rights are presented, such as the right of good administration (Art. II-101 TCE), the right of access to documents (Art. II-102 TCE) and the freedom of movement and residence for nationals of third countries legally resident in the territory of a Member State (Art. II-105(2) TCE).

According to Article II-101(1) TCE 'every person has the right to have his or her affairs handled impartially, fairly and within a reasonable time by the institutions, bodies, offices and agencies of the Union'. This right includes the right to be heard, to have access to his or her file and the obligation, for EU institutions, bodies, offices and agencies, to give reasons for their decisions.[45] Article II-101(3) TCE refers to the principles of contractual and non-contractual responsibility of the Union, the substance of which is at present included in Article 288 TEC. Paragraph 4 recalls that every citizen 'may write to the institutions of the Union in one of the languages of the Constitution and must have an answer in the same language.'[46]

Article II-102 TCE corresponds with the principle of Article 255(1) TEC on the right of access, for any citizen of the Union, to documents of certain institutions. However, the scope of the principle of transparency has been widened, to the extent that the right of access is no longer limited to documents of the European Parliament, the Council and the Commission, but concerns the documents of all institutions, bodies, offices and agencies of the Union 'whatever their medium'.

The freedom of movement and residence of nationals of third countries legally resident in the territory of a Member State is listed in Article II-105(2) TCE, which is immediately after the reference to the freedom of every citizen of the Union to move and reside freely within the territory of the Member States, the subject-matter of the present Article 18(1) TEC. Therefore, from the way citizen's rights have been elaborated in this Title it follows that the scope of (the rights of) European Citizenship has been extended.

The fourth and fifth references to European Citizenship are to be found in Part III of the EU Constitution. Title II of Part III (Arts. III-123 to 129 TCE) provides for operational provisions on which measures to implement the principles of 'Non-discrimination and Citizenship' can be based. Apart from the con-

---

[43] It is remarkable to note that Part II of the EU Constitution is still called 'The Charter of Fundamental Rights of the Union' and is accompanied by a preamble.

[44] For example Art. II-99 TCE deals with the right to vote and to stand as a candidate at elections to the European Parliament; Art. II-100 TCE with the right to vote and to stand as a candidate at municipal elections; Art. II-103 TCE with the European Ombudsman; Art. II-104 TCE with the right to petition; Art. I-105 TCE with the freedom of movement and of residence; and Art. II-106 TCE with diplomatic and consular protection.

[45] Art. II-101(2) TCE.

[46] The principle which at present is included in Art. 21(3) TEC.

cept of European Citizenship also the two non-discrimination provisions present-ly included in Part One of the EC Treaty – Articles 12 and 13 TEC – are includ-ed in this title of the EU Constitution. Subsection 1 (*The European Parliament*) of Section 1 (The Institutions) in Chapter I (Provisions governing the Institu-tions) of Title VI (The functioning of the Union) recalls the existence of the right to petition, respectively, the European Ombudsman: Articles III-334 and 335 TCE.

Thus, from the – in some respects somewhat confusing – way that European Citizenship has been elaborated in the EU Constitution, one gets the impression, first of all, that the concept has been given more impetus and attention compared to the present situation in the EC Treaty. A further observation is that European Citizenship has found its place (in Art. I-8 TCE) in the context of the respect to be paid, by the Union and its institutions, to *fundamental and human rights*. Then, by presenting the citizen in the context of the *democratic principles* to be respected by the Union (Title VI of Part I TCE), the intention has clearly been to create more understanding among citizens concerning what the European Union is doing. Furthermore, from the set of *citizen's rights* included in the Charter of Fundamental Rights (Title V of Part II TCE) it may be concluded that the scope of European Citizenship has been extended.

All in all, it appears that, through its presentation in the EU Constitution, Eu-ropean Citizenship as a concept has been strengthened and promoted as a princi-ple of EU law of major importance. In fact, now it also tends to overlap – at least partly – with the other, more political, concept of a *Citizen's Europe* which is aimed at bringing the ordinary citizens closer to the European Union.

## 7.    THIRD COUNTRY NATIONALS

A moment ago it was observed that a reference to the freedom of third country nationals to travel and reside in a Member State was included in the EU Consti-tution, under 'Citizens Rights'.[47] Is it imaginable that they – citizens of third countries having a lawful residence in one of the Member States – will be grant-ed European Citizenship, or at least certain rights covered by that concept?

Here, clearly a distinction has to be made between family members – of an EU citizen – having the nationality of a third state, and third country nationals who possess an autonomous right of residence in one of the Member States as primary beneficiaries.

### 7.1    Family Members of EU Citizens

Family members of an EU citizen having the nationality of a Member State can already profit from certain rights and facilities. Here the contents of Regulation

---

[47] *Supra*, para. 6.

1612/68 and, once Directive 2004/38 will have full legal effect, the equivalent provisions of that directive are of importance. More in particular the principle of equal treatment is the key element.[48]

Now, in a number of recent Court decisions the situation of family members possessing the nationality of a third country has been further strengthened. In the Court's case law family members – the partner and/or children of a EU benefi-ciary – have been protected by fundamental rights, notably the principle regard-ing *respect for family rights* of Article 8 of the European Convention for the Pro-tection of Human Rights and Fundamental Freedoms.

An example is the Court's decision of 11 July 2002 in the *Carpenter* case.[49] Mary Carpenter was a national of the Philippines. She visited the United King-dom and married a UK national who ran a business selling advertising space in medical and scientific journals. For the purpose of his business Mr Carpenter travelled to other Member States.[50] In the proceedings the argument was put for-ward that this case did not present any link to any of the situations envisaged un-der Community law, the so-called 'internal' situation doctrine. However, the Court rejected this argument and ruled that Mr Carpenter was availing himself of the right freely to provide services guaranteed by Article 49 TEC.[51] The Court concluded that Article 49 TEC, read in conjunction with the fundamental right to respect for family life, must be interpreted as precluding a refusal, by a Member State of origin of a provider of services established in that Member State who provides services to recipients established in other Member States, of the right to reside in its territory for that provider's spouse who is a national of a third coun-try.

Another example is the Court's decision of 23 September 2003 in the *Akrich* case.[52] Akrich was a Moroccan citizen who was granted leave to enter the United Kingdom on a one month tourist visa. However, he was convicted of attempted theft and the use of a stolen identity card. Whilst residing unlawfully in the Unit-ed Kingdom, he married a British citizen who established herself in Ireland as a worker. Akrich joined his wife in Ireland, but he did not possess a right of resi-dence there. With his wife he later returned to the United Kingdom where he ap-plied for entry clearance as the spouse of a UK citizen.[53] The national authorities refused to grant him such a right. The Court found that Akrich did not enjoy the

---

[48] In Art. 24(1) of Directive 2004/03 it is said:

'Subject to such specific provisions as are expressly provided for in the Treaty and secondary law, all Union citizens residing on the basis of this Directive in the territory of the host Member State shall enjoy equal treatment of that Member State within the scope of the Treaty. The ben-efit of this right shall be extended to family members who are nationals of a Member State and who have the right of residence or permanent residence.'

[49] ECJ, judgment of 11 July 2002, Case C-60/00, *Carpenter* [2002] *ECR* I-6279.

[50] Paras. 13-14.

[51] Paras. 28-29.

[52] ECJ, judgment of 23 September 2003, Case C-109/01, *Akrich* [2003] *ECR* I-9607.

[53] Paras. 29-34.

rights provided for in Article 10 of Regulation 1612/68 because he had not resided lawfully on the territory of a Member State, in his case, Ireland.[54] However, the Court added that the UK authorities, in assessing the application by the spouse to enter and remain in that Member State, must nonetheless take into consideration the right to respect for family life under Article 8 of the European Convention for the Protection of Human Rights and Fundamental Freedoms, provided that the marriage is genuine.[55] It was left to the national court to make the final appreciation in this case.

Although not referring explicitly to Article 8 of the European Convention, in this context also the Court's decision of 25 July 2002 in the case *MRAX* (*Mouvement contre le racisme, l'antisémitisme et la xénophobie*) can be mentioned.[56] In this case the Court, *inter alia*, came to the conclusion that a Member State cannot send back at its border a third country national who is married to a national of a Member State and attempts to enter its territory without being in possession of a valid identity card or passport (or, if necessary, a visa) where he is able to prove his identity and the conjugal ties and there is no evidence to establish that he represents a risk to the requirements of public policy, public security or public health within the meaning of Article 10 of Directive 68/360 and Article 8 of Directive 73/148.[57] In this decision the Court, while examining the legality of sanctions imposed by a Member State in situations of such an unlawful stay, invoked the principle of *proportionality* on more than one occasion.[58]

In the Court's case law there are even examples of cases where the discussion is primarily focused on the position of third country nationals (family members of an EU citizen).

The Court's decision of 17 September 2002 in the *Baumbast and R.* case is such an example.[59] The discussion concerned the right of residence of children and the (former) partner – of a EU citizen – having the nationality of a third country who, however, was the primary carer of those children. In view of the importance of the 'integration' objective of the principle of free movement of persons, the Court concluded that children must have the possibility of going to school and pursuing further education in the host Member State as is expressly provided in Article 12 of Regulation 1612/68.[60] As to the position of the primary carer for the children having the nationality of a third country, the Court felt that if such a parent were refused the right to remain in the host Member State during the period of their children's education that might deprive those children of a right which is granted to them by the Community legislature. In this context ref-

---

[54] Paras. 50 et seq.
[55] Para. 58.
[56] ECJ, judgment of 25 July 2002, Case C-459/99, *MRAX* [2002] *ECR* I-6591.
[57] Para. 61.
[58] See for example paras. 61, 78 and 90.
[59] See *supra* n. 12.
[60] Paras. 30-31 respectively 61/62.

erence was made to Article 8 of the European Convention.[61] The Court concluded that the children concerned had the right to be accompanied by the person
who is their primary carer and, accordingly, that that person is entitled to reside
with them in that Member State during their studies.[62]

A similar approach was followed by the Court in its decision of 19 October
2004 in the *Chen* case, already mentioned.[63] However, whereas in this case the
mother had a third country nationality, the child possessed the nationality of a
Member State. Thus the child was entitled to invoke the rights of European Citizenship, more particularly Article 18 in conjunction with Article 12 TEC.[64]

## 7.2    Long-term Residents and Directive 2003/109 of 25 November 2003

Another category of third country nationals concerns those people who possess a
proper right of residence in one of the Member States, as primary beneficiaries.
In such a situation the question arises whether 'long-term residents' having the
nationality of a third country as well as their family members, should not be
granted certain civil and political rights as developed for EU citizens within the
framework of European Citizenship. More in particular, two aspects are relevant
here: the right of (free) movement within the European Union and the right to
vote and to stand as a candidate for local, regional and/or national elections.

Obviously the situation of a third country national as the primary beneficiary
of a right of (free) movement within the European Union has to be discussed in
the context of Title IV of (Part III of) the EC Treaty, as introduced by the Amsterdam Treaty, where rules concerning, *inter alia*, the asylum and immigration
policy of the European Community are to be found. More in particular, paragraphs 3 and 4 of Article 63 TEC are of relevance here.[65] Now, concerning the
principle of movement of third country nationals, having a right of residence in a
Member State, the European Union has recently adopted a legislative instrument.
The relevant decision is Council Directive 2003/109 of 25 November 2003 concerning the status of third country nationals who are long-term residents.[66] The
directive is based on both provisions mentioned, paragraphs 3 and 4 of Article
63 TEC. According to the regime of the directive Member States shall grant
long-term resident status to third-country nationals who have resided legally and
continuously within their territory for *five years* immediately prior to the submis-

---

[61] Paras. 71-72.
[62] Para. 73.
[63] See *supra* n. 25.
[64] Paras. 25-26 to be read in conjunction with para. 45.
[65] Art. 63(3) TEC concerns measures on immigration policy, more in particular concerning
conditions of entry and residence (a) and illegal immigration and illegal residence (b). Art. 63(4)
TEC concerns measures defining the rights and obligations under which nationals of third countries who are legally resident in a Member State may reside in other Member States.
[66] *OJ* (2004) L 16/44.

sion of the relevant application (Art. 4(1)). The deadline for the transposition of the directive expires on 23 January 2006 (Art. 26).

As conditions for acquiring long-term resident status the directive requires (a) stable and regular resources which are sufficient to maintain himself/herself and the members of his/her family without recourse to the social assistance system of the Member State concerned and (b) health insurance in respect of all risks normally covered for the country's own nationals in the Member State concerned (Art. 5). Also the Member States may require third country nationals to comply with integration conditions, in accordance with their national law (Art. 5(2)).

An important component of the directive concerns the functioning, also in this context, of the principle of *equal treatment*. In Article 11(1) of the Directive it is stated that long-term residents shall enjoy equal treatment – compared to the nationals of the host Member State – as regards:

a. 'access to employment and self-employed activity;
b. education and vocational training, including study grants in accordance with national law;
c. recognition of professional diplomas;
d. social security;
e. tax benefits;
f. access to goods and services;
g. freedom of association and affiliation and membership of an organization representing workers or employers;
h. free access to the entire territory of the Member State concerned.'

Paragraphs 2 to 4 of Article 11 provide for certain limitations and restrictions of the principle of equal treatment.[67] Be that as it may, at least similar rights and benefits as included in Regulation 1612/68 and attributed to EU citizens, have been granted to long-term residents having the nationality of a third country.

With respect to the right of (free) movement to other Member States, Article 14(1) of the directive states that a long-term resident shall acquire the right to reside in the territory of a Member State other than the one which granted him/her the long-term residence status, for a period extending to three months provided that certain conditions are met. In this respect it is said – in Article 14(2) – that a long term resident may reside in a second Member State: (a) to exercise an economic activity in an employed or self-employed capacity; (b) to pursue studies or vocational training; (c) for other purposes. Apart from certain nuances and exceptions[68] the Member State may also require the persons concerned to pro-

---

[67] Para. 2 allows for the application of equal treatment in cases where the registered or usual place of residence of the long-term resident, or that of family members for whom he/she claims benefits, lies within the territory of the Member State concerned. Para. 3 concerns limitations to access to employment or self-employed activities in cases where these activities are reserved for nationals and where there are language requirements. Para. 4 allows Member States to limit equal treatment in respect of social assistance and social protection to core benefits.

[68] See the categories mentioned in paras. 3-5 of Art. 14.

vide evidence that they have (a) 'stable and regular resources' as well as (b) 'sickness insurance' (Art. 15(2)). Also the host Member State may require third country nationals to comply with immigration measures, in accordance with its national law (Art. 15(3)). The exception to this principle concerns the situation of a third country national who has already been required to comply with integration conditions in his/her first Member State of stay.[69]

Thus, although it is clear that long-term residents having the nationality of a third country do not possess an absolute right of free movement within the territory of the Union, in essence their status is not so different compared to the situation of EU workers and independents.

As to the question of whether or not to grant European Citizenship, or at least certain civil or political rights, to long-term residents in the EU having a third country nationality there are, on the one hand, arguments to do this. Indeed, the possession of citizenship can only contribute to the objective of integration in the society of the host Member State. More in particular, one could think at the right of vote and the right to stand as a candidate in local elections.[70] On the other hand, there may be political reservations in taking this step. Politically, this is certainly a sensitive area. That having been said, in several Member States – such as the Netherlands – long-term residents having the nationality of whatever country have for a long time already had a right to vote and to stand as a candidate in municipal elections.[71]

Therefore, is it not imaginable that an EU instrument granting such a right to long-term third country nationals will be adopted, if not now then at least in the (near) future? It is clear that the EU Constitution has missed the opportunity to take such an important step towards the integration of all people, whatever their nationality, in the environment where they live and to contribute, physically and financially, to the benefit of its citizens. Also there is no reference to such a prerogative in the Hague Programme.[72] Now we have to wait for a new opportunity in the future.

---

[69] Second sub-paragraph of Art.15(3). In the third sub-paragraph it is said that the persons concerned may still be required to attend language courses.

[70] Thus, the equivalent of Art. 19(1) TEC.

[71] The duration of residence in the Dutch case is five years. See for the overall Dutch situation the 'Wet van 29 augustus 1985 tot wijziging van de Kieswet en de Gemeentewet' [Act of 29 August 1985 amending the Elections Act and the Local Government Act], *Staatsblad* (1985) p. 478, to be read in conjunction with Art. 130 of the Dutch Constitution as amended in 1983.

[72] See *supra* n. 36. In para. III.1.5 it is only said that 'a comprehensive approach involving stakeholders at the local, regional, national, and EU level' is essential. Also para. 38 on immigrant integration policy in the European Council's latest conclusions, those of 16/17 December 2004 (Doc 16238/04 of 17 December 2004), is drafted in global terms.

## 8.    CONCLUDING REMARKS

European Citizenship, introduced by the Maastricht Treaty, was originally considered to be mainly a political concept. However, the Court of Justice in its case law has given the concept a proper meaning and interpretation.

More in particular, by stressing the nationality aspect and – for EU citizens – European Citizenship as a consequence, the Court, through the application of the principle of equal treatment, has extended the scope of beneficiaries of free movement within the European Union, more in particular to categories of non-economically active EU nationals. In its interpretation the Court has also mitigated the requirement of having one's own resources as a condition for a lawful stay and residence in a host Member State. The Court's case law is in particular relevant for students, one of the categories of non-economically active EU citizens.

As to the further development and/or broadening of European Citizenship rights it is theoretically possible to extend, with regard to EU citizens, the right to vote and to stand as a candidate to elections at the regional level and, even, to elections at the national level. However, this idea has not been upheld in the EU Constitution.

On the other hand, the EU Constitution presents European Citizenship in a broader context compared to the present situation. First of all, citizenship is referred to in the discussion concerning 'Democracy in the EU' where certain principles are included, such as the principle of democratic equality, the principle of representative democracy, the principle of participatory democracy, the social dialogue, transparency and the protection of personal data. Furthermore, the EU Constitution has included citizens' rights in the Charter on Fundamental Rights. In doing so, the EU Constitution has extended the scope of European citizenship rights to areas other than the ones mentioned at present in Part II TEC. Examples are the right to good administration, the right to access documents and, even, the freedom of movement and residence for nationals of third countries legally resident in the territory of a Member State.

From the way European Citizenship is presented and elaborated in the EU Constitution, one may conclude that the concept is more and more linked to the concept of a 'Citizen's Europe', the public debate aiming to bring the ordinary citizen closer to the EU and its institutions.

A final question is whether European Citizenship, or at least certain civil and political rights, cannot also be granted to third country nationals. It is clear that third country nationals who are family member of an EU citizen can already enjoy certain rights and facilities on the same footing as nationals of the host Member State. The situation may be viewed differently when one considers the status of third country nationals having a long-term resident status in one of the Member States. Nonetheless, while recognizing that an identical status compared to EU citizens is not indicated, one may argue that long-term residents should be able to profit at least from some of the privileges nowadays possessed by EU citizens, for example the right to vote in elections for the local government. Here the objective of the integration of people, whatever their nationality, in their local environment is important.

Be that as it may, it is to be expected that European Citizenship (in close connection with the concept of a Citizen's Europe) will play a role of primary importance in the process of European integration in the future. In fact a role which is similar to the one played – in the 1960s, 1970s, and 1980s – by the 'Internal Market' objective of the EC Treaty which, indeed, at that time was the key objective of the European Community. This development may illustrate the gradual development of the Union, from an economic entity of interest primarily for the Member States and business, to a political one in the context of which the ordinary citizen occupies a central position.

Obviously such a development is to be welcomed. It can only but contribute to solid popular support for the process of European integration and, as such, constitute an important factor to guarantee its continuation in the future.

# THE EUROPEAN OMBUDSMAN AND THE EU CONSTITUTION

## P. Nikiforos Diamandouros[*]

### 1. INTRODUCTION

I shall begin this article by explaining what an ombudsman is, how the ombudsman institution has spread and developed and the relationship between ombudsmen and the courts. I shall then describe the European Ombudsman's role in the Convention and the provisions of the EU Constitution that relate to the Ombudsman. Finally, I shall consider the Charter of Fundamental Rights and explain why ombudsmen, including ombudsmen in the Member States, have a key role to play in the Charter's implementation.

### 2. WHAT IS AN OMBUDSMAN?

#### 2.1 The Basic Role

The basic function of an ombudsman is to investigate and report on complaints against public authorities. The world of ombudsmen is diverse, but there are certain generally recognised criteria that every ombudsman should meet. These are: independence; fair procedure; public accountability; and effectiveness. As well as exercising a control function over public authorities, ombudsmen are also a resource to help improve the quality of public sector management, especially by dealing with the underlying systemic problems that give rise to complaints.

#### 2.2 The Development of the Ombudsman Institution

The first ombudsman office was created in Sweden in 1809 to check the legality of public officials' actions. During the next century and a half, just two more countries established ombudsmen with general competence: Finland in 1919 and Denmark in 1955.

---

[*] European Ombudsman.

*D. Curtin, A.E. Kellermann and S. Blockmans, eds., The EU Constitution: The Best Way Forward?*
© 2005, *T.M.C. Asser Instituut, The Hague.*

In the 1960s and early 70s, a first wave of global expansion began when older democracies such as Norway, New Zealand, the UK and France set up ombudsmen. They did so in order to tackle citizens' problems with public administration, which expanded and took on new roles in the 20th century, especially after the Second World War, when the welfare functions of the state grew dramatically.

In two subsequent waves of global expansion, ombudsmen were established in many newer democracies as part of their commitment to respect human rights and the principle of democracy:

- From the mid-1970s onwards, ombudsmen were established in post-authoritarian states, such as Spain, Portugal and Greece in Europe and in many countries of Latin America.

- After 1989, ombudsmen were established in post-totalitarian states; that is, in countries formerly ruled by communist regimes.

This sequence of development is reflected in different names: *Ombudsman*; *Commissioner for Administration*; *Médiateur*; *Defensor del Pueblo*; *Human Rights Ombudsman*; *Commissioner for Civil Rights*. It also means that the work of contemporary ombudsmen, including the European Ombudsman, is based on three overlapping and mutually supportive elements: legality, good administration and human rights.

## 2.3    The European Ombudsman

The Maastricht Treaty established the European Ombudsman in 1993 to enhance relations between citizens and the Union level of governance. The European Ombudsman is competent to deal with maladministration in the activities of Community institutions and bodies. The institutions are, of course, listed in the Treaty but the category of 'bodies' is open-ended and has grown significantly in recent years as new agencies have been established. The lodestar of the European Ombudsman's work, especially as regards legality and human rights, is the case law of the Court of Justice and the Court of First Instance. This brings me to an important general point about the relationship between the work of ombudsmen and that of the courts.

## 2.4    Ombudsmen and the EU Courts

The rule of law and respect for individual rights cannot be guaranteed unless there is a strong and independent judiciary. Where this precondition is met, however, ombudsmen can also play a valuable role in empowering citizens, providing redress and raising the quality of public administration. To explain why this is so, it is useful to compare some of the different characteristics of the courts and ombudsmen. Decisions of courts are binding and can provide authoritative interpretations of the law. However,

- rules of procedure are strict and complex;

- proceedings are often lengthy and expensive;

- a court case is usually a zero-sum game: that is, one side wins and the other loses; and, finally,

- courts can act only when a case is brought before them.

On the other hand:

- ombudsmen have flexible and informal procedures. This is possible because an ombudsman normally has no power to make legally binding decisions. (Nor is such a power necessary: where the rule of law and democracy are strong, public authorities usually follow an ombudsman's recommendations);

- they can act relatively quickly and cheaply, normally with no cost to the complainant;

- they can promote positive-sum outcomes that benefit both the complainant and the public authority; and finally,

- ombudsmen can be proactive as well as reactive. For example, they can take initiatives to deal with systemic problems in the public administration. They can also organise information campaigns to inform citizens about their rights and how to use them.

The importance of the courts in upholding the rule of law and individual rights means that it is essential not to overload them with unnecessary cases. Ideally, therefore, going to court should be the last, not the first, resort for a citizen who has a problem with the public authorities.

Where ombudsmen exist, citizens can choose the non-judicial remedy of the ombudsman as an alternative to going to court. This widens access to justice and strengthens both the rule of law and the quality of democracy. This analysis of ombudsmen and of different remedies informed the European Ombudsman's main proposals for the EU Constitution.

## 3. THE CONVENTION, THE EU CONSTITUTION AND OMBUDSMEN

### 3.1 The European Ombudsman's Main Proposals

The European Ombudsman participated as an Observer in both the Convention chaired by Valéry Giscard d'Estaing, which drafted the EU Constitution, and in the earlier Convention (chaired by Roman Herzog) which drafted the Charter of Fundamental Rights, proclaimed at Nice in December 2000. In both Conventions, the Ombudsman pushed for the deliberations to focus not just on power structures, but also on citizens.

As regards the judicial protection of human rights, the Ombudsman supported both the Union's accession to the European Convention on Human Rights and a legally binding Charter of Fundamental Rights, arguing that the two should be seen as complementary, not as alternatives. The EU Constitution does indeed provide for both these types of protection.

The Ombudsman also emphasised that good administration is essential for citizens to be able to enjoy their rights as an everyday reality and called for the EU Constitution to provide for a law on good administration that would apply to all the Union institutions and bodies. Such a law would implement the citizen's right to good administration, contained in Article II-101 TCE[1] and put an end to the present confusing situation, in which different Union institutions apply different codes of good administration.

As Commissioner De Palacio pointed out in the European Parliament's debate on the Ombudsman's Annual Report (25 September 2003), this call has been answered in Article III-398 TCE, which provides for European laws to ensure an open, efficient and independent European administration. Furthermore, the Secretary General of the European Commission, Mr O'Sullivan, has mentioned 2006 as a possible date for the Commission to bring forward a draft proposal for such a law. Finally, the Ombudsman called for the EU Constitution to set out clearly the remedies available to citizens if their rights under Union law are not respected, including both the right to go to a national court and the right to an effective non-judicial remedy.

### 3.2    The European Ombudsman's Place in the EU Constitution

As regards the role of the European Ombudsman, the outcome was very positive. In Part I of the EU Constitution, the European Ombudsman is mentioned in both Article I-10 of the title on citizenship and fundamental rights (Title II) and Article I-49 of the title on the democratic life of the Union (Title VI). The Ombudsman thus constitutes the link between the Union's commitments to human and fundamental rights and its democratic commitments and aspirations. Article I-49 TCE also makes clear that the European Ombudsman is elected by the European Parliament, rather than appointed. This change better reflects reality, as well as having symbolic importance for the Ombudsman's independence. Furthermore, the demise of the 'pillar' structure of the Union means that the Ombudsman's mandate is broadened to include all the Union Institutions, bodies, offices and agencies. The articles on the European Ombudsman in the Charter of Fundamental Rights (Art. II-103 TCE) and in Part III of the EU Constitution (Art. III-335 TCE) also incorporate these changes.

---

[1] The numbering of articles is as in the final version of the Treaty establishing a Constitution for Europe, document CIG 87/2/04 REV 2 (signed on 29 October 2004).

### 3.3 Judicial and Non-Judicial Remedies in the Member States

As regards judicial remedies, Article I-29 TCE answers (if somewhat obliquely) the Ombudsman's call for the EU Constitution to inform citizens of their right to go to a national court. It requires Member States to provide 'remedies sufficient to ensure effective legal protection in the fields covered by Union law.' However, neither the Convention nor the IGC found time to act on proposals to strengthen non-judicial remedies in cases where Member States fail to comply with Union law. Nonetheless, I remain convinced that ombudsmen at all levels have a vital role to play in ensuring the full and correct implementation of Union law, including the Charter of Fundamental Rights, to which I will now turn.

## 4. THE CHARTER OF FUNDAMENTAL RIGHTS

### 4.1 Implementation of the Charter at the Union Level

In relation to the Union level of governance, the European Ombudsman has actively promoted the Charter ever since its proclamation by the European Parliament, the Council and the Commission at the Nice summit in December 2000. In dealing with complaints and in own-initiative inquiries, the Ombudsman has consistently taken the view that failure to respect the rights contained in the Charter is maladministration. The EU Constitution incorporates the Charter as its Part II and explicitly foresees that the Union courts will be called on to interpret the Charter (revised Charter Preamble). Naturally, the European Ombudsman will follow the case law of the Union courts, when it appears.

### 4.2 Implementation of the Charter by the Member States

The Charter is also addressed to Member States 'when they are implementing Union law.' (Art. II-111 TCE). I do not intend to enter into a complex legal debate about the precise meaning of that phrase in its specific context. If necessary, the Court of Justice may, in future, give an authoritative legal interpretation. For present purposes, it is enough to point out that, in general, the concept of implementation includes not only the transposition of Directives (or 'framework laws', as they will become under the EU Constitution) into national law, but also the application of such national law by public authorities in the Member States.

In accordance with the principle of subsidiarity, the task of implementing Union law and policy mostly falls, in fact, on national, regional and local authorities and other public organisations in the Member States. If citizens are to enjoy their Charter rights in practice, therefore, it is essential for the different public authorities of the Member States to follow the Charter even when they are acting under national law, at least if the national law concerned implements Union law.

## 4.3    Remedies against Member States

Rights also depend on the existence of effective remedies. Understandably, citizens who believe that a Member State is not respecting Union law often seek a remedy at the Union level. Some citizens complain to the Commission, in its role as guardian of the Treaty. This can eventually lead the Commission to refer the matter to the Court of Justice under Article 226 of the EC Treaty. Many complainants, however, hope that the Commission will solve their case quickly in the administrative stage of the Article 226 procedure, without going to Court. Citizens also petition the European Parliament concerning infringements. In practice, it often falls to the Commission to examine these cases as well. Finally, many citizens complain to the European Ombudsman against public administrations of the Member States, but such complaints are outside the mandate. My expectation is that when the EU Constitution comes into force and the Charter becomes legally binding, many more citizens are likely to try to bring cases to the Union level. I believe that it would be more effective and in accordance with the principle of subsidiarity for most such cases to be dealt with locally, in the Member State itself. That would also avoid overloading the Commission's Article 226 procedure and the European Parliament's petitions procedure.

## 4.4    The Need to Strengthen Non-Judicial Remedies in the Member States

Citizens who wish to protect their fundamental rights against the public administrations of the Member States can, of course, bring proceedings in national courts. But for reasons that I have already explained, going to court should be the last, not the first, resort for a citizen who has a problem with the public authorities. I also know from experience that few citizens who seek a remedy at the Union level are satisfied by the information that their only recourse is a judicial remedy in the Member State. I therefore firmly believe that an essential element of subsidiarity in remedies is to strengthen non-judicial remedies in the Member States. I am reinforced in this belief by the fact that ensuring full and correct implementation of Union law is not just a matter of providing effective remedies, vital though that is. It also involves the difficult and painstaking task of strengthening the capacity of public authorities of the Member States to follow the law, observe the principles of good administration and respect human rights. Ombudsmen are particularly well suited to combining such reactive and proactive functions and to creating synergies between them. For example, by publicising criteria of good administration (such as the Code of Good Administrative Behaviour that I mentioned earlier) ombudsmen can:

- make their own findings more easily understandable; and

- help both citizens and the administration focus on their mutual expectations in a way that promotes trust and more effective communication.

## 4.5    The Role of the European Network of Ombudsmen

The current situation in the European Union is that there are ombudsmen in all 25 Member States, either at national or regional level or, in some countries – such as Spain – at both levels. For my part, I am working actively to deepen our existing co-operation with them through the European network of ombudsmen. The Network also includes ombudsmen in the candidate states and the wider Schengen area, embracing more than 90 offices in 30 countries. It ensures that complaints are rapidly directed to the competent ombudsman and facilitates the exchange of information about best practices and developments in European law. I am already working with our partners from the Member States in the Network, to assist and encourage them in ensuring the full and correct implementation of Union law. I believe that, with the co-operation of the European Parliament and the Commission, we could put in place, by the time the EU Constitution comes into force, a comprehensive, coherent and effective system of non-judicial remedies in the Member States, to help citizens enjoy their rights under Union law *vis-à-vis* public authorities in the Member States, including their fundamental rights under the Charter. This would:

–    enhance choice for citizens by providing an alternative remedy;

–    strengthen subsidiarity;

–    spare Union institutions from overload; and

–    contribute to administrative capacity building in the Member States, where needed.


## 5.    CONCLUSION

I would like to conclude with, here are a few general reflections about constitutions, which I believe are particularly relevant to the Treaty establishing a Constitution for Europe. Every constitution can be looked at from two perspectives. The first sees it as a way of allocating public authority between different institutions and different territorial levels of government. From this perspective, the constitution can be understood as both the result of competing political forces and as a framework within which political competition takes place. During the Convention that drafted the EU Constitution, we heard a lot of debate from this perspective. We shall no doubt hear more during the process of ratification. Such debate is normal and healthy in any democracy, but it should not exclude the second perspective.

From the second perspective, a constitution is a framework for relations between individuals and public authorities – of all kinds and at all levels of governance. In a *democracy*, the two perspectives are inseparably linked through the idea of *citizenship*. The EU Constitution represents a major step forward along the road of creating a genuine citizenship of the Union, as a complement to national citizenship. The Charter in particular is an instrument with great potential to translate fundamental values and principles into reality by empowering citizens and strengthening democracy at all levels of the Union. To achieve this potential requires *proactive* intervention by institutions, to make citizens aware of the new possibilities opened up for them by the Charter and to encourage and assist public authorities at all levels of the Union to make the rights and aspirations of the Charter the touchstone for their actions. It is towards the realisation of this goal that institutions should strive and, as the European Ombudsman, I pledge myself to work hard for its achievement.

# PART IV

## Expansion of Executive, Judicial and Legislative Powers

# SHARED LEADERSHIP IN THE EU: THEORY AND REALITY

Simone Bunse, Paul Magnette and Kalypso Nicolaïdis[*]

## 1.    INTRODUCTION

The European Union (EU) is characterised by a purposeful diffusion of political authority between supranational and intergovernmental institutions. Based on the ideal of shared leadership, it relies on a delicate institutional balance guarding equality between its ever more diverse members and managing potential tensions between the more and less populated states. Such tensions are present in any federal construct, and have been a key concern since the 'original six' founded the European Coal and Steel Community (ECSC) in 1951.[1]

From its early beginnings the Community method has sought to balance the two key principles of equality and democratic representation. Nonetheless, over time – with successive enlargements predominantly to small states and the extended use of qualified majority voting (QMV) in the Council – the original founding compromise became more contentious. The big countries increasingly fell prey to what some referred to as the 'Gulliver syndrome', picturing themselves as giants potentially held back by a crowd of mini-countries.[2] Since the Nice Treaty negotiations, the division between the big and the small states has become ever more explicit. Thus, the rational of the Convention on the Future of Europe was not only to ensure that preparations for the forthcoming IGC would be more 'broadly based and transparent,' but, crucially, to resolve this increasingly stark divide.[3]

---

[*] Simone Bunse, Nuffield College, University of Oxford; Paul Magnette, Institute for European Studies, Université libre de Bruxelles; and Kalypso Nicolaïdis, St. Antony's College, University of Oxford.
[1] P. Magnette and K. Nicolaïdis, 'Big vs. Small States in the EU: Reinventing the Balance' (Notre Europe, Research Note No. 25 (2003)). M. Kohnstamm and G. Durand, 'Common Nonsense – Defusing the escalating "Big vs. Small" Row' (Brussels, European Police Center (2003)) available at: <http://www.theepc.be/en/default.asp?TYP=SEARCH&LV=279&see=y&PG=TEWN/EN/directa&AI=229&l=>.
[2] P. Magnette and K. Nicolaïdis, 'The European Convention: Bargaining in the Shadow of Rhetoric', 27 *West European Politics* (2004).
[3] European Council (14-15 December 2001) Laeken Declaration (15 December 2001). 'Conclusions of the Presidency. Annex I'. (SN300/1/01 REV 1) available at: <http://europa.eu.int/constitution/futurum/documents/offtext/doc151201_en.htm.>.

---

*D. Curtin, A.E. Kellermann and S. Blockmans, eds., The EU Constitution: The Best Way Forward?*
© *2005, T.M.C. Asser Instituut, The Hague.*

This contribution examines the 'big versus small' divide in the Convention. It shows that rather than rectifying it, the division between the big and the small dominated the final months of the Convention's work and almost resulted in its breakdown. The key questions which the contribution seeks to address are who won and who lost in the Convention and – most importantly – why. It begins by examining the EU's original bargain and how it evolved. Particular emphasis is put on how small state interests were protected and how the sharing out of leadership was ensured. This is followed by an analysis of the Convention's endgame which was dominated by the passionate debate over the future shape of the EU's Council presidency. While the bigs favoured the creation of a permanent Council president, the smalls fiercely defended the rotation principle to guard equality in the EU. The analysis pays particular attention to the leadership resources which both the big and small states had at their disposal, how effectively these were used, and what strategies were applied.

It is argued that despite the EU's ideal of shared leadership which marked its original design and motivated the creation of the Convention, the larger states assumed the key leadership role in the Convention end-game compromising this ideal in case of the European Council presidency. Strong resistance by a large small state coalition led by the Benelux notwithstanding, the Franco-German proposals assumed the dominant position around which a consensus was constructed leading to an outcome that trumped the interests of the smalls. Apart from their material strength, the key resources France and Germany relied on to shape the final outcome were institutional advantages (such as key allies in the Convention Presidium whose procedural power over the negotiations and the outcome was crucial), an alliance with other big states (such as the UK and Spain), and to a lesser extent their reputation. Through their own structural leadership and the Convention chair's forceful leadership (or exploitation of informal powers) they turned their material advantage into bargaining leverage inducing the other states to make concessions. The Benelux countries, in turn, concentrated on generating a united coalition of small states (instrumental leadership) and convincing the bigs of the importance of the equality and shared leadership ideal for the effective functioning of the EU (intellectual leadership). However, given the intensity of the preferences of the bigs, the Presidium's support of the Franco-German compromise, and the hard bargaining atmosphere – besides being in the majority in the Convention – the combination of material and institutional resources with structural leadership proved more successful.

## 2.  THE IDEAL OF SHARED LEADERSHIP: THE EU'S HISTORICAL INSTITUTIONAL BALANCE

The European Community (EC) was founded on two impulses. First, its creators aimed at designing a system based on shared leadership so that size would no longer equal might and temptations of hegemony by any of the big states would be alleviated. Second, while sharing out leadership, this new system denied the full import of sovereign equality between states – one of the most fundamental ways in which the EC diverged from the outset from common standards of international law and institutions. The *de facto* reality was that small states benefited disproportionately from the pooling of sovereignty, both as a way of managing interdependence and of recovering sovereignty on the international scene. To guarantee a fair balance between the bigs and the smalls the Paris Treaty set up three complementary mechanisms: a system of weighted votes in the Council of Ministers; independent supranational institutions; and a rotating rather than permanent Council presidency.

## 2.1    Weighted Votes in the Council of Ministers

Systems of weighted votes try to offer a degree of security for small state interests while giving the largest states a greater say in the decision. The EC's initial system of qualified majority voting is a perfect illustration of this logic of 'regressive proportionality' – a midway house between the principles of 'one country, one vote' and 'one citizen, one vote' reflecting the EU's twin sources of legitimacy. The three large Member States were given 4 votes, Belgium and the Netherlands 2, and Luxembourg 1 vote. This implied that – although over-represented – the largest states were 25 times 'less represented' than the smallest one. A decision could be blocked by 6 votes, i.e., by two large states or one large and at least one small state (Belgium or the Netherlands), but not by a small state alliance or one state by itself. The qualified majority (QM) represented about 70% of the population (see Table 1).

However, this consensus did not last. The 1973 enlargement called for a revision of the original weighting: while the UK received the same votes as the three large EC founders, Denmark and Ireland were given a smaller weight than Belgium and the Netherlands. The four big states now had 10 votes each, Belgium and the Netherlands 5, Denmark and Ireland 3, and Luxembourg 2. The QM changed to 42 out of 58 votes. In practice, this preserved the original logic of a 'blocking minority' of two large or one large and at least one small state. Successive enlargements followed the same logic: Greece in 1981 and Portugal in 1987 were given the same weight as Belgium and the Netherlands, Spain as a quasi-large state received 8 votes (a bargain it later came to resent), Finland in 1995 was given the same weight as Denmark and Ireland, while another category was created for Sweden and Austria, which received 4 votes. A QM subsequently consisted of 62 out of 87 votes; the blocking minority became more complex requiring the coalition of at least two large and two small states, one large and four small, or at least six small states. But the relative scale of representation – with a factor of one to five between the smallest and biggest state – remained unchanged.

In May 2004, Poland, the Czech Republic, Hungary, Slovakia, Lithuania, Latvia, Slovenia, Estonia, Cyprus, and Malta were accommodated into this system. Poland received 8 votes, the Czech Republic and Hungary 5, Slovakia, Lithuania, Latvia, Slovenia and Estonia 3, and Cyprus and Malta 2. The QM

**Table 1. The Evolution of Qualified Majority Voting in the Council of Ministers**

| | Number of Votes in Council of Ministers: | | | | | | | | Representing: | | |
|---|---|---|---|---|---|---|---|---|---|---|---|
| **Bigs** | 1958 EU6 | 1973 EU9 | 1981 EU10 | 1986 EU12 | 1995 EU15 | May 2004 EU25 | Nov. 2004[1] EU25 | 2007[2] (EU27) | Pop. (mil) | % of EU25 | % of EU27 |
| Germ. | 4 | 10 | 10 | 10 | 10 | 10 | 29 | 29 | 82.398 | 18.1 | 17.0 |
| France | 4 | 10 | 10 | 10 | 10 | 10 | 29 | 29 | 60.181 | 13.2 | 12.4 |
| UK | – | 10 | 10 | 10 | 10 | 10 | 29 | 29 | 60.065 | 13.2 | 12.4 |
| Italy | 4 | 10 | 10 | 10 | 10 | 10 | 29 | 29 | 57.998 | 12.7 | 12.0 |
| Spain | – | – | – | 8 | 8 | 8 | 27 | 27 | 40.217 | 8.8 | 8.3 |
| Poland | – | – | – | – | – | 8 | 27 | 27 | 38.623 | 8.5 | 8.0 |
| **Total** | **12 (70.6%)** | **40 (69%)** | **40 (63.5%)** | **48 (63.2%)** | **48 (55.2%)** | **56 (45.2)** | **170 (53%)** | **170 (49.3%)** | **339.482** | **74.5%** | **70.1%** |
| **Smalls** | | | | | | | | | | | |
| Romania | – | – | – | – | – | – | – | 14 | 22.272 | – | 4.6 |
| NL | 2 | 5 | 5 | 5 | 5 | 5 | 13 | 13 | 16.151 | 3.6 | 3.3 |
| Greece | – | – | 5 | 5 | 5 | 5 | 12 | 12 | 10.666 | 2.3 | 2.2 |
| Belgium | 2 | 5 | 5 | 5 | 5 | 5 | 12 | 12 | 10.289 | 2.3 | 2.1 |
| Czech R. | – | – | – | – | – | 5 | 12 | 12 | 10.249 | 2.3 | 2.1 |
| Portugal | – | – | – | 5 | 5 | 5 | 12 | 12 | 10.102 | 2.2 | 2.1 |
| Hungary | – | – | – | – | – | 5 | 12 | 12 | 10.045 | 2.2 | 2.1 |
| Sweden | – | – | – | – | 4 | 4 | 10 | 10 | 8.878 | 2.0 | 1.8 |
| Austria | – | – | – | – | 4 | 4 | 10 | 10 | 8.188 | 1.8 | 1.7 |
| Bulgaria | – | – | – | – | – | – | – | 10 | 7.538 | – | 1.6 |
| Slovakia | – | – | – | – | – | 3 | 7 | 7 | 5.430 | 1.2 | 1.1 |
| Denmark | – | 3 | 3 | 3 | 3 | 3 | 7 | 7 | 5.384 | 1.2 | 1.1 |
| Finland | – | – | – | – | 3 | 3 | 7 | 7 | 5.191 | 1.1 | 1.1 |
| Ireland | – | 3 | 3 | 3 | 3 | 3 | 7 | 7 | 3.924 | 0.9 | 0.8 |
| Lith. | – | – | – | – | – | 3 | 7 | 7 | 3.593 | 0.8 | 0.7 |
| Latvia | – | – | – | – | – | 3 | 4 | 4 | 2.349 | 0.5 | 0.5 |
| Slovenia | – | – | – | – | – | 3 | 4 | 4 | 1.936 | 0.4 | 0.4 |
| Estonia | – | – | – | – | – | 3 | 4 | 4 | 1.409 | 0.3 | 0.3 |
| Cyprus | – | – | – | – | – | 2 | 4 | 4 | 0.772 | 0.2 | 0.2 |
| Lux. | 1 | 2 | 2 | 2 | 2 | 2 | 4 | 4 | 0.454 | 0.1 | 0.1 |
| Malta | – | – | – | – | – | 2 | 3 | 3 | 0.400 | 0.1 | 0.1 |
| **Total** | **5 (29.4%)** | **18 (31%)** | **23 (36.5%)** | **28 (36.8%)** | **39 (44.8%)** | **68 (54.8%)** | **151 (47%)** | **175 (50.7%)** | **145.220** | **25.5%** | **29.9%** |
| QM | 12 (70.6%) | 41 (70.7%) | 45 (71.4%) | 54 (71.1%) | 62 (71.3%) | 88 (71%)[3] | 232 (72.3%)[3] | 258 (74.8%)[3] | – | – | – |
| BM | 6 (35.3%) | 18 (31%) | 19 (30.2%) | 23 (30.3%) | 26 (29.9%) | 37 (29.8%) | 90 (28%) | 88 (25.5%) | – | – | – |
| **Total** | **17** | **58** | **63** | **76** | **87** | **124** | **321** | **345** | **484.702** | **100** | **100** |

[1] Nice rules enter into force; [2] Expected accession of Bulgaria and Romania; [3] Cast by a majority of Council Members on a proposal from the Commission

threshold was raised from 62 to 88 and the blocking minority from 26 to 37 votes. This implied that the 6 biggest states with a total of 56 votes representing almost 75% of the EU population needed to generate another 32 votes (support by at least six smalls) to get a proposal adopted. Blocking a proposal, in turn, required at least 8 smalls representing only 18.7% of the EU population. This allocation, however, was even shorter-lived than the previous arrangements. With the growing number of 'smalls', favouring them to 'equal out' size differences became more contentious. Put simply, the 'bigs' feared being held hostage by the 'smalls'. Thus, the Nice Treaty, whose institutional provisions have been in force since November 2004, redesigned the EU's traditional voting system by changing three parameters: the revision of weights (the number of votes of the big states increased from five to almost ten times that of the smallest member); the majority threshold (raised from 71 to 74%); and the adoption of additional voting criteria. Acting upon a Commission proposal, the votes must be cast by a majority of the Member States; otherwise the Council requires votes by at least two-thirds of the members. In addition, the QM must represent at least 62% of the total EU population.

Above all, this was the first instance of revision of the relative weight of Member States since the Treaty of Rome. Most candidate countries could be associated with existing groups of states, and be given the same number of votes: the Czech Republic and Hungary were equated with Belgium, Portugal, and Greece; Bulgaria with Sweden and Austria; the three Baltic states and Cyprus with Luxembourg. And France strongly refused the claims of a much larger unified Germany and preserved a unique category for the big ones, in the name of the solidarity between the founding states. New categories were created for Romania and Malta.

In a nutshell, the Nice bargain achieved two results: the emergence of Spain and Poland almost on a par with the 4 big states; the maintenance of the relative weights of the now '6 bigs' who now commanded ten rather than five times more votes than the smallest ones. Overall, the new arrangements changed the weightings slightly in favour of the big states, as quantitative studies show and brought the system closer to the principle of one person, one vote than in the original 1958 bargain.[4] Unsurprisingly the Irish Prime Minister Bertie Ahern stated recently 'if [he] had to depend on Ireland's weighted vote to promote our interests in the Council, [he] would not bother to turn up.'[5]

---

[4] See, for example, R. Baldwin and M. Widgren, 'The Draft Constitutional Treaty's Voting Reform Dilemma (CEPS Policy Briefs No. 44 (November 2003)) available at: <http://www.ceps.be>; R. Baldwin, et al., 'Nice Try: Should the Nice Treaty be ratified?', 11 *Monitoring European Integration* (CEPR 2001); and T. Raunio and M. Wiberg, 'Winners and Losers in the Council: Voting Power Consequences of EU Enlargments', 36 *Journal of Common Market Studies* (1998) pp. 549-562.

[5] Ahern, cited in T. Brown, 'Achieving Balance: Institutions and Member States' (Federal Trust Online Paper, No. 1/04 (2004)). In addition, under QMV it is usually understood that big states retain an informal veto – but certainly not small states.

## 2.2    The Independence of the EU's Supranational Institutions

Similarly, supranational law and institutions are supposed, disproportionately, to serve weaker actors and have also been essential to obtain a degree of equality between the EU Members. The independent supranational Commission was granted the monopoly on the right to initiate Community legislation and make proposals to the Council of Ministers. The intergovernmental Council of Ministers has to accept them before becoming law and can in the majority of cases only amend them unanimously – a provision that grants the Commission considerable agenda-setting power.[6] The European Parliament (EP) gradually developed into an independent co-legislator alongside the Council. The relative power of these three institutions depends on the underlying legislative procedure (co-decision, co-operation, or consultation) and voting arrangements.[7] Finally, the European Court of Justice (ECJ) was set up to interpret the treaties and to bind all Member States equally to EU law. In fact, the ECJ is probably the most independent of the EU institutions. By establishing early on the principles of supremacy and the direct effect of Community law the ECJ gave itself the power to deliver judgments countering the position of big Member States. While there is a lively academic debate as to the extent to which the Court has actually done so, there is little doubt that small countries have benefited from its case law.[8] This combination of functions of the EU institutions and the independence of the Commission, EP, and ECJ were to ensure that size would not be mathematically related to influence.

Interestingly, although the Commissioners were explicitly prohibited to '[either seek or take] instructions from any government,'[9] small states initially feared potential 'dirigisme' and Franco-German dominance.[10] It was their insistence that led to the creation of the Council representing the Member States. However, the rule of collegiality within the Commission has prevented the Commissioners from systematically defending their member state's interest.[11] The Commission has therefore developed the reputation of being a guarantor of the 'general interest' against the weight of the large states. Thus, small states have generally come to see it as their strongest ally and defender of minority interests,

---

[6] This holds in all cases where qualified majority voting (QMV) applies.

[7] See, for example, G. Tsebelis, 'The Power of the European Parliament as a Conditional Agenda Setter', 88 *American Political Science Review* (1994) pp. 128-139.

[8] See, for example, E. Stein, 'Lawyers, Judges, and the making of a Transnational Constitution', 75 *American Journal of International Law* (January 1981) pp. 1-27; A. Burley and W. Mattli, 'Europe before the Court: A Political Theory of Legal Integration', 47 *International Organization* (Winter 1993) pp. 41-76; J. Weiler and U. Haltern, 'The Autonomy of the Community Legal Order – Through the Looking Glass', 37 *Harvard International Law Journal* (1996).

[9] ECSC Art. 9; EEC. Art. 157.

[10] S. George, *Politics and Policy in the European Community* (Oxford, Oxford University Press 1991) p. 3.

[11] J. Joana and A. Smith, *Les commissaires européens* (Paris, Presses de Sciences Po 2002).

while big states tend to assert their power in the Council's various layers and sub-structures, which emerged as intergovernmentalism strengthened.

In addition, the composition of the Commission explains, in part, its support by the small countries. Each small state was guaranteed one Commissioner, while the large states have traditionally had two Commission posts. Despite this strongly digressive rule of proportionality in the Commission, this asymmetry did not tip the balance of support. The fact that the Commission has always included one member for each state is not merely understood in terms of representation, but as a guarantee that the peculiar situation of the small states can be understood in the college. The Irish Minister for Foreign Affairs explained that if 'the Irish public has a strong sense of the importance of the Commission as a guarantor of fair play and of the common interest' it is not 'that commissioners act as national representatives, but that there is around the table a fair appreciation of the concerns of individual Member States'.[12] For smaller states, who always fear that their colleagues from the large states are unaware of their peculiarities, this is a particularly important aspect.

Since the Nice Treaty entered into force each Member State sends one Commissioner to the college theoretically putting big and small on an equal footing.[13] However, the Nice Treaty further stipulated that once the EU consists of 27 states, the number of Commissioners should be less than the number of Member States. Instead, they should be chosen according to a rotation system based on the principle of equality and reflecting the demographic and geographical range of all states.[14] While bigger states can compensate for the lack of a Commissioner through their weight in the other EU institutions, smaller countries will find themselves at a greater disadvantage. In short, here, too, representation is moving away from the equality principle.

De facto inequality is also visible in the EP. The attribution of seats in the EP is digressively proportional. While favourable for the big states, it offers few advantages to small states. Most small states are either three or four times less represented in the EP than the big ones. Although the overall representation of small states increased from 24% in 1958 to 40% in 2004 with subsequent enlargements, the big states' share is still 60% (see Table 2).[15] Nonetheless, the EP's more fluid nature offers small states the possibility of forming ad hoc coalitions within transnational political groups. Thus, smaller state representatives tend to promote their interest better in the EP than in a rigid intergovernmental Council. Such cost-benefit calculations explain their defence of the Commission-EP pair.

---

[12] B. Cowen, 'Speech at the European Policy Centre (Brussels, 3 April 2003) in l'Union européene', 24/2 Journal of European Integration, pp. 139-164.

[13] Big states often hold the most important Commission portfolios. The new Barroso Commission may be a notable exception.

[14] Treaty of Nice, Protocol on enlargement, Art. 4, Provisions concerning the Commission.

[15] This will decrease further should Romania and Bulgaria join in 2007 and with the entering into force of the Constitutional Treaty.

**Table 2. The evolution of the Composition of the European Parliament**

| Bigs | Number of MEPs: | | | | | | | | | Representing: | | |
|---|---|---|---|---|---|---|---|---|---|---|---|---|
| | 1958 | 1973 | 1976 | 1981 | 1986 | 1991 | 1995 | 2004 | 2007 | % of MEPs | % of EU25 | % of EU27 |
| Germany | 36 | 36 | 81 | 81 | 81 | 99 | 99 | 99 | 99 | 13.5 | 18.1 | 17.0 |
| France | 36 | 36 | 81 | 81 | 81 | 81 | 87 | 78 | 72 | 10.7 | 13.2 | 12.4 |
| UK | - | 36 | 81 | 81 | 81 | 81 | 87 | 78 | 72 | 10.7 | 13.2 | 12.4 |
| Italy | 36 | 36 | 81 | 81 | 81 | 81 | 87 | 78 | 72 | 10.7 | 12.7 | 12.0 |
| Spain | - | - | - | - | 60 | 60 | 64 | 54 | 50 | 7.4 | 8.8 | 8.3 |
| Poland | - | - | - | - | - | - | - | 54 | 50 | 7.4 | 8.5 | 8.0 |
| **Seats (%)** | **76%** | **73%** | **79%** | **75%** | **74%** | **75%** | **68%** | **60%** | **57%** | **60%** | **~75%** | **~70%** |
| **Smalls** | | | | | | | | | | | | |
| Romania | - | - | - | - | - | - | - | - | 33 | - | - | 4.6 |
| NL | 14 | 14 | 25 | 25 | 25 | 25 | 31 | 27 | 25 | 3.7 | 3.6 | 3.3 |
| Greece | - | - | - | 24 | 24 | 24 | 25 | 24 | 22 | 3.3 | 2.3 | 2.2 |
| Belgium | 14 | 14 | 24 | 24 | 24 | 24 | 25 | 24 | 22 | 3.3 | 2.3 | 2.1 |
| Portugal | - | - | - | - | 24 | 24 | 25 | 24 | 22 | 3.3 | 2.3 | 2.1 |
| Czech R. | - | - | - | - | - | - | - | 24 | 20 | 3.3 | 2.2 | 2.1 |
| Hungary | - | - | - | - | - | - | - | 24 | 20 | 3.3 | 2.2 | 2.1 |
| Sweden | - | - | - | - | - | | 22 | 19 | 18 | 2.6 | 2.0 | 1.8 |
| Austria | - | - | - | - | - | | 21 | 18 | 17 | 2.5 | 1.8 | 1.7 |
| Bulgaria | - | - | - | - | - | - | - | - | 17 | - | - | 1.6 |
| Slovakia | - | - | - | - | - | - | - | 14 | 13 | 1.9 | 1.2 | 1.1 |
| Denmark | - | 10 | 16 | 16 | 16 | 16 | 16 | 14 | 13 | 1.9 | 1.2 | 1.1 |
| Finland | - | - | - | - | - | | 16 | 14 | 13 | 1.9 | 1.1 | 1.0 |
| Ireland | - | 10 | 15 | 15 | 15 | 15 | 15 | 13 | 12 | 1.8 | 0.9 | 0.8 |
| Lithuania | - | - | - | - | - | - | - | 13 | 12 | 1.8 | 0.8 | 0.7 |
| Latvia | - | - | - | - | - | - | - | 9 | 8 | 1.2 | 0.5 | 0.5 |
| Slovenia | - | - | - | - | - | - | - | 7 | 7 | 1.0 | 0.4 | 0.4 |
| Estonia | - | - | - | - | - | - | - | 6 | 6 | 0.8 | 0.3 | 0.3 |
| Cyprus | - | - | - | - | - | - | - | 6 | 6 | 0.8 | 0.2 | 0.2 |
| Lux. | 6 | 6 | 6 | 6 | 6 | 6 | 6 | 6 | 6 | 0.8 | 0.1 | 0.1 |
| Malta | - | - | - | - | - | - | - | 5 | 5 | 0.7 | 0.1 | 0.1 |
| **Seats (%)** | **24%** | **27%** | **21%** | **25%** | **26%** | **25%** | **32%** | **40%** | **43%** | **40%** | **~25%** | **~30%** |
| **Total** | **142** | **198** | **410** | **434** | **518** | **536** | **626** | **732** | **732** | **100** | **100** | **100** |

Source: Bunse (forthcoming DPhil thesis, University of Oxford)

## 2.3    Avoidance of a Permanent Presidency

The principle of equality and the ideal of shared leadership is exemplified most 'purely' by the rotating Council presidency.[16] Upon its creation, small countries feared that if they gave the EC a single figurehead at the top, this person would unavoidably be in the sway of the big and powerful. Thankfully, such a fear chimed with that of big country heads of state and government who wanted to avoid the emergence of an autonomous leader that could have undermined their own prestige. There was also widely shared agreement that a permanent presidency would risk generating rivalry with the young Commission. Thus, the original model established a system of equal rotation among the governments of the Member States to chair the different formations of the Council of ministers followed regardless of size, economic power, or merit.[17]

The rotation principle allowed the Member States equal access to an institution which – rather unexpectedly – evolved from a 'fairly passive [manager]'[18] and mere administrative function into a crucial agenda setter, a promoter of political initiatives, and a compromise shaper.[19] Enabling states to make diplomatic contributions independent of their political and economic weight,[20] the office has been particularly important for the smalls:

'The most positive aspect of the rotating presidency is that it gives us a chance to hold an influential role and that you manage to get totally different people to look at the same issue which you move into the spotlight.'[21]

The fact that the EU's small states attribute greater importance to the presidency than the big states also shows itself in public opinion polls. In the period from 1986-2004 for which data on this question exists, almost 72% of the interviewees in small states attached high importance to the Council presidency,

---

[16] For a discussion of the value of the rotating Council presidency see S. Bunse, 'The Value of Rotating Council Presidency: Small State Entrepreneurship in the EU' (forthcoming DPhil thesis, Nuffield College, Oxford University).

[17] H. Wallace, 'The Presidency: Tasks and Evolution', in C. O'Nuallain and J.-M. Hoscheidt, *The Presidency of the European Council of Ministers; Impacts and Implications for National Governments* (London, Croom Helm in association with the European Institute of Public Administration 1985) p. 2 and M. Westlake, *The Council of the European Union* (London, Cartermill 1995) p. 37.

[18] H. Wallace and G. Edwards, 'The evolving Role of the Presidency of the Council', 52 *International Affairs* (1976) p. 536.

[19] E.J. Kirchner, *Decision-making in the European Community – The Council Presidency and European Integration* (Manchester, Manchester University Press 1992); Westlake, *supra* n. 17; F. Hayes-Renshaw and H. Wallace, 'Executive Power in the European Union: The Functions and Limits of the Council Ministers', 2 *Journal of European Public Policy* (1995) pp. 559-582; P. Sherrington, *The Council of Ministers – Political Authority in the European Union* (London, Pinter 2002).

[20] See *Financial Times* (4 December 2000).

[21] Greek Official, European Parliament (26 April 2004) in Bunse *supra* n. 16.

while only 64% of the citizens in the bigger countries considered the presidency important. The lowest levels of people considering the presidency important were recorded in Germany with 45% and 55% during the 1994 and 1999 presidencies respectively and France (52% in 2000). The highest shares of the population regarding the presidency as important were found in Portugal and Greece with above 80% during past presidencies.[22] Unsurprisingly, proposals to replace the rotating presidency with a permanent EU president (see below) were to cause an outcry by the small Member States.

Overall, at each treaty revision the question of size became more apparent and the EU's initial model ever more complex. While successive enlargements led to a progressive 'representational deficit' of the group of bigs in the EU, in terms of equality they have retained and further strengthened their greater weight in the EU's decision-making system. The principle of pure equality was only applied in the case of the rotating Council presidency. Whether and why this trend is continuing can be seen from the Convention's end-game and the EU's future institutional set-up.

3.    POWER POLITICS IN THE CONVENTION: THE SMALL VERSUS BIG DIVIDE

Amongst the key rationales behind the creation of the Convention was to tackle the increasing small versus big cleavage more effectively than previous intergovernmental conferences (IGCs) had done and to find a new bargain to reconcile the principles of equality and proportional democratic representation in the EU. This was, *inter alia*, to be achieved by transforming the Convention into a more representative body that would openly debate all the issues and interests at stake. Thus, its members (105 altogether) included not only government representatives, but also members of national parliaments, the European Parliament (MEPs), and Commission representatives. Similarly, the candidate states were granted government and parliamentary representatives.[23] The Economic and Social Committee (Ecosoc), the European social partners, the Committee of the Regions and the European Ombudsman were invited as observers.

The ideal of sharing out leadership was also present in the Convention. All states regardless of their size were given the same number of seats (one government representative and two national parliamentarians). In addition, all parties could present proposals, suggest amendments, and try to rally support for them in the Convention. Finally, rather than a system of weighted votes, the Laeken declaration established that decision-making in the Convention would rest on 'consensus'. Thus, theoretically a majority could have represented a very small minority of the European population. In addition, the fact that each component of

---

[22] Eurobarometer 60, available at: <http://europa.eu.int/comm/public_opinion/standard_en.htm.>.
[23] Their only restriction was not to obstruct any emerging compromise.

the Convention was to form part of a final consensus, gave them a potential collective veto. Unsurprisingly, small states had supported the idea of a Convention from the outset – they had good reasons to think that the Convention process would strengthen their position compared to the previous IGCs at which their capacity to shape the final outcomes had been marginal with only a theoretical recourse to the veto.[24]

The Convention was headed by a presidium consisting of a chair (the former French President Valery Giscard d'Estaing), two vice chairs (the former Italian and Belgian prime ministers Giuliano Amato and Jean-Luc Dehaene), and 9 other Convention members. The latter included representatives of the governments holding the Council presidency during the Convention and two representatives each from national parliaments, the EP, and the Commission. In addition, the Convention's representative of the Slovene Parliament was invited on behalf of the candidate countries.

The Presidium's role was defined as 'lending impetus to the Convention and providing it with a basis on which to work.'[25] To do so it was granted considerable procedural powers including preparing draft agendas for each plenary session and working group and a Convention Secretariat (under the former head of the British civil service, John Kerr) to assist it. However, this Convention composition and operating mode failed to strengthen small state bargaining power and narrow the big-small divide over institutional issues. Once the EU's institutions were tackled, the Convention members soon divided along this line, reproducing a classic feature of former intergovernmental negotiations. Two proposals reflected the big versus small cleavage in the Convention particularly clearly and competed for the dominant position.

## 3.1    The ABC Proposal of a Permanent President versus improving the *Status Quo*

Contrary to the Community's original bargain the first proposal advocated the election of a full-time European Council presidency from among former heads of government for a period of up to 5 years. It was initially put forward by a three big state coalition: former Spanish Prime Minister Jose Maria Aznar, British Prime Minister Tony Blair, and French President Jacques Chirac (hence the ABC proposal).[26] Its proclaimed rationale was to enhance the effectiveness of the Council's work by having a full-time person in charge of managing it; to ensure greater continuity in terms of priority and long-term planning; and to give a more permanent face to the EU in the rest of the world. Although progress in and out-

---

[24] A. Moravscik and K. Nicolaïdis, 'Explaining the Treaty of Amsterdam: Interests, Influence and Institutions', 37 *Journal of Common Market Studies* (1999) pp. 59-85.

[25] Available at: <http://european-convention.eu.int/praesidium.asp?lang=EN>.

[26] Both Blair and Aznar have been tipped as possible candidates for the job, although they denied any interest in the position.

side the Convention addressed the last two issues through setting up annual as well as multi-annual Council work programmes[27] and the creation of a European Foreign Affairs minister, the first rationale remained paramount.

The second proposal came from the opposition to a permanent presidency: the self-styled 'friends of the Community method' – later referred to as the group of smalls –which had met since April 2002 to flesh out common positions across issues. Over time, the group comprised between 16 and 19 countries, with the Benelux taking the lead in the presidency debate.[28] Their counterproposal was presented in December 2002 and was broadly supported by the group of smalls.[29] In addition to prioritising the strengthening of the Community method, electing the Commission president by the EP, and enhancing the Commission's executive powers, its key focus was the defence of the rotation principle to guard equality in the EU's future institutional design.

According to them the Council presidency could only be reformed, if the new rules were safeguarding 'the principle of equal treatment of all Member States, just as the balance between the institutions of the Union.' The proposal of a European Council President from outside the circle of its members was unacceptable as – in their view – 'it did not come up to these conditions.'[30] To enhance the Council's effectiveness the Benelux suggested another approach: a clearer distinction between the executive and legislative functions of the Council. Executive functions (the coordination of national policies) should be chaired by the Commission while rotation would be maintained at European Council level and the specialised ministerial Councils performing legislative functions.

Not inconsequential, politicians as well as the media framed the issue of the Council presidency as that of 'Presidency of the Union'. This ambiguous semantics conveyed both the intent of the bigs and the fears of the smalls. For the bigs, this new president of the European Council should indeed come to be seen as the president of the Union as a whole reflecting the role of the revamped European Council as the superior authority in the EU, directing and overseeing the work of other institutions. For the opposing small states, as per the original bargain this was exactly the outcome to be avoided: the concentration of power in a single

---

[27] See, for example, Seville Council Conclusions.

[28] In its fullest configuration, the group included all Member States and candidate countries except the six big states, Romania and Greece – the latter became an observer when it took on the EU presidency. The three Benelux countries, however, played an ambivalent role in this dynamic, sometimes posing as the leaders of this group when putting forth their early proposal, sometimes following a more autonomous line in order to position themselves as a mediating force in the Convention. This twofold strategy may reflect their dual identity, on the one hand as the traditional promoters of small countries' interests since the creation of the EC, on the other hand 'the Benelux', an almost-big-country, a founding member with a greater claim to leadership than all the small newcomers.

[29] Denmark and Sweden were more sceptical.

[30] Benelux Memorandum (4 December 2002) European Convention Secretariat (11 December 2002) CONV 457/02, CONTRIB 171, available at: <http://www.gouvernement.lu/salle_presse/actualite/2002/12/04memorandum/memorandum.rtf>.

individual leading the EU in the name of the most powerful heads of state in the EU.


## 4.     THE WINNERS AND THE LOSERS: RESOURCES AND STRATEGIES

Who, then, were the winners and the losers in this debate? What resources did they have at their disposal and what strategies did they use? Leadership in the EU and IGC negotiations has long been provided by a Franco-German axis although its strength has varied throughout history and its nature seems to be changing. This did not differ much in the case of the Convention, partly because it did not replace IGCs and in fact took place in the shadow of the following IGC, i.e., the veto power of the Member States. It is therefore no surprise that the bargaining space, i.e., the set of settlements potentially acceptable to the Convention, were bounded by the positions and bottom lines of the most powerful Member States and that the very salient issues were firmly kept under their control. Once concrete issues were put on the table, the representatives of the governments loyally defended their interests – as did most of the national parliamentarians nominated by the governments. By the autumn of 2002 they started to build coalitions and invoke their veto in the pending IGC.[31] The other members, anticipating the IGC, adapted their behaviour to this constraint.

Not only did the Member States take the lead, at the same time the parliamentarians were largely ineffective. The political parties were unable to develop coherent visions and positions, except in a few specific instances for example related to symbolic ideological gains (mention of the 'social market economy' for the socialists).[32] But the big parties only had a superficial unity and on most issues were unable to overcome their divisions and build coalitions beyond the *status quo*. For most representatives, party political or component identity was not the primary determinant of their positions in the Convention. They saw the role of party groups as channels to exchange information rather than forums to co-ordinate positions.[33]

Thus, the Convention was overall – particularly in institutional and policy issues – not radically different from IGCs and much of its end-game was dominated by the kind of hegemonic compromises that have characterized EU politics since its inception.

---

[31] In most states, one of the 2 national parliamentarians was drawn from the opposition. But this did not mean that they did not defend national interests. The British conservative MPs, for example, were more critical than the representative of the government helping them to play on the 'domestic constraint.'

[32] See *supra* n. 2

[33] P. Berès, 'Une constitution pour la grande Europe', 36 *Notes de la Fondation Jean Jaurès* (2003).

### 4.1    The Hegemonic Compromise: The Franco-German 'Dual Presidency'

The 'Franco-German compromise' was put forward by the two countries on the occasion of the 40th anniversary of their bilateral friendship (*Élysée*) treaty in January 2003. Shortly before presenting their joint institutional proposals, in October 2002, France and Germany had replaced their government representatives with their foreign ministers increasing their political weight in the Convention. Their compromise sought to reconcile the ABC proposal with aspects from the Benelux proposal that were also supported by Germany. Germany did not defend the rotating Presidency, but sought to strengthen the Commission. Although the Franco-German compromise was not formally put on the Convention agenda and generated widespread opposition within it, it immediately became a focal point for subsequent debates. The contribution included the controversial creation of what became referred to as a 'dual EU Presidency' with a permanent European Council President elected from amongst its members and a directly elected Commission President by the EP. Permanent chairs would also be created for foreign affairs, Ecofin, the Eurogroup, and justice and home affairs (JHA).

From the outset France and Germany relied upon a number of resources that were instrumental in turning its proposal into the focal point. First and most importantly, they found a crucial ally in Valéry Giscard d'Estaing. At the January 20 and 21 plenary which served as a first exploration of institutional questions Giscard reacted favourably calling their compromise 'a positive proposal [that is] going in the right direction (...) guaranteeing the stability of EU institutions'.[34] He was personally much closer to the Franco-German compromise than to the Benelux proposals and sensitive to the British position which – while supporting the permanent Council Presidency – was initially sceptical about the election of the Commission President. His detractors recalled the fact that he had become the Convention's chair on the insistence of Chirac, Blair, and German Chancellor Gerhard Schroeder. In addition, he himself 'created' the European Council in 1974 and would therefore naturally want to make it the apex of the European system. They pointed out, furthermore, that this dual presidency set-up resembled the peculiar French political system in which the president is the 'leader of the nation' and the 'ultimate arbitrator of the national interest', while the prime minister heads the government.[35] Finally, they argued that his two foremost goals have been to support the claims of big countries and to weaken the Commission. His defenders, in turn, retort that this only appeared to be the case because he tried to ensure that 'his' Constitution would not be radically altered by the IGC, and therefore the most powerful Member States. Whatever the motivation, at some point before the official tabling of the draft articles on insti-

---

[34] See Convention plenary (20-21 January 2003) available at: <http://www.europarl.eu.int/europe2004/index_en.htm.>.

[35] V. Wright, *The Government and Politics of France* (London, Routledge 1989).

tutions, he chose to take sides and to support the idea of a permanent Council Presidency.

Giscard's and the Presidium's support were crucial because its composition, functions, procedural control, and operating style gave it the necessary legitimacy and influence to shape the Convention's final outcome. As Laeken had left the process and procedures of the Convention undefined, Giscard had ample room for manoeuvre. During the first three months members were invited to 'present their views on the EU' and listen to civil society associations. On this basis, Giscard presented what he called an issue-specific 'synthesis' reducing the scope of the discussion, and set up 'working groups' on controversial topics to 'study' the subject in-depth. Finally, after the reports of the working groups had been discussed in plenary sessions, the Presidium presented actual draft articles to the Convention which were supposed to mirror the substance of working group reports and reactions of the plenary sessions. Members then suggested amendments leading to revised proposals by the Presidium. But, crucially, while the Convention was supposed to remain sovereign in this process, the Presidium acted as the interpreter of the dominant view and was the sole drafter of the actual text presented to the floor. Giscard fully exploited his formal and informal powers assuming the major directing and leadership role. As Allen[36] finds, he 'monopolised reporting of the work of the Convention to both Member States and the public' , 'it was usually Giscard's or Kerr's summary of proceedings that formed the ongoing basis for further negotiation', and he cleverly 'created controversies (...) or negotiating positions that were designed to be conceded in return for consensus on more important items.' [37] In fact, it was Giscard who determined that no voting would take place in the Convention, that a single text would be agreed rather than options proposed, how consensus and the majority was to be defined, and when a consensus existed. This gave him much leverage to steer the result towards his most preferred option. Crucially, as his definition of consensus rested essentially on the Member States' population size rather than the number of Member States, the Franco-German compromise was guaranteed a dominant position in the drafting process.[38]

The UK's and Spain's support of a permanent European Council president (they advocated an even stronger president than the Franco-German compromise) were a second key resource. In addition, Italy supported a strong 'Mr Eu-

---

[36] D. Allen, 'The Convention and the Draft Constitutional Treaty', in F. Cameron, ed., *The Future of Europe* (London, Routledge 2004).

[37] Allen *supra* n. 36, at p. 24. Interestingly, Ludlow finds that the Convention which drafted the Charter of Fundamental Rights only succeeded because its chair Roman Herzog was able to dominate the process, see P. Ludlow, *A View from Brussels; A Commentary on the EU: 2004 and beyond* (Brussels, Centre for European Policy Studies 2001).

[38] In addition, perhaps daunted by its highly divisive nature or as a strategic means to exert pressure to compromise, it was Giscard who decided not to put the EU's future institutional design on the Convention agenda until the very end.

rope.'[39] Once on board, the countries which supported the idea of a permanent presidency represented the largest part of the European population – as Giscard pointed out in various interviews. Before the plenary, he argued that the EU now comprised three categories of states: the four largest ones, with a population of more than forty million inhabitants, which, together, amount to 74% of the EU population; eight medium-sized countries, with a population between 8 and 16 million people, which represent 19% of the population; and eleven small states which, together, only include 7% of the population. Some weeks later, at the Athens European Council, he explicitly drew the consequences of this analysis: since those who reject the idea of a permanent president for the Council only represent a quarter of the EU population, they should not be allowed to prevent the formation of a 'consensus' (which, in Giscard's mind, seemed to mean a very large majority). With such an argument, Giscard contradicted the principle of equality among conventioneers he had supported so far.

It is also noteworthy that Spain was amongst the Presidium's three government representatives. So was Denmark, which was the only country not to join the small country camp in their defence of the rotating presidency. In addition, it proved difficult for the smalls to split the big country coalition promoting the permanent presidency. Thus, the big country camp remained strong – the only wedge appeared on QMV and the Commission composition when Spain and Poland, joined quietly by some new members, started waging a 'give Nice a chance' campaign towards the end. This position later explained the difficulties of the IGC and the failure of the December 2003 Brussels Summit.

A third resource on which the Franco-German axis could rely was its past reputation and legitimacy. As Cameron argues, the EU as a whole has usually reaped beneficial results from the Franco-German initiatives – a prominent example being European and Monetary Union (EMU).[40] Particularly, Germany had in the past frequently defended small state interests and the legitimacy of the Franco-German compromise was enhanced as – apart from the presidency – it contained important elements that were in line with small state suggestions. As seen above, the election of the Commission President by the EP, for example, reflected Benelux suggestions and had broad support in the Convention. Crucially, the British position evolved in this regard. Apparently, its traditional opposition to replacing a Commission President chosen by the Member States with an elected one could be traded off against the 'strategic prize' of a stronger leader representing EU governments on the world stage. As Peter Hain, the British government representative, put it to his Parliament:

'in the end there will have to be an agreement and a necessary process of adjustment by all parties. We have, for example, been willing to look at, with certain very big safeguards, electing the Commission President through some method, provided that

---

[39] *The Guardian* (24 January 2003).
[40] F. Cameron, *The Future of Europe* (London, Routledge 2004) p. 12.

does not involve being hostage to a particular political faction and provided that the outcome is one that the Council can accept. So it is not something we sought and we remain deeply sceptical about it, but if, as part of the end game, getting an elected President of the Council, which is very much a priority for us, involves doing something with the Commission President with those very important safeguards that I mentioned, then that is something that we might have to adjust to.'[41]

Moreover, a consensus had emerged on the double-hatted foreign affairs minister as included in the Franco-German proposal and supported in the autumn by a narrow majority in plenary even if the precise division of tasks (in particular in terms of external representation) between a European Council President and the proposed European Foreign Minister in charge of the EU's Common Foreign and Security Policy were unclear under the Franco-German plan and remained so in the Convention's draft treaty.

To sum up, the strategy France and Germany relied upon was fourfold: a) uniting their resources to provide direction in the Convention over the EU's future institutional set-up; b) fully exploiting its positional resources such as access to and support by the Convention Chairman and its Presidium in order to move its proposal into the dominant position; c) bringing the UK and Spain on its side; and d) inducing the smalls to make concessions on the permanent presidency in return for an elected Commission president and European foreign minister.

## 4.2    The Small State Rebellion

However, the small states (particularly Belgium, Luxembourg, Ireland, Finland, Austria, the Netherlands, and Portugal) reacted in a very hostile manner to the Franco-German compromise.[42] In addition, politicians from the ten Central and Eastern European countries, as well as national parliaments, the European Com-

---

[41] P. Hain, 'Interview in the European Affairs Committee of the House of Commons' (25 March 2003) available at: <http://www.publications.parliament.uk/pa/cm200203/cmselect/cmeuleg/63-xxvi/3032502.htm.>.

[42] A Benelux position issued on the same day confirms and summarises these criticisms:
'*En ce qui concerne le Conseil européen, le Benelux demeure favorable au maintien de la rotation au niveau du Conseil européen et aussi pour les Conseils spécialisés. Il réitère son opposition au principe d'une présidence élue, à temps plein et en dehors du Conseil européen, qui risque de modifier l'équilibre institutionnel, surtout au détriment de la Commission et de provoquer par conséquent une confusion de compétences ainsi qu'une situation de rivalité entre institutions. Le Benelux estime qu'un acteur européen supplémentaire sur la scène internationale est susceptible d'apporter la confusion dans la représentation de l'UE dans les différentes enceintes internationales*'. 'Prise de position des Premiers Ministres et des Ministres des Affaires étrangères du Benelux suite à la Contribution franco-allemande à la Convention' (Brussels, 21 January 2003) available at: <http://europa.eu.int/constitution/futurum/documents/contrib/cont210103_fr.pdf>. See also similar statements published by the Finnish government: Finnish Ministerial Committee for EU Affairs (17 January 2003) 'Extract from the Government report to Parliament on Finland's position regarding the future of the EU and issues that have emerged in the work of the Convention', available at: <http://europa.eu.int/constitution/futurum/documents/other/oth170103_en.pdf>.

mission, and the EP were sceptical. At the January plenary on institutional issues most Conventioneers regretted a state of affairs where positions were adopted in advance and the Convention was transformed into an intergovernmental conference. Liberal Democrat British MEP Andrew Duff talked about a 'cut and paste' compromise putting divergent views side by side without reconciling them. Dutch Christian Democrat MEP Hanja Maij-Wegen announced for the record that 64 speakers had spoken against the dual-Presidency plans, 11 in favour, and 15 had remained neutral.[43] Others counted 55 speakers against, 18 in favour, and 15 somewhat against.[44] Thus, the proportion against the appointment of a president of the European Council at that point was roughly 3 to 1.

To rally support for their own proposals the Benelux tried to generate a coherent small state coalition that comprised up to 19 states and convince the others of the shortcomings of the dual presidency and the value of the rotation principle (intellectual leadership). Their arguments included some of the same concerns raised in the original bargain, such as the importance of avoiding the creation of two competing power centres (the Commission and Council). In addition, the lack of a clear division of labour between the two presidents and mechanisms to mediate between them were perceived as fraught with risks. Further, delegates argued that the plan of a dual Presidency could unbalance the position of the High Representative/Minister for Foreign Affairs and would fall short of bringing the EU closer to its citizens. The second set of arguments rested on the potential damage a dual presidency could have for the EU's institutional balance. The small state coalition tried to convince the bigs that a permanent European Council President would undermine the role of the Commission by turning it into the secretariat for such a president and confining it to managing the internal market. Third, the proposal was criticised as inconsistent. On what grounds it was asked, did its promoters believe that EU heads of states and governments would recognise the authority of one among them, a former peer most likely from a big Member State. This was all the more true with regard to foreign policy in the context of the Iraq War. Would a former Prime Minister – the likely pedigree of a European Council president – have the political clout to represent the EU on the world stage? Would the French accept being represented by a British citizen in Washington or *vice versa*?

The smaller countries' most radical argument against the dual presidency proposal was, however, that the rotating presidency had for almost fifty years been the symbol of equality between the EU's Member States. Not only would the Council President most likely be selected from among the bigger countries but he, whoever he might be, would be the big countries' voice and marginalise the smalls. This would endanger the future functioning of the EU which rests on

---

[43] Press Release (21 March 2003) available at: <http://www.europarl.eu.int/europ2004/textes/verbatim_030121_Summary.htm.>.

[44] G. Grevi, *Gloves off: The Going gets tough in the Convention* (Brussels, European Police Centre 2003).

shared leadership and harmonious relations between the bigs and the smalls. On similar grounds, Giscard's logic of consensus was fiercely rejected. It introduced in the procedure of the Convention a majoritarian logic (as in majority of population rather than Member States), which was alien to the EU's traditional *modus operandi*, had not been foreseen by the Laeken mandate, and had not governed their work so far. If this became the Convention's rule, all the minorities could feel that the process does not respect their rights, and this could ruin the legitimacy of the whole enterprise. In the run-up to the formal debates on institutions, they issued a paper at the end of March to reiterate their common stance in favour of the community method.[45] Most importantly, they spelled out clearly where the distinction between big and small states ought to be relevant and where not: yes, demographic factors are relevant for representation in the European Parliament and to voting weights in the Council of Ministers; no, they should not lead to 'any hierarchy of Member States' or 'differentiate between them in terms of their entitlement to involvement in the operations of the institutions'. On the Council, while they acknowledged less than full consensus, this meant that a rotating presidency ought to be the predominant aspect of a new system.

At a meeting in Luxembourg in early April, the smalls confirmed their rejection of the permanent Council Presidency. At the Athens meeting of the European Council on 16 April 2003, each country laid out its argument once again with little or no visible attempt to bridge the existing divide between big and small countries. However, their apparent unity was not perfect and became increasingly fragile. Not all aspects of the Benelux counterproposal enjoyed the coalition's support. For example, contrary to the Benelux compromise, the other small countries continued to support the maintenance of rotation for the General Affairs Council rather than its chairing by the President of the Commission. Some also opposed the chairing of the Foreign Affairs Council by the Foreign Affairs minister, arguing that the latter could not chair a body that was supposed to hold him accountable. This weakened the position of the Benelux and the weight of their counterproposal.

The unity of the coalition of smalls weakened further when – despite the weight of their arguments – neither the big states reconsidered their position nor Giscard changed his strategy and small state concerns about the permanent presidency were pushed more and more into the background. In view of the looming conflict, the Benelux countries produced an updated proposal which the other 16 small countries did not officially go along with. In addition, another option for consideration in the plenary (the election of the president of the European Council by universal suffrage or an electoral college) was put forward by Greek Foreign Minister George Papandreou. The proposal had little chance to fly in the short run but was meant, in part, to reintroduce the central consideration of dem-

---

[45] 'Reforming the Institutions: Principles and Premises' (CONV 646/03 (28 March 2003)).

ocratic legitimacy in the Convention debate. If the Convention was to get rid of democratically-elected prime ministers and heads of states to head the European council, the least it should do was to give the new figurehead a democratic pedigree. Moreover, such an election would give the president a source of legitimacy separate from the Commission and therefore reduce the potential rivalry between the two bodies by making the Council president a more supranational figure. Papandreou's proposal drew some support from Brutton, the Irish representative and a couple of other conventioneers. Most importantly, it served to signal in plenary that there was no full agreement in the Presidium.

However, rather than fulfilling their objectives, i.e., question Giscard's 'consensus' on the permanent presidency and the broad features of the Franco-German compromise, the increasing heterogeneity of viewpoints towards the end called for strong leadership in order to conclude the Convention and prevent its failure. This was provided by Giscard and the Presidium who shaped the final compromise.

### 4.3    The Final Compromise: Trumping the Smalls

The Presidium's draft compromise resembled the Franco-German compromise and ignored the key criticisms of the smaller countries. While the Presidium tried to constrain Giscard somewhat and a number of points in its proposal deviate from Giscard's initial draft, the main reforms opposed by small and medium states were left in: a smaller Commission, a Commission president nominated by the Council rather than the Parliament, and the abolition of the rotating presidency.[46] The smalls were too loose on all sides; particularly the abolition of the rotating presidency meant that the shared leadership ideal was compromised in the European Council. It is therefore no surprise that after Giscard had presented this proposal, the Benelux published a very hostile letter, regretting the method used by Giscard presenting his own ideas, and the fact that he had not taken their position into consideration.[47]

The final compromise was reached in the very last hours of the Convention, in June 2003. By applying the 'single negotiating text' approach and bypassing threats of a veto, the Presidium played an important role in shaping the final outcome.[48] It leveraged its hybrid nature as a secretariat/mediator and as a college to the fullest. On the one hand, like presidencies in IGCs, it acted as an organiser and as a mediator with the support of the Convention's Secretariat, seeking to forge a compromise on a step-by-step basis. But it chose to do so, not by leaving

---

[46] Magnette and Nicolaïdis, *supra* n. 1.

[47] 'Lettre des trois représentants du Benelux à la Convention européenne, Jacques Santer, Louis Michel et Gijs de Vries, au président de la Convention, Valéry Giscard d'Estaing au sujet des propositions de réforme des institutions' (Brussels, 25 April 2003) available at: <http://europa.eu.int/constitution/futurum/documents/other/oth250403_fr.htm>.

[48] Magnette and Nicolaïdis, *supra* n. 2.

options open until a last minute package deal but by submitting a single negotiating text. This text, in turn, became the reference or *status quo*, with the burden of proof being put on the dissenters. More often then not, after the submission of the initial draft articles, the Secretariat in its explanatory comments was able to pit one set of amendments against another, and represent its own initial version with only cosmetic alterations. Since, on the other hand, the Presidium was a collective organ, a college rather than a single presiding Member State, it had enough authority to impose its viewpoints as 'consensual' or at least 'the best possible compromise'. This made it harder for the rest of the Convention to question its proposals. In this context, potential vetoes were forestalled and actual ones ignored.

These informal tactics worked in reaching a 'consensus', but they also left a definite 'bad taste' among many delegates, which in the end might have deprived the Presidium proposal from the kind of legitimacy that a more negotiated text would have. By debating in absolute secrecy, without displaying the textual basis for its own sessions, the Presidium conveyed the idea that the grounds for its decisions were not purely normative. Moreover, within the Presidium itself, the Chair acted with an iron fist, controlling relations with the Secretariat and often submitting proposals to his colleagues a few hours before discussion. By requiring that once a topic had been tabled in the Presidium, members were not allowed to present amendments for debate in the plenary, he sought to signal consensus even where it did not exist. It is little wonder, then, that these provisions never commanded the support of a majority of Member States in the Convention, with obvious implications for the IGC.

The failure of the Brussels Summit in December 2003 revealed the limits of this strategy: while France and Germany strongly supported the Convention text which strengthened their own power, Spain and Poland continued to oppose the new system of weighting votes, a majority of the small states refused to abandon their 'representation' in the Commission, and the presidency continued a thorny issue. Although a dozen compromises were put on the table, the solution adopted by the Convention by consensus proved very fragile. The Convention's attempt to surpass the intricate logic of intergovernmental bargains proved short-lived.


5.    CONCLUSION

European integration has been based on a sophisticated concept of shared leadership to manage its inherent tension between large and small countries – a trait the EU shares with all federal experiences. Three mechanisms in particular preserved the basic principle of equality among Member States, while giving to the larger ones a preponderant role: the system of weighed votes in the Council, the role and composition of the EU's supranational institutions, and the rotating presidency.

Successive enlargements have made these mechanisms ever less adapted to the functioning of the Union. As the number of small states has grown much more rapidly than the number of large states, the institutions which guaranteed equality among states have seemed less defendable to the larger ones. By the time the Convention was convened, a new bargain was needed to reconcile the principles of equality among states and proportional democratic representation in the EU.

However, the Convention did not manage to narrow the divide between large and small states – quite the contrary. Agreeing on such a new bargain proved highly difficult and conflictual, making the small-big cleavage more visible than ever before. At the centre of the conflict was the reform of the rotating Council Presidency which had been the only institutional mechanism in the EU that guarded equality in its pure form and which — due to its increasing importance and influence – was much appreciated by the smalls. While most of the large states tried to strengthen the role of the European Council (and thus the role of governments) in the decision-making process by providing it with a permanent chair, most of the small states defended the existing EU institutions and the rotation principle of the Council Presidency.

To bridge the fierce differences over the EU's future institutional set-up France and Germany put forward a compromise which immediately turned into the focal point. The reasons why include their material leadership resources, alliance with other big states, and reputation, but most crucially their proposal enjoyed support by the Convention chair Giscard d'Estaing who provided the key draft of the Constitutional Treaty. This seems to confirm that the ability of actors to successfully provide leadership increases with the level of their involvement in, or access to, the drafting process.

Despite a large opposing small state coalition led by the Benelux, their 'numerosity' did not translate into bargaining power. Given that Giscard had defined the majority in terms of population size rather than in absolute terms, the smalls had to resort to intellectual leadership strategies, i.e., convincing the big state coalition of the value of rotation and attempting to change big state preferences. However, the logic of the negotiations in the Convention and its outcome were primarily governed by the initial distribution of preferences and their intensity.[49] Thus, this strategy was doomed to failure. In the hard bargaining atmosphere strong structural leadership had to be applied to push governments towards an agreement and to ensure that the Convention would not break down. Thus material and positional leadership resources, which the smalls lacked, proved most important and the final compromise trumpeted the interests of the smalls. The large states won the permanent presidency of the European Council compromising the principle of equality for the EU's most powerful guiding institution, while the smalls won the election of the Commission President by the EP requested by Germany, and managed to preserve some form of rotation in the Council and in the composition of the Commission. Whether this compromise will preserve the balances of the Union, despite all the criticisms it generated, remains to be seen.

---

[49] Magnette and Nicolaïdis, *supra* n. 2.

# THE UNSTOPPABLE ADVANCE OF THE EUROPEAN COUNCIL

## Jan Werts[*]

### 1.    FORMULATION OF THE PROBLEM

This article will try to outline the unstoppable advance of the European Council, and its effects on the Institutions of the European Union. Furthermore, we shall analyze the background of this important development. In 1991 a study of this phenomenon led to the following safe conclusion:

> 'Contrary to expectations, shortly after its emergence, the European Council worked its way into the Community's decision-making process, *without deeply undermining the institutional balance*: the position of the European Commission, the European Parliament, and the Council of Ministers'.[1]

–   Is this important conclusion still valid today?
–   What changes did the 1992 Treaty on the European Union (TEU) introduce?
–   How does the European Council operate in practice today?
–   What is the relationship between the European Council and the Institutions of the Union?
–   Finally, what will be the impact of the recently agreed introduction of a semi-permanent President of the European Council?

### 2.    FROM PARIS (1974) VIA MAASTRICHT TO BRUSSELS (2004)

The creation of the European Council was a compromise. Agreement was reached in 1974 in Paris, during the Meeting of the Heads of Government of the Community, presided over by French President Valéry Giscard d'Estaing. This was 'a real triumph for advocates of intergovernmental co-operation,' going

---

[*] European Media Correspondent in Brussels. Jan Werts has covered European Council meetings since their beginning in 1975. He obtained his Doctorate in 1991 at the Vrije Universiteit Brussels with his thesis entitled 'The European Council'.
[1] J. Werts, *The European Council* (Amsterdam, T.M.C. Asser Instituut/Elsevier Science 1992) (Doctoral thesis) p. 297.

*D. Curtin, A.E. Kellermann and S. Blockmans, eds., The EU Constitution: The Best Way Forward?*
© 2005, T.M.C. Asser Instituut, The Hague.

hand in hand with the promise of a democratically-elected Parliament with legal powers 'as a Federalist countermove'. The creation was necessary, because the Community had stagnated after the prosperous 1960s, during which its economic integration had made headway. The Council of Ministers no longer succeeded in taking the decisions envisaged.

The European Council was created in order to improve the functioning of the Institutions, especially that of the Council of Ministers. It can be argued that the success of the Council depends to a great extent upon the manner in which it is able to fit itself into the Union's decision-making process. The Council was legally laid down in the Single European Act (SEA) of 1986. Article D of the 1992 TEU extends the rule as from the SEA: 'The European Council shall provide the Union with the necessary impetus for its development and shall define the general political guidelines thereof'. This description fits all three pillars of the Union. In the Constitutional Treaty this task is widened to define the Union's 'general political directions and priorities'. With this not very detailed definition of its powers, the European Council is largely free to operate as it wishes. Its role deliberately having been left vague, the European Council's evolution has been shaped, above all, by practical political necessities and the wishes of the Heads of Government.[2]

The composition of the European Council remained unchanged since 1974: the Heads of State or Government and the President of the European Commission. They are 'assisted', according to the TEU, by the Ministers for Foreign Affairs (FMs) of the Member States and by a member of the European Commission, usually the Commissioner for External Affairs. However, in the Constitutional Treaty in the articles regarding the European Council, neither the FMs nor the Ministers of Finance are mentioned. This is in line with the classic aspiration of France to strengthen further the position of the Heads of State and Government. According to Article 21(3) TCE, the members of the European Council, when the agenda so requires, 'may decide each to be assisted by a minister and, in the case of the President of the Commission, by a member of the Commission'.

During the negotiations in Maastricht on the setting up of an Economic and Monetary Union (EMU), the Finance Ministers (the EcoFin) secured the right to 'participate in European Council meetings'.[3] As a result, if matters regarding the EMU are on the agenda, which is mostly the case, the EcoFin members are invited. In the very important financial, economic, social and budgetary area the EcoFin has with this addition taken over the coordinating role from the FMs.

At its creation in 1974 it was expressly stated that the European Council would not change the process of political decision-making.[4] There was no indi-

---

[2] In this article 'Heads of Government' stands for the European Council composed of the 'Heads of State or Government of the Member States and the President of the Commission'.

[3] Declaration No. 4 annexed to the Final Act on the occasion of the signature of the TEU.

[4] *Eighth General Report EC* (1974), Communiqué Meeting of the Heads of Government of the Community (Paris 9-10 December 1974) p. 297.

cation whatsoever, then, that the European Council would turn into a decision-shaping and decision-making body. Certainly, therefore, the Heads of Government are in the European Council bound by the rules laid down in the Treaties and their ancillary procedures, when they choose to act as Council of Ministers. Our study, completed in 1991, taught us that the Heads of Government neverthe-less, right from the beginning, took decisions as a 'supreme arbitrator' or '*instance d'appél*' regarding matters which were left unsolved by the Council of Ministers. That has not changed since.

However, the European Council, both in its operational approach and in its composition, clearly differs from the Council of Ministers, which acts as the 'regular' decision-making body. The Heads of Government cleverly sidestep their handicap of not being in fact the decision-making Council of Ministers. In many cases they present their agreement concerning an issue as a 'political ac-cord'. Shortly after the European Council meeting, such an accord is put on a le-gal footing by the Council of Ministers and the other Institutions, often without even changing one iota in the text. In this way the European Council creates a two-phase decision-making process: politically in the European Council and le-gally in the Council of Ministers. This way the checks and balances procedure, governing lawmaking in the Union via the Institutions, is being pushed aside.

The role of the European Council has been reinforced with the TEU of 1992. By virtue of Title V TEC the Common Foreign and Security Policy (CFSP) be-longs to the prerogatives of the European Council. A novelty was the clauses of ex Article 109 J (2), (3) and (4) and 109 K 2 TEC, where the Council 'meeting in the composition of Heads of State or Government' shapes the EMU (in other words without the participation of the President of the Commission). A third novelty in Maastricht was Article 103(2) where the European Council in the guise of the Council of Ministers every year discusses the 'broad guidelines' of the economic policies of the Member States.

Furthermore, there is the formation of the representatives of the Member States, which on the basis of Article 109 A(2) TEC and 158 TEC decides on im-portant appointments and Article 216 TEC where it determines the seat of the In-stitutions. Examples are the appointments within the framework of the European Central Bank (ECB) and the President of the Commission. To sum up: the green light from the European Council is required for two exceptionally essential ac-tivities of the Union: EMU and CFSP.

In April 2003, Valéry Giscard d'Estaing as Chairman of the European Con-vention launched his remarkable Draft Institutional Proposals. He wanted to up-grade the European Council substantially. Giscard proposed to the Convention that the European Council be elevated to an official Institution. The European Council was to get a President, to be appointed by the Heads of Government for a period of 2,5 years, renewable once. The new president would 'prepare, chair and drive' the activities of the European Council, ensure its continuity and, moreover, represent the EU in the wider world. That signified the end of the six-month rotating Presidency.

The smaller Member States see a risk of incoherence between the President of the European Council and the Commission President, whose areas of responsibilities both overlap and fall within the scope of the Executive branch. In particular this concerns the preparation of and follow-up to European Council decisions. Moreover, a semi-permanent President affords the prospect of a new layer of administration around his person, having functions that are partially exercised by the Commission. The co-ordination between the two Presidents may prove to be difficult. The new President, according to the smaller Member States, embodies a strategy for the larger Member States to run the Union via an informal inner circle.

The entire approach was contrary to the philosophy of a Europe based on the famous Community Method.[5] The smaller Member States predicted that the envisaged 'twin-presidency' would encroach on the powers of the Commission:

'The European Council will be dominating, its chairman will receive a prominent role. The Commission's role as a self-steering and independent political force will be devaluated to become that of a dependent administrative secretariat. (...) The semi-permanent President will undermine the influence of the smaller Member States. He will be one voice too many in external matters.'[6]

However, in the course of the negotiations on the Convention, the smaller Member States reluctantly had to accept the idea of a semi-permanent President. Otherwise the larger Member States would have scuppered the entire Convention. As a concession to the smaller Member States it was agreed that the new President would receive a more restricted job description than Giscard d' Estaing and the largest Member States had proposed. In 2004 the Intergovernmental Conference laid down the whole foregoing upgrading of the European Council in the Constitutional Treaty.


3.     NEW DEVELOPMENTS IN THE FUNCTIONING OF THE EUROPEAN COUNCIL

Since the 1984 Fontainebleau meeting in particular, on many occasions important activities were undertaken and problems of the Union were solved in the European Council. Sometimes this required complicated negotiations, which often went on for several days and nights. Politically the European Council is today the highest and the leading body of the EU. The Heads of Government as the highest representatives of national sovereignty deal with, if desired, every main

---

[5] This means, briefly, decision-making after a proposal by the Commission, co-decision or an opinion by the Parliament, and a final decision in the Council of Ministers.

[6] Our translation from 'De Conventie: een tussenstand', Governmental note from the Dutch FM J.G. de Hoop Scheffer and State Secretary for European Affairs A. Nicolaï, No. 28 473 of 7 March 2003, at the request of MP F. Timmermans.

item and each detail of both the institutional and the extensive substantive law area of the Union, as well as with intergovernmental and bilateral issues which arise. Its Founding Father, Jean Monnet,[7] therefore called his creation the 'Provisional European Government'.

Already in our 1991 analysis we outlined twelve tasks. They include issues within and outside the scope of the Treaties. But it did not stop there. The European Council went on to muscle in on the preparatory work of some activities of the Institutions relating to important issues. Sometimes the European Council even takes on the task of supervising the execution of its own decisions. Take, for example, the 2000 Lisbon meeting. It is extremely interesting to see how the Lisbon European Council introduced an entirely new working method.

The meeting in Lisbon chose, according to the Conclusions, as a strategic target for the EU, 'to become the most competitive and dynamic knowledge-based economy in the world'. This process 'will be underpinned by the European Council taking on a pre-eminent guiding and co-ordinating role'. It is based on the 'effective monitoring of progress' towards the 'new strategic goal' via 'a new open method of co-ordination'. Since Lisbon, the aim of the yearly European Council Spring meeting is to tackle the most important socio-economic problems (such as economic reform, full employment and social cohesion).

Here the European Council operates as the ultimate political centre of the Union. Apart from setting the agenda, the future make-up and the policy of the Union, the Heads of Government gave themselves the task of the execution and the supervision thereof. By so doing the European Council emphasised in Lisbon its readiness to absorb tasks from the Commission as well as the Parliament and the Council. This occurred without any form of discussion with these Institutions.

In Lisbon Europe moved unnoticed in an intergovernmental direction, without a Treaty amendment. During the final Press conference the acting European Council President talked on the basis of the Conclusions about 'the new open method of co-ordination at all levels, coupled with a stronger guiding and co-ordinating role for the European Council'. He noted 'a true revolution in our working methods, (…) hinging between national policies around European objectives'. In short 'an effective method of co-ordination'.

### 3.1 An Overview of the wide Sphere of Activities of the European Council:[8]

– A review of the Treaties in 1986, 1991, 1997, 2001 and 2004 in the role of an Intergovernmental Conference (IGC);

---

[7] Werts, op. cit. n. 1, at pp. 64-67.
[8] Here we refer to the European Council in one of its different compositions.

- The settlement of complicated accession negotiations in Dublin and Brussels in 1984 (with Spain and Portugal), in Corfu 1994 (with Austria, Finland and Sweden) and in Copenhagen 2002 (with Cyprus, the Czech Republic, Estonia, Latvia, Lithuania, Hungary, Poland, Slovakia, Slovenia and Malta);

- The consensual adoption of the multiannual financial framework of the Union since 1988. It was repeated in Edinburgh in 1992 and subsequently in Berlin in 1999, once again for a seven-year period. The agreed spending limits went side by side with important (and difficult to agree upon) policy changes to the Structural Funds and the Common Agricultural Policy, which are by far the biggest budget items. At the same time the complicated problem of burden-sharing among the individual Member States was addressed;

- The Treaty of Amsterdam brought the important task of authorising of closer or enhanced cooperation initiatives between the Member States ex Article 11 TEC;
    - The Treaty of Amsterdam introduced moreover Article 7 TEU. The Heads of State or Government can identity a 'serious and persistent breach by a Member State' of the fundamental rights as stipulated in Article 6 TEU.
    - The drawing up of requests addressed to the Institutions;

- The drawing up of requests addressed to the Institutions;

- The initiation of a considerable amount of secondary legislation;

- The laying down of a common approach to politically sensitive institutional issues. See Edinburgh 1992 as an example. The meeting had to find an explanation as to how to work with the principle of subsidiarity;

- The discussion of urgent national internal problems. During the Laeken meeting (2001), for instance, the Austrian Chancellor, Wolfgang Schüssel, demanded an extension of the ecopoint system. Austria used this system in order to restrict the transit flow of heavy goods vehicles through the environmentally sensitive Alps. Schüssel threatened to prevent the enlargement of the Union with the Eastern European countries, if he did not get his way. He got his way;

- The discussion of undesirable conditions and situations in other EU Member States in order to enforce changes. An example was the inflationary linking of wages and salaries to price development in Belgium, at the time the only Member State to do so. Prime Minister Wilfried Martens, returning from the 1981 Maastricht Summit to Brussels, used the Conclusions for home consumption, in order to clarify the intolerability of the link. Another example is President Chirac's fierce criticism of the liberal Dutch drugs policy at the 1995 Cannes Summit;

–   Sometimes the European Council puts the brakes on European integration. It does so by tempering the plans, ambitions and expectations of the European Commission, the European Parliament and some governments. During the meetings of Dublin (in October 1996) and Biarritz (in 2000) it became crystal clear that the envisaged Treaty of Amsterdam (1997), and later the Treaty of Nice (2001), would present few novelties. The time was not yet right.[9]

–   The setting up of thematic meetings about one single subject. In this way, elements from the TEU and the TEC are turned into policy. In Finnish Tampere (1999) a special meeting was organized to work out the Area of Freedom, Security and Justice of the TEU. There were the aforementioned Employment meeting in Luxembourg (1997) and Lisbon (2000) to create the most competitive society in the world;

As the Conclusions of their meetings show, the Heads of Government expanded with the European Council the function of creating their own rules, to develop their own assignments, committees, task forces and initiatives on the basis of experience.

This incomplete outline also shows some of the tasks which the European Council has taken over from the Union's Institutions during the course of the years.

4.    THE RELATIONSHIP BETWEEN THE EUROPEAN COUNCIL AND THE INSTITUTIONS

4.1    **The Parliament**

The European Council and Parliament are antipodes. The first represents the Member States of the Union; the latter represents the citizens. Strasbourg takes note of the European Council, but the opposite rarely happens. There has not been much progress beyond the speech of the President of the Parliament (since 1981) at the start of the European Council meeting, and afterwards the report of the President of the European Council to the plenary in Strasbourg (since 1987). As an Institution, the Parliament does not have a grip on the activities of the intergovernmental European Council. A new and interesting development was the withdrawing by the incoming President of the Commission, José Manuel Barroso, of his proposed team of Commissioners on October 27, 2004. Under

---

[9] The winding down of over-ambitious expectations regarding the Union (in particular those of some interested parties) via the European Council also took place at the November 1997 Employment European Council in Luxembourg. Commission proposals for the creation of twelve million new jobs were swept off the table. This happened under a reference to the principle of subsidiarity.

Parliament's pressure the Italian and Latvian governments had to replace their original nominees and Barroso, moreover, had to reshuffle two portfolios. Here we saw a conflict between Parliament and some members of the Council, with as its main issue the composition of the European Commission

The European Council curtailed the Parliament as the budget authority. The European Council fixes the financing of the Union in detail, every seven years. This working method interferes with the authority of the Parliament, which, according to Article 272 (ex. 203) TEC, makes up the budget authority, together with the Council of Ministers. But is there any other way? The European Parliament is, as it should be at any rate, supranational through and through and the European Council is intergovernmental. In short, Parliament and Council remain in different spheres.

## 4.2   The Commission

According to the Treaties, the Commission is the initiating body. In practice, things are different. The Commission agrees that only some ten percent of its proposals relate to proper initiative.[10] Nowadays it is the European Council which initiates. It is customary for the European Council to ask the European Commission, but also sometimes simply to request or even to instruct it, to present proposals or develop certain issues and projects. Anyone who studies the relationship between the European Council and the Commission over the years will reach the conclusion that the Commission is in fact clearly subservient. The refrain is similar at every meeting, as the Conclusions show. This undermines the Commission's position of independence.

Experience shows that the role of the Commission in meetings depends to a large extent on the input of its President. Jacques Delors (1985-1995) dominated the meetings. Delors personally introduced the subjects to the Heads of Government. Together with Chancellor Kohl and President Mitterrand, Delors was the chief actor in completing the big projects of his era: the Single European Act (1986), the Internal Market (1993), the EMU and Enlargement. Delors saw the meetings as an instrument to realize his own political ideas. The influence of the Commission President clearly diminished after 1995, with the appointments of Jacques Santer and later Romano Prodi, both 'low profile'.

Initially the Commission made no proposals at all to the European Council. It elaborated its questions as if they were based on Article 208 TEC (ex 152 TEC). Only since Maastricht (1991) has the Commission issued proposals regarding the most important projects to the European Council. This started, as laid down in the TEU, with the EMU. Subsequently the Commission also sent proposals to the European Council regarding the other major project: Enlargement of the Union with thirteen countries.

---

[10] *Agence Europe* (14 September 2002) p. 5.

The underlying (but not often expressed) motivation of the Commission to deal with the European Council in this way is that its initiating task may be undermined in the legal sense, but that its proposals henceforth enjoy the support of the highest political leaders. Thanks to the emergence of the European Council, the Heads of Government delved into the 'nitty gritty', the complicated technical details. The actual fact that the European Council regularly commands the Council of Ministers to settle certain Commission proposals reinforces the Commission. It has used the European Council in a certain sense in order to *'retirer pour mieux sauter'*. Today, one may conclude that the emergence of the European Council has upgraded and strengthened the position of the Commission in the Union's decision-making machinery. The European Council and the Commission now form a tandem which drives decision-making.

## 4.3    The Council of Ministers

The intended globalisation of European action through the European Council had an important impact on the Council of Ministers. Through the arrival of the European Council the 'ordinary' Council of Ministers has politically lost its key role. The real political debates no longer take place there. The Treaty states that the Council of Ministers has the decision-making authority. This occurs in the General Affairs and External Relations (GAERC) and the Specialised Councils (e.g., EcoFin, Agriculture, or Transport). The European Council regularly commands – sometimes even imposing a deadline – the completion of a certain Regulation, or Directive. The Council of Ministers duly obeys. Nowadays, even governments receive orders!

Until 'Maastricht' 1991, the proposition in my earlier mentioned thesis was valid, namely that 'all decisions of the European Council, insofar as they lead to legislation, must be incorporated in Community legislation through the action of the Institutions involved, with the Council of Ministers to the fore'. Today, however, the European Council often operates as the decision-making body, sometimes in the composition of the Heads of State or Government and acting by a qualified majority. Yet in various situations the legal status and the enforceability of its decisions remain unclear. They include a raft of purely political decisions, varying from 'soft law' to texts with the character of 'hard law'.

## 5.    THE RELATIVE MEANING OF THE TREATY ESTABLISHING A
CONSTITUTION FOR EUROPE

The starting point of the Treaty establishing a Constitution for Europe is an active Union, despite the membership of 25+ Member States. For this, the Union requires a power centre in which all Member States are represented at the highest level. Their President, the semi-permanent President of the European Council, will become the figurehead of Europe. He or she will, for example, be the one phoning President George W. Bush during a political crisis. Conceivably, the reverse will be the case.

The big countries, especially France and the UK, but also Germany, like to play the game via the European Council. That will certainly be the case in a Union with 25 or more Member States of which two thirds belong to the category 'smaller'. Despite the fierce resistance of most smaller Member States, the European Council turned during the recent IGC into an Institution of the Union. The smaller Member States, aided by the European Commission, have in the Convention succeeded in dismantling the intended powerful Bureau of the President, proposed by the big Member States. But nothing prevents the future semi-permanent President of the European Council from establishing new structures in order further to consolidate his position. Therefore the earlier mentioned, so-called 'restricted job description' in the Constitutional Treaty merely amounted to symbol politics in order to appease the protesting smaller Member States.

Exactly the same thing happened at the creation of the European Council in 1974, as outlined earlier. Then, there was no indication whatsoever that the European Council would turn into a decision-shaping and decision-making body. The opposing Benelux countries were assured that nothing would change the decision-making process. It was explicitly stressed that the existing decision-making process would be maintained and even reinforced.

Yet the decision-making process changed profoundly. As described under section 3, the European Council, in the practice of its actions, has for years gone much further than the tasks laid down in the TEU. These tasks are: to provide the Union with the necessary impetus for its development and to define its general political direction and priorities. Right from the beginning in 1975, the Heads of Government took decisions as a 'supreme arbitrator' or '*instance d'appel*', regarding matters which had left the Council of Ministers in a stalemate. Moreover, since 1978 they develop all the important political projects. It started with the European Monetary System, which was created in Copenhagen in 1978.

In other words, it cannot be denied that the European Council on paper keeps its role both vague and broad, but in practice manifests itself fully, including concerning matters of detail. This process is now bound to repeat and reinforce itself. As happened with the European Council in 1974, the upcoming Treaty Establishing a Constitution for Europe offers the new semi-permanent President (Art. 22(2) TCE) a job description capable of broad interpretation. Given the example of the development of the European Council, the long-term President will undoubtedly give his job the maximum weight and scope. As the leading figure, the so-called 'President of the European Union' will be afforded the necessary space and authority.

The emergence and the success of the European Council reveal the fact that the Institutions of the Union possess neither the legitimacy, nor the power, nor the administrative authority to serve the EU as an integrating framework. The intergovernmental working method which took its place was often also the result of the good personal relationships between the political leaders of the (big) Member States. For many years the driving forces were 'buddies'. Chancellor

Schmidt and President Giscard d'Estaing in the 1970s, Chancellor Kohl and President Mitterrand in the 1980s, and more recently the Prime Ministers Silvio Berlusconi (Italy), Tony Blair (UK) and José Maria Aznar (Spain).

Propelled by national interests, this phenomenon has spurred the European Council to great results. Remember, for instance, the EMU with the euro and at the same time the Enlargement with Central and Eastern Europe. Without the ceaseless input, during many years, of the Heads of Government leaders these gigantic projects would never have been realised simultaneously and perfectly on schedule. Apparently, given their success, the Heads of Government do have the mandate of the citizens to administer the EU.

The Heads of Government regularly take it upon themselves to solve the biggest problem that plagues the Union at a particular moment. Often it concerns a question which has occupied the Commission and the Council of Ministers for months, and left them in a stalemate. The European Council then tackles such a problem during an extended and exhausting (night) session, sometimes a marathon session. This often happens after the Council of Ministers has deliberated extensively.

The preparatory work by the Commission and the Ministers for Foreign Affairs, in particular via the Committee of Permanent Representatives (Coreper), must offer a chance of agreement in order to succeed. This preparatory work is essential to the success of the meeting, as experience has shown. The second condition is the existence of a deadline, forcing the European Council to succeed. At crucial moments like these, the European Council is more or less obliged to reach a compromise, given among other things the traditional overwhelming publicity surrounding this occurrence.

More than once (for instance in Maastricht 1991, Amsterdam 1997, Berlin 1999 Nice 2000, and Brussels 2004) we have seen the exhausted and visibly rundown Heads of Government limping from the 'arena' between six and nine o'clock in the morning; entirely washed out, yet eager to defend the results when faced with 'their' national media. We do not know of any example of such an exhausting European Council meeting having ended in failure. They do find a solution, always. The positive effect on European integration of this persistent and total dedication of the highest national political leaders, time and time again, can hardly be overestimated.

# THE EVOLUTION IN THE ROLE AND POWERS OF THE EUROPEAN COMMISSION

## Michel Petite and Clemens Ladenburger[*]

### 1. INTRODUCTION

It is an adventurous exercise to attempt a survey of the future role of an Institution. History recalls that human factors, external yet unknown parameters, always distort natural trends. And this is relevant for the future role and powers of the Commission under the new Treaty establishing a Constitution for Europe (hereafter: the EU Constitution). We will attempt to reduce the risk involved by concentrating on some of the most important points, rather than trying to draw a complete picture based on an exhaustive analysis. After some introductory remarks on the scope of this report, the substance will be presented while following two simple themes: continuity and change.

In the interests of brevity, this report focuses on those rules of the EU Constitution that deal directly with the role and powers of the Commission. There are two further aspects which cannot be examined here, although they should certainly be borne in mind, given their obvious relation to the way in which the Commission will perform its role under the EU Constitution:

– First, this report will have to leave aside issues related to the Commission's composition and internal functioning, as well as the method of designating its members and, in particular, its President. Needless to say, however, the corresponding rules provided for in the EU Constitution will be crucial for the Commission's legitimacy and authority, and hence for the manner in which the Commission will be able to assume its tasks. As in the past, the place which each of the institutions can occupy in constitutional practice depends not only on what the founding texts expressly state concerning their tasks, but also on their internal efficiency and on their political weight as perceived by the other actors and – not least – by citizens. How they are composed and organised is pivotal in this respect.

---

[*] Michel Petite is Director-General of the Legal Service of the European Commission and Clemens Ladenburger is a member of that Service. All opinions expressed in the article are personal.

*D. Curtin, A.E. Kellermann and S. Blockmans, eds., The EU Constitution: The Best Way Forward?*
© 2005, T.M.C. Asser Instituut, The Hague.

- Secondly, we will concentrate on the evolution of the Commission's own core tasks and powers. We will not be able to go into any depth concerning the evolution of the powers of the other institutions and bodies, which are dealt with in other reports. But as is well known, the Union's institutional architecture is marked not so much by a system of strict separation of powers, but by a constant interplay between the institutions participating in and contributing to each other's functions. Therefore, changes to the tasks and powers of other institutions – and the EU Constitution contains some tasks and powers which are by far more profound than those concerning the Commission itself – will inevitably have significant repercussions on how the Commission will in practice perform its functions. To mention merely some examples:

  - The European Parliament's radically expanded right to give its consent to practically all major international agreements, and in particular in trade policy,[1] will certainly influence the methods and procedures to be followed by the Commission when negotiating these agreements.

  - The new possibilities offered in Article III-362 TCE (the current Art. 228 TEC) for more rapid procedures leading to Court of Justice sanctions against Member States persisting in infringements will obviously impact on the Commission's infringement policy.

  - The new role played by national parliaments in subsidiarity control will entail, for the Commission, a new experience of direct dialogue with national parliaments in pursuing the legislative procedures.

  - And, of course, the relationship of the newly created President of the European Council with the Commission President and the Union Minister for Foreign Affairs will certainly be amongst the most important open questions of future constitutional practice.

Thus, the three reports presented in this session of the Conference must necessarily be seen as complementary and interrelated, and a panel discussion on all three of them will no doubt yield further insights into each institution's role under the EU Constitution.

2.    CONTINUITY: THE COMMISION'S MISSIONS ARE CONFIRMED

  1) Perhaps the most important finding of this report is also a very simple one. The EU Constitution fully confirms and consolidates all the classic

---

[1] See Art. III-325(6)(a)(v) combined with Art. III-315(2). For a speculative comment on this rule, see M. Petite, 'Avis de temps calme sur l'article 189 A paragraphe 1: point d'équilibre entre le droit d'initiative de la Commission et le pouvoir décisionnel du Conseil' 3 *Revue du Marché Unique Européen* (1998) p. 197.

core functions of the Commission which have so far marked, in the first pillar, its pivotal role for the Community method:

– The Commission continues to have an exclusive right of initiative in all instances where this right previously existed. For European legislation, the EU Constitution now expressly enshrines that exclusive right as a general constitutional principle and constitutive element of the legislative procedure (Arts. I-26(2) and I-34 TCE). The corollary rule requiring unanimity in the Council for any amendment of a Commission proposal is also completely maintained (Art. III-395(1) TCE).

– The Commission's executive functions are preserved. That is true for the execution of the budget, for the adoption of 'derivative' acts based on secondary law – one area where, as we shall see, the Commission's role will be enhanced through the new instrument of delegated regulations, and also for the various instances in which the current EC Treaty itself assigns to the Commission the role of regulatory and/or administrative execution of Community law, particularly in the area of competition and State aids.[2]

– The Commission retains, without limitation, its role as the guardian of the Treaty.

– In external relations the Commission will represent the Union and negotiate agreements on its behalf, in all areas where it presently fulfils these tasks for the Community (see below).

2) A valuable achievement of the EU Constitution is that in Article I-26[3]

---

[2] As a consequence of the new system of non-legislative acts enshrined in Art. I-35 TCE, the EU Constitution, in the section on competition in Part III, now expressly recognises the Commission's power to adopt regulations which are based directly on the Treaty and which do not constitute acts of implementation of the Council Regulations which precede them (Arts. III-165(3), III-168(4) TCE). The reason for this is that in these cases of block exemption regulations, the regulatory substance is wholly laid down in the Commission regulation; the preceding Council regulations could therefore not easily be regarded as legal bases for 'implementing acts', within the meaning of Art. I-37 TCE. On the new system of legal instruments and the distinction between legislative and non-legislative acts in particular, see C. Ladenburger, 'Towards a Post-national Constitution – Federal, Confederal or Genuinely Sui-generis? Introductory Comments on the Convention Method, and on some Features of an improved Constitutional Charter', *Revue europeenne de droit public* (2004) pp. 75 et seq. (in particular pp. 97-100).

[3] 'The Commission shall promote the general interest of the Union and take appropriate initiatives to that end. It shall ensure the application of the Constitution, and measures adopted by the institutions pursuant to the Constitution. It shall oversee the application of Union law under the control of the Court of Justice of the European Union. It shall execute the budget and manage programmes. It shall exercise coordinating, executive and management functions, as laid down in the Constitution. With the exception of the common foreign and security policy, and other cases provided for in the Constitution, it shall ensure the Union's external representation. It shall initiate the Union's annual and multiannual programming with a view to achieving interinstitutional agreements.'

TCE of its truly 'constitutional' first Part; it finally provides a handy, accurate and comprehensible definition of these main functions of the Commission, just as it does for each of the other institutions. In order to measure the resulting gain in visibility and clarity, not least for citizens wishing to grasp the basic features of the system from reading the EU Constitution, it suffices to compare Article I-26 TCE with the wording of the present Article 211 TEC, a provision mixing essential elements with secondary platitudes and marked by a number of clumsy, bureaucratic and uninspiring formulae. But the value of this wording in Article I-26 TCE certainly goes beyond a political façade: notwithstanding the fact that the authors of the EU Constitution decided not to formally establish a legal hierarchy between its various Parts, crystallising the core functions of the Commission in a single provision in Part I (just as Arts. I-20, I-21, I-23, I-29 to I-31 TCE do for the other institutions), Part I clearly conveys a legal and political message. These functions belong to the constitutional bedrock of the Union. They mark the rule; any derogatory provisions in Part III are exceptions and will be interpreted narrowly. In future rounds of the EU Constitution's amendment these core functions are likely to be considered and defended as lasting principles guiding any reform, placing the burden of proof on those who wish to modify them or include derogations. The express recognition of the exclusive right of initiative follows the same intention and might be hoped to have the same effect: the Exceptions in Part III to that constitutional principle are not likely to proliferate in future negotiations, but rather to disappear over time.

3) When looking back at the deliberations of the Convention, one should not forget that this result, a complete confirmation of the Commission's tasks, could by no means be taken for granted at the beginning of the process. Rather, there was intense and fascinating public debate, conducted not only on the floor of the Convention, but even more so by the various actors of civil society accompanying the Convention – academia, think-tanks, pro-European movements and other groups. Virtually every element of the Union's current institutional architecture was called into question, and some rather revolutionary ideas were put on the table:

– At the centre of that debate was the question whether a true single 'European government' could be created, combining all the executive functions currently exercised in part by the Commission and in part by the Council. The panoply of proposals included models aimed at drastically reducing the current role of one of the two institutions: whether that of the Commission, to a mere technical administration managing Community policies and a secretariat facilitating the Council's and Parliament's action, or that of the Council, to a mere second legislative Chamber. The Convention members realised quickly that all these proposals would pose threats to the essence of the present Community method, and the quite stark clashes of interest between Member States attracted by one tendency or another led the Convention to search for consensus in the middle, through, in principle, confirmation of the *status quo* of a mixed executive power.

– It should not be forgotten that the Commission initially demonstrated openness to participate without taboos in such a reflection on the restructuring of the Union's executive: as President Prodi stated in his address to the Convention at its opening, the Commission was ready to renounce part of its current roles, for example in the field of competition, in order to focus on enhanced core governmental missions. All this also became obsolete when it appeared that Convention members basically preferred to confirm the *status quo*.

– The most revolutionary concepts, sometimes tabled in an elaborate form, were those providing *de facto* for a merger of the executive functions of the Council and the Commission. It is interesting to note that a trace of this idea did survive in the form of the Union Minister for Foreign Affairs, the Vice President chairing the External Relations Council, the one groundbreaking institutional innovation devised by the European Convention and never before contemplated in an IGC (see below). There was certainly no chance of success for the occasional proposals to generalise that model by conferring the Presidency of the various council formations to the competent Commissioners. But it should not be forgotten that one further major step in that direction, i.e., the suggestions to have the Commission (Vice) President chair the General Affairs Council, was close to being accepted at the end of the Convention, in the run-up to a compromise package on the permanent European Council President. One level higher, the 'top merger solution', i.e., one Union President presiding at the same time over the European Council and the Commission, was also backed in the Convention by a group of prominent members, and the EU Constitution was finally designed to leave that possibility open, should the time be ripe in the future.[4]

– Some more traditional topics of discussion also reappeared on the floor of the Convention, such as proposals to abolish the monopoly of initiative of the Commission and to grant such a right equally to the Parliament (or to Member States). It took relatively little pedagogic effort and plenary discussion to convince Convention members that the functioning of the national legislative process is not transposable to that at Union level.[5]

---

[4] See Art. I-22(3) TCE, permitting *e contrario* a President holding another Community office.

[5] However, some parliamentarians, in the very last minute of the Convention, successfully pushed for including the instrument of a 'citizens' initiative'. Although the wording of Art. I-47(4) TCE resembles that of Art. III-332 TCE (the current Art. 192(2) TEC) on the right of Parliament to invite the Commission to table a proposal, and it is thus clear that the invitation is not binding

   – One last area in which one might regret that the IGC, despite promising initiatives in the Convention, finally came back almost to the *status quo* as regards the Commission's powers, is the Economic and Monetary Union, and notably the task of surveillance of budgetary discipline. Against some reticence on the part of government representatives, the Convention had at least led to the modest step of giving the Commission a genuine right of proposal, amendable only by unanimity, in the first steps of the excessive deficit procedure.[6] At the last minute, however, the IGC reversed even that modest step.

In sum, the basic continuity marking the EU Constitution's rules on the role and powers of the Commission is the result of several factors at work in the Convention, the IGC, and surrounding public debate. It is due in part to pedagogic efforts to raise awareness, in the Convention and beyond, of the virtues of the existing Community method, but also in part to conflicting tendencies amongst various Member States that prevented both a drastic reinforcement and a weakening of the Commission. Finally, as regards more revolutionary models, there was perhaps a certain lack of vision and convergence amongst Member States on the direction of the European project, combined, to be sure, with a real scarcity of time to evaluate properly the chances and the risks of these models.

## 3.    AREAS OF CHANGE

Without any pretension to being exhaustive, three main areas will be presented below where the EU Constitution will entail changes in the Commission's role and powers. We will start with a seemingly very specific amendment to the classical Community method which might, however, have great practical impact. We will then assess a rather remarkable extension of that method to new areas, and will finish with an area of true institutional innovation.

### 3.1    Executive Rulemaking, in particular through delegated Regulations

In certain areas of modern society marked by technology and rapid change, all contemporary parliaments are increasingly faced with the difficulty of keeping pace with developments and of having insufficient expertise to make the sound and timely judgments needed for proper lawmaking. This has resulted in a long-

---

on the Commission, it remains to be seen whether the citizens' initiative might not in practice work as a more serious constraint upon the latter's right of initiative.

   [6] I.e., for the finding that an excessive deficit exists and for addressing recommendations, see paras. 6 and 7 of the current Art. 104 TEC. That all subsequent steps should in any event continue to be decided on the basis of simple Commission recommendations was undisputed.

standing trend towards delegated executive rulemaking. At the Community level, the need to resort to that technique is felt even more urgently given the relatively cumbersome legislative process. At the same time, it has become clear over time that the instrument offered by the present Treaty, i.e., Comitology, does not fully suffice to meet that need: it is criticised for a lack of transparency, and the Parliament as co-legislator hesitates to use it for matters of importance since it has no really effective control over its exercise.

The EU Constitution's response to that problem is the instrument of delegated regulation (Art. I-36 TCE): the legislator may delegate to the Commission (and only to it) the power to enact such regulations to supplement or amend certain non-essential elements of European laws or framework laws. Both branches of the legislator may retain some control, whether by the possibility of 'revoking' a regulation enacted by the Commission, or by deferring its entry into force by a period during which they may object. This is in fact the first express recognition of a delegated power of the Commission to engage in delegated executive rulemaking; and yet in practice the same power has already so far existed as part of the concept of 'implementing acts' adopted under the Comitology procedures in accordance with Articles 202, 3rd indent, and 211, 4th indent TEC.

The EU Constitution, however, does not replace the present concept of implementing acts with that of delegated acts, nor does it set out with precision how the concept of 'delegated regulation' and 'implementation' in Articles I-36 and I-37 TCE relate to each other. While, particularly for lawyers from Roman legal systems, the conceptual distinction is in principle familiar, the way it is set out in the EU Constitution certainly leaves a considerable margin to the legislator to determine, in the political process, whether to use one or the other technique in a given case. One might expect that wherever the Parliament is involved as co-legislator, it will henceforth systematically insist that delegated regulations be used rather than the regulatory Comitology procedure, whereas individual decisions – even those of great importance such as in the context of managing funds – will continue to be taken in Comitology. At the same time, and that is the main effect which Article I-36 TCE was designed to achieve, the Commission will be entrusted with delegated executive rulemaking to a far greater extent, since the Parliament, given its rights of control pursuant to Article I-36(2) TCE, will more readily agree to unburden the legislative procedure and delegate important regulatory powers, even in politically sensitive areas (cf., regulation of the financial markets addressed in the well-known 'Lamfalussy report' of 15 February 2001[7]).

How, exactly, will the mechanisms of control referred to in Article I-36(2) TCE work, and how much leeway will the Commission have when using the new instrument? That is yet another point on which the EU Constitution leaves much room for institutional practice. Without wishing to engage in speculation, one might assume that the Member States will attempt to set up within the Council a system allowing, similarly to Comitology, a control of delegated regulations

---

[7] Available at: <http://europa.eu.int/comm/internal_market/securities/lamfalussy/index_en.htm.>.

prior to their entry into force, although their possibilities of intervention might not be identical given that the Council may halt such a regulation only by qualified majority. The Parliament, conversely, scores a tremendous gain in potential control as compared with the present situation, though all depends on how efficiently it manages to organise itself, given its workload in legislation. It might turn out that Parliament's influence will be felt by the Commission only in rare cases of particular political sensitivity, where the threat of a negative vote with absolute majority under Article I-36(2) TCE can be credibly made. Be that as it may, the main point is that the EU Constitution strengthens the capacity of the Commission to perform its rulemaking tasks with complete accountability and transparency, for the benefit of the Union as a whole.

As to those categories of derived acts which will remain covered by the traditional concept of 'implementing acts' and hence by Comitology, the EU Constitution may also bring about some change. Compared to Article 202 TEC, Article I-37 TCE offers some conceptual clarification: it is now undoubtedly the Legislator that confers implementing powers (and not the Council as the 'primary executive branch' which would cede some of its power to the Commission as the 'auxiliary executive', as some had interpreted Art. 202 TEC) to, as a rule, the Commission, while granting it to the Council must be confined to 'specific duly motivated cases'. More significantly, the present Comitology Decision, so far adopted unanimously by the Council alone, is converted into ordinary legislation (i.e., co-decision of the Parliament and the Council), which will allow the Parliament to leave a distinctive mark on the organisation of Comitology. And, on one point that has not been widely noted, Article I-37(2) TCE now speaks of 'control by *Member States* of the Commission's exercise of implementing powers. [emphasis added].' That reference to Member States, which is not in Article 202, 4th indent TEC, of course covers the representatives of Member States sitting in the Committees. But will that wording still permit an intervention by the Council, as presently in the administrative and regulatory Comitology procedure, substituting itself in the last instance for the Commission in adopting an implementing act? This is yet another open question on which the three institutions will have to form a view.

## 3.2    The 'Communitarisation' of the Third Pillar

No doubt the greatest increase in the Commission's responsibilities will result from the rather spectacular step in the EU Constitution to 'communitarise' *de facto* the present Third Pillar. Indeed, the EU Constitution extends, but for a few derogations of limited scope, the classical rules and procedures of Community law to the area of police and judicial cooperation in criminal matters within the framework of the 'Area of Freedom, Security and Justice' – a policy area that will occupy a most prominent place in the EU Constitution.[8]

---

[8] For a more detailed analysis see C. Ladenburger, 'Police and Judicial Cooperation in Criminal Matters in the Draft Constitution for Europe', 1 *Europarättslig Tidskrift* (2004) p. 45.

How did it become possible for the European Convention to reach consensus on this step, and for the IGC to preserve essentially such consensus? In a nutshell, the answer is that, against the backdrop of citizens' particularly high expectations for European action in this field, the shortcomings of the intergovernmental, international law oriented approach of the present Third Pillar (Arts. 29 to 42 TEU) were all too patent. Decision-making procedures in this area are hampered by the rule of unanimity in a Council overloaded by Member State initiatives following more the national priorities of the day than any genuine European interest. They give birth to instruments often tailored so as to ensure that no Member State's law has to change, and which either enter into force only years later, if ever (i.e., conventions), or lack direct effect and any monitoring of transposition and implementation in the Member States (i.e., decisions and framework decisions), because there is no guardian of Treaty obligations. In addition, the complex pillar structure forces comprehensive political initiatives to be artificially split up into various instruments of different legal effect. And, finally, there is a deficit in legitimacy due to the absence of parliamentary involvement in the decision-making and the severe restrictions of judicial control pursuant to Article 35 TEU.

Against this background, the Convention members decided, and the IGC confirmed, that it was not promising to attempt a further remodelling of the intergovernmental system set up in Maastricht and revised in Amsterdam, but that only the Community method offered adequate solutions.

For the Commission, this radical change of system will, *inter alia*, have the following consequences:

– The Commission's right of initiative is considerably strengthened. Although the EU Constitution does not entirely eliminate the possibility of Member State initiatives, it requires such initiatives to be tabled by a quarter of the Member States (i.e., 7 States in a Union of 25 to 28 members) jointly (Art. III-264 TCE). In practice it may be expected that Member States will rarely attempt to put together such a large group for an initiative, particularly in the co-decision procedure with the European Parliament which will govern virtually all matters of criminal law.

– The Commission will replace the Council Presidency in the role of negotiator of international agreements – and such negotiation of agreements is of growing political importance in this field, as can be seen from the Union's agreements with the US on extradition and on judicial assistance in criminal matters, negotiated in the wake of 11 September 2001.

– The EU Constitution's normal rules on delegated rulemaking and implementing acts (see point 3.1 *supra*) will apply in this field. As a rule the Commission and not the Council, as is often the case today, will be called upon to adopt such acts. While the Council might be expected, in areas such as operational police cooperation where it will continue to be the sole primary legislator, to confer implementing powers on itself 'in duly justified specific cases' (Art. I-37 (2) TCE), it certainly would not be permitted to do so for an entire policy area such as police cooperation.

–   The normal budgetary rules will be extended to this area; there will be no more possibility of Member State financing as practised today, for instance, in the case of Europol. The Commission will execute the budget in all instances; and it will have to devise rules replacing the present arrangements of Member State financing.

–   The Commission will be able to open infringement proceedings before the Court of Justice against Member States. For the effective realisation of the 'Area of Freedom, Security and Justice' this is one of the most significant innovations. The task will be particularly delicate, bearing in mind that the Commission will not only have to monitor the effective transposition of future framework laws (but also of the numerous existing 'framework decisions') in national criminal law, but also to ensure full respect of fundamental rights in areas covered by Union law. Both are however indispensable if Member States are to be expected to cooperate in mutual trust in a single European judicial area in which classical extradition procedures and the like have no further place.

–   Finally, the Commission's central role, as foreseen in the EU Constitution, in setting up and managing 'enhanced cooperation' between a smaller number of Member States, will apply without exception also to such schemes of cooperation in criminal law (and one might expect them to occur more frequently here than elsewhere). This means that, unlike today, the Commission will acquire an exclusive power to submit a scheme of enhanced cooperation to the Council for establishment or to reject it,[9] and that it will have a primary role in the process of authorising the subsequent joining in such a scheme by other Member States.

In sum, this breakthrough in the Convention represents much more than simply the extension of the normal Community (or now: Union) method to yet another field of policy. The challenge for the Commission will be enormous. It will be to make that method work in an area still perceived as lying at the heart of traditional notions of national sovereignty, and marked by the particular attention of national parliamentarians and the public. Consequently, the Commission will, for instance, have to develop new practices of dialogue with national parliaments, but also to use its best legal expertise and sensitivity, in drafting Union law and then acting as its guardian, on questions that it has so far largely stayed out of. And it will be expected to offer imaginative solutions in the legislative initiatives

---

[9] It appears, however, that that power does not exist in the case of an 'automatic' establishment of enhanced cooperation after a Member State has resorted to the 'emergency brake' mechanism in the field of approximation of criminal law and no other solution has been found, see Arts. III-270(4) and III-271(4) TCE, *in fine*.

that the EU Constitution requires it to table on various complex topics: conferring operational powers on Europol and developing Eurojust, adapting the rules
on decision-making, budgeting, and judicial control of these Union bodies, creating the evaluation arrangements contemplated in Article III-260 TCE, and even
setting up a European Prosecutor's Office.

## 3.3    External Relations

The field of external relations, and Common Foreign and Security Policy (CFSP)
in particular, was the second area where Convention members realised that institutional change would be necessary in the interest of a more efficient Union
policy. However, unlike the 'Area of Freedom, Security and Justice', it was politically unrealistic simply to resort to the classic recipes of the Community
method. Willing to tackle the present shortcomings, the Convention and then the
IGC resorted instead to innovation, by overcoming the rigid pillar structure
while nonetheless maintaining an intergovernmental specificity of the CFSP, and
by introducing the office of the Union Minister for Foreign Affairs. That is why
this area is probably the one where the impact of the EU Constitution on the
Commission is the least certain. In any event a fundamental distinction will continue to apply, though now under the umbrella of a single Union law governed
by common principles, between the classic 'Community' external relations and
the CFSP.

In external relations other than the CFSP, i.e., those of the present Community, the Commission's functions are preserved and strengthened: it retains an
exclusive right of initiative, in particular to propose international agreements
other than those related exclusively or principally to the CFSP and to monetary
policy, and negotiates those agreements;[10] it manages programmes and funds under the Union's budget, including those serving the implementation of the 'civil'
side of the CFSP. A highly significant step is the provision in Article I-26(1)
TCE stipulating that the Commission ensures the Union's external representation
in all matters except the CFSP and cases expressly laid down in the EU Constitution (i.e., monetary policy); this will apply in all international organisations and
put to rest a question so far often controversial between the institutions and the
Member States.

In the CFSP, the new decisive actor will be the Minister for Foreign Affairs.
The Commission will lose its own present shared right of initiative to him. In a
similar vein the current Council Presidency will lose its role of representing the
Union's CFSP externally; instead that role will be fulfilled by him, and by the
President of the European Council at the level of Heads of State (see Arts. III-

---

[10] Although Art. III-325 TCE merely refers to the 'negotiator' or 'negotiating team of the
Union', it is clear from para. 3 of that article and Art. I-26(1) TCE that this means: the Minister
for agreements relating exclusively or principally to the CFSP, and the Commission for all other
cases.

296 and I-22 TCE). The Minister will likewise negotiate international agreements relating exclusively or principally to the CFSP. Finally, he will chair the Foreign Affairs Council.

The novel institutional experience will of course result from the fact that this Minister will be a full member of the Commission (and one of its Vice Presidents), with all the rights and duties of a Commissioner. The idea was officially launched by R. Prodi in a speech to the Parliament in October 2000,[11] and although it was initially met by a great deal of scepticism in governmental quarters, it nevertheless became, during the Convention, the only game in town. In the fulfilment of some of his functions, the Minister will however not, or only partially, be bound by 'Commission procedures'. Thus, the College of Commissioners will not provide him with any instructions as to his actions as Chairman of the Foreign Affairs Council. He will carry out the Union's CFSP 'as mandated by the Council'[12] and the College will not be able to bind him by diverging mandates or directions. Nonetheless, he will be subject to full political responsibility for all his actions vis-à-vis the Commission President and the Parliament, and need their confidence as much as that of the Council.[13] In fact, the Minister stands for a partial merger of the Union's two executive institutions, given that the tasks of a Commissioner are combined with the function of chairing the Council. It is clear that this imaginative institutional construction will raise interesting legal questions, on which we cannot go into in any depth here and to which the Commission and the other institutions will have to find viable solutions once the Minister is in office.

The same can be said of the External Action Service, which is to be established by a Council decision to be adopted upon a proposal from the Union Minister for Foreign Affairs after consulting the European Parliament and after obtaining the consent of the Commission. The EU Constitution describes its function as assisting the Minister in fulfilling his mandate and mentions its recruitment sources, but for the rest leaves its organisation and functioning to the aforementioned Council decision. In due course, that decision and subsequent

---

[11] *Bulletin of the EU* No. 10/2000, pp. 149-153.

[12] One question in this connection arises from the fact that the Constitution in Art. I-28(2) TCE attributes the function of carrying out the CFSP to the Minister himself, and thus neither to the Council nor to the Commission as such, but apparently does not contemplate the possibility for the Minister himself to take any formal legal acts such as decisions (see Art. I-35(2) TCE, mentioning only the Council, the Commission and the Central Bank). Such taking of formal legal acts is, however, at least in the context of classic Community policies, the backbone of any 'carrying out' of a policy, and a need for this may also be shown in the CFSP where only the Council appears expressly authorised to take decisions, see Arts. III-295(2), III-297 and III-298 TCE.

[13] The Minister is, as part of the College, subject to the same possibility of a parliamentary motion of censure as any other Commissioner; although Art. I-26(8) TCE requests him only to resign from his Commission office in that case, Art. I-26(5) and (6) and Art. I-28(4) TCE mean that he must be replaced in all his functions in such a case. In the case of a loss of confidence, the President of the Commission can ask the Minister to resign, but needs the approval of the European Council.

practice will therefore have to deal with three types of issues of great institutional significance for the Commission that, again, we can only mention in passing here:

- the tasks and areas of activity of that Service, as related to those of the current Directorates-General of the Commission fulfilling external relations tasks;

- the definition of the political strings of command governing the action of that Service;[14]

- the precise administrative status and affiliation of that Service – an exercise for which some precedents may be found in current interinstitutional practice,[15] though they may not be functionally and politically quite comparable.

However, apart from these interesting questions for the future one should not forget what appears as the main progress of the EU Constitution in this area: it will render obsolete a series of institutional disputes arising presently from the existence of competing actors (Commission, High Representative, Presidency) and different legal regimes and decision-making procedures (in particular, international agreements of the Union under Arts. 24 TEU vs. those of the Community under Art. 300 TEC). Above all, it will provide enormous potential for more consistent external action on the part of the Union. In this spirit, we do not intend to participate in speculative discussions whether the introduction of the Minister for Foreign Affairs will work more to strengthen the institutional profile of the Commission or of the Council. Instead, we are confident that the Minister will be able to work constructively in both institutions. He will help the Commission become a privileged place for the conception of an efficient and consistent Union external policy across the present pillars, just as much as, in his capacity as chairman of the Council, he will greatly enhance that institution's authority and efficiency as the decision-maker in external policy.

---

[14] Although the Constitution in Art. III-328 TCE mentions 'Union delegations' as a separate concept without referring to the External Action Service, it may be assumed to intend those delegations to form part of this Service. Thought will therefore have to be given to how best to square the provisions on administrative organisation in Art. III-328 TCE (stipulating that external representation is carried out by the Union delegations, and placing them under the authority of the Minister) with the institutional principle expressed in Art. I-26 TCE that outside the CFSP the Commission represents the Union externally.

[15] The Joint Interpretation Service 'SCIC', the Office of Publications, the European Personnel Selection Office.

## 4.    CONCLUSION

The EU Constitution's primary message as regards the role and powers of the Commission is one of continuity and consolidation: the Commission's traditional functions have all been confirmed, and it thus very largely retains its pivotal place in the characteristic interplay of the institutions that is the essence of the Community method. It is to be welcomed that Part I of the EU Constitution now contains strong formulae defining these functions and enshrining them as a constitutional bedrock. This contributes to making the Union's political system understandable for citizens, and consolidates an institutional model from which any future rounds of Treaty amendment will not easily depart. That is the result of three years of passionate discussion preparing, marking and accompanying the work of the Convention and the IGC. In both *fora* forces attracted by an intergovernmental dilution of the Community method were confronted by other forces aiming at establishing the Commission as the sole executive centre of a more integrated Union. Far-reaching plans for a merger or concentration of the two current executive powers, the Council and the Commission, in particular did not have any realistic chance of success, in the absence of sufficient time to evaluate them properly, as well as in view of the fundamental divergences amongst Member States on the direction of the European project.

The EU Constitution will, however, entail some new institutional challenges for the Commission: in the area of executive rulemaking it develops and enriches the classical Community method particularly by the new instrument of delegated regulation. It extends that method fully to the future key policies serving the creation of an 'Area of Freedom, Security and Justice', leading the Commission and the other institutions to new frontiers so far associated exclusively with the national state. Finally, in external relations it expressly entrusts the Commission with the Union's external representation in all matters outside the CFSP, and strengthens the latter policy by introducing the Minister for Foreign Affairs, thus opening new opportunities for a more efficient and consistent Union policy – opportunities of which the Commission and the Council, and the Minister working in each of them, should make best use in a spirit of loyal cooperation.

The benchmark of success of institutional reform is whether it results in an overall system in which each institution can perform its core missions in greater consistency, clarity and legitimacy than before. Our conclusion is that this can be said of the EU Constitution as far as the Commission is concerned, and that the Community method, with the central role it provides for the Commission as the promoter of the general European interest, has been preserved and extended.

# THE EXPANDING ROLE OF THE EUROPEAN PARLIAMENT

Ricardo Passos*

## 1.  INTRODUCTION: THE IDEA OF A CONSTITUTION — FROM SPINELLI TO GISCARD D'ESTAING

Twenty years ago, the European Parliament adopted a resolution containing a 'draft Treaty establishing the European Union' based on the so-called Spinelli draft. On 14 February 1984 this resolution was adopted by a large majority (237/ 31/43). Many of the ideas developed in this resolution were considered unrealistic at that time. Yet, not many years later – 20 years is not a long period in such an important political evolution – the Union now has a real Constitution, which actually took on board some of the provisions of the Spinelli draft.

Indeed, in these last 20 years, after the creation of its 'Committee on Institutional Affairs' in 1981, the European Parliament has constantly tried to influence the shaping of the Union. It has insisted on the need for more clarity, efficiency, democratic accountability and the protection of the fundamental rights of citizens. To that effect, Parliament always proposed to reinforce the Community method as opposed to the Intergovernmental method.

With the constant defence of this set of principles, Parliament has adopted a series of resolutions of great importance in recent years, in particular before and after each IGC.[1] More recently, the Member States also realised that, in the light

---

* Head of Division, Legal Service, European Parliament. The views expressed in this paper are personal and do not necessarily coincide with the positions adopted by the European Parliament.

[1] Parliament systematically adopted resolutions before the successive IGCs in order to influence their work; it also adopted after each IGC a resolution evaluating the results achieved. Hereafter the resolutions before and after the respective IGCs are enumerated.
   – Single European Act
   . Resolution of 14 February 1984: report and draft Treaty Spinelli (*OJ* (1984) C 77/33).
   . Resolutions of 16 January 1986: report Planas (*OJ* (1986) C 36/144) and of 17 April 1986 (*OJ* (1986) C 120/96).
   – Treaty of Maastricht
   . Resolutions on the basis of report by D. Martin of 14 March 1990 (*OJ* (1990) C 96/114), 11 July 1990 (*OJ* (1990) C 231/97) and of 22 November 1990 (*OJ* (1990) C 324/219).
   . Resolution of 7 April 1992: report Martin (*OJ* (1992) C 125/81).
   – Treaty of Amsterdam
   . Resolutions of 17 May 1995: report D. Martin/Bourlanges (*OJ* (1995) C 151/56) and of 13 March 1996: report Duff/Maij-Weggen (*OJ* (1996) C 96/77).

*D. Curtin, A.E. Kellermann and S. Blockmans, eds., The EU Constitution: The Best Way Forward?*
© 2005, *T.M.C. Asser Instituut, The Hague.*

of an enlargement with very important political and geographical implications, a mere adaptation of the existing Treaties would not respond to the expectations created for citizens aiming in particular at clarifying the Union's nature, its values and competencies and at the same time increasing its democratic accountability and efficiency.

The Treaty of Nice was largely considered insufficient and its Declaration 23 called for a deeper and wider debate about the future of Europe and indicated, *inter alia*, the following issues to be tackled in a forthcoming IGC:

- a more precise delimitation of powers between the Union and the Member States;
- the status of the Charter of Fundamental Rights;
- a simplification of the Treaties without changing their meaning; and
- the role of the national parliaments in the European architecture.

In its resolution of 31 May 2001, after the adoption of the Treaty of Nice, Parliament noted that 'the negotiations on the Treaty of Nice demonstrated, as in the case of the Amsterdam Treaty, that the purely intergovernmental method has outlived its usefulness for the purpose of revising the Treaties, as the governments eventually implicitly recognised when they adopted Declaration 23'.[2] Parliament therefore claimed that the holding of a new IGC should be based on a radically different process which should be transparent and open to participation by the European Parliament, the national parliaments and the Commission and that the IGC should initiate a constitutional development process. In this respect, Parliament took the view that a Convention should be established with a similar remit and configuration to the Convention which drew up the Charter of Fundamental Rights, 'the task of which should be to submit to the IGC a constitutional proposal based on the outcome of an extensive public debate and intended to serve as a basis for the IGC's work'.[3]

In its resolution of 29 November 2001, Parliament developed its previous resolution and added to the issues indicated in Declaration 23 the following:

- the incorporation of the CFSP into the Community pillar,
- the recognition of the legal personality of the Union,

---

- Resolution of 19 November 1997: report Méndez de Vigo/Tsatsos (*OJ* (1997) C 371/99).
- Treaty of Nice
- Resolutions on the basis of report Dimitrakopoulos/Leinen of 18 November 1999 (*OJ* (2000) C 189/222), 3 February 2000 (*OJ* (2000) C 309/85) and of 13 April 2000 (*OJ* (2001) C 40/409); Resolution of 31 May 2001: report Méndez de Vigo/Seguro (*OJ* (2002) C 47E/108).

[2] *Supra* n. 1, Resolution of 31 May 2001, para. 5.
[3] *Idem*, para. 39.

- the consolidation within the EC Treaty of the Charter of Fundamental Rights,

- the elimination of the democratic deficit that characterises the EMU at present and the establishment of a well-balanced economic and monetary system,

- the establishment of a common police, judicial and criminal policy (in particular the merging within the Community framework, recognition of the full jurisdiction of the Court of Justice, the integration of Europol into the Union's institutional framework and the establishment of a European Public Prosecutor's Office).

Parliament underlined, moreover, that if the Union institutions are to operate more democratically and more effectively, the following items should be included for debate:

- the system for nominating the Presidencies of the European Council, the General Affairs Council and the Council meeting sectorally,

- simplification of legislative procedures and co-decision as the general procedure,

- the removal of the distinction between compulsory expenditure and non-compulsory expenditure,

- the introduction of a hierarchy of Community acts,

- the involvement of the Parliament in the common trade policy and in external economic relations,

- the election of the Commission by the European Parliament and the nomination of the members of the Court of Justice and of the Court of First Instance by the Council, acting by qualified majority vote with the assent of the European Parliament.[4]

This long list of items may be considered as Parliament's road-map for the IGC 2003/2004.

In fact, the European Council in the Laeken Declaration of 15 December 2001 took many of them as issues to be tackled by the Convention.[5] It is also true that during the elaboration of the EU Constitution by the Convention,

---

[4] Resolution of 29 November 2001 on the constitutional process and the future of the Union (*OJ* (2002) C 153/310); reporters: J. Leinen and M. de Vigo, A5-0368/2001, para 4.

[5] For a complete view of the preparation of the Laeken Declaration and the discussions of the Convention in particular on the institutional issues, see the excellent article by P. Magnette, 'La constitutionnalisation des traités européens: forces et limites de la "méthode conventionnelle"', in *Une Constitution pour l'Europe*, Réflexions sur les transformations du droit de l'Union européenne (éditions Larcier 2004) pp. 24-51.

Parliament's Delegation insisted on the above-mentioned items.[6] Indeed, some of Parliament's reports were exclusively aimed at influencing the work of the Convention and some had an undeniable influence, like, for example, the report of Mr Carnero on the legal personality of the Union, the report of Mr Lamassoure on the division of competencies and the report of Mr Bourlanges on the typology of acts and the hierarchy of norms.

On 24 September 2003, Parliament adopted its resolution on the draft Treaty establishing a Constitution for Europe containing its opinion on the convening of the IGC.[7] In this article a full account has been given of Parliament's resolutions of 29 November 2001 and of 24 September 2003 on the Constitution established by the Convention. These are the most recent official positions adopted by the European Parliament and when, throughout the paper, reference is made to Parliament's position, this refers to these resolutions. In the meantime, on 9 December 2004, the Constitutional Affairs Committee adopted a report drawn up by Mr Mendez de Vigo (former Member of the Convention) and Mr Corbett evaluating the draft Constitution as adopted by the IGC.[8] On the basis of this report, on 12 January 2005 Parliament adopted a resolution on the Treaty establishing a Constitution for Europe (PA_TA(2005)004). This resolution provides a very positive evaluation of the EU Constitution. Parliament considers that its tries to achieve a Constitution since its first direct election has been crowned by the success of the Convention, which prepared the draft using a democratic, representative and transparent method. Parliament believes that the EU Constitution

---

[6] The main reports adopted by Parliament relating to subjects under discussion in the Convention are the following:
- Resolution of 16 March 2000: report Duff/Voggenhuber on the drafting of a European Union Charter of Fundamental Rights (*OJ* (2000) C 377/329).
- Decision of 14 November 2000: report Duff/Voggenhuber on the approval of the draft Charter of Fundamental Rights (*OJ* (2001) C 223/74).
- Resolution of 23 October 2002: report Duff, on the impact of the European Union Charter of Fundamental Rights and its future status (*OJ* (2003) C 300E/432).
- Resolution of 29 November 2001: report Leinen/Méndez de Vigo on the European Council of Laeken and the future of the Union (*OJ* (2002) C 153/310(E)).
- Resolution of 25 October 2001: report Poos on the reform of the Council (*OJ* (2002) C 112/317(E)).
- Resolution of 14 March 2002: report Carnero González on the legal personality of the European Union (*OJ* (2003) C 47/594(E)).
- Resolution of 7 February 2002: report Napolitano on the relationship between the European Parliament and the national parliaments in the framework of the European integration (*OJ* (2002) C 284/322 (E))
- Resolution of 16 May 2002: report Lamassoure on the division of competencies between the European Union and the Member States (*OJ* (2003) C 180/493(E)).
- Resolution of 17 December 2002: report Bourlanges on the typology of acts and the hierarchy of norms in the European Union (*OJ* (2004) C 31/126).
- Resolution of 14 January 2003: report Napolitano on the role of regional and local powers in the European Union (*OJ* (2004) C 38E/167).
- Resolution of 24 September 2003: on the draft Treaty establishing a Constitution for Europe and opinion of the European Parliament on the convening of the IGC (*OJ* (2004) C 77E/255).

[7] *OJ* (2004) C 77E/255; Rapporteurs: Gil-Robles Gil-Delgado and Tsatsos, doc. A5-0299/2003.

[8] PE 347.119v02.

is a good compromise and a vast improvement on the existing treaties and hopes that all Member States will be in a position to achieve ratification by mid-2006. In that respect, it suggests that the Member States, when distributing the EU Constitution, make a clear distinction between the elements already in force in the existing treaties and the new provision introduced by the EU Constitution, with a view to informing the debate. This resolution was adopted by 500 Members in favour, 137 against and 40 abstentions.

In the present contribution, the focus will be on the main changes contained in the EU Constitution concerning the European Parliament, albeit sometimes in a summary and incomplete manner.[9] These changes are those contained in the official document adopted by the IGC as published in the *Official Journal of the European Union*.[10] Even if it is not feasible to discuss here all the changes contained in the Constitution, the following items seem of particular relevance:[11]

- The institutional framework and, in particular, the relationship between the European Parliament and the Commission;

- The simplification of instruments and procedures, the establishment of the principle that co-decision is the legislative procedure generally applicable and the progress made in the area of Justice and Home Affairs;

- The expansion of the consent procedure and the future involvement of the Parliament in the Commercial Common Policy (CCP);

- The financial provisions.

## 2.  THE INSTITUTIONAL FRAMEWORK AND IN PARTICULAR THE RELATIONSHIP BETWEEN THE EUROPEAN PARLIAMENT AND THE COMMISSION

With some exceptions (in particular concerning CFSP and the appointment of members of the Court of Justice and of the Court of First Instance[12]), most of the

---

[9] It goes without saying that the items selected in this paper do not cover all the subjects that could be analysed within the perspective of the European Parliament. One example is the important implications stemming from the incorporation of the Charter of Fundamental Rights and the accession of the Union to the European Convention on Human Rights, which is one of the requests made by Parliament, but which is not developed in this article.

[10] When this article was drafted the last texts available were Documents CIG 87/04 and 87/04 ADD 1, both from 6 August 2004. In the meantime, the official text has been published in *OJ* (2004) C 310/1-474. The articles referred to are those contained in the official version.

[11] It is understood that this selection of items is a personal choice.

[12] Concerning the appointment of Judges, the Convention and the IGC maintained the current system (appointment by common accord of the Member States). Yet, a novelty has been introduced, which is worth mentioning: before the decision is taken, an independent committee shall give an opinion on the adequacy of the candidates to be appointed Judges or Advocates General. The role of this advisory committee may very well be of great importance in the future. Parliament is entitled to appoint a member to this committee. Indeed, such idea has recently been

modifications entailed in the EU Constitution concerning the institutional framework were welcomed by Parliament. It regretted, however, that the proposal by
the Convention to create a separate 'Legislative Council' was not eventually endorsed by the IGC.

Regarding the election of the President of the European Council, Parliament
raised some reservations. It took the view that 'the election of the President of
the European Council cannot in itself solve all the current problems affecting the
functioning of that institution and could entail unforeseeable consequences for
the institutional balance of the Union.'[13] In this respect, Parliament considered
that 'the role of the President must be strictly limited to that of a chairperson in
order to avoid possible conflicts with the President of the Commission or the
Union Minister for Foreign Affairs and not to endanger their status or encroach
in any way on the Commission's role in external representation, legislative initiative, executive implementation or administration.'[14]

Concerning the election of the President of the Commission and the vote of
consent, the EU Constitution mentions the word 'election' and no longer 'approval' by the Parliament and reinforces the political guidance of the President
over the Commission.[15]

Article I-27 TCE now explicitly requires that the name of the appointee shall
reflect the result of the European elections. The designation of Mr José Manuel
Durão Barroso as a candidate for the Commission's Presidency illustrates this
new rule, even if it is not yet legally binding. Indeed, the President of the political group with most Members within the European Parliament (EPP-DE Group)
said openly and clearly, before the name of the candidate President of the Commission was announced, that his group could only accept a candidate belonging
to his political group.

According to Article I-27(2) TCE, the President, the Union Minister for Foreign Affairs and the other members of the Commission shall be subject as a body
to a vote of consent by the European Parliament. Yet, in practical terms, Parlia-

---

used for the first time for the appointment of members of the European Union Civil Service Tribunal
(see *OJ* L 50 of 18 January 2005, appointing members of a Committee responsible for drawing
up a list of candidate judges of this Tribunal).

[13] See Parliament's Resolution of 24 September 2003, *supra* n. 6, para. 20.

[14] According to Kokott and Rüth there is a risk of a threat to the institutional balance, because the President of the European Council:

'will not only potentially conflict with the role assigned to the Commission President, but
also with that of the newly created Foreign Minister, which would lead to new tensions in external representation at a moment when precisely this problem was supposed to be remedied by the
merger of the functions of the High Representative and the Commissioner for External Relations.'

J. Kokott and A. Rüth, 'The European Convention and its Draft Treaty establishing a Constitution for Europe: Appropriate Answers to the Laeken Questions?', 40 *Common Market Law Review*
(2003) p. 1327.

[15] In this respect it could be recalled that Parliament's representatives in the Convention were
adamantly opposed to the idea of a Congress, as proposed by President Giscard d'Estaing almost
until the end of the Convention.

ment can veto one or several of the individual candidates, if it is prepared to sacrifice the whole Commission. Such a situation actually occurred on 27 October 2004 with the Barroso I Commission. Fearing that Parliament would vote against the Commission as submitted the day before, Mr Barroso decided not to submit his Commission for Parliament's approval on 28 October 2004 and asked for more time 'to consult with the European Council further'. On 4 November 2004, the Council submitted a new list of persons whom it proposed for appointment as members of the Commission. In this list two candidates who were subject to strong criticism from Members of Parliament during the hearings and the debate of the presentation of the Commission were not included. Mr Barroso submitted a new Commission to the European Parliament on 18 November 2004, which was approved.

By conveying the message that it was not willing to approve the Barroso I Commission, Parliament showed clearly that it intends to play its political role fully. Already, in his first speech to the House on 14 September 2004, the newly elected President of Parliament, Mr. Josep Borrell, stressed that the process of consent was not to be considered as a mere formality. On the other hand, Parliament's consent reinforces considerably the legitimacy of the Commission. In its Resolution of 18 November 2004 concerning the election of the Barroso II Commission, Parliament welcomed 'the democratic and legal validity of the approval process and the essential contribution it makes to building the good working relationship between the Commission Parliament that the Union needs'.[16] The difficulties with the election of the Barroso I Commission also made clear the complexity of his task *vis-à-vis* the Member States, when the latter insist on presenting a particular candidate. The Convention's draft seemed more appropriate in this regard, because according to Article 26(2), each Member State would establish a list of three persons, whom it considered qualified, leaving the President with a margin of appreciation on the eventual choice to be proposed to the Parliament.

It is regrettable that even if Article I-27 TCE mentions the word 'election' concerning the President of the Commission, the final decision on the appointment of the Commission belongs to the European Council (para. 2). Is this a pure formality or can the Council still have a margin of appreciation? One can argue that it is rather a 'formal decision', because it is taken 'on the basis' of Parliament's consent.

Article I-28 TCE concerns the role of the Union Minister for Foreign Affairs, who will be appointed by the European Council, with the agreement of the President of the Commission. He shall preside over the Foreign Affairs Council and be, at the same time, Vice-President of the Commission.[17] The hybrid nature of

---

[16] Resolution of the European Parliament on the election of the new Commission, see Texts adopted on that date, PA_TA(2004) 0063.

[17] For further developments see P. Ponzano, 'La réforme des Institutions de l'Union européenne dans le cadre de la Constitution', 1 *Revue du Droit de l'Union européenne* (2004) pp. 25-38.

his tasks may raise difficulties for coherently and efficiently conducting the Union's external actions, and a division of tasks with the President of the European Council and the President of the Commission may be delicate to achieve.

As far as his relations with the Parliament are concerned, it is worth recalling that, as with all the other Commissioners, he shall be subject to a vote of consent by the European Parliament (which was not foreseen in the first drafts of the Convention). Also, he shall resign if the President of the Commission so requests, but in accordance with the procedure set out in Article I-28 TCE (decision of the European Council, acting by qualified majority, with the agreement of the President of the Commission). His status is thus different from the other members of the Commission. This may raise a problem of interpretation concerning the existing framework agreement on relations between the European Parliament and the Commission. According to this agreement:

> 'the Commission accepts that, where the European Parliament expresses lack of confidence in a Member of the Commission (subject to political support for such a view, in terms both of substance and of form), the President of the Commission will consider seriously whether he should request that Member to resign.'(para. 10).[18]

In some cases, a 'grey zone' will occur and it may be complex to determine with clarity if he should act in his quality as Minister or as Vice-President of the Commission (example: negotiation of international agreements in areas relating at the same time to CFSP and to other policies on which the Commission is fully competent). It is true that 'the Union shall ensure consistency between the different areas of its external action and between these and its other policies' (Art. III-292(3) TCE) and that the Union negotiator depends on the subject of the agreement envisaged (Art. III-325(3) TCE). Only the experience and possibly the personality chosen to exercise these ambivalent functions will indicate if this

---

[18] See Rules of Procedure of the European Parliament, Annex XIII. In its Resolution on the election of the new Commission of 18 November 2004 (see *supra* n. 16), Parliament called for the existing Framework Agreement between the Parliament and the Commission to be reviewed and updated as soon as possible on the basis of the commitments made by Mr Barroso. As for the resignation of an individual Member of the Commission, Parliament requested that it should be included in the new agreement that if it votes to withdraw confidence (subject to political support for such a view, in terms both of substance and form), the President will consider seriously whether he should request that Member to resign and that the President shall either require the resignation of that Member or justify his refusal to do so before Parliament (para. 5(a) of the abovementioned resolution). Following this resolution, a new Framework Agreement between the Parliament and the Commission will be adopted in June 2005 (see draft report of Mr Jo Leinen of 8 April 2005 (PE 355.690v02.00), which was adopted by the Committee on Constitutional Affairs on 10 May 2005). On the political responsibility of the Commission, the draft agreement states that 'each Member of the Commission shall take political responsibility for action in the field which he or she is in charge, without prejudice to the principle of Commission collegiality' (para 1); and 'if Parliament decides to express lack of confidence in a Member of the Commission, the president of the Commission, having given serious consideration to that decision, shall either request that Member to resign or explain his or her decisions to Parliament.' (para 3).

was an improvement and contributed to the consistency of the Union's external action or if it rather makes things more complex (the risk that he acts as a 'Trojan horse').[19] This post certainly requires high political authority and, at the same time, great institutional sensitivity.[20] It is expected that the European Parliament will exercise careful scrutiny over the way in which the Minister will conduct his responsibilities.

3.   SIMPLIFICATION OF INSTRUMENTS AND PROCEDURES AND THE ESTABLISHMENT OF THE PRINCIPLE THAT CO-DECISION IS THE LEGISLATIVE PROCEDURE GENERALLY APPLICABLE

### 3.1   Simplification of Instruments and Procedures

With the successive revisions of the Treaties, the number of instruments has increased considerably. As a result, it became particularly difficult to distinguish precisely the means of action through which the Union could exercise its powers. The existing Treaties do not even define the legal scope of a number of instruments. As a well known Judge said, 'the overall picture is one of vagueness and of legal uncertainty.'[21] Having noted that the Union instruments were fifteen and that the reason for this proliferation was that the authors of the Treaty on the European Union wished to clearly mark out the new areas of CFSP and JHA in different ways, the Convention was firmly determined to rectify this and simplify both the instruments and the procedures. This work was rather successful and instead of the existing fifteen instruments, the Constitution now only has six. In the same context, the introduction of a hierarchy of norms between legislative and executive acts[22] and the explicit recognition of the primacy of the Constitution and of Union law over the law of the Member States are worth stressing.

---

[19] J. Schoo, 'Das institutionelle System aus der Sicht des Europäischen Parliaments', in J. Schwarze, ed., *Der Verfassungsentwurf des Europäischen Konvents* (Baden-Baden, Nomos 2004) p. 73.

[20] K. Hänsch, 'Die Verfassung für die Europäische Union – nach der Regierungskonferenz', 7 *Zeitschrift für Europarechtliche Studien* (2004) p. 10.

[21] K. Lenaerts, 'How to simplify the Instruments of the Union?' (Paper submitted on 17 October 2002 to the Convention Working Group IX on 'Simplification', WG IX, WD 07) p. 2, available at: <http://european-convention.eu.int/docs/wd9/4352.pdf>. See also, S. van Raepenbusch, 'Les instruments juridiques de l'Union', in *Commentaire de la Constitution de l'Union européenne* (Institut d'Etudes Européennes (2005)) pp. 203-218.

[22] Although not defined as such in the EU Constitution, the hierarchy of norms corresponds to the following order: Constitution, European laws and framework laws, European regulations adopted as delegated acts, European regulations and decisions adopted directly under the Constitution, European regulations and decisions adopted as implementing acts (see K. Lenaerts and D. Gerard, 'The Structure of the Union according to the Constitution for Europe: The Emperor is getting dressed', 29 *European Law Review* (2004) p. 289).

The novelty – which eventually received a large consensus within the Convention and the IGC – is the creation of a new instrument: the 'delegated acts'. These acts will flesh out the detail or amend certain elements of a legislative act, under some form of authorisation defined by the legislator. This type of instrument applies where the legislator feels that essential elements in a given area, as defined by it, necessitate a legislative development which can be delegated. Article I-36(1) TCE defines the 'Delegated European Regulations' and stipulates that 'the essential elements of an area shall be reserved for the European law or framework law and accordingly shall not be the subject of a delegation of power'. The second paragraph of this provision establishes the conditions for such a delegation: the possibility for the European Parliament to revoke the delegation or to object to its entering into force. This should enable Parliament to concentrate on the political aspects of laws, delegating technical aspects to the Commission.[23] It will also improve its role in the supervision of comitology.

### 3.2    Co-decision is the Ordinary Legislative Procedure

The other, rather more important, development for the European Parliament is the consecration in Article I-34 TCE of the basic principle that the ordinary legislative procedure is the co-decision procedure, as described in Article III-396 TCE. According to the final report of the Working Group IX on simplification, chaired by Professor Amato, 'the democratic legitimacy of the Union is founded on its States and peoples, and consequently an act of legislative nature must always come from the bodies that represent those States and peoples, namely the Council and the Parliament'.[24]

The logical consequence of this is a very important extension of cases where co-decision will apply. With the EU Constitution in force, the Council will take many more decisions by qualified majority voting (QMV) and Parliament's powers of legislative co-decision will have been multiplied. The number of areas of co-decision increased by forty-five and now cover over seventy legal bases.

In fact, during the Convention, there was a clear perception that, with a Union composed of more than twenty-five Member States, retaining unanimity voting in the Council would inevitably mean gridlock in the areas concerned. The most obvious example that experts put forward related to Justice and Home Affairs (JHA) (provisions where unanimity is generally required, conventions concluded in accordance with Article 34 TEU lacking ratification by Member States, framework decisions like the one concerning the European arrest warrant without direct effect).[25]

---

[23] A. Duff, 'An Interim Reflection on the European Convention and the Intergovernmental Conference', in *A Constituição Europeia: Que novas perspectivas para a União Europeia?* (Lisbon, Europa – Novas Fronteiras, Centre d'information Jacques Delors (2003)) p. 23.

[24] See the final report of Working Group IX on Simplification of 29 November 2002, CONV 424/02, p. 2.

[25] See the contribution by G. de Kerchove to the Working Group X 'Freedom, Security and

Although Parliament attaches great importance to the extension of QMV in the Council and welcomes the fact that the new 'ordinary legislative procedure' will become the general rule, it also underlined the need for further extensions of QMV and co-decision in the future.[26] In this context, it approved the introduction of the *passerelle* clause. According to this clause, where the Constitution provides for European laws or framework laws to be adopted by the Council in accordance with a special legislative procedure, the European Council may adopt a European decision allowing for the adoption of such acts in accordance with the ordinary legislative procedure (Art. IV-444(2) TCE).

In its above-mentioned Resolution of 24 September 2003, Parliament expressed its concern regarding the unsatisfactory answers given to certain fundamental questions concerning, in particular, the suppression of the requirement of unanimity in the Council in certain vital areas.[27]

In some cases the EU Constitution introduced an 'emergency break' clause – which was not envisaged by the Convention – enabling the Member States to refer a matter to the European Council, where they consider that a draft European Framework law affects a fundamental aspect of their legal system. This applies in matters on the establishment of minimum rules concerning, *inter alia*, the mutual admissibility of evidence between Member States or the rights of individuals in a criminal procedure (Art. III-270 TCE) or the definition of criminal offences and sanctions (Art. III-271 TCE). Such a clause exists also where a fundamental aspect of the national social security system is at stake (Art. III-136 TCE). After discussion, the European Council shall, within four months – the period during which the co-decision procedure is suspended – either refer the draft back to the Council (and the legislative procedure continues) or request the Commission to submit a new proposal (and the original draft falls).

This procedure may present a serious risk of slowing down, and even blocking, the legislative process just because the proposal is not agreeable to a single Member State. In a Union with 25 Member States or more such a risk is real. Proposals will probably be watered down in order to gain acceptance from all Member States and to avoid enhanced co-operation. Furthermore, this clause may also have a chilling effect on the Commission and may indirectly affect its margin of discretion, when the latter submits a legislative proposal in the areas concerned. Finally, it is rather surprising that, while a co-decision procedure is pending, the European Council is entitled to intervene, when in principle it shall not exercise legislative functions (Art. I-21 TCE). It is needless to point out that, in the meantime, the European Parliament is completely out of the picture and

Justice', on 13 November 2002, Working Document 35, pp. 1-8, available at: <http://european-convention.eu.int/docs/wd10/6112.pdf>. See the same author with A. Weyembergh, 'Quelle Europe pénale dans la Constitution?', in *Commentaire de la Constitution de l'Union Européenne* (Institut d'Etudes Européennes (2005)) pp. 317-354.

[26] See the Resolution of 24 September 2003, *supra* n. 6, paras. 5, 16, and 18.

[27] Ibid., para. 29.

loses any influence in the outcome of this procedure. For these reasons, it is not surprising that this provision was the object of long discussions and opposition by some Member States within the IGC for it brings elements of democratic deficit that existed in the past (Luxembourg Compromise, Ioaninna).

### 3.3    The Progress made in the Area of Justice and Home Affairs

The improvements to the functioning of the area of JHA in the EU Constitution are without doubt one of its main achievements. QMV and co-decision were extended to most issues and the typical 'Third Pillar' instruments (conventions, framework decisions, common positions) were suppressed or replaced by the new legal instruments. Also, the EU Constitution foresees the principle of the jurisdiction of the Court of Justice (legality control and preliminary rulings). The text adopted by the Convention provided for the exclusion of the review of the validity or proportionality of operations carried out by law-enforcement services for the maintenance of law and order and internal security is limited to the sole co-operation in criminal matters, 'where such action is a matter of national law' (Art. III-283 of the text adopted by the Convention). This last element was likely to reduce even more the restriction assigned to the Court's jurisdiction, so that it would remain competent to rule on any Member State action aimed at implementing measures decided at Union level. Unfortunately this sentence was deleted by the IGC and does no longer exists in the final version (see Article III-377 TCE). Nonetheless, one can say that this evolution is closely linked to the proposed 'communitarisation' of police and judicial co-operation in criminal matters.[28]

On border checks, asylum and immigration, the EU Constitution establishes the principle of solidarity and fair sharing of responsibility, including its financial implications, between the Member States (Art. III-268 TCE). European laws or framework laws shall establish measures concerning the gradual establishment of an integrated management system of external borders (Art. III-265(2)(d) TCE). The word 'gradual' has been stressed. Indeed, this provision provides the legal basis needed for the adoption of measures such as promoting co-operation, training, exchange of information and financial solidarity. The possible creation of a common European border guard unit has been considered as a possibility, but rather in the long term.

On co-operation in the field of civil law, the discussion within the Convention (Working Group X) was in particular to apply QMV and co-decision to all aspects of family law with cross-border implications. The majority however believed that in this field, the Council should act by unanimity, after consulting the European Parliament. A *passerelle* clause was also foreseen and in the future the Council may decide (by unanimity after consulting the Parliament) on those aspects of family law with cross-border implications which may be the subject of

---

[28] Lenaerts and Gerard, *supra* n. 22, at p. 303.

acts adopted by the ordinary legislative procedure (Art. III-269 TCE). This was the last possible compromise.

Concerning judicial co-operation in criminal matters, the Convention was deeply concerned that citizens need to be certain that action against serious cross-border crime is taken in all Member States and that such crime is punished strictly across the Union. In that respect, the Convention proposed a certain degree of approximation of substantive criminal law 'concerning the definition of criminal offences and sanctions in the areas of particularly serious crime with cross-border dimensions resulting from the nature of such offences or from a special need to combat them on a common basis' (Art. III-172(1) of the text adopted by the Convention). The Convention further delineated the scope of action by an enumeration in the EU Constitution of those types of crime that are considered to have a transnational dimension. It also stipulated that the Council, acting by unanimity, and after the consent of the European Parliament, may adopt a decision adding other crimes to this list, in order to respond adequately to changing patterns of crime. These provisions adopted by the Convention were not modified by the IGC (see Art. III-271(1) and (2)). The IGC however inserted a new provision, the so-called emergency break clause (already criticised in this article) foreseeing the referral by a Member State of the legislative proposal to the European Council where this Member State considers that the proposal 'would affect fundamental aspects of its criminal justice system' (Art. III-271(3) TCE). In the case of a deadlock, the possibility of enhanced co-operation is envisaged, under certain conditions.

The same approach applies to the approximation of laws of criminal procedure (Art. III-270(3) TCE). During the Convention (Working Group X), experts gave evidence that the need for approximation of certain elements of criminal procedure was widely recognised by practitioners and perhaps more urgently than approximation of substantive criminal law.[29] Article III-270 TCE (which corresponds to Art. III-171 of the Convention's text) provides for the setting of common minimum rules on the admissibility of evidence between Member States, the rights of individuals in criminal procedure (building on the standards enshrined in the ECHR, as reflected in the Charter) and the rights of victims of crime. The Council can subsequently, by unanimity and after obtaining the consent of the European Parliament, identify other elements of procedure on which minimum rules are required to facilitate mutual recognition (Art. III-270(2)(d) TCE).

The Convention and the IGC gave more operational powers to Eurojust than those established in the Treaty of Nice (Art. 31 TEU). According to Article III-273 TCE, Eurojust's tasks may include 'the initiation of criminal investigations, as well as proposing the initiation of prosecutions conducted by competent authorities, particularly those relating to offences against the financial interests of

---

[29] See the final report of Working Group X on 'Freedom, Security and Justice', CONV 426/02 of 2 December 2002, p. 11.

the Union'. In these prosecutions 'formal acts of judicial procedure shall be carried out by the competent national officials'. This provision should not, in principle, exclude the national member of Eurojust, to the extent that he has received such competence.[30] The European law determining Eurojust's structure and field of action should also 'determine arrangements for involving the European Parliament and the national parliaments'. This gives a large margin of discretion to the legislator, taking into account the specific nature of this body and the necessity of its complete independence.

From Eurojust, the Council may establish a European Public Prosecutor's Office (EPP) in order to combat crimes affecting the financial interests of the Union. This Office is established by a European law of the Council acting unanimously after obtaining the consent of the European Parliament (Art. III-274(1) TCE). In its resolutions and during the Convention, Parliament insisted on having in the Constitution a provision already creating the EPP. Members of the Convention, namely those in Working Group X, were divided on this issue. Some considered that the case had not been sufficiently made to justify an EPP. They questioned in particular its jurisdiction and its relationship with the national competent authorities (the national Public Prosecutor, the judiciary and the police) and opposed any reference to the EPP in the Constitution. The compromise was to make this reference, but to foresee a subsequent decision taken by the Council to establish the EPP.

Since this decision should be taken unanimously, this process may take years. Possibly, in order to facilitate this initiative, Article III-274 TCE limits the scope of the EPP's jurisdiction: while the Convention mentioned 'serious crime having cross-border dimension, as well as crimes affecting the interests of the Union' (Art. III-175 of the text adopted by the ConventionTCE), the EU Constitution stipulates 'crimes affecting the financial interests of the Union'(Article III-274(1) TCE). On one point there was apparently a consensus: the EPP should not be a 'new' institution. That is the reason why the evolution envisaged is from Eurojust. This leaves open the future structure of the new Office, which could be singular or collegial. It can be expected that in the forthcoming years, Parliament will bring pressure with a view to establishing the EPP, being particularly worried about the issue of fraud concerning the EU budget.

## 4.    THE EXPANSION OF THE CONSENT PROCEDURE

Parliament's role has also been increased by the expansion of the consent procedure in general[31] and in particular regarding the conclusion of international

---

[30] Ibid., p. 19.

[31] The cases on which the European Parliament will be consulted under the consent procedure have been multiplied, in cases of great political significance, like the following:
   – flexibility clause: Art. I-18 TCE;

agreements. The future involvement of Parliament in the implementation of the common commercial policy (CCP) is very important in this context.

## 4.1    The Consent of the European Parliament for the Conclusion of International Agreements

The EU Constitution maintains the consent of the European Parliament for association agreements, for those establishing a specific institutional framework or with important budgetary implications for the Union (Art. III-325 TCE). The novelty is that the consent procedure is required for agreements covering fields to which the ordinary legislative procedure will apply (Art. III-325(6)(a),(v) TCE).

This implies two major changes as to the current Treaties:

–    Firstly, the consent procedure will be required even when the agreement does not entail an amendment to an act adopted under the co-decision procedure. Thus, agreements concerning the common commercial policy – as the measures defining the framework for implementing this policy are adopted by ordinary legislative procedure[32] – will require Parliament's consent. The consent procedure can also apply to agreements with third countries and international organisations concerning development co-operation, humanitarian aid and economic, financial and technical co-operation.

–    Secondly, with the abandonment of the pillars, the consent procedure will also be required for international agreements concerning judicial co-

---

–  multi-annual financial framework: Art. I-55 TCE;
–  accession of a candidate State: Art. I-58 TCE;
–  suspension of certain rights resulting from Union membership: Art. I-59 TCE;
–  agreement on voluntary withdrawal from the Union: Art. I-60 TCE;
–  measures to combat discrimination: Art. III-124 TCE;
–  addition of new rights: Art. III-129 TCE;
–  first provisions on the Structural Funds and the Cohesion Fund: Art. III-223 TCE;
–  minimum rules on specific aspects of criminal procedure: Art. III-270(2)(d) TCE;
–  minimum rules concerning the definition of criminal offences and sanctions on other areas of crime than those indicated in para. 1: Art. III-271(1) TCE;
–  creation of a Public Prosecutor's Office and possible extension of its powers: Art. III-274(1) and (4) TCE;
–  international agreements mentioned in Art. III-325(6) TCE;
–  enhanced co-operation excepting fields of exclusive competence and CFSP: Art. III-419(1) TCE;
–  ordinary revision procedure – decision of the European Council not to convene a Convention: Art. IV-443(2) TCE;
–  simplified revision procedure: Art. IV-444 TCE.

[32] See M. Cremona, 'The Draft Constitutional Treaty: External Relations and External Action', 40 *Common Market Law Review* (2003) p. 1364.

operation in criminal matters (Arts. III-270 and III-271 TCE). In the present treaties, Parliament is not consulted on the conclusion of such agreements (Arts. 24 and 38 TEU). Parliament's involvement in this area is particularly welcomed considering that international agreements on co-operation are essential to combat terrorism, trafficking in human beings and sexual exploitation of women and children, illicit drug trafficking and organised crime[33] (see, for example, the agreement with the USA on extradition and on judicial assistance in criminal matters).

## 4.2    The Involvement of Parliament in the Common Commercial Policy

Contrary to the current situation, where Parliament is not even consulted, the latter will play a much more important role in external commercial policy in the future. Indeed, Parliament will not only establish (in co-decision) the measures defining the framework for implementing the CCP, but will also be more closely involved in the negotiation of international agreements and its consent will be required.

As for its legislative competence, it goes without saying that the measures concerned must be legislative by nature. In other words, Parliament will participate in the drafting of acts of general application (e.g., acts like the current regulation on anti-dumping, the regulation on a generalised system of preferences, the regulation on obstacles to free trade), but Parliament's participation is not foreseen for acts that do not have a legislative nature (acts of the Commission deciding on anti-dumping rights in a specific case). As for the negotiation of agreements, Article III-315(3) TCE stipulates that the Commission shall report 'regularly' to a special committee (appointed by the Council and corresponding to the former '133 Committee') and to the European Parliament 'on the progress of negotiations'. This is something that is not specifically required for the other international agreements (see Art. III-325 TCE).

More importantly, this creates a legal obligation for the Commission to inform the Parliament, which may be considered an 'essential procedural requirement', within the meaning of Article III-365(2) TCE, subject to judicial control by the Court of Justice, and, in any case, Parliament may consider refusing to give its consent if it considers that it had not been sufficiently informed on the progress of the negotiations. The Council therefore needs to monitor the respect

---

[33] A declaration has been adopted by the IGC concerning the conclusion of international agreements relating to the area of freedom, security and justice. According to this declaration:

'the Conference confirms that Member States may negotiate and conclude agreements with third countries or international organisations in the areas covered by sections 3, 4 and 5 of Chapter IV of Title III of Part III of the Treaty establishing a Constitution for Europe insofar as such agreements comply with Union law'. This declaration was put forward by Member States wishing to maintain the possibility to conclude international agreements particularly in the area of family law. This declaration does not, in any way, affect the rights of the European Parliament to be consulted under the assent procedure, as is foreseen in Art. III-325(6)(v) TCE.

of this obligation by the Commission before it concludes the agreement. Parliament will no doubt play an active role in this field in the future and, in the light of this perspective, in July 2004 it set up a parliamentary committee responsible for external commercial policy.

## 5.    THE FINANCIAL PROVISIONS

Concerning the Union's finances an attempt at simplification was made. A separate title has been included in Part I containing the budgetary and financial principles (Art. I-53 TCE), the Union's own resources (Art. I-54 TCE), a multi-annual financing framework (Art. I-55 TCE) and the annual budget (Art. I-56 TCE). These provisions are then developed in Part III (Arts. III-402 to III-415 TCE).

### 5.1    The Convention's Proposals

The Convention proposed a global system for the financial provisions, based on a three-tier approach: own resources, financial perspectives (Multi-annual Financial Framework, hereafter MFF) and the annual budget. Under this system:

–   on own resources, the Council would decide by unanimity and its law has to be approved by all the Member States before entering into force (Parliament is merely consulted); the modalities would be adopted by the Council by QMV, with the consent of the European Parliament (Art. 53 of the draft adopted by the Convention);

–   on MFF, the Council would decide by QMV with the consent of the Parliament (Art. 54, idem.);

–   on the annual budget, the distinction between compulsory expenditure and non-compulsory expenditure would be abolished. The budget would be adopted jointly by the Parliament and the Council through a simplified procedure: one reading in each institution followed by the convening of a Conciliation Committee if an agreement was not reached. Parliament would have the final word if the two institutions did not achieve an agreement under certain circumstances (Art. 310, idem.).

### 5.2    The IGC's Provisions

The provisions contained in the Convention's text were considerably modified by the IGC. The so-called 'ECOFIN proposals'[34] followed another approach: all the aspects of own resources would be decided by the Council by unanimity

---

[34] Informal meeting of ECOFIN, proposals submitted in October 2003 to the Presidency of the European Council.

(Parliament only consulted), the MFF would be approved by the Council acting by unanimity (Parliament only consulted) and the budget would be decided by a so-called 'strict co-decision procedure' whereby in the event of a failure to reach an agreement between Parliament and the Council, the lowest amount proposed would be retained. These proposals would reduce Parliament's powers considerably: practically no influence in the decision on own resources and on MFF and no real negotiation on the budget. After proposals made by the Italian Presidency[35] and Irish Presidency,[36] the IGC adopted the following system:

-   own resources: law of the Council acting unanimously approved by all the Member States (Parliament merely consulted); the Council shall lay down (by QMV) implementing measures insofar as this is provided for in the law on own resources (consent of Parliament) (Art. I-54 TCE);

-   MFF: law of the Council, acting unanimously, after the consent of Parliament (Art. I-55(2) TCE). The European Council may, unanimously, authorise the Council to act by QMV when adopting the law laying down the MFF;

-   annual budget: at the stage of the Conciliation Committee, if Parliament rejects the joint text while the Council approves it, a new draft budget shall be submitted by the Commission. If Parliament approves the joint text while the Council rejects it, Parliament may decide to confirm all or some of its first reading amendments; where a Parliament amendment is not confirmed, the position agreed in the Conciliation Committee on the budget heading subject to the amendment shall be retained.

## 5.3    Evaluation of these Provisions

The MMF provision does not exist in the current Treaty. However, since 1988 inter-institutional agreements have been concluded providing for financial perspectives and accessory rules on the budgetary procedure. Thus, the insertion of this provision in the Constitution is not a complete surprise and can rather be considered as a codification of this inter-institutional *acquis*, even if the procedure is different: consent of Parliament instead of negotiations on equal terms. Parliament has stated that its power to approve the MFF presupposes the rapid opening of inter-institutional negotiations, in addition to the Intergovernmental Conference on the structure of this framework and the nature of the constraints on the budgetary procedure; it also stressed that the MFF should leave the budgetary authority with significant room for manoeuvre during the annual procedure.[37]

---

[35]  IGC 60/03, ADD 1.
[36]  IGC 78/04.
[37]  Resolution of 24 September 2003, *supra* n. 6, para. 28.

Concerning the annual procedure, Parliament will no longer have the final word on the budget, except if the Council itself rejects the joint text of the Conciliatory Committee. Actually, the emphasis will be placed on the negotiations in the Conciliatory Committee with the unavoidable time pressure involved. On the other hand, this procedure gives the Commission more power than before, since the mutual veto at conciliation requires the Commission to propose a new budget.[38] This allows the Commission 'conditional agenda-setting power over the budget'. This being said, in its Resolution of 12 January 2005 on the Treaty establishing a Constitution for Europe (P6_TA(2005)0004), Parliament:

'welcomes the fact that citizens will have greater control over the European Union's action by increased democratic accountability, notably due to the following improvements: (...) (f) a new budgetary procedure will require the approval of both the Council and the European Parliament for all European Union expenditure, without exception, thus bringing all expenditure under full democratic control'; (g) (...)'.

In this context, Parliament decided recently to set up a temporary committee on policy challenges and the budgetary means of the enlarged Union 2007-2013.[39] This temporary committee was composed of fifty members and was chaired by the President of the Parliament. Its mandate was, *inter alia*, to 'define the European Parliament's political priorities for the future financial perspective both in legislative and budgetary terms and to make an estimate of the financial resources to be allocated to the European Union expenditure for the period 2007-2013'. Its Rapporteur was Mr Reimer Böge (EPP). On 10 May 2005, the temporary committee adopted its final report which should be voted by the Parliament in June 2005. In this report, the committee considers, *inter alia*, that:

'the enlarging European Union should have appropriate financial resources to match the scale of its rising political ambitions and to meet its growing responsibilities at home and abroad; insists further that all expenditure from the EU budget should be designed to add European value to the public expenditure of Member States, and that the principle of subsidiarity should be strictly respected over spending decisions in the field of non-exclusive competence – in particular the criterion that EU action does, by reason of its scale or effects, better achieve the objectives of the Union.' (para. 1).

The committee states further it is:

'aware of the difficult political, economic and social context in several Member States, but recalls that the EU budget has increased by 8.2% between 1996 and 2002, while the average increase in national budgets (EU-15) has been 22.9%; (...); takes

---

[38] See J. Schoo, 'Finanzen und Haushalt', in J. Schwarze, ed., *Der Verfassungsentwurf des Europäischen Konvents* (Baden-Baden, Nomos Verlagsgesellschaft 2004) pp. 127-137.
[39] Resolution of 15 September 2004, PE 347.436.

the opportunity to point out that the ceiling of own resources decided in 1993 for 15 Member States has remained unchanged since then, i.e. 1.31% of EU GNI for commitment appropriations and 1.24% of EU GNI for payment appropriations; recalls that the level of the EU budget currently accounts for under 2.5% of aggregate public spending in the Union compared to an average of 47 % of EU GNI for total public spending.' (para. 5).

## 6.    CONCLUSION

At a time of great political significance – the ending of the division of the European continent – and of uncertainty, it is indeed of crucial importance that the IGC adopted a Constitution shaping a simplified and unified structure for the Union. This text is the result of long debates and negotiations, first among the *Conventionnels* and then among the Member States. It cannot thus satisfy everybody. Some would have preferred that the Convention should have had the true status of *pouvoir constituant,* omitting the subsequent phase of the IGC. This is maybe a respectable point of view but is just not realistic, at least in 2004. It may be recalled that, contrary to the wishes of some, the Convention actually delivered a 'Constitution',[40] as a result of a large consensus, without containing options on the more delicate political issues and this text was the point of departure for the IGC's work (and not the existing Treaties).

The EU Constitution contains compromises and is certainly not a perfect text. It represents, however, a substantial improvement in many respects compared with the present Treaties. In many respects the position of the European Parliament has been considerably reinforced. Due to its political long-standing coherent strategy and to the efforts deployed by its members during the Convention, Parliament obtained some important concrete results. In order to evaluate them, it suffices to consider the contents of the resolutions cited in the introduction to this article and the number of requests actually satisfied by the Convention and eventually by the IGC.

The main improvements may be summarised as follows:

a)    The Convention process and the involvement of the European Parliament, the national parliaments, the Commission and the civil society as a whole had such an impact that in the future no relevant modification of the Constitution shall take place by the traditional intergovernmental method; the setting up of a Convention shall be mandatory to that effect, and this already constitutes a major achievement in terms of democracy and the involvement of citizens in the Union's life;

---

[40] On the political importance of the acceptance of the word 'Constitution', see Kokott and Rüth, *supra* n. 14, at pp. 1319-1320.

b)  The EU Constitution corresponds to a new phase in European integration, during which the European Union will consolidate its legal order into a constitutional order binding on its Member States and citizens, even if the Constitution is ultimately approved in the form of a classical international treaty;[41]

c)  The incorporation of the Charter of Fundamental Rights identifies the citizens with the European project and is an expression that the Union will rule its actions in respect of a body of principles shared by the Member States and the European peoples;

d)  The election of the Commission by the European Parliament will reinforce its political control over the Commission and increase the democratic legitimacy of the latter;

e)  With the explicit recognition of a single legal personality, the unification of the existing treaties and the abolishment of the pillar structure, the EU Constitution calls for a single legal entity, 'The Union', based on a unitary system of normative acts, provides more clarity and reinforces the external action of the Union;

f)  By generalising the co-decision procedure (the ordinary legislative procedure) and by extending majority voting in particular in the area of JHA, the EU Constitution has improved the consistency and the effectiveness of the Union, as well as its democratic accountability by the reinforcement of Parliament's role;

g)  By simplifying the existing legal instruments and procedures and by establishing a clearer division of competencies between the Union and the Member States, the EU Constitution increases legal certainty and transparency concerning 'who does what by which means' at Union level.[42]

It is now up to the peoples of Europe, by referendums or by their legitimate representatives, to decide whether they believe that this Constitution should be adopted. They will take this decision freely and openly throughout the territory of the Union. This is already an enormous achievement. As in our democratic States, also concerning Europe, the future is now in the hands of our fellow citizens. Let us hope that the debate on ratification will be sincere, ambitious and truly on the European issues at stake.

The European Parliament by a large majority (500/137/40) conveyed a clear message to the national parliaments and to the public opinion in general in its

---

[41] European Parliament resolution of 24 September 2003 on the draft Treaty establishing a Constitution for Europe and the European Parliament's opinion on the convening of the IGC, A5-0299/20003, see the adopted texts of 24 September 2003.
[42] Lenaerts and Gerard, *supra* n. 22, at p. 322.

Resolution of 12 January on the Treaty establishing a Constitution for Europe by endorsing the Constitutional Treaty and 'wholeheartedly' supporting its ratification.[43]

---

[43] PA_TA(2005)0004, para. 6.

# EXPANSION OF EXECUTIVE, JUDICIAL AND LEGISLATIVE POWERS – A CONTRIBUTION TO THE DEBATE

## Christiaan W.A. Timmermans[*]

In this contribution I would like to raise three points:

1. 'Improving the efficiency and quality of EU legislation' has been the subject of repeated debate. Seven years ago, that is in 1997 under the previous Dutch presidency, the Asser Institute organised another of its well-reputed international colloquia, that time on 'Improving the quality of legislation in Europe'.[1] On that occasion also, the session in which I intervened was chaired by Advocate General Francis Jacobs. At the time we had fierce discussions on setting up a European Council of State or at least an expert committee for vetting the quality of draft European legislation (the tiny experts committee headed by Tim Koopmans), on improving the internal quality control procedures of Parliament, the Council and the Commission, and on improving the subsidiarity test by elaborating tools of impact assessment with regard to legislative proposals. It might be interesting to consider what has been done in the meantime with regard to improving the quality of Union legislation. Space is lacking in order to do this, but nevertheless a few points can be made:

- No initiatives have been taken to set up a European Council of State or a new scrutiny committee.[2] The Constitutional Treaty is also silent in that regard. However, that need not be regretted in my view.

- On the other hand, one has the impression that a great deal of work has been done at grassroots level to set in place and improve procedures and instruments to reinforce quality control: an interinstitutional agreement on better lawmaking was adopted in 2003[3] in following up an action plan on simplifying and improving the regulatory environment of 2002.[4] In 2001

---

[*] Judge of the Court of Justice of the European Union.
[1] A.E. Kellermann, et al., eds., *Improving the Quality of Legislation in Europe* (The Hague, Kluwer Law International 1998).
[2] But see G. Sandström, 'Knocking EU Law into Shape', 40 *CMLRev.* (2003) pp. 1307-1313.
[3] *OJ* (2003) C321/1.
[4] COM (2002) 278 final.

*D. Curtin, A.E. Kellermann and S. Blockmans, eds., The EU Constitution: The Best Way Forward?*
© 2005, T.M.C. Asser Instituut, The Hague.

a Commission communication was published on the codification of the *acquis communautaire*[5] and in 2002 the Commission adopted a communication on impact assessment.[6] The development of one single tool of integrated impact assessment could certainly have a positive effect, also in rendering the subsidiarity test more meaningful and its application in individual cases better motivated. However, this new method of impact assessment is not yet fully operational. In this regard the Constitutional Treaty might provide an important impetus for the Commission to live up to the commitments it has undertaken in the various recent documents which I mentioned, notably as to the impact assessments. Indeed, the mechanisms provided for by the protocols on national parliaments and on subsidiarity and proportionality requiring the immediate information of national parliaments concerning draft legislative proposals to trigger also a scrutiny by national parliaments in respect of subsidiarity allowing them to submit reasoned opinions to the Union institutions and, as a measure of last resort, also the possibility for Member States to resort to the Court in order to appeal against a European legislative act because it breaches the principle of subsidiarity might prompt the Commission to take very seriously indeed the commitments as to the motivation of its legislative proposals with regard to respecting the subsidiarity principle.

To conclude on this point: I think that sufficient literature voicing excellent intentions has been produced and that now the moment has arrived to put all this into practice. As Francis Jacobs concluded seven years ago: 'what is needed is not major reforms; rather, more care in the legislative process, more rigour, above all more concern for the consumer – whether judge, practitioner or citizen.'[7] These words are still as true as when they were spoken seven years ago.

2.  I would like to react to what Mr. Werts[8] has said in his article on the relationship between the European Council and the Commission. On the one hand, Mr. Werts concludes that the Commission is clearly subservient to the European Council because often the European Council in its conclusions is requesting the Commission to take initiatives, to present proposals on specific subjects, trespassing in doing so on the Commission's exclusive right of initiative. On the other hand, however, he states that it is easier for the Commission to get its proposals through the Council once it has the backing of the European Council. He even concludes that the European Council and the Commission form a tandem which drives decision-making. If that were true, the subservience of the Commission would be a lesser evil, it would be a *'reculer pour mieux sauter'*.

---

[5]  COM (2001) 645 final.
[6]  COM (2002) 276 final.
[7]  Loc. cit. n. 1 at p. 17
[8]  See the article by J. Werts' on pp. 3-20.

In my view, the importance of the role of the Commission and its impact on the decision-making of the European Council are mainly dependent on the substantive input the Commission is able to produce in the deliberations of the European Council, and more particularly the quality of that input. Good personal relations between officials in the preparatory process of European Council meetings also play an important role. The European Council provides a privileged platform for the Commission to obtain the green light for its initiatives and to get backing from the highest political level in the Union, so as to trigger the formal decision-making process and bring that process to a successful end.

Will the Constitutional Treaty change this relationship between the Commission and the European Council? It might. First of all, there is the permanent President of the European Council. Obviously good cooperation between that President and the President of the Commission, also on the level of their aides, will be important. For the Commission, to be able to continue playing its role as initiator and being allowed to make its input in the decision-making process of the European Council, it will be essential that the President of the European Council will not be able to develop his own executive arm, his own administration which would then necessarily be competing with the Commission. Fortunately, the Constitutional Treaty in its final version does not provide for that. We have to wait and see how this will develop in practice.

There is a second point on which the Constitutional Treaty might entail changes for the relationship between the European Council and the Commission, this time an important change limited to the area of external relations, but in itself worrying enough. I refer to Article III-293 TCE. This article formalises the decision-making process of the European Council in the field of external relations. The European Council will decide on the basis of a recommendation from the Council. This recommendation by the Council to the extent that it covers areas to which the Community method of decision-making applies, will have to be based on a Commission proposal. This formalization of the European Council decision-making procedure might hamper the direct access of the Commission to the European Council and make it more difficult for it to play its role in acting, as Jan Werts phrased it, in tandem with the European Council, driving the decision-making.

3. This brings me to my third and final point. One of the institutional headaches caused by the pillar structure of the Maastricht Treaty has been how to ensure the coherence of the Union's external action at the same time applying to the various areas of external action the very different decision-making procedures, and more particularly how to prevent the Community method in the field of external relations from being driven out or overarched by the intergovernmental method of CFSP decision-making. I refer to the issue of cross-pillar decision-making.

Part of the solution which the Constitutional Treaty brings to this problem is to introduce (following, by the way, a suggestion of the European Commission itself) the function of the Union Minister for Foreign Affairs with his double-hatted allegiance to the Commission and the Council, depending on the area of external action which will be involved. One of the main tasks of the minister according to Article I-28 TCE is to 'ensure the consistency of the Union's external action'. That is more easily written down than put into practice. One might expect the Union minister to feel occasionally like Goethe's Doctor Faust: '*Zwei Seelen wohnen, ach, in meiner Brust, Die eine will sich von der andern trennen*'.

When Michel Petite and Clemens Ladenburger write in their paper 'that this imaginative institutional construction will raise interesting legal questions'[9] I cannot but agree, adding perhaps that this might be an understatement. They regard as the main progress of the Constitution in the area of external Union action that it will render obsolete institutional disputes arising notably from different legal regimes and decision-making procedures. I think that this sketches a rather rosy picture. It is precisely in the field of external relations that the EU Constitution upholds the so utterly divergent decision-making procedures of CFSP and, to put it in shorthand, the Community method. With one important exception which I shall mention shortly, the Constitutional Treaty requires these divergent procedures – for instance co-decision and, in the field of CFSP, the in principle unanimous Council decision-making without a Commission proposal and without a substantive role for the European Parliament – to be fully respected (Art. III-308 TCE). So in spite of the abolition of the pillar structure which is certainly a good thing, these divergences in procedures will remain and, at the same time, I expect the institutional battles to protect the Community method.

I would like to make two final remarks in that respect: first, the Constitutional Treaty provides for a European external action service, set up to assist the Union Minister for Foreign Affairs in fulfilling his mandate (Art. III-296(3) TCE). I hope that this action service will only cover the area of CFSP and not the areas of 'Community competence'; in other words, that a transfer to this European external action service of the present services of the Commission in areas like commercial policy, development cooperation and others, is not intended.

Secondly, I would like to come back to cross-pillar decision-making. Under the present Union Treaty, as far as I know, institutional practice has avoided the adoption, in the area of external relations, of decisions based at the same time on a legal basis from the Community Treaties and the second and third pillar, such a combination being highly questionable from an institutional point of view, not only because of divergences in the relevant decision-making procedures but also the different nature of the legal instruments available under the various pillars. In this respect, the Constitutional Treaty brings about a very important innovation, but clearly in my view to the detriment of the Community method. I refer again to Article III-293 TCE which formalises the decision-making of the European Council in the field of external action. If I read this article correctly, it allows the European Council to adopt, upon a recommendation from the Council, European

---

[9] See the article by M. Petite and C. Ladenburger on p. 320.

decisions establishing external policies to be followed with regard to specific countries or on particular thematic issues, covering all the areas of external action. The Council recommendation will have to be adopted while respecting the procedures applying to the areas concerned. That means that CFSP decision-making might have to be combined with co-decision. But in the end the European Council will decide unanimously. This is cross-pillar (cross-area) decision-making as far as the adoption of the Council recommendation is concerned, with the final decision of the European Council being of an intergovernmental nature. Does this not closely resemble the institutional model of the famous (for some infamous) Fouchet plan from the early 1960s?[10] Not entirely, because the Council, in drawing up its recommendation in cases where Community competences are concerned, will need a Commission proposal and will have to respect the role of the European Parliament. Moreover, it might not be excluded that the Court might at least have jurisdiction concerning these European Council decisions to the extent that they cover areas of Community competence and have external effects. So the Constitutional Treaty might add to the institutional complexity of the Union the concept of mixed decisions. I may add that the Constitutional Treaty also appears to provide for cross-area Treaty Making by the Union (Art. III-227 TCE).

All this is sufficient to employ a new generation of European law specialists.

---

[10] See C.W.A. Timmermans, 'The Uneasy Relationship between the Communities and the Second Union Pillar: Back to the Plan Fouchet?', 1 *Legal Issues of European Integration* (1996) p. 61.

# SOME REFLECTIONS ON THE EXPANSION OF EXECUTIVE, JUDICIAL AND LEGISLATIVE POWERS

## Stanislaw Biernat[*]

In this brief article I have decided to present several rather casual reflections and observations on the alterations to the legislative, executive and judicial powers of the EU, as introduced by the Constitutional Treaty.

First, a general remark: the issue of to what extent the Constitutional Treaty is 'the treaty' and to what extent it is 'the constitution' has often been the subject of discussion. The space available restricts any elaboration of this topic, however. I will therefore merely observe that the issue of specific Union powers and ties between them is undoubtedly associated with the 'constitutional' aspect of the new Treaty. Laying down the means of governance and defining the roles for particular powers are surely matters to be regulated in the constitutions of the Member States and should thus be treated likewise in such a complex organization which the EU certainly is. The way in which governance is set out should ensure the simultaneous pursuance of various values, such as efficiency, but also democracy, accountability, and many others.

How should the institutional changes envisaged by the Constitutional Treaty be assessed compared to the present status determined by the EU and EC Treaty? Actually the changes are essential, although not revolutionary. They could not be of the latter category because of the way in which the Constitutional Treaty was developed and because of the diverse contradictory interests involved in the process. Other articles in this publication describe the most important novelties of the Constitutional Treaty, such as conferring the European Council with the status of an institution of the Union, separating the office of the European Council President, as well as that of the Union Minister for Foreign Affairs.

The attempt made in the Constitutional Treaty to separate legislative and executive functions should be stressed. This occurred through dividing the legal acts of the Union's institutions into legislative and non-legislative categories. The reason behind this distinction between the acts seems to be not the introduction of the division of powers among the institutions of the Union, but much more an attempt to simplify legal instruments and procedures, as well as provid-

---

[*] Professor at the Jagiellonian University, Krakow; Jean-Monnet-Chair of European Law.

*D. Curtin, A.E. Kellermann and S. Blockmans, eds., The EU Constitution: The Best Way Forward?*
© 2005, T.M.C. Asser Instituut, The Hague.

ing a more evident indication of the nature of specific instruments. Also of major importance was definitely the intention to strengthen the Parliament further, which is seen as the democratic factor in the Union, as well as extending the co-decision procedure, which is to become the basic legislative procedure. This has been expressed by referring to it as an 'ordinary legislative procedure'. All legis-lative procedures, according to the Constitutional Treaty, are to be transparent and carried out in public.

Indirectly, one might infer from the reform of the legal instruments that the drafters of the Constitutional Treaty have introduced a division of powers within the framework of the institutional system of the Union. In line with the distinc-tion between legal acts that I have just mentioned, the Parliament and the Coun-cil could be classified as the legislative power whereas the Commission is the executive power. Such a conclusion would nevertheless fail. On the one hand, the Council performs certain executive functions. On the other hand, the Com-mission will be able to issue delegated regulations based on the delegations con-tained in European laws or European framework laws. The Constitutional Treaty places these regulations in the category of non-legislative acts. However, in their contents as well as their general and abstract nature, the Commission's delegated regulations will actually be a manifestation of law-making functions. It seems that some so-called implementing acts of the Commission could be similarly re-ferred to. One can notice that 'legislation' according to the Constitutional Treaty is not a synonym for 'law-making'. The latter notion has a broader scope. The former refers, on the other hand, not so much to the normative character of legal acts but to the features of the Union institutions participating in the process of establishing these acts and to the features of the legislative procedure.

Hence it will not be possible unambiguously to ascribe particular institutions of the EU to either legislative or executive bodies in the traditional sense known in constitutional theory also after the Constitutional Treaty comes into force. Such a conclusion may disappoint those who would like to see the European Union as an organization having more features which are characteristic of states. Actually there are no reasons to be disappointed. Firstly, in modern states the di-vision of powers does not occur in a pure form either. Secondly, the institutional arrangements in the EU should be assessed not from the point of view of the pu-rity of theoretical structures, but rather in the context of the values (mentioned earlier) to which it has to adhere, such as efficiency, democracy, accountability, etc.

The constitutional alterations in the institutional solution in the EU are often the outcome of (frequently contested) political decisions. The controversies per-tain to the desirable direction of the Union's development, for example the one resulting from the dilemma between supranational v. intergovernmental models. Viewed from this perspective, the evaluation of institutional reform introduced by the Constitutional Treaty is equivocal. The powers of the European Council and its President strengthen the intergovernmental trend in the Union. The same pertains to the Council of Ministers. Yet, the series of treaty alterations regarding the decision-making procedures in the Council, as developed in the Constitutional Treaty, which involve a more widespread procedure of adopting acts by qualified majority voting are the manifestation of the Community method of integration. It is interesting to see a similar procedure envisaged in the Constitutional Treaty for the European Council, although with a limited scope.

In turn, the increased role of Parliament in the legislative process and to some extent in the budget procedure (especially as far as the Multi-annual Financial Framework is concerned) put forward in the Constitutional Treaty is a manifestation of supranational (at the same time – democratic) elements developing in the Union.

It is generally difficult to place some of the institutional reforms envisaged in the Constitutional Treaty within the discussed categories. The office of the Union Minister for Foreign Affairs represents such a difficult case. It is linked by functional and organizational ties with the European Council and the Council of Ministers as well as with the Commission.

In its turn, the Commission is considered to be an institution reflecting the supranational nature of the Union. Its present position has been preserved by the Constitutional Treaty and even strengthened in the area which is now the third pillar as well as in the area of external relations, except for the CFSP. Concerns have been voiced, however, that the Commission's role, as well as that of its President in drawing up the Union's strategy, will be undermined after the Constitutional Treaty comes into force, particularly after the institutionalization of the European Council and its President. Such a threat is indeed real and may change the balance of power to some extent and perhaps also impair the efficiency of the EU's functioning. In this context, opinions have been voiced that the legitimization and position of the President of the Commission and, indirectly, the whole Commission, will be made stronger through the solution adopted in the Constitutional Treaty (Art. I-20(1) TCE), namely the fact that the President of the Commission is elected by the Parliament. Pursuant to Article I-27 TCE the European Council, acting by qualified majority, shall propose to the European Parliament a candidate for President of the Commission.

I personally doubt whether the discussed provisions of the Constitutional Treaty actually bring about much novelty. It seems that this change has more to do with terminology rather than content, certainly when compared to the EC Treaty now in force. It is worth reiterating that, according to Article 214(2) TEC, the Council, when meeting in the composition of Heads of State or Government and acting by qualified majority, shall nominate the person it intends to appoint as President of the Commission; the nomination shall be approved by the European Parliament. As shaped by the provisions of the Constitutional Treaty, the European Council, being already officially a Union institution, is essentially the equivalent of the Council, meeting in the composition of Heads of State or Government. The competences of the Parliament to elect the President of the Commission, as provided for in the Constitutional Treaty, are not considerably different from the recent competence to approve him or her, in the case when the European Council presents only one candidate. Although the new provision of Article I-27 TCE obliges the European Council to take into account the elections for the European Parliament and to organize appropriate consultations, it is obvious that even now, without such an explicit obligation, the composition of the Parliament is being taken into consideration by the leaders of the Member States and unofficial consultations do in fact take place.

In essence, the Member States will wield at least the same influence over the appointment of the President of the Commission as will the Parliament, and principally an even greater influence.

My contribution has not dealt with the judiciary. I will only remark that after the Constitutional Treaty comes into force, I expect the Court of Justice of the European Union to assume a major role in the interpretation of new institutional provisions. One may foresee that the distinction between legislative and non-legislative acts as well as the division of powers to issue such acts may become contentious matters. In a broader perspective, with the Constitutional Treaty already in force the institutional balance will seem somewhat different than before. This may bring about the necessity for the Court of Justice of the European Union to step in as an arbitrator in disputes between political institutions; something which has also occurred in the past. One should note that the ECJ has acted very skillfully in this capacity, e.g., dealing with the controversy between the Commission and the Council concerning the Economic and Monetary Union.

# PART V

## Access to Justice and the EU Constitution

# THE WORKLOAD OF THE EU COURTS AND THE CITIZEN'S RIGHT TO HAVE ACCESS TO A JUDGE

## Denis Waelbroeck[*]

What model do we want for the European Union? Ought the European Union to remain a mere Union of States and institutions in which individuals may face obligations, but may not challenge them in court (at least in a number of cases)? Or ought those affected by its acts be able normally to submit the question of their legality to a judge and, if that were so, would the Community not gain in terms of its legitimacy?

This question, which is central to the current constitutional debate, will be dealt with in this article. I will not deal with other major changes with a significant impact on the citizen's right to a judge such as the incorporation into the Constitution of the Charter of Fundamental Rights, providing that the Union shall seek accession to the European Convention on Human Rights, extending the jurisdiction of the Court in the area of freedom, security and justice, etc. These changes, which are most welcome, will be addressed by others.[1]

## 1. THE BACKGROUND

In the judgments rendered by the Court of First Instance in the *Jégo-Quéré* case[2] and by the Court of Justice in *Unión de Pequeños Agricultores* (hereinafter *UPA*),[3] both courts disagreed fundamentally as to how this question ought to be

---

[*] Partner, Ashurst Brussels; Professor at the Université Libre de Bruxelles and the College of Europe, Bruges.

[1] See the article by Rick Lawson in this book, pp. 377-395.

[2] CFI, judgment of 3 May 2002, Case T-177/01, *Jégo-Quéré* v. *Commission* [2002] *ECR* II-2365.

[3] ECJ, judgment of 25 July 2002, Case C-50/00 P, *Unión de Pequeños Agricultores* v. *Council and Commission* [2002] *ECR* I-6677. See on this judgment, e.g., P. Cassia, *L'accès des personnes physiques ou morales au juge de la légalité des actes communautaires* (Paris, Dalloz 2002) pp. 1045 et seq.; Fl. Malvasio, under CFI, 3 May 2002, *Jégo-Quéré*, *supra* n. 2, and ECJ, 25 July 2002, *UPA*, *AJDA* (2002) pp. 867 et seq.; R. Mehdi, 'La recevabilité des recours formés par des personnes physiques ou morales à l'encontre d'un acte de portée générale: l'aggiornamento n'aura pas lieu…', 39 *Revue trimestrielle de droit européen* (2003) pp. 23-50; F. Berrod and F. Mariette, 'Le pourvoi dans l'affaire *Unión de Pequeños Agricultores* v. *Council*; le retour de la procession d'Echternach', *Europe* (2002) p. 11; R. Barents, 'Een midzomernachtdroom op de Kirchberg',

---

*D. Curtin, A.E. Kellermann and S. Blockmans, eds., The EU Constitution: The Best Way Forward?*
© 2005, T.M.C. Asser Instituut, The Hague.

approached. Where the Court of First Instance in *Jégo-Quéré* ruled in favour of opening up the access of individuals to the Community courts, the Court of Justice – in its *UPA* judgment – confirmed its traditional and more restrictive approach on access to the EU Courts.

In this judgment, the Court of Justice, in line with its *Plaumann* case law,[4] required an individual who is affected by the contested act by reason of certain attributes which are peculiar to him or by reason of circumstances which differentiate him from all other persons and thus distinguish him individually to prove that the act was directed directly against him in particular. In other words, the admissibility of an action for annulment brought by an individual applicant depends on the latter's ability to prove that the disputed act is not purely of a general nature but contains in fact individual decisions of which he is the addressee (i.e., the act – though normative 'in form' – should be shown to contain, 'in fact', a disguised decision against the applicant).

Even the fact that the applicant is part of a closed class of economic actors concerned by the act is not sufficient. The applicant has to show that it is his specific situation that justified the adoption of the act. In order to be able to dispute the legality of an act, the applicant, rather than undergoing the 'effects' of the act, should be its 'object'.

Admittedly, in the last couple of years the EU Courts have slightly broadened the conditions of admissibility for actions for annulment. Thus, applications have been allowed not only when the act was adopted 'taking into consideration' the applicant's particular situation, but also in the event that the institution adopting the act was 'under a duty, pursuant to specific legal provisions, to take into account the specific situation of the applicant and failed to do so.'[5] The difficulty of this new case law is, however, that it has never been easy to determine its exact scope of application and in practice the courts have remained very strict in their approach.[6]

It is against this background that Advocate General Jacobs – after having been invited by the Court, following a plenary hearing, to examine the possibilities of reconsidering the existing case law – delivered his opinion in the *UPA* case on

---

*SEW* (2003) p. 8; P. Gilliaux, 'L'arrêt, *Unión de Pequeños Agricultores:* entre subsidiarité juridictionnelles et effectivité', 39 *Cahiers de Droit Européen* (2003) p. 177 et seq.; J. Hamer, 'Neueste Entwicklungen in europäischen Rechtsschutzsystem', 35 *Juristische Arbeitsblätter* (2003) pp. 666 et seq.

[4] ECJ, judgment of 15 July 1963, Case C 25/62, *Plaumann* v. *Commission* [1963] *ECR* 116.

[5] CFI, judgment of 14 September 1965, joined Cases T-480/93 and T-483/93, *Antillean Rice Mills et al.* v. *Commission* [1995] *ECR* II-2305; ECJ, judgment of 15 February 1996, Case C-209/94, *P. Buralux et al.* v. *Council* [1996] *ECR* I-615; ECJ, judgment of 16 May 1991, Case C-358/89, *Extramet Industries* v. *Council* [1991] *ECR* I-2501 which even accepts – this has remained so far an exception – that an applicant may challenge a general act if this act causes serious prejudice to him or her.

[6] See, e.g., ECJ, judgment of 10 April 2003, Case C-142/00 P, *Commission* v. *Nederlandse Antillen* [2003] *ECR* I-3483, paras. 71 et seq. (See para. 3 of the Opinion of Advocate General Jacobs in Case C-50/00 P, *supra* n. 3).

21 March 2002. In this opinion, the Advocate General concluded that the current conditions of admissibility are indeed too strict and not in line with those of most Member States of the EU and that:

> 'an individual should be regarded as individually concerned within the meaning of the fourth paragraph of Article 230 EC by a Community measure where, by reason of his particular circumstances, the measure has, or is liable to have, a substantial adverse effect on his interests.'[7]

When assessing the admissibility of an action for annulment introduced by an individual applicant, only the 'effects' of the measure on the situation of the applicant and its importance should be established and the applicant no longer has to establish that he was the 'cause' or the 'object' of the disputed act.

Moreover, on 3 May 2002 – and even before the Court of Justice ruled in the *UPA* case – the Court of First Instance (in a five-judge composition) in its no less spectacular *Jégo-Quéré* judgment followed largely the same reasoning as the Advocate General, making it clear that the existing case law on Article 230(4) TEC is indeed too strict and it proposed instead an entirely new admissibility criterion:

> '(…) in order to ensure effective judicial protection for individuals, a natural or legal person is to be regarded as individually concerned by a Community measure of general application that concerns him directly if the measure in question affects his legal position, in a manner which is both definite and immediate, by restricting his rights or by imposing obligations on him. The number and position of other persons who are likewise affected by the measure, or who may be so, are of no relevance in that regard.'

Following this judgment and Advocate General Jacobs' opinion in the *UPA* case, expectations were high that the time had come for a significant broadening of the conditions of admissibility for actions for annulment. However, these expectations were buried on 25 July 2002, in the *UPA* case, when the Court of Justice found, instead, that the interpretation of the notion of individual interest:

> 'cannot have the effect of setting aside the condition in question, expressly laid down in the Treaty, without going beyond the jurisdiction conferred by the Treaty on the Community Courts.'

As stressed by the Court:

> 'According to the system for judicial review of legality established by the Treaty, a natural or legal person can bring an action challenging a regulation only if it is concerned both directly and individually.'

---

[7] See paras. 85 et seq. of the Opinion of Advocate General Jacobs in Case C-50/00 P, *supra* n. 3, *ECR* I-6707.

Neither the reasons given in the opinion of Advocate General Jacobs in the *UPA* case, nor the Court of First Instance's judgment in the *Jégo-Quéré* case, altered the Court of Justice's stance on this issue. Moreover, if the brief nature of the *UPA* judgment left any doubts as to the Court's intention – and notably as to the possibility of certain future developments[8] – these doubts disappeared following a series of judgments rendered by the EU Courts confirming that the notion of 'individual interest' has remained unchanged, or, if anything, has become even stricter than in the past.[9]


2.      THE EU CONSTITUTION


In parallel with these judicial developments and prompted by the formal invitation contained in the *UPA* judgment to consider a possible change in Article 230(4) TEC, a debate was launched within the European Convention resulting in a revised wording of the Article (Art. III-365(4) TCE), stating as follows:

---

[8] See my doubts at the time in D. Waelbroeck, 'Le droit au recours juridictionnel effectif des particuliers. Trois pas en avant, deux pas en arrière', 38 *CDE* (2002) pp. 3 et seq.

[9] See, e.g., ECJ, judgment of 10 April 2003, Case C-142/00 P, *Commission* v. *Nederlandse Antillen* [2003] *ECR* I-3489, where the Court quashed a decision of the CFI by giving a restrictive reading of the *Antillean Rice* jurisprudence; ECJ, judgment of 10 December 2002, Case C-312/00 P, *Commission* v. *Camar* [2002] *ECR* I-11355; CFI order of 6 May 2003, Case T-321/02, *Paul Vannieuwehuyze-Morin* v. *Parliament and Council* [2003] nyr; CFI, judgment of 14 November 2002, Case T-94/00, *Rica Foods* v. *Commission* [2002] nyr; CFI, judgment of 3 April 2003, Case T-114/02, *BaByliss S.A.* v. *Commission* [2003] *ECR* II-1279; CFI, order of 8 August 2002, Case T-155/02 R, *VVG International* v. *Commission* [2002] *ECR* II-3239; CFI, order of 21 March 2003, Case T-167/02, *Etablissements Toulorge* v. *Parliament and Council* [2003] *ECR* II-1111; CFI, order of 30 April 2003, Case T-155/02, *VVG International* v. *Commission* [2003] *ECR* II-1949; CFI, judgment of 26 February 2002, Case T-17/00, *Rothley and Others* v. *European Parliament* [2002] *ECR* II-579; and on appeal ECJ, judgment of 30 March 2004, Case C-167/02 P [2004] nyr, finding inadmissible an appeal brought by the MEPs against an act of the Parliament defining the rights and obligations of MEPs in anti-fraud measures; CFI, order of 6 September 2004, Case T-293/02, *SNF SA* v. *Commission* [2004] nyr, rejecting an appeal against a directive limiting the use of polyacrymalides in cosmetic products, thereby affecting severely the position of the applicant and six other manufacturers of these products within the Community and rendering their patents useless; CFI, order of 6 May 2003, Case T-45/02, *DOW Agrosciences* v. *Parliament and Council* [2003] *ECR* II-1973, finding that the fact that the applicant held a marketing authorisation for products using substances affected by a decision establishing a list of priority substances is not sufficient to individualise him in the same way as an addressee of the act; CFI, order of 29 April 2002, Case T-339/00, *Bactria* v.*Commission* [2002] *ECR* II-2287 and on appeal ECJ, order of 12 December 2003, Case C-258/02 P [2003] nyr, declaring inadmissible an application for the annulment of a Regulation identifying a substance for review although the contested regulation imposed detailed and direct obligations on the applicant and did not require Member States to take additional measures to comply. See also the Opinion of Advocate General Jacobs of 10 July 2003 in Case C-263/02 P, *Commission of the European Communities* v. *Jégo-Quéré & Cie S.A.* [2004] nyr, and the judgment of the ECJ in that case of 1 April 2004, nyr. To be noted also – in a more favourable way – the judgment of the CFI of 30 September 2003, in Case T-243/01, *Sony Computer Entertainment* [2003] nyr, which gives a broad interpretation of Art. 230(4) TEC, similar to the *Extramet* precedent, *supra* n. 5.

'Any natural or legal person may, … [under the same conditions as Community insti-tutions or Member States], institute proceedings against an act addressed to that person or which is of direct and individual concern to him or her, and against a regu-latory act which is of direct concern to him or her and does not entail implementing measures.'[10]

The EU Constitution thus contains two amendments to the present text of Article 230(4) TEC:

–    First, the proposal no longer restricts the types of acts which an individual can challenge, namely acts of which he is the addressee or acts which concern him directly and individually. An individual applicant is no longer required to show that the act amounts to a genuine decision or a disguised decision 'taken in the form of a regulation.'

–    Secondly, the individual can also attack any 'regulatory' (i.e., non-legisla-tive) acts which are of direct concern and which do not entail implement-ing measures, and this means that any individual interest no longer has to be shown.


3.     COMMENTS ON THE AMENDMENTS

As I had the opportunity to indicate in the past,[11] these two amendments, though undeniably progress, remain in many ways unsatisfactory.

As to the first of these proposed amendments it is mostly 'cosmetic' and merely codifies existing case law. Indeed, the Court already accepted long ago that an individual applicant can challenge not only disguised decisions taken in the form of a regulation but also purely legislative acts (i.e., even genuine direc-tives[12] or genuine regulations[13]). In several judgments, the Court thus made clear that it is not the form but the actual nature of the act which is important when assessing the admissibility of an action for annulment.[14] In other words, whilst the proposed reformulation of Article 230(4) TEC is certainly to be welcomed as

---

[10]  The current version of Art. 230(4) TEC reads as follows:
'Any natural or legal person may, under the same conditions, institute proceedings against a decision addressed to that person or against a decision which although in the form of a regulation or a decision addressed to another person is of direct and individual concern to the former.'
[11]  See D. Waelbroeck, 'Vers un accès plus ouvert à la justice communautaire', in P. Magnette, ed., *La Grande Europe* (Brussels, Editions de l'Université de Bruxelles 2004) pp. 223 et seq.
[12]  ECJ, order of 23 November 1995, Case C-10/95 P, *Asocarne* [1995] *ECR* I-4149; or more recently, CFI, order of 10 September 2002, Case T-223/01, *Japan Tobacco* v. *Parliament and Council* [2002] *ECR* II-3259.
[13]  ECJ, judgment of 18 May 1994, Case C-309/89, *Codorniu* v. *Council* [1994] *ECR* I-1887.
[14]  ECJ, judgment of 31 March 1971, Case C-22/70, *Commission* v. *Council (ERTA)* [1971] *ECR* 274.

it does away with any ambiguity in its present wording, it is difficult to see that it really changes anything in practice.

In contrast the second proposed amendment constitutes a clear broadening – although still a relatively modest one – of the conditions for access to judicial proceedings as compared with the present situation. One common aspect of the regulations disputed in *Jégo-Quéré* and *UPA* was indeed their lack of any implementing measures. As a result, in the absence of any challengeable act at national level, individuals adversely affected by these directly applicable EU acts had no means of challenging their legality before the national courts. The only solution open to them was to infringe the law, be prosecuted before the national courts and then to dispute the legality of the acts as a defence. In several judgments, the EU courts had to recognise that the applicant in such cases had no remedy before his own national courts. They claimed, however, that it was not for them to change the wording of the Treaty. The new proposed wording of Article 230(4) TEC is accordingly designed henceforth to allow individuals directly affected by a regulatory act which does not entail implementing measures to challenge it directly before the Court of First Instance. In such a case, they do not have to establish any 'individual interest.' It is sufficient for them to establish a 'direct concern' (i.e., under the current case law a direct causality between the act and the applicant). This proposal is thus certainly an improvement on the present situation, though I still find it unsatisfactory for two reasons.

First of all, the amendment concerns only mere 'regulatory acts'. This is ambiguous and could be understood as excluding genuine legislative acts or 'law' as the legislator should be immune from any form of judicial review exercised upon the request of an individual applicant.[15]

If this is the view, this is clearly at odds with the right to an effective remedy before a Court as now formally enshrined in the Charter of Fundamental Rights[16] and would, moreover, be regrettable for a number of other reasons, and in particular because:

a) it would go against the general tendency in a growing number of countries of submitting the legislator's acts to judicial review;

b) it would ignore the fact that judicial review contributes greatly to the quality of legislative work in a way which is different but no less decisive than the democratic control exercised by a directly elected parliament;

---

[15] In their article on pp. 171-179 of this book, however, Armin von Bogdandy and Jürgen Bast take a wider view of the term 'regulatory act' as referring to any act of a general nature. I agree that such an interpretation appears more in line with the objective of effective judicial protection enshrined in Art. II-107(1) TCE.

[16] See Art. II-107 TCE; the 'Explanation' to the Charter, however, specifies that this right to an effective remedy 'has not been intended to change the system of judicial review laid down by the Treaty, and particularly the rules relating to admissibility for direct actions before the courts.' See also Art. II-112(2) according to which 'rights recognized by this Charter for which provision is made in other parts of the Constitution shall be exercised under the conditions and within the limits defined by these relevant Parts.'

c)  it would make no sense in the Community system where the legality of acts, both of a legislative and regulatory nature, can always be disputed indirectly by individuals via a request for a preliminary ruling or by way of an action for damages.

The system therefore – if it is to be read as excluding the possibility to challenge such acts directly in court – appears unduly restrictive and in many ways lacks the necessary internal coherence.

Secondly, the amendment only applies where an act does not require any implementing measures. Where the contested Community acts are subject to implementing measures, the view seems to be that it is sufficient to improve the remedies available before the national court as the latter in any event can (or indeed must, depending on the case) refer a request for a preliminary ruling to the Court of Justice.

This was at least the view of the Court of Justice in the *UPA* judgment, i.e., that:

> 'the Treaty in its Articles 173 and 184 [now Arts. 230 and 241 EC] on the one hand and Article 177 [now Art. 234 EC] on the other hand have established a complete system of judicial review aimed at ensuring the control on the legality of the acts of the institutions assigning to the Community judge.'[17]

The Court, in other words, is of the opinion that the various types of remedies and procedures set out in the above articles complement each other in creating a 'complete system of judicial review'. In compliance with Article 10 TEC, the Court simply takes the view that 'it is up to the Member States to provide for a system of rights of appeal and procedures which allows for the safeguarding of the right to an effective legal protection.'[18]

Apparently for the same reasons, the EU Constitution adds to the present wording of Article 220 TEC (Art. I-29(1) TCE) a paragraph stating that 'Member States shall provide remedies sufficient to ensure effective legal protection in the fields covered by Union law.'

All this seems to suggest that in order to allow for a complete system of judicial review it suffices for the national jurisdictions to ensure the possibility of a remedy challenging the legality of a Community act 'thereby eliminating any gaps in the system'.

This, however, ignores the fact that, in such a system, individual applicants have to wait for the national implementation of a measure in order to challenge it before the national courts, which then have to refer the question of the validity of the Community rule back to the Court of Justice as they are themselves at the same time denied any competence to rule thereon (*Foto-Frost* case law).

---

[17] See para. 40 of the judgment.
[18] See para. 41 of the judgment.

Moreover, it ignores that the reference for a preliminary ruling does not constitute a remedy, in the proper sense of the term, to which an applicant is entitled, but rather a simple procedure of co-operation between judges. In the context of this procedure, the applicant does not have any direct access to the Court but is entirely dependent on the goodwill of the national judge who can always (and often will) refuse such reference or – even if the judge proceeds to make such a reference – may formulate the question poorly or ineffectively (or indeed sometimes fail to ask the important questions). In addition, in several cases, the questions are not asked at an early stage of the procedure, but only after one or two appeals, if at all. Therefore the parties will often be forced to engage in long judicial procedures to have their rights upheld in a particular case.

There are, in addition, several other practical problems,[19] such as the fact that:

- national procedures differ and often do not provide an adequate remedy (e.g., only few national legal systems allow for purely declaratory actions in respect of national legislation and outside the context of any concrete dispute,[20] which results, in the absence of such declaratory actions, in applications which are being initiated too late; it is difficult to see how the Court of Justice could impose on Member States the introduction of such a remedy without contradicting its own case law which requires an interest that is real and certain);

- mostly, national proceedings can only be initiated following the adoption of national implementing measures and not as from the date of publication of the damaging Community act (although the principle of legal certainty requires rapid remedies);[21]

- it is only when the national judge has doubts as to the legality of Community law that he should proceed to a reference (which – given that refer-

---

[19] For a more complete description of the problems that may arise, see H. Schermers and D. Waelbroeck, *Judicial Protection in the European Union*, 6th edn. (The Hague, Kluwer 2001) paras. 899-912 and para. 1005.

[20] See in the United Kingdom the system of 'declaratory relief' which allows private applicants which may one day be harmed by a rule to examine its compatibility with the law, even in the absence of an interest that is certain and present. See on this question and on the difficulties of introducing such remedies in other Member States, the study by P. Gilliaux, loc. cit. n. 2, p. 187.

[21] See, however, ECJ, judgment of 10 December 2002, Case C-491/01, *British American Tobacco* [2002] *ECR* I-11568, para. 40 according to which

'The opportunity open to individuals to plead the invalidity of a Community act of general application before national courts is not conditional upon that act's actually having been the subject of implementing measures adopted pursuant to national law. In that respect, it is sufficient if the national court is called upon to hear a genuine dispute in which the question of the validity of such an act is raised indirectly.'

See also P. Nihoul, 'Vie du Droit: Le recours des particuliers contre les actes communautaires de portée générale', *JTDE* (2003) pp. 38-43.

ences are seldom popular – potentially discourages him from questioning the validity of the act) and only a national court of last resort is in principle under a duty to make a preliminary reference (but there is no sanction in the case of – all too frequent – non-compliance);

– arbitration tribunals cannot request a preliminary ruling (*Nordsee* case law) although they themselves are prohibited from declaring a Community act illegal (*Foto-Frost* case law);

– the reference for a preliminary ruling does not allow parties to exchange pleadings and cannot be appealed. Moreover, if the question is too general, institutions and Member States will not be sufficiently informed of the problems to be discussed; etc.

It is clear, therefore, that a decision on validity will mostly never intervene at all or when it does, will do so too late.

Finally, it should be stressed that the system thus envisaged can cause a significant multiplication of applications in different Member States with the risk of contradictory decisions. This can be easily demonstrated by way of a practical example taken from the recent case law.

In *Etablissements Toulorge* v. *Parliament and Council*,[22] the applicant, a compound feed manufacturer (joined by 245 other competing manufacturers[23]) had sought to dispute – following the *Jégo-Quéré* judgment – the legality of a Community directive imposing on all compound feed manufacturers the obligation to make public the list of ingredients contained in their products as well as their exact percentage and therefore to make public their secret recipes.[24] The directive, as such, dispossessed them of years of cost-intensive research. They claimed that this had been done without any convincing objective justification relating to public health or otherwise. Following the *UPA* judgment, the Court of First Instance had no choice but to declare the action for annulment inadmissible[25] as being directed against a normative act which did not concern the applicants 'individually'.[26] The applicants were referred back to the national courts of the various countries where they were active. The system thus obliges the economic operators concerned – in this case generally SMEs – to challenge the national imple-

---

[22] See CFI, order of 21 March 2003, Case T-167/02, *Etablissements Toulorge* v. *Parliament and Council* [2003] *ECR* II-1111.

[23] See CFI, Case T-321/03, *Juchem and 244 others* v. *Council and Parliament*, pending.

[24] Directive 2002/2/EC of the European Parliament and of the Council of 28 January 2002 amending Council Directive 79/373/EEC on the circulation of compound feeding stuffs and repealing Commission Directive 91/357/EEC. *OJ* (2002) L 063/23-25.

[25] The action for damages, however, remained pending.

[26] The Court of First Instance considers that the right to the know-how concerning secret recipes is not a sufficiently 'specific' right, thus emphasizing once more the uncertain nature of the *Antillean Rice* case law referred to in n. 5.

menting measures in the twenty-five Member States of the Union (and in several Member States effectively even in their regional subdivisions given that the competence to implement directives often belongs to regional entities).[27] In addition, in order to avoid the secret know-how from becoming public knowledge, these operators, instead of having one single summary procedure at the Community level, must obtain injunctive relief in all Member States of the Community in order to obtain effective protection for their right (if the know-how becomes public in one State, it loses its secrecy everywhere and thus no longer enjoys any protection).

In the absence of any other solution, proceedings had therefore – in this case – to be introduced by the compound feed manufacturers throughout the European Union before national courts which then had to refer the case back to the Court of Justice. Interim relief has so far been obtained first in England, followed by similar decisions in Scotland, Northern Ireland and Wales, thereafter in France, Italy, the Netherlands, Germany, Ireland and all other Member States where it was requested (some procedures are still pending and new ones are being introduced as soon as implementing measures are adopted in the various Member States).[28]

It is important to note that – not too surprisingly – the English High Court expressed some perplexity at the fact that the question of the legality of a directive had been submitted to it at all, asking itself whether 'an application for an interim injunction suspending operation of the relevant provision of the Directive in the meantime should not itself more appropriately be made to the Court in Europe.' Given the judgment of the Court of First Instance in the *Toulorge* case,[29] the High Court recognised, however, that the applicant had in fact no choice but 'to claim the alleged invalidity of Community measures of general application before a national court and then ask it to make a reference to the European Court of Justice for a preliminary ruling as to validity.'[30] The High Court itself thus had no other choice but to examine the merits of the application.

The High Court then ruled that the directive was *a priori* manifestly disproportionate and that its application was going to cause an 'enormous economic impact on compound feed manufacturers'[31] and suspended the English implementation measure. Since the High Court was not itself competent to declare the

---

[27] In the United Kingdom, for instance, discrete actions had to be filed by the compound feed manufacturers in England, Scotland, Northern Ireland and Wales.

[28] See *infra* n. 34.

[29] See *supra* n. 22.

[30] Judgment of 6 October 2003. See *R* (on the application of ABNA limited & others) v. *The Secretary of state for Health and others* [2004] *EuLR* 88; and [2003] *EWHC* 2420 (Admin).

[31] According to the High Court, 'In all the voluminous materials put before me, it is very difficult to see just where the public health safety justification to justify [the Directive] could be.' The Court concluded that 'there are cogent and powerful arguments that the provisions of the Directive are invalid.'

directive illegal, it – rightly – referred to the Court of Justice a request for a pre-liminary ruling on its validity.[32]

In practice, this means that the EU courts will nevertheless have to decide on the legality of the directive – after having themselves, a couple of months earlier, declined jurisdiction to rule on this question on a direct application for annul-ment from 246 companies. Strikingly, the whole system therefore does not re-move any workload from the Court of Justice, but only leads to a meaningless 'judicial carrousel' with unnecessary costs and burdens for applicants and na-tional courts.

Moreover, whilst the High Court has meanwhile suspended the English imple-menting measures,[33] this does not eliminate the problems existing in the other Member States. Indeed, it is necessary for the applicants to introduce – and win – prior to the entry into force of the implementing measures in each Member State, applications for the suspension of such measures[34] (in Italy, the applicants

---

[32] ECJ, Case C-453/03, *ABNA and others*, pending.

[33] See *All England Reporter* (October 2003) *R* (on the application of *ABNA Ltd. and others*) v. *Secretary of State for Health and others*.

[34] As stressed by the English judge,

'were I to grant interim relief applicable to England, compound feed manufacturing compa-nies trading in other European jurisdictions would (unless the national courts of these jurisdic-tions also grant interim suspensory relief) be required to disclose percentage listings and thereby potentially reveal their own trade secrets whereas English companies would not have that expo-sure.'

Meanwhile, the French implementing measure was suspended by the French *Conseil d'Etat* on 29 October 2003 (in Cases 260768, 261833 and 261034) because of the irreparable damage to be suffered and the apparent lack of public health reasons justifying the rule. Strangely enough, the *Conseil d'Etat* decided not to refer the matter to the ECJ, as the English High Court had already done. On 30 October 2003, the High Court of Scotland likewise suspended the Scottish implemen-tation measure, followed on 5 November 2003 by the High Court of Wales and on 7 November 2003 by the High Court of Northern Ireland. On 30 October 2003, the administrative Court of Lazio refused to suspend the Italian implementation measure, the measure being regarded as justified. On appeal, however, the Council of State of Italy provisionally suspended the Italian measure on 5 November 2003. On 11 November 2003, a formal decision to suspend the measure was taken by the Italian Council of State in Cases *Spr Fratelli Martin* and *Cargill Srl* and a question was referred to the ECJ (Cases C-11/04 and C-12/04). In Spain, an application to declare the measure in breach of the Constitution has been declared inadmissible by the Supreme Court on 22 April 2004 and enforcement actions have been commenced by the authorities against infringing com-panies. In the Netherlands, the measure was suspended by the Dutch Administrative Court in The Hague on 22 April 2004, and questions were referred to the ECJ (Case C-194/04). In Ireland, the Irish High Court suspended the implementing measures on 26 April 2004 until the ruling of the ECJ on the existing referrals. In Germany, there are various supervision decisions from the ad-ministrative courts in Düsseldorf (3 May 2004), Hamburg, and Dresden, but the procedure is still pending. In Slovenia, the National Constitutional Court has suspended the implementation mea-sures until the ECJ has ruled on the references. In Portugal, the procedure is still pending. Sev-eral Member States – although they have implemented the directive, have accepted that they will not enforce its provisions *vis-à-vis* the companies concerned, so as to avoid useless procedures. In other Member States, appeals are still to be filed. In others, there are no possibilities of appeal and companies will therefore have to infringe the law, be sued, and then to argue the illegality of the measure.

failed at first instance and then succeeded on appeal; the procedure is still pending in a number of Member States). Knowing that the Court of Justice has always objected to national procedural rules which made it 'impossible or excessively difficult' for parties to pursue their claim under the law, one can only wonder whether such a principle of 'effectiveness' of remedies only applies to national courts and not to the Court of Justice.

Therefore, it is rather fallacious to argue that the preliminary procedure on validity compensates for the lack of any direct action for annulment and that there are no gaps in the system of judicial review.[35]

## 4.    EXCESSIVE WORKLOAD FOR THE COURTS

The title of this article not only refers to 'the citizen's right to have access to a judge' but also to 'the workload of the EU courts'. I will therefore also discuss whether any opening of the conditions of standing will lead to an excessive workload for the Courts. This is indeed a perfectly legitimate concern as only a court that has the time to deal with its workload offers the judicial protection desired by the parties.

In this regard, it should first be stressed that Advocate General Jacobs in the *UPA* case has convincingly demonstrated that the increase in the workload should in all likelihood remain within reasonable limits.[36] This observation is based on the experience of Member States having themselves recently broadened the conditions for the admissibility of an application. It does not seem credible, therefore, that – as claimed by some authors – the desired enlargement of the conditions for admissibility would result in 'tens of millions of actions brought by individuals'.[37]

Moreover, the idea is not, and has never been, to introduce any sort of *actio populars*, but merely to ensure a reasonable broadening of the conditions for admissibility (along the lines suggested by Advocate General Jacobs, or by the Court of First Instance in *Jégo-Quéré*). Moreover, since actions for annulment have to be brought within strict time-limits (in the interest of legal certainty), this in itself should also prevent a flood of cases.

---

[35] This was, for instance, the main argument of the President of the ECJ in defending on 17 February 2003 the current system as being adequate before the Convention. According to him: '*S'agissant, en quatrième lieu, de la question des recours directs des particuliers contre des actes de portée générale des institutions, la Cour estime que le système actuel, fondé sur le principe de la subsidiarité en ce sens que ce sont notamment les juridictions nationales qui sont amenées à protéger les droits des particuliers, satisfait aux exigences essentielles d'une protection juridictionnelle effective des droits des justiciables, y compris des droits fondamentaux.*'

[36] See the Opinion of Advocate General Jacobs in Case C-50/00 P, *supra* n. 3.

[37] See P. Nihoul, loc. cit. n. 21, p. 40; See also D. Hanf, 'Talking with the Pouvoir Constituant in Times of Constitutional Reform: the European Court of Justice on Private Applicants' Access to Justice', 10 *Maastricht Journal of European and Comparative Law* (2003) pp. 265-290.

I would finally like to comment that if the Court itself is correct as to the justifications for the restrictions on the conditions for admissibility (i.e., that it is not problematic as all issues of validity are in any event placed before it by national courts under the *Foto-Frost* case law), it is unclear whether there would ever be any problem relating to an increased workload. Indeed:

– if the Court is right – *quod non* – in claiming that the Community legal system at present does not contain any gaps, all issues of validity being in any case placed before it through the preliminary reference system (as they should be pursuant to the *Foto-Frost* case law), then the number of cases should not increase, but simply change in nature (i.e., become direct actions before the Court of First Instance rather than references for a preliminary ruling to the Court of Justice). The present system only ties up the Court with requests for a preliminary ruling which could be avoided if a direct action – this time before the Court of First Instance - were possible within strict time-limits. It should be noted in this respect, moreover, that the number of references for a preliminary ruling on the validity of Community acts remains in any event very limited;

– if the Court, however, is incorrect in claiming that there are no gaps (as I believe), the conclusion does not change. Indeed, even if a reasonable broadening of the conditions were to bring about an increase in workload (undoubtedly of a reasonable nature and at the level of the Court of First Instance and not of the Court of Justice), then it is clear that workload-related issues should not justify the denial of access to justice. Moreover, in terms of economy of procedure, it seems preferable to have one centralised remedy instead of twenty-five or more decentralised remedies.

Finally, it may be added that if the admissibility conditions were to be more flexible, less energy would be spent by the Courts (and the parties) on examining pleas of inadmissibility.[38]

## 5. MAY THE SOLUTION ULTIMATELY COME FROM THE EUROPEAN COURT OF HUMAN RIGHTS?

Whatever the reasons for the strict attitude taken by the Court of Justice and the Constitution may be, it is clearly more and more unrealistic to expect any solution to this problem from within the Community. One may however wonder whether a solution might not be found outside the Community, namely from the European Court of Human Rights.

---

[38] For those reasons, one can only wonder whether, at least for some political institutions, the workload of the Court is not in reality a good excuse to create a system allowing them to escape judicial control.

As is well known, although the Community is not a party to the Convention, this does not mean that the Member States could not nevertheless be held responsible for Community acts before the European Court of Human Rights.[39]

Whether the present system of the admissibility of Article 230(4) TEC is at all compatible with the European Convention on Human Rights is more than doubtful, however.[40] Recently, the European Court of Human Rights has indicated that the procedure for a preliminary ruling, which does not offer individuals direct access to the competent jurisdiction, is not a genuine remedy within the meaning of Article 35 of the European Convention on Human Rights. If this is so, it follows, however, that this procedure is also not a substitute for a right of access to justice.[41] Nor does, in my view, the national judge offer the necessary remedy, given that he does not have the power to declare an EU act invalid (*Foto-Frost* case law).

In this regard, it is not without interest that, shortly after the *UPA* judgment, the European Court of Human Rights rendered an important judgment on the minimum conditions for access to justice which confirms the previous case law and also confirms current doubts as to the compatibility of the Community system with the standards required by the European Convention on Human Rights.

In the *Posti* case,[42] the Finnish government restricted the fishing rights of two applicants. The applicants were not allowed to challenge the measure before the national courts and they challenged this absence of remedies before the European Court of Human Rights as being illegal in respect of a tribunal within the meaning of Article 6 of the Convention.

---

[39] See ECtHR, judgment of 18 February 1999, Appl. No. 24833/94, *Matthews* v. *The United Kingdom*; see also, Appl. No. 56672/00, *Senator Lines*, in this case, the application brought against 15 Member States for a breach of the Convention by EU Institutions was ultimately declared inadmissible as the breach had meanwhile been remedied and the applicant was no longer a 'victim'. See also Appl. No. 45036/98, *Bosphorus* v. *Ireland*, available at: <www.echr.coe.int.> (go to Judgment and decisions – search the case law - HUDOC – make sure that Decisions, Judgments, Reports and Resolutions' boxes on the left are checked). Moreover, Art. I-9(2) TCE provides that the Union shall seek accession to the European Convention for the Protection of Human Rights and Fundamental Freedoms.

[40] See D. Waelbroeck and A.M. Verheyden, 'Les conditions de recevabilité des recours en annulation des particuliers contre les actes normatifs communautaires à la lumière du droit comparé et de la Convention des droits de l'homme', *CDE* (1995) p. 399.

[41] ECtHR, judgments of 23 January 1999, Appl. No. 44677/98, *Mayo Alvarez* v. *Spain*; of 4 May 1999, Appl. No. 41974/98, *Kutcherenko* v. *Ukraine*; of 28 July 1999, Appl. No. 22774/93, *Immobilière Saffi* v. *Italy*; of 15 June 2000, Appl. No. 25723/94, *Erdogan* v. *Turkey*; of 11 October 2001, Appl. No. 34896/97, *Graxi* v. *Italy*.

[42] See ECtHR, judgment of 24 September 2002, Appl. No. 27824/95, *Posti and Rahko* v. *Finland*, paras. 53-54. Although the ECtHR in this case refers to the conditions of admissibility of Art. 230(4) TEC, the reasoning indicates that Art. 6 of the Convention is much broader than the current case law in support of its argument of the ECJ. See, *inter alia*, the reference to the *Extramet* judgment as an example of what ought to be the rule, although – as we know – this case has so far remained the exception in the application of Art. 230(4) TEC. See *supra* n. 5.

As regards the applicability of Article 6 of the Convention, the European Court observed that:

> 'the Convention is intended to safeguard rights which are "practical and effective" as opposed to "theoretical" or "illusory" (...) It follows that where a decree, decision or other measure, albeit not formally addressed to any individual natural or legal person, in substance does affect the "civil rights" or "obligations" of such a person or of a group of persons in a similar situation, whether by reason of certain attributes peculiar to them or by reason of a factual situation which differentiates them from all other persons, Article 6 § 1 may require that the substance of the decision or measure in question is capable of being challenged by that person or group before a "tribunal" meeting the requirements of that provision.'

Pursuant to Article 6 of the Convention, every individual should have access to a judge 'determining his civil rights and obligations'. In the *Posti* judgment, in order to come to the conclusion that the applicants had the right to be heard by the tribunal, the European Court limited itself to establishing that a fishing right existed which was not conditioned by legislative amendments but which had effectively been limited by the decree, the validity of which was contested by the applicants. The consequence seems to be that an individual should have access to a judge in the event that an act – even of a general nature – affects his rights in a way which was not explicitly provided for at the time when these rights were granted.

After the *Posti* judgment, which again openly called into question systems of access to justice which are too restrictive, the compatibility of the Community system of remedies laid down in Article 230(4) TEC with the Convention, seems more questionable than ever.


6.    CONCLUSION

The debate on access to justice within the Community is developing with remarkable speed focusing on an area which is becoming increasingly relevant in view of the daily extension of Community competence. The proposals for the EU Constitution, however, contribute insufficiently to the improvement of the present situation following the disappointing *UPA* judgment. It is therefore uncertain that any progress will be achieved in this area in the immediate future, unless – as I hope – the European Court of Human Rights were to decide that the system is incompatible with Articles 6 and 13 ECHR.

# THE EXPANDING ROLE OF THE NATIONAL COURTS AND THE EU CONSTITUTION

## Jutta Limbach[*]

Not only politics, but also jurisdiction can contribute to breathing much needed life into the EU Constitution. The European Court of Justice, for instance, has ensured, inspired by the spirit of the Treaties, the uniform validity of European Community law in the Member States. As early as in 1963, the court held that European Community law not only addresses the Member States, but can directly impose obligations, and confer rights, on the individual. This principle of 'direct effect' has been assessed as the 'Big Bang' by which the Community came into being as a community of law. The ECJ has also consolidated the protection of fundamental rights. In doing so, it has invoked the constitutional traditions that are common to all Member States as well as the European Convention on Human Rights and has made reference to these legal sources as general principles of Community law. Later on, this formulation was incorporated into the Treaty establishing the European Union.

The national courts have not been in a position to further develop the law of the European Economic Community, and the law of the European Union, in the same manner. The fact that, in spite of this, the national courts have made an important contribution to the further development of Community law results from the situation where the above-mentioned fundamental decisions by the European Court of Justice have been delivered in proceedings for a preliminary ruling pursuant to the former Article 177 TEC (now Art. 234 TCE) that were initiated by national courts. Also the national courts have shaped the profile of the rule of law principle in European law. Also in the future, they can make a contribution to the EU Constitution taking a concrete form.

The national courts' competences will not be modified by the EU Constitution. It is, and will be, their task to apply the law of the European Union to the extent that it directly affects the legal relationships between the citizens and the state or among the citizens themselves. The principle of the direct applicability of EU law, its 'direct effect', is undisputed today. Moreover, Article I-6 TCE explicitly establishes that the Constitution, and the law adopted by the Union's in-

---

[*] President of the Goethe Institute and former President of the Federal Constitutional Court of Germany.

*D. Curtin, A.E. Kellermann and S. Blockmans, eds., The EU Constitution: The Best Way Forward?*
© 2005, T.M.C. Asser Instituut, The Hague.

stitutions, 'shall have primacy over the law of the Member States', provided that when enacting the respective legislation, the European Union's organs have acted within the framework of the competencies that have been assigned to them. The national courts themselves must ascertain the legal principles of EU law, which are applicable with priority. This means, from the point of view of university law faculties, that this area of the law should in the future be a compulsory subject.

Also the national courts have to take into account in their decisions the principles of conferral, of subsidiarity and of proportionality (Art. I-9(1) TCE). Where they have doubts concerning the constitutionality of secondary EU law or as regards the interpretation of primary or secondary EU law, they must refer their questions to the European Court of Justice. The ECJ has to answer these questions by way of a preliminary ruling in the interest of the uniform validity of EU law. Especially during the first years of the EU Constitution, it will be decisive that the European courts and the national courts should determine, in a cooperative spirit, the possibilities and the limits of the competences under constitutional law in an understandable and transparent manner.

The national courts will also have to use the law of the EU Constitution as a standard of interpretation for those provisions of national law that have been enacted in order to implement EU law. In this context, the provisions of the Charter of Fundamental Rights of the Union are of particular importance. Pursuant to its Article II-111 TCE, they are addressed to the Member States, and thus to the national courts, but only when they implement EU law. The provisions of the Charter are judicially cognisable only in the interpretation of executive acts taken by institutions and bodies of the Union and in ruling on their legality.

In this context, an insight that has been developed by the German Federal Constitutional Court applies here: fundamental rights are not only defensive rights against interference by a public authority. These provisions of the Charter, in their entirety, are at the same time objective principles that have an effect on law-making, and on the application of the law. No provision of secondary EU law and of the national law that is enacted to implement secondary EU law may contradict the Charter, and each of these provisions should be interpreted in the spirit of this system of values.

In the Charter, we encounter many classical and familiar fundamental rights of liberal origin. However, the EU Constitution is not only about Europe as a liberal project. It is true that the Treaties conceived and constituted the European Union mainly as a confederation of states that served economic cooperation. By contrast, social policy did not matter in this context. The abundant use of socio-political imperatives and the incorporation, within the Constitution, of a part that is dedicated to social policy indicate that a change in direction is intended. The EU Constitution claims to give the European Union also a social dimension apart from the liberal one. Pursuant to Article I-3(3) TCE, it strives to achieve a social market economy, highly competitive and aiming at full employment and social progress. Moreover, the Charter formulates, under the title 'Solidarity', social fundamental rights and political aims. For instance, every person is conferred with a right to fair and just working conditions and a right to protection against unjustified dismissal. The Union also recognises and respects the entitlement to social security benefits and social services providing protection in cases such as maternity, illness, old age or the loss of employment.

Are these rights individual rights that are enforceable by legal action, or are they only political directives, in spite of the fact that they are referred to as 'rights'? Some Members of the European Parliament indeed advance the opinion that the EU Charter was intended not only to establish social policy aims but also to confer personal rights.[1] At present, there is an intensive discussion among constitutional law scholars about the question of whether social fundamental rights have the quality of norms and whether they are enforceable by legal action. What is discussed is not only the tense relationship between freedom and social security. Both principles are also interrelated, and they are mutually dependent. The political liberty rights as well as the rights of social participation are part of the functional foundations of democracy, because someone who has neither an income nor a home will hardly be able to participate actively in political processes.

Irrespective of the characterisation under the law that the provisions of the Title 'Solidarity' may be given, Article II-112(5) TCE makes it clear what the significance of these provisions for the courts exactly is: the provisions of the Charter are judicially cognisable only in the interpretation of executive acts taken by institutions and bodies of the Union and in ruling on their legality. The reverse conclusion of this is that the national courts may not decree social claims by individuals *vis-à-vis* the institutions and bodies of the European Union. As a general rule, the protection that is intended by the norms of the Charter will only be achieved through acts by the legislative bodies and the executive power, but not primarily through the courts.

All the same, the social provisions of the Charter may not be underestimated. As an aid to interpretation they can also serve to incorporate social features into capitalism. The right to protection against unjustified dismissal can, for instance, play a role where the dismantling of protection against dismissal is discussed. It is often alleged that less protection against dismissal means more jobs. The social fundamental right that is enshrined in the Charter could motivate the competent court to investigate whether this allegation can be proven in the event that the existing safeguards under labour law are indeed curtailed by law.

---

[1] N. Dimmel, 'Grundrechte und Grundsicherung – Zur Bedeutung der sozialen Grundrechte in der Grundrechtecharta der Europäischen Union für die Entwicklung der sozialen Sicherheit in Österreich', in F. Matscher, ed., *Erweitertes Grundrechtsverständnis*, Schriften des Österreichischen Instituts für Menschenrechte, Vol. 8 (Kehl am Rhein, Engel 2003) pp. 219 et seq.; T. Marauhn, 'Das Grundrecht auf Zugang zu den Leistungen der sozialen Sicherheit – Anmerkungen zur Normkategorie der sozialen Grundrechte', ibid., pp. 2476 et seq.; G. Malinverni, 'Die Sozialrechte in der Schweiz', ibid., pp. 289 et seq.

The national courts will have to take account of the fact that the EU Constitution has brought together market economy aims with the principle of social compensation. It will also be their task to harmonise, in a wise manner, the liberty rights and the rights of social participation in the legal area of the European Union.

# THE IMPACT OF THE EU CONSTITUTION ON THE RELATIONSHIP BETWEEN STRASBOURG AND LUXEMBOURG

Rick Lawson[*]

## 1. INTRODUCTION: THE EU CONSTITUTION AND FUNDAMENTAL RIGHTS

For more than 30 years academics and politicians have discussed the position of fundamental rights in the legal order of the European Communities and the Union. They have argued for and against EU accession to the European Convention on Human Rights; they have advocated or opposed a separate bill of fundamental rights.

One might be tempted to say that these issues have finally been settled, now that the text of the EU Constitution has been agreed upon: Article I-9 TCE provides for Union accession to the European Convention on Human Rights (ECHR), whereas Part II incorporates the Charter of Fundamental Rights. It would seem, therefore, that a solid framework for the protection of fundamental rights in the EU legal order has been put in place.

Likewise the relationship between the European Court of Justice (the ECJ in Luxembourg) and the European Court of Human Rights (the ECtHR in Strasbourg) – which is the topic of the present contribution – appears to have been settled. The Luxembourg Court is, and will continue to be, the only court that is competent to rule on the interpretation and validity of Community law; the Strasbourg Court has, and will continue to have, the last word on the interpretation and application of the rights and freedoms guaranteed by the ECHR. Two major changes will occur – albeit that they are both of a somewhat symbolic nature: Luxembourg will have a written set of fundamental rights to refer to (but it has managed quite well so far with its unwritten set of general principles), and the jurisdiction of the Strasbourg Court will expressly include the Union (but even at present the Union is not completely outside its jurisdiction, as we will see later on).

So is this the 'end of history' for fundamental rights? Not quite. To begin with, the EU Constitution remains to be adopted. Secondly, it may be true that

---

[*] Prof. Dr. R.A. Lawson, Faculty of Law, University of Leiden, the Netherlands.

*D. Curtin, A.E. Kellermann and S. Blockmans, eds., The EU Constitution: The Best Way Forward?*
© 2005, T.M.C. Asser Instituut, The Hague.

Article I-9 TCE asserts that the Union 'shall' accede to the European Convention, but this formulation[1] conveniently ignores that accession will require agreement from the other side as well: the Council of Europe and its 46 Member States. Admittedly, the Council of Europe has repeatedly indicated that it would welcome EU accession, and the new Protocol 14 to the ECHR contains a clause to this end: 'The European Union may accede to the Convention'. The explanatory memorandum, however, warns us that this does not settle the matter:

> 'It should be emphasised that further modifications to the Convention will be necessary in order to make such accession possible from a legal and technical point of view. (...) At the time of drafting of this protocol, it was not yet possible to enter into negotiations – and even less to conclude an agreement – with the European Union on the terms of the latter's possible accession to the Convention, simply because the European Union still lacked the competence to do so. This made it impossible to include in this protocol the other modifications to the Convention necessary to permit such accession. As a consequence, a second ratification procedure will be necessary in respect of those further modifications, whether they be included in a new amending protocol or in an accession treaty.'[2]

It remains to be seen how this 'second ratification procedure' will proceed. It will be interesting to watch the negotiations that will precede the EU's accession: some non-EU Member States, such as Turkey and Russia, may believe that they have an interesting bargaining chip here.

However, these are more or less technical issues, and they are hopefully of a temporary nature. Rather than focussing on the technicalities that are involved in EU accession to the ECHR, this paper will approach the relationship between the ECJ and the European Court of Human Rights from a somewhat different perspective. It adopts the perspective of an individual (a natural or legal person) who alleges that his fundamental rights have been violated. The responsibility may reside with domestic authorities or with the institutions of the Union. As we will see, his/its claim may end up being considered by the European Court of Human Rights or rather be brought before the European Court of Justice. It follows that four different situations may exist:

---

[1] As in doc. CIG 87/2/04 of 29 October 2004. Interestingly, the Draft Treaty as presented by the Convention had used more cautious terms: 'the Union *shall seek* accession' (doc. CONV 850/03, 18 July 2003). The very first draft of this provision (Art. 5 as it then was) was even less enthusiastic: 'the Union *may* accede' (doc. CONV 528/03, 6 February 2003).

[2] Protocol 14 to the Convention for the Protection of Human Rights and Fundamental Freedoms, amending the control system of the Convention (CETS No. 194; adopted 13 May 2004), Explanatory Memorandum, paras. 101-102, available at: <http://conventions.coe.int/Treaty/ EN/ Reports/Html/194.htm.>.

|                         | Cases before ECtHR        | Cases before ECJ              |
| ----------------------- | ------------------------- | ----------------------------- |
| Alleged violations by   | category 1                | category 4                    |
| domestic authorities    | *(e.g., Tyrer)*           | *(e.g., Grogan)*              |
| Alleged violations by   | category 2                | category 3                    |
| EU Institutions         | *(e.g., Senator Lines)*   | *(e.g., Baustahlgewebe)*      |

This paper will seek to explore the 'inter-institutional' dimension of each of these four categories – that is, the extent to which the relationship between Strasbourg and Luxembourg is an issue in these cases – and will seek to assess the impact, if any, of the entry into force of the Treaty establishing a Constitution for Europe.

## 2.    CATEGORY 1 – STRASBOURG REVIEWS COMPLAINTS ABOUT DOMESTIC AUTHORITIES

The first category represents the conventional form of European human rights litigation: an individual believes that one of his rights under the ECHR has been violated by his national authorities and, after exhausting domestic remedies, brings a complaint before the European Court of Human Rights in accordance with Article 34 ECHR. The classic example (but one could mention hundreds of others) is *Tyrer* v. *the UK*: a boy complains that the use of judicial corporal punishment is incompatible with the prohibition of degrading punishment (Art. 3 ECHR).[3]

For obvious reasons this scenario is the least problematic one in terms of the institutional interaction between the Council of Europe and the European Union (or between Strasbourg and Luxembourg): there is none. In addition, it is plain that neither the entry into force of the EU Constitution as such, nor the EU's accession to the ECHR, would affect this situation. Also after the EU has become a party to the ECHR, its Member States would continue to be held accountable for human rights violations allegedly committed by their own authorities.

One might speculate whether this clear-cut division of labour may change in the long run. As is well known, the Strasbourg Court faces an ever-increasing backlog of cases. The reforms introduced by Protocol 11 led to an enormous rise in the Court's output, but despite all improvements the Court is still overwhelmed by the number of fresh complaints. It remains to be seen whether the new set of procedural reforms introduced by Protocol 14 will be sufficient to cure this problem. If it turns out that the Court is simply unable to cope with

---

[3] ECtHR, judgment of 25 April 1978, Appl. No. 5856/72, *Tyrer* v. *UK*, *Series A 26*. All cases can be found through the 'HUDOC' search engine at the Court's website: <www.echr.coe.int.>.

100,000 cases per year (the number of applications that is commonly predicted for 2008 or 2010), then it will become inevitable to reconsider the judicial infrastructure of Europe. This might entail new roles for Strasbourg and Luxembourg and perhaps some sort of division of labour. But again, this is a matter for speculation.

For the time being we have more pressing questions. The image that Strasbourg reviews acts of domestic authorities and that Luxembourg is not concerned at all, may have to be adjusted in two respects. In the first place, EU law may be challenged indirectly, that is in cases against EU Member States that implement EU law. In the second place, the principles that the European Court of Human Rights develops in its case law may affect the Union, simply because they will be difficult for the Union institutions (including the ECJ) to ignore.

Let us first take a closer look at 'indirect' challenges of EU law. Strasbourg has adopted a straightforward approach towards situations where Contracting Parties act in order to execute international obligations, for instance under an extradition treaty with a third country, and where they are said to violate fundamental rights:

'Under Article 1 of the Convention the member States are responsible for all acts and omissions of their domestic organs allegedly violating the Convention, regardless of whether the act or omission in question is a consequence of domestic law or regulations or of the necessity to comply with international obligations.'[4]

Thus, in the well-known case of *Soering* the Court did not hesitate to rule that the extradition of the applicant to the USA would violate Article 3 ECHR, even though the British decision to extradite him was taken in accordance with a bilateral extradition treaty with the US.[5] It is difficult to avoid the conclusion that an EU Member State is accountable for human rights violations by its own authorities whilst implementing EU law. Indeed, in *Cantoni* the Strasbourg Court reviewed the quality of French rules relating to the sale of medicinal products, without attaching any significance to the fact that these rules had been adopted in order to implement an EC directive:

'The fact, pointed out by the Government, that Article L 511 of the Public Health Code is based almost word for word on Community Directive 65/65 does not remove it from the ambit of Article 7 of the Convention.'[6]

Accordingly an EU Member State may find itself caught between Luxembourg (which may interpret its obligations under EU law in a certain fashion) and

---

[4] ECommHR, 9 February 1990, Appl. No. 13258/87, *M. & Co.* v. *FRG*, *DR* 64, p. 144; 33 *Yearbook ECHR* (1990) p. 51.

[5] ECtHR, judgment of 7 July 1989, Appl. No. 14038/88, *Soering* v. *UK*, *Series A 161*.

[6] ECtHR, judgment of 15 November 1996, Appl. No. 17862/91, *Cantoni* v. *France*, *Reports* 1996-V p. 1617, para. 30.

Strasbourg (which may find that the domestic authorities, in following the ECJ's case law, violate the ECHR). An interesting example is offered by the case of *Bosphorus Airlines,* which is currently pending in Strasbourg. The case concerns the seizure by the Irish authorities of an aircraft which Bosphorus had leased from Yugoslav Airlines JAT. When the aircraft was in Ireland for maintenance, in 1993, it was seized under an EC Regulation which implemented the UN sanctions against the Federal Republic of Yugoslavia (Serbia and Montenegro). Bosphorus challenged the retention of the aircraft. During the proceedings, the Irish Supreme Court referred a preliminary question to the ECJ on whether the aircraft was covered by the relevant Regulation. The answer was in the affirmative: the ECJ considered that the general interest outweighed the individual rights of Bosphorus.[7] Subsequently, the Supreme Court had little choice but to apply the decision of the ECJ and reject Bosphorus's appeal. The aircraft was the only one ever seized under the relevant EC and UN regulations.

Bosphorus then brought a complaint in Strasbourg under Article 1 of Protocol No. 1 (protection of property), arguing that it had to bear an excessive burden resulting from the manner in which the Irish State applied the sanctions regime and that it suffered significant financial loss. Four years later, in September 2001, the Strasbourg Court held a hearing on the admissibility and merits of the application, following which the case was declared admissible.[8] More than two years later the Chamber relinquished jurisdiction in favour of the Grand Chamber. In May 2004 the President of the Court gave the European Commission leave to intervene as a third party, and in September 2004 the Court decided to devote a *second* hearing to the case. The unusual length of the procedure suggests that the case is considered as highly sensitive.

How to approach cases like these? From the Strasbourg perspective the most logical thing would be to stick to its doctrine that the High Contracting Parties are responsible for all acts and omissions of their organs, regardless of whether the conduct in question happens to involve the execution of EU law. Interestingly, EU law points in the same direction, since Article III-435 TCE (currently Article 307 TEC) makes clear that the Member States' obligations under the European Convention on Human Rights shall not be affected by EU law. But the extreme care that the European Court of Human Rights displays in *Bosphorus* suggests that Strasbourg is not too eager to follow that approach. One can only speculate about the reasons. Perhaps the Strasbourg Court prefers to avoid an unequivocal ruling and rather waits until the Union accedes to the ECHR. Once that has happened, it will be possible to bring cases such as *Bosphorus* against both the Member State concerned *and* the Union. In that scenario they could each defend 'their part' of the case in their own right.

---

[7] ECJ, judgment of 30 July 1996, Case C-84/95, *Bosphorus* v. *Minister for Transport, Energy and Communications and others* [1996] *ECR* I-3953.

[8] ECtHR, decision of 13 September 2001, Appl. No. 45036/98, *Bosphorus Airways* v. *Ireland*, nyr.

Let us now turn to the second way in which the decisions that the European Court of Human Rights takes in 'conventional' cases may have an impact on EU law. Clearly it is to some extent inevitable that the decisions of the European Court of Human Rights transcend the concrete cases in which they are delivered. The interpretations that the Court develops in one case will be relevant in others, as the Court observed already in 1978:

> 'The Court's judgments in fact serve not only to decide those cases brought before the Court but, more generally, to elucidate, safeguard and develop the rules instituted by the Convention, thereby contributing to the observance by the States of the engagements undertaken by them as Contracting Parties.'[9]

Even though there is no formal system of *stare decisis*, legal certainty and the principle of equality require the Court to follow its own precedents unless cogent reasons force it to reconsider its position. In its recent *Pretty* judgment, the Strasbourg Court recalled:

> 'The applicant's counsel attempted to persuade the Court that a finding of a violation in this case would not create a general precedent or any risk to others. It is true that it is not this Court's role under Article 34 of the Convention to issue opinions in the abstract but to apply the Convention to the concrete facts of the individual case. However, judgments issued in individual cases establish precedents albeit to a greater or lesser extent and a decision in this case could not, either in theory or practice, be framed in such a way as to prevent application in later cases.'[10]

For the ECJ this means that it may be confronted with Strasbourg jurisprudence that was developed in cases unconnected to EU law, and that is 'spilling over' to cases that do matter to the EU. To give a concrete example: if the Strasbourg Court finds that Article 8 ECHR (the right to respect for private life, family life, home and correspondence) extends to business premises and may be invoked by legal persons – as it did in *Colas Est* v. *France*[11] – then this finding is bound to have an effect on EU law, for instance on the procedural dimension of competition law.[12]

Of course the Union is in this respect in the same position as any High Contracting Party that is not involved in a case where new standards are developed: one can only wait and see what Strasbourg comes up with. Yet, after accession, it will be easier for the EU to intervene in cases pending before the Court. This

---

[9] ECtHR, judgment of 18 January 1978, Appl. No. 5310/71, *Ireland* v. *the UK, Series A 25*, para. 154.

[10] ECtHR, judgment of 29 April 2002, Appl. No. 2346/02, *Pretty* v. *UK, Reports* 2002-III, p. 155, para. 75.

[11] ECtHR, judgment of 16 April 2002, Appl. No. 37971/97, *Colas Est* v. *France, Reports* 2002-III, p. 105.

[12] ECJ, judgment of 22 October 2002, Case C-94/00, *Roquette Frères* [2002] *ECR* I-9011, para. 25.

would allow the Union to point the Court's attention to the significance, from the perspective of EU law, of the legal questions before it.

## 3.    CATEGORY 2 – STRASBOURG REVIEWS COMPLAINTS ABOUT EU INSTITUTIONS

Our second category relates to cases where the European Court of Human Rights is asked to address alleged violations by institutions of the European Union. Clearly the EU is not, for the time being at least, a party to the ECHR. Complaints addressed against the EC or the EU are therefore simply rejected since cases can only be brought against the High Contracting Parties.

However, this situation has not prevented claims about the Union from being brought in Strasbourg: applicants tried to bring a complaint against the Member States instead. It is likely that similar complaints will be lodged in the near future. In deciding these cases, the position of the Convention bodies has evolved and continues to evolve.

Two scenarios may be distinguished at the outset. The first one involves complaints addressed against all Member States, the argument being that the Member States may be held collectively or individually responsible for violations of the Convention by Community institutions – for instance an alleged violation of privacy by the European Commission. The second scenario involves complaints addressed against a particular Member State, not so much for its own conduct but for acts of the Union in connection with that State – for instance an allegedly unreasonable amount of time taken by the ECJ to issue a preliminary ruling in a case pending before the domestic court of a particular Member State. Whereas the former group represents attempts to establish a 'pure' form of Member State responsibility, it will be noted that there is a rather thin line between the latter group and the *Cantoni* and *Bosphorus* type of cases that we discussed above.

Interestingly, in one of its very first decisions – in 1958! – the European Commission of Human Rights observed that if a State party to the ECHR concludes another international agreement which disables it from performing its obligations under the Convention, it will be answerable for any resultant breach of its obligations thereunder.[13] Since there is no reason to assume that this principle does not apply to international agreements establishing an international organisation, the Commission's decision seemed to open the door to 'Member State responsibility' for the conduct of international organisations. Indeed, in the 1980s the Commission dealt with a series of cases in which it expressly left open the possibility that the Member States are answerable for violations of the ECHR by Community institutions. All cases were rejected, however, on other grounds.[14]

---

[13] ECommHR, decision of 10 June 1958, Appl. No. 235/56, *X & X. v. FRG*, 2 *Yearbook ECHR* (1958-1959) p. 300.

[14] See, e.g., ECommHR, decision of 9 December 1987, Appl. No. 11123/84, *Tête v. France*,

In 1990 the Commission changed its position. In the well-known case of *M. & Co.*, which was addressed against Germany, the Commission found that the transfer of powers to an international organisation is not incompatible with the Convention provided that within that organisation fundamental rights receive an 'equivalent protection'.[15] The ECJ was considered to offer this 'equivalent protection'. The principle established by *M. & Co.* was later applied to a fairly large number of cases concerning alleged Community violations: all these complaints were rejected without much ado. Thus the claim that domestic authorities should review Community measures prior to their implementation was consistently rejected – to accept it would, of course, present a serious obstacle on the road of European integration. Likewise in *Pafitis*, a case concerning the reasonable-time requirement of Article 6 ECHR, the Court refused to take into consideration the time needed by the ECJ for delivering a preliminary ruling. The Court observed that 'to take it into account would adversely affect the system instituted by Article 177 of the EEC Treaty and work against the aim pursued in substance in that Article'.[16]

Thus judicial restraint characterised the first Strasbourg decisions concerning Member State responsibility for Community action. In 1999, however, the European Court seemed to take a more assertive approach. In *Matthews* the Court observed that:

> 'The Convention does not exclude the transfer of competences to international organisations provided that Convention rights continue to be 'secured'. Member States' responsibility therefore continues even after such a transfer.'[17]

The facts of the case were atypical, though, and a more straightforward decision of the Strasbourg Court was needed. That need still exists. In the case of *Guérin* a French company brought a complaint against the 15 Member States for a judgment delivered by the ECJ – but the complaint was rejected as manifestly ill-founded.[18] Then the case of *Senator Lines* seemed destined to become the leading case in this area; it was assigned to the Grand Chamber of the European Court of Human Rights. The applicant in the case was a German company that complained of a breach of the right to a fair trial (Art. 6 ECHR) by the Court of

---

*DR* 54, p. 76; ECommHR, decision of 19 January 1989, Appl. No. 13539/88, *Dufay* v. *EC and its Member States*.

   [15] ECommHR, decision of 9 February 1990, Appl. No. 13258/87, *M. & Co.* v. *FRG*, *DR* 64, p. 144; 33 *Yearbook ECHR* (1990) p. 51.

   [16] ECtHR, judgment of 26 February 1998, Appl. No. 20323/92, *Pafitis a.o.* v. *Greece*, *Reports* 1998-I, p. 457, para. 95.

   [17] ECtHR, judgment of 18 February 1999, Appl. No. 24833/94, *Matthews* v. *the UK*, *Reports* 1999-I, p. 251, para. 32.

   [18] ECtHR, 4 July 2000, Appl. No. 51717/99, *Guérin Automobiles* v. *les 15 Etats de l'Union Européenne*, nyr. The Court unanimously considered the application inadmissible, without deciding whether it was competent *ratione personae* to hear the complaint.

First Instance and the European Court of Justice. Like in *Guérin* Senator Lines' application was directed against the 15 Member States of the European Union, the argument being that the Member States may be held collectively or individually responsible for violations of the Convention by Community institutions. Unfortunately the case was declared inadmissible in March 2004 on factual grounds.[19]

Subsequently it was the case of *Emesa Sugar* v. *the Netherlands* which squarely raised the question to what extent an individual Member State may be held responsible for ECJ decisions which are implemented by the domestic courts or by other authorities. Emesa was involved in litigation before a Dutch court. Pursuant to Article 234 TEC, the Dutch court referred questions to the European Court of Justice for a preliminary ruling. When the case was pending before the ECJ, after the Advocate General had delivered his Opinion, Emesa sought leave to submit written observations in order to respond to the Advocate General's submissions. The Statute of the ECJ and its Rules of Procedure make no provision for this. However, Emesa based its request on the right to a fair trial, as laid down in Article 6 ECHR. More in particular Emesa relied on well-established case law of the Strasbourg Court according to which the concept of a fair hearing implies the right to adversarial proceedings. This requires that the parties to criminal or civil proceedings must have the opportunity to have knowledge of and comment on all evidence adduced or observations filed, with a view to influencing the court's decision.[20] Interestingly, the Strasbourg Court has determined in a series of cases, the first of which dates from 1991, that this principle also applies to the submissions of the Advocates General before the highest national jurisdictions.[21] Emesa took the view that this case law also applies to the Opinion delivered before the ECJ by the Advocate General and accordingly sought leave to reply to it.

In deciding on this request,[22] the ECJ first reiterated that fundamental rights form an integral part of the general principles of Community law and confirmed the special significance of the European Convention. The Court then examined the status and role of the Advocate General within the Community's judicial system. The Court concluded that the case law of the European Court of Human Rights 'does not appear to be transposable to the Opinion of the Court's Advocates General'. It remains to be seen whether the grounds advanced by the ECJ

---

[19] ECtHR, decision of 10 March 2004, Appl. No. 56672/00, *Senator Lines GmbH* v. *Austria a.o.*, nyr.

[20] See, e.g., ECtHR, judgment of 18 March 1997, Appl. No. 21497/93, *Mantovanelli* v. *France*, *Reports* 1997-II, p. 436, para. 33; ECtHR, judgment of 3 March 2000, Appl. No. 35376/97, *Krcmár* v. *Czech Republic*, para. 40.

[21] See, among many authorities, ECtHR, judgment of 30 October 1991, Appl. No. 12005/86, *Borgers* v. *Belgium, Series A 214-B*, paras. 26-29; ECtHR, judgment of 20 February 1996, Appl. No. 19075/91, *Vermeulen* v. *Belgium, Reports* 1996-I, p. 224, paras. 29-30.

[22] ECJ, Order of 4 February 2000, Case C-17/98, *Emesa Sugar (Free Zone) NV* v. *Aruba* [2000] *ECR* I-665.

are convincing,[23] but in any case leave to submit written observations in response to the AG's Opinion was dismissed.

Following the preliminary ruling of the ECJ, the Dutch court decided the case accordingly. Emesa then brought a complaint in Strasbourg against the Netherlands in lieu of the Communities proper. The main argument was that the Netherlands were responsible for the fact that the Dutch court, in applying the ECJ's preliminary ruling, relied on a judgment delivered in breach of Article 6. The judgment in the case of *Pellegrini* seems to suggest that this argument may be successful:

'The Court notes at the outset that the applicant's marriage was annulled by a decision of the Vatican courts which was declared enforceable by the Italian courts. The Vatican has not ratified the Convention and, furthermore, the application was lodged against Italy. The Court's task therefore consists not in examining whether the proceedings before the ecclesiastical courts complied with Article 6 of the Convention, but *whether the Italian courts*, before authorising enforcement of the decision annulling the marriage, *duly satisfied themselves that the relevant proceedings fulfilled the guarantees of Article 6. A review of that kind is required where a decision in respect of which enforcement is requested emanates from the courts of a country which does not apply the Convention.* Such a review is especially necessary where the implications of a declaration of enforceability are of capital importance for the parties.'[24]

The same standard may apply to preliminary rulings too, since the ECJ – as we will see in the next session – does not 'apply the Convention': Luxembourg has always been careful to emphasise that it only draws 'inspiration' from the 'guidelines' supplied by the Convention and by the judgments of the European Court of Human Rights.

In January 2005 the Court decided *Emesa*.[25] Just like in *Guérin* and *Senator Lines*, it rejected the complaint on grounds that were not connected to the issue of 'Member State responsibility'. The Court noted that the domestic proceedings in *Emesa* concerned custom duties. Since this did not involve the determination of 'civil rights and obligations', the Court considered that the whole case fell outside the substantive scope of Article 6 ECHR. The complaint was therefore

---

[23] For a more detailed discussion, see the author's annotation in 37 *Common Market Law Review* (2000) pp. 983-990, and D. Spielmann in 43 *Revue trimestrielle des droits de l'homme* (2000). See also the later case of *Kress,* following which it seems difficult to support the ECJ's position in *Emesa* (ECtHR, judgment of 7 June 2001, Appl. No. 39594/98, *Kress* v. *France, Reports* 2001-VI, p. 1).

[24] ECtHR, judgment of 20 July 2001, Appl. No. 30882/96, *Pellegrini* v. *Italy, Reports* 2001-VIII, p. 353, para. 40 [emphasis added]. Cf., *mutatis mutandis,* ECtHR, judgment of 26 June 1992, Appl. No. 12747/87, *Drozd & Janousek* v. *France & Spain, Series A 240,* para. 110; ECtHR, judgment of 14 December 1999, Appl. No. 37019/97, *A.M.* v. *Italy, Reports* 1999-IX, p. 45, para. 26.

[25] ECtHR, decision of 25 January 2005, Appl. No. 62023/00, *Emesa Sugar* v. *the Netherlands.*

rejected *ratione materiae*. This outcome is somewhat surprising: if the case was inadmissible for this obvious reason, then why did the Court 'communicate' it to the Dutch Government at all? Why did it invite the European Commission to intervene? It is also interesting to recall that the ECJ itself did not deny the applicability of the right to a fair trial, as laid down in Article 6 ECHR, in *Emesa*.

Are there still any lessons that one might draw from this case law? Quite apart from the outcome of specific cases, there is an element of unfairness in cases where EU Member States are being held responsible for situations that are to a considerable extent beyond their control. The Dutch government has very little to say about the way in which the ECJ regulates its procedure. If all Member States are involved in a case, as in *Senator Lines*, they may have a difficult time in agreeing on a common line of defence. Conversely, for the EU it is difficult to stand by as cases like *Senator Lines* and *Emesa* are pleaded in Strasbourg: they are in reality about the EU. Finally, for the applicant it may be somewhat intimidating to have to bring proceedings against a group of States. For all these reasons, EU accession to the European Convention has to be welcomed.

4.    CATEGORY 3 – LUXEMBOURG REVIEWS COMPLAINTS ABOUT EU
      INSTITUTIONS

Ever since the ECJ's landmark judgments in the cases of *Handelsgesellschaft* and *Nold*,[26] in the early 1970s, the Union is in a process of accepting and acknowledging that it is bound by fundamental rights. The case law is well-known[27] and may be summarised as follows:

> '... according to settled case-law, fundamental rights form an integral part of the general principles of law, whose observance the Court ensures. For that purpose, the Court draws inspiration from the constitutional traditions common to the Member States and from the guidelines supplied by international treaties for the protection of human rights on which the Member States have collaborated or to which they are signatories. The ECHR has special significance in that respect.'[28]

Recent decisions show that this is still a very dynamic branch of case law. Take for instance *Baustahlgewebe* in which the Court found a Community violation of

---

[26] ECJ, judgment of 17 December 1970, Case C-11/70, *Internationale Handelsgesellschaft mbH* v. *Einfuhr- und Vorratsstelle für Getreide und Futtermittel* [1970] *ECR* 1125, para. 4; ECJ, judgment of 14 May 1974, Case C-4/73, *J. Nold* v. *Commission of the European Communities* [1974] *ECR* 491, para. 13.

[27] For an overview, see B. de Witte, 'The Past and Future Role of the European Court of Justice in the Protection of Human Rights', in Ph. Alston, ed., *The EU and Human Rights* (Oxford, Oxford University Press 1999) pp. 859-897.

[28] ECJ, judgment of 10 July 2003, Joined Cases C-20/00 and C-64/00, *Booker Aquaculture a.o.* v. *The Scottish Ministers* [2003] *ECR* I-7411, para. 65; references to earlier case law omitted.

fundamental rights for the first time in history, or *Connolly* on the freedom of expression of EU civil servants, or again *Roquette Frères* where the Court accepted that the Commission must comply with the requirements of the right to respect for private life when searching business premises.[29]

Although the common constitutional traditions were the first source of fundamental rights to be recognised by the ECJ, its importance seems to have diminished over the years.[30] Instead the ECJ has increasingly referred to the ECHR and to the jurisprudence of the European Court of Human Rights. It should be added that the ECJ has also based itself on other human rights instruments, albeit to a lesser extent.[31]

The principles established in the Court's case law were reaffirmed in the preamble to the Single European Act, then incorporated in the Treaty of Maastricht (Art. F(2) TEU) and then in the Treaty of Amsterdam (Art. 6(2) TEU). The only difference is that the reference to *other* human rights instruments, which has always been maintained in the Luxembourg case law, never made it to the Treaty texts. The explanation will probably be that the drafters preferred a shorter reference to the sources of fundamental rights. Be that as it may, Article I-9(3) TCE provides:

'Fundamental rights, as guaranteed by the European Convention for the Protection of Human Rights and Fundamental Freedoms and as they result from the constitutional traditions common to the Member States, shall constitute general principles of the Union's law.'

Our first conclusion should therefore be that the ECHR will still be one of the sources of fundamental rights when the EU Constitution enters into force.

Yet it is also true that the Court has always been careful to state that it only draws 'inspiration' from the 'guidelines' supplied by human rights treaties. Clearly the Court did not and does not consider itself bound by these treaties, as the following quote illustrates:

---

[29] ECJ, judgment of 17 December 1998, Case C-185/95 P, *Baustahlgewebe* v. *Commission of the European Communities* [1998] *ECR* I-8417, para. 29; ECJ, judgment of 6 March 2001, Case C-274/99 P, *B. Connolly* v. *Commission of the European Communities* [2001] *ECR* I-1611, para. 37; ECJ, judgment of 22 October 2002, Case C-94/00, *Roquette Frères SA* [2002] *ECR* I-9011, para. 25.

[30] It is a telling detail that the 'Black Monday' draft treaty presented by the Dutch presidency in 1991 (which was subsequently vetoed) did not refer to constitutional traditions at all. Draft Article G(2) provided: 'The Union shall respect the rights and freedoms as recognized in the European Convention for the Protection of Human Rights and Fundamental Freedoms' (see *Europe Documents* No. 1746/1747 of 20 November 1991).

[31] For a reference to the ESC, see ECJ, judgment of 2 February 1988, Case C-24/86, *V. Blaizot* v. *University of Liège and others* [1988] *ECR* 403, para. 17. For references to the ICCPR, see ECJ, judgment of 18 October 1989, Case C-374/87, *Orkem* v. *Commission of the European Communities* [1989] *ECR* 3351, para. 31, and ECJ, judgment of 17 February 1998, C-249/96, *Grant* v. *South-West Trains Ltd* [1998] *ECR* I-650, para. 44. For a reference to an ILO Convention, see ECJ, judgment of 8 April 1976, Case C-43/75, *Defrenne* [1976] *ECR* 474, para. 20.

'... Article 6(1) of the EHRC provides that (...) everyone is entitled to a fair and public hearing (...). *The general principle of Community law* that everyone is entitled to
fair legal process, *which is inspired by those fundamental rights* (...) is applicable in
the context of proceedings brought against a Commission decision imposing fines on
an undertaking for infringement of competition law'. [32]

Likewise the ECJ keeps some distance when it refers to individual judgments of
the Strasbourg Court:

'(...) the reasonableness of such a period must be appraised in the light of the circumstances specific to each case and, in particular, the importance of the case for the person concerned, its complexity and the conduct of the applicant and of the competent
authorities [see, *by analogy,* the judgments of the European Court of Human
Rights].'[33]

Meanwhile the Charter of Fundamental Rights of the EU was adopted, as a political document, in Nice in December 2000.[34] As is well known, the Charter contains a wide variety of rights: civil and political rights, economic, cultural and
social rights. Its text reveals a certain amount of ambiguity: some provisions are
expressly directed to the EU; others are not addressed to any authority in particular, but relate to policy areas where the Union has little or no competence. Be
that as it may, the Charter combines classic and innovative provisions, from the
prohibition of slavery to the right to good administration – in short, it is an attempt to formulate the 'state of the art' in human rights.

Following the Charter's proclamation, the Commission announced that it
would take the Charter into account when drafting legislation.[35] Yet in the Luxembourg case law the Charter's role is less than prominent. Presumably because
of its soft law nature, the ECJ has refrained from applying it, although the Court
of First Instance and a number of Advocates General had no difficulty in doing
so.[36] But it is quite predictable that the incorporation of the Charter into the Con-

---

[32] ECJ, judgment of 17 December 1998, Case C-185/95 P, *Baustahlgewebe* v. *Commission
of the European Communities* [1998] *ECR* I-8417, paras. 21-22, emphasis added; references to
earlier case law omitted.

[33] Ibid. para 29.

[34] *OJ* (2000) C 364/01. On the Charter, see J.-Y. Carlier and O. de Schutter, *La Charte des
droits fondamentaux de l'Union européenne* (Brussels, Bruylant 2002); W. Heusel, ed., *The Charter
of Fundamental Rights and Constitutional Development in the EU* (Cologne, Bundesanzeiger 2002);
P. Eeckhout, 'The EU Charter of Fundamental Rights and the Federal Question', 39 *CMLRev.*
(2002) pp. 945-994; J.W. Sap, *Het EU-Handvest van de Grondrechten: De opmaat voor de Europese
Grondwet* (Deventer, Kluwer 2003); J. Meyer, ed., *Kommentar zur Charta der Grundrechte der
Europäischen Union* (Baden-Baden, Nomos 2003).

[35] See SEC (2001) 380/3: 'any proposal for legislation and any draft instrument to be adopted
by the Commission will therefore, as part of the normal decision-making procedures, first be
scrutinised for compatibility with the Charter'.

[36] Contrast, for instance, the Opinion of AG Léger with the Court's ruling in ECJ, judgment
of 6 December 2001, C-353/99 P, *Council of the European Union* v. *H. Hautala* [2001] *ECR*
I-9567 and I-9594.

stitutional Treaty will change the *status quo*. Once the EU Constitution enters into force, there is nothing to prevent the ECJ from applying the Charter. Likewise it will be even more difficult than it is today to ignore the Charter in the legislative process.

In her article, Judge Limbach raises a number of interesting questions about the nature of the rights contained in the Charter, and their significance for the ECJ and national courts.[37] I, for my part, will limit myself to raising one question:[38] will the interpretation of the Charter's rights and freedoms be in line with the jurisprudence of the European Court of Human Rights? For sure Article II-112(3) TCE does state that 'corresponding' provisions of the Charter and the European Convention shall have the same meaning. But this may not be sufficient to prevent diverging interpretations in practice. It is interesting in this respect to recall the case of *Emesa*. In that case the ECJ did not deny the applicability of the right to a fair trial, as laid down in Article 6 ECHR. Nor did it express any doubts concerning the position taken by the Strasbourg Court. The rejection of Emesa's request resulted from the fact that the ECJ distinguished its own situation from that of the courts of the Member States. Arguably, this decision was based on an interpretation that is not shared by the Strasbourg Court. It is plain that a similar scenario may occur under the EU Charter.

In all fairness it should be added that *Emesa*, to the extent that it deviates from the Strasbourg case law, is an exceptional case. In recent years the ECJ has been increasingly prepared to refer to the jurisprudence of the European Court of Human Rights. The judgments in *Baustahlgewebe*,[39] *Krombach*[40] and *Österreichischer Rundfunk*[41] may serve as illustrations.

However, applicants may still feel that the ECJ erred when interpreting fundamental rights and, indeed, on occasion it may deliberately decide not to follow the Strasbourg case law.[42] Again, the accession of the EU to the ECHR would be most welcome, since it would allow parties to apply to the Strasbourg Court if they believed that the ECJ misinterpreted rights that are also protected under the European Convention. For that very same reason it would be most unfortunate if,

---

[37] See the article by Jutta Limbach on pp. 373-376 of this book.

[38] See for a number of other questions my contribution to the 'launch issue' of the *European Constitutional Law Review*: 'Human Rights after the Adoption of the EU Constitution: The Best is yet to come', 1 *European Constitutional Law Review* (2005) pp. 27-37.

[39] *Supra* n. 29, para. 29.

[40] ECJ, judgment of 28 March 2000, Case C-7/98, *Krombach* v. *André Bamberski* [2002] *ECR* I-1935, para. 39.

[41] ECJ, judgment of 20 May 2003, Case C-465/00, *Österreichischer Rundfunk* [2003] *ECR* I-4989, paras. 73 et seq.

[42] See, for instance, CFI, judgment of 20 April 1999, Joined Cases T-305/94, T-306/94, T-307/94, T-313/94 to T-316/94, T-318/94, T-325/94, T-328/94, T-329/94 and T-335/94, *Limburgse Vinyl Maatschappij a.o.* v. *Commission* [1999] *ECR* II-931, para. 420:

'The fact that the case-law of the European Court of Human Rights concerning the applicability of Article 8 of the ECHR has evolved since the judgments in *Hoechst*, *Dow Benelux* and *Dow Chemical Ibérica* therefore has no direct impact on the merits of the solutions adopted in those cases'.

on the occasion of EU accession to the Convention, a mechanism were devised to prevent individuals from bringing a complaint before the European Court of Human Rights on the sole ground that their case has already been examined by the ECJ.

## 5.     CATEGORY 4 – LUXEMBOURG REVIEWS COMPLAINTS ABOUT DOMESTIC AUTHORITIES

Perhaps the most interesting and sensitive questions of a constitutional nature are raised in connection to our fourth and last category of cases, where the ECJ examines human rights compliance by the Member States. Are the Member States obliged, *as a matter of EU law,* to respect fundamental rights? Which fundamental rights? Beneath the surface there are other questions: should the EU develop its own human rights policy in order to actively promote human rights in the Member States? Do the EU institutions have a role to play in supervising domestic compliance with human rights standards? Can they take measures, or should they be able to do so, if a Member States violates human rights? Should the capacity of the Union to involve itself with domestic human rights be limited to situations where violations threaten to disturb the internal market? Or should *any* violation of human rights be a concern to the Union? If so, how does this relate to the activities of the Council of Europe, and in what way will this affect the position of the European Court of Human Rights? What is the impact of the introduction of European citizenship, the creation of an 'Area of Freedom, Security and Justice', and the incorporation of the Charter?

Like in the 'first dimension' discussed above, it was the ECJ that initiated this discussion. The Court decided in the late 1980s that the general principles of Community law, including fundamental rights, do not only bind the institutions, but also the Member States where they implement Community law.[43] It later added that the same applies if Member States restrict the common market freedoms (free movement of workers, of services, of goods, of capital): any such restriction should be in conformity with human rights.[44] It later adopted a more general formula, as a result of which the present state of the case law can be summarised as follows:

'(...) according to the Court's case-law, where national legislation falls *within the field of application of Community law* the Court, in a reference for a preliminary ruling, must give the national court all the guidance as to interpretation necessary to enable it to assess the compatibility of that legislation with the fundamental rights whose observance the Court ensures.'[45]

---

[43] ECJ, judgment of 13 July 1989, Case C-5/88, *Wachauf* v. *Bundesamt für Ernährung und Forstwirtschaft* [1989] *ECR* 2609, para. 19.

[44] ECJ, judgment of 18 June 1991, Case C-260/89, *ERT* [1991] *ECR* I-2925, para. 43.

[45] ECJ, judgment of 25 March 2004, Case C-71/02, *Karner* v. *Troostwijk GmbH*, nyr., para. 49, emphasis added.

It is worth observing that it may be easier, and therefore more attractive, for individual applicants to try and get their human rights claim before the ECJ than before the European Court of Human Rights: any court, even at first instance, can refer preliminary questions to the Luxembourg Court, whereas Strasbourg can only be accessed after a lengthy process whereby all domestic remedies are exhausted. The individual may not be bothered too much by the fact that an *authentic* interpretation of the ECHR can only be obtained in Strasbourg: he will happily rely on any 'European' ruling in his favour. And if the ECJ happens to rule against him, he can always exhaust domestic remedies and try his luck in Strasbourg. One might object that this accumulation of applications will lead to very long procedures – but the possibility already exists and is actually being used by individuals.[46] Accordingly, the same case may be subsequently examined by the ECJ and the European Court of Human Rights – which, in turn, raises the issue of possibly diverging interpretations of human rights standards.

That risk was already highlighted by the UK government in the case of *Watson & Belmann* (1976). As to the question whether the ECJ should review if Italian rules relating to the registration of foreigners complied with the ECHR, the UK observed:

> 'Any exercise of overlapping jurisdiction by the institutions established by the Convention and by the Court of Justice of the European Communities could give rise to confusion and conflict. The generalized and somewhat imprecise language of the Convention and of the exceptions to which most of the rights set out in Section I thereof are subject can give rise to questions of construction which fall with the ultimate jurisdiction of the institutions created by the Convention. Similarly, it is for those institutions alone to make a ruling on a national measure which is contrary to the Convention but compatible with Community law.'[47]

Behind this argument was a more general sentiment that the ECJ ought not to review national measures for their compliance with human rights standards. In response to this proposition Advocate General Trabucchi stated that the ECJ could not examine alleged infringements of fundamental rights by a State body 'to the same extent to which it could do so in reviewing the validity of Community acts'.[48] The issue was left undecided in *Watson & Belmann*. But some ten years later the ECJ did assume the power to review domestic measures from a human rights perspective, provided that they are 'within the scope of Community law'. The ECJ never adopted AG Trabucchi's suggestion that the fundamental

---

[46] For an example (apart from *Bosphorus,* etc., mentioned above), compare ECJ, judgment of 16 December 1992, Case C-206/91, *Koua Poirrez* [1992] *ECR* I-6685, with ECtHR, judgment of 30 September 2003, Appl. No. 40892/98, *Koua Poirrez* v. *France.*

[47] ECJ, judgment of 7 July 1976, Case C-118/75, *Watson & Belmann* [1976] *ECR* 1207, at p. 1191. Note that the quote offers support for the concept of 'Member State responsibility' discussed in para. 3 *supra.*

[48] Opinion in Case C-118/75, *supra* n. 47, at p. 1207.

rights test should not be equally demanding when national measures are under review.

The result is a constant flow of cases, usually through the preliminary rulings procedure, where it was alleged that national authorities violate human rights. A well-known example is *Grogan* which involved the Irish prohibition of information about abortion facilities abroad.[49] But many other examples can be added: *Demirel* on the German decision to expel the spouse of a Turkish worker, *Cinétèque* on the French restrictions of the sale of videotapes of films, *Konstantinidis* on the way in which German authorities transcribed a Greek name, *Kremzow* on the consequences for a criminal conviction of the finding that the trial had been unfair – and more recently cases such as *Carpenter* and *Baumbast* on the free movement of persons and their family members, *Österreichischer Rundfunk* and *Lindqvist* on the right to privacy, *Booker Aquaculture* on the absence of financial compensation following the destruction of fish infected by a contagious disease, and *Karner* on the compatibility with the freedom of expression of Austrian restrictions on advertisements.[50]

It is conceivable that these individual cases may be supplemented by infringement procedures (Art. 226 TEC), whereby the Commission prosecutes a Member State for failing to respect fundamental rights that fall within the field of application of Community law.[51] Apart from specific obligations under Community law to respect fundamental rights (such as the prohibition of discrimination of Arts. 12 and 13 TEC), a more general legal basis to take action against domestic violations can be found in Article 7 TEU. This provision allows for measures against Member States if there is a serious and persistent breach of the fundamental values on which the EU is based, notably human rights. The procedure of Article 7 TEU was enhanced by the Treaty of Nice, following the crisis surrounding the participation of the right-wing *FPÖ* in the Austrian government. Action may now be taken if there is 'only' a serious risk that things may go wrong in a Member State. The arrangement of Article 7 TEU returns in Article I-59 TCE.

Back to the ECJ and its role *vis-à-vis* the Member States in the field of fundamental rights. The newest fashion in this branch of jurisprudence is that *Member States* invoke fundamental rights in order to justify policies which might other-

---

[49] ECJ, judgment of 4 October 1991, Case C-159/90, *Grogan* [1991] *ECR* I-4741.

[50] ECJ, judgment of 30 September 1987, Case C-12/86, *Demirel* [1987] *ECR* 1417; judgment of 11 July 1985, Joined Cases 60-61/84, *Cinétèque* [1985] *ECR* 2627; judgment of 30 March 1993, Case C-168/91, *Konstantinidis* [1993] *ECR* I-1191; judgment of 29 May 1997, Case C-299/95, *Kremzow* v. *Republik Österreich* [1997] *ECR* I-2629; judgment of 11 July 2002, Case C-60/00, *Carpenter*, nyr.; judgment of 17 September 2002, Case C-413/99, *Baumbast*, nyr.; judgment of 20 May 2003, Joined Cases C-465/00, C-138/01 and C-139/01, *Österreichischer Rundfunk*, nyr.; judgment of 6 November 2003, Case C-101/01, *Lindqvist*, nyr.; judgment of 10 July 2003, Joined Cases C-20/00 and C-64/00, *Booker Aquaculture a.o.*, nyr.; judgment of 25 March 2004, Case C-71/02, *Karner* v. *Troostwijk GmbH.*, nyr.

[51] On that issue see COM (2003) 606 final, pp. 8 et seq.

wise be deemed incompatible with EU law. An early example was offered by the Dutch 'media cases' where the Netherlands government sought to rely on Article 10 ECHR in order to defend restrictions applying to broadcasting corporations.[52] More recently the Austrian Government successfully invoked its obligations under Article 11 ECHR in order to justify its permission for a demonstration on the public highway which hampered the free movement of goods.[53] And in October 2004 the ECJ accepted that German authorities prohibited the commercial exploitation of 'laser games' on the ground that these games, to the extent that they simulate the killing of human beings, are incompatible with human dignity, as protected by Article 1 of the German Constitution.[54]

What would the adoption of the EU Constitution mean for this category of cases? Two observations may be made. First, it may be expected that the 'human rights profile' of the European Union will be enhanced by the incorporation of the Charter of Fundamental Rights. It is not difficult to predict that as a consequence more human rights cases will be brought before the ECJ[55] and that the same issues may be examined by the ECJ and the European Court of Human Rights – which in turn raises the issue of possibly diverging interpretations of human rights standards. The EU Constitution does not offer a remedy to prevent this. The solution will have to be found in 'good neighbourliness' between Strasbourg and Luxembourg, whilst respecting the independence and different missions the two European Courts.

Second, if one examines the developments in this area so far, the overall trend would seem to be one of growing acceptance that the EU has a legitimate interest in securing adequate respect for human rights in its Member States – either through judicial procedures before the ECJ or through political pressure on the basis of, eventually, Article 7 TEU. Yet the '*Watson & Belmann* sentiments' of the mid-1970s re-emerged when the Charter of Fundamental Rights was negotiated. Article 51(1) of the Charter (Art. II-111(1) TCE) provides:

> 'The provisions of the Charter are addressed to the institutions, bodies, offices and agencies of the Union with due regard to the principle of subsidiarity *and to the Member States only when they are implementing Union law* [emphasis added].'

---

[52] ECJ, judgment of 25 July 1991, Case C-353/89, *Commission* v. *the Netherlands* [1991] *ECR* I-4097. See also ECJ, judgment of 9 October 2001, Case C-377/98, *Netherlands* v. *Parliament and Council* [2001] *ECR* I-7079. On the latter case see esp. the Opinion of AG Jacobs, para. 197:

'...the rights invoked by the Netherlands are indeed fundamental rights, respect for which must be ensured in the Community legal order. The right to human dignity is perhaps the most fundamental right of all, and is now expressed in Article 1 of the Charter of Fundamental Rights [....]. It must be accepted that any Community instrument infringing those rights would be unlawful'.

[53] ECJ, judgment of 12 June 2003, Case C-112/00, *Schmidberger* v. *Republik Österreich* [2003] *ECR* I-5659.

[54] ECJ, judgment of 14 October 2004, Case C-36/02, *Omega Spielhallen*, nyr.

[55] For a very recent example, illustrating the high expectations (of individuals and domestic courts, it would seem), see Case C-328/04, *Vajnai Attila*, pending.

The formula 'when they are implementing Union law' reflects current practice only to a very limited extent. Was it a mistake to which no consequences should be attached, or is it a deliberate attempt to roll back the existing case law of the ECJ? Many of the cases mentioned above did not concern the implementation of EU law, but related to very diverse situations which were considered to fall 'within the field of application of Community law'. It remains to be seen if the ECJ will adapt its jurisprudence and follow the more narrow wording of Article 51(1) Charter (Art. II-111(1) TCE). There is no legal obligation to do so: on the basis of Article I-9(3) TCE the ECJ could simply continue to review national measures 'within the scope of Community law'.

## 6.    SOME FINAL OBSERVATIONS

The EU Constitution provides in Article I-9 for Union accession to the European Convention on Human Rights, whereas Part II incorporates the Charter of Fundamental Rights. The first impression is that this arrangement settles the relationship between the European Court of Justice and the European Court of Human Rights. But our review, in addition to emphasising the importance of EU accession, suggests that there are some outstanding issues. The two European Courts will have to devise ways to minimise the risks of diverging interpretations that might be detrimental to both. In addition, it will be very interesting to see if the ECJ develops in the direction of a human rights court, not only with respect to the institutions but also *vis-à-vis* the Member States, and if so, how this will affect the balance between Strasbourg and Luxembourg. To be continued.

# THE EXPANDING JURISDICTION OF THE EU COURT OF JUSTICE

## Ad Geelhoed[*]

## 1. INTRODUCTION

Since the entry into force of the EEC Treaty in 1958, the organisation of the Community judiciary has twice been the subject of revision at Treaty level. The Single European Act of 1986 introduced the possibility of attaching a Court of First Instance (CFI) to the European Court of Justice (ECJ). In 1988 this resulted in the establishment of such a court with jurisdiction limited mainly to hearing and determining direct actions brought by natural and legal persons. The rapid increase in the workload of both the Court of Justice and the Court of First Instance in the 1990s led to the considerably more drastic adaptation by the Treaty of Nice. The main changes were the following:

- the Court of First Instance acquired competence, in principle, to hear at first instance all direct actions, including those brought by Member States or institutions;

- the possibility was created to give the CFI jurisdiction to deliver preliminary rulings, in specific areas laid down by the Statute;

- it was made possible to provide the CFI with jurisdiction for other classes of actions or proceedings;

- the possibility to create judicial panels to hear and determine at first instance certain classes of actions or proceedings brought in specific areas.

Two important characteristics of the changes introduced by the Treaty of Nice are that they constitute the first step in the development from a Community jurisdiction towards a Community judicial system and, linked to this, that they provide for a remarkable degree of flexibility in the implementation of the Treaty provisions concerned. Much has been left to further regulation in either the Statute of the Court of Justice or decisions to be taken by the Council of Ministers.

---

[*] First Advocate General at the Court of Justice.

*D. Curtin, A.E. Kellermann and S. Blockmans, eds., The EU Constitution: The Best Way Forward?*
© 2005, *T.M.C. Asser Instituut, The Hague.*

I will refrain, in this context, from commenting on the – important – adaptations to the Community system of judicial control introduced by the Treaty of Nice. Many others have already done this in an excellent manner before me. The central question which I will discuss is whether the post-Nice Community judicial system – disregarding the need for a few small adaptations – is equipped to meet the growing demand for legal protection in a European Union organised on the basis of the Constitutional Treaty, signed on 29 October 2004. As will be explained in more detail below, this not only concerns the quantitative growth of the demand for legal protection in an ever growing European Union which is, *inter alia*, characterised by creeping 'juridification' of internal relationships within the Union. It also relates to changes in the qualitative composition of that demand. These changes are the result of fundamental decisions taken in the revision of the Treaty, such as the decision to fully 'communitarise' the third pillar. Though less conspicuous, the so-called second and third degree effects of the integration process itself may prove to be equally significant in the longer term. These may generate further demands in respect of the organisation of the implementation and application of Community law, and, as time goes by, in respect of the Community judicial system, on the other hand.

I will first deal in more detail with the factors which may influence the quantitative growth of the demand for legal protection within the European Union. Next, I will discuss the – considerable – changes in the qualitative composition of that demand. On this basis, I will then attempt to provide an answer to the question whether the Treaty of Nice offers sufficient possibilities for the development of a judicial system which can accommodate the growing and changing demand for legal protection, on the one hand, and which provides adequate guarantees for maintaining the quality and unity of judicial decisions within the Community.

## 2.    THE GROWTH IN THE DEMAND FOR LEGAL PROTECTION

Statements on the quantitative growth in the demand for legal protection within the Union can only be speculative. However, a number of factors may be identified which are relevant to that development.

### 2.1    The growing Size of the Union

This factor may be self-evident, but it is impossible to establish, even approximately, a precise relationship between the growth of the Union in terms of inhabitants and the growth in the demand for legal protection by the Community Courts. The recent experiences with the enlargement of the Union following the accession of Finland, Austria and Sweden are illustrative in this respect. Although these three Member States have a long tradition of adhering to the rule of law, all of which have a highly developed judicial system, the number of cases referred by national courts for a preliminary ruling by the Court of Justice differs strongly. Various explanations are offered for this, each of which may give a partial indication of the underlying reasons for these striking differences, but which, taken together, lead to the inevitable conclusion that making more precise statements on the relationship between the enlargement of the Union and the growth in the demand for legal protection in the Community remains a difficult matter: legal traditions which are more geared towards solving legal conflicts through mediation rather than litigation; the degree to which economic relations have become 'juridified'; a judicial organisation with few or with many specialised courts; national judges' knowledge of Community law and their preparedness to recognise the Community law aspects of the cases before them and their consequences, etc.

Once national courts have crossed the threshold of unfamiliarity with and the uncertainty of applying Community law, it might be possible, very cautiously, to establish a correlation between the level of prosperity in the Member States and the demand for legal protection at Community level. The growth of prosperity tends to lead to both the 'juridification' of economic relations and an increase in the intensity of cross-boundary transactions. In both cases the relevance of Community law in the national society also increases.

Focusing more on the recent, more sizable enlargement of the Union and in the light of the foregoing, a spasmodic increase in the number of cases coming to the ECJ and the CFI is not as such to be expected. It is more likely that these numbers will increase gradually following an initial delay.

## 2.2    Changes in the Scope of the Union's Powers

Since the Single European Act, the scope of the powers of the European Union has frequently been extended, sometimes quite drastically. The great majority of the extension of powers was in the field of so-called policy integration, the most important component of which is, by far, the Economic and Monetary Union. To the extent that these powers are restricted to coordination or to supplementing action taken by the Member States, measures taken pursuant to them up until now have not unduly burdened the Community courts. As these powers are primarily aimed at achieving greater coordination between the Union and the Member States and are strongly discretionary in character, it is unlikely that they will give rise to litigation. The situation is different for new powers, which further define the exercise of rights and duties of citizens and enterprises within the Union. Examples of this may be found in the area of social policy (following Maastricht and Amsterdam) and environmental policy (ever since the Single European Act). Secondary legislation in these fields of competence has indeed led to a significant increase in the workload of the Court of Justice. This is also likely to be the case in respect of the interpretation and application of the voluminous secondary legislation (to be) based on Articles III-257 to III-277 TCE on the area of freedom, security and justice. Whether and to what extent this will also be the case in respect of the Charter of Fundamental Rights contained in Part II of that Treaty remains to be seen and is more difficult to predict. Probably, questions on the validity, interpretation and application of acts of the Union will be presented from the perspective of basic rights. As a result of this, the Court of Justice's role as a constitutional court will be more highlighted, in a quantitative sense as well.

The distribution and division of powers between the Union and the Member States has been regulated in a sharper and more comprehensive manner in Articles I-9 to I-17 TCE than is currently the case in the Treaty on the European Union. This explicit and detailed constitutionalisation of the division of powers within the Union, which is also a politically sensitive issue within the Member States, will, I expect, give rise to more case law than at present in a more heterogeneous Union. The remarkable increase, since the *Tobacco Advertising* case,[1] in the number of cases on questions of competence, would seem to be a prelude to such a development.

## 2.3    Legislative Activity in the Union

The demand for legal protection is strongly determined by the legislative activity of the Union. Good examples of secondary legislation which resulted in a significant increase in cases coming before the Community courts are provided by Directive 89/104[2] on the harmonisation of trade mark law and Regulation 40/94[3] on the Community trade mark. The extensive activity of the Union legislature in the field of intellectual property in a wider sense will certainly lead to the broadening of the stream of direct actions and preliminary references. As a result both the Court of Justice and the Court of First Instance will be confronted with noticeable problems of capacity.

It is more difficult to predict the effects of the decentralisation in the application and enforcement of Community competition law envisaged by Regulation 1/2003[4] on the cooperation between the Court of Justice and the national courts in the context of the preliminary reference procedure. However, it would seem to me safe to accept that these effects will prove to be significant.

On the whole, it is not easy to predict which impact the secondary legislation of the Union will have on the demand for legal protection by the Community courts. Thus, Directive 85/374[5] on product liability, which is extremely broad in scope *ratione personae*, potentially covering every consumer, has led to comparatively little case law. In contrast, there is a good deal of case law on Directive 77/187[6] on the safeguarding of employees' rights in the event of transfer of

---

[1] ECJ, judgment of 5 October 2000, Case C-74/99, *Imperial Tobacco Ltd and Others* [2000] *ECR* I-8599.

[2] *OJ* (1989) L 040/1-7.

[3] *OJ* (1994) L 011/1-36.

[4] *OJ* (2003) L 001/1-25.

[5] *OJ* (1985) L 210/29-33.

[6] *OJ* (1977) L 061/26-28.

undertakings, although it is clearly more limited in scope as far as the group of interested persons is concerned. It would be worthwhile to analyse more systematically the effects of the content and scope of Community secondary legislation on the demand for legal protection which it generates.

In general, the structure of the Community legal order, which requires the involvement of the competent national – legislative, executive and judicial – authorities for the implementation, application and enforcement of Community measures, rather complicates the carrying out of this analysis. The development of the Court's case law on the Sixth VAT Directive[7] over the years is illustrative of how in the vertically structured Community legal order the demand for legal protection arises with a certain delay. Secondary Union legislation does not always lead to an increase in cases being brought before the national and Community courts. The significant adaptations to both the system of the common agricultural policy and the legal instruments used for its implementation since the beginning of the 1990s have had as a – welcome – side-effect that the volume of case law on agricultural matters is now more in proportion with its economic significance. Perhaps a more general conclusion may be drawn from this observation: the more Community legislation interferes, both in depth and in detail, with the economic activities of market participants, the more it will generate a disproportionate demand for legal protection.

## 2.4  Judicial Activity in the Union

Every supply creates its own demand. This basic economic truth also applies to the fundamental role which the Court of Justice has played in, e.g., defining the autonomous character of the Community legal order and in its systematic and extensive interpretation of the basic Treaty provisions on the four freedoms. It is quite easy to infer from the case law that a quantitative correlation exists between the 'landmark' judgments and the series of subsequent judgments in which the ECJ elaborates upon and further defines the perspectives which it has opened up. Out of the many rather obvious examples I would refer only to the sometimes searching evolution of the case law from *Dassonville*[8] to *Keck and Mithouard*.[9] This may be described as an Odyssey which, together with *Keck*, has not yet found its Ithaca, although sometimes the opposite is suggested, or hoped for.

A more recent example is the exploration, started with *Baumbast*,[10] of the essence or core of the right of residence for EU citizens within the territory of the Member States laid down in Article 18(1) TEC. The proven lure of such a land-

---

[7] *OJ* (1977) L 145, pp. 1-32.

[8] ECJ, judgment of 11 July 1974, Case C-8/74, *Dassonville* [1974] *ECR* 837.

[9] ECJ, judgment of 24 November 1993, joined Cases C-267/91 and C-268/91, *Keck and Mithouard* [1993] *ECR* I-6097.

[10] ECJ, judgment of 17 September 2002, Case C-413/99, *Baumbast and R* [2002] *ECR* I-7091.

mark judgment is apparent from cases such as *Chen*[11] and *Bidar*[12] which are still pending before the Court.

Again, judgments such as *Decker*[13] and *Kohll*[14] may be regarded as jurisprudential comets which carry many other judgments in their trails.

The interpretation of secondary Community legislation also regularly leads to a substantial sequel in the case law. A good example of this is provided by Directive 77/187,[15] which was mentioned earlier. The broad interpretation given by the Court of Justice to the concept 'transfer of undertakings' resulted in ever more questions being referred to the Court by national courts based on factual situations which differed in certain respects. Other examples of this phenomenon can easily be provided.

Finally, the extent to which the assistance of the Court of Justice is invoked is influenced in a structural manner by the importance which the Court attaches to the preliminary reference procedure of Article 234 TEC in guarding unity and equality in the interpretation and application of Community law. Despite all criticism, the Court has not up until now diluted the wine it served in the *Cilfit*[16] judgment. It is not unthinkable that this somewhat timorous attitude of the Court, can be explained by the fact that with each subsequent round of enlargement of the Union, national courts in the new Member States had (and still have) to become acquainted with Community law. Although it may be understandable that the Court wishes the learning curve of the judicial bodies in newly acceded Member States to be as steep as possible, this entails 'more advanced' courts in the 'old' Member States unnecessarily contributing to the heavy workload of the Court by their preliminary references.

## 2.5    Conclusion

This fleeting exploration leads to the inevitable conclusion that the demands on the Community courts will grow significantly in the medium and longer term, i.e., between five and ten years. This should be taken into account in designing the future judicial architecture of the Union. Mere incremental adaptations may provide some alleviation in the short term, but they cannot provide a lasting solution to this problem.

---

[11] ECJ, judgment of 19 October 2004, Case C-200/02, *Zhu and Chen*, nyr.

[12] ECJ, Case C-209/03, *Bidar*, pending.

[13] ECJ, judgment of 28 April 1998, Case C-120/95, *Decker* v. *Caisse de maladie des employés privés* [1998] *ECR* I-1831.

[14] ECJ, judgment of 28 April 1998, Case C-158/96, *Kohll* v. *Union des caisses de maladie* [1998] *ECR* I-1931.

[15] See *supra* n. 6.

[16] ECJ, judgment of 6 October 1982, Case C-283/81, *Cilfit* v. *Ministero della Sanità* [1982] *ECR* 3415.

3. QUALITATIVE CHANGE IN THE DEMAND FOR LEGAL
   PROTECTION

Until recently substantive Community law was mainly public economic law
(*droit public économique, Wirtschaftsrecht*), which was aimed at the establishment and proper functioning of the internal market and taking into account qualitative conditions based on public interest. The implementation of the legal
provisions adopted for that purpose – for the greater part Union legislation transposed into national law by national legislatures – is entrusted to the competent
national authorities who operate under the judicial supervision of the national
courts. The unity required at the level of the Union in the interpretation and application of Union law is ensured by the cooperation between the Court of Justice and the national courts in the context of the preliminary reference procedure
of Article 234 TEC. This procedure occupies a central position in the judicial
structure of the Union. In considering the, in retrospect, surprising success of the
preliminary reference procedure as the centrepiece of the judicial structure
within the Union, it is often overlooked that this procedure was potentially successful from the outset due to the economic-instrumental character of the original Community legislation and the decentralised implementation and application
of these rules. In part, it replaced comparable national economic legislation, in
part it imposed restrictions on the national legislature in shaping its policy instruments for conditioning and shaping market processes. In this context the preliminary reference procedure was often regarded as an annoying incident in legal
proceedings, particularly by national administrative authorities. However, as
long as the preliminary reference procedure did not take up more time than was
reasonable, it was accepted as being necessary. The interests of legal unity and
equality within the internal market were considered as outweighing the complications which the results of that procedure could have for national economic
policy and law. In public economic law which is characterised not so much by
ethical preferences, but by choices of a more instrumental nature, the supremacy
of substantive Community law, as interpreted by the Court of Justice, was accepted relatively easily, even where this had significant choices for existing national legislation and national policies based thereon. Again, looking back, it is
fascinating to observe that the Court's case law in the 1970s under the preliminary reference procedure on the free movement of goods and services and the
freedom of establishment met with such little resistance. This is even more so as,
in that period in particular, the liberal tendency of this case law was diametri-
cally opposed to the national economic policies of the Member States which
were strongly focused on the national economic context.

Compared to the first 35 years of its existence as the European Economic
Community, the European Union in the past 15 years has undergone three fundamental changes. Firstly, as a result of the establishment of the EMU, in addition
to market integration, policy integration – in the form of the coordination of economic and budgetary policy – has become much more important. The institutional consequences of this have still not been sufficiently thought out and the

Constitutional Treaty does not remedy this either. As this enhanced area of policy integration has not had any direct consequences for the demand for legal protection, I will not deal with it any further in this context.

Secondly, the structure of competences of the Union will change fundamentally following the complete absorption of the subjects which previously fell within the ambit of the third pillar. Both the 'communitarisation' of national migration policy and law and the competence to strengthen and deepen cooperation in the field of criminal law affect areas which are considered as belonging to the heart of the national legal order. On the one hand, these areas are frequently characterised by the expression of nationally determined ethical and political preferences. On the other hand, the exercise of public powers in these areas is subject to the observance of a closely-knit framework of national and supranational fundamental rights. And rightly so, as the exercise of public powers in the fields of migration and criminal law may have far-reaching consequences for the citizens concerned. The dynamics of the integration process, however, has resulted in these powers, which were closely guarded for a long time by the Member States, having become less effective. That is immediately clear in the case of migration law, where the expansion of the *internal* free movement of persons, as a result, in part, of the case law of the Court of Justice, has led to the necessity of creating homogenous substantive and procedural rules for *external* free movement of persons in order to prevent undesirable shifts in cross-boundary movements. The authors of the Schengen Agreement and the implementation agreements already recognised this fact. The connection between the two aspects of free movement is also acknowledged in the recent case law of the Court of Justice.[17]

As regards substantive and procedural criminal law in general, the need for more unity is clearly less apparent. As far as the great majority of criminal offences are concerned, the effectiveness required of national criminal law can be ensured by improving the efficiency of the traditional forms of cooperation between national justice authorities. An exception obviously has to be made for those types of criminal behaviour which are directly linked with the increasing intensity of cross-boundary movements within the Union.

This all leads to the conclusion that national migration law, for the greater part, will soon have to be 'communitarised', whereas Union legislation will come to affect national practice in respect of certain types of crime. Both these developments will influence the demand for legal protection in a qualitative sense: where legal certainty is at issue in cases involving the status of persons or the legality of using certain coercive measures, such as imprisonment, the speed with which a final decision is rendered co-determines the quality of the administration of justice.

---

[17] ECJ, judgment of 23 September 2003, Case C-109/01, *Akrich* v. *Secretary of State for the Home Department* [2003] *ECR* I-9607.

Thirdly, the growing dynamism of cross-border movement within the Union may call into question the self-evident nature of responsibility for the application of Union law being entrusted to the national authorities. Particularly in situations in which intensive cooperation between national authorities is a precondition for an adequate application of the rules concerned and where differences in the application of legislation could have serious economic and social repercussions, the Union cannot restrict its role to supervision at a distance. This observation, firstly, applies to monitoring and administrating cross-border movements with third countries, such as customs and border controls. But for how long will the present decentralisation of prudential supervision of financial services remain compatible with the factual integration of capital markets within the EMU? Be that as it may, the great social risks resulting from distortions in the application of Union legislation within the completed internal market, must necessarily lead to greater homogencity in a unitary structure for applying Union legislation. The sharp distinction between Community legislation, on the one hand, and national application, on the other, will fade away. The inevitable question which then arises is whether it is so obvious to leave the task of ensuring legal protection in respect of decisions taken in the context of such a *de facto* 'communitarised' application practice to the national courts. Is it not more logical in such a situation to create direct access to the Union courts?

The last two of the three qualitative changes in Union law referred to above raise the issue of the tenability of the preliminary reference procedure itself. In the one situation, the question is whether this procedure, as a step in national legal proceedings, is compatible with the procedural efficiency required in criminal and migration cases. In the other situation, it may degenerate to a somewhat artificial detour in the chain of legislation and implementation which has become ever more 'communitarised'. Both changes will be felt particularly in a field such as migration law in which adequate legal protection requires cases to be dealt with expeditiously and in which both legislation and application will become Community matters. In view of the empirical fact that this field of law in particular is characterised by a relatively large demand for legal protection, the question as to the tenability of the preliminary reference procedure will be most acute.

## 4.    THE JUDICIAL ARCHITECTURE OF THE UNION

In view of the expected continuation of the growth for legal protection and of the qualitative changes of that demand, various scenarios may be envisaged in respect of the possible developments.

### 4.1    The Internal Efficiency of the Courts

In the short term, covering a time span of the next five to ten years, it may be expected that the possibilities created by the Treaty of Nice will be used to the

full. This can be done in various ways, each of which may result in the extension
of the capacity of the centralised dual structure of the Court of Justice and the
Court of First Instance.

The first method consists of adopting measures to improve the internal effi-
ciency of the institution. These include measures such as shortening the reports
for the hearing, being selective about the cases in which the Advocate General
presents an Opinion (now possible under Art. 20(5) of the Statute of the Court of
Justice); using as much as possible the possibility under Article 104(3) of the
Rules of Procedure to rule on preliminary references by reasoned order; drafting
Opinions in so-called 'pivotal' languages (French, German, English, Spanish and
Italian) and translating only the most relevant sections of the orders referring
preliminary questions. These measures, together with sharper monitoring of internal deadlines, may result in a certain growth in the Court's capacity for dealing with cases, which should become visible in the requisite shortening of the
time needed to rule on cases. However, if the volume of cases coming to the
Court continues to increase, these gains in capacity will be used up relatively
quickly.

The second group of possible measures concerns the reallocation of direct actions and preliminary references between the Court of Justice and the Court of
First Instance. This possibility, which was created by the Treaty of Nice, has already been used in that the CFI has been empowered to hear direct actions
against decisions of the Commission, the Court of Auditors, the European Central Bank and independent Union bodies, subject to a right of appeal to the Court
of Justice on points of law only. It should be pointed out, however, that although
this may initially relieve the Court of Justice of some of its workload, it obviously considerably contributes to an increase of that of the CFI. If, as may be
expected, appeals are lodged in a fairly large proportion of the cases decided at
first instance, this reallocation will ultimately culminate in an increase of the
Court of Justice as a whole! Given the present sizeable workload of the CFI, the
reallocation will have to be accompanied by making rigorous use of the possibility opened up by the Treaty of Nice to attach judicial panels to the CFI in certain
specific areas (Art. 220(2) TEC). One such specific area might be trade mark
law, or more generally, intellectual property law. Article 224 TEC also offers a
certain amount of organisational elasticity by permitting more than one judge per
Member State to be appointed to the CFI. Up until now, there has been a certain
reticence in using the possibility created by Article 225(3) TEC to grant the CFI
jurisdiction to hear and determine questions referred for a preliminary ruling in
certain areas. This reticence is based, on the one hand, on the empirical fact that
questions of principle relating to the Community legal order may also arise in
more technical cases on, e.g., Regulation 1408/71[18] on social security or the
Sixth VAT Directive and, on the other hand, on the fact that there are undeniable
substantive links between the various fields of Union law.

---

[18] Consolated version *OJ* (1997) L 28, pp. 1-54.

My personal view is that these objections will have to be set against the greater risks posed to the quality of the Community order by congestion within the Court. In that case it should be considered whether to empower the CFI to hear certain categories of preliminary references, particularly in fields in which the CFI already has jurisdiction to hear appeals from judicial panels.

However, although these measures – and other measures which could be made possible by a few adaptations to the Statute and the Rules of Procedure – are absolutely necessary, in due course they will prove to be insufficient to solve the underlying problem. The significant activity, at present, of the Union legislature in the areas of migration law and cooperation in the field of criminal law, will most probably lead, following a certain delay, to a significant rise in the number of requests for preliminary rulings. Once Article III-369 TCE has entered into force, the Court will be obliged to rule on these questions 'with the minimum of delay'. Presuming that the Court is already completely burdened, applying this provision will have crowding out effects, which will become visible in the extension of the time needed to rule on preliminary references in other cases. If this indeed proves to be the case, the question as to the judicial architecture of the Union will have to be raised once again.

## 4.2    The Judicial Architecture of the Future: Some Possible Models

In the longer term, both the size and the composition of the demand for legal protection within the European Union will cause the framework created by the Treaty of Nice to burst. Depending on the activism of the Union legislature and the future additional enlargements of the Union, that horizon may be closer or further away. However, that uncertainty forces us to think about the judicial architecture within the Union post-Nice now. On the whole there are four possible models for that architecture:

– a model which builds upon the Nice model, the traditional centralised model with increased differentiation by area of law;

– a model which retains the main features of the present system, but which provides for a more or less extensive degree of territorial decentralisation in certain fields of Union law;

– a model which preserves the main features of the present system in respect of the areas of law which traditionally fell within the ambit of the first pillar and in respect of the Court's constitutional role, but which provides for territorially decentralised specialist Union courts in areas where it may be expected that the implementation and application stage will become increasingly 'communitarised'; such decentralised Union courts would deal with actions against decisions of the administrative authorities applying Union law at first instance, subject to review by the CFI;

– a more radical variant of the previous one was presented by the current Minister of Justice of the Netherlands, J.P.H. Donner: building upon the

idea of establishing a Community service charged with the application of
migration and customs law and the idea of creating Union criminal law
restricted to a number of types of criminal offences with concomitant
police and justice infrastructure, such a system of decentralised Union
courts could constitute the foundation of a judicial organisation in the
Union modelled on the American system of federal jurisdiction.

Objections of a practical, legal and political nature may be raised against each of
these models. The most important objection against the first model is that it does
not really offer a solution to the problems resulting from the expected qualitative
shift in the demand for legal protection. As a side remark: for how long will it be
possible to keep intact the centralisation in Luxembourg of the administration of
justice within the Union in *all* cases in a European Union which one day may
stretch from Trabzon to Oporto?

The main objection against the second model, which provides for a certain
degree of decentralisation – restricted to certain areas of law – is that it entails
risks for the unity of law within the Union. This is also the main reason why the
Court of Justice in the past has rejected this idea. However, in addition, it does
not really resolve the intrinsic flaws which the preliminary reference procedure
has in certain fields.

The third model may be criticised as it is based on the presumption that the
implementation and application of parts of the Union law would be transferred to
Community level. The Member States explicitly were not (yet) prepared to take
this step in the framework of the Constitutional Treaty. The same applies *a fortiori* to the fourth model.

It would be more fruitful, in my view, to start with the question of what each
model offers in providing a structural solution to the problems with which the
Court of Justice is going to be faced in the light of foreseeable future developments in law and policy. Viewed from that perspective, the third model would
appear to be the most attractive. It is flexible from the organisational point of
view (and therefore easily adaptable to the demand for legal protection); it provides a solution for the flaws of the preliminary reference procedure in the field
of migration law (and criminal law); it offers sufficient guarantees for ensuring
legal unity and it leaves enough room to the Court to enable it to fulfil its fundamental role as a constitutional court.

# CONSTITUTIONALIZING EFFECTIVE REMEDIES: TOO MUCH ON EU COURTS, TOO LITTLE ON NATIONAL COURTS

## Arjen W.H. Meij[*]

## 1.    INTRODUCTION

The Constitutional Treaty[1] does not provide major changes to the EU judicial system as compared to the post-Nice situation. Even so, the return to a single system following the abandonment of the pillar structure, exceptions being limited to the CFSP area and police actions, may be considered an important step. The twofold structure divided between the EU courts, on the one hand, and the national courts, on the other, linked by the preliminary ruling mechanism, is retained.

The court system naturally follows the implementing structure of the EU legal order. In this regard the Constitutional Treaty does not make fundamental choices modifying the present system to any degree, the present system being largely based on the implementation of EC law by the national administrative and enforcement authorities as well as the national courts. Lately, however, opposing tendencies may be observed in this respect. To the extent that Regulation 1/2003 refers decision making on exemptions from the cartel prohibition under the present Article 81(3), TEC primarily to the private parties concerned and secondarily to the national cartel authorities, it decentralizes judicial protection in competition cases to the national courts. By contrast, the creation of a single Community trade mark to be registered by one central Office (for harmonization in the internal market) gives rise to substantial litigation concentrated in the Community courts. Similarly, centralisation of several procedures for authorizing the marketing of dangerous substances, such as in medicaments, foodstuff additives and pesticides, gives rise to a shift of litigation from the national courts to the Community courts. Even if, short of treaty guidance, decisions on centralizing or decentralizing the implementation of common policies appear to be

---

[*] Judge, Court of First Instance of the European Union. The opinions expressed are personal.
[1] Treaty establishing a Constitution for Europe, also referred to as TCE, doc. CIG 87/2/04 REV 2, signed in Rome, 29 October 2004.

*D. Curtin, A.E. Kellermann and S. Blockmans, eds., The EU Constitution: The Best Way Forward?*

taken pretty much on an *ad hoc* basis, their consequences in terms of the organization of the administration of justice should not be underestimated.

In line with the principle henceforth designated as the 'conferral' of competences, as explicitly maintained in Article I-11 TCE, the general characteristic of the court system remains that the EU courts exercise specifically conferred jurisdiction as provided by the Constitutional Treaty, and the national courts have jurisdiction in all remaining litigation, in particular in cases concerning the application of Union law between private parties and as against Member States' authorities. Until recently, direct jurisdiction concerning private litigants, as opposed to indirect jurisdiction resulting from preliminary references, was conferred on the EU courts in direct actions against the Community institutions and pursuant to the odd arbitration clause concluded under Article 238 TEC (Art. III-374 TCE). A striking new development in this respect is provided by Article 229A TEC, introduced by the Treaty of Nice and reposited in Article III-364 TCE, in that it allows the EU courts to be given direct jurisdiction concerning Community industrial property rights in cases between private parties. Such conferral of jurisdiction has been proposed, alongside the creation of a specialised court under Article 225A TEC (Art. III-359 TCE), for the Community patent which has, for some time now, been on the verge of being adopted. It may largely depend on the number of cases instigated whether administering justice as between private parties in a multilinguistic international setting will provide satisfactory results.

## 2.    EFFECTIVE REMEDIES

The Constitutional Treaty seems to acknowledge, slightly more so than the existing treaties hitherto, the twofold structure of the judicial system, divided as it is between the EU courts, on the one hand, and the national courts, on the other. In its first paragraph Article I-29 TCE refers to the Court of Justice of the EU, which properly includes the Court of Justice as the supreme branch of the institution, and a General Court intriguingly resembling the present Court of First Instance and specialised courts. In rather familiar wording these EU courts are entrusted with the task of ensuring that the law is observed in the interpretation and application of the Constitution. In a second phrase the same paragraph makes an indirect reference to the national courts of the Member States, without, however, explicitly entrusting them with a similar task. Instead, this second phrase addresses itself to the Member States, instructing them to 'provide remedies sufficient to ensure effective legal protection in the fields covered by Union law', much in the vein of a similar phrase used by the ECJ in the *UPA* case[2] in order to underline the complementary character of remedies in national

---

[2] ECJ, judgment of 25 July 2002, Case C-50/00 P, *Unión de Pequeños Agricultores* v. *Council and Commission* [2002] *ECR* I-6677, para. 41.

courts and those in the EU courts. Plainly in the nature of international law, just as the EC Treaty, the Constitutional Treaty addresses only the Member States as such, not a particular branch of their constitutional system such as the courts.[3] Consequently, the legal basis of the national courts' role in applying Union law must continue to be inferred from the Member States' general duty to ensure the fulfilment of their obligations under Union law, as reappears in Article I-5(2), together with the loyalty principle.

The instruction directed to the Member States to provide effective legal protection coincides with the right to an effective remedy as provided by the integrated Charter in Article II-107 TCE. The latter provision reflects a general principle of Union law enshrined in the Court's case law. The explanation appended to this provision refers in particular to the *Johnston*[4] and *Heylens*[5] case law. This principle being of a general nature, it supposedly concerns both levels of jurisdiction, in the EU courts and the national courts. Coupled with the idea of effective legal protection in Article I-29 TCE, it would appear to have a broader scope than only access to a court and to extend to the whole of the Court's case law on the principle of effectiveness. It may then serve as a background for two observations on the judicial system as provided in the Constitutional Treaty, a first to the effect that the Treaty contains too much as regards the EU courts and a second emphasizing that it purports too little as regards national courts.

## 3.    TOO MUCH DETAIL ON DIRECT ACTIONS

If the Constitutional Treaty does not change much of the judicial system as such, neither does it demonstrate evidence of any reflection upon how it should be arranged. Albeit in a large variety of ways, constitutions usually regulate such fundamental issues as the position and structure of the courts in the institutional system they create, general access, procedural principles, the position of the judges and eventually fundamental rights. Understandable as it may be that the EC Treaty at the time also arranged the forms of action, conditions of admissibility, grounds of appeal, powers of judgment and many other elements of procedure and organization, one may wonder whether it is still appropriate to determine all such modalities on a constitutional level. Even if modifying the Statute of the Court and the Rules of Procedure has become slightly less cumbersome since the Treaty of Nice, experience under the EC Treaty has shown a degree of rigidity, most recently in the *UPA* judgment already referred to, which may not quite be in line with the needs of legal practice or, for that matter, of present society. Some considerations may illustrate this need for some degree of flexibility.

---

[3] Note, however, the role conferred on national parliaments by Art. I-11 TCE, para. 3 and the related protocol, in respect of compliance with the principle of subsidiarity.

[4] ECJ, judgment of 15 May 1986, Case C-222/84, *Johnston* [1986] *ECR* 1651.

[5] ECJ, judgment of 15 October 1987, Case C-222/86, *Heylens and Others* [1987] *ECR* 4097.

Strikingly, the explanation appended to Article II-107 TCE sets out that the inclusion of the right to an effective remedy in the 'charter' part of the Constitutional Treaty is not intended to change the system of judicial review, particularly the rules relating to admissibility for direct actions, except for certain amendments, such as the provision of a right of appeal against regulatory acts in Article III-365(4) TCE. This explanatory comment could hardly express more eloquently the assumption it implies that the principle of effectiveness may indeed require a further adaptation of the system. It is perhaps an understatement to suggest that the *Plaumann*[6] formula for the admissibility of actions for annulment has more or less outlived itself, in that it seems to require disproportionate amounts of time and effort from counsel and judges equally and continues in its application to give rise to frequent criticism. Who would want to work another 40 years with the *Plaumann* criterion? It would, however, appear that the accommodating effort, on account of the *Jego Quéré/UPA* saga, to provide in the equivalent provision of Article 230 TEC (Art. III-365 TCE) an action for annulment open to private applicants 'against a regulatory act which is of direct concern to him or her and does not entail implementing measures', only solves half the problem and may give rise to fresh questions.[7] A simple and balanced solution, more closely in line with approaches functioning satisfactorily on national courts' level, would be to strike the criterion of individual concern from the fourth paragraph of Article 230 TEC. As a matter of fact, the condition of direct concern, properly interpreted and applied, may appropriately fulfil the useful parts of the individualitycriterion, but do away with its rigidity. This might allow for a limited broadening of the present *Plaumann* standard, including a restrictive approach towards acts of a general nature, without opening the floodgates to waves of unnecessary actions, as is often feared. The pending proposal for a Council regulation implementing the Aarhus Convention[8] on Community level in a way also confirms the need for more flexibility. This UN convention requires, more specifically, access to justice in environmental matters, for members of the public having a sufficient interest, providing adequate and effective remedies. As the present criteria under Article 230 TEC do not allow for a right of access to justice in environmental matters for every natural and legal person, the proposal limits legal standing to certain environmental organisations at the European level, the so-called 'qualified entities'. Apart from the question whether Article 230 TEC allows secondary legislation to fill in its admissibility requirements, the proposal thus purports to implement the Aarhus Convention in a rather artificial manner.

---

[6] ECJ, judgment of 15 July 1963, Case C-25/62, *Plaumann* v. *Commission* [1963] *ECR* 116.

[7] See R. Barents, 'The Court of Justice in the Draft Constitution', 11 *Maastricht Journal of European and Comparative Law* (2004) pp. 130 et seq.

[8] 'Proposal for a regulation of the European Parliament and of the Council on the application of the provisions of the Aarhus Convention on Access to Information, Public Participation in Decisionmaking and Access to Justice in Environmental Matters to EC Institutions and Bodies', *COM* (2003) 622 (final).

Admittedly, as the jurisdiction of the EU courts is based on the principle of specific attribution of powers, the EU Constitution needs to provide, in broad terms, the categories of cases which they may hear, preferably by reference to parties rather than acts or actions, much in the vein of the third paragraph of Article I-29 TCE. This provision might indeed, under c), have said 'rule in other cases provided for in a European Law'. Legislators are perfectly able to draft a proper system of judicial protection, implementing fundamental provisions to that effect in a constitution. Even if present developments in the need for legal protection may point to a gradual shift from objective review of the legality of Community acts to more emphasis on the protection of subjective rights as against EU institutions, this brief comment does not purport to contend that the present system should immediately be abandoned. The permanent EU legislator may, however, be slightly more sensitive to the need for change and adaptation than incidental drafters of treaty texts.

## 4.  TOO LITTLE ON NATIONAL COURTS

On the other hand, those who have framed the Constitutional Treaty have missed a historical opportunity to provide an explicit legal basis for the role of national courts in the application of Union law. In the course of preparations for the Treaty of Nice a suggestion to that effect, to be inserted in Article 234 TEC, was made by the Due report,[9] prepared at the time for the Commission, but it was not taken up by the IGC on that occasion. As mentioned above, no tradition has so far developed for EU Treaty texts to address a particular branch of government instead of the Member States as such. Article I-5(1) TCE expressly pledges respect for the national identities inherent in the Member States' fundamental political and constitutional structures. And if the Court in its preliminary rulings frequently addresses the national courts directly, in particular with regard to their obligation to provide effective legal protection to individuals under EC law, it may have limited, but never given up the principle of the institutional autonomy of the Member States.

However, laying down in the Constitutional Treaty the national courts' mandate to apply and properly give effect to Union law within the sphere of their jurisdiction does not, in my view, in any way infringe upon national institutional autonomy as regards the national court system. Express recognition on the Union constitutional level of the national courts' duty to apply and give effect to Union law, confirms that this duty is not merely an obligation following on from Article I-5(2) TCE, but reflects a proper mandate of those courts within the sphere of their competences according to their national laws. It would also confirm that the EU courts and the national courts each fulfil complementary roles in a single

---

[9] O. Due, et al., 'Report by the Working Party on the Future of the European Communities' Court System', available at: <http://europa.eu.int/comm/dgs/legal_service/docs/due_en.pdf>.

system of judicial protection of the Union. In this perspective it would seem appropriate to provide in Article I-29(1) TCE, alongside the EU courts' mandate, that the national courts of the Member States shall ensure that the law is observed in the interpretation and application of the Constitution and secondary Union Law in all cases where relevant within their jurisdiction. The instruction to the Member States, in the present text of the same paragraph, to 'provide remedies sufficient to ensure effective legal protection' is of a different nature, directed as it is to the Member States and assuming only implicitly the position of the courts themselves.

It may be argued that recognition of the role of national courts on the constitutional treaty level would change nothing but appearances,[10] as this role already follows from the present treaty texts, *inter alia*, from Article 10 TEC (Art. 5(2) TCE). This comment purports to sustain, on the contrary, that the creation of a Treaty foundation for the role of national courts is of more than symbolic value. It would rather appear as the logical keystone rounding off a construction, admittedly developed in standing case law, by vesting the national courts with an autonomous co responsibility and thus mobilizing them in view of the effective application of the law of the Union. It would also facilitate national courts in new as well as old Member States in their duty to make critical assessments of national laws and administrative action in the light of Union law, and eventually to disapply national laws. Furthermore, explicit reference to the national courts' mandate under Union law provides a proper foundation for appropriate actions to support national courts in acquiring the necessary equipment, information infrastructure and expertise to fulfil their EU mandate. Essentially, projects such as *Eurinfra* set up in the Netherlands in order to specifically provide the Dutch courts with an expertise and database infrastructure on European law, are of fundamental, as it were constitutional, interest at the EU level, as a means to secure effective cooperation within the single court system of the Union and to promote sufficient coordination between courts to counterbalance growing administrative networks. A coherent judicial system of a twofold structure, on EU and national level, requires a consistent twofold constitutional foundation.

---

[10] Cf., in an outstanding and comprehensive dissertation on the mandate issue, M. Claes, *The National Courts' Mandate in the European Constitution* (Oxford, Hart 2005) p. 577.

# SOME THOUGHTS ON ACCESS TO JUSTICE WITHIN THE EUROPEAN CONSTITUTIONAL FRAMEWORK

## Piet Van Nuffel[*]

When the Treaty establishing a Constitution for Europe (hereinafter: the EU Constitution) will enter into force, it will supplement the national constitutional arrangements as a common constitutional framework within whose confines each Member State will organise its own domestic legal order. In the fields covered by Union law, the constitutional arrangements of the Member States are to provide 'remedies sufficient to ensure effective legal protection'.[1] In addition, it remains for the Court of Justice of the European Union to ensure 'that in the interpretation and application of the Constitution the law is observed'.[2] This paper provides some thoughts on this division of judicial tasks, in particular the role attributed in the European constitutional framework to the national courts and the restrictions placed on the jurisdiction of the European Court of Justice (ECJ). Since the ECJ has an exemplary role to play in providing access to justice, this article lingers on some elements that might be relevant to the evaluation of the Court's effectiveness, while wondering whether the linguistic factor has any role to play in this connection.

## 1.     ACCESS TO JUSTICE BEFORE THE NATIONAL JUDICIARIES

Access to justice depends not only on 'access to the judiciary' but, in the first place, on good governance and general compliance with the law both at the national level and at the level of the Union. The codification in the EU Constitution of important judge-made principles of Union law such as the principle of primacy and the obligation to ensure effective judicial protection will strengthen the position of Union law within the national constitutional systems. Even though

---

[*] Legal secretary at the Court of Justice of the European Union. All views expressed in this article are personal.

[1] See Art. I-29(1) TCE, subsection 2.

[2] Art. I-29(1) TCE, subsection 1. The 'Court of Justice of the European Union' will be the common denominator for the ECJ (in the EU Constitution named 'the Court of Justice'), the Court of First Instance (henceforth the 'General Court') and specialised courts.

*D. Curtin, A.E. Kellermann and S. Blockmans, eds., The EU Constitution: The Best Way Forward?*
© 2005, T.M.C. Asser Instituut, The Hague.

the principle of the primacy of Community law has by now turned into one of the cornerstones of the Community legal order, the fact that it will be expressly recognised in Article I-6 TCE should not be underestimated. If the EU Constitution is to be ratified, the incorporation of this jurisprudential principle into a Treaty text will indeed turn the principle into an obligation of international law to which Member States have expressly committed themselves.

In an enlarged Union, the preliminary ruling procedure remains, more than ever, the backbone of the constitutional system of judicial protection. The threshold to refer questions to the ECJ should therefore be as low as practically possible. This is important in the Member States that recently acceded to the Union, as their judiciary has to be encouraged to search for the correct application of Union law, involving, where necessary, references to the ECJ for a clarification of the applicable Union law. However, the same *rationale* still applies in the 'older' Member States, where some judges may not yet feel familiar with Union law and may have to overcome a certain hesitation to refer questions to the ECJ.

It does not serve effective judicial protection to refrain national courts' access to the preliminary ruling procedure, such as precluding 'lower' courts from referring to the ECJ, as is the case for Title IV of the EC Treaty. Since questions of Union law must be dealt with at the earliest possible occasion, one should avoid any false impression that a preliminary reference to the ECJ is an action of 'last resort' of the same kind as an application to the European Court of Human Rights.

The better option is to lower the threshold for access to the ECJ while providing the latter with appropriate means to reply swiftly to any increase in references for a preliminary ruling. Any mechanisms allowing the ECJ to formulate a swift reply to references should be encouraged. One should mention in this respect the practice of the registry of informing the referring court about precedential cases that may be sufficient for its question to be answered as well as the increasing use of orders. However, the ECJ should never install an almost mechanical recourse to orders that reply to a reference by referring to existing case law: the ECJ should not be discouraged from 'changing its mind'.

## 2.    CONSTITUTIONAL LIMITS TO THE ECJ'S JURISDICTION

In a 'Union based on the rule of law' any limit to the jurisdiction of the ECJ should be compensated by effective judicial protection at the national level (see Art. I-29(1) TCE). However, the EU Constitution leaves some questions unanswered:

a)    Are the conditions for introducing direct actions such as amended by Article III-365(4) TCE (action against a 'regulatory act which is of direct concern to [the individual] and does not entail implementing measures') of the kind to guarantee 'effective judicial protection'? In any case, Union law should dispense with the situation whereby a remedy against an executive act is available only if the person concerned is willing to first infringe the law. In that respect, the possibility to challenge 'regulatory acts' that do not need implementing measures should certainly be welcomed. The term 'regulatory' act in Article III-365(4) TCE does not fit in with the distinction drawn in the EU Constitution between legislative and non-legislative acts. On the basis of the activities of the Convention, commentators tend to agree that the clause allowing actions to be brought against 'regulatory acts' will not allow individuals to bring a direct action against legislative acts, not even if that act does not entail implementing measures. How then to ensure effective judicial protection? One could argue that the obligation for the Member States 'to provide remedies sufficient to ensure effective legal protection in the fields covered by Union law' (Art. I-29(1) TCE) requires them to create a remedy for individuals to challenge Union acts against which there is no recourse at Union level (e.g., by means of a declaratory action). If that would not be possible, one may wonder why the ECJ would not see it as its mission to ensure judicial protection at Union level, e.g., by giving a broader interpretation to the term 'regulatory acts' than the participants in the Convention may have foreseen. In this respect, would it not be possible for the ECJ to ensure judicial protection against legislative and executive acts of the Union whenever the referring court makes clear that effective judicial protection is absent at the national level? The risk of overburdening the ECJ's workload is not so great since, even if there would have been a remedy available at the national level, the *Foto-Frost* case law would anyhow have required the national court involved to refer to the ECJ where the legality of a Union act is at stake.[3]

b)  What about judicial protection in the Common Foreign and Security Policy (CFSP)? Article III-376 TCE will enable the ECJ to review the validity of 'European decisions of the Council providing for restrictive measures against natural and legal persons'. That clause cannot be considered as merely confirming the existing courses of action against (Community) acts implementing CFSP sanctions. It implies that the European decisions themselves, even though based on CFSP provisions, will be challengeable as to their effects on natural and legal persons.

c)  How about the existing limit to the ECJ's jurisdiction with respect to the validity or proportionality of police and law-enforcement operations and the exercise of national powers with respect to law and order and the safeguarding of internal security? Article 35(5) TEC introduced such a restriction with respect to police and judicial cooperation in criminal mat-

---

[3]  ECJ, judgment of 22 October 1987, Case C-314/85, *Foto-Frost* v. *Hauptzollamt Lübeck-Ost* [1987] *ECR* 4199.

ters, which has been maintained for the same field in Article III-377 TCE.[4] On the face of it, such a clause recognises a protected sphere of national sovereignty. One may wonder, however, whether the European constitutional framework allows it to play that role. Where the European Court of Justice is asked to ensure that the law is applied in the interpretation and application of Union law, 'the law' to be ensured also encompasses the rights and freedoms of any person affected by Union law. Where the Court is asked to interpret a provision of Union law with a view to having it applied by national courts, it may have to clarify that provision by indicating possible courses of action at the national level that would be incompatible with Union law, taking into account the fundamental freedoms that Member States have to respect in their application of Union law. Without actually speaking out on the validity of specific law-enforcement operations of the Member States, the Court's ruling may thus contain precise indications on the proportionality or legality of such operations.

3.    MAKING THE ECJ A(N) (EVEN) BETTER COURT?

The ECJ has an exemplary role to play not only in matters of Union law but also in striving towards 'good governance'. In this respect, the criteria to evaluate the Court's effectiveness can be described as relating either to 'quality' or to 'speed'.

a)   As to quality, outsiders are better placed to evaluate. However, two elements may be mentioned. First, the screening of candidate-judges, which is foreseen in Article III-357 TCE, should be applauded. This scrutiny will be carried out by a panel composed of former members of the Court and national magistrates and lawyers, one of whom has to be proposed by the European Parliament. It may be expected that this panel will question candidate-judges not only on their past experiences but also on the views held with respect to specific legal or other issues. In this way, the scrutiny procedure may emphasise the 'political' role of judges. In my view, that should not necessarily be seen as a negative point. After all, the application and interpretation of the law is not a neutral exercise and the legal community has a right to know which views are shared by the judges who will later participate in the rule-making process within the ECJ. Secondly, as to the creation of judicial panels, it should be highlighted

---

[4] Art. 64 TEC contains a similar clause where it states that the Treaty Title on visas, immigration, asylum and other policies related to the free movement of persons 'shall not affect the exercise of the responsibilities incumbent upon Member States with regard to the maintenance of law and order and the safeguarding of internal security'.

that specialisation may be good for certain aspects, for example where the examination of facts and the screening of complex decision-making processes is concerned, but such specialisation is not necessarily an asset in areas where the rules to be applied do not have a limited scope but have direct links with the fundamental principles of EU law, such as the application of the competition rules.

b)  As to speed, efforts have been made at the level of the ECJ to improve the existing situation, in particular through extended working in chambers and enhanced recourse to orders. One other idea to make better use of resources within the Court would be to integrate the involvement of the Advocate General in the debate before the Court (e.g., by having an opinion rendered before the hearing) rather than having such involvement closing that debate.

c)  Striking a balance between 'quality' and 'speed' is a decision with obvious political consequences: deliberating in chambers may accelerate the overall handling of cases but does not guarantee that a significant number of judges are involved in the handling of any single case. It should be noted that since the most recent enlargement, every judge is only involved in a relatively small minority of the cases.[5] In any particular case, it is thus most probable that the judge of the Member State concerned will not be sitting. One should see the scrutiny of candidate-judges also against this background. Having passed that scrutiny, all judges sitting in a case will indeed know that their authority is not only based on the proposal of candidate-judges by a national government but on an explicit peer-review of their qualifications. The legitimacy that all judges derive from such scrutiny may facilitate the acceptance of decisions by private parties and national governments who practically lose the guarantee that 'their' judge will be sitting in a case.[6] In the same way as striking a balance between quality and speed, it is a political decision to judge the overall 'efficiency' of the ECJ: that judgment requires both 'quality' and 'speed' to be set off against the resources made available to the Court.

---

[5]  According to Art. 221 TEC, the ECJ sits in chambers of three or five judges or in a Grand Chamber or, exceptionally, as a full Court. Since 1 May 2004, the Grand Chamber consists of thirteen judges (see Art. 16 of the ECJ's Statute as amended by Council Decision 2004/404/EC, Euratom of 19 April 2004, (*OJ* (2004) L 132/1), whereas its decisions are valid if at least nine judges are sitting. Decisions of the full Court are valid if at least fifteen judges are sitting (see Art. 17 of the ECJ's Statute).

[6]  It should be clear, however, that there has never been any right to have a specific Judge sitting in a case. Art. 18 of the ECJ's Statute provides, on the contrary, that a party may not apply for a change in the composition of the Court or of one of its chambers on the grounds of either the nationality of a Judge or the absence from the Court or from the chamber of a Judge of the nationality of that party.

For example, proceedings may be accelerated if more resources would be given to recruit translators and correctors.

d)  Is the linguistic regime playing any role in this respect? As to the relationship between the ECJ and the legal community, there should be no doubt that the regime of translating the most important judgments into all the official languages is the most efficient way. One should indeed not neglect that 'translation costs' arise whenever a person is asked to interpret a document in a language which is not his or her mother tongue or is asked to translate such document for other persons. Whenever such translation costs are not borne (once) at the level of the ECJ, they have to be borne several times more at a decentralised level. This does not imply that any single judgment should be published in all languages. For voluminous competition judgments, it may indeed be sufficient to have only extracts published, as is already the current practice. However, if judgments are to be published, translations in all the official languages should be available at the Union level, so as to reduce the translation costs that inevitably follow within the Member States. As to the regime of the working language, it should be pointed out that any change from French to English or to French and English would not necessarily improve the overall speed or the quality of the work. However, any such change would, without doubt, have specific positive effects, e.g., where English is the language of the case, and more particularly, to extend the possibilities for the recruitment of judges and their staff.

## 4.    PUTTING THE CONSTITUTIONAL FRAMEWORK INTO PRACTICE

The above-mentioned thoughts may already indicate that in the field of Union law, just as in any other area of the law, ensuring access to justice is not only a matter of constitutional design, but depends even more on good governance by all the authorities involved and on the political willingness to allocate sufficient resources to these authorities. In this respect one can only encourage the national judiciary and the European Courts to maintain their close contacts and to strive together towards an even better performing system of access to justice. For the citizen, of course, the success of the constitutional framework will be measured rather through whether or not administrative action at national or European level may avoid having any judiciary involved and, if that cannot be avoided, through the swiftness by which justice may be delivered.

# PART VI

## The Impact of the EU Constitution on selected Member States and neighbouring Countries

# THE IMPACT OF THE EU CONSTITUTION ON THE NATIONAL CONSTITUTIONS: FOCUSING ON THE NETHERLANDS' CONSTITUTIONAL DEBATE

Alfred E. Kellermann[*]

## 1. INTRODUCTION

So that the European citizen can better understand the contents and objectives of the EU Constitution it is useful to analyze the differences between the EU Constitution and the national constitutions, as well as its impact on the national constitutions themselves. For our analysis we will take the Dutch Constitution as well as the possible impact of the EU Constitution on Dutch constitutional practice as a concrete example. A simple analysis will show, for example, that the EU Constitution will increase citizens' rights and, conversely, will not reduce their rights nor replace their national constitution. Receiving more and, at the same time, losing nothing might convince citizens to approve of the EU Constitution in a national referendum.

I hope to be able to clarify this with the following two questions and answers, focusing mainly on the Dutch situation: 1) Will the impact of the EU Constitution have as a consequence that we can abolish national constitutions? 2) If the EU Constitution does not reduce the need for the national constitutions, what impact can we expect? The adaptation or approximation of national constitutions?

## 2. WILL THE IMPACT OF THE EU CONSTITUTION HAVE AS A CONSEQUENCE THAT WE CAN ABOLISH NATIONAL CONSTITUTIONS?

In order to be able to answer this question, it is important that every European citizen is aware of the differences between both constitutions. The Dutch Constitution, compared with the EU Constitution, demonstrates the following differences:

---

[*] Senior Legal and Policy Advisor and Visiting Professor in the law of the EU at the T.M.C. Asser Institute.

*D. Curtin, A.E. Kellermann and S. Blockmans, eds., The EU Constitution: The Best Way Forward?*
© 2005, T.M.C. Asser Instituut, The Hague.

1) The EU Constitution deals with a territory of 25 Member States with approximately 500 million citizens as well as their associations with overseas countries and territories. The text has 21 authentic languages. The
   Netherlands Constitution deals only with the territory of the Netherlands,
   with approximately 16 million citizens, and its overseas territories. The
   Dutch Constitution has been drafted in one language only.

2) The first Dutch Constitution dates from 1814, with amendments in 1815,
   1840, 1848, 1887, 1917, 1922, 1953, 1956, 1983, 1995 and 2002, whereas
   the not yet ratified text of the EU Constitution dates from 29 October
   2004.

3) The EU Constitution contains four Parts and, in total, 464 articles:
   –  Part I: Objectives, fundamental rights and citizenship, Union
      competences, the Union's institutions and bodies, the democratic life
      of the Union, the Union's finances, the Union and its immediate envi-
      ronment, Union membership (59 arts.).
   –  Part II: The Charter of Fundamental Rights of the Union (54 arts.).
   –  Part III: The Internal and external Policies and functioning of the
      Union: internal market, economic and monetary policy and policies in
      other areas (social, agricultural, environmental, consumer protection,
      transport etc.) (342 arts.).
   –  Part IV: General and final provisions (9 arts.).

4) The Dutch Constitution contains 8 Chapters and, in total, 142 articles and
   it regulates the establishment and powers of the institutions of the state
   (the Monarchy, the Government, the Ministers, the States General, the
   Council of State, the General Auditor's Office, the Judiciary, as well as
   the functioning of these bodies concerning legislation, the government
   and the administration of justice. Further, the powers and tasks of the
   lower regions of government such as the provinces, the municipalities,
   and the district water boards are also dealt with. The details are regulated
   in State Acts.

5) Nationality and citizenship.
   The Dutch Constitution, according to Article 7, requires that an Act
   should provide the necessary conditions and criteria for Dutch nationality.
   This was done most recently by the statute law of 1984. The old rule that
   the child receives the nationality of the father has been replaced by the
   rule that the child has Dutch nationality if the father or the mother has
   Dutch nationality (Art. 3). Union citizenship, as mentioned in the EU
   Constitution, is however additional to national citizenship; it will not replace it (Art. I-10(1) TCE). Union citizenship does not give the citizen the
   right to acquire the nationality of another EU Member State. European
   Citizenship, as introduced by the Maastricht Treaty, was originally considered to be only a political concept. However, the Court of Justice, as

we can read in the contribution by Prof. Dr. Jaap de Zwaan[1] to this colloquium book, has given the concept a proper meaning and interpretation.

However, Union Citizenship gives Dutch nationality an extra new dimension and provides the Dutch citizen with the following additional
rights as mentioned in Article I-10(2):

(a) 'the right to move and reside freely within the territory of the Member
    States;
(b) the right to vote and to stand as candidates in elections to the European Par-
    liament and in municipal elections in their Member State of residence, under
    the same conditions as nationals of that State;
(c) the right to enjoy, in the territory of a third country in which the Member
    State of which they are nationals is not represented, the protection of the dip-
    lomatic and consular authorities of any Member State on the same conditions
    as the nationals of that State;
(d) the right to petition the European Parliament, to apply to the European Om-
    budsman, and to address the institutions and advisory bodies of the Union in
    any of the Constitution's languages and to obtain a reply in the same lan-
    guage.'

6) Priority or primacy of Community law.
   The relationship between the Community legal order and the national legal order is regulated, as far as priority is concerned, in Articles 93 and 94
   of the Dutch Constitution: 'treaty provisions that, according to their content, are generally binding, have priority over national legislative provisions'.

   However, in Article I-6 TCE primacy is not limited to general binding
   provisions as is the case in the Dutch Constitution: 'the Constitution and
   law adopted by the institutions of the Union in exercising competences
   conferred on it shall have primacy over the law of the Member States'.

   Moreover, Community law has priority over national constitutions, in the
   sense that a Member State can not appeal against the national constitutional provisions which form an obstacle to the implementation of Community law as decided by the European Court of Justice in Case 100/77.[2]

From our enumeration of the differences, it follows, globally speaking, that national constitutions regulate two kinds of matters and issues: Matters which are
only regulated in the national constitutions such as *the division of power between
the national institutions and the conditions for receiving the nationality of a state*
and issues which are regulated in the national as well as in the EU Constitution

---

[1] See the article by J. de Zwaan on pp. 245-264.
[2] ECJ, judgment of 11 April, Case C- 100/77, *Commission* v. *Italy* [1978] *ECR* 879.

such as *the relationship between the international or Community legal order and the national legal order.* In the first example, the national constitutional text will provide the final answer, in the second example, in my opinion, it is the EU Constitution which will have the last word and national constitutional texts that do not comply with the EU constitutional provisions should be adapted accordingly or they should limit themselves to only a reference to Article I-6 TCE.

The answer to our first question, therefore, is that the national constitutions – in our example the Dutch Constitution – should not be abolished; they should rather be amended or adapted.

The EU Constitution does not reduce rights, on the contrary it provides the national citizen with additional rights as mentioned in Article I-10(2) TCE. However, we must remember that European Citizenship has already existed since the Treaty of Maastricht, but the EU Constitution has strengthened these Citizenship rights and presented them in a broader context compared to the present situation. For example, the EU Constitution included citizens' rights in the Charter of Fundamental Rights.

A condition for receiving these extra rights is that the European citizen acquires the respective nationality according to the provisions of his national constitution. If one does not have the nationality of one of the EU Member States, one does not therefore acquire European citizenship.

If the EU Constitution does not abolish the national constitution, gives the citizen additional rights and, conversely, does not reduce that citizen's rights, is that not a convincing clarifying argument to vote in favour of an EU Constitution? This is just one example of the advantages of an EU Constitution. There are, however, many more short-term and long-term advantages and disadvantages, which we will not elaborate upon in this brief contribution. For example, sometimes the approximation of laws can reduce the citizen's rights; however, the benefits from approximation are much greater than the losses.

3.    IF THE EU CONSTITUTION DOES NOT REDUCE THE NEED FOR
      THE NATIONAL CONSTITUTIONS, WHAT IMPACT CAN WE
      EXPECT? THE ADAPTATION OR APPROXIMATION OF NATIONAL
      CONSTITUTIONS?

Although the national constitutional provisions will generally not be replaced by the EU Constitution and as we still need national constitutions in the Member States, the adaptation and approximation of the national constitutional provisions will, on the other hand, be necessary for several reasons. These reasons are not only based on the EU Constitution, but also on many other considerations like stimulating the equal legal effect of Community law in all the EU Member States. However, after the ratification of the EU Constitution, in some countries by means of a referendum, in other countries by parliamentary assent, we may expect an extra incentive for the process of adapting and approximating the national constitutions.

## 3.1    The Netherlands' Constitutional Debate

It is interesting to mention that the ratification of all Treaty amendments since the conclusion of the 1957 EC Treaty of Rome has been implemented in the Netherlands by the Netherlands Parliament alone. For the Constitutional Treaty, however, it was considered whether a consultative referendum should be held, based on an Interim Law which entered into force in 2002. Although this initiative was formally and legally possible from a constitutional point of view before this time, this option was now made possible for the first time in Dutch history. Before enumerating the reasons for approximating or adapting national constitutional texts in general, in our answer to the second question we will focus on the situation in the Netherlands and will discuss the position of the EU Constitution in the Netherlands' constitutional debate.

In the deliberating years 2002/2003 and 2003/2004 the European Convention and the EU Constitution have often been on the political and judicial agenda in the Netherlands. In Document 2003/2004, 28.473, no. 35[3] the Opinion of the Dutch Council of State of 13 June 2003 and the follow-up report of 26 September 2003 have been included. Both the opinion and the report concern topics which refer to the results of the European Convention on the Future of Europe.

On 4 June 2003 the Dutch Government requested an 'Opinion' from the Council of State on the expected developments of the EU Constitution for the Dutch legal order. Since the European Communities and the Union, from a substantive point of view, have for a long time already had a 'Constitution', now, for the first time, this will also be established formally in a written constitution. Therefore the evaluation by the Council of State does not include an evaluation as to whether a transfer of state powers is necessary, but more especially whether the EU Constitution satisfies the requirements of a democratic legal society: legal certainty and equality; democratic legitimacy and public accountability; efficiency and effectiveness. As far as accession to the European Convention for the Protection of Human Rights and Fundamental Freedoms is concerned, this does not result in a new transfer of sovereignty, but more specifically in better coordination between the activities of the EU and the European Court of Human Rights (ECtHR ) concerning Human Rights protection.

The draft Constitution is, in the 'Opinion of the Council of State', only a codification and continuation of the legal European developments and it does not interfere and conflict with the Dutch Constitution. The draft Constitution will, however, have an impact on the interrelationship between the national institutions. The Dutch Government agrees with the Council of State in that the EU Constitution does not bring about a new transfer of state powers, but merely a continuation of the old trend and a restructuring of existing powers. The Dutch Government also agrees with the Council of State that the EU Constitution dem-

---

[3] Hand. II 2003/2004 28.472, no. 35.

onstrates that the continuation of the existing *acquis communautaire* is the objective. This follows from Part IV, which regulates the replacement of the EC and EU Treaties as well as the reference to the contents of the Court of Justice Decisions.

In order to prevent the overburdening of the ECJ with the preliminary rulings procedure, the Council of State suggests that the national referring courts should annex a tentative answer to their preliminary questions. A second suggestion from the Council of State is that the ECJ can subsequently select the provisional preliminary national court decisions.

The 'Opinion of the Council of State' further refers to suggestions for improving the coordination in the Netherlands for the preparation of Community policies and legislation between the ministries (CoCo)[4] as well as the coordinated implementation of Community legislation (ICER).[5]

Next the Council of State focuses on the inclusion of the Charter of Fundamental Rights in Part II of the EU Constitution. As a consequence, the Charter provisions will have legal force. The Charter is not directed towards the national legal orders, but refers to Union and European Community law and its implementation by the Member States. In Articles II-111 and II-112 TCE a differentiation is made between 'rights' and 'principles'. The inclusion of the Charter of Fundamental Rights within the EU Constitution has an added legal value, which characterizes the EU Constitution as a real constitution with fundamental rights. The Dutch Government prefers the accession of the EU to the ECHR for equal treatment between the EU and the other Member States of the Council of Europe. The procedures before the ECJ can then be considered as a final remedy in the sense of Article 35, first sentence, of the European Convention on Human Rights.

### 3.2   Consultative Referendum – Why should a Referendum be held?

Why prepare a proposal for a law on holding a consultative referendum? The Dutch Government explains, in its general comment, that in the EU Constitution special powers are granted regarding criminal law and external policies as well as the inclusion of fundamental rights. It is not just another Treaty amendment, and therefore a greater involvement on the part of citizens is necessary. A referendum is the solution. By drafting a proposal for a law on holding a consultative referendum, the Government envisages strengthening and improving the legitimacy of the decision-making on the Constitutional Treaty, by looking to the citizens for advice.

---

[4] CoCo: Nederlandse Coördinatiecommissie voor Europese Integratie en Associatieproblemen [Dutch Coordination Commission for European Integration and Association Problems].

[5] ICER: Interdepartementale Commissie Europees Recht [Interdepartmental Commission on European Law].

The Council of State took a positive stance and agreed with the consultative referendum as an adapted form of consulting the citizens. However, a minority opinion was put forward by one Council Member, Richard Lauwaars. He was of the opinion that a consultative referendum is not very useful, as a negative referendum result would not be accepted by the Dutch government, as the Netherlands cannot accept to withdraw from the European Union.[6]

The 'Protocol on the role of National Parliaments in the European Union', annexed to the Constitutional Treaty, will have an impact on the working methods of the Dutch Parliament. Especially Article 3 et seq. of the Protocol which determines, *inter alia*, that National Parliaments may send to the Presidents of the European Parliament, the Council and the Commission a reasoned opinion on whether a draft European legislative act complies with the principle of subsidiarity. This will lead to joint meetings and deliberations between the first and second chamber of the Parliament. The Government has not yet considered whether these united meetings and joint deliberations will lead to a Dutch constitutional amendment, whereas, for example, in France the reinforced role of the national parliament will lead to an adaptation of the French Constitution.[7]

### 4.     CONCLUDING REMARKS

After a *tour d'horizon* of the Netherlands constitutional debate, in a general concluding overview we will provide our opinion on the reasons for the approximation or adaptation of national constitutional texts along the lines of the EU Constitution in the near future:

1)  For some national constitutions an adaptation might be necessary in order to be able to ratify the EU Constitution. These constitutions must, for example, include a text on the transfer of state powers to an international organization, powers which should be exercised jointly with the EC and EU. Without such provisions, EU Member States otherwise risk a constitutional complaint. This could happen, for example, in the case of Malta. As the Maltese Constitution does not include such an article, the question arises whether Malta's Accession Treaty with the EC and EU could not be declared invalid by a Maltese national court.

2)  The role of national constitutions is, at the EU level, often underestimated by politicians, while it is overestimated at the national level. At the EU level the example is the Irish 'no' in the referendum on the Nice Treaty.

---

[6] See also, L.F.M. Besselink and S. Prechal, 'Kroniek van het Europees en Nederlands constitutioneel recht', ['A Chronicle of European and Dutch Constitutional Law'] 79 *Nederlands Juristenblad* [*Netherlands Law Journal*] (2004) p. 506.

[7] Delegation pour l'Union Europeenne, Compte Rendu No. 107 of the Meeting of 15 December 2004 of the Assemblee Nationale, p. 3.

At the national constitutional level, there are two difficulties. The constitutional provisions of some Member States have not been sufficiently adapted to facilitate the full effect of Community law. However, by constructive dialogue the difficulties have been overcome by judicial ingenuity and by constructive dialogue between the European Court of Justice and the national courts. Several national supreme courts still hesitate to recognize the primacy of Community law unconditionally and find no adequate basis in the national constitution to do so.

3)  The approximation of national constitutions, with more or less uniform legal language, terminology and concepts, is necessary to produce the identical legal effect of Community law in all EU Member States. This will improve references between national constitutions and the EU Constitution. For the primacy of Community law, the national legislators could limit themselves to including a reference to Article I-6 TCE in the so-called European Chapter of the national constitutional texts.

4)  There was already a need to adapt national constitutions, because some national constitutional provisions were contrary to the provisions of the Nice Treaty (for example, on citizenship, voting rights or extradition of one's own nationals, and transfer of land and real estate by non-residents). Nowadays the special and new provisions of the EU Constitution will require the adaptation of many national constitutions. For example, the French Constitutional Court decided on 19 November 2004 that the French Constitution must be altered before the EU Constitution can be ratified in France. The necessary revisions will take place at the beginning of 2005, allowing for the possibility of a referendum in the first half of 2005. The Constitutional Court decided that certain parts of the EU Constitution that 'affect the essential conditions for the exercising of national sovereignty' will require a change in the national law before being ratified. The Court cited justice and foreign policy as the main areas requiring changes to the constitution.

   The increased powers that national parliaments will have if the EU Constitution is ratified and enters into force also require a change to the French Constitution, as the role of the French parliament must be defined by the Constitution. And the judges decided that the Treaty does not contradict the first article of the French Constitution – that France is a secular Republic. However, the stated primacy of EU law over national law does not require a change to the French Constitution, and neither does the inclusion in the EU Constitution of the Charter of Fundamental Rights.

   In my opinion it still makes a difference that primacy is stated in the EU Constitution. Judges can change their minds or their opinions. However, the Constitutional Treaty text is rigid and can only be changed by unanimity among all the Member States.

5)  Adaptation of national constitutions is a *perpetuum mobile*, just like the *acquis communautaire* of the EU Constitution is a moving target. There-

fore, it is necessary that the national constitutions become more flexible, and that the amendment procedures are simplified. Many national constitutions are rigid and in this way form an obstacle to a dynamic European integration process. If, for example, we need a national referendum for every amendment to a complicated Treaty text, this may result in unexpected and unpleasant outcomes for further European integration. Constitutional lawyers are, on average, rather conservative, in the sense that national constitutions are considered holy and rigid, meriting complicated amendment procedures.

6) The way in which some national constitutional texts deal with the European integration process is rather poor from a political and a psychological point of view. For example, the Dutch Constitution does not refer to the EC and/or EU at all. In my opinion, in the near future in the national constitutional texts references to the EU Constitution should be required. This approach will improve the transparency and the coherence of the Community legal order, as required by the EU Constitution. An obligation for the Member States to refer in the provisions of their national constitutions to the respective provisions of the EU Constitution will be the starting point for a confederation!

Another suggestion to improve the coherence of the Community and the national legal order could be realized by including a text, similar to that of the Canadian Constitution of 1982, stating that (if we replace 'Canada' with 'European Union'): 'The European Union Constitutional Law includes the constitutions of all Member States as interpreted by their highest Courts'. It would guarantee constitutional integration as well as constitutional and legal pluralism. Such an adaptation of national constitutions, which is a bottom-up approach, could make Europe more effective and closer to the citizens.

The answers to our second question are rather extensive and of a legal-constitutional character. The answers do not concern the citizen directly and are, moreover, more of interest to politicians, members of parliament, government representatives, academics and constitutional lawyers. These considerations will not motivate and convince the average European citizen to vote 'yes' in a referendum, as they do not always understand the technical complicated relationship between the EU Constitution, the *acquis communautaire* and the national constitutions.

# SOME POINTS CONCERNING THE EU CONSTITUTION FROM A HUNGARIAN PERSPECTIVE

Jenö Czuczai*

## 1. INTRODUCTION

It is beyond any doubt that the Treaty establishing a Constitution for Europe,[1] as signed on 29 October 2004 in Rome, contains a great deal of political compromises. That is why one may recognize in the finally adopted legal text of the EU Constitution that there are many linguistic and/or sometimes even substantial incoherencies in this Treaty,[2] a Treaty which is undoubtedly unique by its very nature as well as by its structure and content. One thing, however, is important and very positive in my opinion, namely that the voice of the new Member States has been to a large extent heard in many fields of the new EU Constitution, and this is not by accident. The representatives of the new Member States could participate in the workings of the Convention almost as full members as well as after the Convention, and, in the context of the Intergovernmental Conference (IGC), the new Member States had already had a very influential role because of the unanimity rule for the adoption of the new EU founding Treaty. This contribution tries briefly to discern and explore the main elements of those compromises which to some extent, or maybe even fully, reflect, in the European Convention, the proposals elaborated either by one or by many new Member States during either the Convention and/or the IGC. The article also attempts, however, to point out those elements of the new EU founding Treaty which cannot be welcome from the point of view of many of the new Member States. Sometimes I even have to address certain points and solutions which are enshrined in the EU Constitution from a critical but analytical approach. Finally, this contribution will deal with the ratification process of the signed EU Constitution from the point of view of why some of the new Member States have already ratified the new EU founding Treaty so quickly and almost without any substantial social and/or pro-

---

* Vice-President of the European Law Academy, Budapest. All the views expressed and/or opinions developed in this paper reflect exclusively the personal views of the author.
[1] See, Treaty establishing a Constitution for Europe (hereinafter referred to as the EU Constitution or TCE), as published in the *OJ* (2004) C 310/1.
[2] See for further elaboration on this, Jan Wouters's article on pp. 163-169 of this book.

*D. Curtin, A.E. Kellermann and S. Blockmans, eds., The EU Constitution: The Best Way Forward?*
© 2005, T.M.C. Asser Instituut, The Hague.

fessional debate thereon at the national level. Certainly, I will primarily base my research and findings on the topic based on Hungarian experiences and concerns in terms of the new EU constitution-making process, because, by adopting a broader comparative legal dimension in Central and Eastern Europe, I would inevitably exceed the purpose of this article.

## 2.  SOME POSITIVE POINTS CONCERNING THE EU CONSTITUTION

According to the official Hungarian position,[3] Hungary welcomes the Treaty establishing a Constitution for Europe as adopted by the European Council under the Irish Presidency and finally signed by all the Member States in Rome in October 2004. In the official commentaries on the EU· Constitution, the experts from a Hungarian point of view tend to underline the following elements of the new EU founding Treaty as being absolutely positive as far as our country is concerned:

–  As is well known, for Hungary one of the most important points to be addressed under the IGC was the protection of minority rights. Hungary made several proposals in this respect to the IGC.[4] Finally, a compromise was agreed upon among the Member States, textually resulting in Article I-2 TCE under the heading of 'The Union's values'. It reads as follows:

   *'The Union is founded on the values* of respect for human dignity, freedom, democracy, *equality*, the rule of law and *respect for human rights, including the rights of persons belonging to minorities.* These values are common to the Member States in a society in which pluralism, non-discrimination, tolerance, justice, solidarity and equality between women and men prevail.' (emphasis added).

---

[3] See, *inter alia*, P. Györkös, 'Politikai megállapodás az Alkotmányos Szerződésről – az Ir elnökség mérlege' ['Political Compromise on the EU Constitutional Treaty – the Results achieved under the Irish Presidency'] 4-5 *Európai Tükör* (Budapest, 2004 July-August) pp. 166-170; Árpád Gordos-Bálint Ódor, 'Az Európai Alkotmányos Szerződés születése' [The Birth of the New EU Constitutional Treaty] (Budapest, HVG Orac Ltd. 2004) or A. Müller, 'Az Európai Alkotmány által létrehozott uniós jog – és intézményrendszer' [The EU Legal and Institutional System, created by the EU Constitution] 6 *Európai Jog* (2004) pp. 3-7.

[4] J. Szájer, '"Unity In Diversity" Proposal for the Representation of National and Ethnic Minorities in the Institutional System of the EU Committee of National and Ethnic Minorities (CONEM)' (Brussels, CONV 580/03, Contrib. 258) availablet at: <http://register.consilium.eu.int/pdf/en/03/cv00/cv00580en03.pdf>. Similarly see, P. Balázs, et al., 'Le respect des minorités et la structure constitutionelle européenne' (Brussels, CONV 639/03, Contrib. 286) available at: <http://register.consilium.eu.int/pdf/en/03/cv00/cv00639en03.pdf>; P. Medgyessy, 'Discours du Premier Ministre de la Hongrie, Session de l'Assemblée parlementaire du Conseil de l'Europe' (2 October 2003) available at: <http://www.coe.int/T/F/Com/Dossiers/Sessions-AP/sept-2003/>; P. Medgyessy, 'Discours du Premier Ministre de la Hongrie á l'inauguration de la Conférence Intergouvernementale de l'Union Européenne' (7 October 2003); and finally see, 'Proposition de la Présidence, Conclave ministériel de Naples' (doc. CIG 52/03 ADD1).

This italicised wording is not totally satisfactory (from the perspective of the protection of minority rights), but, in the given circumstances, that was the maximum that the Hungarian delegation could achieve. As seen, the text clearly rejects, however, the collective rights' approach (it only talks of 'rights of persons belonging to minorities') as it does not sufficiently clarify whether the above provision concerns 'ethnic and national minorities' (despite the fact that this has been the main Hungarian concern, as is well known) or, indeed, which minorities!? It uses only the very vague term of 'minorities' which in fact includes every type of minority from Moslems to Roma issues and even to homosexuals (as special group minorities), etc., which means that the proper meaning remains a matter of interpretation. That was not really the Hungarian aim in terms of its original proposals on this question, especially if one looks at Article II-81 TCE, a provision which also only addresses the issue under 'non-discrimination based on special grounds' from an individualistic approach, namely: 'Any discrimination based on *any ground* such as (…) *membership of a national* minority (...) shall be prohibited'.

Moreover, there is an in-built discrepancy or contradiction between the wording of Articles I-2, II-81 and III-124 TCE, especially taking into account the enumerated areas intended for protection. While Articles I-2 and II-81 TCE talk about the protection of rights of persons belonging to minorities, although in different contexts, Article III-124 TCE does not mention the issue at all, which is a real problem! This provision can be found under Part III, Title II TCE under the heading of 'Non-discrimination and citizenship' and reads as follows:

'Without prejudice to the other provisions of the Constitution and within the limits of the powers assigned by it to the Union, *a European law or framework law of the Council may establish the measures needed to combat discrimination based* on sex, racial or ethnic origin, religion or belief, disability, age or sexual orientation. The Council shall act unanimously after obtaining the consent of the European Parliament'. (emphasis added).

Why, then, is the special ground of 'based on membership of a national minority' not mentioned in the enumeration of the above-quoted Article III-124 TCE in order at least to make a harmonious correlation between the effective implementation of Article II-81 TCE in this respect and the proper application of the other Articles, referred to above, in terms of the protection of minority rights *vis-à-vis* the non-discrimination principle?[5] Some experts maintain that this is most probably because the most influential 'big Member States', like France, Germany, etc., did not want to allow the possibility also to legislate in the future on minority rights issues at the EU level, possibly and primarily for financial and budgetary reasons.

---

[5] See C. Hillion, 'Enlargement of the EU – The Discrepancy between Membership Obligations and Accession Conditions as regards the Protection of Minorities', 27 *Fordham International Law Journal* (2004) pp. 715-740, in particular on pp. 738 et seq.

That is why when Hungary ratified the Treaty establishing a Constitution for Europe on 23 December 2004 (as the second Member State after Lithuania), in the promulgating Parliamentary decision[6] the Hungarian Parliament made the following two statements:

'With respect to Article I-2 of the Constitutional Treaty, a provision which makes reference – among the Union's values – to the rights of persons belonging to minorities, the Hungarian Parliament, taking this fact into consideration, sees the following as providing guidance in this respect: based on Article I-2 TCE, *the protection of national and ethnic minorities' rights has become the constitutional principle of the Union*. According to the Hungarian Parliament the mentioned *Article I-2 TCE also covers the joint (collective) exercise of rights* of persons belonging to national and ethnic minorities. According to the Hungarian Parliament the principle of full equality as well as the application of the non-discrimination principle does not contradict the legality of measures aimed at preventing and avoiding situations in which national and ethnic minorities suffer discrimination. It is the opinion of the Hungarian Parliament that the Constitutional Treaty and its provisions on non-discrimination reflect the essence of the Union's fundamental principles and exclude any kind of uncertainty in terms of discrimination. The enumeration that can be found under Article II-81 TCE also excludes any discrimination in the light of the application of Articles III-117[7] and III-122 TCE.[8] The Hungarian Parliament supports the position that, in light of Article III-124 TCE, Community legislation should be initiated on combating any discrimination based on national and ethnic origin and in order to assist in preventing that such communities could be discriminated against based on these grounds. The Hungarian Parliament believes that the Community legislation will in the future promote the full and proper implementation of the Union's common values in this respect.'[9]

---

[6] See Parliamentary Resolution No. 133/2004 (XII.23) on the ratification by the Republic of Hungary of the Treaty establishing a Constitution for Europe, adopted by overwhelming majority (97%) on 20 December 2004.

[7] Art. III-117 TCE reads as follows:
'In defining and implementing the policies and actions referred to in this Part, the Union shall take into account requirements linked to the promotion of a high level of employment, the guarantee of adequate social protection, the fight against social exclusion, and a high level of education, training and protection of human health.'

[8] Art. III-122 TCE reads as follows:
'Without prejudice to Articles I-5, III-166 and III-238, and given the place occupied by services of general economic interest as services to which all in the Union attribute value as well as their role in promoting its social and territorial cohesion, the Union and the Member States, each within their respective competences and within the scope of application of the Constitution, shall take care that such services operate on the basis of principles and conditions, in particular economic and financial conditions, which enable them to fulfil their missions. European laws shall establish these principles and set these conditions without prejudice to the competence of Member States, in compliance with the Constitution, to provide, to commission and to fund such services.'

[9] Unofficial translation by the author. See, 'Resolution of the Hungarian Parliament' (No. 133/2004 (XII.23)), point 2.

All the above-quoted unilateral understanding of the Hungarian Parliament may be evidence that in the application and interpretation of the relevant TCE provisions on the protection of minority rights, Hungary will take into account its original approach and perceptions concerning these rights as common values of the enlarged EU, provided, of course, that the EU Constitution will indeed enter into force.

In the light of what has been said above and in conclusion, I nevertheless think that Article I-2 TCE, as finally adopted by the IGC in terms of its content, is more than nothing and should be welcomed in particular by a new Member State having almost three million compatriots living outside the borders of the country (most of them even outside the current EU).[10]

– From a Hungarian academic point of view, one may also welcome Article I-5(1) TCE in the new EU founding Treaty, which reads as follows:

'The Union shall respect *the equality of Member States* before the Constitution as well as their national identities, inherent in their fundamental structures, political and constitutional, inclusive of regional and local self-government. It shall respect their essential State functions, including ensuring the territorial integrity of the State, maintaining law and order and safeguarding national security'.[11] (emphasis added).

This is important for Hungary, but maybe even for other new Member States, in the light of avoiding any possible scenario/formation of so-called 'second-class membership', which has been one of the main fears in these countries of Central and Eastern Europe in terms of acceding to the EU.[12] In my view this

---

[10] See, in more detail, J. Czuczai, 'The EU Charter: Is it a New Accession Condition of a Post-Nice Effect?', IV/4 *Európa 2002* (Budapest, December 2003) pp. 22-31.

[11] This 'equality of Member States' concept is also preserved under Art. I-26(6) TCE when it is stipulated:

'As from the end of the term of office of the Commission referred to in paragraph 5, the Commission shall consist of a number of members, including its President and the Union Minister for Foreign Affairs, corresponding to two thirds of the number of Member States, unless the European Council, acting unanimously, decides to alter this number. The members of the Commission shall be elected from among the nationals of the Member States *on the basis of a system of equal rotation between the Member States*. This system shall be established by a European decision adopted unanimously by the European Council and on the basis of the following principles: (a) *Member States shall be treated on a strictly equal footing* as regards determination of the sequence of, and the time spent by, their nationals as members of the Commission; consequently, the difference between the total number of terms of office held by nationals of any given pair of Member States may never be more than one, (b) subject to point (a), each successive Commission *shall be so composed as to reflect satisfactorily the demographic and geographical range of all the Member States.*' (emphasis added.)

This wording is advantageous for Hungary as one of the nine small new Member States and also, I should think, for many other new Member States too.

[12] See, for example, 'Convention on the future of Europe. Contributions of the Representatives of the Romanian Government September 2002-February 2003' (Bucharest 2004, MoEI) in

provision also provides a better articulated division at the EU primary law level between what is an EU competence and what remains exclusively and/or partly within Member States' competences, the latter – as stipulated in the above-mentioned new article of the EU Constitution – having even to be *expressis verbis* respected by the EU in the future!

– Article I-26(5) TCE can also be welcomed and it reads as follows:

'The first *Commission* appointed under the provisions of the Constitution [that means from 2009] *shall consist of one national of each Member State*, including its President and the Union Minister for Foreign Affairs who shall be one of its Vice-Presidents'.

This is also a great achievement for the smaller Member States (and we must not forget that out of the 10 new Member States, nine are small, the only 'big' one being Poland).

– Another very important provision for Hungary and many other Member States is Article I-11(2) TCE, in particular the following sentence: 'Competences not conferred upon the Union in the Constitution *remain with the Member States*'. This is the first time – concerning proposals of the new Member States – that such an important principle has been *expressis verbis* laid down at treaty-based, primary law level.

– I also welcome Chapter III in Part I of the EU Constitution, which is about 'enhanced cooperation'. This is in particular from three points of view: (a) it must be welcomed that: Enhanced cooperation *'shall be open at any time to all Member States, in accordance with Article III-418'* (Art. I-44(1) 2nd indent TCE). (b) 'Acts adopted in the framework of enhanced cooperation shall bind only participating States. *They shall not be regarded as part of the acquis which has to be accepted by candidate States for accession to the Union'* (Art. I-44(4) TCE). (c) *'The Commission and the Member States participating* in enhanced cooperation *shall ensure that they promote participation* by as many Member States as possible' (Art. III-418(1) 2nd indent TCE, plus in general, Arts. III-416-423 TCE). This last element is brand new, but is an extremely important novelty within the EU Constitution for the purpose of putting the principle of solidarity firmly into practice in this area as well as the so-called 'catching-up' doctrine *vis-à-vis* the less developed new Member States in the course of further deepening the European integration process.

– Hungarian officials – similar to, for instance, Ireland, the U.K. or Poland, etc. – think that it is a positive development in the new EU founding Treaty that the common security and defence policy has remained subject to the the unanimity rule (see Arts. III-309-312 and III-422(3) TCE).

---

particular pp. 18 et seq. on the 'Definition and repartition of competences between the Member States and the EU'.

– I consider it satisfactory that in terms of the legal acts of the Union under Title V of Part I of the EU Constitution ('Exercise of Union Competence') the Union legal order will be better framed and better structured by the TCE as opposed to the current system in this respect.[13] From a structural as well as functional points of view a remarkable constitutional development at the EU level is the incorporation of the new Title VI of Part I of the EU Constitution into the refounding Treaty (under the heading of 'The Democratic Life of the Union'). This new Title VI will be a great challenge in terms of implementation for both the 'old' as well as the 'new' Member States. For the new Member States this is especially in the context of the 'Europan identity-building process' as well as in relation to the 'further democratisation process' already in a post-accession reality.

– A special concern in many new Member States is what defines the relationship with their neighbours after accession? In particular Hungary is concerned about this, since it is a Member State with no less than seven neighbours, four of whom are not yet EU Member States, and of these four, two will not be joining the EU in the foreseeable future despite the fact that within the territories of these two countries there is a remarkably large Hungarian minority (Ukraine and Serbia and Montenegro). That is why a Hungarian academic may also be satisfied with the new TCE Article, namely Article I-57 which reads as follows:

'1. The Union shall develop a special relationship with neighbouring countries, aiming to establish an area of prosperity and good neighbourliness, *founded on the values of the Union* and characterised by close and peaceful relations based on cooperation.'

The reference to the values of the Union means that the 'protection of the rights of persons belonging to minorities' is also included, namely also that of the national and ethnic minorities.

– Many new Member States may finally welcome the adoption of the Charter and the fact that it will have become Part II of the EU Constitution and therefore also binding on the Member States when implementing EU law (Art. II-111 TCE). Article I-60 TCE on 'Voluntary withdrawal from the Union' should also receive a positive response from the new Member States as during the EU accession-driven constitutional adaptation process in many new Member States the issue of 'withdrawal from the EU' has drawn special attention in the parliamentary debates, as is the case, for example, in Slovakia.[14] Finally, it must be welcomed how significantly the solidarity principle is ad-

---

[13] See in more detail, K. Lenaerts, 'A Unified Set of Instruments', 1 *EU Constitutional Law Review* (2005) pp. 57-61.

[14] See, for example, J. Czuczai, 'Constitutional Preparation for EU Accession in the New Central and Eastern European Member States', in J. de Zwaan, et al., eds., *The European Union – An ongoing Process of Integration. Liber Amicorum A.E. Kellermann* (The Hague, T.M.C. Asser Press 2004) p. 274.

dressed (in several places) in the EU Constitution, thereby strengthening the future image of a 'Social Europe' in terms of the enlarged EU (for example: Arts. I-43, I-48 and III-329 TCE). In this respect special attention should be devoted to the new Article I-43 TCE ('Solidarity clause') which reads as follows:

'1. *The Union and its Member States shall act jointly in a spirit of solidarity if a Member State is the object of a terrorist attack or the victim of a natural or man-made disaster.* The Union shall mobilise all the instruments at its disposal, including the military resources made available by the Member States:
(a) – prevent the terrorist threat in the territory of the Member States,
    – protect democratic institutions and the civilian population from any terrorist attack,
    – assist a Member State in its territory, at the request of its political authorities, in the event of a terrorist attack.
(b) assist a Member State in its territory, at the request of its political authorities, in the event of a natural or man-made disaster.'

One may think of the recent natural disaster in Slovakia at the High Tatra, etc., when welcoming this new guaranteed understanding of solidarity in a concrete founding Treaty provision.

3.    SOME CRITICAL REMARKS ABOUT THE EU CONSTITUTION

– First of all, I am not happy with the title of the new EU founding Treaty. I think that it is unfortunate that it is called as a 'Constitution' because, in my view, this Treaty is not a 'Constitution' primarily because the EU is not a 'state' (a federal state), and normally a constitution belongs to 'statehood' (as a basic law). Secondly, from a sociological and/or psychological point of view, it is not useful to call this document a 'Constitution' because, normally, the citizens of the Member States are not even aware of their own (national) constitution, so how could one expect them to know more about the so-called supranational 'EU Constitution'? This title is therefore, in my opinion, discouraging and to some extent misleading, which is disadvantageous in particular from the point of view of the national courts and other law enforcement bodies of the (new) Member States.[15] Another open question is on which

---

[15] I think that the judiciaries of the new Member States would apply this refounding Treaty of the EU more readily and with greater enthusiasm if it was called something other than a Constitution. This is because the judges and the other law-enforcement bodies in most of the new Member States – as practice shows – do not even apply their own national constitutions, and now there is a desire to implement something even beyond their national constitutions, something which is also called an 'EU Constitution' which can easily be perceived to be a kind of 'Super-Constitution' overriding their own national constitutions! It seems to me that maybe such a double 'over-constitutionalised' horizon will be too complicated and too highly-sophisticated for ordinary lawyers, like judges, civil servants or prosecutors, etc., in many new Member States, especially in the

points does this (re)founding new Treaty of the EU address the whole of 'Europe'? How, and based on which legal and moral grounds, can the 25 current Member States of the EU stipulate and/or address anything on behalf of all the European States, the number of which is at least 46 taking into consideration that the Council of Europe currently has 46 Member States?[16]

– Another possible criticism derives from the fact that this new refounding Treaty of the EU is in fact a 'constitutional cocktail'. In my view, the first two Parts are of a constitutional nature (significance), whereas the Parts III and IV are rather of a founding Treaty character. This means that the first two Parts should have been formulated in a separate 'Constitutional Charter' (maybe attached as a Protocol to the main Treaty), whereas the other two Parts (Part III-IV TCE) should have continued to function as an interstate multilateral founding Treaty. This distinction might have significance in terms of how the two different documents could be amended in the future. In my view, the Constitutional Charter-one part could also only have been amended unanimously in the future, whereas the other two Parts (the current Parts III-IV TCE) could have been amended by either a 4/5 or a 2/3 majority of the ratifying Member States. The present solution in this respect does not seem to be reasonable and satisfactory according to many pragmatic points and concerns raised by experts, for example from the European University Institute in Florence, including many from the new Member States (see Arts. IV-443-445).[17]

– I believe that a further shortcoming (weakness) of this Constitution is that it does not contain interpretative provisions at the begining. This is important especially if we consider that this Constitution is in fact a product of hard-earned political compromises, meaning that it therefore contains many vague and over-politicised terms. One of the clearest examples of this very vague, but somehow legislative vocabulary is the sometimes really confusing use of the term 'law' in the language of the TCE. For example, Article I-6 TCE reads as follows: 'The Constitution and *law* adopted by the institutions of the Union in exercising competences conferred on it shall have primacy *over the law* of the Member States'. But what does 'law adopted by the institutions of the Union' actually mean? In fact the Union institutions adopt legal (regulatory, legislative/non-legislative, delegated, executive and/or implementing)

---

eyes of all those lawyers who have been trained under the former so-called socialist legal culture!

[16] An interesting question for further interdisciplinary research of the EU Constitution could be to what extent does the Treaty address all the peoples of Europe (see the preamble of Part II TCE), or to what extent does it in its title *expressis verbis* aim to establish a Constitution for the whole of Europe?

[17] See, A. Albi and P. Van Elsuwege, 'The EU Constitution, National Constitutions and Sovereignty: An Assessment of a "European Constitutional Order"', 29 *ELR* (2004) pp. 741 et seq., in particular the literature referred to in footnotes 5-6. A good example of the need for this distinction is Art. III-129 TCE.

acts and other measures, but not 'law' in the singular! Also what is the meaning of 'the law of the Member States'? Does it also include, for example, the national constitutions of the Member States? These are not questions which are easy to answer.[18]

Similarly, we can still encounter the term 'law' in plenty of places in the EU Constitution, such as, for example, in Article I-33 TCE, which refers to 'European *law*' and 'European framework *law*' or Article I-5(1) TCE, which also stipulates that the Union shall respect the Member States' essential state functions, including 'maintaining *law* (...)'. Alternatively under Article I-29(1) TCE the term 'law' is already differently addressed, namely: 'The Court of Justice of the European Union (...) shall ensure that in the interpretation and application of the Constitution *the law* is observed', whereas later under Article I-29(3)(b) the Constitution-maker addresses 'only' the 'Union *law*' in terms of the preliminary ruling procedure! An interesting novelty can be found in Article I-29(1) 2nd indent, namely: 'Member States shall provide remedies sufficient to ensure effective legal protection in the fields covered by *Union law*'. It remains to be seen what the difference is between 'Union law' under Article I-29(1) 2nd indent, and the term 'the law' under the same Article, but used in the 1st indent. It should also be noted that the term 'Union law' is used in Part II TCE, for example under Article II-111(1) or Article II-87-88, etc., whereas under Article I-9(3) TCE[19] the term Union's law is already referred to, but without any further clarification. Another problematic *terminus technicus* is the term 'act' and/or 'regulatory act' as used, for example, under Article III-365(4) TCE. What is the difference between these two terms? Perhaps they should be clarified by the ECJ when interpreting Union law? All these terminological discrepancies might result in some difficulties when attempting a proper, consistent and coherent translation of these terms into the national official languages of many Member States, including the new members (see, for example, the recent language and thus the translation problems in terms of the EU Constitution in Latvia, etc.).[20]

– There are some minor inconsistencies in the EU Constitution which should be given some critical attention. For example, Article I-19 TCE which reads as follows: 'The Union shall have an institutional framework which shall aim to (...) – serve its interests, those of its citizens and those of the Member States'.

---

[18] See, J. Czuczai, op. cit. n. 14, in particular on pp. 273-276.

[19] It reads as follows:

'Fundamental rights, as guaranteed by the European Convention for the Protection of Human Rights and as they result from the constitutional traditions common to the Member States, shall constitute general principles of *the Union's law*' (emphasis added).

[20] Art. I-36 TCE reads as follows:

'European laws and framework laws may delegate to the Commission the power to adopt delegated European regulations to supplement or amend *certain non-essential elements* of the law or framework law (...)*The essential elements of an area* shall be reserved for the European law or framework law and accordingly shall not be the subject of a delegation of power'.

I do not see why the interests of the Member States and of the nationals of the Member States as citizens of the Union should be so clearly and expressly separated and distinguished from each other, especially in the context of constitutionally (re)designing, to a certain extent, the reformed European Union institutional framework and taking into account the fact that the new refounding Treaty of the EU has placed its citizens at centre stage (with regard to its primary activities). Another example of built-in inconsistency can be found in Article II-112 TCE which stipulates:

'3. Insofar as this Charter contains rights which correspond to rights guaranteed by the Convention for the Protection of Human Rights and Fundamental Freedoms, the meaning and scope of those rights shall be the same as those laid down by the said Convention (...)'.

And what about the permanent practice of the European Court of Human Rights in this respect? Why is it not referred to at all in the above-mentioned TCE Article, especially if we consider that the EU is pushing the candidate countries very strongly to adopt, in full, the permanent practice of the European Convention on Human Rights in Strasbourg and even the Commission is regularly monitoring this.[21] Finally, a great achievement of the EU Constitution, beyond doubt, is the adoption of the Protocol on the application of the principles of subsidiarity and proportionality, and especially the introduction of the new mechanism in terms of how national Parliaments can finally bring a matter before the ECJ provided that – at least as they see it – the principle of subsidiarity has been violated by the EU institutions.[22] The main problem, however, is that the national Parliaments do not have *locus standi* before the ECJ according to the refounding Treaty of the EU as well as the Protocol, and thus they will very much depend on the will of the Member States' governments if they wish to exercise this new possibility provided for by the new Protocol, which is a really delicate situation.

– I would also like to point out the fact that, in my view, the EU Constitution establishes, to a large extent, only an 'empty shell' constitutional framework for the refounded EU because, according to my calculations, there are more than 200 authorizing provisions therein for the adoption – for the purpose of implementing the Constitution – of further European laws, framework laws, decisions, etc., the number of which is therefore numerous and indeed re-

---

But what is meant by the 'essential elements' or 'non-essential elements' of a regulatory area where the EU has legislative competence? This is not defined at all in the EU Constitution. In my opinion at least an enumerative list of these elements (essential *vis-à-vis* non-essential) should have been provided in an interpretative provision by the TCE itself, if not for other reasons then for the sake of legal certainty, since the EU is based on the principle of the rule of law.

[21] See, P. Birkinshaw, 'A Constitution for the EU? A letter from Home', 10 *European Public Law* (2004) pp. 57-84, in particular on pp. 79 et seq.

[22] See Protocol A.2. in *OJ* (2004) C 310/207-210, in particular Art. 7-8.

markable. For example, as far as the comitology regime is concerned, Article
I-37(3) TCE referes to certain future European laws which will lay down, in
advance, the rules and general principles concerning the mechanisms for
Member State control of the Commission's exercise of implementing powers.
Similarly, there are authorizations for further EU legislation, for example, in
the fields of 'The principle of participatory democracy' (Art. I-47(4) TCE) or
the 'Transparency of the proceedings of Union institutions, bodies, offices
and agencies' (Art. I-50(3) 2nd indent TCE), or the 'Protection of personal
data' (Art. I-51(2) TCE), or the Union's finances (Arts. I-54(3)-(4), I-55(2),
etc.) or in terms of European Prosecutorship (Art. III-274(1) TCE) and this
long list could be extended. But what happens if these 'implementing', constitutionally important, subsequent European legal acts will not be adopted on
time (because of the uninanimity requirement, or the lack of Parliamentary
consent, etc.), or merely with a substantial delay? Will the EU Constitution
remain fully implemented from the very day of its entry into force without
these legal acts on the part of the Union? Will this not create, at least in certain areas, some sort of legal uncertainty?

– Finally, as far as Part III TCE is concerned, I think that it is even more complicated and sophisticated than the current text of the TEC with the so many
cross-references between the different Parts of the EU Constitution.[23] This
means that in this respect the goal of the Laeken Declaration on the Future of
Europe, namely to simplify the new refounding Treaty of the EU (with regard
to its language, structure, drafting, etc.) and to make it more readily comprehensible for the citizens of the Union in order to stimulate the situation where
the European citizens are increasingly closer to the refounded EU, thereby
placing them at the heart of its constitutionalising activities,[24] seems not to
have been met by the final product of the Treaty.

## 4.   THE RATIFICATION PROCESS IN THE MEMBER STATES

As mentioned above, in Hungary Parliament has already ratified the EU Constitution on 20 December 2004 after Lithuania, which already ratified as the first
Member State on 11 November 2004. In the meantime Slovenia has also ratified
the Treaty establishing a Constitution for Europe on 1 February 2005.[25] The first

---

[23] See, M. Dougan, 'The Convention's Draft Constitutional Treaty: Bringing Europe to its Lawyers', 28 *ELR* (2003) pp. 763-793.

[24] See the Preamble of the Charter of Fundamental Rights of the EU in Part II TCE, which reads as follows:

'The Union *'places the individual at the heart of its activities*, by establishing the citizenship of the Union and by creating an area of freedom, security and justice'.

[25] See 'Spain gives a Good Demonstration of how to support the New Constitution', in *Népszava* ['The Voice of the People', a Hungarian daily newspaper] (11 February 2005) p. 9.

three countries that have ratified the EU Constitution are new Member States. One may pose the question whether this is only by accident? One could even add a second question as to why the majority of the new Member States do not consider it important to have an in-depth social dialogue on the new Treaty and – except for Poland and the Czech Republic – a referendum?

Personally, I was of the firm opinion that the new EU founding Treaty should be ratified by a nationwide referendum in Hungary too, the result of which would bind the Budapest Parliament.[26] Unexpectedly, on a cold morning in December last year, however, I heard on the radio that Parliament had already ratified it (within two weeks, with only six hours' debate). This was really a surprise to me. Similarly, I heard that in Lithuania the ratification had taken place on the last working day of the outgoing Parliament in Vilnius just before the general elections, in fact without any discussion as to its merits, although there were many more 'no' votes than in Budapest.

I think one possible answer to the above questions might be taken from the historical experiences in the constitutional developments, learned by and in the Central and Eastern European new Member States before the Berlin wall fell. In the former so-called socialist system in this part of Europe there were very nicely worded constitutions in force which were patterned almost literally on the so-called Stalinist Constitution of 1936 of the former Soviet Union.[27] The main characteristic of these constitutions was, however, that they remained largely on paper, because the state and its organs and the people did not take them seriously. The existence of such a mentality even today in Central and Eastern Europe in terms of constitutional behaviour cannot in general be excluded. That leads me to conclude that maybe certain political circles in the given countries might have thought that the new Treaty establishing a Constitution for Europe (still on paper) would either never enter into force (because it would fail to be ratified by referendums in certain other Member States) or if it did enter into force as scheduled (by November 2006), then in practice at the national level it would have no real significance, since it can be stated that in general from the point of view of the ordinary people even the national constitutions might have no real relevance and that is why most citizens in these countries in fact know nothing even about their own national constitutions in Central and Eastern Europe, let alone the EU Constitution! In this respect it would prove to be a positive lift-off for the whole ratification process in Europe if at least some of the new Member States could ratify the EU Constitution very quickly at the beginning of the ratification process. I may agree with this last perception, but only in a wider European context,

---

[26] See, interview with J. Czuczai, 'A Referendum on the New EU Constitution in Hungary', in *Világgazdaság* ['The World Economy', a very popular Hungarian daily business journal] (1 October 2004) p. 3.

[27] See in more detail, J. Czuczai, 'Transition from State Economy into Market Economy. The Hungarian Experiences', in A. Petchsiri, et al., eds., *Comparative Regional Integration: ASEAN and the EU* (Bangkok, Chulalongkorn University, European Studies Series Vol. 2 (2002)) pp. 160-181, in particular on pp. 166 et seq.

and exclusively with the aspect of encouraging others. In no way, however, do I agree with the perception that the new EU Constitution will anyhow remain only a document on paper in the enlarged EU. I rather want to see it as a Constitutional Treaty in action!

5.    CONCLUDING REMARK

In answering the question posed by the 34th Asser Colloquium on European Law, 'The EU Constitution: the best way forward?', I may conclude by saying that even if it is not the best way forward, it is nevertheless a reasonably good and promising way forward in order to further deepen and widen the reunification process of Europe in the 21st century for the benefit of all of us, Europe's current and future citizens.

# THE CONSTRUCTION OF THE EUROPEAN UNION: RECOMMENDATIONS FROM A BALKAN PERSPECTIVE

**Duško Lopandić**[*]

The former French President Francois Mitterrand used to compare the establishment of the European architecture with the building of medieval cathedrals: it was the work of generations. In modern Europe, every new generation of politicians and lawyers had to add some additional chapels – or chapters – to the former framework of this legal cathedral. With the adoption of the Treaty establishing a Constitution for Europe, the question today may be the following: are we seeing the end of this endeavor? Can we speak of the construction finally taking shape and therefore coming to an end?

Overall, we can say that the Treaty establishing a Constitution for Europe presents a serious effort to transform the European Union into a real political union of countries sharing a 'common destiny'. The Treaty also presents an endeavour to establish a much clearer and potentially a more efficient (though a very complex) structure – a kind of peaceful, democratic, legal 'Empire' – both for its citizens and for the rest of the world. In the field of foreign relations, the EU will, in principle, act in a clearer and much more consistent way, while the scope of its activities will expand.

There are those who criticize the shortcomings of the Constitutional Treaty. However, overall I think that the general opinion of the legal experts is a positive one. The EU Constitution is indeed a step in the right direction. It would not be a catastrophe, but it would be a pity and a setback for the whole European construction if the voters in some national referenda were to reject the EU Constitution. So, my first suggestion would be a strong recommendation to accept the EU Constitution.

The second question which is relevant to the process of future EU construction concerns a possible enlargement *fatigue*, due to the probability of additional problems connected to the recent 'big bang' enlargement. Some European decision makers may think in terms of the 'end of history'. In fact, the thesis could be that the historic mission of the European construction has come to an end with the inclusion of the majority of Central and European countries belonging to the former Warsaw Pact. According to this point of view, 'Europe' (i.e., the EU)

[*] PhD, Assistant Minister for External Economic Relations, Republic of Serbia.

*D. Curtin, A.E. Kellermann and S. Blockmans, eds., The EU Constitution: The Best Way Forward?*
© 2005, T.M.C. Asser Instituut, The Hague.

should now halt its enlargement process and should concentrate instead on its own energy and resources.

There is a tendency, and this can be seen in the debate on Turkey's proposed membership, to introduce some new, additional elements into the process of EU accession. This will mean that the process may even become longer and more complicated.

I am strongly opposed to this point of view. In fact, the logic of enlargement is still strong. The EU may be, in a way, the victim of its own success, but it would be counterproductive and even politically disastrous to stop the process of enlargement before its logical end – while a number of European countries in South-eastern Europe are still actively involved in this process. The same logic as was applied to Central Europe should be extended to South-eastern Europe (i.e., the Balkans, including the former Yugoslav republics).

So my second recommendation would be that the EU should continue, with even greater gusto, the process of enlargement.

The great responsibility and challenge lies with ten new EU Members. They should *in the first instance* work on the implementation of EU *acquis* obligations and *prove* that the enlargement was a success. Moreover, they should support in every way (politically, technically, etc.) the process of further enlargement.

Let me now turn to a more regional perspective. We may wonder how these changes will affect the Western Balkan countries, which, for the time being, have been omitted from the EU enlargement process, or how these changes will affect my country: Serbia and Montenegro (SaM).

The EU Constitution envisages that it should come into force on 1 November 2006, the year that should mark the end of the current EU enlargement process to attain 27 Member States. Negotiations with Romania and Bulgaria have been completed and they will become Members of the European Union in January 2007.

The Western Balkan countries are, as we know, 'potential candidates'. Croatia and Macedonia have already submitted their applications for EU membership. Negotiations with Croatia will probably start in March 2005 (provided there is full cooperation with ICTY). In addition, Turkey will also start negotiations for membership.

The EU Constitution has not introduced changes in provisions and criteria as regards conditions for EU membership. The only novelty is the introduction of provisions that envisage a procedure for countries that want to *leave* the European Union.

However, we cannot forget all the possible pitfalls and difficulties lying on the road towards applying the *acquis,* including the new *Constitutional acquis*, to the new members of the Union. Although the formal criteria for EU membership have not changed, there is no doubt that with each EU enlargement the tasks for the future membership candidates become more complex. To put it simply, the so-called *acquis communautaire* corpus has become larger, and its structure and the way it functions have become more complex. At the time when Spain entered the EU (in the 1980s), the total number of all EC regulations amounted to some

40,000 pages in length. This volume is now probably over 100,000 pages, not to mention that the competencies have spread to new sectors.

One of the difficulties the countries of the Western Balkans will face will be to deal simultaneously with the *new* and the *old acquis,* i.e., the legal system established under the EU Constitution will function *in parallel* with the previous *acquis.*

Consequently, although the principle of future membership for the Western Balkan countries will not be at stake, becoming an EU member is becoming increasingly complex and time consuming, which could be because the EU is facing other complex issues, such as Turkish membership, etc.

Serbia and Montenegro are notoriously lagging behind in the institutional approximation to the EU, which is largely (if not exclusively) the result of our internal dispute as to whether we should join the EU together or separately. Signing the Stabilization and Association Agreement (SAA) with the EU is uncertain because the Feasibility Report on the SAA negotiations has been delayed for almost a year. This situation endangers the country's vital interests in the long-term and is not sustainable. However, bearing in mind the newly established European Partnerships between the EU and the Western Balkan countries, and the so-called 'twin-track procedure' for Serbia and Montenegro, the process of becoming closer to the EU has not been stopped and constitutional co-operation could be established relatively quickly. The 'twin-track' approach to the negotiations for SAA (i.e., separate negotiations with Serbia and with Montenegro on some trade and economic issues) will facilitate overall process.

We believe that Serbia and Montenegro could make up for the lost time in the process of institutional approximation if it submits a formal application simultaneously with the signing of the Stabilization and Association Agreement with the EU. There is a precedent, as this is exactly what Slovenia did in 1996, thus managing to 'get on the train' of the EU membership negotiations. As for Serbia and Montenegro, a desirable deadline for the membership application/signing the SAA could be as early as 2006. The second half of this decade could therefore be used for the acceleration of reforms and the more rapid adoption of the *acquis,* so that the membership negotiations could finish around the end of this decade or a few years later.

# THE EU CONSTITUTION AND ITS IMPACT ON RELATIONS WITH THE RUSSIAN FEDERATION[*]

Mark Entin[**]

## 1.    INTRODUCTION

Has one ever heard an expert or a politician saying the following? 'Look here. Russia has not taken part in the elaboration of the EU Constitution. Russia will not exert any influence on its ratification and entry into force. Generally speaking, it has nothing to do with this internal act of the European Union. It does not make any difference to Russia whether the European Union has a Constitution or not. Developments inside the European Union are of no interest to its great Eastern neighbour.' Let us imagine that such a statement has been made. Could it be true? Is there any need to study the impact which the EU Constitution may have on legal and political developments in the Russian Federation? Are the developments inside the European Union of any interest to Russia? Is the European Union interested in exerting an influence upon the developments inside the Russian Federation? Let us seek some obvious, and not so obvious, answers.

Formally, the above statement contains nothing illogical in itself. Unfortunately, it could well have been made. The rationale for this is that the Russian Federation is not a member of the European Union. The author of such a statement could argue that Russia has no intention of joining the EU in the foreseeable future. For its part, the European Union is not ready even to discuss such a possibility.

According to the leaders of the Russian Federation and its political elite, Russia does not need to become a member of any supranational entity. Russia has its own national interests which it is able to protect. It has its own culture and historical heritage that it will try to preserve.[1] The state bodies and the population

---

[*]  This article has been prepared within the framework of the TACIS project on the establishment of the Russian-European Center of Economic Policy (RECEP).

[**] Professor of international law at the Moscow State Institute (University) of International Relations; Director of the MGIMO Institute of European Law. The author worked as a diplomat in Strasbourg for many years and is the author of numerous books, manuals and research articles on the law of international organizations, the European Union, EU institutions, human rights and world politics.

[1] See, e.g., С. Кара-Мурза, Здравый смысл, Литературная газета, 9 - 15 июня 2004 г.,

---

D. Curtin, A.E. Kellermann and S. Blockmans, eds., The EU Constitution: The Best Way Forward?
© 2005, T.M.C. Asser Instituut, The Hague.

must rebuild the country and confirm its stature as a global actor relying entirely on its own forces. The leaders of the Russian Federation and its political elite think that Russia has enough strength and resources to develop as a self-sufficient power. The challenges of globalization do not impede this and the limitations and constraints of interdependence can be put to one side.

Of course, they have come to this conclusion not without hesitation. They had different aspirations in the early and mid-1990s. But the situation was different at that time. It has changed drastically now. The ideas have changed accordingly.

There is no need to judge the position of the Russian political elite. It does not matter whether it is right or wrong, whether it is based on realistic calculations or selfish attitudes. What is important is that this position is the way it is. It is just a matter of fact.

It is also evident that for the European Union Russia is a third country.[2] The European Union never considered Russia as its close ally. All the grand words and pompous political declarations about a strategic partnership must be taken at their true value. The European Union never thought about attracting Russia to EU membership. It was not the case when the Partnership and Co-operation Agreement was drafted. It is even less so now.[3]

In accordance with Jacques Delors' theory of European circles, Russia lies beyond the European Union area of vital interests. A number of reasons were advanced on different occasions to explain why Russia has no vocation to become a member of the EU. It is a common belief now in the EU capitals that Russia is too large to be integrated. Russia is a continent in itself. It is larger than all the EU countries taken together. It has thousands of kilometers of borders with China and other Asian states. Russia has a huge population. If it is admitted to the European Union, the balance of power will be shifted towards it. Russia has so many internal problems. The war in Chechnya is not over. There are very wide economic disparities between the regions. It has not resolved contradictions

---

no. 23 (5975). – C. 10 [S. Kara-Murza, 'Common Sense', 23 *Literaturnaya Gazeta* (9-15 June 2004) (5975) p. 10].

[2] In this respect the EU Constitution changes nothing. The mere fact that its neighbourship provisions (Title VIII Art. I-57 TCE, 'The Union and its Neighbours') precede those on membership and are inserted in Part I of the EU Constitution and not in Part III dealing with external relations does not mean that Russia or other EU neighbours receive a special status. It does not mean that they cease to be third countries for the European Union. For the opposite view see the report on legal harmonization by A.E. Kellermann, 'Membership of the European Internal Market without being an EU Member State: A Comparison of EU-Norway, EU-Switzerland and EU-Russia Relations, with special Focus on the Experiences with Approximation of Legislation. What will be the Best Way Forward for the Russian Federation?', available at: <http://www.recep.ru>.

[3] See, e.g., M. Vahl, 'Just Good Friends? The EU – Russia "Strategic Partnership" and the Northern Dimension' (Brussels, CEPS Working Document no. 166 (March 2001)) available at: <http://www.ceps.be>; Эмерсон М. Слон и Медведь: Европейский союз, Россия и их ближнее зарубежье [M. Emerson, 'An Elephant and a Bear: European Union, Russia and their Near Abroads' (Brussels, CEPS Paperback Books 2001)].

between different ethnic and religious groups present on it soil. It is better for the European Union to keep a distance between Russia and itself. Russia is too independent. It will be very difficult for the European Union, if possible at all, to absorb it. Recently, it has become fashionable to blame Russia for drifting away from common European values.[4]

All these perceptions are not persuasive.[5] There are many historical and cultural facts contradicting them. Russia has made an enormous contribution to European culture. It liberated Europe, hand in hand with other nations, from fascism. It suffered unprecedented losses to free itself from communist rule.

From time to time it is difficult to distinguish between the genuine beliefs that Russia must not be considered a friendly nation and the speculations hiding the lack of will on the part of the European Union to have closer ties with Russia.[6]

In any case, we have no other choice but to take it for granted that the European Union and Russia are entirely autonomous political entities. They do not consider political integration to be necessary or plausible. They take decisions concerning their internal development and external policy independently, following their own national interests, without paying much attention to the opinion of the other side.

If this is so, let us repeat our initial question and ask ourselves once more whether all that means that the EU Constitution is of no interest to Russia and

---

[4] See, e.g., Putin's 'Russia. A Special 14-page Survey', 371 *The Economist*, No. 8376 (22-28 May 2004). Zbigniew Brzezinski even insisted that 'Putin's regime in many ways is similar to Mussolini's Fascism'. See Z. Brzezinski, 'The Fleeting Appeal of Moscow's Mussolini', *The Moscow Times* (22 September 2004) p. 10. The famous French author Maurice Druon expressed an entirely opposite view. According to him, Russia will never return to communist structures and ideology. French leftist parties and trade unions are now more Marxist than Russia. But Russia has no options other than to be an autocratic democracy. See Дрюон М. Поможем России победить терроризм, который постепенно добирается до всех нас, Известия, 27 сентября 2004 г. - С. 4 [M. Druon, 'Let us help Russia to crush Terrorism which is gradually reaching us all', *Izvestia* (27 September 2004) p. 4].

[5] Let us consider, for example, the issue of a 'huge population'. In Russia it is steadily decreasing. The gap between Russia and other big European countries is becoming less and less pronounced. See, e.g., 'World Population Prospects: The 2002 Revision and World Urbanization Prospects: The 2001 Revision' (Population Division of the Department of Economic and Social Affairs of the United Nations Secretariat) available at: <http://esa.un.org/unpp>; Население России 2002. Десятый ежегодный демографический доклад, Под ред. А.Г. Виневского. - М.: книжный дом 'Университет', 2004. – С. 173 – 195 [A. Vishnevsky, 'Population of Russia 2002. The Tenth Annual Demographic Report' ("oscow, Book House 'Universitet' (2004)) pp. 173-195]; ноябрь - декабрь 2004 г. - С. 28 – 46 [A. Vishnevsky, 'Alternatives to Migration Strategy', 2 *Russia in Global Politics* (2004) pp. 28-46].

[6] See, e.g., Россия и Европейский Союз: переосмысливая стратегию взаимоотношений, Под ред. А.Мошеса; Моск. Центр Карнеги; Фин. Ин-т междунар. Отношений. - М.: Гендальф, 2003. – 119 [A. Moshes, ed., 'Russia and the European Union: Rethinking the Relationship Strategy' (Special FIIA – Carnegie Moscow Centre Report 2003)] available at: <http://www.upi-fiia.fi/english/publications/upi_report/reports/FIIA-CarnegieReport2003.pdf>.

will have no impact on its internal and foreign policies. No, it does not mean that. Although the Russian Federation and the European Union are far away from any kind of political integration, membership of the EU is not on the agenda and there is no intention on either side to touch upon this issue, the EU Constitution is nevertheless of great relevance to the Russian Federation, to its state bodies, political elite and population as a whole.

A great deal of attention was paid by the Russian mass media to the work of the last Intergovernmental Conference and the Convention for the Future of Europe which preceded it. Many articles with an analysis of the draft Constitution appeared in scientific journals and various magazines.[7] The process of ratification will be under the scrutiny of the Russian mass media on a permanent basis.

Russia is a part of Europe. The European Union is its main player. It is very important for the Russian elite and the Russian population to know and understand in what direction the European Union will evolve. The EU Constitution provides them with a fairly clear answer.

Russia is a European Union neighbour. The EU Constitution contains a special article on the EU neighbourhood policy (Art. I-57 TCE). The fact that the neighbourhood policy is enshrined in the EU Constitution increases its political and institutional status. It becomes a constant factor in the EU-Russia relationship.

The EU Constitution establishes a set of requirements addressed to those states which the European Union considers to be its current or future foreign partners or even strategic partners. The enumeration of these requirements in the Constitution may drastically change the EU's external policies, its relationship with third countries and international organizations and its international environment. Of course, all this will have a tremendous impact on the EU-Russia relationship.

## 2.    RUSSIAN INTEREST FOR THE EU'S CONSTITUTIONAL PROCESS

The coverage by the Russian mass media of the work of the Intergovernmental Conference which drew up the text of the Treaty establishing a Constitution for Europe was reminiscent of that in the 25 countries of the European Union. It focused, as was the case in the Member States, on a limited number of issues causing differences among these States. That is why the general knowledge of the EU Constitution in Russia was distorted. The general public and to some extent the political and legal communities associated it with a more or less compromise solution for disputes on the allocation of votes, rules for majority voting, the extension itself and the (lack of) reference to the word 'God' in the preamble. It will

---

[7] See, e.g., *Europe, Contemporary Europe, Moscow Journal of International Law, Russian Justice, Russian State and Law.*

take a great deal of time and effort to explain to the public the true meaning of the EU Constitution and its impact both on the European Union and on the Russian Federation.

Now, the attitude in Russia to the EU Constitution, its meaning and future consequences has started to change. A serious analysis has taken preference over the former information notices and brief articles of a speculative nature.[8] Academic circles, political and non-governmental organizations have organized a number of international conferences to discuss the main features of the EU Constitution. Heavyweight magazines, as well as weekly and daily newspapers publish comments on issues related to the EU Constitution written by eminent lawyers and well-known politicians. Federal and regional TV and radio stations broadcast special programmes and debates on the anticipated internal developments in the European Union.[9]

The live radio and TV discussions on the EU Constitution demonstrated that the general public was eager to understand why the European Union had decided to provide itself with a constitutional act and whether or not it will drastically change its nature, as well as whether the EU will undergo a transformation into a federal state when the EU Constitution enters into force. The audience asked questions about the Convention on the Future of Europe and the Intergovernmental Conference, the working procedures they had used and the rules under which they had been established and had been functioning, as well as the role they had played in the elaboration of the EU Constitution. The proverbial person in the street wanted to obtain answers to a number of key questions. Among them were questions concerning the efficiency of the EU structures, the overwhelming influence of the EU bureaucracy on decision-making, the EU's readiness to respect the principles of sovereignty and equality of Member States, the EU's plans and intentions and its ability to meet new challenges, etc.

All this is convincing proof of a genuine interest on the part of the Russian public to everything related to the European Union and, especially, to such new developments in its internal life as the adoption of the EU Constitution. In practice, Russia, its leaders and ordinary people attach tremendous importance to its relationship with the European Union. The explanation for this is as clear as day. Most Russians see themselves as 100% Europeans. They believe that Russia has made a considerable contribution to the might and glamour of the European continent. They believe that the fate of Russia is inseparable from that of the other

---

[8] See, e.g., Энтин Л.М. О проекте Конституции Европейского Союза, Московский журнал международного права, № 1 (53), январь - март 2004 г. – с. 85 - 100 [M. Entin, 'On the Constitution of the European Union', 1 *Moscow Journal of International Law* (53) (2004) pp. 85-100]; Энтин М.Л. Правовые основы внешней политики Европейского Союза, Московский журнал международного права, № 4 (52), октябрь - декабрь 2003 г. – С. 86 – 116 [M. Entin, 'Legal Basis of EU External Policy', 4 *Moscow Journal of International Law* (52) (2003) pp. 86-116].

[9] Among them are popular radio stations such as 'Echo Moskvy', 'Mayak', etc.

part of Europe. Years of communist rule have not changed anything in these perceptions.[10]

The European Union is the Russian Federation's major trade and economic partner. Both of them share a common historical and cultural heritage. Their economies are complimentary. The enlargement has brought the Union to the borders of Russia. Other prerequisites for moving closer to each other exist as well.

There is a common understanding in Russia that positive trends in EU development could be of benefit to Russian business and ordinary people. In contrast, crisis developments in the EU may have a negative effect on the Russian Federation. This attitude throws some light on why people in Russia are interested in what the Union could become in a few years and how it will evolve. The EU draft Constitution contains answers to some of these questions.


3.     THE TRANSFORMATION OF THE EU AND ITS IMPACT ON RUSSIA

The EU Constitution could make the European Union much more powerful and dynamic. It envisages a set of delicately tailored reforms, which are to be put into practice using a step by step approach.

The EU Constitution does not deprive the Member States of their national identity. But it establishes a new balance of competences and powers between Brussels and the States' capitals.

The EU Constitution does not create a new institutional structure for the European Union, but it does introduce considerable changes therein. The European Union will function in a different way with the permanent President of the European Council, the concentration of responsibilities in the hands of the Minister for Foreign Affairs, the nearly equal representation of Member States in the European Commission, the collective running of the Council formations and the strengthening of the European Parliament.

The EU Constitution does not presuppose a departure from the way the policies are conceived in the EU. But their elaboration and implementation, their content and control over their execution will not be the same.

The EU Constitution is designed for about 30 countries. But it envisages a possibility of EU fragmentation into different economic, social, political and military spaces with unpredictable participation and dynamics.

---

[10] See, e.g., 'How to deepen Cooperation between Russia and the European Union? Как углубить сотрудничество России и Европейского Союза?' (Paper – Moscow, 'Russia in United Europe' Committee (2003)); 'On the Measures for the Introduction of a Visa-Free Regime between the Russian Federation and the European Union / Безвизовый режим между Россией и Европейским Союзом' (ЕС доклад – Москва,  Комитет Россия в объединенной Европе [ЕС: 'Roadmap' – Moscow, 'Russia in United Europe' Committee] (2004)).

The EU Constitution will help the European Union to become a more efficient player on the world stage. It will enable the EU to spread over its borders the benefits of good governance, liberty, democracy, security, justice and prosperity.

At the same time, some of these answers are not obvious. The EU Constitution embraces the neo-liberal model of economic development. Free trade, free movement and other key elements of a single market and an economic and monetary union are invigorated. Nevertheless, doubts remain concerning the European Union's approaches towards globalization, the preservation of its proper achievements in the social field, and the transformation of the EU into the most efficient and competitive economy in the world based on knowledge.

The EU countries face very difficult social and economic choices and challenges. All of them need to carry out structural reforms, introduce much more efficient and modern pension schemes and social security systems. These issues are dealt with in the EU Constitution in an elusive and superficial way.

The text envisages the transformation of the EU from an entirely civil economic and political society into a defence, and even a military one. It is not clear whether such a move represents a radical departure from the previous model of EU development or just another step in the same direction. For decades the European communities and the European Union served as an example and a point of attraction for third nations. A military build up within the framework of the Union could be assumed to be preparation for the coercive dissemination of its values and principles.

In Russia, there is an understanding that the EU Constitution is only a design. Everything will depend on how its provisions will be implemented. When this perception is applied to the dynamics of the EU-Russia relationship, it is usually emphasized that real politics must take into consideration the internal developments both in the Russian Federation and in the European Union as well as the bilateral experience they have acquired.

The Russian Federation and the European Union have undergone profound changes. Russia is emerging after many years of crisis with consolidated state institutions and a rapidly evolving economy. It is genuinely interested in strengthening international law, the United Nations and other multilateral tools of international co-operation. It pays more and more attention to improving relations with its neighbours on the basis of equality and mutual benefit. Its strategy consists of projecting across its borders multiple areas of integration, economic growth, stability and internal and external security.

The European Union, after a sequence of transformations, has emerged not only as a common market which it used to be for decades, but as a combination of economic, monetary, social, political and defence communities. Its model of development and its success story being very attractive,[11] non-member countries

---

[11] Ukraine being one of the latest examples.

had been queuing up to accede to the EU. Ten of them recently managed to join the EU. Others are expected to do so in a few years time. To meet the challenges of adaptation the EU constantly modernises its institutions and its primary and secondary law. All this will help the EU to become a more efficient player in its relationship with the Member States and on the world scene.

The relations between Russia and the European Union will have a considerable impact upon future developments on the Eurasian continent, crisis prevention and management, non-proliferation, the international struggle against terrorism, organized crime and illegal migration. Its main features are of the outmost importance to themselves, as well as to the fate of their common neighbours.

The European Union's enlargement was a crucial test for the maturity of the relationship between the Russian Federation and the Union. Both sides have shown a spirit of compromise and responsibility in finding solutions to their differences. When the understanding of how to settle these differences was achieved, the prospects for closer relations and a real strategic RF-EU partnership appeared much brighter.

For many months, the legal, economic, social and financial consequences of the European Union's enlargement continued to fuel contradictions between the Russian Federation and the European Union.[12] Russia had established links, agreements and contracts with candidate countries in different fields, subsequently negatively affected by the enlargement. Moscow insisted on protecting its legally ensured interests. It protested against the EU policy of urging the acceding countries to terminate the agreements duly concluded and in force at that time, without taking into consideration the Russian position. According to Moscow, such a stance was incompatible with the 1969 Vienna Convention on the Law of International Treaties and general principles of international law. Brussels used to reply that the overall consequences of the enlargement would benefit Russia.

EU officials based their position, *inter alia*, on the fact, acknowledged by the Russian side, that the overall level of tariffs for imports of goods of Russian origin to the new Member States should decrease, as of 1 May 2004, from an average of 9% to around 4% due to the application by the enlarged EU of the Common Customs Tariff to imports from Russia.[13] Brussels stressed that Rus-

---

[12] See Последствия расширения Европейского Союза для экономики России. М., Национальный инвестиционный Совет 2004. – 94 с ['Consequences of EU Expansion for Russian Economy' (Moscow, National Investment Council (2004))]. See for conflicting rights and obligations arising from agreements with third countries concluded before 1 January 1958 or for acceding states, before the date of their accession, Art. 307 TEC as referred to by A. E. Kellermann, 'The Impact of EU Enlargement on the Russian Federation', 4 *Romanian Journal for European Affairs* (2004) pp. 5-40.

[13] Joint Statement on EU Enlargement and EU-Russia Relations, adopted on 27 April 2004, available at: <http://europa.eu.int/comm/external_relations/russia/russia_docs/js_elarg_270404.htm>.

sian companies would have access to a broader common market. It will be much easier for them to do business. Trade barriers will become lower. Summing up, the conditions for trade, joint ventures and co-operation will improve.

The EU requested Russia to accept as automatic the extension of the Partnership and Co-operation Agreement to the new Member States. It relied on the PCA provision describing the EU as an entity whose composition must be regarded as its internal matter.

Russia stuck to the opposite point of view. Under the PCA there were signatures of only 15 EU countries with which Russia had entered into an agreement. The enlargement was changing the EU drastically. The extension could be considered only as a result of negotiation.

These contradictions gave rise to tension between the RF and EU. Their relationship was on the verge of disruption. Nevertheless, political realism and wisdom won the day. After unprecedented talks between a large European Commission delegation headed by its President and the Russian Government in Moscow on 21-22 April 2004, the Russian and EU diplomats reached a fair compromise. On 27 April 2004 the Russian Minister for Foreign Affairs, Sergei Lavrov, and his EU and acceding countries' counterparts signed a Protocol to the PCA extending it to the new EU Member States.[14] On the same day the Joint Statement on the EU Enlargement and EU-Russia Relations was issued addressing Russian concerns. It deals with a number of sensitive political and economic issues of crucial importance for RF-EU relations. At the same time, it manages to resolve some acute economic disputes which are of interest to Russian corporate business.

Brussels assumed an obligation to start negotiations with a view to concluding an agreement on facilitating the issuing of visas to Russian and EU citizens on a reciprocal basis and to continue to examine the conditions for visa-free travel as a long-term perspective. For Russia, it is a very sensitive political issue. It concerns everybody. It is considered to be a test of the EU's readiness to create common spaces with Russia in deed and not only in word.

There is another issue worth many billions of euros. The EU confirmed that it does not impose any limits on imports of fossil fuels and electricity from Russia. It recognized that long- term contracts had played and would continue to play an important role in ensuring stable and reliable supplies of Russian natural gas to the EU market.

In an effort to address some major Russian economic concerns Brussels decided to adopt special measures to prevent a sudden sharp negative impact on

---

[14] Protocol to the Partnership and Co-operation Agreement establishing a Partnership between the European communities and their Member States, on the one part, and the Russian Federation, on the other part, to take account of the accession of the Czech Republic, the Republic of Estonia, the Republic of Cyprus, the Republic of Latvia, the Republic of Lithuania, the Republic of Hungary, the Republic of Malta, the Republic of Poland, the Republic of Slovenia, and the Slovak Republic to the European Union, adopted on 27 April 2004.

traditional trade flows from Russia and to reconsider the eventual economic effect of numerous antidumping procedures and procedures incorporating quantitative thresholds (concerning potassium chloride, ammonium nitrate, grain-oriented electrical sheets, silicon carbide, aluminium foil, etc.).

In addition, the EU confirmed that Russian exports of non-alloyed aluminium into Hungary will benefit from a gradual alignment to the Common Customs Tariffs until 1 May 2007, that exports of aluminium manufactured products will be subject to a custom duty rate of around 4% in the enlarged EU and that compensatory tariff adjustments accorded in the context of EU enlargement through modifications of the EU tariff schedule will be applied on an MFN basis to the advantage of Russian exporters.

The EU agreed to increase the Russian overall steel exports quota by 438,000 tons by the end of 2004, reflecting traditional Russian exports to acceding countries, and to adapt, consequently, the Russia-EU agreement on trade in certain steel products.

The Member States were allowed to continue authorizing on a case by case basis the operation of noisy Russian aircraft following the EU enlargement.

The EU confirmed that the current contracts on the supply of nuclear materials with the acceding countries, persons and undertakings would remain valid and it agreed to start negotiations on an agreement on trade in nuclear materials.

The Joint Statement of 27 April 2004 also highlighted the issue of Kaliningrad.

## 4.   FUTURE PARTNERSHIP

The settlement of numerous disputes, enshrined in the Statement, as well as the conclusion of the marathon negotiations on the conditions for Russian accession to the WTO paved the way for accelerated work on common spaces or, rather, eliminated the obstacles. Both parties officially acknowledged that the enlargement offers new opportunities for further strengthening their partnership.

### 4.1   Common Spaces

This partnership is to take shape through the creation of a number of common spaces. These future common spaces are the Common European Economic Space (CEES), the common space of freedom, security and justice, the common space of external security and the common space of research and education, including cultural aspects.

Later this year, the 15th Russia-EU Summit in Moscow is expected to discuss a draft road-map for achieving this aim. The experience to be gained in implementing the approved road-map will pave the way for a new legal framework for RF-EU relations. It will enrich the Russian Federation and the European Union neighbourhood policies in many ways. In their turn, the neighbourhood policies will exert considerable influence on RF-EU relations.

In the future, they will be reshaped taking into consideration a new constitutional provision on the neighbourhood policy and adjustments that the EU Constitution will bring to the functioning of the European Union.

The decision to create four common spaces was taken a little more than two years ago at the St. Petersburg RF-EU 2003 Summit. The 12th Russia-EU Summit held in Rome on 6 November 2003 agreed to intensify efforts to fulfil this decision. A strong determination to produce concrete results was expressed.[15] The first results were scrutinized in The Hague at the end of 2004 with the aim of adopting in Moscow a road-map for creating common spaces later this year. The initial proposals prepared by the EU were tabled at the 13th Russia-EU Summit held in Moscow on 21 May 2004. But the Russian side expressed a wish to produce a more pragmatic and result-oriented version.

Russia and the EU have been working on the concept of a Common European Economic Space since 2001.[16] The Rome Russia-EU Summit endorsed the work done and welcomed the concept.[17] Before the end of the current year it must be transformed into a road-map of concrete measures to achieve tangible results as early as possible. It is a difficult task. The existing concept is rather vague. It defines only a number of principles and guidelines for the activities that can be implemented in the short term. More specific objectives are to be discussed and set at a later stage.

The EU concept 'Wider Europe: new neighbourhood' advising the EU's neighbours to follow the EU model of society and offering them some benefits of the enlarged common market does not clarify the matter.[18] This document is not entirely compatible with the European Commission Communication on EU-Russian relations of 9 February 2004, outlining the means which the Commission considers to be the most effective in establishing the common spaces.

In accordance with the concept of the CEES, its main goals consist of giving the economic integration a further boost, enhancing general prosperity on both sides, improving standards of living, increasing the protection of human health

---

[15] 12th EU-Russia Summit Joint Statement (Rome, 6 November 2003) No. 13990/03 (Press Release no. 313) p. 2, available at: <http://ue.eu.int/ueDocs/cms_Data/docs/pressdata/en/er/77845.pdf>.

[16] The decision to establish a joint High-Level Group (HLG) to elaborate the concept of the CEES was taken at the Russia-EU Summit in October 2001. Five months later the Co-operation Council of the PCA provided the HLG with a mandate to elaborate a concept for a closer economic relationship between the RF and EU by October 2003.

[17] Annex I 'The Common European Economic Space (CEES) – Concept paper' to the Joint Statement of the 12th EU-Russia Summit, *supra* n. 13, at pp. 5-9.

[18] See См. Грушко А.В. Российский взгляд на концепцию Широкой Европы. Россия и Евросоюз: добрососедство без права на родство? - М.: Комитет 'Россия в объединённой Европе' 2004 – С. 22-32 [A.V. Grushko, 'Russian Approach to "Wider Europe" Concept', *Russia and European Union: Good neighbourliness without the Right to Kinship Relationship?* (Moscow, 'Russia in United Europe' Committee. (2004)) pp. 22-32].

and well being, as well as of the environment, and, ultimately, serving 'the purpose of political stability in the region and worldwide'.[19] How are these goals to
be achieved? The concept responds accordingly: through mutual commitments, a
well structured basis, a high degree of regulatory and legislative convergence,
trade and investment facilitation, and boosting business and investor confidence
in the predictability and transparency of rules.[20]

The CEES is understood as an open and integrated market between the RF
and EU. To create it, the partners should undertake to enhance the mutual openness and compatibility of their economies and to develop interconnected infrastructure networks. They will use as a basis the implementation of common,
harmonized or compatible rules and regulations, legislative approximation, trade
facilitation, competition rules and intellectual, industrial and commercial property rights.

The CEES will aim to cover substantially all sectors of the economy. It will
focus on eliminating obstacles and creating opportunities for cross-border trade
in goods and services, establishing the operation of companies, the movement of
capital and related aspects of the movement of persons.[21]

The work on the conceptualisation of three other common spaces lagged
somewhat behind. The working groups on these spaces were created quite recently. Nevertheless, they are very active. All of them have been working very
hard on the respective road-maps. It is important that they may build on a vast
practical experience of co-operation on both sides in combating terrorism, organized crime and financial fraud, joint actions on the international scene and
implementing joint scientific and technical projects. In this sense the results of
the group on common scientific and educational space are significant. It managed to achieve agreement on the road-map in this sphere in advance of all other
groups. But the Russian proposal to adopt it and not to wait for the agreements
on other road-maps was not supported by the European Union.

It is obvious that the scope of the four common spaces 'should be broader
and deeper in comparison with the WTO and PCA provisions'.[22] What does it
imply in legal terms? The document on the concept of the CEES suggests that
the new bilateral agreements should be formalized by way of protocols attached
to the PCA or could take the form of self-standing agreements as the case may
be. The existing dispute settlement mechanism under the PCA will 'be considered for use as long as it corresponds to the provisions of the new agreements'.[23]

---

[19] Annex I, *supra* n. 13, at p. 6.
[20] Ibid.
[21] Ibid., at p. 8.
[22] Ibid., at p. 7.
[23] Ibid., at p. 9.

## 4.2   European Neighbourhood Policy

The main purpose of the common spaces of the European Union and the Russian Federation consists of consolidating stability, security and prosperity in Europe and transforming it into a united continent without dividing lines.

The EU neighbourhood policy has the same purpose. Its inclusion in the EU Constitution will have a direct impact on how the relationship between the European Union and Russia is tailored.

It will have an even more direct impact on Russia's closest neighbours. It implies that the political situation in the area of the CIS (Commonwealth of Independent States) countries could undergo important changes.

A sudden disruption of historical economic, industrial, trade and cultural and scientific ties between the former republics of the Soviet Union was a terrible blow to the young economies of the newly independent states. Each of them had to adapt to a new situation, to proceed with reforms and reconstruction on their own. Only recently have the tendencies of integration started to gain momentum. Mutual interests of the CIS countries in a free access to each other's markets, developing mutually beneficial joint ventures, joining efforts to contain the ever-growing threats of radicalism, terrorism and organized crime reinforce these tendencies.

During the 1990s the CIS countries signed dozens of virtual agreements which nobody was in a hurry to implement. Now, they are much more prepared to get down to work on real plans, programmes and hard law treaties bringing their people and economies closer. The necessary political will seems to be there. It is strongly encouraged by the pressing needs to make their economies more competitive. Free trade and common integration areas comprising different formations of CIS countries are perceived as feasible.

Russia does its best to promote such tendencies. Moscow is the focus of these events. It uses its influence and might to enhance the integration between the CIS countries. Top Russian officials have advanced crucial initiatives to this end.

What about the European Union? What is its position? What does it think and intend to do about it? For some years the European Union will be entirely preoccupied with internal readjustments caused by the new wave of enlargement. It will need much more money than it currently has in order to cope with the newly acquired internal disparities. Nevertheless, the Union will try to be very active concerning its 'near abroad'. The EU has partnership and co-operation agreements with the majority of CIS countries. It thoroughly monitors everything that is happening on their territories. It provides them with economic help. Brussels is massively present in their internal political life. It exerts influence on them through other international organizations. Their elites strive for the wealth and prosperity of Western Europe.

On previous occasions, the European Union demonstrated a rather negative attitude towards the CIS countries' intentions to put into practice the integration endeavours of different magnitudes. The EU leaders had the feeling that all other

European nations should follow the European Union model of development, which is likely to suit them best. To do this properly, they must install friendly governments in office, strengthen economic links with the West, implement westernisation policies and introduce EU legislation in their internal legal order. Accordingly, Brussels considered the CIS integration initiatives as impeding these ideal perspectives.[24]

However, political perceptions may change with time. The progress in establishing four European spaces for Russia and the European Union and updating the EU concept of a Wider Europe creates new attitudes and opportunities. Let us hope that they will benefit the integration processes in the CIS area.

European scholars and political scientists have been discussing the main features of the Wider Europe strategy from the beginning of this decade. Debates on this subject were closely connected with the EU enlargement. Many prominent politicians contributed to the debate. On 5 December 2002, speaking in Brussels at an academic conference, the European Commission President, Romano Prodi, for example, advanced a set of ideas about 'A Policy of Proximity'. He argued that in order to have 'a ring of friends', the European Union will 'have to offer more than partnership and less than membership' to neighbouring states 'sharing everything except the institutions'.[25]

Anticipating the coming enlargement, the General Affairs Council in April 2002 requested the European Commission and the High Representative for Common Foreign and Security Policy 'to work out the ideas on the EU relations with its neighbours'. Five months later an informal meeting of foreign ministers noted their initial five-page outline. The Copenhagen European Council in December 2002 confined itself to stating: 'the Union remains determined to avoid new dividing lines in Europe and to promote stability and prosperity within and beyond the new borders of the Union'. In March 2003, the European Commission sent to the Council and the European Parliament the first full Communication 'Wider Europe – Neighbourhood: A New Framework for Relations with our Eastern and Southern Neighbours'.[26] The Council and then the European Council agreed with the Commission's approach. They approved the principles and objectives of the EU's external activities in relation to its 'near abroad'. On this basis the European Commission elaborated a document on the new neighbourhood instrument. In May 2004 it tabled the latest Communication entitled 'European Neighbourhood Policy. Orientation Document'.[27] The concept of a Wider Europe was broadened to encompass the Caucasian states. It was definitively renamed as the European Neighbourhood Policy (ENP).

---

[24] See N. Gvosdev, 'Russia, its Neighbors and EU Expansion', *The Moscow Times* (6 May 2004) p. 8.

[25] Cited by W. Wallace, 'Looking after the Neighbourhood: Responsibilities for the EU - 25' (Notre Europe, Policy Paper no. 4 (July 2003)) p. 5, available at: <http://www.notre-europe.asso.fr/IMG/pdf/Policypaper4.pdf>.

[26] COM (2003) 104 final.

[27] COM (2004) 373 final.

The essence of the ENP is to offer neighbouring states incentives to co-operate and all possible advantages short of membership linked to the fulfilment of political, economic and administrative conditions. The incentives include growing benefits from a stepbystep increase in participation in the EU internal market, in the area of freedom, security and justice, and policies in the field of energy, transport, ecology, innovation, social cohesion etc. The preparation for receiving such benefits is backed by modest financial aid. The conditions are elaborated at length. They are of three types. First of all, the dependent states must stick to democratic and market-oriented reforms. Secondly, they are expected to control migration and combat corruption, drug and human trafficking and other forms of organized crime. Thirdly, they assume an obligation to support the EU initiatives aimed at conflict settlement and its struggle against terrorism, WMD proliferation and other global threats as they are perceived by the European Union. The decisions on whether this or that neighbouring country can live up to the level of the commitments are taken by Brussels. It is the ultimate judge as to whether this or that neighbouring country deserves benefits and of what kind. It is also up to Brussels to upgrade treaty relations with its partners when it deems this to be necessary. The ENP is to be implemented through the well-known mechanisms of bilateral action plans, 'working within a differentiated framework which responds to progress made by the partner countries in the defined areas'.

The ENP is the European Union's external action initiative containing mostly a description of how bilateral relations between the EU and each and the whole range of its neighbours are to be organized. At the same time it has an important regional dimension. The ENP inherited this from the Union's policies towards its Mediterranean neighbours.

The EU has a long history of Mediterranean policy implementation. Its origin could be traced back to the beginning of the 1970s. In November 1995 the EU and Mediterranean countries decided to give it a fresh start and the Barcelona Process was launched. According to the conclusions of some EU experts, its results were rather meagre.[28] In 2000 and two years later the Marseilles and then the Valencia Euro-Mediterranean Conferences had to repeat the call for the reinvigoration of the Barcelona Process. Despite all its failures and shortcomings the Process is valuable because it provides the parties with a multilateral context for co-operation.

The first European Commission Communication on the ENP is quite explicit about the importance of the regional dimension of co-operation when it deals with developing relations with the Mediterranean countries. It emphasizes the

---

[28] 'Any assessment of the prospects for a coherent neighbourhood policy;' – writes W. Wallace – 'must (…) start with a sober reflection on the relative failure of Mediterranean policies since the 1970s'. He continues: 'Despite the Barcelona process and the adoption of a 'Common Strategy' towards the Mediterranean during the last Portuguese EU Presidency, the EU as a collective actor still lacks a coherent foreign policy towards North Africa', *supra* n. 13, at pp. 13-14.

need for creating a common free trade area. It invites these countries to do their utmost to step up regional co-operation using all the tools they have at their disposal. It assures them that the EU will support regional networks of co-operation and will do this by political and financial means. But the paper on Wider Europe is evasive on the subject of regional co-operation when it deals with intensifying EU relations with the Western CIS countries.

The second Communication is a little more balanced. It seeks to overcome some of the shortcomings of the previous one. It pays tribute to the importance of regional co-operation between the EU Southern as well as Eastern neighbours. Four priority areas are identified. They are linked to economic and social policies, ecology, justice and home affairs, and to civil society formation. The Council of Europe, Council of Baltic Sea States, and Black Sea Economic Co-operation are cited as examples.

However, the European Commission has failed to make a decisive step in the right direction. The May 2004 Communication does not mention any of the CIS integration projects. This is a pity. Russia and other CIS countries will have to persuade Brussels to support them. It is a challenge, but it is worth doing.

There is another valuable proposal which Brussels has not retained. Some of the EU scholars put forward the idea of designing a framework for an economic and political association within which the neighbourhood countries 'can act as effective partners of the EU rather than as dependents'.[29] According to them:

'a Free Trade Area for Europe and the Mediterranean, with common institutions comparable to those of the European Economic Area, would have a more acceptable balance between internal and external priorities. Now the task for the Commission and for member governments is to define the structure and capabilities of such a free trade area in more detail, pulling together the parallel processes of Mediterranean and Eastern association, of energy dialogues, cross-border regional co-operation and proposals for improved transport links into a package that offers worthwhile incentives for neighbouring states to welcome a framework for multilateral co-operation.'[30]

Maybe in today's Europe such a proposal is too ambitious. It is future-oriented. It is too difficult to implement. But this proposal has the wisdom of addressing problems in a comprehensive way. It could be retained for creating compatible sub-regional and pan-European co-operation. It might pave the way for combining the integration efforts of the CIS countries with the intention to create common spaces or neighbourhood links with the EU.

In any case, such a proposal is no more innovative than the adoption by the European Council of the EU Constitution. Whether or not it can be taken on board by the European Union, depends to a large extent on the relationship between the European Union and the Russian Federation, on its possible evolution and strengthening its legal basis.

---

[29] Ibid., at p. 29.
[30] Ibid., at pp. 29-30.

## 4.3    Partnership and Cooperation Agreement

It may be expected that the EU Constitution would have a direct impact on legal developments in the Russian Federation. The European Union and Russia have committed themselves to promote gradual rapprochement and integration of their social and economic structures through the creation of a number of common European spaces as was described above. To achieve such a target, instruments of legal adaptation and approximation are to be used. It is impossible to move closer to each other and to establish a true working strategic partnership without bringing legal systems, legislation and case law closer as well.

Now the legal framework for the relationship between Russia and the EU is made in the PCA and a few bilateral agreements on specific issues – steel, textiles, scientific co-operation, etc. The PCA is a flexible legal instrument. Very important changes have been introduced in the PCA, without formally amending it, by the Summit decision to streamline the political dialogue and launch the work of the Russia-EU Permanent Partnership Council. The latter is considered a much more efficient and transparent tool of co-operation management. Its first session took place on 27 April 2004, in Luxembourg at the level of ministers for foreign affairs.

Other major changes were introduced in the PCA, without formally amending it, by the EU's unilateral decision to consider Russia as a country with a market economy and its incorporation in the EU internal legislation. Russian political and business communities have been exerting tough pressure on the EU and its Member States to take such a decision for many years.

The legal framework is further developed and consolidated by both bilateral and unilateral political instruments. An outstanding role in this connection is played by the Summit joint declarations. They are used to strengthen co-operation, establish its main priorities, highlight new future-oriented aims and proceed with indicative planning. Both Russia and the EU consider them as a means of updating the PCA. The 12th Russia-EU Joint Statement is indicative in this respect. According to it, both sides have agreed to intensify 'efforts to fulfil the decision to create common spaces between the EU and Russia, *building on the PCA and the Joint Statement of the St. Petersburg Summit*'.[31]

Practical aspects of co-operation are tackled by unilateral strategies adopted by the EU and Russia. Recently the EU has started to rely more and more on European Commission Communications. They concern EU-Russian relations, neighbourhood policies etc.

All these internal and international instruments are useful for providing legal and political grounds for day to day co-operation, although they are full of contradictions and incompatibilities. But they fall short of assuring the aim of

---

[31]  12th EU-Russia Summit Joint Statement, *supra* n. 13, at p. 2.

launching real integration and extending the common market and the area of freedom, security and justice beyond the EU borders.

What is needed in a legal perspective is to proceed with a gradual approximation of the RF and EU legislation and the elaboration of a legal framework adapted to the aim of creating four common spaces combined with additional updating of the PCA or the elaboration of an agreement of a new type.

The recent RF-EU joint declarations are somewhat controversial regarding the PCA. The PCA is continually mentioned as a legal basis or a framework for further fostering bilateral relations. At the same time, it is acknowledged that when creating common spaces the RF and EU must go beyond the PCA provisions.

The expert community in Russia has a strong feeling that the PCA is entirely outdated. Many of them believe that the PCA does not correspond even to the existing level of the relationship. It must be renegotiated and replaced by a new generation treaty – maybe, a treaty on strategic partnership. When? The sooner the better.

One of the most concise expressions of this belief can be found in a short book on this very subject written by a well-known Russian political scientist from the Russian Academy of Sciences Institute of Europe, U. Borko.[32] Borko explains that the PCA played a useful and positive role in the past. It helped the RF and EU to establish a new kind of relationship. It provided both sides with very valuable experience. But it belongs to the past. It was conceived ten years ago. At that time everything was different.

Since the launching of the partnership both Russia and the EU have undergone profound changes. Their relationship has become much broader and more mature. Europe is now facing new challenges. There is a greater need for RF and EU co-operation on a world scale. But the PCA is silent on these issues. It contains provisions made obsolete by life itself, for example, on institutional structures of co-operation management, on assisting Russia, on a transitional economy, etc. The PCA vision of the goals of the partnership is too narrow. Many PCA provisions will not be implemented. It is not a reliable vehicle for going ahead with the establishment of four common spaces...

The opposite point of view is also quite popular. Many lawyers from EU countries share this view. It can be found, for instance, in the lecture delivered by Alfred E. Kellermann at the MGIMO Conference on the RF-EU Relationship on 11 May 2004. He stated directly and clearly:

'The PCA may be considered a relatively successful formula in the EU external policy. It is certainly a reliable legal instrument for sustaining long-term relations

---

[32] Борко Ю., Европейскому Союзу и России необходимо Соглашение о стратегическом партнёрстве. – М. Пробел-2000, 2004. – 56 А. [U. Borko, 'European Union and Russia need an Agreement on Strategic Partnership' (Moscow, Probel (2000, 2004))]. The Committee 'Russia in United Europe' published it at the beginning of June 2004.

with the Russian Federation. The PCA is designed to bring Russia to the gateway of the world market economy. It offers access of goods of the Russian Federation to the European market and opens many opportunities for the EC financial and technical assistance. Principles of free trade, reciprocity and fair competition are the core to the fulfilment of the objectives of the agreement. The chance is given to build a solid institutional framework for a political dialogue with the EU. Furthermore, Russian companies can rely on non-discriminatory treatment should they want to establish themselves in the EU. Russia is encouraged to approximate its laws to those of the EU (…)' [33]

Officials from the EU are much closer to this approach than to the one shared by U. Borko and some other Russian political scientists. According to them, the potential of the PCA is not exhausted. The fact that the Agreement is not applied properly does not mean that it is not a good legal instrument. The parties must be blamed for any shortcomings in the implementation. They are responsible for not applying the PCA properly and effectively and not for the PCA itself. It is much more reasonable to try to achieve better results relying on the existing treaties instead of neglecting them and advancing new proposals.

Brussels reminds Moscow that Russia is not yet a member of the WTO. Russia will join not earlier than in 2006. The PCA gives both sides an opportunity to apply WTO standards and regulations to their bilateral relations. Its usefulness in this sense is beyond doubt. And it will remain very useful as an appropriate and stable legal basis for RF-EU relations for some time.

### 4.4    Rethinking the Partnership

The PCA was concluded for a period of 10 years. It will expire in 2007. Until then, no new treaty of such complexity could be negotiated.

This may be true. Nevertheless, it is obvious that the establishment of common spaces requires new thinking, new legal tools and new approaches to the adaptation and approximation of Russian legislation and legal practice to the process of European integration. Russian lawyers should do all this. They should work in close co-operation with their colleagues from EU countries. But at the same time they must take into consideration the needs and aspirations of all nations of the Commonwealth of Independent States.

The main requirement is that the future legal grounds for creating common spaces should be compatible with and support achieving the goals of establishing efficient integration spaces comprising the interested CIS countries.

To make them compatible, special attention must be given to the provisions of the EU Constitution concerning partnership relations and membership. In both

---

[33] A.E. Kellermann, 'The Impact of EU Enlargement on the Russian Federation' (Materials of the MGIMO Conference 'Political, economic and legal aspects of the relationship between Russia and the European Union' (11 May 2004)). For an elaborated version of these materials see A.E. Kellermann, 'The Impact of EU Enlargement on the Russian Federation', *supra* n. 10.

cases, the text of the EU Constitution insists that to be eligible for the status of an EU partner, a candidate for membership or a Member State, the country must uphold the same values which are shared by the EU and on which the European Union is based.

The inclusion of these requirements in the EU Constitution has a symbolic meaning. At the same time, there are no grounds for believing that they will not be put into practice. The legal nature of the European Union and other provisions of the EU Constitution ensuring that the EU institutions and Member States must abide by all its norms will force the Union to construe its relations with third countries in a predetermined manner.

Traditionally, the leaders of the Russian Federation, the Russian political elite and political scientists used to believe that the relationship between Russia and the European Union may evolve according to three different scenarios. They must be quite sure that there is a choice between integration, co-operation and confrontation. Only recently have such beliefs been questioned. Some Russian authors started to explain that the choice is much more limited. Either Russia becomes a true strategic partner of the European Union, continues democratic reforms and assigns itself the aim of political, legal, economic and social integration with the EU or it will drift towards a 'cold peace' or confrontation. The scenario of co-operation is nothing more than a mirage. It pushes both sides towards the policies of deterrence and tough competition which are inconsistent with partnership relations.[34]

The relevant provisions of the EU Constitution stating that the European Union will only establish relations of partnership with democratic nations are self-explanatory.


5.    CONCLUDING REMARKS

In conclusion, it must be mentioned that the EU Constitution does not exclude any option as far as future relations between Russia and the European Union are concerned. Russia is a European state. If Russia upholds the common values of the EU, then – formally – nothing will preclude it from becoming a member of the European Union. Now, this is impossible to imagine, but anything may change with the passing of time. Meanwhile, it is essential to use all the opportunities contained in the EU Constitution to improve relations between Russia and the European Union.

---

[34] See Энтин М. Л. Возможно ли сотрудничество между Россией и Европейским Союзом? (Европейская безопасность: события, оценки, прогнозы. Центр по изучению проблем европейской безопасности Института научной информации по общественным наукам) №. 14, 2004г. – С.4-8 [M. Entin, 'Is Cooperation between Russia and the European Union Possible?' (European Security: Events, Evaluations and Forecasts, Center for European Security Problems of the Institute of Information on Social Sciences) no. 14 (2004) pp. 4-8].

Let us not forget that the Russian Federation and the European Union share a common historical and cultural heritage. Their economies are complimentary. They have similar approaches to many international and global issues. They need each other. They must work together for consolidating stability, security and prosperity in Europe and transforming it into a united continent free from dividing lines. The ghosts of the cold war, confrontation and deep mutual distrust should be banished from European politics.

If Russia and the European Union succeed, they will create an entirely new political reality. Its embryos could be found in mutual commitments to promote further rapprochement and gradual integration of social and economic structures of the enlarged EU and Russia through the creation of a number of common spaces between them. Both Russia and the European Union need to use this historic opportunity and to create, with the participation of other CIS countries, an area of integration, stability and prosperity embracing all European nations.[35] Both sides must cooperate closely and intensively. Better coordination and consistency of EU external actions as envisaged in the EU Constitution will be of use for moving in this direction.

As we see, the assumption put forward at the beginning of this article has turned out to be incorrect. The EU Constitution will have a major impact on Russian politics and internal legal developments in many ways. Let us hope that its influence will be beneficial for the relationship between Russia and the EU and will pave the way towards their mutual political integration.

---

[35] In this connection I would like to recall the words of the former President of the Soviet Union Mikhail Gorbachev:

'Almost two decades ago, I called for the building of a common European home, an idea that became central to perestroika's new political thinking. In the years that followed, decisive steps were taken to make it a practical reality... Today, a great deal hinges on where Europe goes from here. It can head towards new dividing lines or towards a truly united Europe that includes Russia. A Europe that embraces Russia is the only Europe that could become a credible partner to the United States, China and other emerging powers.' *The Moscow Times* (6 May 2004) p. 8.

# ANNEXES

# WELCOME ADDRESS AT THE 34TH ASSER INSTITUTE COLLOQUIUM ON EUROPEAN LAW 'THE EU CONSTITUTION: THE BEST WAY FORWARD?'

**Frans Nelissen**[*]

Your Excellencies, distinguished colleagues, friends, ladies and gentlemen,

On behalf of the Asser Institute for International Law I welcome you here at the Kurhaus in Scheveningen, The Hague for the 34th Asser Colloquium on European Law: 'The EU Constitution: the Best Way Forward?'.

So, welcome to The Hague, the City of International Law, including EU Law. Close to us here, on the edge of the North Sea, there are more than thirty international organizations, among which quite a few deal with the law, including EU law: for example, organizations like Europol and Eurojust. The Hague is sometimes even called 'The Legal Capital of the World' because of this.

Speaking on behalf of the Asser Institute I can safely say that – as a research institute with its focus on international and EU law – we find ourselves in a luxurious position in the middle of all these organizations and in the middle of so many practitioners and experts in the field.

Together with the Dutch law faculties and their specialists in international and EU law, which we, being an interuniversity institute, represent here in The Hague, our goal is to carry out research and to disseminate the results thereof via publications and academic meetings and conferences like this one.

I believe that we find ourselves – embedded in this international legal atmosphere – in a good environment to discuss the best way forward for the EU, including your views on the EU Constitution.

This conference takes place at a moment in time when the Netherlands holds the EU Presidency, which marks the occasion and provides us with the possibility to make a relevant and timely contribution to the ongoing debate on the European Constitution. On the agenda is the question whether the European Constitution improves democracy, transparency and the efficiency of the European Union's decision-making process, also in the light of the EU enlargement process.

We will also deal with topics such as the perspectives of European citizenship, the exercise of Union Competence and the process of ratification and eventual exit options.

---

[*] Director, T.M.C. Asser Institute.

D. Curtin, A.E. Kellermann and S. Blockmans, eds., *The EU Constitution: The Best Way Forward?*
© 2005, T.M.C. Asser Instituut, The Hague.

The Conference offers a forum for debate on the EU Constitution with contributions from more than 60 invited experts from the European institutions (the Parliament, the Court of Justice, the Council and the Commission) and representatives of the Parliaments, Governments, the judiciary and universities from the 25 Member States and five candidate states, alongside the United States of America, Switzerland and Russia. The last-mentioned state is a perfect example of the Widening European process.

After 16 months of debate and deliberation, and more than 7,000 proposed amendments, the efforts of the so-called European Convention have resulted in a final draft treaty, presented at the Brussels Convention in June last year. The Convention includes, among other things, a bill of rights, a foreign Minister and even a President of the European Council.

On the 18th of June this year the European Constitution was agreed upon at the European Council. It was decided that the draft constitution should also be signed by the new Member States immediately after joining the EU in May of this year.

Now we need to convince the European citizens and the national parliaments in the 25 Member States to ratify the new constitution.

I express my sincere hope that this international Asser Conference – with a large representation from the ten new Member States and from Bulgaria, Croatia, Romania and Turkey as candidate countries, and finally Serbia and Montenegro as a pre-candidate country – will provide many arguments for ratifying the European Constitution.

I wish you an interesting and stimulating Conference.

# THE EU CONSTITUTION: IMPROVING DEMOCRACY?

**Thom de Graaf**[*]

Ladies and gentlemen,

What good will the European Constitution do for Europe's citizens? The question strikes me as being highly relevant, considering that referendums on that Constitution will be held over the next two years in many EU Member States, including the Netherlands.

You may already have made up your mind on this issue. Some may still be hesitating about voting for or against. But for most people, the European Constitution is hardly an everyday concern. Most people have not even started comparing the alternatives. So I would like to make it clear why I think the citizens of Europe should say 'yes' to the European Constitution. And maybe I can convince some undecided voters.

Formally speaking, the European Constitution is not a constitution at all, but a treaty between states. However, it does contain the main elements of a constitution in the classic sense: democracy, the rule of law, fundamental rights, citizenship and the separation of powers. The only thing missing from the list is national sovereignty. And there is a good reason for that; the European Constitution is not intended to create a nation-state.

The traditional features which I have just mentioned are very much in the spirit of the Laeken Declaration of 2001, which set us on the road to the European Convention. That declaration stressed the goals of democracy, transparency and efficiency. This brings me to two questions. With those goals in mind, how do we judge the final document that emerged from negotiations? And how will the treaty deliver more democracy, transparency and efficiency to the public?

Here is an initial, general conclusion. Entirely in the spirit of the Laeken Declaration, major steps have been taken towards a more transparent, democratic and efficient European Union. Although I should add that, as far as I am concerned, this treaty is not the end of the line for European integration. It is still not perfect, to use a understatement. But in any case, there can be no question that the Constitution is an improvement over the current treaties. For example, it explicitly emphasises the importance of getting the public actively involved in the

---

[*] Deputy Prime Minister of the Netherlands.

*D. Curtin, A.E. Kellermann and S. Blockmans, eds., The EU Constitution: The Best Way Forward?*
© 2005, T.M.C. Asser Instituut, The Hague.

European Union. It also promotes more transparent decision-making within the EU. This could do a great deal to narrow the gap between the public and Brussels, which will be a major task for the EU in the years ahead. The president designate of the European Commission, José Manuel Barroso, recently said that 'the biggest challenge we face is not the Euro-scepticism of the few, but the Euro-apathy of the many.' I could not agree with him more.

More transparency, more democracy and more efficiency. But the constitution will also put an end to the legal maze that the European Union has become. I am referring to the two existing foundational treaties and the whole range of amendments piled on top of them. And what exactly is the difference between the Union and the Community? We will never have to grapple with that troublesome question again, because there will be *one* European Union with a well-defined legal personality.

The next point is an important one. The European Constitution will promote democracy. The new powers of the European Parliament in the lawmaking process will be entirely to our benefit. In general, the European Parliament will have the right of co decision whenever European laws or framework laws are adopted. It will have that right in thirty-three *more* cases than it does now, an example of this is asylum policy. And its authority will extend to the entire annual budget, whereas up to now it has only had a final say about non-mandatory spending.

So is that the end of the line? Not as far as I am concerned. In the future, even more authority should be transferred to the European Parliament. For example, the Constitution will not give it the power to dissolve the Council of Ministers or to discharge individual members of the Council. I believe a true control organ is essential to a vital democracy. We are not quite that far yet, but the Constitution will move us in the right direction.

The Constitution will also get national parliaments more closely involved in decision-making. The key instrument is an early warning procedure, in which national parliaments can ask European lawmakers to reconsider proposals if they conflict with the principle of subsidiarity. We call it 'showing a yellow card'. The goal is to bring the decision-making process as close to the public as possible.

Greater transparency in decision-making is an important part of making Europe more democratic. How can the public get a clearer view of what is going on? The Dutch government fought hard for transparency in the negotiations. And we made some progress. Under the new Constitution, both the European Parliament and the Council will hold public meetings to discuss draft legislation. I am looking forward to seeing the European Union's twenty-five agriculture, education or transport ministers debating on television or on the Internet! How would our own finance minister, Gerrit Zalm, hold up against his German colleague, Hans Eichel, and how well would the French minister Nicolas Sarkozy perform? We would love to see that!

Still, besides *seeing* what goes on, the public should also have a chance to *take part*. That is why the principle of participatory democracy has also been given a place in the Constitutional Treaty. The approach which the treaty takes is that the European institutions give citizens and representative organisations the tools to express their views, in a range of forums and on the Internet. That approach creates opportunities for public debate on the European Union and its record. For example, I sometimes sit in front of my computer and chat with members of the public about the policy decisions I have made. Doing that forces you to express yourself clearly and concisely. And that is another important element of transparency.

The jewel in the crown of participatory democracy is the citizens' initiative introduced in the treaty. For the first time, citizens will be able to ask the Commission to submit a proposal on a legislative issue that matters to *them*. Strict conditions will have to be met, though not nearly as strict as the conditions currently in place for calling a referendum in the Netherlands. A citizens' initiative can lead to new legislation but can also be used as a corrective mechanism to ask the Commission to withdraw existing rules. We are witnessing the birth of the European popular referendum. It almost seems as though the EU is more open to government reform than the Netherlands. If you are aware of my political background, you will not be surprised that I am pleased by that development. The Netherlands is certainly not leading the way in this area. But who knows – maybe it will follow in Brussels' footsteps!

Constitutions are created to protect individual freedom. And fundamental freedoms must have a place in every Constitution. So I am very pleased that the Charter of Fundamental Rights of the Union has been incorporated in full in Part II of the European Constitution. Above all, the Charter is directed at the European institutions. Another important point is that the scope for individual access to the European Court of Justice in Luxembourg has been expanded. That gives individual citizens legal protection against restrictive measures, which the Council can take against natural or legal persons. In particular, this concerns measures in order to combat terrorism. It is a good thing that the Council will have this power, especially in today's world, but it is just as important for individuals to have the opportunity to subject the lawfulness of these measures to judicial review.

I am also very pleased that the Constitution will make it possible for the European Union to accede to the European Convention on Human Rights. That will allow individuals to hold the European Union to account if they feel their human rights have been violated. Since the EU is taking on more and more features of a state, it seems to me that this is a very important move. And so I hope that accession to the Convention can take place in the very near future.

I started out by asking what good will the European Constitution do for Europe's citizens? I would answer that it does them a great deal of good. The benefits to the public include greater democracy, fundamental rights, transparency and effectiveness. It may not be perfect, and it may not go far enough, but it is a major step forward. And that is why I hope that in the upcoming national referendums, European citizens will cast a decisive vote in favour of their new Constitution. Right now, it is the best way forward.

# COLLABORATION ON CRIMINAL LAW AND THE EU CONSTITUTION

**Piet Hein Donner**[*]

Ladies and gentlemen,

The Dutch are currently involved in a debate on who is the greatest Dutchman of all time, a debate that has already kept the UK and Germany busy. You see, we move with the times and with the main cultural trends in Europe. I am glad to be able to inform you that at least two lawyers have figured on the long list: T.M.C. Asser and Grotius. So our host tonight, the Asser Institute, can feel proud. I am sorry, however, to have to report to you that neither of these persons appear on the final short list of ten names.

The Dutch will probably choose William of Orange as the greatest Dutchman. This is a very European choice. By choosing a German, who lived for most of his life in Brussels and who was incarnated in a principality in the south of France, the Dutch will enhance their European credentials. At the same time it is a very Dutch choice, because most Dutchmen confronted with the question of who is the greatest Dutchman, instinctively think of themselves. So by choosing a German as the greatest Dutchman, they can continue to think in secret: 'well; I am of course, the greatest Dutchman, because he really was a German'.

Personally, I think there are other eligible candidates, like, for example, Desiderius Erasmus, the fifteenth century theologist, humanist, philosopher and writer. But he also had some particular notions, like: 'Women, you cannot live with them, you cannot live without them.' And since, as you all know, you cannot become a European Commissioner with that kind of notion, you most certainly cannot become the greatest Dutchman of all time.

I mention this phenomenon of a contest to establish who is the greatest national hero, because it is a symptom of our times. The more the world is globalizing, the more Europe is integrating, the more desperate we cling to these vestiges of national diversity and our separate past. In the Netherlands we even had a public debate on the question of whether some candidates should posthumously be naturalised in order to be able to compete. Luckily this discussion was so short-lived that the European Commission could not even start an infracture pro-

---

[*] Minister of Justice of the Netherlands.

*D. Curtin, A.E. Kellermann and S. Blockmans, eds., The EU Constitution: The Best Way Forward?*
© 2005, T.M.C. Asser Instituut, The Hague.

cedure for discrimination. Anyway, I consider it to be a serious omission that the right of every European citizen to stand in any national fame contest was not included among the 50 fundamental rights in the charter. With so many fundamental rights, one more or less does not really make any difference.

The point I really want to make, is that these contests show that we are still a long way from a common European feeling. Worse than this: we are moving away from it. The more our societies are integrating through intensive social, economic and cultural intercourse and through ever expanding cross-border contacts, the more people feel insecure and threatened, and will look for security and identity in past national pride and achievements. As a result, people turn against the notion of the Union, because it is identified as the cause of all insecurity and change. That will be the real issue in the time to come; convincing people that the Union is not the cause of all social ills, but rather the instrument and institutional framework that creates the possibility of coming to grips with these ills.

And convince them we will have to, if we want the new Constitutional Treaty to be accepted. And it must be accepted. Not because it is the best treaty imaginable, and it is most certainly not a constitution (it will only become a constitution if more than two thirds of the articles are deleted and the remaining articles can be amended by a two thirds majority). The Treaty has to be accepted because it is the bare minimum we need in order to manage our internal relations within the European Union. To live together in peace in society requires a government; to protect, to act and to settle conflicts. Due to technical, economic and political changes we have come to live so close together in Europe, that we cannot live together in peace without a basic governmental structure to bind us all and to act in the common interest, to settle conflicts and to protect the commonwealth. Without it we would slowly revert to a state of growing irritation, permanent insecurity and deepening mutual suspicion. Not by commission, but by omission; because each of our states has progressively lost the capacity to cope independently with the problems of modern society, and will therefore try to solve them at the expense of neighbouring countries. Helmut Kohl once predicted that without the European Union, Europe would revert to war within half a century. The recent history of the former Yugoslavia has proven him wrong; it takes an even shorter period.

The main impulse behind the European Union is no longer the aspiration to create additional possibilities, but to restore lost capacities. This is particularly true in the area of Justice and Home Affairs, an area which is, at the same time, the main battlefield in the coming years on which to re-conquer the support of the European populations. Because cooperation in this area affects the elementary feeling of feeling secure in society without undue restraints. A feeling that is not simply restored by adopting a constitutional text, but by much arduous work and slow progress in transforming the core business of our national states into a semblance of effective cooperation and the capacity to act in common.

European states are increasingly confronted with problems and phenomena with which they can no longer cope separately: cross-border crime; illegal trade in all its guises, cigarettes, drugs and people, even children. Similarly, European states have during these past thirty years come to accept that they are incapable of dealing separately with modern migration and waves of international refugees. And these past years have made it clear that terrorism is a threat that has to be faced in common.

This is the real motive behind an evolution in which a subject that only twenty years ago was considered by friend and foe to be the exclusive territory of the Member States, is now one of the main topics in the forthcoming European Council. Some think that the political choice to shift border controls from the internal to the external borders has singularly promoted the process of police and judicial cooperation. But even the Schengen process was in reality based on the implicit recognition by Member States of their growing incapacity to guarantee adequate controls at their mutual borders. It is the reason why the Schengen *acquis* was rapidly accepted by almost all the other Member States and has since been incorporated into the EU *acquis*.

The scope of Union involvement has not stopped growing in the subsequent treaties of Maastricht, Amsterdam and Nice. In the framework of the Tampere Programme of 1999 the basis has been laid for a European immigration and asylum policy, for simplified procedures for police and judicial cooperation, for judicial coordination on the basis of mutual recognition, for joint police investigations and for the concentration of procedures. Europol and Eurojust have since been set up.

A fortnight ago the principles of a new multi-annual Justice and Home Affairs programme were accepted in this same building. The realisation of the so-called Hague programme will imply a new fundamental step in achieving a situation in which internal borders and national jurisdictional boundaries are no longer an obstacle to law enforcement, anti-terrorism protection and cross-border litigation, while Member States will integrate their controls and asylum and immigration policies at the external borders.

And it does not stop there. Major issues still have to be addressed before a real constitutional phase is achieved; a situation of stable cooperation in which an equilibrium exists between the different interests involved. A major issue will be how to realise effective and integrated operational capacity in the fight against organised cross-border crime and in prosecuting serious crimes. Should this be realised by a progressive harmonization of substantive and procedural criminal law? In other areas harmonization has been the solution for many problems in the Union. But in this area harmonization does not solve much. Resistance will be great, because national populations are often very attached to their national criminal law which is a reflection of particular social problems and national characteristics. Changing criminal law, therefore, often corrodes the feeling of security and violates the sense of propriety, if it is not considered an outright violation of the rule of law. But even apart from this resistance, the harmonization of criminal law will not solve the problem of cooperation. Crime is not fought by laws, but by actual police operations, prosecution and trial. Even if the whole of criminal law would be uniform, jurisdictional limits would still be the same. Effective prosecution and the trying of cross-border crime therefore requires a common jurisdiction rather than the harmonization of national criminal law.

Another aspect that will have to be dealt with urgently is the organisation of the European judiciary. The enforcement of immigration and criminal law will, as a rule, involve national judges. As this enforcement will progressively be regulated by European law the possibility of asking prejudicial questions will exist in almost all cases. Given the almost unavoidable delays in answering prejudicial questions, this could effectively nullify the useful effect of any policy, or the effect of legal protection, because justice delayed is justice denied. The progressive involvement of the European Union in this area therefore requires an urgent reorganisation of the European jurisdiction and a solution for the language problem.

I hope I have made clear that cooperation in the area of justice and home affairs is still in a stage of full development. Some people are worried that the process seems to be impelled more by the actual need of fighting criminality and terrorism, than by the respect of freedoms and rights. Some think that a clear picture of the goals and what ought to be achieved in this area should be given first. But as my favourite for the most famous Dutchman, Erasmus, once said: 'if you keep thinking about what you want to do or what you hope will happen, you do not do it, and it will not happen.' We have to move forward because we cannot fail the challenges of modern society and we have to find answers to the fears and the need for protection of modern man.

The Constitutional Treaty speaks of an area of freedom, security and justice. At first sight this seems to be a string of political platitudes intended to make people feel good. Freedom, security and justice; who could be against them? But what do they mean? At a closer look, each of the terms has a broader meaning. Freedom is not only freedom in terms of the absence of fear, oppression or want. Freedom also relates to the collective capacity to direct our actions and thereby to realise our collective destiny. 'Security' does not only imply a common ward against threats, but also the sense of security in our communities which is based, among other things, on familiarity and identification with our diverse legal systems. And justice is not only the impartial enforcement of rights and obligations, but also implies the power to bring about justice and a just society. In this sense the concept of an area of freedom, security and justice evokes a broader and more complex picture. In the tension between the different elements and their extensive meanings lies the mainspring of a balanced and yet innovative development of European policy and law in this area.

# THE PROCESS AND IMPACT OF EU CONSTITUTION-MAKING: VOICE AND EXIT (REPORT OF THE DISCUSSION)

**Steven Blockmans**[*]

1.     INTRODUCTION

On behalf of the T.M.C. Asser Institute for International Law, its director, Frans Nelissen, welcomed their Excellencies and participants to the Kurhaus Hotel in Scheveningen/The Hague for the 34th Asser Colloquium on European Law entitled *The EU Constitution: the best way forward?* Nelissen commemorated the fact that this conference took place at a time when the Netherlands held the EU Presidency (July-December 2004). After 16 months of debate and deliberation, and more than 7,000 proposed amendments, the efforts of the European Convention resulted in a draft Constitutional Treaty which was submitted to the President of the European Council in Rome on 18 July 2003. On 18 June 2004, the Intergovernmental Conference approved a provisional consolidated text of the Treaty establishing a Constitution for Europe. At the time of the Asser Colloquium, the editing of this text was almost complete in view of the formal signing of the EU Constitution in Rome on 29 October 2004 by the Heads of State and Heads of Government of the 25 Member States and of Bulgaria, Romania and Turkey in their capacity as candidate countries and observers to the IGC.

Building upon Nelissen's opening words, Alfred E. Kellermann (T.M.C. Asser Institute) and Deirdre Curtin (University of Utrecht), the two organizers of this Asser Colloquium, set out the main themes of the conference. On the agenda were, *inter alia*, the questions whether the Treaty establishing a Constitution for Europe places the citizen at centre stage and whether it improves democracy, transparency and the efficiency of the European Union's decision-making process, also in the light of the ongoing enlargement process. Topics such as the prospects for EU citizens and the exercise of Union competences under the EU Constitution, as well as the process of ratification of the Constitutional Treaty and possible exit options would all be dealt with.

---

[*] Researcher in the law of the European Union, T.M.C. Asser Institute, The Hague. For the sake of clarity, excerpts from some of the written contributions have been reproduced in this report. It goes without saying that the intellectual property rights over these parts remain with their authors.

*D. Curtin, A.E. Kellermann and S. Blockmans, eds., The EU Constitution: The Best Way Forward?*
© 2005, T.M.C. Asser Instituut, The Hague.

## 2.    THE EU CONSTITUTION: IMPROVING DEMOCRACY?

In his speech to the plenary, H.E. Thom de Graaf, Deputy Prime Minister of the Netherlands, asked what good the EU Constitution will do for Europe's citizens and why they should say 'yes' to that constitution. While recognizing that the EU Constitution is not the end of the line for the European integration process, de Graaf considered it to be an improvement on the current treaties. In his view, major steps have been taken towards a more transparent, democratic and efficient European Union. This could do a great deal to narrow the gap between the public and Brussels, for 'the biggest challenge we face is not the Euro-scepticism of the few, but the Euro-apathy of the many' (*dixit* Barroso).

De Graaf devoted most of his speech to the democratic progress made with the Constitutional Treaty. He pointed out that, if and when the EU Constitution enters into force, the European Parliament will have the right of co-decision whenever European laws or framework laws are adopted and that its authority will extend to the entire annual budget. According to the Deputy Prime Minister, even more authority should in the future be transferred to the European Parliament for it to become a true 'control organ', essential for a vital democracy. Another improvement is that national parliaments will become more closely involved in EU decision-making because they will be able to ask the European legislator to reconsider proposals if they conflict with the principle of subsidiarity ('showing a yellow card'). Another approach which the Constitutional Treaty takes is that the EU institutions give citizens and representative organisations the tools to express their views on the EU and its record, in a range of forums and on the Internet. For de Graaf, the jewel in the crown of participatory democracy is the citizens' initiative introduced in the EU Constitution. For the first time, citizens will be able to ask the Commission to submit a proposal on a legislative issue that matters to *them*. Strict conditions will have to be met, although not nearly as strict as the conditions currently in place for calling a referendum in, for example, the Netherlands. A citizens' initiative can lead to new legislation but can also be used as a corrective mechanism to ask the Commission to withdraw existing rules. According to de Graaf, we are witnessing the birth of the European popular referendum.

De Graaf concluded his speech by saying that, while the EU Constitution may not be perfect and may not go far enough, it is a major step forward. He expressed the hope that, in the upcoming national referendums on the ratification of the EU Constitution, European citizens would cast a decisive vote in favour of *their* new Constitution. That, in his view, would be the best way forward.[1]

---

[1] At the end of the speech, Tom Eijsbouts presented H.E. de Graaf with the first copy of the new *European Constitutional Law Review*, published by T.M.C. Asser Press.

3.    THE PROCESS OF EU CONSTITUTION-MAKING AND THE VOICE
      OF THE CITIZENS

Before delivering his keynote speech, Joseph H.H. Weiler picked up on
Kellermann's plea that the participants to the conference should turn to the task
of convincing citizens to ratify the Constitutional Treaty. Weiler disagreed. The
role of academics is to offer contrasting views on the Constitutional Treaty, from
different perspectives and with different normative inclinations. Collectively,
academics are neither the Bureau de Recherche of the European Union, nor an
extension of its Spokesman's Office. Academia is one of the important custodi-
ans of a story that is being taught. It puts an important culture in place, as well as
a yardstick for the future, in controlling the myth and telling the narrative.

   Weiler presented a thesis which is at the core of these remarks: 'the defining
feature of Europe's new Constitution is a word, an appellation. It is not the content of the Treaty establishing a Constitution for Europe which gives it epochal
significance but the fact that an altogether unremarkable treaty amendment has
been given the grand name 'Constitution'.' According to Weiler, the word has
had, and will continue to have, an enormous political impact – positive and negative – on the process of adopting the EU Constitution and on its subsequent life.
But it is not only a political impact which the word imparts. Weiler predicted
that it will become a tool for understanding some of the core conceptual implications which Europe's particular constitutional choice implies.

   In a mental exercise, Weiler asked the participants to imagine the new TCE,
as presented for ratification in the twenty five EU Member States, with the word
'Constitution' excised from all the places in which it appears and to question
themselves what it is that they would find. The conclusion is fairly obvious: it
does not look like a constitution (Weiler referred to the size and weight of the
document and made the comparison with the American Constitution) and it does
not read like a constitution. Instead of making reference to the ultimate constitutional authority underpinning the document (the People), the opening phrase of
the document now before Europe's peoples is the very same as that used since
the very first Treaty establishing the European Coal and Steel Community in
1951: 'His Majesty the King of the Belgians (...)', followed by the long list of
heads of state and heads of government. The non-initiated reader would be forgiven if he believed that he was reading the standard opening of an international
treaty. He would be forgiven if the same opinion were formed by going to the
end of the document: 'This Treaty shall be ratified by the High Contracting Parties in accordance with their respective constitutional requirements. The instruments of ratification shall be deposited with the Government of the Italian
Republic', followed by '[in witness whereof], the undersigned plenipotentiaries
have signed this Treaty (...).'

   Substantively speaking, the document contains for the most part just that
what one had hoped to see in the Treaty of Amsterdam, and certainly in the
Treaty of Nice in the countdown to enlargement of the Union: a sensible, though
far from radical amendment of the institutional architecture and decision-making

processes of the Union; some meaningful but equally non-radical nods towards the further democratization of the above; the Charter of Fundamental rights; the codification of the constitutional *status quo*; and some sensible clarification of language. The treaty revision procedures have been interestingly amended to provide a multi-tier process: Convention plus IGC; IGC without Convention; decision of the European Council alone. But, significantly, from a constitutional point of view, all three processes are, in conventional thinking, not typical of constitutions but rather of treaties. They all require unanimity among the governments of the high contracting parties and ratification by national procedures in all Member States.

Hence, if one omits the lexical addition to this document of the word 'constitution', one will find a post-enlargement 'Treaty of Nice *bis*.' Put differently by Weiler: if the Nice IGC had come up with the identical material content of the EU Constitution, it would have been welcomed as a sensible adaptation of the treaties establishing the European Union to enlargement. Materially not more significant than the Treaty of Maastricht (with the creation of the EMU) and institutionally not more consequential than the Single European Act (with the introduction of qualified majority voting), no one would have used any superlatives to describe its content, it would have attracted limited public attention or debate in most Member States, it would certainly not have generated the numerous referendums, and there would have been no talk of the need for a constitution – 'no Convention, no European Philadelphia, no Constitution-speak, but at best a good old treaty masquerading as a constitution.'

However, even if the current text is no more than Nice *bis*, the fact is that a Nice *bis* was necessary to adapt the Union's constituent treaties to the reality of enlargement. And the only way to get there was to change the rules about change. No longer an IGC which failed to deliver both in Amsterdam and Nice, but the differently constituted Convention. Weiler had considered the Convention to be the true innovation, but ended up holding a sober view on the legitimacy of the drafting process. For, except for the Christian roots debate, the European Convention was unable to galvanize public opinion around the process. Also, the Convention could have come up with a compact and more audacious document. Maybe the Convention was a missed opportunity because it morphed into a hybrid IGC. Foreign Ministers and other powerbrokers jumped in once it became apparent that this process was going to deliver something that the previous IGCs had failed to do and that once a text emerged it would be difficult to change it radically. They believed, or had to make-believe, that they were not simply redrafting Nice but doing something far more transcendent. On this reading the treaty had to masquerade as a constitution for the result to be achieved.

It may well be that the constitutional commotion was a *conditio sine qua non* in arriving at an indispensable text. But by the same token, the EU Constitution might become the victim of its own hype. According to Weiler, the latter is not necessarily a bad thing, 'for the project of elites to be rejected every now and again by popular will, can be a salutary experience.' Symbolically, the rejection of the Constitutional Treaty (in one or more of the referendums organized by Member States) will be a huge victory for European democracy, for it will force a sense of honesty upon the heads of state and heads of government towards their constituencies. Moreover, it will constitute a lesson in one of the little understood disciplines of democracy, namely that when qualified majority rules apply, as is almost always the case with constitutional amendment, there is a need for the majority to convince the minority and not to ride over it roughshod.[2]

4.    THE PROCESS OF RATIFICATION AND THE EXIT OPTIONS: A
      LEGAL PERSPECTIVE

In his speech, Bruno de Witte provided a legal dimension to Weiler's last observations. He asked participants what the best way forward would be for the EU Constitution in the case of a so-called 'ratification crisis'. As said by de Witte, the text prepared by the Convention and adopted by the IGC contains a gigantic but unavoidable gamble caused by the fact that the entry into force of the Constitutional Treaty is subject to the same rigid legal conditions as the Treaties of Maastricht, Amsterdam and Nice before. Since the new Treaty is an amendment of the existing EC and EU Treaties (the Constitutional Treaty aims to repeal those treaties, but a repeal is just the extreme form of an amendment), the revision procedure described in Article 48 TEU necessarily applies. Thus, the new treaty will, *normally speaking*, only enter into force if approved by all the Member State governments in the framework of an IGC and if ratified by all states according to their constitutional requirements. The latter condition multiplies the chances of an *accident de parcours* comparable to, or worse than, what happened with the Treaty of Maastricht in Denmark and with the Treaty of Nice in Ireland. In neither of these two cases did the other Member States, or the EU institutions, officially argue that the other Member States could go ahead without the recalcitrant state. They managed to find a 'soft law' solution which did not modify the agreed text but enabled these two countries to approve the revision treaty in a second referendum, so that the EU legal rules for entry into force were entirely respected. This time around, the argument that the majority of states should be able to go ahead with a Treaty revision even in the absence of some countries' ratification has been openly made, on three different occasions: during the work of the Convention, after the European Council of December 2003 that failed to conclude the IGC, and after Tony Blair's announcement that the United Kingdom would submit the Constitutional Treaty to a referendum. De Witte briefly

---

[2] Weiler developed three scenarios to prove his point. Scenario 1: a small and non-critical number of Member States reject. Scenario 2: the number and composition of the rejection front is such that the project is defeated. Scenario 3: the EU Constitution secures ratification by referendums in all or even a majority of Member States. For an elaboration, see pp. 10-11 in Weiler's contribution.

reviewed the political considerations made on those occasions, *inter alia*, by paraphrasing Giscard d'Estaing, who had stated unpromisingly that if a large majority of the citizens of Europe and of the Member States approve the EU Constitution, problems would arise for the states that refused to ratify it and not for the Constitution itself.[3] De Witte pointed out that the text of the Constitutional Treaty is not so militant at all. Declaration No. 30 *on the ratification of the Treaty establishing a Constitution for Europe* states that 'if, two years after the signature of the Treaty establishing a Constitution for Europe, four fifths of the Member States have ratified it and one or more Member States have encountered difficulties in proceeding with ratification, the matter will be referred to the European Council.' In this way, Declaration No. 30 only states the obvious, namely that the European Council deals with any serious problem arising in the path of European integration. But it also expresses the hope that, if such a situation will occur, the European Council will be able to devise a cunning plan to save the Constitutional Treaty despite the opposition expressed in some parts of the Union's territory.

De Witte agrees with Weiler and many others that it is quite possible that something will indeed go wrong during the national ratification phase, because (presumably) the treaty will be rejected in a referendum in at least one of the Member States. The most likely candidate for causing such difficulties is the United Kingdom, but since its referendum is scheduled only for 2006, it is quite possible that a ratification crisis may erupt earlier on in other countries: in Denmark or Ireland (the earlier culprits), in France or the Netherlands, or perhaps in the Czech Republic or Poland. In view of the volatility of national electorates, there are plenty of unknown national political constellations as regards the referendums. What, then, are the legal scenarios which are available, under the present – EU and international – rules, for dealing with such a ratification crisis? At the outset of his analysis, de Witte discarded two legally unviable options: (a) the partial entry into force of the EU Constitution and the creation of an 'Enhanced Union' between the willing Member States, whereby the latter also remain members – together with the unwilling states – of the old EU; and (b) 'refoundation', whereby the signature of the Constitutional Treaty leads to the abolition of the old EU and the 'refoundation' of the Union on a new legal, i.e., the Constitutional Treaty. The first option is not feasible because the European revision treaties deal with an organization that already exists, comprising Member States which have existing rights and obligations. Allowing for the partial ratification of a revision treaty (such as the Constitutional Treaty) would lead to different circles of members, some bound by the new and the old rules, and others by the old rules only. The EU institutions could not function under the new and old rules simultaneously, so the revision must necessarily apply to all states or to none of them. The 'Giscard' argument – the second option – cannot be

---

[3] See V. Giscard d'Estaing, 'Vite, la Constitution de l'Europe!', *Le Monde* (10 July 2004).

made because the states who would want to move ahead would have nothing to hang on to as long as the Constitutional Treaty itself has not properly entered into force in accordance with the rules of Article 48 TEU. The repeal of the old treaties presupposes, and is preceded by, the entry into force of the new treaty, not the other way around. Under the current rules of Article 48 TEU, *all* Member States must give their agreement to the changes.

According to de Witte, the most orthodox scenario in the case of a clear failure by one or more Member States to ratify the Constitutional Treaty is that the European Council acknowledges that the Constitutional Treaty will not enter into force and that the relations between the Member States (and the legal position of the EU institutions and the citizens) will continue to be governed by the EC and EU Treaties as last amended by the Treaty of Nice and the Accession Treaties (the *'Nice Plus' scenario*). The European Council could decide to immediately set in motion a new treaty revision process, governed by Article 48 TEU. In the meantime, there would be ample scope for tinkering with the current post-Nice Treaty regime, so that the contents of the Constitutional Treaty need not be completely dropped. This could be done in, essentially, two different ways: through the application of parts of the Treaty by means of secondary law (see, e.g., the formal enactment of a Constitutional Treaty innovation under current law with the establishment of the European Defence Agency[4]) or mere institutional practice (some of the new policy competences added by the Constitutional Treaty could be exercised by using the residual powers clause of Article 308 TEC),[5] and through the use of forms of closer cooperation, both inside and outside the Union. In view of the restrictions imposed by the Nice regime for enhanced cooperation within the Union, the states wishing to move ahead in accordance with the content of the Constitutional Treaty could also launch forms of cooperation between smaller groups of Member States outside the EU institutional framework, but membership of the EU imposes certain legal constraints on the scope and content of such cooperation.

Rather than admit defeat and proceed on the basis of the Nice Treaty, the European Council could also decide to face the misgivings emerging from a ratification crisis in one or more countries, while trying to keep the Constitutional Treaty alive. This is the *'voice' scenario*, in which the views of the dissenters are taken into account by the supporters of the Constitutional Treaty with a view to achieving a mutually acceptable compromise. The first option is to try to accommodate the dissenting state (or its dissenting electorate) within the bounds of the Constitutional Treaty as agreed by all governments at the IGC (cf., what hap-

---

[4] Council Joint Action 2004/551/CFSP of 12 July 2004 on the establishment of the European Defence Agency, *OJ* (2004) L 245/17. Recital 6 of the Joint Action mentions that the Agency 'is also envisaged in the draft [TCE]'.

[5] Such informal applications of the TCE would require the agreement of all the Member States. And, of course, informal application of an unratified TCE would increase even further the present opacity of the EU system and would therefore run counter to one of the main objectives which the TCE was set to achieve, that of increasing simplicity and transparency.

pened after the unsuccessful Danish Maastricht and Irish Nice referendums). Whether this 'vote-again scenario' could be repeated in the case of a new ratification crisis depends very much on the circumstances. On previous occasions, the crisis was caused by a single and small Member State and after rejection of the Treaty by a rather small margin of votes. If the Constitutional Treaty were to be rejected in a large Member State, or in more than one Member State, or by a huge majority of the electorate, then an easy accommodation would be more difficult. What one could envisage, then, is to go one step further and embark upon a true *renegotiation* of the Constitutional Treaty, the object of which would be to accommodate the concerns that provoked rejection in one or more countries (provided that one could identify such concerns with sufficient precision) by modifying the text of the treaty. Since the Constitutional Treaty has come into legal existence upon its signature in October 2004, renegotiation would mean drawing up another treaty that would replace the Constitutional Treaty as well as revise the current EC and EU Treaties. That new treaty could either, if the disagreement relates to specific policies, provide opt-outs for the recalcitrant state(s) without modifying the content for the other states, or, if the disagreement relates to the general principles or the institutional reforms, it would have to change the relevant rules for all Member States. All Member States would then have to lodge a new act of ratification, which would require a new approval by their national parliaments but probably not a new referendum in countries where a referendum on the (original) Constitution had already been successful. The delay involved in all this could be mitigated, possibly, by resorting to the *provisional application* of the Constitutional Treaty as originally agreed at the IGC (see Art. 25 VCLT), but only when coupled with ongoing negotiations to save the essence of the Constitutional Treaty.

If the Member States which agree to ratify the Constitutional Treaty do not, or cannot, listen to the 'voice' of the recalcitrant states, then the opposite scenario could be considered, namely that of one or more (or most) Member States exiting from the EU as we know it, so as to enable the Constitutional Treaty to come into operation (*the withdrawal scenario*). Article I-60 TCE allows for the unilateral withdrawal from the Union by a Member State, subject only to some procedural conditions. This withdrawal clause is obviously not applicable before the TCE itself has entered into force and would therefore not be available, as such, in the case of a ratification crisis. The withdrawal from the EU by a non-ratifying Member State is therefore a matter to be dealt with under current EU and international law. In the absence of an express withdrawal clause in the current EC and EU Treaties, the general rule of Article 56 VCLT could be invoked. This article holds that a treaty which contains no express provision on withdrawal is not subject to withdrawal 'unless (i) it is established that the parties intended to admit the possibility of denunciation or withdrawal; or (ii) a right of denunciation or withdrawal may be implied by the nature of the treaty.' Apart from unilateral withdrawal, Article 54 VCLT allows a state to terminate a treaty if all its co-contracting parties agree to that. This hypothesis is more likely to arise in the context of the Constitutional Treaty. The withdrawal of a Member

State would, however, not directly pave the way for the entry into force of the Constitutional Treaty. Article IV-447 TCE makes entry into force conditional upon ratification by *all* the signatory states. A Member State cannot be excluded or forced to withdraw by the other Member States against its own will. The threatening words of Giscard d'Estaing that a non-ratifying state would create a problem for itself and not for the Constitutional Treaty are legally wrong. What would be needed is a combination of two legal texts: (a) an agreement in which all Member States accept the withdrawal of the Member State X and organize the future relations between that state and the remaining Member States; and (b) a treaty concluded between the remaining Member States in which they adopt a *Constitutional Treaty-bis*, which is identical to the original TCE, with the exception of all the articles referring directly or indirectly to the withdrawing state. Both these legal texts would have to be approved by the national parliaments, but would probably not have to be submitted to a referendum.

De Witte explored another form of withdrawal, namely the scenario whereby the remaining Member States could decide to collectively withdraw from the EU (including the EC) and reconfigure a new organization, which he called the 'Enhanced Union'. That would leave the original rump-EU unable to function in the absence of most of its Member States. The withdrawing states would have to justify their action on the basis mentioned in Article 62 VCLT, namely that a fundamental change of circumstances makes it impossible for them to continue as parties to the original EC and EU Treaties. More particularly, they would have to argue that the original objectives of the treaties can no longer be achieved and require the kind of *saut qualitatif* provided by the Constitutional Treaty. De Witte finds this argument very dubious given the fact that the content of the Constitutional Treaty is not so radically different from the TEC and TEU in their post-Nice version. However, the most compelling argument against the legal validity of this scenario is that it would allow, in an indirect but effective way, the objective of excluding the recalcitrant state (which is unlawful) to be achieved. At the very least, the break-away states would have a duty to negotiate adequate terms for their future relations with the state(s) left behind, who could not be accused of having breached their existing treaty obligations.

In conclusion, de Witte remarked that none of the described scenarios are easy and that all of them require complicated legal arrangements that would be difficult to explain to the European citizens. The feasibility of the various options would depend on where the ratification crisis originates and how many states and voters are involved therein. The fact that the legal scenarios depend closely on the political constellation of the day explains why many commentators flatly distinguish between a legal and a political approach to this matter. Many of the statements calling for the Constitutional Treaty to go ahead in case of a ratification crisis indicate that such an initiative should not be stopped by 'legal technicalities'. In other words, the 'vanguard states' could also choose to 'ignore the law' and sweep away the current EU and international law rules if this were needed to extricate themselves from a ratification crisis and pursue their most cherished political goals and interests. Such a revolutionary move requires strong political resolve and close cohesion among the members of the break-away group. In the absence of such revolutionary spirit, de Witte considers it a good idea to keep an eye on the legal technicalities, and patiently explore the resources these can offer.

5.    REFERENDUMS ON THE CONSTITUTIONAL TREATY: CITIZEN'S VOICE?

In the panel discussion following the opening speeches, Anne Peters (University of Basel) devoted attention to the fact that, legally speaking, the 10 or so projected referendums on the EU Constitution are not genuine European referendums in the sense that they do not have their legal basis in EU law, even if this was proposed by nearly half of the members of the Convention. The Member States' referendums on the Constitutional Treaty have their legal basis in domestic law. Peters explained some of the differences in the timing, procedure, thresholds and legal status of the referendums. She pointed out that the desirability of a European referendum or of parallel referendums in the Member States might depend on the legal quality and on the political importance of the text which is at issue. According to Article I-1 TCE 'this Constitution [reflects] the will of the citizens and the States of Europe'. In this quotation, two assertions are relevant for the issue of referendums. The first is its auto-qualification as a constitution, the second is the text's reference to the will of the citizens. Peters considered the qualification of the text of 29 October 2004 as a 'constitution' to be appropriate, although she asserted that the document is, technically speaking, a hybrid between a contract and a constitution. On the contract side, she noted that the text comes in the form of an interstate treaty under public international law and that its contents, ratification and future amendments are based on unanimous agreement between the contracting parties. On the other hand, the text also fulfils typical functions of a constitution, such as the organization of the polity, the containment of political power, and the embodiment of basic values. It contains some typical constitutional contents such as rules on the powers of the institutions, programmatic provisions on the objectives of the Union, and justifying principles such as fundamental rights, democracy, and transparency. But neither the legal qualification as a constitution, nor the text's reference to the will of the citizens as its normative basis requires those citizens to pronounce their will by means of a referendum. Likewise, does it not necessarily mean that its adoption requires an amendment of the adopting Member States' constitutions. This is important, because in many Member States a constitutional amendment must be approved by a mandatory referendum (e.g., in Denmark or Ireland). However, the assessment whether the adoption of the Constitutional Treaty requires a national constitutional amendment is for the Member States to take individually and depends on the national constitution.

In the remainder of her presentation, Peters discussed some of the specific legal benefits from the European referendums: they ensure a direct democratic foundation of the Constitutional Treaty; encourage citizens' engagement and identification with the polity; foster transnational movements (NGO-coalitions, etc.); encourage more openness, substantial communication (less ideology), and may ultimately allow for more social learning. On the other hand, she warned against some caveats. Firstly, the fact that only parallel referendums (as opposed to a genuinely European referendum) will take place can be viewed as a *de facto* realization of the federal concern: votes will be counted separately per Member State and disapproval in one country will block the entry into force of the Constitutional Treaty. Thus, while parallel referendums seem appropriate because the EU is a transnational federal polity, the requirement of approval in the sub-entities is an anti-majoritarian element in relation to the entire polity, because the voters in one or several sub-entities may be able to overrule the overall majority. Secondly, most of the ten referendums were initiated either by the government or by the majority in parliament. They therefore do not have a really critical function (and certainly had no preventive effect), but they rather serve as an acclamatory tool. Thirdly, and in Peters' eyes most crucially, the referendums on the EU Constitution confer a purely 'genetic' legitimacy, which is, as a matter of principle, weak. Constitution-making does not happen in one big bang, but is a process over time. In contrast, the isolated act of popular approval relates only to the status quo and cannot justify a constitution (for all times to come). The most important factor of the legitimacy of a constitution is not its mode of creation, but its performance and continuing popular support. Both can be verified only *ex post*. 'Social legitimacy' in the sense of acceptance and diffuse support, and output legitimacy, that is the actual performance of the constitution and fulfilment of constitutional functions, do not (directly) depend on the genesis of the constitution. Therefore, Peters' overall conclusion is that the parallel referendums will not contribute much to the legitimacy of the Constitutional Treaty.

6.    CONTRIBUTIONS TO THE DEBATE

During the discussion, Leonard Besselink (University of Utrecht) asked whether it would be feasible to have a renegotiation of the Constitutional Treaty in the case of non-ratification by one or more Member States. Would it not be difficult to isolate the issues for renegotiation, i.e., to decide what is 'constitutional' and what is not? De Witte recalled that similar questions were addressed in the cases of the negative referendums in Denmark and Ireland. With relative ease, the Member States then defined and agreed on the issues that were taken back to the drawing board and put back to a popular vote.

Fabian Amtenbrink (University of Groningen) remarked that the Constitutional Treaty would become subject to referendums in a number of, but by no means all Member States. To the extent that these referendums also fulfil the function of legitimising the future EU Constitution, the question arises in what ways the lack of such referendums in all Member States will result in an imbalance of legitimacy. Given the constitutional restraints in some Member States with regard to introducing referendums, prescribing referendums in all Member States or otherwise demands – in broad terms – enhanced public scrutiny in the individual and this does not seem to be a realistic option. Yet, in place thereof, the EU Constitution would have been a good opportunity to introduce a single Europe-wide referendum. Even if such a referendum would not have had any legally binding effect, its symbolic meaning could have boosted the legitimacy of the Constitutional Treaty. Weiler added to this by saying that national parliamentarians in the Convention spoke on their own behalf – they had no 'red lines' to take into account and did not act as representatives, as 'members' of national parliaments. In this sense, opportunities were lost in the constitution-making phase. It would, for example, have been audacious to propose a uniform (European) electoral process for the European Parliament.

Jo Shaw (University of Manchester) agreed that national parliaments, as institutions, were indeed not very active during the Convention. But to discard national parliamentary influence altogether would be going too far. In her view, Weiler had made a profound understatement of the representational value of national MPs, especially since no single Member State or parliamentary interest exists. She referred to the different party caucuses in the Convention. On the ratification procedure of the Constitutional Treaty, Shaw defended the view of campaigning academics as herself, especially to counter anti-democratic statements and behaviour in the United Kingdom. The circumstances in which the holding of a referendum was announced in April 2004 by Prime Minister Tony Blair have already given rise to much media comment. There was, however, no debate in the Cabinet about the proposal before it was announced in Parliament. It would appear to have been a tactical move on the part of Blair with a view to the performance of his party in both the European Elections of 2004, and the anticipated General Election of May 2005, and to remove a tactical weapon regarding the role of plebiscitary democracy from his political opponents.

Deirdre Curtin (University of Utrecht) did not agree with the exceptionality of the UK referendum, as similar problems are present in other Member States as well – albeit perhaps less outspoken. Shaw stated that the main point is that national interests and sensitivities should be taken into account in the run-up to and the aftermath of the referendums. She predicted that the ratification process for the Constitutional Treaty would be very difficult. Although the European Parliament has called for a consolidated and coordinated approach to ratification, in practice each of the ratification processes is likely to be a national issue, contextualised in different ways by European issues and especially the relationship between each Member State, its partners and the EU institutions. According to Shaw, the most that is likely to occur is that there may be a coordinated information and communication campaign, in which the European Parliament plays a central role. Ratification will be drawn out at least into 2006, and possibly well beyond, especially if one or more Member State holds more than one referendum. In that case, the question will arise as to the timing of the next enlargement of the EU. Should Bulgaria and Romania accede on the basis of the Nice settlement and ratify the Constitutional Treaty later? Or should accession be delayed until the Constitutional Treaty comes into force, so that the national accession referendums themselves are conducted on the basis of the Constitutional Treaty? Unless the entire Constitutional Treaty project has already foundered by that time, the British referendum is likely to be held in the first half of 2006 – after the General Election of May 2005, after the end of the UK Presidency (second half of 2005), and before the beginning of the World Cup Finals in June 2006 – '(…) you try holding a referendum on EU-related matters in the United Kingdom during a major football tournament to be held in Germany, especially when England believed it was robbed of the 'right' to host the tournament (…).'

Shaw concurred with de Witte's objective presentation of the legal scenarios in the wake of a non-ratification of the Constitutional Treaty in one or more Member States. She pointed out that it cannot be doubted that all of the mentioned scenarios, which to a greater or lesser extent are conceivable or likely, raise interesting questions of principle for the EU. There remains uncertainty, however, as to what the treaty basis of the European Union will be in the future (EU Constitution or Treaty of Nice), whether it will or will not be faced with a substantial *crise existentielle* in the event of ratification difficulties, and what its membership configuration might be in five or ten years time. The answer to the question of 'treaty or constitution', alluded to by previous speakers, is probably both mixed and contingent, since the EU displays in some respects a multitude of faces at different times and in different fields of its activity. This would not be fundamentally changed by the Constitutional Treaty despite its formal abandonment of the Maastricht pillar system, and its creation of legal personality for the EU as a whole. In some respects, in both its internal and external dealings, the EU continues to be treated by others and indeed acts as an international organization. In other respects, especially with regard to some of the implications of European integration for citizens and residents of the Member States, it has at least a quasi-constitutional force and effect. These aspects would be greatly reinforced by the formal adoption of the Charter of Fundamental Rights as a constitutive and binding element of the EU legal order, notwithstanding the restrictive effects of the so-called 'horizontal clauses'. Ironically, the very fact that the Constitutional Treaty will be subject to referendums in so many Member States (albeit, as Peters explained, not a single common ratification referendum which would allow the citizens of the Member States to act as an incipient common European political *demos*, as well as acting as separate national *demoi*) does reinforce its constitutional character, since it is difficult to imagine why something which is essentially merely an international arrangement between sovereign states ought otherwise to involve the invocation of so many acts of popular sovereignty.

In his intervention, Peter-Christian Müller-Graff (University of Heidelberg) briefly developed three theses on topics related to the process and impact of 'EU Constitution-making' in the light of 'voice' and 'exit'. As to the first thesis, Müller-Graff stated that the Constitutional Treaty masters the conceptually paradoxical task of combining the idea of a constitution with that of exit. The creation of a text which uses in one part of its self-description the word 'constitution' evidently raises expectations which are different from those connected to a treaty, even if the text, in legal terms, projects a treaty. Hence the combination of both terms will be and is already a source for public misunderstanding. Nevertheless the idea of a Constitutional Treaty is not necessarily a paradox in itself as far as legal perception is concerned, but a correct description of the creation and control mechanisms of public powers by an international treaty. Müller-Graff agreed with Weiler that skipping the word constitution implies no categorical novelty for such a legal understanding: the document remains a treaty.

Müller-Graff's second thesis is that the exit-option of non-ratification is full of paradoxes and incalculable effects. He made three observations in this respect. Firstly, in the projected ratification procedure (Art. IV-447 TCE), the reasonable unanimity principle gives every Member State the choice between consent or exit concerning the establishment of the new Union. Hereby the inclusion of the voice of the citizens is variable, as it depends upon the specific constitutional requirements of every Member State. This is a rational consequence of the basic concept that the Constitutional Treaty does not imply a self-constitutionalisation of a European polity, but is a Treaty. Secondly, in legal terms, the exit-option in the ratification procedure is limited and paradoxical. The rejection of the Constitutional Treaty does not end the adherence to the *acquis* currently in force. For example, the provisions on the internal market and the EMU remain basically unchanged in the new text. Hence those who reject the Constitutional Treaty will find themselves to be legally bound by the core content of the rejected text. And thirdly, in political terms, the exit-option in the case of non-ratification is incalculable and ambiguous in its long-term consequences. Müller-Graff referred to the remarks made in this respect by de Witte and Shaw.

The last thesis put forward by Müller-Graff is that in the case of ratification of the Constitutional Treaty the existence of the exit clause can have an ambiguous effect on the voice of a Member State. Again, three aspects were mentioned as relevant. Firstly, the impact of the so-called 'constitution-making' procedure on the future political reality, when seen in the light of 'voice and exit', may materialize in the degree of implementation and durability of the new text: the stronger the voice of the Member States and the citizens is provided for and perceived by the addressees within three areas of decisions, namely within the 'making' period, within the new framework of decision-making, and within the amendment procedures of the Constitutional Treaty, the more durable the impact of the new text on political reality can be expected. Secondly, there are many differentiated channels and weights of voice on all three of the just mentioned levels.[6] And thirdly, there is the ambiguous effect of the voluntary withdrawal option (Art. I-60 TCE) on the weight of the voice of a Member State. On the one

---

[6] See para. 3.2 of Müller-Graff's contribution to this book.

hand, it may enhance its weight as long as the other Member States are willing to continue the member configuration of the Union. If they are not, then the existence of the exit-option may persuade them to give less political weight to the voice of a certain Member State by implicitly or even explicitly pointing to the possibility of voluntary withdrawal provided for by the Constitutional Treaty. On the other hand, this situation may paradoxically shape an overall prudent use of the voice of a Member State in the regular decision-making procedures and hence contribute to the stability of the future member configurations of the EU.

After briefly speculating on the terms of 'treaty' and 'constitution', Evgeni Tanchev (Constitutional Court of Bulgaria) outlined the main strands of thought presented in his written contribution on the problem of the legitimacy and legitimation of the EU Constitution in the context of contemporary constitutional pluralism. In a first part of his contribution, Tanchev compares the EU Constitution, the first non-stately constitution in human civilization, to the full-fledged constitutionalism of nation states. After that, he looks at the EU Constitution's legitimacy and legitimation within different methods of integration (community, intergovernmental, federal). In the final part of his contribution, EU Constitution legitimacy is compared to the emerging phenomena that mark the beginning of a global constitutional order. Tanchev's main conclusion is that it is inadequate to draw from and build upon the foundations of legitimacy of previous constitutional developments to tackle the problem of the legitimacy and legitimation of the (making of the) EU Constitution. The EU Constitution challenges the well-established constitution-making patterns in 18th century political theory constructs of participatory democracy. Other legitimation instruments are necessary to study the problem.

Ion Gâlea (Ministry of Foreign Affairs of Romania) agreed with Peters on the fact that a popular vote confers legitimacy from a 'genetic' point of view, but not from the point of view of reflecting the will of future generations. The EU Constitution will be a living instrument and the tool for revision will therefore be important. In this respect, Müller-Graff observed that the teleological interpretation is the dominant method used by the European Court of Justice. Together with the opinions of the Advocates General, the views of the Court can carry a lot of weight in order to interpret the EU Constitution in the light of future needs and circumstances. Gâlea also asked about the character of the future right of withdrawal from the Union. The main principle governing the law of treaties – applicable to the Treaty establishing a Constitution for Europe – is *pacta sunt servanda*. Thus, withdrawal is possible only if the Constitutional Treaty itself or the Vienna Convention on the Law of Treaties allows for this. The question therefore arises whether this right is 'inherent', like the right of self-defence, or whether it is somehow based on the will of the parties involved. Several speakers touched upon this point by referring to Article 56 VCLT and said that the matter might ultimately be decided upon by the Member States together.

# TRANSPARENCY AND LEGAL INSTRUMENTS IN THE EU CONSTITUTION (REPORT OF THE DISCUSSION)

**Wouter van Ballegooij**[*]

## 1.    INTRODUCTION

As chairperson, Jenö Czuczai (European Law Academy, Budapest) opened plenary session II with the remark that on the topic of transparency and legal instruments the devil was really in the detail. He cited an article by Lenaerts in the newly published *European Constitutional Law Review*:

'Under the EC and EU Treaties, the Union uses no less than 15 different instruments, some having the same appellation but entailing different legal effects, others being rarely used. This diversity has contributed to the development of an obscure patchwork of norms with ill-defined scope, legal effects and institutional origin. That situation consequently limits democratic control over governance at the European level.

The Constitution reorganizes the Union's instruments, under Title V of Part I, and is inspired by the crucial distinction between legislative and executive acts, which are common to all Member State legal systems. It clarifies the separation of powers at the European level and enables the establishment of a true hierarchy of norms, which, however, is not defined as such in the Constitution. In view of the peculiarities of the Union's institutional system, the Constitution proposes an innovative distinction between legislative (article I-33) and non-legislative acts (article I-34)'[1]

Czuczai agreed with Lenaerts in that the Convention came up with the innovative distinction between legislative and non-legislative acts. The question to be answered by plenary session II was whether the new instrument called 'European law' met the expectation created by this notion.

## 2.    NEW LEGAL INSTRUMENTS

Jürgen Bast (Max Planck Institute, Heidelberg) raised the question whether the EU Constitution meets the expectations it had raised by employing the term 'Eu-

---

[*]  Researcher in EU Law, T.M.C. Asser Institute, The Hague. For the sake of clarity, excerpts from some of the written contributions have been reproduced in this report. It goes without saying that the intellectual property rights over these parts remain with their authors.

[1]  K. Lenaerts, 'A Unified Set of Instruments', 1 *European Constitutional Law Review* (2005) pp. 57-61.

*D. Curtin, A.E. Kellermann and S. Blockmans, eds., The EU Constitution: The Best Way Forward?*
© 2005, T.M.C. Asser Instituut, The Hague.

ropean law'. Or did this discourse form part of a purely symbolic constitutionalism? If the latter was the case, one might perceive a 'European law' as an element of what the political scientist Karl Loewenstein in the 1950s called a 'semantic constitution', i.e., a constitution that is unwilling to effectively shape and limit public power, constituted elsewhere.

Bast discussed a number of legal characteristics which a 'European law' is expected to show:

- *Act of Parliament.* A law derives its claim to higher legitimacy from its conceptual assignment to a parliamentary procedure. Article I-34(1) TCE does indeed employ co-decision, but Article I-34(2) TCE provides for various exceptions called 'special legislative procedures'. Whenever the Constitutional Treaty, in Part III, so provides, the Council acts as a legislator that does not necessarily need to reach agreement with parliament. *In sum*, the Constitutional Treaty does not always provide for European laws to be subject to parliamentary co-decision, and cannot therefore in all cases claim legitimacy as an act adopted under parliamentary responsibility.

- *Supremacy of law.* A law is supposed to meet the expectation of being the (almost) supreme law of the law, ranking only below the Constitution but prevailing over other instruments enacted under that Constitution. A hierarchy of norms is, to date, essentially foreign to Union/Community law. Since the Union's institutions are bound to act within their respective powers a hierarchy of norms is not required since possible conflicts of norms are, at least in principle, already solved by the horizontal order of competences. One would expect this system to be overthrown by the concept of European law, but Part I of the EU Constitution does not provide an article to this extent. We are therefore referred to the individual empowering provisions of Part III. This leaves us with the strange situation that European regulations (agriculture) may prevail over interfering European laws.

- *Domain of the law.* This concept refers to the subject areas reserved for rule-making by way of laws. As a rule, interference with fundamental rights is only permissible on the basis, or by order, of a law. Overall, one may technically designate the sum of the empowering provisions of Part III of the EU Constitution which provide for European laws and framework laws as the 'domain of the law' under the Constitutional Treaty. This notion, however, does not meet the expectation that the domain of the European law extends to an area of specifically protected fundamental rights. In European constitutional law the chapter on legal instruments is still not interlinked with that on fundamental rights protection.

- *Shielding against the judiciary.* In most national constitutional systems, the law enjoys a high degree of shielding against the judiciary. Not so in the EU. Despite the wording of Article 230(4) TEC, all instruments are subject to legal review if the contested provisions are of direct and individual concern to the plaintiff. Under Article III-365(4) TCE a plaintiff may now challenge 'regulatory acts' which directly concern him. Bast submitted that the TCE provisions on legal protection should be construed in the light of the right to an effective remedy (Art. II-107(1) TCE). Any act of general application (including legislative acts) should therefore be considered as possibly constituting a 'regulatory act' within the meaning of Article III-365 TCE.

– *Openness to the public and transparency.* Constitutional rules applicable solely to 'legislative acts' concern the transparency of the rule-making process, its openness to the public. Hence, the line which the Constitutional Treaty draws between legislative and non-legislative acts is relevant, both in legal and in political terms, since this delimitation concerns the appropriate level of public scrutiny. Bast submitted that only a careful analysis of Part III of the EU Constitution can determine whether this distinction between legislative and non-legislative acts is based on reasonable criteria. Part III provides us with a blurred picture as to the division between legislative and non-legislative acts (see, for instance, state aid (Art. III-169 TCE), the customs code (Art. III-151(5) TCE) and administrative cooperation in the area of freedom, security and justice (Art. III-263 TCE)). It seems as if the drafters of the EU Constitution purposely excluded these competences from the domain of European law/ public scrutiny.

Bast concluded that the new set of legal instruments and transparency rules introduced by the Constitutional Treaty are a welcome development. Their application, however, hinges on the distinction between legislative and non-legislative acts in Part III. Bast concluded that the EU Constitution is a 'nominal' constitution, a third type of constitution in Loewenstein's classification:

> 'The primary objective of the nominal constitution is educational, with the goal, in the near or distant future, of becoming fully normative and actually governing the dynamics of the power process instead of being governed by it.'

## 3.    EXECUTIVE ACTS AND CONTROL MECHANISMS

Michelle Everson (Birbeck College, London) approached the new legal instruments from a governance perspective. She reiterated that when talking about the European Union, its institutions and the Constitutional Treaty one should bear in mind that the entire EU constitutional polity is in dispute. This realization makes it difficult to apply traditional constitutional principles, such as control and the rule of law to the European Union. In Everson's view, one has to accept that the legitimacy of EU action is largely dependent upon normative considerations (factual legitimacy, efficacy and accountability). Executive action is taken in the public interest, but how do we explain this in the context of the European Union? Is there really something like an EU public interest? Everson stressed that one can however definitely speak of political administration when discussing governance in the EU context. As a consequence one would have to go in search of ways to make this administration politically accountable. This, however, is a normative task. The Constitutional Treaty is not a normative document, it is merely an empty shell. Everson saw it as the task of lawyers to put disputed principles into action.

In response to Everson's last suggestion, Czuczai proposed that the first European Law should be on the comitology system. He pointed out that one of the main achievements of the Constitutional Treaty is the abolition of the pillar system. What practical implications would this have for collaboration in the area of freedom, security and justice?

4.    OPERATIONAL COLLABORATION ON JUSTICE, SECURITY AND
      POLICING IN THE CONSTITUTIONAL FRAMEWORK

In his speech, Steve Peers (University of Essex) focused on the operational control of activities in the areas of justice, security and policing in accordance with the Constitutional Treaty's provisions. He distinguished two levels:

- parliamentary control when legislation is adopted based on the notion that coercive powers should be governed by parliament; and

- accountability (judicial, ombudsman) once operations are carried out to ensure that the rule of law is upheld plus that there are remedies.

Peers stressed the enormous difficulty in scrutinizing the actions of EU-level agencies and organizations and operational collaboration between police, judicial and customs authorities. The new multi-annual programme for Justice and Home Affairs (Hague Programme) contains a number of new cross-border policing measures. These result in an increase of police exercises across borders. The European Parliament and national parliaments are not sufficiently involved in scrutinizing the measures taken. Under the current third pillar, the European Parliament only has a right to be consulted on proposed legislation. The position of national parliaments differs from Member State to Member State. The Council only scrutinizes the activities of Europol and Eurojust to a limited extent. It is very difficult to assess what goes on at these agencies.

In commenting on the Constitutional Treaty, Peers first paid attention to the notions of Freedom, Security and Justice in Article III-257 TCE. He noted that the 'Justice' concept in this article seems to be limited to civil Justice. Article III-263 TCE allows for administrative cooperation by executive acts. Peers pointed out that intrusive measures like the setting up of a European Criminal Records database could be set up without effective scrutiny and control. In general, however, the Constitutional Treaty enhances the role of the European Parliament and the European Court of Justice in this area. We are dependent upon the European Parliament in particular to put in place effective control mechanisms.

Czuczai followed up the presentation by Peers by reminding the audience that the drafters of the Constitutional Treaty had the task of simplifying the EU's treaty structure. Now we have a Constitutional Treaty consisting of three parts. Can we still make sense of their interrelationship?

## 5.    DRAWING THE THREADS TOGETHER FROM PARTS I AND III OF THE EU CONSTITUTION

Jan Wouters (Leuven University) reminded the audience that in earlier versions the Constitutional Treaty only contained two parts, with Part I containing the constitutional structure (institutional architecture, etc.) and Part II containing the legal basis (type of competence, acts and procedures). The IGC upheld this architecture. Wouters raised two questions related to drawing the threads together from Parts I and III of the Constitutional Treaty:

(1)    What has been the guiding principle to deal with certain issues in the first part and other issues in the third part?

(2)    What is the result of these choices for their relevance and revision procedure?

In its September 2003 opinion on the outcome of the IGC, the Commission already pointed out that the Constitutional Treaty lacks any logic as to why certain provisions were inserted in Part I and others in Part III. A good example is the provision dealing with eligibility requirements for Commission members that features in Part I whereas the eligibility requirements for judges were placed in Part III. The same incoherence may be detected for substantive provision, for instance on fundamental freedoms, that are scattered over Parts I, II and III.

As to the implications for relevance and revision, Wouters showed his surprise at the fact that there is now a difference in the revision procedure for Parts I and III. Perhaps this may be explained by the fact that certain provisions of Parts I and III are so closely interlinked that a different amendment procedure would make no sense. There is however a simplified revision procedure applicable to the internal market and more surprisingly the area of freedom, security and justice.

Wouters concluded by saying that the actual relationship between Parts I and III is not what it should have been. Part III is built on a combination of old and new (rewritten) provisions. An important opportunity was missed to change certain Community provisions.

6.    PANEL AND GENERAL DISCUSSION

In a reaction to the presentation by Everson, Deidre Curtin (University of Utrecht) expressed some reservations as to the use of the words 'political administration' when discussing EU governance. She also noted, however, an increase in executive power in the European Union, which is also reflected in the Constitutional Treaty. The Commission has indeed become more politicized. Both the Commission and the Council are delegating policies to agencies. Certain top-down accountability measures were put in place, but we are lacking coherent action. Everson agreed with Curtin's analysis. However, she stuck to the words political administration when describing EU governance, since both the Council and the Commission and even their agencies were overtly political in their actions. This required new approaches to ensure accountability.

In his presentation, Piet Eeckhout (King's College London) focused on the legal instruments of the Common Foreign and Security Policy. Are they legal? Are they law? He stated that this would surely have to be the case if a Constitution provides for them. Did Article I-6 TCE on the supremacy of Union law apply? Eeckhout consequently addressed the relationship between the provisions on the legal instruments in Part I and the CFSP provisions in Part III. In discussing the changes which the Constitutional Treaty brings about, Eeckhout mentioned the fact that the EU will now officially be endowed with legal personality. There will also be an integrated procedure for concluding international agreements. The ECJ will have competence, though it is limited to measures against persons. Eeckhout wondered whether the Court would not be competent to decide whether CFSP decisions were reasoned.

Jörg Monar (University of Sussex) took a realist stance on the Constitutional Treaty. In his view this treaty is all about power. Monar called transparency a crucial aspect in the exercise of public power. He raised four questions:

(1)   How much power is exercised at EU level?

(2)   What is the power exercised (for sustainable development for instance)?

(3)   How is the power actually exercised (reduction of the number of legal instruments)? And

(4)   a fundamental question: who exercises the power?

In his presentation, Siniša Rodin (University of Zagreb) linked transparency in the European Union to legitimacy. He pointed out that discrepancies still exist between East and West. Central and Eastern Europe have only recently moved from authoritarian to rational discourse. In Rodin's view, transparency is indispensable for rational discourse not only at the European level, but also at the level of Member States. According to Rodin this means much more for new Member States, because they do not have long experience with rational discourse.

Rodin was critical of the 2000 Transparency Regulation, which refers to citizens of the Union as its beneficiaries. (Citizens of) candidate countries and third countries are not mentioned, neither is there any reference to external relations. Rodin wondered what message this document sends to candidate countries. Was it that transparency has a different meaning and effect according to the country one comes from?

Ramses Wessel (University of Twente) posed two questions to Eeckhout. First, Wessel recalled Eeckhout referring to the CFSP competences in the Constitutional Treaty as 'undefined'. The Treaty indeed gives no indication as to which of the fixed categories the CFSP competences belong. On the other hand, Wessel thought most people would agree that we are dealing with a mixed competence, in which both the Member States and the Union work closely together. Ironically, the treaty-making competence in this area at the same time seems to imply an exclusive competence on the side of the Union. After all, all 35 treaties concluded on the basis of Article 24 TEU are only concluded by the Union; the Member States are not a party to any of these treaties. In EC law this would be a clear indication of an exclusive competence, following from the supranational nature of the Community. Wessel asked how one should interpret this phenomenon under EU law. Wessel's second question concerned the supremacy of CFSP acts. It seemed that these acts, for the larger part, remained beyond the Court's jurisdiction. In terms of their effect in the national legal orders, however, the Constitutional Treaty does not seem to make a distinction between the various Union acts. Wessel wondered whether one could argue that at least within the national legal orders one should not make a distinction between CFSP and other Union acts.

Eeckhout responded to Wessel's first question by stating that there are no grounds to conclude that provisions of CFSP would have no primacy under the Constitutional Treaty's provisions. The only argument against such a conclusion would be that CFSP measures are not law. An unequivocal answer to the first question was made impossible, however, by the almost complete lack of jurisdiction of the ECJ in CFSP matters. In response to the second question, Eeckhout pointed to the integration towards one single article for treaty-making. Until then, there had indeed been no mixed agreements under the 2nd and 3rd pillar.

# THE DEMOCRATIC LIFE OF THE EUROPEAN UNION (REPORT OF THE DISCUSSION)

**Nicole Versteegen**[*]

## 1. THE ROLE OF PARLIAMENTS IN THE EU CONSTITUTIONAL FRAMEWORK: A PARTNERSHIP OR RIVALRY?

As a former Member of the European Parliament (MEP) and a present member of the Finnish Parliament, Heidi Hautala gave a concise overview and comparative analysis of where the European Parliament and national parliaments stand in terms of enhancing public scrutiny. As a practitioner Hautala argued in favour of practical co-operation between parliamentarians to enhance public scrutiny. She was moderately positive about the role of national parliaments, which, in her eyes, have a place in the EU decision-making process as they are directly accountable to citizens in the Member States. In line with this, she argued that national parliaments and the European Parliament are moving from competition as to who represents EU citizens, to complementary roles. Nevertheless, she expressed her concerns about the legitimacy gaps in the Council procedures. Although the evolution is ongoing, control of the Council remains a problem for the European Parliament, national parliaments and citizens. However, the fact that citizens have gained some political rights in terms of becoming political subjects to policy-making may pave the way for creating new opportunities for a common European public space. (Insert paper).

## 2. THEORY AND REALITY OF PUBLIC ACCESS TO EU INFORMATION

The presentation by Lorenzo Cotino (University of Valencia) was based upon ten years of research within the Council and the European Commission on the legalization of transparency and the right of access to documents. Cotino's paper converges on the idea that transparency has become the term to represent the public image of the European Union. The picture he gave illustrated that in reality, however, access to EU information has often been insignificant and anecdotal and can hardly serve to legitimize the European Union. (Insert paper).

---

[*] T.M.C. Asser Institute, The Hague.

*D. Curtin, A.E. Kellermann and S. Blockmans, eds., The EU Constitution: The Best Way Forward?*
© 2005, *T.M.C. Asser Instituut, The Hague.*

3.    PERSPECTIVES OF EUROPEAN CITIZENSHIP

Jaap de Zwaan (Erasmus University Rotterdam) described in detail the concept of European Citizenship from an institutional, political and legal perspective. His presentation highlighted the role of treaty makers, legislators and the Court of Justice in the context of a political union as opposed to a purely economic union. De Zwaan's overall impression is that the concept of European Citizenship in the Constitutional Treaty has been given more attention than has been the case until now. Reference can be made to Part II of the EU Constitution. Illustrated by a concise overview of the Court of Justice's jurisprudence, de Zwaan expressed the importance of the Institution in the practical development of the concept of EU citizenship. The ECJ has given European Citizenship its own merits compared to the existing jurisprudence relating to economically active workers. De Zwaan was especially pleased by the innovations brought about by the EU Constitution in the light of the new directive on free movement of persons, covering both economically active and non-economically active EU nationals. In addition, he raised a few thought-provoking statements as to the possibility to grant third country nationals, family members of EU citizens or long-term residents, certain political and civil rights. (Insert paper).


4.    QUESTIONS AND ANSWERS

In reaction to Cotino's speech, Steve Peers (University of Essex) underlined the importance of the link between individual requests for documents and the documents available on the institutions' registers. For example, the creation of the registers developed from the right of individual access pursued through the European Courts, the European Ombudsman and the political process. According to Peers, many of the documents available on the register are only available because of individual requests to release the documents. Therefore he advised Cotino to take into consideration the wider dissemination of documents through non-institution websites, such as websites of NGOs and the press, including summaries of documents that appear in press reports. With regard to participation, Peers pointed to the indirect impact of access to documents upon effective public participation. In addition, he argued that access to documents has assisted the participation of MEPs, national MPs, NGOs, business groups and other members of the public in the debate over EU affairs. Finally, he underlined the usefulness of examining the Constitution's provisions for opening up Council proceedings on legislative matters. In Peers' view, this development is intrinsically important, and could have implications for access to documents. Cotino agreed on the points raised by Peers and emphasized the significant role of the European Ombudsman in improving, controlling and monitoring the electronic transparency and access to documents on, among others, the Internet.

Philipp Kiiver (Maastricht University) referred to Hautala's remarks concerning the way in which parliaments scrutinize the EU policy of their governments.

According to Hautala this can take the form of polarized government, opposition debates or the formation of cross-party consensus to support a coherent national standpoint. In addition, Hautala pointed out that the European Parliament is increasingly treating national parliaments as allies rather than competitors. Kiiver wondered how these two points correlate. He underlined that it may be profitable for the European Parliament to have national parliamentary allies if their views coincide. But he wondered what would happen if the national parliaments' views are not consistent with those of the European Parliament. Kiiver suggested that it is not detrimental to stimulate emphasis on the national interest, in the light of the development towards transnational parliamentarism and the reflection of the European interests in the European Parliament. Hautala responded that especially matters of justice and civil rights could form a basis for cooperation between the European Parliament and the national parliaments. The parliaments may have a common concern for protecting citizens' rights, for example in the context of the disclosure of flight passenger information to the US authorities.

Flora Goudappel (Erasmus University Rotterdam) questioned the official emphasis now placed in the Constitutional Treaty on the role of national parliaments instead of strengthening the position of the European Parliament. She considered this to be a movement away from European integration, which is especially the case when one looks at the Protocol on Subsidiarity as described by Hautala. Goudappel questioned this move towards devolving new powers to national parliaments, while their involvement at present is not functioning in the way it should. Therefore, she preferred strengthening the role of national parliaments in the field of the implementation of EU law. In addition, she argued that an early warning by national parliaments in the case of possible future implementation problems within a national legal system would solve many problems, which now come to the fore too late to effectuate change. A second element of Goudappel's doubts concerned the 'mandating arrangements' as mentioned by Hautala. In her opinion this will very often be a useless exercise when qualified majority voting is involved. She had doubts about the use of such a mandate when the position is outvoted in the Council. She pointed out that the position of the European Parliament could be strengthened with better or closer cooperation with national parliaments.

Hautala agreed with the fact that early involvement by national parliaments is of great importance and welcomed the strengthening of the role of national parliaments in the field of implementing EU law. Referring to the early warning issue, Hautala responded by saying that the fact that national parliaments are more closely involved in this way, will mean that, in practice, they will also check for implementation problems in advance.

5.    THE EUROPEAN OMBUDSMAN AND THE EU CONSTITUTION

Nikiforos Diamandouros (EU Ombudsman) provided a clear statement and vision on the role of the European Ombudsman in the current and future European

Union. As a political scientist, Diamandouros signalled a perceptible shift in the way the European Ombudsman approaches certain issues. He referred to the tendency to expand the Ombudsman's mandate by trying to incorporate a broader principle of maladministration therein. (Insert paper). Diamandouros pointed out that the Code of Good Administrative Behaviour is becoming increasingly the object of concerted efforts to ensure a uniform law in the near future. He fully expected that the European Ombudsman can contribute to the adoption of this law, which will eliminate the concern of overlapping codes. To his mind, the Code is becoming the object of significant interest in a number of Member States. He signalled efforts in trying to incorporate the Code of Good Administrative Behaviour into national legislation, which is major step in enhancing the fight against maladministration. According to Diamandouros, the European Ombudsman is committed to promoting good administration, to stimulate public administration and to see things beyond the terms of strict legality. However, he remained convinced that subsidiarity is a major principle of the European Union. Therefore the main principle should be to provide a broad legal definition of the existing network and likewise to prevent actions that might undermine the principle of subsidiarity.

## 6.    PANEL AND GENERAL DISCUSSION

Gerard van der Wal (Houthoff Buruma, Brussels) provided a thoughtful analysis as a close observer of the European Ombudsman's work. (Insert paper). Tom Eijsbouts (University of Amsterdam) spoke in defence of the European Parliament. His vigorous debate converged on the idea and the power of representation in the European Union. He considered the European Parliament to be a forceful institution for representation. He pointed out that there are many thoughts developing in scholarship and practice to circumvent the European Parliament, but all are doomed to fail if the European Union succeeds in being the centre of political life. Eijsbouts claimed that no political future for the Union is conceivable without the solid capacity of popular representation.

   Steve Peers referred to the two speakers who commented on the need to ensure that non-judicial remedies are available in Member States as regards EC law and human rights. Peers agreed with the speakers and mentioned two practical suggestions. First, he argued that the obligation to do so could be established in EC legislation either by means of horizontal legislation, sectoral legislation or fundamental treaty law; for example, by way of drafting a Code of Conduct on this issue and promoting it. Secondly, he pointed out that the future EU Human Rights Agency could also address the issue, possibly in conjunction with the European Ombudsman.

   Anne Peters (Basel University) referred to Diamandouros' perception that the focus of the Ombudsman will probably be on the protection of human rights. She pointed out that the mandate to enhance the fight against maladministration is limited to the activities of the executive branch. She therefore wondered if enhancing human rights scrutiny falls outside the scope of the European Ombudsman's activities. In addition, she wondered whether there will be an overlap between the newly established network dealing with human rights problems and the activities of the Ombudsman. Rick Lawson (Leiden University) intervened by arguing that there will be no overlap with the activities of the European Ombudsman, as the network does not deal with individual complaints.

Diamandouros assured that all Member States *do* have non-judicial remedies in place and that all States, with the exception of Italy and Germany, have national ombudsmen. Therefore the question should be how to provide better coordination. Referring to the human rights question, Diamandouros argued that the Ombudsman's concern is to ensure that human rights are implicitly present in EU legislation. Legislation has to be in conformity with the European Convention on Human Rights as well as the Charter of Fundamental Rights. Diamandouros cautioned that new democracies tend to overload the national ombudsmen by invoking the Nordic model. As court decisions are not adhered to by the executive, these states argue that their ombudsman should be empowered with prosecutorial functions to ensure that the executive complies. Diamandouros considered this to be a recipe for disaster. An ombudsman cannot be a *panacea* and ought to be regarded as an instrument in the *nexus* of institutions trying to promote the rule of law and democracy.

# EXPANSION OF EXECUTIVE, JUDICIAL AND LEGISLATIVE POWERS (REPORT OF THE DISCUSSION)

## Adam Łazowski and Tamara Takács*

### 1. THE EVOLUTION OF THE ROLE AND POWERS OF THE EUROPEAN COUNCIL

Jan Werts (European Correspondent, Brussels) highlighted crucial issues relating to the European Council: its evolving position in the decision-making process and the institutional balance, the changes brought about by the EU Treaty, and the future impact of the Constitutional Treaty. He compared the initial tasks and the objectives of the European Council with the wording of the Constitutional Treaty, where the definition is much wider and somewhat vaguer in setting priorities. He pointed out that the original model based on the institutional triangle has been increasingly confused by the emergence of the European Council and already in 1991 the European Council seemed to have been a forum for the heads of governments to take decisions regarding questions which had not been resolved by the Council of Ministers. The successive treaty amendments granted increased importance to the European Council. The Treaty on the European Union, for example, entrusted the Council with tasks within the framework of the CFSP and the European Monetary Union. In the European Convention there were strong proposals advocating the substantial upgrading of the European Council. Werts mentioned the proposals for the acknowledgement of the European Council as an official institution and the introduction of the post of a permanent President of the European Council. This latter will obviously have an impact on the Community model, in particular on the character and role of the (President of the) Commission. Werts analysed the trepidations mostly represented by the smaller Member States. Werts emphasized that a very important challenge facing the EU was the accomplishment of the Lisbon Agenda, which entrusts additional important tasks to the European Council. The European Council will operate as the ultimate political centre, having an 'eminent guiding and coordinating' role. Thus, it will have to deal with the most important economic and social problems and manage the execution and supervision of the

* Adam Łazowski is a Senior Researcher in the law of the European Union, T.M.C. Asser Institute; Tamara Takács is a PhD candidate, University of Utrecht and the T.M.C. Asser Institute.

*D. Curtin, A.E. Kellermann and S. Blockmans, eds., The EU Constitution: The Best Way Forward?*
© 2005, T.M.C. Asser Instituut, The Hague.

whole decision-making process. At this point, Werts noticed that, in this way, the European Council would absorb tasks from the Commission, the Parliament and the Council of Ministers, a move which could take place without prior inter-institutional discussion or treaty amendment.

For the future of the European Union, and its Constitutional Treaty, Werts considered that the permanent President of the European Council will *de facto* be the President of the EU. He expected the role and the importance of the European Council to be further strengthened, something Werts saw as the optimal solution in the course of the evolution of the European Union. By relying on his experience as a journalist, he expressed the view that the European Union seems to function as the most effective and functional method of deliberation between the Member States. The necessary preparation prior to such deliberations places the Commission and the Coreper in an important, reinforced position. Thus, Werts adhered to his opinion that the emergence of the European Council is not a weakening element, but rather a welcome addition to the famous Community model.

Moritz Roettinger (European Commission) asked Jan Werts whether the European Council has ever adopted regulations, directives or decisions while acting as the Council of Ministers, something which, in theory, it could do. Werts responded that until 1991, when his study of the European Council ended, there had been no such decisions taken by the European Council in the guise of the Council of Ministers. Nor, since 1991, had he noticed such a practice except for those he had mentioned, which were adopted on the basis of the Treaty on the European Union. Thus, he explained that the European Council takes decisions in a political sense, not in a legal sense – this latter remaining with the Council of Ministers.

Francis Jacobs (Advocate General at the ECJ) made a remark related to the increased role of the Presidency, which in the EU Constitution will operate over a much longer period and will affect the European Council as some of the power would shift in practice. Werts agreed and underlined that he, personally, was shocked by the modification of the Presidency in the past decades, especially since the entry into force of the Treaty on the European Union. He noted that the Presidency has *de facto* become an institution, with a strengthened position to the detriment of the roles of the Commission. Werts regretted this phenomenon.

## 2.    THE EXPANDING ROLE OF THE EUROPEAN PARLIAMENT

Ricardo Passos (Legal Service, European Parliament) firstly reflected on the contributions from the previous day, in particular that of Joseph Weiler, in which he provided some critical comments on the working and the outcome of the European Convention. Passos emphasized that, contrary to Weiler, he believed that the involvement of civil society was effective and very important in the Convention's work. Furthermore, he believed that the negative outcome of the referendums around Europe would not lead to a win-win situation as the Treaty of Nice does not and would not work well with 25 Member States. Therefore, Passos believed that the Treaty of Nice was certainly not the best way forward. As a point of departure for his presentation, Passos highlighted that the important elements in the EU Constitution were intimately related to clarity, efficiency, and democratic accountability. Passos illustrated these elements by providing a long list of achievements, which have an important effect on the functioning of the European Union. These elements would lead to crucial improvements, in three particular areas as far as the European Parliament is concerned. Firstly, the procedure for the approval of the President of the Commission and the open hearings increase the legitimacy of the Commission and the EP's political control there over. Passos expressed the expectation that the votes cast during the next EP elections may possibly influence the composition of the successive college of Commissioners. Secondly, the best achievement by the Convention and the Intergovernmental Conference was in the field of Justice and Home Affairs: the remarkable extension of qualified majority voting, the introduction of the approximation of substantive and procedural criminal law, the strengthening of more operational powers for Eurojust and the perspective of a European Public Prosecutor. And, thirdly, the Common Commercial Policy (CCP) has been modified by the introduction of the co-decision procedure for measures implementing the CCP, and the participation of the EP would be extended in the drafting of acts. Also, the Parliament's consent has been confirmed and the Commission has a new obligation to inform the Parliament and the Council of Ministers. Passos concluded his presentation by reiterating that the time to vote has arrived for the citizens in those Member States which ratify the EU Constitution by a popular referendum. In this context, he pointed out that the organisation of such referendums is very risky, as it is tempting for national politicians to confuse the electorate and to mix up European issues with issues of a national character.

Fabian Amtenbrink (University of Groningen) wondered whether the hopes for raising the consciousness of the citizens relating to the European elections and thus to shape the possible composition of the Commission were not too optimistic taking into account the fact that European political parties still do not exist. He also doubted whether EP elections were really based on genuine European issues. Amtenbrink asked Passos if the EU Constitution marks an improvement in these respects. Passos pointed out that there are provisions in the Constitutional Treaty encouraging European parties, while no mention is made as to how the Member States should organise the European elections and campaign. One has to acknowledge that the Member States very often fail to give a real European dimension to the EP elections campaign, which is another element frustrating a generally higher turnout.

Armin van Bogdandy (Max Planck Institute, Heidelberg) reflected on the presentation by Werts and asked Passos if he shared Werts' opinion that the European Council had evolved very significantly, whereas the European Parliament had not done so. Passos expressed his doubts concerning this issue and stated that an increase in the powers of the European Council would inevitably lead to a decrease in the powers of the European Parliament. Werts joined the discussion by emphasizing that the nature of the two institutions is very different and that they are not easily compared. Van Bogdandy also pointed out that the emergence of the European Council contained an alarming element. From a constitutional-legal point of view it is now an institution with no real lines of responsibility within the constitutional setting in which it is placed. Jan Werts, in his reflection on this point, emphasized that ever since its creation the European Council has been a decision-making body, which has always succeeded in arriving at a compromise, a politically expedient decision, and its decisions are much more publicised than those of any of the other institutions.

3.    THE EVOLUTION IN THE ROLE AND POWERS OF THE EUROPEAN COMMISSION

Clemens Ladenburger (Legal Service, European Commission) started his presentation by emphasizing how difficult it was at this stage to make a judgement as to the evolution of the role and power of the Commission and to envisage developments for the future. The areas of change which he highlighted touched upon the function being exercised by the Commission, and at this point he mentioned how regrettable and strange a phenomenon it was that while there were important debates related to the internal structure and composition of the Commission, there was not enough discussion relating to the composition and election of the members of the Parliament. He also stated that one necessarily had to take into account the repercussions of the evolution of the other institutions such as, for example – as mentioned by Werts, the new office of a permanent President of the European Council. Ladenburger welcomed the comprehensive encapsulation of the functions of the Commission in the Constitutional Treaty, which is not only symbolic, but expresses a concrete politico-legal message: the co-functions of the Commission are the constitutional bedrock of the institutional system. With regard to the actual powers of the Commission, as modified by the EU Constitution, Ladenburger described, firstly, how the Commission's role in executive rule-making had increased, notably with the introduction of instruments of delegated regulation. This may imply a major unburdening of the legislator and a more substantial delegation of implementing rule-making power to the Commission. On this point, he envisaged that the new delegated regulations would, over time, very largely replace the regulatory comitology procedure. For further reflection, Ladenburger raised the dilemma of how the control mechanisms for the Parliament and the Council would work in practice in the new system, and he envisaged, as his point of view, that Parliament's scrutiny over delegated acts will be felt in a small number of politically sensitive areas of delegation. Furthermore, within the Council, the members would probably try to set up a system similar to comitology to be able to follow the Commission's delegated regulation. Another area of change brought about by the EU Constitution is the field of Justice and Home Affairs. Here, Ladenburger reflected on Passos' presentation and emphasized that the *de facto* 'communitarisation' of the third pillar has extended the role and power of the Commission, by opening new possibilities for dialogue with the national parliaments, providing access to infringement procedures also in respect of fundamental rights in criminal procedures. It also sets a challenge for the Community method in an area intimately related to state sovereignty. As for the area of external relations, and the role of the Commission therein, Ladenburger pointed out that it was difficult to determine the exact line between the CFSP and the remainder of external relations: likewise, the respective roles of the new Foreign Minister and the Commissioner for External relations have a vague borderline. The new Foreign Minister will be a member of the Commission, thus he/she needs the confidence of the Parliament and the Commission. According to Ladenburger, such a contradiction can be solved if the Commission allows the Foreign Minister to work constructively, accepting his/her support for becoming a privileged actor in a cross-pillar area.

Piet Eeckhout (King's College, London) pointed out that it is very difficult to draw a line between general foreign policy and other aspects of external relations, and that any meaningful decision will have multiple aspects, as the Commission and the Council – each with their interests – would need to be involved. Eeckhout saw the role of the Foreign Minister as a common denominator; as someone who listens to all institutions involved and comes up with a coherent foreign policy and has it accepted at Commission and Council level. Ladenburger shared this view and drew attention to one potential danger in the new system: in the future, for international agreements, some Member States may claim that the political dimension of the agreement is so great that the CFSP rule of unanimity should apply, whereas currently it is to some extent possible to bring most international agreements under the Community's competence, where qualified majority voting applies. However, he welcomed the fact that the person who would apply the rules and would ensure that they draw the necessary line will be the Foreign Minister himself, because he will chair the Council and will impose the vote when he believes that QMV applies and CFSP aspects are minimal.

## 4.   PANEL DISCUSSIONS

Stanislaw Biernat (Jagellonian University) reflected on the extent to which the new document is a 'treaty' and/or a 'constitution'. According to him, the EU as a complex organisation should have a defined framework of powers and roles, carried out by its institutions, and in this aspect it resembles a national constitutional system of governance. He considers the changes brought about by the Constitutional Treaty to be essential, but not revolutionary, as they are the corollary of a long development and evolution of diverse interests. He drew attention to one of these changes, namely the division of legal acts into legislative and non-legislative acts, which he considered to have been generalized by the attempts to simplify the legal instruments and procedures. Thus, such a division cannot in any way be regarded as an attempt to set up a division of powers between the institutions, and therefore one cannot refer to any of the institutions exercising one particular power. Biernat emphasized the importance of values such as efficiency, democracy and accountability as basic structuring elements in the institutional system. Furthermore, as political decisions, controversial interests determined the path of the EU's development, and he believed that the evolution of institutional powers was equivocal in the Constitutional Treaty. He illustrated this phenomenon by describing the novelties with an intergovernmental or supranational character, which have been enhanced by the Constitutional Treaty. He concluded on this point that in this way the Constitutional Treaty does not bring anything new, and that the modifications lie solely in the terminology. Concerning the judiciary, Biernat expected an increasing role for the ECJ in the interpretation of new institutional provisions after the entry into force of the Constitutional Treaty, with increasing litigation on issues relating to the division of legal instruments and the division of powers. Here the ECJ has proven its skill and capacity to be able to arbitrate in disputes between political institutions.

Victor Duculescu (University of Bucharest) noticed that the notion of separation of powers is difficult to comprehend within the framework of the new Constitutional Treaty. He believed that the institutional architecture was a compromise, and that further European integration would mean more separation of powers. In Romania, the separation of powers is explicit in the Constitution, while he remarked that this is not so in the EU.

Christian Timmermans (a Judge at the ECJ) recalled the debates of the T.M.C. Asser Colloquium in 1997, where proposals were made in favour of a 'European Council of State' or an expert committee to monitor the quality of European draft legislation. None of these particular scrutinizing bodies have been established, which he believed was not regrettable, as other, more appropriate initiatives have been taken on another level: the interinstitutional agreement in 2003, and Commission communications, in particular one on the impact assessment of EU legislation. Relating to the latter, he considered the Constitutional Treaty as a motivating element for increasing the use of the subsidiarity principle by the national parliaments, as laid down in the protocol. As for other institutional issues, Timmermans reflected on what Werts had said about a tandem between the European Council and the Commission in decision-making. Timmermans believed that this was contradictory. Nevertheless, he acknowledged that personal relations in the two institutions have an impact on their cooperation. He emphasized the need for such a good preparation between the President of the Council and that of the Commission. However, this may impede the development of the President of the Council's own administration. Concerning the relationship between the European Council and the Commission in the second pillar, Timmermans referred to cross-pillar decision-making, an important innovation brought about by the Constitutional Treaty, and the introduction of a double-hatted Minister for Foreign Affairs. Analysing the essence of the cross-pillar decision-making, he came to the conclusion that this was to the detriment of the Community method: it combines CFSP decision-making with the co-decision procedure, leaving the final decision to the European Council, a body with an intergovernmental nature. Thus, divergences in the procedure would remain. He also stated that in the limited area of external relations, where the Commission should make the necessary proposals, the formalization of the decision-making procedure largely undertaken by the European Council negatively affects the Commission's position.

# ACCESS TO JUSTICE AND THE EU CONSTITUTION (REPORT OF THE DISCUSSION)

**Tamara Takács**[*]

1.   THE WORKLOAD OF THE EU COURTS AND THE CITIZEN'S RIGHT
     TO HAVE ACCESS TO A JUDGE

Denis Waelbroeck (Université Libre de Bruxelles) welcomed the changes brought about by the EU Constitution, which he considered as significant, providing for better access to justice. Arguing in favour of the Constitutional Treaty, he underlined a number of modifications it has made to the existing treaties, in particular the extension of acts which may be challenged by the individual. From a practitioners' point of view, however, Waelbroeck was less satisfied with the EU Constitution's somewhat timid modifications towards creating a greater access to the EU court for citizens. On this point he referred to his colleagues at the Council of the Bar Associations and Law Societies of the EU (hereinafter: CCBE), who have been fighting for such a fundamentally important reform. Waelbroeck expressed his concerns about the possible consequences of the reforms in the field of judicial control as introduced by the Constitutional Treaty. Such reforms do not satisfy his strongly advocated belief in judicial control and its extension to legislation, as the control introduced by the EU Constitution merely concerns regulatory acts and not acts by the legislature. With reference to the *Foto-Frost* principle, Waelbroeck also criticized the national courts' lack of power to invalidate Community acts and he illustrated the absurdity of this current system with an interesting case taken from his own practice. He related this illustration to the workload of the ECJ by pointing out that the attempt to reduce this workload has been unsuccessful. While rejecting the idea of an *actio popul
aris*, Waelbroeck maintained the importance of wider admissibility, believing that better access to the EU Courts for citizens would confirm the EU's maturity.

---

[*] PhD candidate, University of Utrecht and the T.M.C. Asser Institute.

*D. Curtin, A.E. Kellermann and S. Blockmans, eds., The EU Constitution: The Best Way Forward?*
© 2005, T.M.C. Asser Instituut, The Hague.

2.    THE EXPANDING ROLE OF THE NATIONAL COURTS AND THE EU
      CONSTITUTIONAL SYSTEM

Jutta Limbach (Goethe Institute Munich, former President of the Bundesverfassungsgericht, Karlsruhe) highlighted the way in which the domestic courts can
contribute to realizing the texts of the treaties, and what the position and innovation of the social rights inserted in the Charter of Fundamental Rights could
mean for the European legal community. She illustrated how the ECJ deducted
fundamental theories and principles through its case law, in particular in the field
of the protection of human rights. The role of the national courts in the above-
mentioned development has certainly been the possibility to make use of the preliminary procedure to ascertain the legal principles of EU law. Limbach
emphasized the importance of future cooperation between national courts and the
European courts in the first years of the EU Constitution's existence, in order to
establish a transparent system of theories, competences and the limits of interpretation. She emphasized the use of references to the Charter of Fundamental
Rights in order to establish such limits for interpretation. She pointed to the case
law of the German Federal Court relating to fundamental rights, expanding the
importance of fundamental rights to lawmaking and the application of the law, as
objective principles. Furthermore, she placed the Charter at the heart of the issue,
together with the increasing importance of social policy and the social rights deduced there from. Such a social dimension completes the political dimension of
the EU Constitution, and, indeed, this is in fact enshrined in the Constitutional
Treaty itself. The nature of these rights and their quality as norms are the subject
of ongoing debates, such as their enforceability by legal action. Certainly, they
are part of the functional foundations of democracy, but their protection will primarily be through legislative bodies and the executive. The insertion of such social rights, however, persuades the national courts to investigate the social
dimension of cases, and this may leave the hallmarks of the social dimension on
the harmonisation of fundamental rights.


3.     THE COMPLEMENTARY ROLES OF STRASBOURG AND LUXEMBOURG

In his presentation, Rick Lawson (University of Leiden) analyzed the potential
relations between the Luxembourg and Strasbourg Courts if and when the EU
Constitution enters into force. He described the European Union's enhanced role
in the promotion of human rights since the introduction of Article 7 TEU at
Amsterdam, the newly established network of experts on human rights by the
Commission and, along with these steps, he welcomed the idea of the establishment of a Human Rights Agency. Lawson went on to illustrate the innovations
included in the EU Constitution, such as accession of the Union to the ECHR
and the incorporation of the Charter of Fundamental Rights into the Constitutional Treaty, as well as the possible effects which each of these can have on the
complementarity and involvement of the two courts in reviewing complaints

made against Member States' authorities and complaints against EU institutions. By doing so, he raised the issue of the existing case law of both courts and the cases which are still pending, predicting their possible outcome. The picture he gave illustrates, among other things, how the EU's accession to the ECHR would ensure a minimum protection of human rights and guarantees by the ECJ, similar to that of the Strasbourg Court. He expressed his concerns about the fact that accession to the ECHR could result in 'forum-shopping', and the likelihood of the introduction of certain mechanisms which would lead to a situation where only one court (and that would be Strasbourg) would rule on the human rights dimension of a case. This, he emphasized, would be very unfortunate, not only because there is a significant difference between the reviews carried out by the two courts, but also because it would potentially curtail the competence of the Court in Strasbourg.

4.      QUESTIONS TO THE SPEAKERS AND ANSWERS

Steve Peers (University of Essex) addressed two observations to Rick Lawson. The first observation was related to the complaints in the Union's legal order against Member States or institutions where the individual is not directly involved. With his second remark, Peers emphasized that the importance of general principles is overlooked when talking about human rights protection. However, such principles would complete the list contained in the Charter and thus provide for the recognition of more rights. Rick Lawson reacted to the first remark by illustrating how the DGs at the Commission, in particular the DG for Justice and Home Affairs, deal with complaints by individuals against Member States. He underlined that the civil servants of the DGs review these complaints in the light of the Strasbourg case law. With regard to the second remark, Lawson suggested that, in order to decide the role and place of these principles in human rights protection, one has to determine what the expectations are towards the EU. In particular, if the EU is conceived as a human rights protector at the domestic level then general principles should be strictly considered, but if it respects human rights as an organisation without imposing the concept on its lower components, then the larger picture of the EU will show a different image.

Frits Fliers (Journalist) addressed a question to Jutta Limbach, referring back to her presentation where she allocated the protection of some norms in the Charter to the legislative powers and executive power instead of protection primarily by the courts. Fliers wondered whether such protection would not be better placed and more effectively ensured by the courts instead of politicians. Limbach pointed out that such a different kind of protection, allocated to the legislative and executive power, rather than to the courts, concerns only a special category of rights. These are, in particular, social rights, solidarity or social directives, a term widely used in Germany. In such a category of rights there is no special claim or individual right which one can use to resort to the courts, and even though the courts have the possibility to provide direction, it is the legislative and executive powers which provide for the right mechanism to implement social aims.

Sacha Prechal (University of Utrecht and chairman of the session) posed a question to Rick Lawson, referring back to the three-level human rights protection after potential accession to the ECHR, namely the national, EU, and the ECHR levels. Prechal asked whether such a situation would not lead to an unfortunately extended duration of proceedings for the applicants. Lawson answered in the sense that this phenomenon will not be an explicit consequence of accession to the ECHR, as cases have already been heard in Strasbourg where during the domestic remedies phase preliminary questions had already been directed towards Luxembourg. He believed that the better the quality of preliminary rulings at the ECJ will be, the less need there will be for individuals to exhaust domestic remedies and to litigate in Strasbourg. Denis Waelbroeck, on the other hand, expressed his strong belief in the merits of having one judicial system, in which the unity of jurisdiction is safeguarded by one court at the summit, having a final say on the question. Furthermore, in such a system he sees no risks of 'forum-shopping', because, according to him, proceedings will clearly fall into distinct categories of jurisdiction.

5.     THE EXPANDING JURISDICTION OF THE COURT OF JUSTICE

Ad Geelhoed (Advocate General, ECJ) praised some of the changes made to the judicial system of the EU in the Treaty of Nice. He pointed out that the EU Constitution did not provide for the means necessary to deflate the Court's workload, leaving the possibility that the system would implode in five to ten years' time. In this respect he drew two main lines of possible developments: the quantitative growth of disputes and the qualitative change in the demand for legal protection, the latter being partly the result of creeping juridification. Geelhoed expected such an evolution in particular in migration and criminal law issues in the EU judicial system, envisioning certain consequences for the future architecture thereof. According to Geelhoed, additional effects are likely to generate a further influence on the judicial system and protection of the subjects of EU law. He drew up architectural models which could help to avoid the collapse of the judicial system. One of these was a system of specialized and territorially decentralized courts in areas which are already *communitarised*, where a distinction between EU legislation and national application can hardly be made. He predicted that the Community would become the victim of its own success, and the whole idea of different national authorities dealing with transposing issues would become unsustainable. He considered that the system drawn up in Nice is sufficiently timely to meet the main goal of judicial protection, and some flexibility still exists as such, but thinking of further steps is required.

Gareth Davies (University of Groningen) was concerned about the reform of the preliminary procedure. He highlighted that the major obstacle to this reform is the fact that the European Court of Justice seems to exceed its role by interpreting its functions too broadly. Namely, the Court does not merely interpret the EC Treaty, but it also assesses the facts of a case in detail, failing to respect the division of competences with the national courts. This practice inevitably increases the workload of the ECJ, as national courts are more apt to refer cases based upon a new set of facts. Davies therefore pointed out that reforming the preliminary procedure depends upon the ECJ itself. Geelhoed underlined that there is a gradually forming bond between abstract interpretation by the ECJ and application by the national courts, which centres on how the preliminary questions are formulated. He also stated that new Member States' references to the ECJ are not only a matter of uncertainty, but also that they are a question of seeking comfort in order to justify bringing a ruling against their own administrations.

## 6.    PANEL AND GENERAL DISCUSSIONS

Arjen Meij (Judge at the CFI) emphasized that the modifications in the structure of the future EU judicial system and, in particular, changes to Article 230 TEC will shift the emphasis from the objective review of the legality of a Community act towards emphasis on the protection of individuals' subjective rights. The current system, in the light of this view, is rather rigid, and the retention of such a solution in the Constitutional Treaty is regrettable. Also, inserting the legal basis for national courts applying Union law would have been desirable, not only because it would facilitate the role of these courts in the application of EU law, but also because it would entrust them with a constitutional responsibility and trigger further infrastructural developments in the sphere of technical support (documentation centres, databases, etc.). The latter would result in a secondary coordination mechanism alongside the present preliminary procedure and would facilitate the network between the courts and the national authorities as well.

Vilenas Vadapalas (Judge at the CFI) approached the discussion from the new Member States' perspective, describing the role of the Constitutional Courts of the new Members States in the EU's judicial system. In this system, which is bipolar and where the link between the EU level and the national level is the preliminary preference, the national Constitutional Courts can play a crucial role, having a distinct status in the concept of the state and the rule of law, democracy and the protection of human rights. The future role of these Constitutional Courts is difficult to predict; they may be reluctant to approach the ECJ, but they can also be a crucial link between the ECJ and the national courts. With regard to the Constitutional Treaty itself, Vadapalas drew attention to the introduction of the review of validity for the European decisions of the Council providing for restrictive measures against natural and legal persons, made in the Common Foreign and Security Policy, in particular related to the legality of sanctions. He believed that the ECJ is expected to develop its own doctrine of legal disputes in the future CFSP.

   Piet van Nuffel (Legal Secretary at the ECJ) highlighted some political and
practical aspects of the work and role the European Court of Justice. As for the
political aspects, he sees the ECJ's role in good governance as being essential,
mostly because it provides an example. Therefore, the political scrutiny of the
work of the ECJ should start as early as the recruitment of judges. He emphasized that it is the legal community's interest to recognise the potential of the
candidates. Panels evaluate the candidates, and as the law is never neutral, the
interviewing of candidates should cover general legal views. In this way quality
could be improved. With regard to the speed of the ECJ's work, he suggested
that, like in the CFI, the moment of deliberation should be more concentrated,
meaning that the deliberation of the judges takes place immediately after the
hearing, and that resources should be used effectively. The equilibrium between
these two factors – quality and speed – can be ensured by the above-mentioned
scrutiny of the candidate judges, in particular because with the growing number
of deliberations in chambers, not all judges hear all the cases, and even though
this system certainly contributes to speeding up the procedure, it also increases
the importance of the early scrutiny of future judges ensuring sufficient quality.
Van Nuffel believed that linguistic reforms, such as making the ECJ's working
language English, can be fortunate, enlarging the recruitment of judges and staff;
and legal translation is best and most economically exercised if the costs are concentrated at one level, preferably that of the ECJ.
   Onno Brouwer (Chairman of CCBE's Permanent Delegation to the ECJ) underlined that numerous concerns provided sufficient reason for CCBE representatives to take part in the drafting of the EU Constitution. These concerns were in
particular: the limited access of individuals to justice; the exclusion of certain areas from legality review; and the restricted scope of challengeable acts. These
are the concerns which entrust the CCBE with a particular responsibility to advocate the enhancement of access to justice in all circumstances, and, in this
way, to lend a listening ear to the national bar associations and the courts and to
represent their needs in the Convention. Like other speakers, Brouwer welcomed
some significant progresses brought about by the EU Constitution, but called for
further improvements, such as better cooperation between national and EU
courts. Brouwer supported Geelhoed's proposal for a 5 to 10 year time limit for
bringing about the suggested judicial model in the 'communitarised areas'.


7.    QUESTIONS AND ANSWERS

Tom Eijsbouts (University of Amsterdam) asked Arjen Meij to elaborate on his
suggestion to create a legal basis in the EU Constitution that would codify the
national courts' role as *juges communautaires*. Meij emphasized that the foundations of the national courts in the EU Constitution are vague and therefore debatable. Nevertheless, national courts have the competence and the obligation to
apply Community law, and this is deduced from the case law and the treaties.
Entrusting the national courts with a responsibility or a mandate (Meij empha-

sized that the term used is crucial) would necessitate an increase in the infra-structure of knowledge, facilitated by systems, similar to the one presently func-tioning in the Netherlands, providing for cooperation between judges and the speeding up of the preliminary ruling procedure and the enlargement of capacity, thus supporting the national courts in the application of EU law.

Jenia Peteva (University of Sofia) drew attention to the possibility of and the necessity for NGOs to have legal standing and enjoy judicial protection. She suggested that the specific attitude of the Commission towards private organiza-tions specializing in human rights and humanitarian issues could gradually pro-vide NGOs with legal standing, putting an end to the situation in the case law which distinguishes between NGOs and private organisations specializing in hu-man rights. Meij responded to this remark by referring to the Greenpeace cases, the Aarhus Convention and the current proposal for a regulation to implement it, which would recognize NGOs as qualified entities. This regulation would pro-vide for access to the courts for these qualified entities, and he underlined that such a system created by this proposal would be similar to transparency proceed-ings, the difference being that the question put before the authority may not nec-essarily be challengeable. Meij suggested that one should allow the legislator to deal with such an issue, as it is up to the legislator to amend existing rules and related issues.

Ad Geelhoed reacted to issues raised by Piet van Nuffel, in particular the pre-sentation of opinions of the Advocates General before the hearing in order to speed up the procedure. Geelhoed was not in favour of delivering opinions be-fore hearings, as it would undermine the hearing itself. He emphasized the im-portance of hearings, saying that in 25% of cases he has to change his opinion considerably on the basis of the hearings. Geelhoed suggested a possible solution to the linguistic problems, which would benefit the procedure, and that would be that all the Advocates General should prepare their opinions in English or French, the two languages in which all the members of the Court are proficient, and to present these opinions within a week after the hearing. Related to this is-sue, Brouwer expressed the CCBE's opinion, which considers that the parties should be able to react to the opinion of the Advocate General, thereby not nec-essarily undermining the hearing. Of equal importance are the intervention of Member States and the institutions and the use of *amicus curiae* briefs. Van Nuffel added to his original standpoint the acknowledgement that changing the moment when the opinion is delivered would change the nature of the opinions, but he did not really perceive the consequences mentioned by Geelhoed as being insurmountable obstacles. He considered that, despite the different way of pro-ceeding, the objective should be to support the judges in finding the right solu-tion for the case in question. Concerning the linguistic problems mentioned by Brouwer and the costs of translation, he emphasized the distinction between translation and publication. It is certainly not necessary to publish judgements in every language. According to him, some of the (competition) judgements are not worth translating into in every official language because of their extended length. It should be enough for the legal community to make these judgements available in English and French.

# THE IMPACT OF THE EU CONSTITUTION ON SELECTED MEMBER STATES AND NEIGHBOURING COUNTRIES (REPORT OF THE DISCUSSION)

**Wybe Th. Douma**[*]

Under the chairmanship of Jan Jans (University of Amsterdam) the panel discussed the results of the separate sessions. Jenö Czuczai (European Law Academy, Budapest) summed up and commented upon the second session on transparency and legal instruments in the EU constitutional treaty. He recalled that he started that session by quoting Lenaerts, who considers the new provisions on legal instruments to be an important step forward. However, during the session several significant shortcomings to this part of the EU Constitution were noted. Czuczai discussed some of these, but he still regards the new rules as a positive development, notably because they provide a much more coherent set of legal instruments and because they achieve a much better framed separation of powers and because democracy is strengthened.

Deirdre Curtin then summed up and commented upon session I. This opening session encompassed, *inter alia*, the political aspects of the EU Constitution. In his contribution, the Minister for the Interior described the present situation and the democratic and participatory improvements that will occur once the EU Constitution takes effect, while drawing parallels with developments in the Netherlands and personal internet 'chat' sessions with citizens. Curtin doubted whether the latter could form an example for the EU.[1] She agreed with the speaker that it is not so much the euro-opposition of some but rather the euro-apathy of the many that forms the greatest challenge. Turning to the critical speech by Weiler, Curtin noted that the colloquium would have received far less sponsorship if his title suggestion would have been followed: 'The European Constitution: Victim of its own Hype'. Weiler said he had a sober view of the convention. Curtin would rather label it a harsh view, because contrary to Weiler's assertions a genuine effort seems to have been made to have civil society involved in the process leading up to the Convention (in hearings and in many other ways). Bruno de Witte analyzed what would happen if one or more countries would not ratify.

---

[*] Head of the Section EU Law and Projects Coordinator at the T.M.C. Asser Institute, The Hague.
[1] Several EU Commissioners have in fact already held similar chat sessions on various topics.

*D. Curtin, A.E. Kellermann and S. Blockmans, eds., The EU Constitution: The Best Way Forward?*
© 2005, T.M.C. Asser Instituut, The Hague.

Both he and Weiler seemed to agree that it would not necessarily be a disaster if, for instance, two smaller countries or a group of countries would not ratify. Possibly one would need to live for a while longer with the Treaty of Nice, while already implementing some elements of the EU Constitution. There was some interesting debate on withdrawal. Can a Member State do this now, when withdrawal is not mentioned in the Treaty? According to De Witte, the international framework of the law of treaties would allow for a state to do so. He did raise the question what would happen if several (or even almost all) states would withdraw (leaving behind an empty shell). No final conclusions can as yet be drawn in this respect. Shaw sketched the different, polarized situation in the UK, where euro-sceptics spread a great deal of false information and the need to become involved in the debate is considerable. Anne Peters (Basel) talked about a comparative study of the role of national referenda. Her conclusion was that in this constitutional context the legitimacy benefits are negligible and stressed that the constitution is a result of a process, although from the floor there was some opposition to that view.

Francis Jacob then talked about session IIIB on the efficiency and quality of legislation. He explained that the session had in fact focussed on the developing role of the political institutions and that it had had valuable contributions from the speakers, the panel and from the floor. He highlighted the topic raised in the panel and subsequent discussion of the difficulties in transposing the notion of separation of powers from the national level to that of the EU. Also, Jacob noted that Timmermans was the only speaker examining the issue of the quality of legislation. Referring to the previous Asser Institute colloquium 'The Quality of European and National Legislation and the Internal market'[2] – also inspired by Alfred Kellermann and held seven years ago – he examined whether progress had been achieved since then and which improvements the EU Constitution would bring about in this respect. As an overall conclusion from this session, Jacob stressed that as far as the institutions are concerned, there was a rather positive assessment of the EU Constitution. Although some defects were identified, it was recognised that the EU Constitution would result in greater clarity, greater efficiency and more democratic accountability. Jacob described it as perhaps unlikely that other drafts might emerge which would lead to substantial improvements in those respects. As regards this aspect of the subject, the answer to the question 'The EU Constitution: the best way forward?' seems to be: 'yes'.

Returning to Deirdre Curtin, the well-attended Session IIIA on the Democratic life of the European Union was referred to. It was first of all noted that, in many respects, the topics covered were all well on their way and that the EU Constitution was not terribly crucial. The first speaker in this session was Heidi Hautala and she dealt with the role of national parliaments in the EU. She was

---

[2] That colloquium lead to the publication of the book by A.E. Kellermann, et al., ed., *Improving the Quality of Legislation in Europe* (Kluwer Law International, The Hague 1998).

not convinced of the utility of the new subsidiarity mechanism that gives national parliaments a role in this respect.

The Spanish speaker Lorenzo Cotino (University of Valencia) presented an excellent paper on legal and practical aspects of public access to EU information, noting, for instance, that the amount of information offered online is increasing (for instance the Council is publishing its register on the Internet) and had contributed to a forty-fold increase in the access to information in 2002 compared to the previous years. Curtin regretted that the role of exceptions to public access provisions in practice was not touched upon that much, as this might be one of the key issues in the coming years. After the speech by the European Ombudsman, Nikiforos Diamandouros, a discussion followed on the proliferation of bodies dealing with human rights issues with the risk of fragmentation. Finally in this session, Tom Eijsbouts emphatically defended the European Parliament as the only future of a democratic EU, notably against some MEPs with different views.

The last summing up of and commenting upon a session was done by Sascha Prechal, who started off by noting that the overall assessment of the EU Constitution was not negative, perhaps even positive. Indeed important steps forward had been taken, like the incorporation of the Charter for fundamental rights – making it binding - and the broadening of access to justice for individuals. Another important achievement is the communitarisation of the Third Pillar. There is also a list of concerns, partly because the Constitution did not address some of the persistent problems at all or not adequately, and partly because it created new problems in itself. Two main categories of concern remain, according to Prechal. The first is the judicial architecture of the EU. Within five to ten years the Nice arrangements will probably explode. The EU Constitution did not take up these issues. Advocate General Ad Geelhoed sketched two main lines of development: the quantitative growth of and the qualitative change in the demand for judicial protection. Intermediate solutions were discussed, *inter alia*, where working methods of the ECJ were concerned. All speakers regretted that the EU Constitution had not included the application of European law by national courts. Further, the need for improvements in the field of the review of legislative measures was discussed. Furthermore, it was discussed whether the current system of judicial protection is compatible with Article 6 of the Convention for the Protection of Human Rights. The second main category of concern as regards the Constitution lies in this field. It is expected that the Charter, once it will become a binding instrument, will generate many new cases. Many might be dismissed, as there is uncertainty about the nature of the rights under the Charter, about the scope of its provisions etc. The question is thus whether the Charter is not creating a false picture of the ECJ, thereby becoming another human rights court in Europe? Is the Court sufficiently equipped for such a task? A second problematic area discussed notably by Rick Lawson was the relationship between the Luxembourg Court and the Strasbourg Court. This problem already exists nowadays and will only be reinforced once the EU Constitution enters into force. Indeed a risk of divergent interpretations of similar or the same provisions exists and, until now, no adequate device has been developed to minimise this risk. We will probably end up with a very complex system of human rights protection, of three or perhaps even four levels if we count the traditional international treaties in which only a few specialists will be able to find their way. The participants at the session, including Sascha Prechal, were in favour of accession to the European Human Rights Convention by the EU, while also agreeing on the need to carefully consider how to make the system workable and understandable for the European citizen.

The final Round-table discussion was chaired by Jan Jans and it dealt with the question of the best way forward for the EU. Dusko Lopandic from the pre-accession country Serbia and Montenegro quoted Francois Mitterand who compared the development of the European Union to constructing medieval cathedrals: each generation of politicians and of lawyers would add new chapels or isles. The speaker thought that the general shape of the cathedral was already clear, and the EU Constitution would form an important step towards completing the construction. It would thus be a pity if it would not be ratified by all the Member States, and it seems that most assembled at the Colloquium agree on this. He also stressed that there should not be a stop to deepening or enlarging. The ten new Member States should reassure the old ones that the enlargement was a success, and reassure their population that it was worth becoming a Member of the EU. Only if this enlargement is as successful as the earlier ones, can the development of the EU and further enlargement and deepening continue. Implementation and the understanding of EU law in the new Member States will be of crucial importance. As for those states that could become members in the future, the Tessaloniki Council stressed the possibility for all countries of the Western Balkans to join the EU. Further, he sketched the awkward situation of two legal systems that will appear if the Constitution enters into force: the old rules (notably regulations and directives) and the new ones.

Adam Lazowski (Asser Institute, The Hague) welcomed the fact that the last speaker had stressed the problems that can occur in practice with the old and new *acquis*. The new *acquis* is intellectually extremely interesting and a goldmine for academics. It took quite some effort to explain to Polish judges what directives and regulations are and how to apply them. If they are suddenly faced with a new system which is not very clear in its nature, notably when it comes to implementing regulations and delegated regulations, the effectiveness of Community law might very well suffer, notably in the new Member States. A Working Group from the Convention dealing with sources of law put it as follows: 'nothing is more complicated than simplification.' Lopandic was also struck by the fact that the Convention often stated that its aim was simplification, but in practice the system might be becoming more complicated. He did stress that a structure with so many differences in geographical, political and legal terms might not be able to avoid an elaborated system of rules. Jan Jans added that a decade ago he spoke in Poland about regulations and directives in English while being translated simultaneously into Polish. After the lecture a participant asked why the Community had laws directly applicable which at the same time needs to be transposed into national law – revealing that the translator had used one and the same word for both directives and regulations.

Jaap de Zwaan (Erasmus University Rotterdam) discussed the outcome of the sessions held under the Matra conference in which the new Member States talked about their experiences, notably where it concerned the adaptation of their constitutions – something all the new Member States had done. De Zwaan stressed that also in the old Member States the judiciary needs to participate regularly in courses on new developments in EU law. He was glad that the new Member States were starting to ask for preliminary rulings, notably in the Red Star case touched upon earlier during the conference. As to the role of national parliaments, De Zwaan noted that each of the new Member States has established certain procedures as to how to control what their representatives to the Council are doing. In the majority of cases, one parliamentary committee for European Affairs has been established.

The most important achievement in his view is the restructuring of the structure of the EU, merging the two remaining European organisations into one, the EU having a fully fledged legal personality with, as a result, more uniform and more democratic decision-making procedures and also the idea of a hierarchy of norms and a uniform set of legal instruments - which will need to prove itself in practice. The exception is the Common Security and Defence policy, which remains not a separate pillar, but a small separate room in the building. Also positive is the strengthening of European citizenship, a notion now linked to good governance, transparency, access to documents, etc. If there is a defect to be rectified on a future occasion, then it is the restoration of a distinction between primary and secondary constitutional texts, an issue where the creation of a short constitutional text with protocols was under discussion. Such a short text, composing the main elements of Part I complemented by certain aspects of the Charter on Fundamental Rights and Protocols which could be changed more easily, might still be a better option for the future. As it stands today, the EU Constitution is perhaps not the best way forward, but it is certainly a good way forward.

Jenö Czuczai asked whether it is significant that the official title of the EU Constitution is 'Treaty establishing a Constitution for Europe' and not 'for the European Union'. This is a politically sensitive issue and De Zwaan explained that he would be in favour of interpreting Europe in a very wide manner, thus allowing, in the mid-term or long-term future, those countries respecting minimum requirements (on fundamental rights, the rule of law, good governance, etc.) to share in what we have regarded as benefits, like stability, security and welfare aspects of cooperation. When the EU enlarges to over thirty countries, which in the view of De Zwaan is conceivable, it will be a responsibility for all the participating European countries to reflect on further stages of the European integration process, notably where it concerns the question of what to do with the 'separate room' of the Common Foreign and Security Policy. Many are in favour of complementing what has been accomplished in the economic area with other dimensions, notably where it concerns foreign policy and defence issues.

This will keep the exercise of constructing the European Union integration efforts dynamic.

Ion Galea (Ministry of Foreign Affairs, Romania) asked which incompatibilities exist between the constitutions of states joining the EU and European law, adding that his country has already adapted its constitution with a view to European integration, and about the role of national parliaments under the EU Constitution. De Zwaan pointed out that the particular issue of Romania's compatibility was discussed at one of the earlier sessions, and that in several of the founding Member States (including the Netherlands) there is no reference to the EU in the constitutions. However, there is a reference to sharing responsibilities with international organisations. This is a revolutionary concept for the majority of the new Member States which had only recently gained full independence, and one which is difficult to overcome. This was discussed and the outcome was that there was an insistence that either a reference to the EU (having certain competences or responsibilities) was to be made in the national constitution, or it should contain a provision allowing for the transfer to an international layer with the result that one shares the responsibilities. Jan Jans added that there is still a debate about the Dutch constitution as to whether it is fully in line with European law. As for national parliaments, this is in the first place an internal matter. De Zwaan saw a vital role for them where it concerns the process of bringing the EU citizen closer to the EU, but also in helping the Member States to implement and comply with their obligations under European Law. He agreed with Tom Eijsbouts that it should be left to the EP alone to assist in adopting new European legislation.

# LIST OF ARTICLES

# CHAPTER II
# Economic and Monetary Policy

# CHAPTER III
# Policies in Other Areas

# CHAPTER IV
# Area of Freedom, Security and Justice

## CHAPTER V
## Areas Where the Union May Take Coordinating, Complementary or Supporting Action

## TITLE IV: ASSOCIATION OF THE OVERSEAS COUNTRIES AND TERRITORIES

## TITLE V: THE UNION'S EXTERNAL ACTION

## CHAPTER I
## Provisions Having General Application

## CHAPTER II
## Common Foreign and Security Policy

# INDEX

# LIST OF PARTICIPANTS

Albi, A., Kent Law School, Estonia.

Almer, J., Swedish Institute for European Policy Studies, Sweden.

Amerongen, I. van, T.M.C. Asser Institute, The Netherlands.

Amtenbrink, F., University of Groningen, The Netherlands.

Andras, A., Romania Ministry of Foreign Affairs, Romania.

Andrassy, I., Croation Mission to the EU, Belgium.

Apreutesei, R., Ministry of European Integration, Romania.

Arnold, C., Vrije Universiteit Amsterdam, The Netherlands.

Astapenka, U.A., Belarussian State University, Belarus.

Baciu, L., Leiden University, The Netherlands.

Bakker, P., T.M.C. Asser Institute, The Netherlands.

Balode, E., Ministry of Justice, Latvia.

Barendrecht, M.D., T.M.C. Asser Institute, The Netherlands.

Barnhoorn, L., T.M.C. Asser Institute, The Netherlands.

Baslar, K., Constitutional Court, Turkey.

Bast, J., Max Planck Institute, Germany.

Bastiaans, M.H., T.M.C. Asser Press, The Netherlands.

Berger, M., University of Groningen, The Netherlands.

Bergstrom, C.F., Swedish Institute for European Policy Studies, Sweden.

Besselink, L.F.M., University of Utrecht, The Netherlands.

Betsi, D., Haagse Hogeschool, The Netherlands.

Beukers, T., University of Amsterdam, The Netherlands.

Biernat, S., Jagiellonian University of Cracow, Poland.

Biryukova, E., Russian Federation.

Blockmans, S., T.M.C. Asser Institute, The Netherlands.

Bogdany, A. von, Max-Planck Institute, Germany.

Boot, E., Hogeschool InHolland, The Netherlands.

Borms, K., T.M.C. Asser Institute, The Netherlands.

Bos-Buurman, M., T.M.C. Asser Institute, The Netherlands.

Bos, P.V.F., Barents en Krans, The Netherlands.

Boskovic, V., Government Office for EU Affairs, Slovenia.

Bossche, A.M. van den, Radboud University Nijmegen, The Netherlands.

Boudewijn, R., Clingendael Institute, The Netherlands.

Brink, A. van den, Erasmus University Rotterdam, The Netherlands.

Broeksteeg, J.W.L., University of Maastricht, The Netherlands.

Brommet, J., DAAD, The Netherlands.

Brouwer, O.W., Freshfields Bruckhaus Deringer, The Netherlands.

Burri, S., University of Utrecht, The Netherlands.

Buttigieg, E., University of Malta, Malta.

Capeta, T., University of Zagreb, Croatia.

Choi, T., Leiden University, The Netherlands.

Claes, M., University of Maastricht, The Netherlands.

Cleiren, C.P.M., Leiden University, The Netherlands.

Cojocaru, A., Constitutional Court of Justice, Romania.

Colocolov, N., Russian Federation.

Conlan, P., University of Limerick, Ireland.

Cotino Hueso, L., University of Valencia, Spain.

Coxova, M., Parliamentary Institute, Czech Republic.

Cretu, G., T.M.C. Asser Institute, The Netherlands.

Curtin, D., Utrecht School of Governance, The Netherlands.

Czuczai, J., European Law Academy, Budapest, Hungary.

Damen, L.J.A., University of Groningen, The Netherlands.

Danov, M., T.M.C. Asser Institute, The Netherlands.

Davies, G., University of Groningen, The Netherlands.

Deetman, W.J., The Netherlands.

Diamendouros, P.N., The European Ombudsman, France.

Donner, J.P.H., Ministry of Justice, The Netherlands.

Douma, W., T.M.C. Asser Institute, The Netherlands.

Driessche, I. van den, University of Maastricht, The Netherlands.

Duckwitz, E., Embassy of Germany, The Netherlands.

Duculescu, V., Bucharest University, Romania.

Dun, I. van, T.M.C. Asser Institute, The Netherlands.

Eeckhout, P., King's College London, United Kingdom.

Eijsbouts, W.T., European Constitutional Law Review, The Netherlands.

Ektermane, F., State Chancellery of Republic of Latvia, Latvia.

Eliantonio, M., University of Maastricht, The Netherlands.

Emiliou, N., Permanent Representative Cyprus, Cyprus.

Emmerik, M.L. van, Ministry of Foreign Affairs, The Netherlands.

Entin, M., MGIMO University Institute of European Law, Russian Federation.

Ertuna, T., Erasmus University Rotterdam, The Netherlands.

Everling, U., University of Bonn, Germany.

Everson, M., University of London, United Kingdom.

Feenstra, K., T.M.C. Asser Institute, The Netherlands.

Felgenhauer, H., Europol, The Netherlands.

Ferguson Sidorenko, O., Erasmus University Rotterdam, The Netherlands.

Filoniuk - Krajewska, I., Poland.

Fitori, E., T.M.C. Asser Institute, The Netherlands.

Galea, I., Ministry of Foreign Affairs, Romania.

Galea Raluca, E., Ministry of Justice, Romania.

Gane, E., Ministry of European Integration, Romania.

Geel, L.P.M. van, Ministry of Foreign Affairs, The Netherlands.

Geelhoed, L.A., Court of Justice of the European Union, Luxembourg.

Gerganova, M., Information Centre of the EU, Bulgaria.

Gerven, W. van, University of Leuven, Belgium.

Glikman, O., Russian Federation.

Gonzales, G., T.M.C. Asser Institute, The Netherlands.

Gormley, L.W., University of Groningen, The Netherlands.

Goudappel, F., Erasmus University Rotterdam, The Netherlands.

Graaf, Th.C. de, Ministry of Domestic Affairs, The Netherlands.

Graaf, L.L.M.V. de, Ministry of Foreign Affairs, The Netherlands.

Grinsven, P. van, Clingendael Institute, The Netherlands.

Gul, I.I., T.M.C. Asser Institute, The Netherlands.

Hagard, B.P., European Ombudsman, France.

Hallo, R., Stichting Natuur en Milieu, The Netherlands.

Hamernik, P., Westbohemian University, Pilsen, Czech Republic.

Harteveld, D., University of Tilburg, The Netherlands.

Hautala, H., Parliament of Finland, Finland.

Heida, H.P., Ministry of Domestic Affairs, The Netherlands.

Helander, P., Government Secretariat for EU Affairs, Finland.

Heliskoski, J., Ministry of Justice, Finland.

Hoek, N. van der, T.M.C. Asser Institute, The Netherlands.

Holwerda, J.M., University of Groningen, The Netherlands.

Hoogstraten, S. van, Carnegie Foundation, The Netherlands.

Houdijk, J., Radboud University Nijmegen, The Netherlands.

Houppermans, V.A., Freshfields Bruckhaus Deringer, The Netherlands.

Ignatov, Y., Russian Federation.

Ionea, P.M., Constitutional Court of Romania, Romania.

Ishakoglu, E., Ministry of Justice, Turkey.

Issaeva, M., Russian Federation.

Jacobs, F., Court of Justice of the European Union, Luxembourg.

Jager, J.G. de, The Netherlands.

James, C.D., The Netherlands.

Jans, J.H.,University of Amsterdam, The Netherlands.

Janssen, H.L., Ministry of Domestic Affairs, The Netherlands.

Jarukaitis, I., Ministry of Foreign Affairs, Lithuania.

Jong, M. de, Ministry of Foreign Affairs, The Netherlands.

Joris, T., Université Libre de Bruxelles, Belgium.

Julie, H., European Parliament, Belgium.

Kaddous, C., University of Geneva, Switzerland.

Kalinichenko, P., Russian Federation.

Kavena, M., Parliamentary Institute, Czech Republic.

Keessen, A.M., University of Utrecht, The Netherlands.

Kellermann, A.E., T.M.C. Asser Institute, The Netherlands.

Kennedy, C., Oxford University Press, United Kingdom.

Kiiver, P., University of Maastricht, The Netherlands.

Kisjuhasz, Z., Natav Hungarian Telecommunications LTD, Hungary.

Kiss, K., Hungary.

Kok, S., Vluchtelingenwerk Nederland, The Netherlands.

Komarov, P., Russian Federation.

Koopmans, T., The Netherlands.

Koppen, J.K., NWO/MAGW, The Netherlands.

Korogod, S., Russian Federation.

Korzhova, S., Russian Federation.

Kostrzewa, K., Office of the Committee, Poland.

Krieger, T., T.M.C. Asser Institute, The Netherlands.

Krzysztof, W., University of Wroclaw, Poland.

Kuiper, M.J., College van Beroep voor het Bedrijfsleven, The Netherlands.

Kunova, V., Comenius University, Slovak Republic.

Labine, D., T.M.C. Asser Institute, The Netherlands.

Launay, E., Ministry of Foreign Affairs, France.

Lawson, R., Leiden University, The Netherlands.

Lazowski, A., T.M.C. Asser Institute, The Netherlands.

Lebedik, Y., Academy of Law and Management, Russian Federation.

Lemckert, H., Jongbloed Juridische Boekhandel, The Netherlands.

Licheva, D., Italy.

Limbach, J., Goethe Institute, Germany.

Linarez, A., The Netherlands.

Linde, K. van der, Kluwer Law International, The Netherlands.

Lindgren, G., Ministry of Industry, Sweden.

Lippmann, Th.W.M., Stichting Levi Lassen, The Netherlands.

Loeffen, E., Ministry of Foreign Affairs, The Netherlands.

Lopandic, D., Ministry of International Economic Relations of Serbia, Serbia and Montenegro.

Lotarski, J., University of Sheffield, United Kingdom.

Lueffe, C., Goethe Institute Amsterdam, The Netherlands.

Maduro, M., Court of Justice of the European Union, Luxembourg.

Maggioni, L., Court of Justice of the European Union, Luxembourg.

Magnette, P.,Université Libre de Bruxelles, Belgium.

Manukyan, V., T.M.C. Asser Institute, The Netherlands.

Martonyi, J., Martonyi es Kajtar Baker & McKenzie, Hungary.

Meerten, H. van, Erasmus University Rotterdam, The Netherlands.

Meij, A.W.H., Court of First Instance, Luxembourg.

Meulman, J., Radboud University Nijmegen, The Netherlands.

Monar, J., University of Sussex, United Kingdom.

Moons, B., Chauffeur Geelhoed, The Netherlands.

Morzy, K., Poland.

Mueller-Graf, P.C., University of Heidelberg, Germany.

Nelissen, F.N., T.M.C. Asser Institute, The Netherlands.

Nicolai, A., Ministry of Foreign Affairs, The Netherlands.

Nieminen, L., Academy of Finland, Finland.

Nollen, S., Clingendael Institute, The Netherlands.

Noort, M., Court of Justice of the European Union, Luxembourg.

Nuffel, P. van, Court of Justice of the European Union, Luxembourg.

Ooik, R.H. van, University of Utrecht, The Netherlands.

Ott, A.,University of Maastricht, The Netherlands.

Ouwerkerk, J.G., T.M.C. Asser Institute, The Netherlands.

Paasilehto, S., Institute of International Economic Law, Finland.

Pacheco, J., European Parliament, Belgium.

Papazoglu, M., T.M.C. Asser Institute, The Netherlands.

Passos, R., Legal Service - European Parliament, Luxembourg.

Peers, S., University of Essex, United Kingdom.

Peters, A., University of Basel, Switzerland.

Peters, J.A., The Netherlands.

Peteva, J., University of Sofia, Bulgaria.

Petite, M., European Commission, Belgium.

Piekaar, M., T.M.C. Asser Institute, The Netherlands.

Pitrova, L., Parliamentary Institute, Czech Republic.

Pogacnik, H.P., Slovenia Telecom., Broadcasting and Post Agency, Slovenia.

Pogacnik, M. SECLI, Slovenia.

Poppens, H., Ministry of Economic Affairs, The Netherlands.

Pozhidaeva, M., Russian Federation.

Prechal, S., University of Utrecht, The Netherlands.

Preda, C., Ministry of European Integration, Romania.

Rakic, M., Law Office Stanivkovic & Partners, Serbia and Montenegro.

Raluca Amza, V., Ministry of European Integration, Romania.

Ramos Sole, M., Haagse Hogeschool, The Netherlands.

Ratsiborinskaya, D., Russian Federation.

Ribbelink, O.R., T.M.C. Asser Institute, The Netherlands.

Rodin, S., University of Zagreb, Croatia.

Roettinger, M., European Commission, Belgium.

Romein, S., Erasmus University Rotterdam, The Netherlands.

Sakslin, M., Social Insurance Institution, Finland.

Samardzic, S., Institute for European Studies, Yugoslavia.

Sap, J.W., Vrije Universiteit Amsterdam, The Netherlands.

Schagen, J.A. van, Ministry of Domestic Affairs, The Netherlands.

Schilder, A.E., Ministry of Domestic Affairs, The Netherlands.

Schrauwen, A., University of Amsterdam, The Netherlands.

Senden, L., University of Tilburg, The Netherlands.

Sevenster, H.G., Ministry of Foreign Affairs, The Netherlands.

Shaw, J., University of Manchester, United Kingdom.

Shults, O., Russian Federation.

Siemaszko, M., National Bank of Poland, Poland.

Smits, R., University of Amsterdam, The Netherlands.

Sondore, L., Ministry of Finance, Latvia.

Staicu, V.V., Haagse Hogeschool, The Netherlands.

Starman, M., Ministry of Justice of the Republic of Slovenia, Slovenia.

Steen, I. van der, Ministry of Foreign Affairs, The Netherlands.

Surzhin, A., Russian Federation.

Syllova, J., Parliamentary Institute, Czech Republic.

Takacs, T., T.M.C. Asser Institute, The Netherlands.

Tanchev, E., Constitutional Court, Bulgaria.

Tanja, G., Clifford Chance, The Netherlands.

Tans, O., University of Amsterdam, The Netherlands.

Tarman, Z.D., Turkey.

Tillaart, K. v.d., University of Tilburg, The Netherlands.

Timmermans, C.W.A., Court of Justice of the European Union, Luxembourg.

Todoric, V., Serbian European Integration Office, Serbia and Montenegro.

Tongeren, Ph. Van, T.M.C. Asser Press, The Netherlands.

Tromm, J.J.M., The Netherlands.

Trzaskowski, R., Natolin European Center, Poland.

Uher, D., Office of the Government of the Czech Republic, Czech Republic.

Usacka, A., International Criminal Court, Latvia.

Vadapalas, V., Court of Justice of the European Union, Luxembourg.

Vall, M. van de, University of Tilburg, The Netherlands.

Vehar, P., National Assembly, Slovenia.

Veld, J. van de, Bruylant S.A., Belgium.

Verbiest, R., Nederland Doen Evenementen BV, The Netherlands.

Verburg, J.J.L., Court of Appeal, The Netherlands.

Verheecke, O., European Ombudsman, France.

Verhey, L., University of Maastricht, The Netherlands.

Verhoogt, J.C., University of Utrecht, The Netherlands.

Versteegen, N., T.M.C. Asser Institute, The Netherlands.

Versteegh, C.P., NRC Handelsblad, The Netherlands.

Verwey, D.R., Erasmus University Rotterdam, The Netherlands.

Vig, Z., Central European University, Hungary.

Vloten, M.V. van, Ministry of Health, Welfare and Sports, The Netherlands.

Vostrikov, I., Russian Federation.

Vries, L. de, T.M.C. Asser Institute, The Netherlands.

Waelbroeck, D., Ashurst, Belgium.

Waele, H. de, Radboud University Nijmegen, The Netherlands.

Wageningen, A.C. van, University of Amsterdam, The Netherlands.

Wal, G. van der, Houthoff Buruma, Belgium.

Weiler, J.H.H., New York School, United States of America.

Wentkowska, A., High School of Management & Marketing, Poland.

Werts, J., Media Thema Europa, Belgium.

Wessel, R.A., University of Twente, The Netherlands.

Wilde, E. de, Ministry of Foreign Affairs, The Netherlands.

Wissels, C.M., Ministry of Foreign Affairs, The Netherlands.

Witte, B. de, European University Institute, Italy.

Wouters, J., University of Leuven, Belgium.

Xuereb, P.X., University of Malta, Malta.

Zachariadou, E., The Law Office of the Republic Cyprus, Cyprus.

Zanet, E., Information Community Center, Romania.

Zemanek, J., Charles University, Czech Republic.

Zhivotinskaya, O., Russian Federation.

Zwaan, J. de, Erasmus University Rotterdam, The Netherlands.

**THE FIRST SESSION OF THE ASSER COLLOQUIUM ON EUROPEAN LAW WAS HELD IN 1972. THE FOLLOWING IS A LIST OF SESSIONS HELD SINCE 1972:**

| | |
|---|---|
| 23 March 1972 | Uitvoering Gemeenschapsrecht in de Nederlandse rechtsorde |
| 7 July 1972 | Colloquium of Law Teachers |
| 7 June 1973 | Het onderwijs in het Recht van de Europese Gemeenschappen aan de Nederlandse Universiteiten en Hogescholen |
| 6 September 1974 | De verhouding tussen het onderwijs in het Europees Recht en het onderwijs in andere juridische vakken |
| 11 September 1975 | Rechten van de mens |
| 9 September 1976 | Plaats en taak van een Europees Parlement bij een verdere beleids- integratie op sociaal-economisch gebied in Europa |
| 9 September 1977 | Externe betrekkingen van de Europese Gemeenschappen |
| 7 September 1978 | De Europese politieke samenwerking |
| 6 September 1979 | EEC-Comecon Relations |
| 5 September 1980 | Uitvoering van het Gemeenschapsrecht in Nederland |
| 4 September 1981 | Europeesrechtelijke aspecten van consumentenbescherming |
| 3 September 1982 | De rol van de Europese Gemeenschappen in een Nieuwe Internatio- nale Economische Orde |
| 9 September 1983 | EEG-Handelspolitiek en beschermende maatregelen tegen de invo- er uit derde landen |
| 7 September 1984 | Gedifferentieerde integratie in de Europese Gemeenschappen |
| 5/6 September 1985 | Experiences and problems in applying the preliminary procedure of Article 177 EEC |
| 5 September 1986 | Legal Aspects of technological Development and Cooperation in Europe |
| 4 September 1987 | Europees milieurecht: praktische problemen bij de totstandkoming en uitvoering |
| 9 September 1988 | Fraude in de Europese Gemeenschappen |
| 8 September 1989 | De economische en sociale samenhang in de EG: De Europese structuurfondsen |
| 7 September 1990 | Een Economische en Monetaire Unie (EMU) in Europa: Juridische en constitutionele consequenties |
| 12/13 September 1991 | Free Movement of Persons in Europe: Legal Problems and Experi- ences |
| 4 September 1992 | Onderwijs Europees Recht in Nederland |
| 3 November 1992 | Bijzondere zitting: De BV Nederland op de interne markt |
| 10 September 1993 | Externe bevoegdheden van de Europese Unie |
| 9 September 1994 | Diversiteit van de besluitvorming van de Europese Unie |
| 14-16 September 1995 | Reforming the Treaty on European Union: The Legal Debate |
| 13 September 1996 | Recente ontwikkelingen op het gebied van de rechtsbescherming in de Europese Gemeenschap |
| 5 September 1997 | Ontwikkelingen met betrekking tot Art. 90 EG, mede in verband met de privatisering van Nederlandse publieke ondernemingen |
| 4 September 1998 | Het begrip flexibiliteit in het Verdrag van Amsterdam |
| 10 September 1999 | Recente ontwikkelingen op het gebied van de toepassing van het Europees Kartelrecht |
| 20-23 September 2000 | The constitutional Impact of Enlargement at EU and National Level |
| 7 September 2001 | Europees recht en de decentrale overheid in Nederland en België |
| 6 September 2002 | 'Veiligheid' en het recht van de Europese Unie |
| 12 September 2003 | Europees Burgerschap en de rechtsgevolgen voor de burgers in de EU |
| 13-16 October 2004 | The EU Constitution: The Best Way Forward? |